Frommer's®
Bahamas

Our Bahamas

by Darwin Porter & Danforth Prince

THE BAHAMAS ARCHIPELAGO STRETCHES FROM SOUTH FLORIDA almost to Haiti, comprising more than 700 islands. And the experiences that await you are as diverse as the islands themselves. On Paradise Island, you can order "surf and turf" from a tuxedo-clad waiter; buy Bulgari gems; partake of Las Vegas–style gambling; or sail on a James Bond–style yacht (many 007 films used Nassau and Paradise Island as backdrops). The waters off New Providence Island are dense with gardens of elkhorn coral and the sea floor is a graveyard of shipwrecks that draw boatloads of scuba divers.

Personally, we prefer the tranquil, less developed side of The Bahamas—from the underwater caverns of Lucayan National Park to Bimini's raffish End of the World Bar. If you move south from the megaresorts on Nassau and Paradise Island, you'll discover the Out Islands; here, virtually unchanged, is the kind of natural setting that Columbus and his crew first spotted in the 15th century. If you dream of lying under a sheltering palm tree on a deserted beach with talcum-fine sands, these are the islands to visit—some of them so underpopulated, electricity has yet to arrive.

The photos we've chosen reflect the best of these islands, whether you prefer action, relaxation, or a little of both.

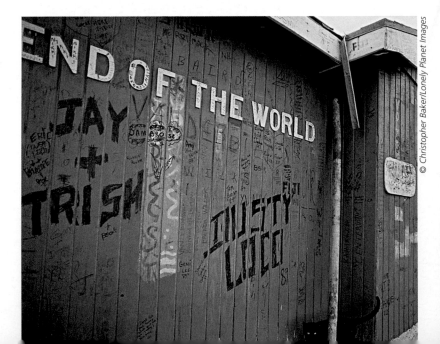

© Christopher Baker/Lonely Planet Images

Bimini's **END OF THE WORLD BAR (left)**, with its sand floor and a back door that opens to the harbor, boasts a storied past; Adam Clayton Powell, the legendary congressman from Harlem, was a fixture here in the 1960s. These days, when the fishing is done, beer-bellied fishermen—each looking like a clone of another former patron, Ernest Hemingway—arrive with their suntanned dates to drink the night away.

Breathtaking **PINK SANDS BEACH (above)** is our favorite in The Bahamas. Its pristine beauty stretches for 5km (3 miles) along Harbour Island's eastern flank. In the wild pirate days, long past, "Calico Jack" Rackham—The Bahamas' most notorious freebooter—raced along this beach clad only in a red kerchief. These days you'll find tranquillity in the beach's northern bird sanctuary and pleasant swimming conditions.

Beginning at 3am on the day after Christmas, revelers in elaborate costumes celebrate **JUNKANOO**. The raucous street parade is an ancient ritual of African heritage that still lives on in The Bahamas and is a symbol of national pride. Some **JUNKANOO MASKS (above)** cover an entire face. This masked man joins stilt, street, and acrobatic dancers, along with clowns and monsters—perhaps a "fly" with red-and-chartreuse eyes and 2.7m (9ft.) wings. The **KING OF JUNKANOO (right)** wears an elaborate headdress, a caparison vest, and a giant hoop skirt made from cardboard and decorated with thin strips of crepe paper meticulously glued on. Part jive, part shuffle, and all dazzling gymnastics, parade participants dance to the syncopated beat of blowing bugles, tin whistles, clanking cowbells, conch shells, and Goombay drums (goat skins stretched over wooden frames).

Take a stroll through Nassau's vast bustling **STRAW MARKET (right),** which dates from 1901, and you'll find all sorts of items made from the top of thatch palm—baskets with colorful embroidery, handbags, hats, tablemats, and even dolls.

The hub of market life from the Out Islands, Potter's Cay lies under the Paradise Island Bridge. **QUEENIE (below)** sells island staples such as papaya, bananas, coconuts, and pineapples. Fishing boats arrive at Potter's Cay, too, to unload their catch of the day, especially snapper and grouper—two mainstays of the Bahamian diet   and the "sexy conch," which Bahamian men view as an aphrodisiac.

The 5.6ha (14-acre) sprawling "water city" at the Atlantis Paradise Island Resort & Casino justifies the resort's hype that "An ocean runs through it." The aquarium here is touted as the largest marine habitat in the world, with more than 100 species of tropical fish, some 14,000 in all. Take a stroll through this Plexiglas walkway at **MARINE PARK (left)**, which provides a unique perspective to see marine life from down below as fish swim overhead.

Paying homage to the "lost continent" of Atlantis, the $850 million, 2,349-room **ATLANTIS PARADISE ISLAND RESORT & CASINO (above)** is a fantasy megaresort. It stands across from Nassau on Paradise Island, the poshest destination in The Bahamas. Atlantis, with a Disney-style replica of a Mayan temple, is not just a resort, but also a water park with marine life, underwater caves, waterfalls, blue lagoons, and a walk-through aquarium.

Built in 1838, this red-and-white banded **LIGHTHOUSE (left)** on Elbow Cay in the Abacos is one of the last hand-turned, kerosene-fueled beacons in The Bahamas. Climb 36m (120 ft.) to the top for a view of dazzling land- and seascapes. Local residents have repeatedly tried to destroy the lighthouse, hoping that ships near Hope Town would wreck on the reefs and they could salvage the profitable cargoes.

"THE CLOISTERS," (below) were once part of a 14th-century monastery near Lourdes, France. Newspaper baron William Randolph Hearst purchased the remains but when dismantled, they were not labeled. Paradise Island developer, Huntington Hartford, grandson of the founder of A&P, hired architects to reassemble the stones; the project took more than a year to complete.

© Angelo Cavalli/SuperStock

© Bill Brooks/Masterfile

The **HORSE-DRAWN SURREY (above)** is still the most romantic way to travel about Nassau. Drivers await passengers in the heart of Rawson Square and tell a colorful living history of Nassau—of all the blood, gore, lore, and legend. You'll pass the grounds of the 1859 Royal Victoria Hotel, once home to a man who inspired Margaret Mitchell to create the character of Rhett Butler in *Gone With the Wind*.

On October 12, 1492, Columbus landed on this frontier island, 122km (200 miles) southeast of Nassau. He named it San Salvador. In 1956, scholar Ruth Durlacher Wolper Malvin placed a lonely cross—known now as the **COLUMBUS MONUMENT (right)**—at what is believed, though disputed, to be the spot where Columbus made landfall.

PINK FLAMINGOS (left)—the graceful national birds of The Bahamas—strike elegant poses in the remote nature reserve of the Inagua National Park. The Romans killed these birds for their tongues—considered the greatest of all delicacies—but they are protected today and are no longer an endangered species. Every spring, flamingos flock to Great Inagua, the most southerly and the third-largest island of The Bahamas, to mate.

At the 16ha (40-acre) **LUCAYAN NATIONAL PARK (above)** on Grand Bahama Island, a wooden path winds through terrain that islanders call the "bush country." Along with rare birds, flora, and fauna, the park's environment ranges from dune-covered beaches to Golden Rock Creek, fed by what is touted as the world's largest underground freshwater cavern system. Bones, pottery, and other artifacts prove that this was a former stomping ground of the Lucayans, who came here to drink from the freshwater springs.

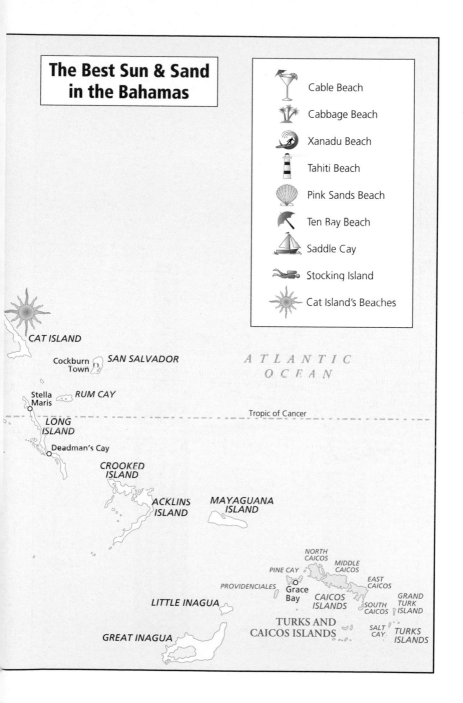

The Best Sun & Sand in the Bahamas

Cable Beach

Cabbage Beach

Xanadu Beach

Tahiti Beach

Pink Sands Beach

Ten Bay Beach

Saddle Cay

Stocking Island

Cat Island's Beaches

CAT ISLAND

Cockburn Town   SAN SALVADOR

ATLANTIC OCEAN

Stella Maris   RUM CAY

Tropic of Cancer

LONG ISLAND

Deadman's Cay

CROOKED ISLAND

ACKLINS ISLAND   MAYAGUANA ISLAND

NORTH CAICOS
MIDDLE CAICOS
PINE CAY
EAST CAICOS
PROVIDENCIALES   Grace Bay   CAICOS ISLANDS
SOUTH CAICOS   GRAND TURK ISLAND
LITTLE INAGUA
TURKS AND CAICOS ISLANDS   SALT CAY   TURKS ISLANDS
GREAT INAGUA

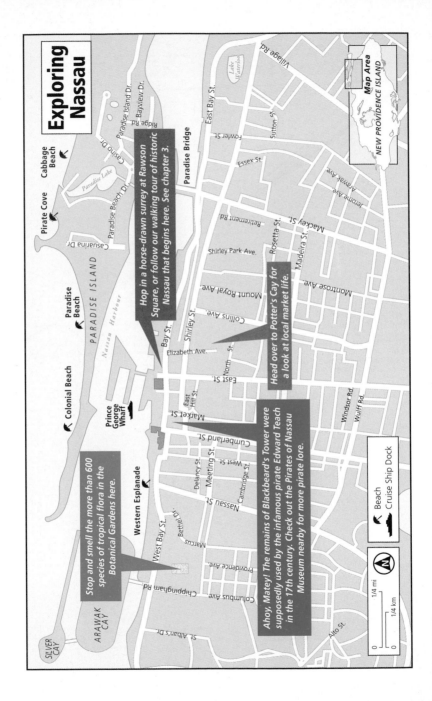

Exploring Nassau

Stop and smell the more than 600 species of tropical flora in the Botanical Gardens here.

Hop in a horse-drawn surrey at Rawson Square, or follow our walking tour of historic Nassau that begins here. See chapter 3.

Head over to Potter's Cay for a look at local market life.

Ahoy, Matey! The remains of Blackbeard's Tower were supposedly used by the infamous pirate Edward Teach in the 17th century. Check out the Pirates of Nassau Museum nearby for more pirate lore.

SILVER CAY
ARAWAK CAY
Western Esplanade
West Bay St.
Bethel D.
Marcus
Providence Ave.
Columbus Ave.
Chippingham Rd.
St. Alban's Dr.
Alto St.
Colonial Beach
Paradise Beach
Paradise Island
Nassau Harbour
Prince George Wharf
Bay St.
Nassau St.
Delancy St.
Meeting St.
West St.
Cumberland St.
Cambridge St.
Market St.
East Hill St.
East St.
North St.
Shirley St.
Elizabeth Ave.
Collins Ave.
Mount Royal Ave.
Shirley Park Ave.
Retirement Rd.
Rosetta St.
Madeira St.
Mackey St.
Montrose Ave.
Jerome Ave.
Arawak Ave.
Essex St.
Fowler St.
East Bay St.
Sutton St.
Village Rd.
Windsor Rd.
Wulff Rd.
Paradise Bridge
Paradise Lake
Paradise Lake
Paradise Beach Dr.
Casuarina Dr.
Casino Dr.
Paradise Island Dr.
Paradise Rd.
Bayview Dr.
Ridge Rd.
Lake Waterloo
Cabbage Beach
Pirate Cove
Paradise Beach

Beach
Cruise Ship Dock

0 1/4 mi
0 1/4 km

Map Area
NEW PROVIDENCE ISLAND

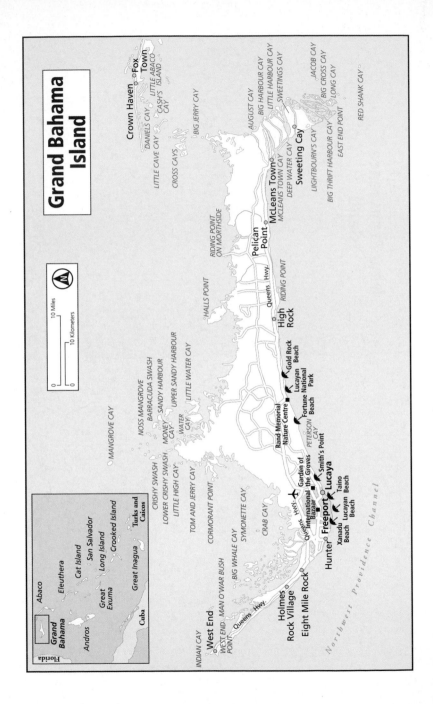

Grand Bahama Island

10 Miles
10 Kilometers

Florida

Abaco
Eleuthera
Cat Island
San Salvador
Grand
Bahama
Andros
Great
Exuma
Long Island
Crooked Island
Turks and
Caicos
Great Inagua
Cuba

INDIAN CAY

West End
WEST END; MAN O'WAR BUSH
POINT
Holmes
Rock Village
Eight Mile Rock
Queens Hwy.
BIG WHALE CAY
SYMONETTE CAY
CRAB CAY
CORMORANT POINT

TOM AND JERRY CAY
LITTLE HIGH CAY
LOWER CRISHY SWASH
CRISHY SWASH
MANGROVE CAY
NOSS MANGROVE
BARRACUDA SWASH
MONEY
CAY
SANDY HARBOUR
UPPER SANDY HARBOUR
WATER
CAY
LITTLE WATER CAY

CROSS CAYS
BIG JERRY CAY

LITTLE CAVE CAY
DANIELS CAY
Crown Haven
Fox
Town
LITTLE ABACO
CASH'S ISLAND
CAY

AUGUST CAY
BIG HARBOUR CAY
LITTLE HARBOUR CAY
SWEETINGS CAY
Sweeting Cay
DEEP WATER CAY
LIGHTBOURN'S CAY
BIG THRIFT HARBOUR CAY
LONG CAY
EAST END POINT
JACOB CAY
BIG CROSS CAY
RED SHANK CAY

McLeans Town
MCLEANS TOWN CAY

Pelican
Point
RIDING POINT
ON NORTHSIDE

HALLS POINT

High
Rock
Queens Hwy.
RIDING POINT

Gold Rock
Beach
Lucayan
Beach
Lucayan National
Park
Rand Memorial
Nature Centre
Fortune
Beach
PETERSON CAY
Garden of
the Groves
Smith's Point
Lucaya
Taino
Beach
Freeport
Hunter
International
Bazaar
Queens Hwy.
Xanadu
Beach
Lucayan
Beach
Beach

Northwest Providence Channel

Frommer's®

Bahamas

2008

by Darwin Porter & Danforth Prince

Here's what the critics say about Frommer's:

"Amazingly easy to use. Very portable, very complete."

—*Booklist*

"Detailed, accurate, and easy-to-read information for all price ranges."
—*Glamour Magazine*

"Hotel information is close to encyclopedic."

—*Des Moines Sunday Register*

"Frommer's Guides have a way of giving you a real feel for a place."
—*Knight Ridder Newspapers*

1807
WILEY
2007

Wiley Publishing, Inc.

About the Authors

As a team of veteran travel writers, **Darwin Porter** and **Danforth Prince** have produced numerous titles for Frommer's, including best-selling guides to Italy, France, the Caribbean, England, and Germany. Porter, a former bureau chief of the *Miami Herald,* is also a Hollywood biographer, and his most recent release is *Howard Hughes: Hell's Angel.* Prince was formerly employed by the Paris bureau of the *New York Times,* and is today the president of Blood Moon Productions and other media-related firms.

Published by:

Wiley Publishing, Inc.

111 River St.
Hoboken, NJ 07030-5774

ISBN: 978-0-470-14568-5
Editor: Jamie Ehrlich
Production Editor: Heather Wilcox
Cartographer: Anton Crane
Photo Editor: Richard Fox
Anniversary Logo Design: Richard Pacifico
Production by Wiley Indianapolis Composition Services

Front cover photo: Rear view of young man doing handstand on beach, Harbour Island
Back cover photo: Facade of a house at Smith Point, Grand Bahama Island.

For information on our other products and services or to obtain technical support, please contact our Customer Care Department within the U.S. at 800/762-2974, outside the U.S. at 317/572-3993 or fax 317/572-4002.

Wiley also publishes its books in a variety of electronic formats. Some content that appears in print may not be available in electronic formats.

Manufactured in the United States of America

5   4   3   2   1

Contents

4 Paradise Island 120

5 Grand Bahama (Freeport/Lucaya) 143

6 Bimini, the Berry Islands & Andros 181

7 The Abacos 206

8 Eleuthera   236

9 The Exumas   260

10 The Southern Bahamas   279

Index   301

List of Maps

An Invitation to the Reader

In researching this book, we discovered many wonderful places—hotels, restaurants, shops, and more. We're sure you'll find others. Please tell us about them, so we can share the information with your fellow travelers in upcoming editions. If you were disappointed with a recommendation, we'd love to know that, too. Please write to:

Frommer's Bahamas 2008
Wiley Publishing, Inc. • 111 River St. • Hoboken, NJ 07030-5774

An Additional Note

Please be advised that travel information is subject to change at any time—and this is especially true of prices. We therefore suggest that you write or call ahead for confirmation when making your travel plans. The authors, editors, and publisher cannot be held responsible for the experiences of readers while traveling. Your safety is important to us, however, so we encourage you to stay alert and be aware of your surroundings. Keep a close eye on cameras, purses, and wallets, all favorite targets of thieves and pickpockets.

Other Great Guides for Your Trip:

Frommer's Portable Bahamas
Frommer's Caribbean
Frommer's Caribbean Cruises & Ports of Call
Frommer's Caribbean Ports of Call

Frommer's Star Ratings, Icons & Abbreviations

Every hotel, restaurant, and attraction listing in this guide has been ranked for quality, value, service, amenities, and special features using a **star-rating system.** In country, state, and regional guides, we also rate towns and regions to help you narrow down your choices and budget your time accordingly. Hotels and restaurants are rated on a scale of zero (recommended) to three stars (exceptional). Attractions, shopping, nightlife, towns, and regions are rated according to the following scale: zero stars (recommended), one star (highly recommended), two stars (very highly recommended), and three stars (must-see).

In addition to the star-rating system, we also use **seven feature icons** that point you to the great deals, in-the-know advice, and unique experiences that separate travelers from tourists. Throughout the book, look for:

Finds	Special finds—those places only insiders know about
Fun Fact	Fun facts—details that make travelers more informed and their trips more fun
Kids	Best bets for kids and advice for the whole family
Moments	Special moments—those experiences that memories are made of
Overrated	Places or experiences not worth your time or money
Tips	Insider tips—great ways to save time and money
Value	Great values—where to get the best deals

The following **abbreviations** are used for credit cards:

AE	American Express	DISC	Discover	V	Visa
DC	Diners Club	MC	MasterCard		

Frommers.com

Now that you have this guidebook to help you plan a great trip, visit our website at **www. frommers.com** for additional travel information on more than 3,500 destinations. We update features regularly to give you instant access to the most current trip-planning information available. At Frommers.com, you'll find scoops on the best airfares, lodging rates, and car rental bargains. You can even book your travel online through our reliable travel booking partners. Other popular features include:

- Online updates of our most popular guidebooks
- Vacation sweepstakes and contest giveaways
- Newsletters highlighting the hottest travel trends
- Online travel message boards with featured travel discussions

What's New in The Bahamas

Big changes are in store for The Bahamas, many of which will be launched in 2008. The major development is occurring both at Cable Beach on New Providence Island outside Nassau and at the mammoth Atlantis Resort on neighboring Paradise Island.

Even sleepy Eleuthera, drowsy for years, is slated to start opening "boutique resorts" in 2008. Otherwise, a great deal of the Out Islands are pretty much as we've described them unless a hurricane hits.

NASSAU/CABLE BEACH Between now and 2009 (possibly 2010), Cable Beach, that shoreline strip of hotels and condos outside Nassau, will experience a building boom. In their grandiose redevelopment plans, Cable Beach promoters are preparing to give the mammoth Paradise Island Resort of Atlantis a run for its money.

There's talk that Cable Beach one day will look as if it were designed by Walt Disney. In 2007, massive multimillion-dollar improvements were made to much of the existing hotel infrastructure. In addition to all the new hotels planned, the existing Wyndham and Sheraton properties will be radically altered. On the charts are new marinas, a redesigned golf course, and even new "lakes."

Even more hotel developments are underway, including a projected reopening of the famous **Compass Point Hotel** on Cable Beach. Owned by Chris Blackwell, founder of Virgin Records, it will offer brightly painted Creole "huts." The **Bob Marley Resort,** a once-private retreat of the reggae star himself and his family, is being converted into a hotel.

On the 92-hectare (230-acre) **Rose Island,** an exclusive retreat 6.4km (4 miles) off the coast of Nassau, the Ritz Carlton chain is planning a deluxe hotel.

For years, **Sun and . . . ,** Lakeview Road at East Shirley Street (© 242/393-1205), was acclaimed as perhaps the finest restaurant on island. In 2006, it made a comeback and has reclaimed its legendary position among local restaurants. As more and more visitors dine only at their hotels, Sun and . . . remains the leading independent choice on New Providence Island, even luring diners from the Atlantis Resort on Paradise Island.

On Cable Beach itself, the opening of **Moso** in the Wyndham Nassau Resort (© 242/327-6200) has created the most media buzz. This is the leading Asian restaurant on island and one of the finest dining choices of the Baha Mar Cable Beach complex. Its Mongolian-style chicken and beef hot pie and its aromatic crispy duck are just some of the many dishes that the Bahamian staff learned how to make with the finesse of the kitchens of the Far East.

PARADISE ISLAND **Chalks International Airways** is no longer flying into Paradise Island from Fort Lauderdale. Air passengers must fly into the recently renamed Lynden Pindling International

Airport on New Providence Island and take a taxi over the bridge to Paradise Island.

Chances are, once on island, a guest will be checking into the rapidly expanding **Atlantis Paradise Island Resort & Casino** (© 242/363-3000). In 2006 and 2007, the resort continued to grow, adding not only more rooms but also additional Water World–type features with a labyrinth of new streams and waterfalls. A 400-unit condo complex is slated for completion by 2009.

Ready in 2007 is the swank **The Cove Atlantis,** Casino Drive (© 242/363-3000), an all-suite hotel that is a semiprivate hideaway within a greater complex. Although much of Atlantis is geared to the family trade, The Cove is strictly an adult retreat. Some of the suites at this posh new address are so large that they are of presidential proportions.

After **Nobu** (© 242/353-3000) opened in the Atlantis Paradise Island Resort's Royal Towers on Casino Drive, it became the most sought-after dining seat in the entire complex. Its cutting-edge take on Asian cuisine has drawn celebrities to its stylish precincts and the culinary genius of the Japanese chef Nobu Matsuhisa, who created all the menu specialties.

Another immediate dining success, **Casa d'Angelo** opened in the Coral Tower at Atlantis on Casino Drive (© 242/363-3000), serving some of the best Italian food in the country in plush, upholstered surroundings. Classic rather than innovative Italian specialties are offered. Dishes are prepared with high-quality ingredients, ranging from carpaccio of tuna to free-range chicken roasted in a wood-fired oven.

GRAND BAHAMA ISLAND A new hotel, **Bell Channel Inn,** Kings Road, Lucaya (© 242/373-1053), is geared mainly to scuba divers but open to all.

Dive packages are available at this resort, which is close to the ocean. Those who stay behind for the day enjoy a solar-heated pool. On-site is a full-service dive shop and a private boat that will take you to some of the best dive sites on Grand Bahama Island, which are only a 5- to 10-minute boat ride from the inn. The on-site Seafood Restaurant & Bar specializes in . . . guess what?

BIMINI Hoteliers on island are concerned about the new U.S. requirements demanding that visitors to The Bahamas must carry a valid passport to enter Bimini, which lies right off the coast of Florida. In former years, vacationers to Florida could show a government-issued photo ID to sail over from Florida for "a taste of The Bahamas," in essence tying in a visit to a foreign country on their Florida holiday. This was one of the most popular trips to be made off the Florida coast. It is estimated that thousands of Florida-bound visitors do not possess a passport. Therefore, the sightseers heading for Bimini are expected to be dramatically curtailed because of this new requirement, which is effective on January 1, 2008.

ELBOW CAY After closing down in 1999 because of damage caused by Hurricane Floyd, **Hope Town Harbour Lodge,** Upper Road, Hope Town (© 242/366-0095), has made a comeback. The property is looking better than ever, and many improvements were made in its restoration, including the addition of hurricane-strength windows and doors, and the installation of private balconies in all the rooms in the main building. Boardwalks and artful landscaping were also part of the deal, along with the restoration of a century-old Butterfly House for rent and the addition of six cottages on the grounds.

ELEUTHERA Outside Gregory Town at Surfers Beach, an informal resort has opened for surfers. Aptly named **Surfers**

Beach Manor (© 242/335-5300), it is a laid-back inn of 11 newly restored and air-conditioned cottages, featuring affordable rates and a Bahamian cuisine.

Big developments are on the way for this chain of islands. In the summer of 2006, groundbreaking began on the **Current Club** at the southernmost tip of North Eleuthera, and the old Club Med at Gregory Town is being turned into a boutique hotel called **French Leave Resort.** Construction began in 2007 on the site of this former Club Med, which was destroyed by a hurricane.

EXUMAS News of a malaria outbreak here in the summer of 2006 damaged tourist prospects to these beautiful islands, which are particularly popular with yachties from Florida. At least 60 people, mostly locals, tested positive for this potentially fatal disease. The Bahamian government increased mosquito control, among other measures. Before coming here, the prudent might want to check the website of the **Centers for Disease Control and Prevention** (www.cdc.gov/travel).

In another development, the major resort in The Exumas, **Four Seasons Resort Great Exuma** at Emerald Bay (© 242/366-6800), has been much improved and has worked out its kinks that became apparent upon its opening. It is now running smoothly and has added El Cielo, an on-site restaurant that is the finest in the archipelago, serving a refined Italian cuisine.

SAMPSON CAY This remote island in the Exumas is the site of **Sampson Cay Club** (© 242/355-2034), which has been considerably improved. The furnishings in the bedrooms have been upgraded, and two units are right on the beach. Rentals have outdoor showers as well as their own dinghy docks. Also, the staff now rents 3.9 and 5.1m (13- and 17-ft.) whalers, as well as Hobie cats.

LONG ISLAND Long the leading resort of this remote island, **Cape Santa Maria Beach Resort,** at Cape Santa Maria (© 242/338-5273), has added eight new beachfront villas, each with luxury appointments, to its complex. The resort has also upgraded its amenities and improved its cuisine. Of course, it still has that fabulous beach frontage.

1

The Best of The Bahamas

The Bahamas is one of the most geographically complicated nations of the Atlantic. A coral-based archipelago, it is composed of more than 700 islands, 2,000 cays (pronounced "keys," from the Spanish word for small islands), and hundreds of rocky outcroppings that have damaged the hulls of countless ships since colonial days.

The Commonwealth of The Bahamas came into being in 1973 after centuries of colonial rule. After Great Britain granted The Bahamas internal self-rule in 1964, the fledgling nation adopted its own constitution but chose not to sever its ties with its motherland. It has remained in the Commonwealth, with the British monarch as its head of state. In the British tradition, The Bahamas has a two-house Parliament, a ministerial cabinet headed by a prime minister, and an independent judiciary. The queen appoints a Bahamian governor-general to represent the Crown.

As The Bahamas moves deeper into the millennium, the government and various investors continue to pump money into the tourism infrastructure, especially on Paradise Island, across from Nassau, as well as Cable Beach adjoining Nassau. Cruise-ship tourism continues to increase, and a more upscale crowd is coming back after abandoning The Bahamas for many years in favor of other Caribbean islands such as St. Barts and Anguilla.

When Hubert Ingraham became prime minister in 1992, he launched the country down the long road toward regaining its market share of tourism, which under Prime Minister Lynden Pindling had seen a rapid decline. Exit polls revealed some first-time visitors vowing never to return to The Bahamas under the administration of the notorious Pindling, whose government had taken over a number of hotels and failed to maintain them properly.

When Ingraham took over as prime minister, however, he wisely recognized that the government wasn't supposed to be in the hospitality business and turned many properties back over to the professionals. After a painful slump, tourism in the post-Pindling era is booming again in The Bahamas, and more than 1.6 million visitors from all over the world now flock here annually. In the capital of Nassau, it's easy to see where the government's money is being spent: on widened roads, repaved sidewalks, underground phone cables, massive landscaping, sweeping esplanades, a cleanup campaign, and additional police officers walking the beat to cut down on crime.

Perry Gladstone Christie, prime minister from 2002–07, continued to carry out those same policies to better Nassau. Ingraham was reelected prime minister in May 2007.

Unlike Haiti and Jamaica, The Bahamas has remained politically stable and made the transition from minority white rule to black majority rule with relatively little tension.

Economic conditions have slowly improved here as well. You do not see the wretched poverty in Nassau that you see in, say, Kingston, Jamaica, though many poor residents do still live on New Providence Island's "Over-the-Hill" section, an area where few tourists venture to visit (although the neighborhood is gritty and fascinating).

Nassau really is the true Bahamas. You'd think a city so close to the U.S. mainland would have been long since overpowered by American culture. Yet, except for some fast-food chain outlets, American pop music, and Hollywood films, Nassau retains a surprising amount of its traditionally British feel. (By contrast, Freeport/Lucaya on Grand Bahama Island has become almost completely Americanized, with little British aura or Bahamian tradition left.)

The biggest changes have occurred in the hotel sector. Developers have vastly expanded the Atlantis Resort on Paradise Island, turning it into a virtual water world. Even more expansions have been announced, to be completed in 2009 and beyond. The Hilton interests have developed the decaying old British Colonial in Nassau, restoring it to life.

And Grand Bahama Island is in an interesting state of flux. Hotels along the entire Lucayan strip are being upgraded.

If there's a downside to this boom, it's the emphasis on megahotels and casinos—and the corresponding lack of focus on the Out Islands, which include the Abacos, Andros, Bimini, Cat Island, the Exumas, Long Island, and San Salvador. Large resort chains, with the exception of Four Seasons and Club Med, have ignored these islands; most continue to slumber away in relative seclusion and poverty. Other than the Four Seasons megaresort that opened in the Exumas, development in the drowsy Out Islands has been minor. The very lack of progress here will continue to attract a certain breed of adventurous explorer, the one who shuns the resorts and casinos of Paradise Island, Cable Beach, and Freeport/Lucaya. Little change in this Out Islands-versus-the-rest situation is anticipated in the immediate future, except for the island chain of Eleuthera, which is planning to open several boutique hotels in the near future.

There's another trend to note in The Bahamas. After a long slumber, the government and many concerned citizens here have awakened to eco-tourism. More than any government in the Caribbean except perhaps Bonaire, this nation is trying to protect its ecology. If nothing else, residents realize this will be good for tourism because many visitors come to The Bahamas precisely for its natural wonders.

Government, private companies, and environmental groups have drawn up a national framework of priorities to protect the islands. One of their first goals was to save the nearly extinct West Indian flamingo. Today about 60,000 flamingos inhabit Great Inagua Island. Other programs aim to prevent the extinction of the green turtle, the white-crowned pigeon, the Bahamian parrot, and the New Providence iguana.

Although tourism and the environment are bouncing back, many problems still remain for this archipelago nation. While some Bahamians seem among the friendliest and most hospitable people in the world, others—particularly those in the tourist industry—can be downright hostile. To counter this, the government is working to train its citizens to be more helpful, courteous, and efficient. Sometimes this training has been taken to heart; at other times, however, it still clearly has not. Service with a smile is not assured in The Bahamas.

Drug smuggling remains a serious problem, and, regrettably, there seems to be no immediate solution. Because the country is so close to U.S. shores, it is often used as

The Best Beaches of The Bahamas

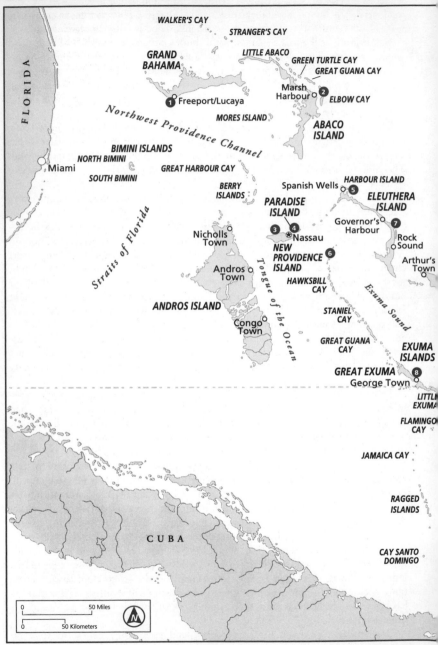

THE BEST BEACHES
Cabbage Beach **4**
Cable Beach **3**
Cat Island's Beaches **9**
Pink Sands Beach **5**
Saddle Cay **6**
Stocking Island **8**
Tahiti Beach **2**
Ten Bay Beach **7**
Xanadu Beach **1**

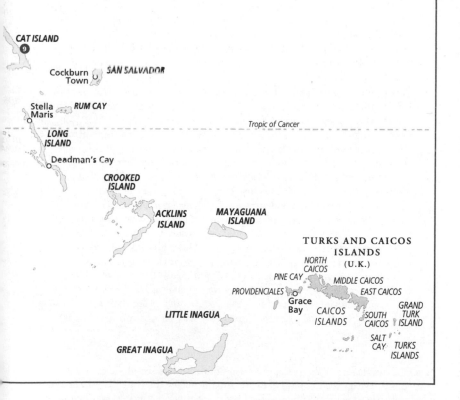

ATLANTIC

OCEAN

CAT ISLAND

Cockburn   *SAN SALVADOR*
Town

Stella   *RUM CAY*
Maris
                                    Tropic of Cancer
LONG
ISLAND

Deadman's Cay

*CROOKED
ISLAND*

*ACKLINS
ISLAND*   *MAYAGUANA
ISLAND*

                            TURKS AND CAICOS
                                ISLANDS
                        NORTH   (U.K.)
                        CAICOS
                    PINE CAY   *MIDDLE CAICOS*
        PROVIDENCIALES   *EAST CAICOS*
                    Grace
                    Bay   *CAICOS*   *GRAND
                            ISLANDS   *SOUTH   TURK
LITTLE INAGUA   *CAICOS*   *ISLAND*

                                    *SALT
                                    CAY*   *TURKS
GREAT INAGUA   *ISLANDS*

Beaches 101: Paradise Island, Cable Beach & More

In The Bahamas, the issue about public access to beaches is a hot and controversial subject. Recognizing this, the government has made efforts to intersperse public beaches near private ones, where access would otherwise be impeded. Although megaresorts discourage nonguests from easy access to their individual beaches, there are so many public beaches on New Providence Island and Paradise Island that all a beach lover has to do is stop his or her car (or walk) to many of the unmarked, unnamed beaches that flank these islands.

If you stay in one of the large beachfront resorts, all you need to do is leave the grounds of the hotel and head for the ocean via the sand in front the resort. But if your accommodation is not beachfront or you want to explore another beach, here are a few details:

Cabbage Beach 𝑅𝑅. On Paradise Island, this is the real showcase, with broad, white sands that stretch for at least 3km (2 miles). Casuarinas, palms, and sea grapes border it. While it's likely to be crowded in winter, you can find a little more elbowroom by walking to the northwestern stretch of the beach. You can reach Paradise Island from downtown Nassau by walking over the bridge, taking a taxi, or boarding a ferryboat at Prince George Dock. Cabbage Beach does not have public facilities, but you can patronize one of the handful of bars and restaurants nearby and use their restrooms Technically, you should be a customer, even if that means buying only a drink, even a Coca-Cola.

Cable Beach 𝑅𝑅. No particular beach is actually called Cable Beach, yet this is the most popular beachfront on New Providence Island. Instead of an actual beach, Cable Beach is the name given to a string of resorts and beaches that lies in the center of New Providence's northern coast, attracting the most visitors. This beachfront offers 6.5km (4 miles) of soft white sand, and the types of food, restaurants, snack bars, and watersports offered at the hotels lining the waterfront vary. Calypso music floats to the sand from hotel pool patios where vacationers play musical chairs and see how low they can limbo. Vendors wind their way among sunblock-slathered bodies. Some sell armloads of shell jewelry, T-shirts, beach cover-ups, and fresh coconuts for sipping the sweet "water" straight from the shell. Others offer their hair-braiding services or sign up visitors for water-skiing, jet-skiing, and banana boat rides. Kiosks advertise parasailing, scuba diving, and snorkeling trips, as well as party cruises to offshore islands. Waters can be rough and reefy, then calm and clear a little farther along the shore. There are no public toilets here because guests of the resorts use their hotel facilities. If you're not a guest of the hotel or a customer, you are not supposed

a temporary depot for drugs shipped from South America to Florida. The Bahamas previously developed a tradition of catering to the illicit habits of U.S. citizens as well; during the heyday of Prohibition, long before cocaine, marijuana, and heroin were to use the facilities. The Cable Beach resorts begin 4.8km (3 miles) west of downtown Nassau. Even though resorts line much of this long swath of beach, there are various sections where public access is available without crossing through private hotel grounds.

Caves Beach. On the north shore, past the Cable Beach Properties, Caves Beach lies some 11km (6¾ miles) west of Nassau. It stands near Rock Point, right before the turnoff along Blake Road that leads to the airport. Since visitors often don't know of this beach, it's another good spot to escape the hordes. It's also a good beach with soft sands. There are no toilets or changing facilities.

Delaporte Beach. Just west of the busiest section of Cable Beach, Delaporte Beach is a public access beach where you can escape the crowds. It opens onto clear waters and boasts white sands, although it has no facilities. Nonetheless, it's an option.

Goodman's Bay. This public beach lies east of Cable Beach on the way toward the center of Nassau. Goodman's Bay and Saunders Beach (see below) often host local fundraising cookouts, where vendors sell fish, chicken, conch, peas 'n' rice, or macaroni and cheese. People swim and socialize to blaring reggae and calypso music. To find out when one of these beach parties is happening, ask the staff at your hotel or pick up a local newspaper. There is a playground here, plus toilet facilities.

Paradise Beach 𝕽𝕽. On Paradise Island, this is one of the best beaches in the entire area. The white sandy beach is dotted with *chikees* (thatched huts), which are perfect when you've had too much of the sun. Mainly used by guests of the Atlantis Resort (p. 122), it lies at the far western tip of the island. If you're not a resident, access is difficult. If you're staying at a hotel in Nassau and want to come to Paradise Island for a day at the beach, it's better to go to Cabbage Beach (see above).

Saunders Beach. East of Cable Beach, this is where many islanders go on the weekends. To reach it, take West Bay Street from Nassau in the direction of Coral Island. The beach lies across from Fort Charlotte, just west of Arawak Cay. Like Goodman's Bay (see above), it often hosts local fundraising cookouts open to the public. These can be a lot of fun. There are no public facilities.

Western Esplanade (also called Junkanoo Beach). If you're staying at a hotel in downtown Nassau, such as the British Colonial Hilton (p. 75), this is a good beach to patronize close to town. The narrow strip of sand is convenient to Nassau and has toilets, changing facilities, and a snack bar.

outlawed, many Bahamians grew rich smuggling rum into the United States. Things have improved, but you'll still see stories in the newspapers about floating bales of marijuana turning up in the sea just off The Bahamas' coastline and such.

Though this illicit trade rarely affects the casual tourist, it's important to know that it is a factor here—and so, armed with this knowledge, don't agree to carry any packages to or from the U.S. for a stranger while you're visiting. You could end up taking a much longer vacation on these islands than you had ever imagined.

1 The Best Beaches

See also "Beaches 101: Paradise Island, Cable Beach & More" box on p. 8.

- **Cable Beach** (New Providence Island): The glittering shoreline of Cable Beach has easy access to shops, casinos, restaurants, watersports, and bars. It's a sandy 6.5km-long (4-mile) strip, with a great array of facilities and activities. See p. 80.

- **Cabbage Beach** (Paradise Island): Think Vegas in the Tropics. It seems as if most of the sunbathers dozing on the sands here are recovering from the previous evening's partying, and it's likely to be crowded near the mega-hotels, but you can find a bit more solitude on the beach's isolated northwestern extension (Paradise Beach), which is accessible only by boat or on foot. Lined with palms, sea grapes, and casuarinas, the sands are broad and stretch for at least 3km (2 miles). See p. 137.

- **Xanadu Beach** (Grand Bahama Island): Grand Bahama has 97km (60 miles) of sandy shoreline, but Xanadu Beach is most convenient to Freeport's resort hotels, several of which offer shuttle service to Xanadu. There's more than a kilometer of white sand and (usually) gentle surf. Don't expect to have Xanadu to yourself, but if you want more quiet and privacy, try any of the beaches that stretch from Xanadu for many miles in either direction. See p. 168.

- **Tahiti Beach** (Hope Town, the Abacos): Since the beach is so isolated at the far end of Elbow Cay Island, you can be sure that only a handful of people will ever visit these cool waters and white sands. The crowds stay away because you can't drive to Tahiti Beach: To get there, you have to walk or ride a rented bike along sand and gravel paths from Hope Town. You can also charter a boat to reach the beach—which isn't too hard, since the Abacos are the sailing capital of The Bahamas. See p. 219.

- **Pink Sands Beach** (Harbour Island): Running the entire length of the island's eastern side, these pale pink sands stretch for 5km (3 miles) past a handful of low-rise hotels and private villas. A coral reef protects the shore from breakers, making for some of the safest swimming in The Bahamas. See p. 256.

- **Ten Bay Beach** (Eleuthera): Ten Bay Beach lies a short drive south of Palmetto Point, just north of Savannah Sound. Once upon a time, the exclusive Cotton Bay Club chose to build a hotel here because of the fabulous scenery. There may not be facilities here, but now that the hotel has closed, the white sands and turquoise waters here are more idyllic and private than ever. See p. 241.

- **Saddle Cay** (the Exumas): Most of the Exumas are oval-shaped islands strung end to end like links in a 209km (130-mile) chain. One notable exception is Saddle Cay, with its horseshoe-shaped curve near the Exumas' northern tip. It can be reached only by boat but, once achieved, offers an unspoiled setting without a trace of the modern world—and plenty of other cays and islets where you can play Robinson Crusoe for a few hours, if you like. See p. 262.

- **Stocking Island** (the Exumas): One of the finest white sandy beaches in The Bahamas lies off Elizabeth Harbour, the main harbor of the archipelago, close to the little capital of George Town. You can reach Stocking Island easily by boat from Elizabeth Harbour, and the sands of this offshore island are rarely crowded; snorkelers and divers love to explore its gin-clear waters. In addition to its beach of powdery white sand, the island is known for its "blue holes," coral gardens, and undersea caves. See p. 270.
- **Cat Island's Beaches:** The white beaches ringing this island are pristine, opening onto crystal-clear waters and lined with coconut palms, palmettos, and casuarina trees—and best of all, you'll practically have the place to yourself. One of our favorite beaches here, near Old Bight, has a beautiful, lazy curve of white sand. Another fabulous beach lies 5km (3 miles) north of New Bight, site of the Fernandez Bay Village resort. This curvy beach is set against another backdrop of casuarinas and is unusually tranquil. Another good beach here is the long, sandy stretch that opens onto Hawk's Nest Resort & Marina on the southwestern side. None of the Cat Island beaches has any facilities (bring everything you need from your hotel), but they do offer peace, quiet, and seclusion. See "Cat Island," in chapter 10.

2 The Best Diving

- **New Providence Island:** Many ships have sunk near Nassau in the past 300 years, and all the dive outfitters here know the most scenic wreck sites. Other attractions are underwater gardens of elkhorn coral and dozens of reefs packed with underwater life. The most spectacular dive site is the **Shark Wall,** 16km (10 miles) off the southwest coast of New Providence; it's blessed with incredible, colorful sea life and the healthiest coral offshore. You'll even get to swim with sharks (not as bait, of course). See p. 100.
- **Grand Bahama Island:** The island is ringed with reefs, and dive sites are plentiful, including the Wall, the Caves (site of a long-ago disaster known as Theo's Wreck), and Treasure Reef. Other popular dive sites include Spit City (yes, that's right), Ben Blue Hole, and the Rose Garden (no one knows how this one got its name). What makes Grand Bahama Island a cut above the others is the presence of a world-class dive operator, **UNEXSO** (the **Underwater Explorer's Society;** ℂ **800/992-DIVE** or 242/373-1244; www.unexso.com). See p. 172.
- **Andros:** Marine life abounds in the barrier reef off the coast of Andros, which is one of the largest in the world and a famous destination for divers. The reef plunges 1,800m (5,904 ft.) to a narrow drop-off known as the Tongue of the Ocean. You can also explore mysterious blue holes, formed when subterranean caves fill with seawater, causing their ceilings to collapse and expose clear, deep pools. See p. 203.
- **Bimini:** Although Bimini is most famous for its game fishing, it boasts excellent diving, too. Five kilometers (3 miles) of offshore reefs attract millions of colorful fish. Even snorkelers can see black coral gardens, blue holes, and an odd configuration on the sea floor that is reportedly part of the lost continent of Atlantis (a fun legend, at any rate). Divers can check out the wreck of a motorized yacht,

the *Sapona* (owned by Henry Ford), which sank in shallow waters off the coast in 1929. See p. 188.

- **Harbour Island** (Eleuthera): In addition to lovely coral and an array of colorful fish, divers can enjoy some unique experiences here, such as the Current Cut, an exciting underwater gully that carries you on a swiftly flowing underwater current for 10 minutes. Four wrecked ships also lie nearby, at depths of less than 12m (39 ft.), including a barge that was transporting the engine of a steam locomotive in 1865, reportedly after the American Confederacy sold it to raise cash for its war effort. See p. 256.

- **Long Island** (The Southern Bahamas): Snorkeling is spectacular on virtually all sides of the island. But experienced divers venturing into deeper waters offshore can visit underwater cages to feed swarms of mako, bull, and reef sharks. Dive sites abound, including the Arawak "green hole," a blue hole of incomprehensible depth. See p. 291.

- **Lucayan National Park:** This park on Grand Bahama Island is the site of a 9.5km-long (6-mile) underground freshwater cave system, the longest of its type in the world. The largest cave contains spiral staircases that lead visitors into a freshwater world inhabited by shrimp, mosquito fish, fruit bats, freshwater eels, and a species of crustacean *(Spelionectes lucayensis)* that has never been documented elsewhere. On the 16-hectare (40-acre) preserve you'll find examples of the island's five ecosystems— pine forests, rocky coppice, mangrove swamps, whiteland coppice, and sand dunes. Pause to sunbathe on a lovely stretch of sandy beach, or hike along paths where you can spot orchids, hummingbirds, and barn owls. See p. 174.

- **Pelican Cays Land and Sea Park:** Known for its undersea caves, seemingly endless coral reefs, and abundant plant and marine life, this park, 13km (8 miles) north of Cherokee Sound at Great Abaco Island, is a highlight for scuba divers. See p. 213.

- **Exuma Cays National Land and Sea Park:** A major attraction of The Bahamas, this park is the first of its kind anywhere on the planet. The 35km-long (22-mile), 13km-wide (8-mile) natural preserve attracts scuba divers to its 453 sq. km (177 sq. miles) of sea gardens with spectacular reefs, flora, and fauna. Inaugurated in 1958, it lies some 35km (22 miles) northwest of Staniel Cay and 64km (40 miles) southeast of Nassau, and is accessible only by boat. See p. 272.

3 The Best Snorkeling

- **New Providence Island/Paradise Island:** The waters that ring densely populated New Providence Island and nearby Paradise Island are easy to explore. Most people head for the Rose Island Reefs, the Gambier Deep Reef, Booby Rock Channel, the Goulding Reef Cays, and some easily seen, well-known underwater wrecks that lie in shallow water. Virtually every resort hotel on the island offers equipment and can book you onto a snorkel cruise to sites farther offshore. See p. 100 and 138.

- **Grand Bahama:** Resort hotels on the island can hook you up with snorkeling excursions, such as the ones offered by **Ocean Motion Water Sports Ltd.** (℅ **242/374-2425;** www. oceanmotionbahamas.com), which is the best outfitter for snorkeling. In addition, the outlet can connect you with any number of other watersports, from banana boating to waterskiing. The clear water around Grand Bahama is wonderful for snorkeling because it has a rich marine life. Snorkelers are fond of exploring Ben's Cave, a stunning cavern that's part of Lucayan Caves, as well as the coral beds at places like Silver Point Reef and Gold Rock. See p. 172.

- **Bimini:** Snorkelers are enthralled with the black coral gardens that are easily accessible from shore, and the colorful marine life around the island. Sometimes when conditions are right, snorkelers enjoy frolicking with a pod of spotted dolphins. Off North Bimini, snorkelers are attracted to a cluster of huge flat rocks that jut from 6 to 9m (20–30 ft.) out of the water at Paradise Point. The most imaginative snorkelers claim these rocks, which seem hand-hewn, are part of a road system that once traversed the lost continent of Atlantis. See p. 189.

- **Long Island** (The Southern Bahamas): Shallow bays and sandy beaches offer many possibilities for snorkeling, and the staffs at both major resorts will direct you to the finest conditions near their stretches of beach. The southern end of the island is especially dramatic because of its unique sea cliffs. Many east-coast beach coves also offer fantastic snorkeling opportunities. See p. 293.

- **Elbow Cay:** With its 209km (130-mile) string of beautiful cays and some of the best beaches in The Bahamas, the Abacos are ideal for snorkeling, especially in the waters off Elbow Cay. Visibility is often

great because the cay lies close to the cleansing waters of the Gulf Stream. Mermaid Beach, a particularly colorful reef, is a favorite. **Froggie's Out Island Adventures** (© 242/366-0431; www.froggiesabaco.com) provides equipment and the best snorkeling advice. See p. 220.

- **Stocking Island:** George Town is the capital of the Exumas, which is celebrated for its crystal clear waters so beloved by yachties. From George Town, Stocking Island lies across Elizabeth Harbour, which is only 1.6 km (1 mile) away. Stocking Island is a long, thin barrier island that attracts snorkelers who explore its blue holes (ocean pools of fresh water floating on heavier saltwater). The island is also ringed with undersea caves and coral gardens in stunning colors. You'll find that Stocking Island has some of the most gorgeous beaches in the Southern Bahamas. See p. 272.

- **San Salvador:** Following in the wake of Columbus, snorkelers find a rich paradise on this relatively undiscovered island, with its unspoiled and unpopulated kilometers of beaches that are ideal for swimming, shelling, and close-in snorkeling. A week's stay is enough time to become acquainted with only some of the possibilities, including Bamboo Point, Fernandez Bay, and Long Bay, which are all within a few kilometers of Cockburn (the main settlement) on the western side of the island. At the southern tip of San Salvador are some of our favorite places for snorkeling, Sandy Point and nearby Grotto Bay. See chapter 10.

4 The Best Fishing

- **New Providence:** The waters around New Providence teem with game fish. In-the-know fishermen long ago

learned the best months to pursue their catch: November to February for wahoo found in the reefs, June and July for blue marlin, and May to August for the oceanic bonito and blackfin tuna. Nassau is ideal for sportfishing. Most boat charters allow their passengers to start fishing within 15 minutes after leaving the dock. The best outfitter is **Born Free Charters** (© 242/393-4144); anchoring and bottom-fishing are also options. See p. 99.

- **Grand Bahama:** The tropical waters along Grand Bahama lure anglers in search of "the big one" because the island is home to some of the biggest game fish on earth. Off the coast, the clear waters are good hunting grounds for snapper, grouper, yellowtail, wahoo, barracuda, and kingfish. Many fishermen catch dolphin (we mean the mahimahi kind, not Flipper). And Deep Water Cay is a fishing hot spot. The best outfitter is **Reef Tours, Ltd.** (© 242/373-5880). See p. 171.

- **Green Turtle Cay:** The deep-sea fishing possibilities off the coast of this cay draw anglers from all over the world. An abundance of giant game fish as well as tropical fish live in these beautiful waters. Both dedicated fisherman and more casual anglers come to the little island seeking yellowfin tuna, a few dolphinfish, and the big-game wahoo, among other catches. Green Turtle Cay boasts some of the best fishing guides

in The Bahamas, weather-beaten men who've spent a lifetime fishing the surrounding waters. The best place to hook up with one of these guides is **Green Turtle Club** (© 242/365-4070). See p. 229.

- **Treasure Cay:** In the Abacos, some of the best fishing grounds are in the sea bordering this remote island. At the **Treasure Cay Marina** (© 242/365-8250), fishermen from all over the world hire experienced skippers to take them out in their search for barracuda, grouper, yellowtail, snapper, tuna, marlin, dolphinfish, and wahoo. Deep-sea, bottom-, and drift fishing are yours for the asking. The cay's own bonefish flats are just a short boat cruise from the marina. See p. 226.

- **The Exumas:** Anglers from all over America descend on this beautiful archipelago for deep-sea fishing or bottom-fishing. Fishermen hunt for kingfish, wahoo, dolphinfish, tuna, and bonito in the deepest waters off the coastline of the Exumas. Many visitors also fly here just to go bonefishing. Among other outfitters who can hook you up with fishing outings is **Club Peace & Plenty** (© 800/525-2210 or 242/336-2551), which rents the necessary equipment and can arrange experienced guides to accompany you. See p. 267.

5 The Best Sailing

- **Marsh Harbour and Hope Town** (the Abacos): Known among yachties for their many anchorages, sheltered coves, and plentiful marine facilities, the Abacos are considered one of the most perfect sailing areas in the world. You can charter boats of all shapes and sizes for a week or longer, with or

without a crew. See "The Active Vacation Planner" in chapter 2, and p. 212 in chapter 7.

- **The Exumas:** Yachties head to these beautiful sailing waters to see some of the most dramatic coastal scenery in The Bahamas. **The Family Island Regatta,** the most popular boating spectacle in The Bahamas, is held here annually. Most of the recreational boating is in the government-protected **Exumas Cays Land and Sea Park,** an area of splendid sea gardens and rainbow-hued coral reefs that stretches south from Wax Cay to Conch Cay. You can rent motorboats at **Minns Water Sports** (© **242/336-3483**) in George Town. See p. 271.

- **New Providence Island:** Although sailing in the waters off New Providence Island isn't the equal of those yachting favorites the Exumas and the Abacos, boaters can still find many delights. More organized boating excursions are offered in New Providence than anywhere else in The Bahamas, especially by outfitters such as **Barefoot Sailing Cruises** (© **242/393-0820;** www.barefoot sailingcruises.com) and **Majestic Tours Ltd.** (© **242/322-2606**). You can also choose from an array of sunset cruises, such as the ones Flying Cloud (© **242/363-4430**) features aboard its fleet of catamarans. The most popular—and the most scenic—trip is sailing to tranquil **Rose Island,** which is 13km (8 miles) east of the center of Nassau and is reached after sailing past several small uninhabited cays. In addition, **Blue Lagoon Island,** 4.8 km (3 miles) northeast of Paradise Island, is a magnet for boaters, offering seven white sandy beaches along with seaside hammocks. The drawback to this

island, however, is that cruise-ship passengers flock here and many beach buffs like to come over on day trips. See p. 70.

- **Grand Bahama Island:** On the beautiful waters off this large island, you can go sailing aboard *Ocean Wonder* (© **242/373-5880**), which is supposedly the world's largest twin-diesel engine glass-bottom boat. This vessel offers the best and most panoramic picture of underwater life off the coast of Grand Bahama Island—a view most often reserved for scuba divers. You can also go sailing aboard *Bahama Mama,* a two-deck 22m (72-ft.) catamaran, on a Robinson Crusoe Beach Party. The catamaran also sails at sunset on a booze cruise. **Superior Watersports** (© **242/373-7863;** www.superior watersports.com) operates this catamaran. See p. 169.

- **Marsh Harbour:** One of the finest anchorages in the Out Islands is found in Marsh Harbour, which is called "The Boating Capital of The Bahamas." **The Moorings** (© **888/952-8420** or 242/367-4000; www. moorings.com) is one of the leading charter sailboat outfitters in the world and rents boats to sail the waters of the Abacos. Passengers discover white-sand beaches and snug anchorages on uninhabited cays. Sailing here is one of the great experiences of visiting The Bahamas. See p. 213.

6 The Best Golf Courses

- **Cable Beach:** The main draw is the **Cable Beach Golf Course** (© **242/327-1741**). The oldest golf course in The Bahamas, this par-72 green was the private retreat of British expatriates in the 1930s. Today it's managed by a corporate namesake of Arnold

Palmer and owned by Cable Beach casino marketers. Small ponds and water traps heighten the challenge, amid more than 7,040 yards of well-maintained greens and fairways. See "The Active Vacation Planner," in chapter 2, and p. 52.

- **Paradise Island:** Tom Weiskopf designed **Ocean Club Golf Club** (© **242/363-3000;** www.oneandonly resorts.com), an 18-hole, par-72 course, and it's a stunner. With challenges that include the world's largest sand trap and water hazards (mainly the Atlantic Ocean) on three sides, the course has received praise from Jack Nicklaus and Gary Player. For the best panoramic ocean view—good enough to take your mind off your game—play the par-3 14th hole. See "The Active Vacation Planner," in chapter 2, and p. 52.

- **Grand Lucaya, Grand Bahama Island:** Designed by Robert Trent Jones, Jr., **The Reef Course** (© **242/ 373-1333**) opened in 2000. The Bahamian press called it a bit like a Scottish course, "but a lot warmer." The course boasts 6,920 yards of links-style greens. See p. 171.

- **The Exumas:** At long last, the Southern Bahamas has a world-class golf course: **Four Seasons Resort Emerald Bay Golf Club** opens onto the waters of Emerald Bay (© **242/366-6800**). The par-72, 18-hole course was designed by Greg Norman, who created six oceanfront holes. The course is challenging yet not daunting, so it appeals to golfers of various skills. See p. 271.

7 The Best Tennis Facilities

- **Paradise Island:** Well-heeled tennis buffs check into the **One&Only Ocean Club** (© **242/363-2501;** www.oneandonlyresorts.com). Many visitors go there just for tennis, which can be played day or night on their six Har-Tru courts. Guests booked into the cabanas and villas of the club can practically roll out of bed onto the courts. Although beginners and intermediate players are welcome, the courts are often filled with first-class competitors. Tennis is free for guests of the One&Only Ocean Club. The tennis complex at the **Atlantis**

(© 242/363-3000; www.atlantis.com) is more accessible to the general public, with 10 courts (6 regular asphalt and 4 hydro quartz), some lit for night games. See p. 139.

- **Freeport** (Grand Bahama Island): Freeport is another top choice for tennis buffs. The best tennis courts on the island are at the **Ace Tennis Center** at the **Westin & Sheraton at Our Lucaya Resorts,** Royal Palm Way (© **242/373-1333**), with four courts, including one that's grass. See p. 173.

8 The Best Honeymoon Resorts

- **Sandals Royal Bahamian Hotel & Spa** (Cable Beach, New Providence Island; © **800/SANDALS** or 242/ 327-6400; www.sandals.com): This Jamaican chain of couples-only, all-inclusive hotels is a honeymooners' favorite. The Bahamas' branch of the chain is more upscale than many of its Jamaican counterparts, and it offers 27 secluded honeymoon suites with semiprivate plunge pools. Staff

members lend their experience and talent to on-site wedding celebrations; Sandals will provide everything from a preacher to flowers, as well as champagne and a cake. It's more expensive than most Sandals resorts, but you can usually get better prices than the official "rack rates" through a travel agent or a package deal. See p. 83.

Eco-Tourism Highlights of The Bahamas

The Bahamas spreads over 258,998 sq. km (101,009 sq. miles) of the Atlantic Ocean. The largest oceanic archipelago nation in the tropical Atlantic Ocean, it offers miles of crystal-clear waters rich with fish and other marine resources. Its natural attractions include a series of underwater reefs that stretch 1,224km (759 miles) from the Abacos in the northeast to Long Island in the southeast. It has the most extensive systems of blue holes and limestone caves in the world.

And, unlike Puerto Rico, Jamaica, Barbados, and other Caribbean island nations, The Bahamas possesses large areas of undeveloped natural mainland. It all adds up to plenty of opportunity for getting up close and personal with nature.

Start with the reefs. Lying off the coast of Andros, The Bahamas includes approximately 2,330 sq. km (909 sq. miles) of coral reef, comprising the third-largest barrier reef system in the world. Rich with diverse marine life, the reef attracts green moray eels, cinnamon clownfish, and Nassau grouper. When officials realized that long-line fishing threatened this fragile ecology, The Bahamas became one of the first Caribbean countries to outlaw the practice.

The nation's Parliament also passed the Wild Birds Protection Act to ensure preservation of rare bird species. That law has made a big difference: Great Inagua Island now shelters more than 60,000 pink flamingos, Bahamian parrots, and a large portion of the world's population of reddish egrets. These birds live in the government-protected 743 sq.-km (290-sq. mile) Inagua National Park.

And that's not all. The islands of The Bahamas are home to more than 1,370 species of plants, plus 13 species of mammals; the majority of them, it must be said, are bats, but wild pigs, donkeys, raccoons, and the Abaco wild horse also roam the interiors of the nation's islands. You'll see whales and dolphins, including humpback and blue whales and the spotted dolphin, swimming in the sea.

To keep an eye on all this natural wealth and share it with the public, the **Bahamas National Trust** administers 25 national parks and more than 283,279 hectares (699,699 acres) of protected land.

- **One&Only Ocean Club** (Paradise Island; © **800/321-3000** in the U.S. only, or 242/363-2501; www.oneand onlyresorts.com): It's elegant, low-key, and low-rise, and it feels exclusive. The guests include many older honeymoon couples. With waterfalls, fountains, reflecting pools, and a stone gazebo, the Ocean Club's formal terraced gardens were inspired by the club's founder (an heir to the A&P fortune) and are the most impressive in The Bahamas. At the center is a French cloister, with carvings from the 12th century. See p. 127.

- **Old Bahama Bay** (Grand Bahama Island; © **800/444-9469** or 242/ 350-3500; www.oldbahamabay.com): Perfect for honeymooners seeking a quiet hideaway in a boutique-style hotel with cottages adjacent to a marina. The casinos, entertainment, shopping, and dining of Freeport/Lucaya are 40km (25 miles) away, but here you can sneak away for luxury, solitude, and romance. See p. 158.

- **Kamalame Cay** (Staniard Creek, Andros; © **242/368-6281;** www.kamalame.com): You'll need deep pockets to afford one of the most exclusive resorts in the Out Islands, a perfect honeymoon retreat for the couple who wants to escape casinos and resorts. With its 5km (3 miles) of white-sand beaches in both directions, this pocket of posh specializes in luxury and comfort. And don't worry if you've already taken your honeymoon; this is the perfect place to take a second one, or even a third. See p. 197.

- **Green Turtle Club** (Green Turtle Cay, the Abacos; © **242/365-4271;** www.greenturtleclub.com): Romantics appreciate this resort's winning combination of yachting atmosphere and well-manicured comfort. It's small (31 rooms) and civilized in an understated way; the charming, clapboard-covered village of New Plymouth is nearby, accessible by motor launch or, even better, a 45-minute walk across windswept scrublands. See p. 229.

- **Abaco Inn** (Elbow Cay, The Abacos; © **800/468-8799** or 242/366-0133; www.abacoinn.com): For barefoot elegance and romance in the sands, this sophisticated little hideaway is one of the gems of the yachting haven known as the Abacos. Luxury villa suites with sunrise and sunset views are the way to go. You and your loved one should seek out a hammock in the gardens. See p. 216.

- **The Bluff House Beach Hotel** (Green Turtle Cay, the Abacos; © **800/745-4911** or 242/365-4247; www.bluffhouse.com): This place was named because of its location atop a 24m (79-ft.) cliff towering over a pink-sand beach. Its 4.8 hectares (12 acres) front the Sea of Abaco on one side and the harbor of White Sound on the other. The accommodations are very private, with a rustic, seafaring decor that has its own elegance. In addition to rooms, the hotel offers beach and hillside villas, and colonial suites with private balconies that overlook the water. See p. 228.

- **Pink Sands** (Harbour Island, Eleuthera; © **800/OUTPOST** or 242/333-2030; www.pinksandsresort.com): You can have a spectacular getaway at this elite retreat on an 11-hectare (27-acre) beachfront estate owned by Chris Blackwell, the founder of Island Records. Its location on a 5km (3-mile) stretch of private pink sand, sheltered by a barrier reef, is just one of its assets. You can ask for a bedroom that evokes an upscale bordello in Shanghai to put you in a romantic mood, and you can also enjoy the best meals on the island. See p. 251.

- **Stella Maris Resort Club** (Long Island, the Southern Bahamas; © **800/426-0466,** 242/338-2051, or 954/359-8238; www.stellamarisresort.com): Right on the Atlantic, built on the grounds of an old plantation, Stella Maris has become a social hub on Long Island. Sailing is important here, as are diving and getting away from it all. Many of the guests hail from Germany, and they lend the place a European flair. The sleepy island itself is one of the most beautiful in The Bahamas, and honeymooners fit into the grand scheme of things perfectly. See p. 293.

9 The Best Family Vacations

- **Sheraton Cable Beach Hotel** (Cable Beach, New Providence Island; ✆ **800/325-3535** or 242/327-6000; www.sheraton.com): A family could spend their entire vacation on the grounds of this vast resort. There's a pool area that features the most lavish artificial waterfall this side of Tahiti; a health club at the nearby Crystal Palace that welcomes both guests and their children; Camp Junkanoo, with supervised play for children 3 through 12; and a long list of in-house activities that includes dancing lessons. Major changes and redevelopment are planned for this resort. See p. 84.

- **Atlantis Paradise Island Resort & Casino** (Paradise Island; ✆ **800/ATLANTIS** in the U.S., or 242/363-3000; www.atlantis.com): This is one of the largest hotel complexes in the world, with endless rows of shops and watersports galore. Both children and adults will enjoy the 5.6-hectare (14-acre) sea world with waterslides, a lagoon for watersports, white sandy beaches, and underground grottoes, plus an underwater viewing tunnel and 240m (787 ft.) of cascading waterfalls. Its children's menus and innovative, creative children's

programs are the best in The Bahamas and perhaps even in the Caribbean. See p. 122.

- **Best Western Castaways Resort & Suites** (Grand Bahama Island; ✆ **800/780-7234** in the U.S., or 242/352-6682; www.bestwestern.com): Here's a good choice for families on a budget. The pagoda-capped lobby is set a very short walk from the ice-cream stands, souvenir shops, and fountains of the International Bazaar. Children under 12 stay free in their parent's room, and the in-house lounge presents limbo and fire-eating shows several evenings a month. The hotel offers a babysitting service and a free shuttle to Williams Town Beach. See p. 149.

- **Regatta Point** (George Town, Great Exuma; ✆ **800/688-0309** in the U.S. or 242/336-2206; www.regattapointbahamas.com): This resort offers efficiency apartments at moderate prices. On a palm-grove cay, it is family friendly, with its own little beach. Bikes are available, and Sunfish boats can be rented. There's also a grocery store nearby where you can pick up supplies. Many units are suitable for families of four or five. See p. 268.

10 The Best Places to Get Away from It All

- **Green Turtle Club** (Green Turtle Cay, the Abacos; ✆ **242/365-4271**; www.greenturtleclub.com): Secluded and private, this sailing retreat consists of tasteful one- to three-bedroom villas with full kitchens. It opens onto a small private beach with a 35-slip marina, which is one of the most complete yachting facilities in the archipelago. Many rooms open poolside, and there's a dining room

decorated in Queen Anne style. See p. 229.

- **Rock House Hotel** (Harbour Island, off the coast of Eleuthera; ✆ **242/333-2053**; www.rockhousebahamas.com): A glamorous and stylish inn—really, a glorified B&B—this posh little hideaway is drawing more and more of the glitterati to its shores. Set on a low bluff above the harbor, it is tranquillity itself with whimsically decorated bedrooms. No one will find you if you decide to hide out here. See p. 252.

- **Club Med–Columbus Isle** (San Salvador, the Southern Bahamas; © **800/CLUB-MED** or 242/331-2000; www.clubmed.com): This was the first large resort to be built on one of The Bahamas' most isolated islands, site of Columbus's first landfall in the New World. It's unusually luxurious, and unusually isolated, for a Club Med, and it occupies a gorgeous beach. The sheer difficulty of reaching it adds to the get-away-from-it-all mystique. See p. 286.

- **Fernandez Bay Village** (Cat Island, the Southern Bahamas; © **800/940-1905** or 242/342-2018 or 954/474-4821; www.fernandezbayvillage.com): The dozen stone and timber villas of Fernandez Bay Village are the closest thing to urban congestion Cat Island ever sees. There's a funky, thatch-roofed beach bar that'll make you feel like you're in the South Pacific—a great place to enjoy a cold beer each afternoon after you leave the stunning sands and turquoise waters behind for the day. There's only one phone at the entire resort, and your bathroom shower will probably open to a view of the sky. See p. 282.

11 The Best Restaurants

- **Sun and . . .** (Nassau, New Providence Island; © **242/393-1205**) has made a comeback after being closed for many years. Once again, it is the leading independent choice on New Providence Island, serving a finely honed international cuisine. It's a throwback to Nassau in its grand heyday. Originally built in the 1930s as a private residence, it lies in an upscale residential neighborhood east of the center of Nassau. See p. 88.

- **Moso** (in the Wyndham Nassau Resort, Cable Beach, New Providence Island; © **242/327-6200**) is the best Asian restaurant on island. A well-trained staff here has learned the secrets of the cuisines of the Far East, and they dispense an array of some of the best-known and tastiest dishes, including teriyaki specialties. See p. 94.

- **Nobu** (the Atlantis Paradise Island Resort's Royal Towers, Paradise Island; © **242/363-3000**) brings a member of this celebrated chain to The Bahamas. It's the most-talked-about and arguably the best restaurant on island, attracting a string of

celebrities. The setting is glamorous, and the cuisine is top rated, prepared with either market-fresh ingredients or exotic ingredients shipped in. See p. 134.

- **Dune** (in the One&Only Ocean Club, Paradise Island; © **242/363-2501**, ext. 64739): The most cutting-edge restaurant in either Paradise Island or Nassau, Dune is the creation of French-born restaurant guru Jean-Georges Vongerichten, the moving force behind several of New York City's top dining spots. Every dish served here is something special—from shrimp dusted with orange powder to chicken and coconut milk soup with shiitake cakes. See p. 133.

- **Bahamian Club** (Paradise Island; © **242/363-3000**): A notch down from the superb Dune, this establishment is one of the leading restaurants in The Bahamas and our favorite at the sprawling megaresort of Atlantis. Strictly upscale, it presents superb French and international cuisine against a backdrop that evokes the British Colonial era. The restaurant serves the island's finest cuts of meats. See p. 131.

- **Mangoes Restaurant** (Marsh Harbour, the Abacos; ✆ **242/367-2957**): For the best and most authentic Bahamian food in the Abaco chain, head for this welcoming spot, where both visiting yachties and locals flock for the fine cuisine. Order up a conch burger for lunch, then return in the evening for the catch of the day— straight from the sea and grilled to your specifications. The namesake mango sauce really dresses up a plate of grilled pork tenderloin. See p. 211.

- **The Landing** (Harbour Island, Eleuthera; ✆ **242/333-2707**; www. harbourislandlanding.com): This attractive restaurant at the ferry dock has awakened the sleepy taste buds of Eleuthera. Brenda Barry and daughter Tracy feed you well from a choice of international cuisines, often prepared from recipes gathered during world travels. Under mature trees in their garden, you feast on delicious pasta dishes, freshly made gazpacho, pan-fried grouper, or a warm duck salad. See p. 254.

- **Rock House Restaurant** (Harbour Island, Eleuthera; ✆ **242/333-2053**; www.rockhousebahamas.com): On the increasingly chic Harbour Island, the restaurant in the Rock House Hotel serves a superb international cuisine. Its hip bodega aura evokes Miami, but it's thoroughly grounded on the island. At lunch you can get a rock lobster sandwich, but at night the chefs display their culinary prowess with an array of satisfying dishes. See p. 255.

12 The Best Nightlife

- **Cable Beach:** Cable Beach has a lot more splash and excitement than Nassau, its neighbor on New Providence Island, and wandering around Cable Beach is also much safer than exploring the back streets of Nassau at night. The main attraction is the **Wyndham Nassau Resort & Crystal Palace Casino** (✆ **242/327-6200**; www.wyndhamnassauresort.com), with an 800-seat theater known for staging glitzy extravaganzas and a gaming room that will make you think you're smack dab in the middle of Vegas. One of the largest casinos on the islands, the Crystal Palace features 750 slot machines, 51 blackjack tables, nine roulette wheels, seven craps tables, and a baccarat table (we think the Paradise Island casino has more class, though). Despite all the glitter, you can still find cozy bars and nooks throughout the resort, if you'd prefer a tranquil evening. See p. 118.

- **Atlantis Paradise Island Resort's Casino and Discothèque:** Paradise Island has the flashiest nightlife in all of The Bahamas, hands down. Not even nearby Nassau and Cable Beach can come close. Nearly all of the action takes place at the incredible **Atlantis Paradise Island Resort & Casino** (✆ **242/363-3000**; www.atlantis. com), where you'll find high rollers from Vegas and Atlantic City alongside grandmothers from Iowa who play the slot machines when the family isn't looking. It's all gloss, glitter, and showbiz, with good gambling (though savvy locals say your odds of beating the house are better in Vegas). For a quieter night out, you can also find intimate bars, discos, a comedy club, and lots more in this sprawling behemoth of a hotel. See p. 141.

- **Grand Bahama Island:** If you want to gamble, and gamble seriously, head for either Cable Beach outside Nassau or Paradise Island. There is also gambling at Lucaya on Grand Bahama Island, but it's less elaborate. The action takes place at the **Isle of Capri,** at the Westin & Sheraton at Our Lucaya Resorts, Royal Palm Way (© **242/ 373-1333**). The facility also contains a bar and restaurant. See p. 178.

2

Planning Your Trip to The Bahamas

You can be in The Bahamas after a quick 35-minute jet hop from Miami. And it's never been easier to take advantage of great package deals that can make these islands a terrific value.

1 The Islands in Brief

The Bahamian chain of islands, cays, and reefs stretches from Grand Bahama Island, 121km (75 miles) almost due east of Palm Beach, Florida, to Great Inagua, the southernmost island, which lies 97km (60 miles) northeast of Cuba and fewer than 161km (100 miles) north of Haiti.

The most developed islands for tourism in The Bahamas are **New Providence Island,** site of Nassau (the capital) and Cable Beach; **Paradise Island;** and **Grand Bahama,** home of Freeport and Lucaya. If you're after glitz, gambling, bustling restaurants, nightclubs, and a beach-party scene, these big three islands are where you'll want to be. Package deals are easily found here.

Set sail (or hop on a short commuter flight) for one of the **Out Islands,** such as Andros, the Exumas, or the Abacos, and you'll find fewer crowds—and often lower prices, too. Though some of the Out Islands are accessible mainly (or only) by boat, it's still worth your while to make the trip if you like the idea of having an entire beach to yourself. This is really the place to get away from it all.

NEW PROVIDENCE ISLAND (NASSAU/CABLE BEACH) New Providence isn't the largest of the Bahamian Islands, but it's the historic heart of the nation, with a strong maritime tradition and the largest population in the country. Home to more than 125,000 residents, it offers groves of palms and casuarinas; sandy, flat soil; the closest thing in The Bahamas to urban sprawl; and superb anchorages sheltered from rough seas by the presence of nearby Paradise Island. New Providence has the country's busiest airport and is dotted with hundreds of villas owned by foreign investors. Its two major resort areas are Cable Beach and Nassau.

The resort area of **Cable Beach** is a glittering beachfront strip of hotels, restaurants, and casinos; only Paradise Island has been more developed. Its center is the Marriott Resort & Crystal Palace Casino. Often, deciding between Cable Beach and Paradise Island isn't so much a choice of which island you prefer as a choice of which hotel you prefer. But it's easy to sample both, since it takes only about 30 minutes to drive between the two.

Nassau, the Bahamian capital, isn't on a great stretch of shoreline and doesn't have as many first-rate hotels as either Paradise Island or Cable Beach—with the exception of the British Colonial Hilton, which has a small private beach. The main advantages of Nassau are colonial charm and price. Its hotels may not be ideally located, but they are relatively inexpensive; some offer very low prices even during the winter high season. You can base yourself here and commute easily to the beaches at Paradise Island or Cable Beach. Some travelers even prefer Nassau because it's the seat of Bahamian culture and history—not to mention the shopping mecca of The Bahamas.

PARADISE ISLAND If high-rise hotels and glittering casinos are what you want, along with some of the best beaches in The Bahamas, there is no better choice than Paradise Island, directly off the coast of Nassau. It has the best food, the best entertainment, terrific beaches, casinos, and the best hotels. Its major drawbacks are that it's expensive and often overcrowded. Boasting a colorful history yet some unremarkable architecture, Paradise Island remains one of the most intensely marketed pieces of real estate in the world. The sands and shoals of the elongated and narrow island protect the wharves and piers of Nassau, which rise across a narrow channel only 180m (590 ft.) away.

Owners of the 277-hectare (684-acre) island have included brokerage mogul Joseph Lynch (of Merrill Lynch) and Huntington Hartford (heir to the A&P supermarket fortune). More recent investors have included Merv Griffin. The island today is a carefully landscaped residential and commercial complex with good beaches, lots of glitter (some of it tasteful, some of it way too over-the-top), and many diversions.

GRAND BAHAMA ISLAND (FREE-PORT/LUCAYA) The island's name derives from the Spanish term *gran baja-mar* (great shallows), which refers to the shallow reefs and sandbars that, over the centuries, have destroyed everything from Spanish galleons to English clipper ships on Grand Bahama's shores. Thanks to the tourist development schemes of U.S. financiers such as Howard Hughes, Grand Bahama boasts a well-developed tourist infrastructure. Casinos, beaches, and restaurants are now plentiful here.

Grand Bahama's **Freeport/Lucaya** resort area is another popular destination for American tourists, though it has a lot more tacky development than Paradise Island or Cable Beach. The compensation for that is a lower price tag on just about everything. Freeport/Lucaya offers plenty of opportunities for fine dining, entertainment, and gambling. Grand Bahama also offers the best hiking in The Bahamas and has some of the finest sandy beaches. Its golf courses attract players from all over the globe, and the island hosts major tournaments several times a year. You'll find some of the world's best diving here, as well as UNEXSO, the internationally famous diving school. Grand Bahama Island is especially popular with families.

BIMINI One of the smallest islands in The Bahamas, it's close enough to Miami (just 81km/50 miles away) to be distinctly separate from the other islands of the archipelago. Bimini is actually a pair of islands with a total area of 23 sq. km (9 sq. miles); smaller North Bimini is better developed than South Bimini. Luxurious yachts and fishing boats are always docked at the island's marinas. Throughout Bimini, there's a slightly run-down Florida-resort atmosphere mingled with some small-town charm (think old-time Key West, before the cruise-ship crowds ruined it).

Sportfishing here is among the best in the world. Once the setting for Ernest Hemingway's *Islands in the Stream* (see below), Bimini attracts big-game fishers for big-league fishing tournaments. If you'd like to follow in the footsteps of such famous anglers as Zane Grey and Howard Hughes, this is your island. In addition, the scuba diving ranks among the very best in The Bahamas.

(Fun Fact **Hemingway in Bimini**

One of the oddest pieces of real estate in the Atlantic—less than a few hundred feet wide in many places, with a surface area of only 23 sq. km (9 sq. miles)—Bimini has always floated like a magic lure, only 81km (50 miles) from some of the most crowded seashores in the United States. During the 1930s, it was famous as an alter ego to Key West. Soaked with liquor during U.S. Prohibition (Bimini served as a depot for outlawed contraband) and widely known today as a storage depot for illegal drugs, the place has always found itself bathed in controversy. Thanks to novelist Ernest Hemingway, its raunchy, no-holds-barred lifestyle became infamous throughout North America.

Hemingway's first boat (the *Pilar*) was a diesel-powered tub he skippered with fellow writer John Dos Passos for the express purpose of reaching Bimini. One of the bloodiest of his many self-destructive acts occurred off the coast of Bimini when, struggling to aim a revolver at the thrashing jaws of a captured mako shark, he accidentally shot himself in both legs. But don't let that fool you: Hemingway did some serious and successful fishing here. Among the most impressive catches of his life were a 356kg (785-lb.) mako and a 233 kg (514-lb.) tuna, both hauled in off the coast of Bimini.

Some of Hemingway's most famous fistfights happened on Bimini, too— one with wealthy publisher Joseph Knapp, others with a series of black contenders who stood to earn $250 if they could stay in the ring with him for three 3-minute rounds. (No one ever collected the money.)

Hemingway revised the manuscript of *To Have and Have Not* on Bimini in 1937. His evocative description of the seaport in *Islands in the Stream* was Alice Town, Bimini's still-seedy capital.

THE BERRY ISLANDS Lying between Nassau and the coast of Florida, these 30-odd islands—which contain only about 77 sq. km (30 sq. miles) of dry land among them—attract devoted yachters and fishermen. This series of islets, cays, and rows of barely submerged rocks have extremely limited tourist facilities and are geared mostly toward well-heeled anglers, many of whom hail from Florida. Most of the full-time population (about 700 people) lives on Great Harbour. We find these islands a lot classier and more charming than Bimini.

ANDROS Made up of two islands, connected by a series of canals and cays called *bights*, Andros is the largest landmass in The Bahamas. It attracts divers, fishing enthusiasts, and sightseers.

Most of the island is uninhabited and unexplored. The main villages are Nicholl's Town, Andros Town, and Congo Town; all are accessible by frequent boat and plane connections from Miami and Nassau. Lodgings range from large resorts to small, plain guesthouses that cater mainly to fishermen.

The world's third-largest barrier reef lies off the coast of Andros, and divers come from all over the world to explore it. The reef plunges 1,800m (5,904 ft.) at a narrow drop-off known as the Tongue of the Ocean. Bonefishing here is among the best on earth, and Andros is also known for its world-class marlin and bluefin tuna fishing.

Known as the "Big Yard," the central portion of Northern Andros is largely a dense forest of mahogany and pine where more than 50 varieties of orchids bloom. Southern Andros boasts a 103-sq.-km (40-sq.-mile) forest and mangrove swamp. Any hotel can arrange a local guide to give a tour.

THE ABACOS   Though this "island" is often called Abaco, it is actually a cluster of islands and islets. It is a mecca for yachters and other boaters who flock here year-round—particularly in July, when the Regatta Time in Abaco race is held at the Green Turtle Yacht Club. For centuries the residents of the Abacos have been boat builders, although tourism is now the main industry.

With the exception of Harbour Island in Eleuthera, you'll find more New England charm here than anywhere else in The Bahamas. Loyalists who left New England after the American Revolution settled here and built Cape Cod–style clapboard houses with white picket fences. The best places to experience this old-fashioned charm are Green Turtle Cay and Elbow Cay, which are accessible from Marsh Harbour. Marsh Harbour itself houses an international airport and a shopping center, although its hotels aren't as good as those on Green Turtle Cay and Elbow Cay (Hope Town).

Many of the Abaco islands are undeveloped and uninhabited. For the best of both worlds, visitors can stay at resorts on Walker's, Green Turtle, or Treasure cays, and then charter a boat to tour the more remote areas.

ELEUTHERA   Long and slender, this most historic of the Out Islands (the first English settlers arrived here in 1648) is actually a string of islands that includes Spanish Wells and Harbour Island, a chic destination. The length of the island

(177km/110 miles) and the distances between Eleuthera's communities require access via three airports. The island lies about 97 km (60 miles) west of Nassau; frequent flights connect the two. Eleuthera is similar to Abaco, and visitors are drawn to the miles of barrier reef and fabulous secluded beaches.

Gregory Town is the pineapple capital of the island chain. A bit farther south is Surfers Beach, one of the best surfing spots in The Bahamas. Several accommodations are available in this sleepy, slightly budget-oriented section of Eleuthera. The only major resort along the entire stretch of Eleuthera is the Club Med at Governor's Harbour. Other inns are more basic.

At the southern end of the island, **Rock Sound** is in a slump, waiting to see whether the fabled Cotton Bay Club will ever reopen.

Off the coast of Eleuthera, **Harbour Island** offers excellent hotels and food, picket fences, and pastel-colored houses that evoke Cape Cod. The beaches on Harbour Island are famed for their pink sand tinged by crushed coral and shells. Another offshore island near Eleuthera, **Spanish Wells** has extremely limited accommodations, and the residents— descendants of long-ago Loyalists—aren't very welcoming to visitors.

THE EXUMAS   Just 56km (35 miles) southeast of Nassau, this 588km-long (365-mile) string of islands and cays— most of them uninhabited—is the great yachting hub of The Bahamas, rivaling (and some say surpassing) the Abacos. These waters, some of the prettiest in The Bahamas, are also ideal for fishing (bonefishing especially). Many secluded beaches open onto tranquil cays. Daily flights service the Exumas from Nassau, Miami, and Atlanta.

This island chain's commercial center is **George Town** on **Great Exuma,** while

Moments **Slow Boat to the Out Islands**

Delivering goats, chickens, hardware, and food staples along with the mail, Bahamian mail boats greatly improve the quality of life for the scattered communities of the Out Islands. You can book passage aboard these vessels to at least 17 different remote islands. All 30 boats leave from Nassau, and the round-trip takes a full day. For more information, consult an office of **The Bahamas Tourist Office** (see "Visitor Information," below) or the dock master at the Nassau piers at © **242/326-9781** or 326-9772. See "Getting Around The Bahamas," later in this chapter, for additional details.

the Exuma National Land and Sea Park—protected by The Bahamas National Trust—encompasses much of the coastline. The park is accessible only by boat and is one of the major natural wonders and sightseeing destinations of The Bahamas, with an abundance of undersea life, reefs, blue holes, and shipwrecks. Portions of the James Bond thriller *Thunderball* were filmed at **Staniel Cay.** Each year in April, George Town hosts the interisland Family Island Regatta, a major event on the yachting calendar. A big new Four Seasons resort and golf course officially opened in the winter of 2004 at **Emerald Bay** in Great Exuma, bringing a new crowd here. The Four Seasons recently added a deep-water marina with 125 state-of-the-art slips for ocean-going yachts, along with a dock master. A few good inns are also on Great Exuma, centered mainly at George Town, and the locals are very hospitable. You'll feel like you practically have the archipelago to yourself.

THE SOUTHERN BAHAMAS This cluster of islands—with excellent beaches, good fishing, and dive sites—is known for its remoteness on the southern fringe of The Bahamas. **Cat Island** is only a few miles wide and 77km (48 miles) long. It's a lush, sleepy island in the southern Bahamian backwater, a great place to get away from it all.

Tradition holds that **San Salvador** was the first landmass that Christopher Columbus reached during his voyage to the New World in 1492. With its history and good beaches, the island is sure to undergo further development.

The appropriately named **Long Island** stretches for 93km (58 miles). Despite a beautiful landscape—there are high cliffs in the north, wide shallow beaches, historic plantation ruins, and native caves—it has remained off the beaten track. It's not always easy to get here; there are two minor airports with arrivals from Nassau, but flights do not occur daily. Both the Stella Maris Resort Club and the luxurious Cape Santa Maria Beach offer fishing and watersports.

Acklins Island and **Crooked Island** are hard to reach, have limited tourist facilities, and appeal to people who want to escape civilization. The clear waters offshore offer good snorkeling and diving, and you'll have the sandy beaches to yourself. These islands are populated by only a mere 1,000 souls; lodging is available on Crooked Island only.

Set very close to the eastern tip of Cuba, **Great Inagua** is the most southerly island of The Bahamas and the third largest in the nation. Pink flamingos thrive here. For the serious bird-watcher, there is no place else like it in the Caribbean. A handful of no-frills inns provide accommodations.

including Australia, Ireland, and New Zealand, should carry a valid passport.

For information on how to get a passport, go to "Passports" in the "Fast Facts: The Bahamas" section of this chapter—the websites listed provide downloadable passport applications as well as the current fees for processing passport applications. For an up-to-date, country-by-country listing of passport requirements around the world, go to the "Foreign Entry Requirement" Web page of the U.S. State Department at **http://travel. state.gov**.

VISAS

The Commonwealth of The Bahamas does not require visas. On entry to The Bahamas, you'll be given an Immigration Card to complete and sign. The card has a carbon copy that you must keep until departure, at which time it must be turned in. You'll also have to pay a departure tax before you can exit the country (see "Taxes," under "Fast Facts: The Bahamas," later in this chapter).

MEDICAL REQUIREMENTS

For information on medical requirements and recommendations, see "Health & Safety," p. 42.

CUSTOMS
WHAT YOU CAN BRING INTO THE BAHAMAS

Bahamian Customs allows you to bring in 200 cigarettes, or 50 cigars, or 1 pound of tobacco, plus 1 quart of spirits (hard liquor). You can also bring in items classified as "personal effects" and all the money you wish.

WHAT YOU CAN TAKE HOME FROM THE BAHAMAS

Visitors leaving Nassau or Freeport/Lucaya for most U.S. destinations clear U.S. Customs & Border Protection before departing The Bahamas. Charter companies can make special arrangements with the Nassau or Freeport flight services and U.S. Customs & Border Protection for preclearance. No further formalities are required upon arrival in the United States once the preclearance has taken place in Nassau or Freeport.

Collect receipts for all purchases you make in The Bahamas. *Note:* If a merchant suggests giving you a false receipt, misstating the value of the goods, beware—the merchant might be an informer to U.S. Customs. You must also declare all gifts received while abroad.

If you purchased an item during an earlier trip abroad, carry proof that you have already paid Customs duty on the item at the time of your previous reentry. To be extra careful, compile a list of expensive carry-on items and ask a U.S. Customs agent to stamp your list at the airport before your departure.

U.S. Citizens

For specifics on what you can bring back and the corresponding fees, download the invaluable free pamphlet *Know Before You Go* online at **www.cbp.gov**. (Click on "Travel" and then click on "Know Before You Go.") Or contact the **U.S. Customs & Border Protection (CBP),** 1300 Pennsylvania Ave., NW, Washington, DC 20229 (© **877/287-8667**), and request the pamphlet.

Canadian Citizens

For a clear summary of Canadian rules, write for the booklet *I Declare,* issued by the **Canada Border Services Agency** (© **800/461-9999** in Canada, or 204/983-3500; **www.cbsa-asfc.gc.ca**).

U.K. Citizens

For information, contact **HM Revenue & Customs** at © **0845/010-9000** (from outside the U.K., 02920/501-261), or consult their website at **www.hmrc. gov.uk**.

Australian Citizens

A helpful brochure available from Australian consulates or Customs offices is *Know Before You Go*. For more information, call the **Australian Customs Service** at © **1300/363-263,** or log on to **www.customs.gov.au**.

New Zealand Citizens

Most questions are answered in a free pamphlet available at New Zealand consulates and Customs offices: *New Zealand Customs Guide for Travellers, Notice no. 4.* For more information, contact **New Zealand Customs Service,** The Customhouse, 17–21 Whitmore St., Box 2218, Wellington (© **04/473-6099** or 0800/428-786; **www.customs.govt.nz**).

4 When to Go

THE WEATHER

The temperature in The Bahamas averages between 75°F and 85°F (24°C–29°C) in both winter and summer, although it can get chilly in the early morning and at night. The Bahamian winter is usually like a perpetual late spring—naturally, the high season for North Americans rushing to escape snow and ice. Summer brings broiling hot sun and humidity. There's a much greater chance of rain during the summer and fall.

THE HURRICANE SEASON

The curse of Bahamian weather, the hurricane season, lasts (officially) from June 1 to November 30. But there is no cause for panic. More tropical cyclones pound the U.S. mainland than The Bahamas. Hurricanes are actually fairly infrequent here, and when one does come, satellite forecasts generally give adequate advance warning so that precautions can be taken.

If you're heading for The Bahamas during the hurricane season, you might want to visit the National Weather Service at www.nws.noaa.gov.

For an online 5-day forecast anytime, check the Weather Channel at www.weather.com (for free!).

THE "SEASON"

In The Bahamas, hotels charge their highest prices during the peak winter period from mid-December to mid-April, when visitors fleeing from cold north winds flock to the islands. Winter is the driest season.

If you plan to visit during the winter, try to make reservations at least 2 to 3 months in advance. At some hotels, it's impossible to book accommodations for Christmas and the month of February without even more lead time.

SAVING MONEY IN THE OFF SEASON

The Bahamas is a year-round destination. The islands' "off season" runs from late spring to late fall, when tolerable temperatures (see "The Weather," above) prevail throughout most of the region. Trade winds ensure comfortable days and nights, even in accommodations without

---

Avoiding Spring Break

Throughout March and into mid-April, it's spring-break season in the Caribbean for vacationing college and high school students. Expect beach parties, sports events, and musical entertainment; if the idea of hundreds of partying fraternity kids doesn't appeal to you, beware. When you make your reservations, ask if your hotel is planning to host any big groups of kids.

Average Temperatures & Rainfall (in.) in The Bahamas

Month	Jan	Feb	Mar	Apr	May	June	July	Aug	Sept	Oct	Nov	Dec
Temp. °F	70	70	72	75	77	80	81	82	81	78	74	71
Temp. °C	21	21	22	24	25	27	27	28	27	26	23	22
Rainfall (in.)	1.9	1.6	1.4	1.9	4.8	9.2	6.1	6.3	7.5	8.3	2.3	1.5

Note that these numbers are daily averages, so expect temperatures to climb significantly higher in the noonday sun and to cool off a good deal in the evening.

air-conditioning. Although the noonday sun may raise temperatures to uncomfortable levels, cool breezes usually make the morning, late afternoon, and evening more pleasant here than in many parts of the U.S. mainland.

Dollar for dollar, you'll spend less money by renting a summer house or fully equipped unit in The Bahamas than you would on Cape Cod, Fire Island, Laguna Beach, or the coast of Maine.

The off season—roughly from mid-April to mid-December (rate schedules vary from hotel to hotel)—amounts to a summer sale. In most cases, hotel rates are slashed from 20% to a startling 60%. It's a bonanza for cost-conscious travelers, especially families who like to go on vacations together. In the chapters ahead, we'll spell out in dollars the specific amounts hotels charge during the off season.

OTHER OFF-SEASON ADVANTAGES

Although The Bahamas may appear inviting in the winter to those who live in northern climates, your trip may be more enjoyable if you go in the off season. Here's why:

- After the winter hordes have left, a less-hurried way of life prevails.
- Swimming pools and beaches are less crowded—perhaps not crowded at all.
- To survive, resort boutiques often feature summer sales.
- You can often appear without a reservation at a top restaurant and get a table for dinner.

- The endless waiting game is over: no waiting for a rented car, no long wait for a golf course tee time, and quicker access to tennis courts and watersports.
- The atmosphere is more cosmopolitan than it is in winter, mainly because of the influx of Europeans.
- Some package-tour fares are as much as 20% lower, and individual excursion fares may be reduced from 5% to 10%.
- Accommodations and flights are much easier to book.
- Summer is an excellent time for family travel, which is not always possible during the winter season.
- Finally, the best Bahamian attractions—sea, sand, surf, and lots of sunshine—remain absolutely undiminished.

OFF-SEASON DISADVANTAGES

Let's not paint too rosy a picture. Although the advantages of off-season travel far outweigh the disadvantages, there are nevertheless some drawbacks to traveling here in summer:

- You might be staying at a construction site. Hoteliers save their major renovations until the off season. You may wake up to the sound of hammers.
- Single tourists find the dating scene better in winter when there are more visitors, especially unattached ones.
- Services are often reduced. In the peak of winter, everything is fully operational. But in summer, many programs (such as watersports) might be curtailed in spite of fine weather.

THE BAHAMAS CALENDAR OF EVENTS

For specific events, you can call your nearest branch of **The Bahamas Tourist Office** (see "Visitor Information," earlier in this chapter) at ℂ **800/BAHAMAS** or check their website at **www.bahamas.com**.

January

Junkanoo. This Mardi Gras–style festival begins 2 or 3 hours before dawn on New Year's Day. Throngs of cavorting, costumed figures prance through Nassau, Freeport/Lucaya, and the Out Islands. Jubilant men, women, and children wear elaborate headdresses and festive apparel as they celebrate their African heritage with music and dance. Mini-Junkanoos, in which visitors can participate, are regular events. Local tourist offices will advise the best locations to see the festivities.

New Year's Day Sailing Regatta, Nassau and Paradise Island. Three dozen or more sailing sloops, ranging from 5 to 8.5m (16–28 ft.), converge off Montagu Bay in a battle for bragging rights organized by The Bahamas Boat Owners Association. For information, call **242/394-0445.** Early January.

Annual Bahamas Wahoo Championships, Berry Islands. Anglers try to bait one of the fastest fish in the ocean, reaching speeds up to 70 mph. For information, call ℂ **305/234-7386** or visit www.bahamaswahoo.com. Mid-January.

February

The Mid-Winter Wahoo, Bimini. The Bimini Big Game Resort & Marina draws Hemingway look-alikes and other anglers to this winter event that is heavily attended by Floridians. For more information, call ℂ **800/ 737-1007** or contact the tournament director, Leonard Stuart, at the Bimini Tourist Office at ℂ **242/347-3529.** Early February.

Farmer's Cay Festival. This festival is a rendezvous for yachtsmen cruising the Exuma Islands and a homecoming for the people of Farmer's Cay, Exuma. Boat excursions will depart Nassau at Potter's Cay for the festival at 8pm on Friday, then return to Nassau at 8pm on Saturday from the Farmer's Cay Dock. For information, contact Terry Bain in Little Farmer's Cay, Exuma, at ℂ **242/355-4006,** or the Exuma Tourist Office at ℂ **242/336-2430.** First Friday and Saturday in February.

March

Bacardi Billfish Tournament, Freeport. A weeklong tournament attracting the who's who of deep-sea fishing. Headquarters is the Port Lucaya Resort & Yacht Club. For more information, call ℂ **305/234-7386** or visit www. portlucayamarina.com. Mid-March.

April

Bahamas Family Island Regatta, George Town, the Exumas. Featuring Bahamian craft sloops, these celebrated boat races are held in Elizabeth Harbour. There's also a variety of onshore activities, including basketball, a skipper's party, and a Junkanoo parade. Call ℂ **242/336-2430** or check www.georgetowncruisingregatta.org for exact dates and information. Usually third week of April.

Bahamas Billfish Championship. This annual event is divided into four competitions, taking place at four different venues and times, spanning April to June. Anglers can fish any and all of the tournaments taking place at Marsh Harbour (third week of Apr), Harbour Island (first week of May), Spanish Cay (mid-May), and Treasure Cay (first week to second week of June). Since dates vary, contact the **Bahamas Billfish Championship** at Two Oakland Blvd., Suite 195, Hollywood, FL

33020 (✆ **866/920-5577** or 954/
920-5577; www.bahamasbillfish.com).
April to June.

Bahamas White Marlin Open, the
Abacos. This rendezvous off Abaco
draws anglers seeking an action-packed
billfish tournament. The headquarters
is the treasure Cay Resort & Marina.
For more information, call ✆ **800/
275-2260** or 954/920-7877, or visit
www.bahamaswhitemarlinopen.com.
Dates vary.

May

Long Island Regatta, Salt Pond, Long
Island. This event sees some 40 to 50
sailing sloops from throughout The
Bahamas compete in three classes for
trophies and cash prizes. Onshore,
dancing to indigenous "rake 'n' scrape"
music, sporting events, and local food
specialties for sale make for a carnival-
like atmosphere. For more information, call ✆ **242/324-6294.** Late May.

June

Eleuthera Pineapple Festival, Gregory Town, Eleuthera. This celebration
devoted to the island's succulent
pineapple features a Junkanoo parade,
craft displays, dancing, a pineapple
recipe contest, tours of pineapple
farms, and a "pineathalon"—a .5km
(¼-mile) swim, 5.5km (3½-mile) run,
and 6.5km (4-mile) bike ride. For
more information, call ✆ **242/332-
2142.** First week of June.

**Bahamas Summer Boating Fling/
Flotilla.** Boating enthusiasts and
yachters make the 1-day crossing from
Florida to The Bahamas (Port Lucaya's
marina on Grand Bahama Island) in a
flotilla of boats guided by a lead boat.
All "flings" depart from the Radisson
Bahia Mar Resort & Yacht Center in
Fort Lauderdale. For more informa-
tion, contact the **Bahamas Tourism
Center** in Florida at ✆ **800/327-7678**

or 954/236-9292. End of June to
beginning of August.

July

Annual Racing Time in Abaco,
Marsh Harbour. This weeklong regatta
features a series of sailboat races in the
Sea of Abaco. Onshore festivities
include nightly entertainment, cocktail
parties, beach picnics, cultural activities, and a grand finale party. For registration forms and information, contact
the Abaco Tourist Office at ✆ **242/
367-3067.** Early July.

Independence Week. Independence
celebrations are marked throughout
the islands by festivities, parades,
and fireworks. It all culminates on
Independence Day. July 10.

August

Emancipation Day. The first Monday
in August commemorates the emancipation of slaves in 1834. A highlight of
this holiday is an early-morning
"Junkanoo Rushout" starting at 4am
in Fox Hill Village in Nassau, followed
by an afternoon of "cook-outs," cultural events such as climbing a greased
pole, and the plaiting of the Maypole.
First Monday in August.

Cat Island Regatta, Southern Bahamas.
Sleepy Cat Island comes alive in the
weekend of festive events, including
sloop races, live "rake 'n' scrape" bands,
quadrille dancing, old-fashioned contests and games, and local cuisine. Contact the **Regatta Desk** at ✆ **242/
502-0600** in Nassau. Early August.

September

All Abaco Sailing Regatta. Local sailing sloops rendezvous at Treasure Cay
Harbour for a series of championship
races and onshore festivities. Contact
the **Regatta Desk** in Nassau at
✆ **242/502-0600** or in Abaco at
✆ **242/367-3067.** Late September.

October

Discovery Day. The New World landing of Christopher Columbus, traditionally said to be the island of San Salvador, is celebrated throughout The Bahamas. Naturally, San Salvador has a parade every year on October 12.

North Eleuthera Sailing Regatta. Native sailing sloops take to the waters of North Eleuthera, Harbour Island, and Spanish Wells in a weekend of championship races. For information, contact the **Eleuthera Tourist Office** at ✆ **242/332-2142.** Mid-October.

Great Bahamas Seafood and Heritage Festival, Heritage Village, Arawak Cay. A cultural affair, this festival held in October showcases authentic Bahamian cuisine, traditional music, and storytelling. For more information, exact times, and schedule of events, contact the **Ministry of Tourism** at ✆ **242/302-2072.**

November

Guy Fawkes Day. The best celebrations are in Nassau. Nighttime parades through the streets are held on many of the islands, culminating in the hanging and burning of Guy Fawkes, an effigy of the British malefactor who was involved in the Gunpowder Plot of 1605 in London. It usually takes place around November 5, but check with island tourist offices.

Bimini Big Game Fishing Club All Wahoo Tournament. Anglers take up the tough challenge of baiting one of the fastest fishes in the ocean. Headquarters is the Bimini Sands Resort & Marina. For information, contact ✆ **242/373-3500** or 242/347-3407, or visit www.bahamaswahoo.com. Mid-November.

Annual One Bahamas Music & Heritage Festival. This 3-day celebration is staged at both Nassau and Paradise Island to celebrate national unity. Highlights include concerts featuring top Bahamian performing artists, "fun walks," and other activities. For details, contact the **Nassau/Paradise Island Office** at the Ministry of Tourism, ✆ **242/302-2000.** Last week of November.

December

Junkanoo Boxing Day. High-energy Junkanoo parades and celebrations are held throughout the islands on December 26. Many of these activities are repeated on New Year's Day (see "January," above). December 26.

5 Getting There

Lying off the east coast of Florida, the archipelago of The Bahamas is the easiest and most convenient foreign destination you can fly to unless you live close to the Canadian or Mexican borders.

Nassau is the busiest and most popular point of entry (this is where you'll fly if you're staying on Paradise Island). From here, you can make connections to many of the more remote Out Islands. If you're headed for one of the Out Islands, refer to the "Getting There" section that appears at the beginning of each island's coverage later in this book for details.

Freeport, on Grand Bahama, also has its own airport, which is served by flights from the U.S. mainland, too.

Flight time to Nassau from Miami is about 35 minutes; from New York, 2½ hours; from Atlanta, 2 hours and 5 minutes; from Philadelphia, 2 hours and 45 minutes; from Charlotte, 2 hours and 10 minutes; from central Florida, 1 hour and 10 minutes; and from Toronto, 3 hours.

THE MAJOR AIRLINES

From the U.S. mainland, about a half-dozen carriers fly nonstop to the country's major point of entry and busiest airline

Tips **New Security Measures**

Because of increased security measures, the Transportation Security Administration has made changes to the prohibited items list. All liquids and gels—including shampoo, toothpaste, perfume, hair gel, suntan lotion, and all other items with similar consistency—are limited on carry-on baggage and the security checkpoint. Pack these items in your checked baggage. Carrying liquids of any sort to the screening checkpoint will cause you delays and will most likely result in the item being confiscated.

With the ever-changing security measures, we recommend that you check the **Transportation Security Administration**'s website, **www.tsa.gov**, as near to your departure date as possible to make sure that no other restrictions have been imposed.

hub, **Lynden Pindling International Airport** (② 242/377-1759). Some also fly to the archipelago's second-most-populous city of Freeport. Only a handful (see below) fly directly to any of the Out Islands.

American Airlines (② 800/433-7300; www.aa.com) has several flights per day from Miami to Nassau, as well as four daily flights from Fort Lauderdale to Nassau. In addition, the carrier flies three times daily from Miami to Freeport. It also offers three flights daily from Miami to George Town and one flight daily from Miami to Marsh Harbour.

Delta (② 800/221-1212; www.delta.com) has several connections to The Bahamas, with service from Atlanta, Orlando, and New York's LaGuardia.

The national airline of The Bahamas, **Bahamasair** (② 800/222-4262 or 242/377-8451; www.bahamasair.com), flies to The Bahamas from Miami and Fort Lauderdale, landing at either Nassau (with seven nonstop flights daily) or Freeport (with two nonstop flights daily).

US Airways (② 800/428-4322; www.usairways.com) offers daily direct flights to Nassau from Philadelphia and Charlotte, North Carolina.

JetBlue (② 800/JET-BLUE; www.jetblue.com) has one direct flight daily to Nassau, from JFK in New York.

Other carriers include **Continental Airlines** (② 800/231-0856; www.continental.com), which has greatly expanded its link to The Bahamas through South Florida through its regional affiliate, Gulfstream International. Continental operates flights between Fort Lauderdale and Andros Town on Andros, with four round-trip flights each week. The airline also offers daily service from Fort Lauderdale to both George Town and Governor's Harbour. In addition, it maintains frequent links between Fort Lauderdale, Freeport, Marsh Harbour, North Eleuthera, and Treasure Cay. **Twin Air** (② 954/359-8266; www.flytwinair.com) flies from Fort Lauderdale three times a week to Rock Sound and Governor's Harbour, and four times a week to North Eleuthera.

Air Canada (② 888/247-2262; www.aircanada.com) is the only carrier offering scheduled service to Nassau from Canada. Direct flights from Toronto and Montreal leave daily; other flights from Toronto and Montreal, as well as other Canadian cities, make connections in the U.S.

British travelers opt for transatlantic passage aboard **British Airways** (② 800/AIR-WAYS** in the U.S. or 0870/850-9850 in the U.K.; www.britishairways.com), which offers four weekly direct

The Gulf of Mexico & the Caribbean

ATLANTIC OCEAN

Bermuda
(U.K.)

0   300 mi
0   300 km

BAHAMAS

Freeport/
Lucaya

Nassau

Andros Is.

Turks & Caicos
Islands
(U.K.)

Great
Inagua

CUBA

Camagüey

Guantánamo

DOMINICAN
REPUBLIC

HAITI

Port-au-Prince

Santo
Domingo

San Juan

Puerto
Rico
(U.S.)

Virgin Is.
(U.S.)

Virgin Is.
(U.K.)

St. Martin/
Sint Maarten
(France/Neth.)

Anguilla
(U.K.)

ST. KITTS
& NEVIS

Guadeloupe
(France)

ANTIGUA &
BARBUDA

Montserrat
(U.K.)

DOMINICA

Martinique
(France)

ST. LUCIA

BARBADOS

ST. VINCENT &
THE GRENADINES

GRENADA

GREATER ANTILLES

Kingston

JAMAICA

CARIBBEAN SEA

LESSER ANTILLES

Port-of-Spain

TRINIDAD
& TOBAGO

Netherlands
Antilles

Aruba
(Neth.)

Curaçao   Bonaire

Caracas

Maracaibo

Barranquilla

Cartagena

Orinoco

Caroni

GUYANA

Apure

VENEZUELA

PANAMA

Colon

Panama
City

Gulf of
Panama

Cauca

Magdalena

Medellín

San Cristóbal

COLOMBIA

Uraricuera

BRAZIL

flights from London to Nassau. The airline also has at least one flight daily to Miami. From here, many connections are available to Nassau and many other points within the archipelago on several carriers.

FLYING TO THE OUT ISLANDS

Many frequent visitors to The Bahamas do everything they can to avoid the congestion, inconvenience, and uncertain connections of the Nassau International Airport. A couple of U.S.-based airlines offer service directly to some of the Out Islands. **American Eagle** (© **800/433-7300;** www.aa.com) offers frequent service from Miami's International Airport to the Abacos, Eleuthera, and the Exumas. **US Airways** (© **800/428-4322;** www.us airways.com) flies nonstop every day from Fort Lauderdale to Eleuthera, usually making stops at both Governor's Harbour and North Eleuthera. US Airways also flies every day from West Palm Beach to the Abacos, stopping in both Treasure Cay and Marsh Harbour.

Chalk's Ocean Airways (© **877/924-2557;** www.flychalks.com) operates 17-passenger amphibious aircraft that take off and land in waters near the company's portside terminals. From the Florida mainland, a nonstop flight departs for Bimini from Fort Lauderdale International Airport. The flight then continues on to Paradise Island. There's also a one-stop flight from Fort Lauderdale's International Airport to Bimini. (The airline also offers charter flights to virtually anywhere in The Bahamas.)

FLYING FOR LESS: TIPS FOR GETTING THE BEST AIRFARE

- Passengers who can book their ticket either **long in advance or at the last minute,** or who **fly midweek** or **at less-trafficked hours** may pay a fraction of the full fare. If your schedule is flexible, say so, and ask if you can secure a cheaper fare by changing your flight plans.

- Search **the Internet** for cheap fares. The most popular online travel agencies are **Travelocity.com** (www. travelocity.co.uk), **Expedia.com** (www. expedia.co.uk and www.expedia.ca), and **Orbitz.com**. In the U.K., go to **Travelsupermarket** (© **0845/345-5708;** www.travelsupermarket.com), a flight search engine that offers flight comparisons for the budget airlines whose seats often end up in bucket-shop sales. Other websites for booking airline tickets online include **Cheap flights.com, SmarterTravel.com, Priceline.com,** and **Opodo** (www. opodo.co.uk). Meta search sites (which find and then direct you to airline and hotel websites for booking) include **Sidestep.com** and **Kayak.com**—the latter includes fares for budget carriers like Jet Blue and Spirit, as well as the major airlines. **Site59.com** is a great source for last-minute flights and getaways. In addition, most **airlines** offer online-only fares that even their phone agents know nothing about. British travelers should check **Flights International** (© **0800/0187050;** www.flights-international.com) for deals on flights all over the world.

- **Consolidators,** also known as bucket shops, are wholesale brokers in the airline-ticket game. Consolidators buy deeply discounted tickets ("distressed" inventories of unsold seats) from airlines and sell them to online ticket agencies, travel agents, tour operators, corporations, and, to a lesser degree, the general public. Consolidators advertise in Sunday newspaper travel sections (often in small ads with tiny type), in both the U.S. and the U.K. They can be great sources for cheap international tickets. On the downside, bucket-shop tickets are often rigged with restrictions, such as stiff cancellation penalties (as high as 50%–75% of the ticket price). And keep in mind that most of what you see advertised is of limited availability. Several reliable consolidators are worldwide and available online. **STA Travel** (www.statravel.com) has been the world's leading consolidator for students since purchasing Council Travel, but their fares are competitive for travelers of all ages. **Flights.com** (© **800/TRAV-800;** www.flights.com) has excellent fares worldwide, particularly to Europe. They also have "local" websites in 12 countries. **FlyCheap** (© **800/FLY-CHEAP;** www.1800flycheap.com) has especially good fares to sunny destinations. **Air Tickets Direct** (© **800/778-3447;** www.airticketsdirect.com) is based in Montreal and leverages the currently weak Canadian dollar for low fares; they also book trips to places that U.S. travel agents won't touch, such as Cuba.

- Join **frequent-flier clubs.** Frequent-flier membership doesn't cost a cent, but it does entitle you to free tickets or upgrades when you amass the airline's required number of frequent-flier points. You don't even have to fly to earn points; **frequent-flier credit cards** can earn you thousands of miles for doing your everyday shopping. But keep in mind that award seats are limited, seats on popular routes are hard to snag, and more and more major airlines are cutting their expiration periods for mileage points—so check your airline's frequent-flier program so you don't lose your miles before you use them. *Inside tip:* Award seats are offered almost a year in advance, but seats also open up at the last minute, so if your travel plans are flexible, you may strike gold. To play the frequent-flier game to your best advantage, consult the community bulletin boards on **FlyerTalk** (www.flyertalk.com) or go to Randy Petersen's **Inside Flyer** (www.insideflyer.com). Petersen and friends review all the programs in detail and post regular updates on changes in policies and trends.

6 Money & Costs

It's always advisable to bring money in a variety of forms on a vacation: a mix of cash, credit cards, and traveler's checks. You should also exchange enough petty cash to cover airport incidentals, tipping, and transportation to your hotel before you leave home, or withdraw money upon arrival at an airport ATM.

In many international destinations, ATMs offer the best exchange rates. Avoid exchanging money at commercial exchange bureaus and hotels, which often have the highest transaction fees.

CURRENCY

The currency is the **Bahamian dollar (B$1),** pegged to the U.S. dollar so that they're always equivalent. (In fact, U.S. dollars are accepted widely throughout The Bahamas.) There is no restriction on bringing foreign currency into The Bahamas. Most large hotels and stores accept traveler's checks, but you may have trouble using a personal check. It's a good idea to exchange enough money to cover airport incidentals and transportation to your hotel before you leave home.

You can change currencies at a local American Express (© **800/807-6233;** www.americanexpress.com) or Thomas Cook (© **800/223-7373;** www.thomascook.com), or at your bank.

Be sure to carry some small bills or loose change when traveling. Petty cash

> **Tips Easy Money**
>
> You'll avoid lines at airport ATMs by exchanging at least some money—just enough to cover airport incidentals and transportation to your hotel—before you leave home.
>
> When you change money, ask for some small bills or loose change. Petty cash will come in handy for tipping and public transportation. Consider keeping the change separate from your larger bills so that it's readily accessible and you'll be less of a target for theft.

will come in handy for tipping and public transportation. Consider keeping the change separate from your larger bills so that it's readily accessible and you'll be less of a target for theft. In general, prices are about the same as in urban America, but they are less expensive than costs in the U.K. Food is often more expensive, however, since so much of it has to be imported.

ATMs

The easiest way to get cash away from home is from an ATM (automated teller machine). The **Cirrus** (℃ **800/424-7787**; www.mastercard.com) and **PLUS** (℃ **800/843-7587**; www.visa.com) networks span the globe; look at the back of your bank card to see which network you're on, then call or check online for ATM locations at your destination. Know your personal identification number (PIN) and your daily withdrawal limit. Ask your card carrier if your current PIN works in the Bahamas, particularly in the Out Islands. Every card is different, but some need a four-digit rather than a six-digit PIN to withdraw cash abroad.

Many banks impose a fee every time a card is used at a different bank's ATM, and that fee can be higher for international transactions (up to $5/£2.65 or more) than for domestic ones (rarely more than $1.50/80p). On top of this, the bank from which you withdraw cash may charge its own fee. To compare banks' ATM fees within the U.S., use

www.bankrate.com. For international withdrawal fees, ask your bank.

You can also get cash advances on your credit card at an ATM. Credit card companies do try to protect themselves from theft by limiting the funds someone can withdraw outside their home country, so notify your credit card company before you leave home. And keep in mind that you'll pay interest from the moment of your withdrawal, even if you pay your monthly bills on time.

On New Providence Island and Paradise Island, there are plenty of ATMs, including one at the Nassau International Airport. There are far fewer ATMs on Grand Bahama Island (Freeport/Lucaya), but those that are here are strategically located—including ones at the airport and the casino (of course).

Very few ATMs are in the Out Islands. If you must have cash on your Out Island trip, make arrangements before you leave Nassau or Freeport; outside of Freeport, we counted just seven ATMs in the entire remaining Out Islands, including the one at the post office in Marsh Harbour. This situation is fluid, however, and more ATMs may be added in the future.

CREDIT CARDS

Credit cards are another safe way to carry money. They also provide a convenient record of all your expenses, and they generally offer relatively good exchange rates. You can withdraw cash advances from your credit cards at banks or ATMs, but high fees make credit-card cash advances a pricey way to get cash. Keep in mind that you'll pay interest from the moment of your withdrawal, even if you pay your monthly bills on time. Also note that many banks now assess a 1% to 3% "transaction fee" on **all** charges you incur abroad (whether you're using the local currency or your native currency).

TRAVELER'S CHECKS

You can buy traveler's checks at most banks. They are offered in denominations of $20, $50, $100, $500, and sometimes $1,000. Generally, you'll pay a service charge ranging from 1% to 4%.

The most popular traveler's checks are offered by **American Express** (© **800/807-6233** or 800/221-7282 for card holders—this number accepts collect calls, offers service in several foreign languages, and exempts Amex gold and platinum cardholders from the 1% fee.); **Visa** (© **800/732-1322**)—AAA members can obtain Visa checks for a $9.95 fee (for checks up to $1,500) at most AAA offices or by calling © **866/339-3378;** and **MasterCard** (© **800/223-9920**).

Be sure to keep a record of the traveler's checks' serial numbers separate from your checks in the event that they are stolen or lost. You'll get a refund faster if you know the numbers.

American Express, Thomas Cook, Visa, and **MasterCard** offer **foreign currency traveler's checks,** useful if you're traveling to one country or to the euro zone; they're accepted at locations where dollar checks may not be.

Another option is the new prepaid traveler's check cards, reloadable cards that work much like debit cards but aren't linked to your checking account. The **American Express Travelers Cheque Card,** for example, requires a minimum deposit, sets a maximum balance, and has a one-time issuance fee of $14.95. You can withdraw money from an ATM (for a fee of $2.50 per transaction, not including bank fees), and the funds can be purchased in dollars, euros, or pounds. If you lose the card, your available funds will be refunded within 24 hours.

7 Travel Insurance

Buying insurance might make sense because The Bahamas is not necessarily a "safe" destination. Although crimes against individual tourists are rare, your property, if left unprotected, could be stolen. Tour operators, airlines, and cruise ships can all go out of business suddenly, making default insurance a wise move on some Bahamian trips. Trip delay insurance might cover expenses that rise suddenly, as in the event of a hurricane.

Check your existing insurance policies and credit card coverage before you buy travel insurance. You may already be covered for lost luggage, canceled tickets, or medical expenses.

The cost of travel insurance varies widely, depending on the cost and length

of your trip, your age and health, and the type of trip you're taking, but expect to pay between 5% and 8% of the vacation itself. You can get estimates from various providers through **InsureMyTrip.com.** Enter your trip cost and dates, your age, and other information for prices from more than a dozen companies.

TRIP-CANCELLATION INSURANCE

Trip-cancellation insurance will help retrieve your money if you have to back out of a trip or depart early, or if your travel supplier goes bankrupt. Permissible reasons for trip cancellation can range from sickness to natural disasters, to the State Department declaring a destination unsafe for travel.

For more information, contact one of the following recommended insurers: **Access America** (✆ 800/729-6021; www.accessamerica.com), **Travel Guard International** (✆ 800/826-4919; www.travelguard.com), **Travel Insured International** (✆ 800/243-3174; www.travelinsured.com), or **Travelex Insurance Services** (✆ 800/228-9792; www.travelexinsurance.com).

MEDICAL INSURANCE

For travel overseas, most U.S. health plans (including Medicare and Medicaid) do not provide coverage, and the ones that do often require you to pay for services upfront and reimburse you only after you return home. As a safety net, you may want to buy travel medical insurance, particularly if you're traveling to a remote or high-risk area where emergency evacuation might be necessary. If you require additional medical insurance, try **MEDEX Assistance** (✆ 800/732-5309; www.medexassist.com) or **Travel Assistance International** (✆ **800/821-2828;** www.travelassistance.com; for general information on services, call the company's Worldwide Assistance Services, Inc., at ✆ **800/777-8710**).

LOST-LUGGAGE INSURANCE

On flights within the U.S., checked baggage is covered up to $2,500 per ticketed passenger. On international flights (including U.S. portions of international trips), baggage coverage is limited to approximately $9.07 per pound, up to approximately $635 per checked bag. If you plan to check items more valuable than what's covered by the standard liability, see if your homeowner's policy covers your valuables. As an added discretion, you might also ask for baggage insurance as part of your comprehensive travel-insurance package.

If your luggage is lost, immediately file a lost-luggage claim at the airport, detailing the luggage contents. Most airlines require that you report delayed, damaged, or lost baggage within 4 hours of arrival. The airlines are required to deliver luggage, once found, directly to your house or destination free of charge.

8 Health & Safety

STAYING HEALTHY

We list **hospital** and **emergency numbers** under "Fast Facts," in each chapter. Even on the remotest island, you'll find, if not a hospital, a local medicine man (or woman, in many cases). Many Bahamians are fond of herbal remedies. But you don't need to rely on these primitive treatments, as most resorts have either hospitals or clinics on-site.

The major health risk here is not tropical disease, as it is in some Caribbean islands, but rather the bad luck of ingesting a bad piece of shellfish, exotic fruit, or too many rum punches. If your body is not accustomed to some of these foods or they haven't been cleaned properly, you may suffer diarrhea. If you tend to have digestive problems, then drink bottled water and avoid ice, unpasteurized milk, and uncooked food such as fresh salads. However, fresh food served in hotels is usually safe to eat.

The Bahamas has excellent medical facilities. Physicians and surgeons in private practice are readily available in Nassau, Cable Beach, and Freeport/Lucaya. A dozen or so health centers are in the Out Islands. Medical personnel hold satellite clinics periodically in small settlements, and there are about 35 other clinics, adding up to a total of approximately 50 health facilities throughout the outlying islands. (We've listed the names and telephone numbers of specific clinics in the individual island coverage that follows throughout this book.) If intensive or urgent care is required, patients are

Healthy Travels to You

The following government websites offer health-related travel advice:
- **Australia:** www.dfat.gov.au/travel
- **Canada:** www.hc-sc.gc.ca/index_e.html
- **U.K.:** www.dh.gov.uk/PolicyAndGuidance/HealthAdviceForTravellers/fs/en
- **U.S.:** www.cdc.gov/travel

brought by the Emergency Flight Service to **Princess Margaret Hospital** (✆ 242/322-2861) on Shirley Street, Nassau. Some of the big resort hotels have in-house physicians or can quickly secure one for you.

There is also a government-operated hospital, **Rand Memorial** (✆ 242/352-6735), on East Atlantic Drive, Freeport, and several government-operated clinics on Grand Bahama Island. Nassau and Freeport/Lucaya also have private hospitals.

Dentists are plentiful in Nassau, somewhat less so on Grand Bahama. You'll find dentists on Great Abaco Island, at Marsh Harbour, at Treasure Cay, and on Eleuthera. There aren't dentists on some of the remote islands, especially those in the Southern Bahamas, but hotel staff should know where to send you for emergencies.

Contact the **International Association for Medical Assistance to Travelers** (IAMAT; ✆ 716/754-4883, or 416/652-0137 in Canada; **www.iamat.org**) for tips on travel and health concerns in the countries you're visiting, and for lists of local English-speaking doctors. The United States **Centers for Disease Control and Prevention** (✆ 800/394-1945; www.cdc.gov) provides up-to-date information on health hazards by region or country and offers tips on food safety. The website **www.tripprep.com**, sponsored by a consortium of travel medicine practitioners, may also offer helpful advice on traveling abroad. You can find listings of reliable clinics overseas at the **International Society of Travel Medicine** (www.istm.org).

COMMON AILMENTS

EXPOSURE TO THE SUN Getting too much sun can be a real issue in The Bahamas. You must, of course, take the usual precautions you would anywhere against sunburn and sunstroke. Your time in the sun should be wisely limited for the first few days until you become accustomed to the more intense rays of the Bahamian sun. Also bring and use strong UVA/UVB sunblock products.

WHAT TO DO IF YOU GET SICK AWAY FROM HOME

In most cases, your existing health plan will provide the coverage you need. But double-check; you may want to buy **travel medical insurance** instead (see the section on insurance above). Bring your insurance ID card with you wherever you travel.

We list **hospitals** and **emergency numbers** under "Fast Facts" in each chapter.

If you suffer from a chronic illness, consult your doctor before your departure. Pack **prescription medications** in your carry-on luggage, and carry them in their original containers, with pharmacy labels—otherwise, they won't make it through airport security. Carry the generic name of prescription medicines, in case a local pharmacist doesn't know the brand name.

For travel abroad, you may have to pay medical costs upfront and be reimbursed later. See "Medical Insurance," under "Travel Insurance," above.

STAYING SAFE

When going to Nassau (New Providence), Cable Beach, Paradise Island, or Freeport/Lucaya, exercise the same caution you would if visiting Miami. Whatever you do, if people peddling drugs approach you, steer clear of them.

Crime is increasing, and visitors should use caution and good judgment when visiting The Bahamas. While most criminal incidents take place in a part of Nassau not usually frequented by tourists (the "Over-the-Hill" area south of downtown), crime and violence have moved into more upscale tourist and residential areas.

Women, especially, should take caution if walking alone on the streets of Nassau after dark, particularly if those streets appear to be deserted.

In the last year, the U.S. Embassy has received several reports of sexual assaults, including some against teenage girls. Most assaults have been perpetrated against intoxicated young women, some of whom were reportedly drugged. To minimize the potential for sexual assault, the embassy recommends that young women stay in groups, consume alcohol in moderation, and not accept rides or drinks from strangers.

Pickpockets (often foreigners) work the crowded casino floors of both Paradise Beach and Cable Beach. See that your wallet, money, and valuables are well secured.

Travelers should avoid walking alone after dark or in isolated areas, and avoid placing themselves in situations in which they are alone with strangers. Be cautious on deserted areas of beaches at all hours. Don't leave valuables such as cameras and purses lying unattended on the beach while you go for a swim.

If you're driving a rental car, always make sure your car door is locked, and never leave possessions in view.

Hotel guests should always lock their doors and should never leave valuables unattended, especially on beaches. Visitors should store passport/identity documents, airline tickets, credit cards, and extra cash in hotel safes. Avoid wearing expensive jewelry, particularly Rolex watches, which criminals have specifically targeted. Use only clearly marked taxis and make a note of the license plate number for your records.

You're less likely to be mugged or robbed in the Out Islands, where life is generally more peaceful. There are some hotels there that, even today, don't have locks on the doors.

The loss or theft of a passport overseas should be reported to the local police and the nearest embassy or consulate. A lost or stolen birth certificate and/or driver's license generally cannot be replaced outside the United States. U.S. citizens may refer to the Department of State's pamphlets, *A Safe Trip Abroad* and *Tips for Travelers to the Caribbean*, for ways to promote a trouble-free journey. The pamphlets are available by mail from the Superintendent of Documents, U.S. Government Printing Office, Washington, DC 20402; via the Internet at www.gpoaccess.gov/index.html; or via the Bureau of Consular Affairs home page at www.travel.state.gov.

9 Specialized Travel Resources

TRAVELERS WITH DISABILITIES

A disability should not stop anyone from traveling to the Bahamian islands. Because these islands are relatively flat, it is fairly easy to get around, even for persons with disabilities.

Many travel agencies offer customized tours and itineraries for travelers with disabilities. Among them are **Flying Wheels Travel** (© **507/451-5005;** www.flying wheelstravel.com), **Access-Able Travel**

(Tips **Finding an Accessible Hotel**

You can call the **Bahamas Association for the Physically Disabled** (BAPD; ℂ **242/322-2393**) for information about accessible hotels in The Bahamas. This agency will also send a van to the airport to transport you to your hotel for a fee, and can provide ramps.

Source (ℂ **303/232-2979;** www.access-able.com), and **Accessible Journeys** (ℂ **800/846-4537** or 610/521-0339; www.disabilitytravel.com).

Organizations that offer assistance to disabled travelers include **MossRehab** (ℂ **800/225-5667;** www.mossresource net.org), the **American Foundation for the Blind** (AFB; ℂ **800/232-5463** or 212/502-7600; www.afb.org), and **SATH** (Society for Accessible Travel & Hospitality; ℂ **212/447-7284;** www.sath.org). **AirAmbulanceCard.com** is partnered with SATH and allows you to preselect top hospitals in case of an emergency.

Also check out the quarterly magazine *Emerging Horizons* (www.emerging horizons.com) and *Open World* magazine, published by SATH.

TIPS FOR BRITISH TRAVELERS WITH DISABILITIES Contact the Royal Association for Disability and Rehabilitation (RADAR), Unit 12, City Forum, 250 City Rd., London, EC1V 8AF (ℂ **020/7250-3222;** www.radar. org.uk).

GAY & LESBIAN TRAVELERS

Generally speaking, The Bahamas isn't a gay-friendly destination. Think twice before choosing to vacation here. Although many gay people visit or live here, the country has very strict antihomo-sexual laws. Relations between homosexuals, even when between consenting adults, are subject to criminal sanctions carrying prison terms. If you would like to make visiting gay beaches, bars, or clubs part of your vacation, consider South Miami Beach, Key West, or Puerto Rico instead.

Of course, the big resorts welcome one and all, even if forced to do so. For many years, the all-inclusive Sandals Royal Bahamian on Cable Beach refused to accept same-sex couples and booked only heterosexual guests. However, rights groups in Canada and Great Britain lobbied successfully, and the Sandals people found they could no longer advertise their resorts, and their discriminatory policies, in those countries. As a result, Sandals capitulated and ended its previous ban. However, gay and lesbian couples looking for a carefree holiday should seriously consider whether they want to spend their hard-earned dollars in a resort like Sandals that did not voluntarily end its ban against homosexuals until forced to do so by more liberal and far-sighted governments.

Single gays and gay couples should travel here with great discretion. If you're intent on visiting, **The International Gay and Lesbian Travel Association** (IGLTA; ℂ **800/448-8550** or 954/776-2626; www.iglta.org) is the trade association for the gay and lesbian travel industry, and offers an online directory of gay- and lesbian-friendly travel businesses; go to their website and click on "Members."

Many agencies offer tours and travel itineraries specifically for gay and lesbian travelers. Among them are **Above and Beyond Tours** (ℂ **800/397-2681;** www.abovebeyondtours.com), **Now, Voyager** (ℂ **800/255-6951;** www.now voyager.com), and **Olivia Cruises & Resorts** (ℂ **800/631-6277;** www.olivia. com).

Gay.com Travel (© 415/644-8044; www.gay.com/travel or www.outand about.com) is an excellent online successor to the popular *Out & About* print magazine. It provides regularly updated information about gay-owned, gay-oriented, and gay-friendly lodging, dining, sightseeing, nightlife, and shopping establishments in every important destination worldwide.

The following travel guides are available at many bookstores, or you can order them from any online bookseller: *Spartacus International Gay Guide* (Bruno Gmünder Verlag; www.spartacusworld. com/gayguide) and *Odysseus: The International Gay Travel Planner* (Odysseus Enterprises Ltd.); and the *Damron* guides (www.damron.com), with separate annual books for gay men and lesbians.

SENIOR TRAVEL

In The Bahamas, the standard adult rate usually applies to all ages more than 21 years of age. The careful, frugal travel shopper, however, might find some deals if arrangements are made before you go.

Members of **AARP** (formerly known as the American Association of Retired Persons), 601 E St. NW, Washington, DC 20049 (© **888/687-2277**; www. aarp.org), get discounts on hotels, airfares, and car rentals. AARP offers members a range of benefits, including *AARP: The Magazine* and a monthly newsletter. Anyone over 50 can join.

Many reliable agencies and organizations target the 50-plus market. **Elderhostel** (© **800/454-5768**; www.elder hostel.org) arranges study programs for those aged 55 and over. **ElderTreks** (© **800/741-7956**; www.eldertreks.com) offers small-group tours to off-the-beaten-path or adventure-travel locations, restricted to travelers 50 and older. **INTRAV** (© **800/456-8100**; www. intrav.com) is a high-end tour operator that caters to the mature, discerning traveler (not specifically seniors), with trips around the world that include guided safaris, polar expeditions, private-jet adventures, and small-boat cruises down jungle rivers.

Recommended publications offering travel resources and discounts for seniors include the quarterly magazine *Travel 50 & Beyond* (www.travel50andbeyond. com); *Travel Unlimited: Uncommon Adventures for the Mature Traveler* (Avalon); *101 Tips for Mature Travelers,* available from Grand Circle Travel (© **800/959-0405** or 617/350-7500; www.gct.com); and *Unbelievably Good Deals and Great Adventures That You Absolutely Can't Get Unless You're Over 50* (McGraw-Hill), by Joann Rattner Heilman.

FAMILY TRAVEL

The Bahamas is one of the top family-vacation destinations in North America. The smallest toddlers can spend blissful hours on sandy beaches and in the shallow seawater, or in swimming pools constructed with them in mind. There's no end to the fascinating pursuits offered for older children, ranging from boat rides to shell collecting, to horseback riding, hiking, or even dancing. Some children are old enough to learn to snorkel and to explore an underwater wonderland. Some resorts will even teach kids to swim or windsurf.

Most families with kids head for New Providence (Nassau), Paradise Island, or Grand Bahama Island (Freeport). Look for our "Kids" icon, indicating attractions, restaurants, or hotels and resorts that are especially family-friendly. See also "The Best Family Vacations," in chapter 1, for additional recommendations.

Every country's regulations differ, but in general, children traveling abroad should have plenty of documentation on hand, particularly if they're traveling with someone other than their own parents (in which case, a notarized form letter from a parent is often required).

For details on entry requirements for children traveling abroad, go to the U.S. State Department website (http://travel.state.gov).

Recommended family travel websites include **Family Travel Forum** (www.familytravelforum.com), **Family Travel Network** (www.familytravelnetwork.com), **Traveling Internationally with Your Kids** (www.travelwithyourkids.com), and **Family Travel Files** (www.thefamilytravelfiles.com).

WOMEN TRAVELERS

Should a woman travel alone to The Bahamas? Opinions and reports vary. A woman traveling alone in such countries as Jamaica faces certain dangers, and safety is often an issue. Women traveling alone in The Bahamas rarely encounter aggressive, potentially dangerous behavior from males and are usually treated with respect. However, some Bahamian men may assume that a woman traveling alone is doing so in order to find a male partner. To avoid such unwanted attention, dress a bit conservatively and don't go wandering the streets of Nassau unescorted at night. It's always advisable to wear a cover-up to your swimsuit when leaving the beach and heading into town. For additional details, see "Staying Safe," earlier in this chapter, on p. 44.

Women Welcome Women World Wide (5W; © 01494/465441; www.womenwelcomewomen.org.uk) works to foster international friendships by enabling women of different countries to visit one another (men can come along on the trips; they just can't join the club). It's a big, active organization, with more than 3,500 members from all walks of life in some 70 countries.

Also check out the award-winning website **Journeywoman** (www.journeywoman.com), a "real life" women's travel-information network where you can sign up for a free e-mail newsletter and get advice on everything from etiquette to safety; or the travel guide *Safety and Security for Women Who Travel,* by Sheila Swan and Peter Laufer (Travelers' Tales, Inc.), offering common-sense tips on safe travel.

AFRICAN-AMERICAN TRAVELERS

Black Travel Online (www.blacktravelonline.com) posts news on upcoming events and includes links to articles and travel-booking sites. **Soul of America** (www.soulofamerica.com) is a comprehensive website, with travel tips, event and family-reunion postings, and sections on historically black beach resorts and active vacations.

Agencies and organizations that provide resources for black travelers include **Rodgers Travel** (© 800/825-1775; www.rodgerstravel.com) and the **African American Association of Innkeepers International** (© 877/422-5777; www.africanamericaninns.com). For more information, check out the following collections and guides: *Go Girl: The Black Woman's Guide to Travel & Adventure* (Eighth Mountain Press), a compilation of travel essays by writers including Jill Nelson and Audre Lorde; *The African American Travel Guide,* by Wayne Robinson (Hunter Publishing; www.hunterpublishing.com); *Steppin' Out,* by Carla Labat (Avalon); *Travel and Enjoy Magazine* (© 866/266-6211; www.travelandenjoy.com); and *Pathfinders Magazine* (© 215/438-2140; www.pathfinderstravel.com), which includes articles on everything from Rio de Janeiro to Ghana, as well as information on upcoming ski, diving, golf, and tennis trips.

SINGLE TRAVELERS

Single tourists often find the dating scene better in The Bahamas during the winter when there are more visitors, especially unattached ones.

Frommers.com: The Complete Travel Resource

For an excellent travel-planning resource, we highly recommend **Frommers. com** (www.frommers.com), voted Best Travel Site by *PC Magazine*. We're a little biased, of course, but we guarantee that you'll find the travel tips, reviews, monthly vacation giveaways, bookstore, and online-booking capabilities thoroughly indispensable. Among the special features are our popular **Destinations** section, where you'll get expert travel tips, hotel and dining recommendations, and advice on the sights to see for more than 3,500 destinations around the globe; the **Frommers.com Newsletter,** with the latest deals, travel trends, and money-saving secrets; our **Community** area, featuring **Message Boards,** where Frommer's readers post queries and share advice (sometimes even our authors show up to answer questions); and our **Photo Center,** where you can post and share vacation tips. When your research is finished, the **Online Reservations System** (www.frommers. com/book_a_trip) takes you to Frommer's preferred online partners for booking your vacation at affordable prices.

On package vacations, single travelers are often hit with a "single supplement" to the base price. To avoid it, you can agree to room with other single travelers or find a compatible roommate before you go, from one of the many roommate-locator agencies.

TravelChums (© 212/787-2621; www.travelchums.com) is an Internet-only travel-companion matching service with elements of an online-personals-type site, hosted by the respected New York–based Shaw Guides travel service. Many reputable tour companies offer singles-only trips.

For more information, check out Eleanor Berman's guide *Traveling Solo: Advice and Ideas for More Than 250 Great Vacations* (Globe Pequot), with advice on traveling alone, either solo or as part of a group tour.

10 Sustainable Tourism/Ecotourism

Each time you take a flight or drive a car, CO_2 is released into the atmosphere. You can help neutralize this danger to our planet through "carbon offsetting"—paying someone to reduce your CO_2 emissions by the same amount you've added. Carbon offsets can be purchased in the U.S. from companies such as **Carbon fund.org** (www.carbonfund.org) and **TerraPass** (www.terrapass.org), and from **Climate Care** (www.climatecare.org) in the U.K.

Although one could argue that any vacation that includes an airplane flight can't be truly "green," you can go on holiday and still contribute positively to the environment. You can offset carbon emissions from your flight in other ways. Choose forward-looking companies that embrace responsible development practices, helping preserve destinations for the future by working alongside local people. An increasing number of sustainable tourism initiatives can help you plan a family trip and leave as small a "footprint" as possible on the places you visit.

Responsible Travel (www.responsible travel.com) contains a great source of sustainable travel ideas run by a spokesperson for responsible tourism in the travel industry. **Sustainable Travel International** (www.sustainabletravelinternational.org) promotes responsible tourism practices and issues an annual Green Gear & Gift Guide.

You can find eco-friendly travel tips, statistics, and touring companies and associations—listed by destination under "Travel Choice"—at the TIES website, www.ecotourism.org. Also check out **Conservation International** (www. conservation.org), which, with *National Geographic Traveler,* annually presents **World Legacy Awards** (www.wlaward. org) to those travel tour operators, businesses, organizations, and places that have made a significant contribution to sustainable tourism. **Ecotravel.com** is part online magazine and part ecodirectory that lets you search for touring companies in several categories (water-based, land-based, spiritually oriented, and so on).

In the U.K., **Tourism Concern** (www. tourismconcern.org.uk) works to reduce social and environmental problems connected to tourism and find ways of improving tourism so that local benefits are increased.

The **Association of Independent Tour Operators** (**AITO;** www.aito.co. uk) is a group of interesting specialist operators leading the field in making holidays sustainable.

For information about the ethics of swimming with dolphins and other outdoor activities, visit the **Whale and Dolphin Conservation Society** (www. wdcs.org) and **Tread Lightly** (www.tread lightly.org).

11 Staying Connected

INTERNET ACCESS AWAY FROM HOME
WITHOUT YOUR OWN COMPUTER

In lieu of the cybercafe that exists in most cities today, in The Bahamas you may have to rely on the good graces of your hotel to get your e-mail.

To see whether there are any cybercafes in your destination, check **www.cyber captive.com** and **www.cybercafe.com**. Aside from formal cybercafes, most **youth hostels** and **public libraries** have Internet access. Avoid **hotel business centers** unless you're willing to pay exorbitant rates.

Most major airports now have **Internet kiosks** scattered throughout their gates. These give you basic Web access for a per-minute fee that's usually higher than cybercafe prices.

WITH YOUR OWN COMPUTER

More and more hotels, cafes, and retailers are signing on as Wi-Fi (wireless fidelity) "hot spots." Mac owners have their own networking technology: Apple AirPort. **T-Mobile Hotspot** (www.t-mobile.com/ hotspot) serves up wireless connections at more than 1,000 Starbucks coffee shops nationwide. **Boingo** (www.boingo.com) and **Wayport** (www.wayport.com) have set up networks in airports and high-class hotel lobbies. IPass providers (see below) also give you access to a few hundred wireless hotel lobby setups. To locate other hotspots that provide **free wireless networks** in cities around the world, go to **www.personaltelco.net**.

For dial-up access, most business-class hotels throughout the world offer dataports for laptop modems, and a few thousand hotels in The Bahamas now offer free high-speed Internet access. In addition, major Internet service providers

Online Traveler's Toolbox

Veteran travelers usually carry some essential items to make their trips easier. Following is a selection of handy online tools to bookmark and use.

- **Airplane Food** (www.airlinemeals.net)
- **Airplane Seating** (www.seatguru.com and www.airlinequality.com)
- **Maps** (www.mapquest.com)
- **Time and Date** (www.timeanddate.com)
- **Travel Warnings** (http://travel.state.gov, www.fco.gov.uk/travel, www.voyage.gc.ca, or www.smartraveller.gov.au)
- **Universal Currency Converter** (www.xe.com/ucc)
- **Visa ATM Locator** (www.visa.com), **MasterCard ATM Locator** (www.mastercard.com)
- **Weather** (www.intellicast.com and www.weather.com)

(ISPs) have **local access numbers** around the world, allowing you to go online by placing a local call. The **iPass** network also has dial-up numbers around the world. You'll have to sign up with an iPass provider, who will then tell you how to set up your computer for your destination(s). For a list of iPass providers, go to www.ipass.com and click on "Individuals Buy Now." One solid provider is **i2roam** (www.i2roam.com; ✆ **866/811-6209** or 920/233-5863).

Wherever you go, bring a **connection kit** of the right power and phone adapters, a spare phone cord, and a spare Ethernet network cable—or find out whether your hotel supplies them to guests. See "Electricity" in the "Fast Facts: The Bahamas" section below.

CELLPHONE USE

The three letters that define much of the world's wireless capabilities are GSM (Global System for Mobiles), a big, seamless network that makes for easy cross-border cellphone use throughout Europe and dozens of other countries worldwide. In the U.S., T-Mobile, AT&T Wireless, and Cingular use this quasi-universal system; in Canada, Microcell and some Rogers customers are GSM; and all Europeans and most Australians use GSM. If your cellphone is on a GSM system and you have a world-capable multiband phone, such as many Sony Ericsson, Motorola, or Samsung models, you can make and receive calls across civilized areas around much of the globe. Just call your wireless operator and ask for "international roaming" to be activated on your account. Unfortunately, per-minute charges can be high—usually $1 to $1.50 (55p–80p) in Western Europe and up to $5 (£2.65) in places like Russia and Indonesia.

For many, **renting** a phone is a good idea. (Even worldphone owners will have to rent new phones if they're traveling to non-GSM regions, such as Japan or Korea.) While you can rent a phone from any number of overseas sites, including kiosks at airports and at car-rental agencies, we suggest renting the phone before you leave home. North Americans can rent one before leaving home from **InTouch USA** (✆ 800/872-7626; www.intouchglobal.com) or **RoadPost** (✆ 888/290-1616 or 905/272-5665; www.roadpost.com). InTouch will also, for free, advise you on whether your existing phone will work overseas.

Buying a phone can be economically attractive, as many nations have cheap prepaid phone systems. Once you arrive at your destination, stop by a local cellphone shop and get the cheapest package; you'll probably pay less than $100 (£53) for a phone and a starter calling card. Local calls may be as low as 10¢ (5p) per minute, and, in many countries, incoming calls are free.

Wilderness adventurers, or those heading to less-developed countries, might consider renting a **satellite phone ("satphone").** It's different from a cellphone, in that it connects to satellites and works where there's no cellular signal or ground-based tower. You can rent satellite phones from RoadPost (see above). InTouch USA (see above) offers a wider range of satphones, but at higher rates. Per-minute call charges can be even cheaper than roaming charges with a regular cellphone, but the phone itself is more expensive. As of this writing, satphones were outrageously expensive to buy, so don't even think about it.

12 Packages for the Independent Traveler

Before you search for the lowest airfare on your own (see earlier in this chapter), you may want to consider booking your flight as part of a package deal—a way to travel independently but pay group rates.

A package tour is not an escorted tour, in which you're led around by a guide. Except by cruise ships visiting certain islands, the option of being escorted around six or so Bahamian islands on an escorted tour does not exist.

Package tours are simply a way to buy the airfare, accommodations, and other elements of your trip (such as car rentals, airport transfers, and sometimes even activities) at the same time and often at discounted prices.

One good source of package deals is the airlines themselves. Most major airlines offer air/land packages, including **American Airlines Vacations** (℗ 800/321-2121; www.aavacations.com), **Delta Vacations** (℗ 800/654-6559; www.deltavacations.com), **Continental Airlines Vacations** (℗ 800/301-3800; www.covacations.com), and **United Vacations** (℗ 888/854-3899; www.unitedvacations.com). Several big **online travel agencies**—Expedia, Travelocity, Orbitz, Site59, and Lastminute.com—also do a brisk business in packages.

Liberty Travel (℗ 888/271-1584; www.libertytravel.com) is one of the biggest packagers in the U.S. Northeast, and it usually boasts a full-page ad in Sunday papers. There's also **TourScan, Inc.,** 1051 Boston Post Rd., Darien, CT 06820 (℗ 800/962-2080 in the U.S.; www.tourscan.com), which researches the best-value vacation at each hotel and condo.

For British travelers, package tours to The Bahamas can be booked through **Kuoni Travel,** Kuoni House, Dorking, Surrey RH5 4AZ (℗ 01306/744-442; www.kuoni.co.uk), which offers both land and air packages to destinations such as Nassau and Freeport, and to some places in the Out Islands. They also offer packages for self-catering villas on Paradise Island.

For an all-inclusive package, **Just-A-Vacation, Inc.,** 15501 Ebbynside Court, Bowie, MD 20716 (℗ 301/559-0510; www.justavacation.com), specializes in all-inclusive resorts on the islands of The Bahamas, plus other destinations in the Caribbean, including Barbados, Jamaica, Aruba, St. Lucia, and Antigua. **Club Med** (℗ 888/WEB-CLUB; www.clubmed.com) has various all-inclusive options throughout the Caribbean and The Bahamas.

Travel packages are also listed in the travel section of your local Sunday newspaper. Or check ads in the national travel magazines, such as *Arthur Frommer's* *Budget Travel Magazine, Travel & Leisure, National Geographic Traveler,* and *Condé Nast Traveler.*

13 The Active Vacation Planner

The more than 700 islands in the Bahamian archipelago (fewer than 30 of which are inhabited) are surrounded by warm, clear waters—ideal for fishing, sailing, and scuba diving. (Detailed recommendations and the costs of these activities are previewed under the individual destinations listings.) The country's perfect weather and its many cooperative local entrepreneurs allow easy access to more than 30 sports throughout the islands. For sports-related information about any of the activities listed below, call © 800/32-SPORT.

WATERSPORTS

FISHING   The shallow waters between the hundreds of cays and islands of The Bahamas are some of the most fertile fishing grounds in the world. Even waters where marine traffic is relatively congested have yielded impressive catches in the past, although overfishing has depleted schools of fish, especially big-game fish. Grouper, billfish, wahoo, tuna, and dozens of other species thrive in Bahamian waters, and dozens of charter boats are available for deep-sea fishing.

Frontiers International (© 800/245-1950 or 724/935-1577; www.frontierstrvl.com) features fly- and spin-fishing tours of The Bahamas and is a specialist in saltwater-fishing destinations. In addition, reef fishing, either from small boats or from shorelines, is popular everywhere, with grouper, snapper, and barracuda being the most commonly caught species.

Specialists and serious amateurs of the sport often head for any of the following destinations.

The island of **Bimini** is known as the "Big-Game Fishing Capital of the World." Here anglers can hunt for the increasingly elusive swordfish, sailfish, and marlin. For tournament listings, see the "Calendar of Events," earlier in this chapter. Bimini maintains its own Hall of Fame, where proud anglers have their catches honored. World records for the size of catches don't seem to last long here; they are usually quickly surpassed.

Walker's Cay in the Abacos and **Chub Cay** in the Berry Islands are famous for both deep-sea and shore fishing. Some anglers return to these cays year after year. Grouper, jacks, and snapper are plentiful. Even spearfishing without scuba gear is common and popular.

Andros boasts the world's best bonefishing. Bonefish (also known as "gray fox") are medium-size fish that feed in shallow, well-lit waters. Known as some of the most tenacious fish in the world, they struggle ferociously against anglers who pride themselves on using light lines from shallow-draft boats. **Andros Island Bonefishing Club** in North Andros (© 242/368-5167; www.androsbone

---

Tips A Warning to Poachers

It is illegal to take sponges or turtles from Bahamian waters. The Ministry of Agriculture, Fisheries, and Local Government also keeps a close eye on crayfish (spiny lobster) and prohibits the export of conch meat. Stone crab cannot be caught within 3km (2 miles) off Bimini or Grand Bahama.

fishing.com) specializes in fishing adventures off some of the most remote and sparsely populated coastlines in the country.

SAILING   The Bahamas is one of the top yachting destinations in the Atlantic. Its more than 700 islands and well-developed marinas provide a spectacular and practical backdrop for sailing enthusiasts. For a listing of frequent regattas, see the "Calendar of Events," earlier in this chapter. The mini archipelago of the **Abacos** is called "The Sailing Capital of the World." You might think it deserves the title until you've sailed the **Exumas,** which we think are even better.

Don't be dismayed if you don't own a yacht. All sizes and types of crafts, from dinghies to blue-water cruisers, are available for charter, and crew and captain are optional for experienced sailors. If your dreams involve experiencing the seagoing life for an afternoon or less, many hotels offer sightseeing cruises aboard catamarans or glass-bottomed boats, often with the opportunity to snorkel or swim in the wide-open sea.

The Abacos have many marinas. The best arrangements for boating can be made at **Abaco Bahamas Charters** (© **800/626-5690** or 242/366-0151; www.abacocharters.com) and at the **Moorings** (© **888/952-8420** or 727/535-1446; www.moorings.com). In the Exumas it's difficult to rent boats because most yachters arrive with their own.

SCUBA DIVING   The unusual marine topography of The Bahamas offers an astonishing variety of options for divers. Throughout the more than 700 islands are innumerable reefs, drop-offs, coral gardens, caves, and shipwrecks. In many locations, you may feel that you are the first human ever to explore the site. Since fewer than 30 of the Bahamian islands are inhabited, you can usually dive in pristine and uncrowded splendor.

Andros Island boasts the third-largest barrier reef in the world. Chub Cay, in the Berry Islands, and Riding Rock, San Salvador, also offer premium spots to take a plunge in an underwater world teeming with aquatic life. The intricate layout of the Exumas includes virtually every type of underwater dive site, very few of which have ever been explored. The Abacos, famous for its yachting, and the extensive reefs off the coast of Freeport are also fabulous dive sites.

Freeport, incidentally, is home to the country's most famous and complete diving operation, **UNEXSO** (© **800/992-DIVE** or 242/373-1244; www.unexso.com). It offers a 5.2m-deep (17-ft.) swimming pool where divers can work toward certification, and the popular "Dolphin Experience," in which visitors are allowed to pet, swim, snorkel, and dive with these remarkable animals.

You can easily learn to dive for the first time in The Bahamas. Lots of Bahamian hotels offer resort courses for novices, usually enabling a beginner to dive with a guide after several hours of instruction. You'll probably start out in the swimming pool for your initial instruction and then go out with a guide from the beach. A license (called a certification card, or "C" card) proving the successful completion of a designated program of scuba study is legally required for solo divers. Many resort hotels and dive shops offer the necessary 5-day training course. Participants who successfully complete the courses are awarded certifications by diving organizations such as PADI or NAUI.

For useful information, check out the website of the Professional Association of Diving Instructors (PADI) at www.padi.com. You'll find a description of the best dive sites and a list of PADI-certified dive operators. *Rodale's Scuba Diving Magazine* also has a helpful website at www.scubadiving.com. Both sites list dive-package specials and display gorgeous color photos of some of the most beautiful dive spots in the world.

SEA KAYAKING If you want to explore the pristine Exumas National Land and Sea Park, a spectacular natural area consisting of 365 mostly uninhabited cays that may be more impressive than anything in the Caribbean, **Ecosummer Expeditions** is your best bet. They'll take you on sea-kayaking itineraries that allow lots of time to enjoy the area's white-sand beaches and numerous reefs. You can also snorkel along the way. A 9-day trip leaving from Nassau costs $1,695. For more information, contact Ecosummer at P.O. Box 177, Clearwater, BC, Canada V0E 1N0 (© **800/465-8884** or 250/674-0102; www.ecosummer. com).

Another sea-kayaking outfit is **Ibis Tours** (© **914/409-5961**; www.ibistours. com).

OTHER ACTIVITIES

BIKE & SCOOTER RENTALS Most biking or scooter riding is done either on New Providence Island (Nassau) or on Grand Bahama Island; both have relatively flat terrain. Biking is best on Grand Bahama Island because it's bigger, with better roads and more places to go. Getting around New Providence Island is relatively easy once you're out of the congestion of Nassau and Cable Beach. In Nassau many hotels will rent you a bike or motor scooter.

On Grand Bahama Island, you can rent bikes at most big hotels (see chapter 5 for phone numbers and addresses of hotels). You can also rent motor scooters starting at about $45 (£24) per day. The tourist office at Freeport/Lucaya will outline on a map the best biking routes.

In the Out Islands, roads are usually too bumpy and potholed for much serious biking or scooter riding. Bike-rental places are almost nonexistent unless your hotel has some vehicles.

GOLF The richest pickings are on Grand Bahama Island. The **Reef Course** is the first new golf course to open in The Bahamas since 1969. Designed by Robert Trent Jones, Jr., it features water along 13 of its 18 holes. The oldest course on Grand Bahama Island is the **Lucayan Golf Course,** a wooded course with elevated greens and numerous water hazards designed for precision golf. See chapter 5 for details, and also refer to "The Best Golf Courses," in chapter 1.

Quality golf in The Bahamas, however, is not restricted to Grand Bahama Island. The **Cable Beach Golf Course** is the oldest golf course in the country. The widely publicized **Ocean Club Golf Club** has unusual obstacles—a lion's den and a windmill—which have challenged the skill of both Gary Player and Jack Nicklaus. It also boasts the world's largest sand trap. See chapters 3 and 4 for more information, and also refer to "The Best Golf Courses," in chapter 1.

A spectacular Greg Norman–designed course opened in Great Exuma, part of the massive new **Four Seasons** resort. See chapter 9.

Golf is also available at a course in the Abacos at the **Treasure Cay Golf Club.** The design is challenging, with many panoramic water views and water obstacles. See chapter 7 for more information.

HIKING The Bahamas isn't the greatest destination for serious hikers. The best hiking is on Grand Bahama Island, especially in **Lucayan National Park,** which spreads across 16 hectares (40 acres) and is some 32km (20 miles) from Lucaya. A large map at the entrance to the park outlines the trails. The park is laced with trails and elevated walkways. The highlight of the park is what may be the largest underground cave system in the world, some 11km (6¾ miles) long. Spiral steps let you descend into an eerie underground world.

Also on Grand Bahama Island, the **Rand Memorial Nature Centre** is the second-best place for hiking. It offers some 40 wooded hectares (99 acres) that you can explore on your own or with a tour guide. A .75km (½-mile) stretch of winding trails acquaints you with the flora and fauna that call Grand Bahama home, everything from a native boa constrictor to the Cuban emerald hummingbird, whose favorite food is the nectar of the hibiscus.

HORSEBACK RIDING   The best riding possibilities are at **Pinetree Stables** on Grand Bahama Island (© **242/373-3600** or 305/433-4809; www.pinetree stables.com). Its escorted eco-tour trail rides are especially interesting. Rides are offered two times a day Tuesday through Sunday; be sure to book rides a few days in advance. See chapter 5 for more information.

Virtually the only place on New Providence Island (Nassau) that offers horseback riding is **Windsor Equestrian Centre & Happy Trails Stables**, Coral Harbour (© **242/362-1820;** www. windsorequestriancentre.com), which features both morning and afternoon trail rides and requires a reservation. These tours include transportation to and from your hotel. The trail rides are guided through the woods and along the beach. See chapter 3 for more information.

Horseback riding is hardly a passion on the other islands.

TENNIS   Most tennis courts are part of large resorts and are usually free for the use of registered guests during the day. Charges are imposed to light the courts at night. Nonguests are welcome but are charged a player's fee; they should call in advance to reserve. Larger resorts usually offer on-site pro shops and professional instructors. Court surfaces range from clay or asphalt to such technologically advanced substances as Flexipave and Har-Tru.

New Providence, with more than 80 tennis courts, wins points for offering the greatest number of choices. At least 21 of these lie on Paradise Island. Also noteworthy are the many well-lit courts at the Radisson Cable Beach Hotel. See chapters 3 and 4. After New Providence, Grand Bahama has the largest number of courts available for play—almost 40 in all. See chapter 5. Within the Out Islands, tennis courts are available on Eleuthera, the Abacos, the Berry Islands, and the Exumas. See chapters 6, 7, 8, and 9 for more information.

14 Getting Around The Bahamas

If your final destination is Paradise Island, Freeport, or Nassau (Cable Beach) and you plan to fly, you'll have little trouble reaching your destination. However, if you're heading for one of the Out Islands, you face more exotic choices, not only of airplanes, but also of other means of transport, including a mail boat, the traditional connecting link in days of yore.

As mentioned, each section on one of the Out Island chains has specific transportation information, but here's a general overview.

BY PLANE

The national airline of The Bahamas, **Bahamasair** (© **800/222-4262;** www. bahamasair.com), serves 19 airports on 12 Bahamian islands, including Abaco, Andros, Cat Island, Eleuthera, Long Island, and San Salvador. Many of the Out Islands have either airports or airstrips, or are within a short ferry ride's distance of one. You can usually make connections to these smaller islands from Nassau.

BY RENTAL CAR

Many travelers don't really need to rent a car in The Bahamas, especially those who are coming for a few days of soaking in the sun at their resort's own beach. In Nassau and Freeport, you can easily rely on public transportation or taxis. In some of the Out Islands, there are a few car-rental companies, but most rental cars are unusually expensive and in poor condition (the roads are often in the same bad state as the rental cars).

Most visitors need transportation only from the airport to their hotel; perhaps you can arrange an island tour later, and an expensive private car won't be necessary. Your hotel can always arrange a taxi for you if you want to venture out.

You may decide that you want a car to explore beyond the tourist areas of New Providence Island, and you're very likely to want one on Grand Bahama Island.

Just remember: Road rules are much the same as those in the U.S., but you *drive on the left.*

For the Out Islands, turn to the relevant "Getting Around" sections of the chapters that follow to determine if you'll want a car (you may want one to explore on Eleuthera or Great Abaco Island); perhaps you'll stay put at your resort but rent a car for only 1 day of exploring.

The major U.S. car-rental companies operate in The Bahamas, but not on all the remote islands. We always prefer to do business with one of the major firms if they're present because you can call ahead and reserve from home via a toll-free number, they tend to offer better-maintained vehicles, and it's easier to resolve any disputes after the fact. Call **Budget** (© 800/472-3325; www.budget.com), **Hertz** (© 800/654-3001; www.hertz.com), **Dollar** (© 800/800-3665; www.dollarcar.com), or **Avis** (© 800/331-1084; www.avis.com). Budget rents in Nassau and Paradise Island. Liability insurance is compulsory.

"Petrol" is easily available in Nassau and Freeport, though quite expensive. In the Out Islands, where the cost of gasoline is likely to vary from island to island, you should plan your itinerary based on where you'll be able to get fuel. The major towns of the islands have service stations. You should have no problems on New Providence or Grand Bahama Island unless you start out with a nearly empty tank.

Visitors may drive with their home driver's license for up to 3 months. For longer stays, you'll need to secure a Bahamian driver's license.

As you emerge at one of the major airports, including those of Nassau (New Providence) and Freeport (Grand Bahama Island), you can pick up island maps that are good for routine touring around those islands. However, if you plan to do extensive touring in the Out Islands, you should go first to a bookstore in either Nassau or Freeport and ask for a copy of **Atlas of The Bahamas.** It provides touring routes (outlined in red) through all the major Out Islands. Once you arrive on these remote islands, it may be hard to obtain maps.

BY TAXI

Once you've reached your destination, you'll find that taxis are plentiful in the Nassau–Cable Beach–Paradise Island area and in the Freeport/Lucaya area on Grand Bahama Island. These cabs, for the most part, are metered—but they take cash only, no credit cards. See "Getting Around" in the chapters on each island that follow for further details.

In the Out Islands, however, it's not so easy. In general, taxi service is available at all air terminals, at least if those air terminals have "port of entry" status. They can also be hailed at most marinas.

Taxis are usually shared, often with the local residents. Out Island taxis aren't metered, so you must negotiate the fare before you get in. (Expect to pay a rate of around $20/£11 per hour.) Cars are often old and badly maintained, so be prepared for a bumpy ride over some rough roads if you've selected a particularly remote hotel.

BY MAIL BOAT

Before the advent of better airline connections, the traditional way of exploring the Out Islands—in fact, about the only way unless you had your own vessel—was by mail boat. This service is still available, but it's recommended only for those who have lots of time and a sense of adventure. You may ride with cases of rum, oil drums, live chickens, or even an occasional piano.

The boats—19 of them composing the "Post Office Navy" under the direction of the Bahamian Chief of Transportation—are often fancifully colored, high-sided, and somewhat clumsy in appearance, but the little motor vessels chug along, serving the 30 inhabited islands of The Bahamas. Schedules can be thrown off by weather and other causes, but most morning mail boats depart from Potter's Cay (under the Paradise Island Bridge in Nassau) or from Prince George Wharf. The voyages last from 4½ hours to most of a day, sometimes even overnight. Check the schedule of the particular boat you wish to travel on with the skipper at the dock in Nassau.

This is a cheap way to go: The typical fare from Nassau to Marsh Harbour is $45 (£24) per person, one-way. Many of the boats offer two classes of passenger accommodations, first and second. In first class, you get a bunk bed; in second, you may be entitled only to deck space. (Actually, the bunk beds are usually reserved for the seasick, but first-class passengers on larger boats sit in a reasonably comfortable enclosed cabin.)

For information about mail boats to the Out Islands, contact the **Dock Masters Office** in Nassau, under the Paradise Island Bridge on Potter's Cay (© **242/393-1064**).

BY CHARTERED BOAT

For those who can afford it, this is the most luxurious way to see The Bahamas. On your private boat, you can island-hop at your convenience. Well-equipped marinas are on every major island and many cays. There are designated ports of entry at Great Abaco (Marsh Harbor), Andros, the Berry Islands, Bimini, Cat Cay, Eleuthera, Great Exuma, Grand Bahama Island (Freeport/Lucaya), Great Inagua, New Providence (Nassau), Ragged Island, and San Salvador.

Vessels must check with Customs at the first port of entry and receive a cruising clearance permit to The Bahamas. Carry it with you and return it at the official port of departure.

The Yachtsman's Guide to The Bahamas (Tropical Island Publishers) covers the entire Bahamas. Copies are available at major marine outlets and bookstores, and by mail direct from the publisher for $40 U.S., plus postage: Tropical Island Publishers, P.O. Box 12, Adelphia, NJ 07710 (© **877/923-9653;** www.yachtsmansguide.com).

Experienced sailors with a sea-wise crew can charter **"bareboat"** (a fully equipped boat with no crew). You're on your own, and you'll have to prove you can handle it before you're allowed to take out such a craft. You may want to take along an experienced yachter familiar with local waters, which may be tricky in some places.

Most yachts are rented on a weekly basis. Contact **Abaco Bahamas Charters** (© **800/626-5690** or 242/366-0151; www.abacocharters.com) or the **Moorings** (© **888/952-8420** or 727/535-1446; www.moorings.com).

15 Tips on Accommodations

The Bahamas offers a wide selection of accommodations, ranging from small private guesthouses to large luxury resorts. Hotels vary in size and facilities, from deluxe (offering room service, sports, swimming pools, entertainment, and so on) to fairly simple inns.

There are package deals galore, and they are always cheaper than "rack rates." (A rack rate is what an individual pays if he or she literally walks in from the street. These are the rates we've listed in the chapters that follow, though you can almost always do better—especially at the big resorts.) It's sometimes good to go to a reliable travel agent to find out what, if anything, is available in the way of a land-and-air package before booking a particular accommodation. See section 12, "Packages for the Independent Traveler," earlier in this chapter, for details on a number of companies that usually offer good-value packages to The Bahamas.

There is no rigid classification of hotel properties in the islands. The label "deluxe" is often used (or misused) when "first class" might have been a more appropriate term. "First class" itself often isn't. For that and other reasons, we've presented fairly detailed descriptions of the properties so that you'll get an idea of what to expect. However, even in the deluxe and first-class resorts and hotels, don't expect top-rate service and efficiency. When you go to turn on the shower, sometimes you get water and sometimes you don't. You may even experience power failures.

The winter season in The Bahamas runs roughly from the middle of December to the middle of April, and hotels charge their highest prices during this peak period. Winter is generally the dry season in the islands, but there can be heavy rainfall regardless of the time of year. During the winter months, make reservations 2 months in advance if you can. You can't book early enough if you want to travel over Christmas or in February.

The off season in The Bahamas—roughly from mid-April to mid-December (although this varies from hotel to hotel)—amounts to a sale. In most cases, hotel rates are slashed a startling 20% to 60%. It's a bonanza for cost-conscious travelers, especially for families who can travel in the summer. Be prepared for very strong sun, though, plus a higher chance of rain. Also note that hurricane season runs through summer and fall.

MAP VS. AP, OR DO YOU WANT TO GO EP?

All Bahamian resorts offer a **European Plan (EP)** rate, which means that you pay for the price of a room. That leaves

---

What the Hotel Symbols Mean

As you're shopping around for your hotel, you may see the following terms used:

- **AP (American Plan):** Includes three meals a day (sometimes called full board or full pension).
- **EP (European Plan):** Includes only the room—no meals.
- **CP (Continental Plan):** Includes continental breakfast of juice, coffee, bread, and jam.
- **MAP (Modified American Plan):** Sometimes called half-board or half-pension, this room rate includes breakfast and dinner (or lunch instead of dinner, if you prefer).

you free to dine around at night at various other resorts or restaurants without restriction. Another plan preferred by many is the **Continental Plan (CP)**, which means you get a continental breakfast of juice, coffee, bread, and jam included in a set price. This plan is preferred by those who don't like to look around for a place to eat breakfast.

Another major option is the **Modified American Plan (MAP)**, which includes breakfast and one main meal of the day, either lunch or dinner. The final choice is the **American Plan (AP)**, which includes breakfast, lunch, and dinner. At certain resorts you will save money by booking on either the MAP or AP because discounts are granted. If you dine a la carte often for lunch and dinner, your dining costs will be much higher than if you stay on the MAP or AP.

Dining at your hotel at night cuts down on transportation costs. Taxis especially are expensive. Nonetheless, if dining out and having many different culinary experiences is your idea of a vacation and you're willing to pay the higher price, avoid AP plans or at least make sure the hotel where you're staying has more than one dining room.

One option is to ask if your hotel has a dine-around plan. You might still keep costs in check, but you can avoid a culinary rut by taking your meals in some other restaurants if your hotel has such a plan. Such plans are rare in The Bahamas, which does not specialize in all-inclusive resorts the way that Jamaica or some other islands do.

Before booking a room, check with a good travel agent or investigate on your own what you are likely to save by booking on a dining plan. Under certain circumstances in winter, you might not have a choice if MAP is dictated as a requirement for staying there. It pays to investigate, of course.

THE RIGHT ROOM AT THE RIGHT PRICE

Ask detailed questions when booking a room. Specify your likes and dislikes. There are several logistics of getting the right room in a hotel. In general, back rooms cost less than oceanfront rooms, and lower rooms cost less than upper-floor units. If budget is a major consideration with you, opt for the cheaper rooms. You won't have a great view, but you'll save your money for something else. Just make sure that it isn't next to the all-night drummers.

Of course, all first-class or deluxe resorts feature air-conditioning, but many Bahamian inns do not, especially in the Out Islands. Cooling might be by ceiling fans or, in more modest places, the breeze from an open window, which also brings the mosquitoes. If sleeping in a climate-controlled environment is important to your vacation, check this out in advance.

If you're being your own travel agent, it pays to shop around by calling the local number given for a hotel and its toll-free number, if it has one. You can check online and call a travel agent to see where you can obtain the best price.

Another tip: Ask if you can get an upgrade or a free night's stay if you stay an extra few days. If you're traveling during the "shoulder" periods (between low and high season), you can sometimes get a substantial reduction by delaying your travel plans by a week or 10 days. For example, a $300 (£159) room booked on April 12 might be lowered to $180 (£95) by April 17, as mid-April marks the beginning of the low season in The Bahamas.

Transfers from the airports or the cruise dock are included in some hotel bookings, most often in a package plan but usually not in ordinary bookings. This is true of first-class and deluxe resorts, but rarely of medium-priced or budget accommodations. Always ascertain whether transfers (which can be expensive) are included.

When using the facilities at a resort, make sure that you know exactly what is free and what costs money. For example, swimming in the pool is nearly always free, but you might be charged for use of a tennis court. Nearly all watersports cost extra, unless you're booked on some special plan such as scuba package. Some resorts seem to charge every time you breathe and might end up costing more than a deluxe hotel that includes most everything in the price.

Some hotels are right on the beach. Others involve transfers to the beach by taxi or bus, so factor in transportation costs, which can mount quickly if you stay 5 days to a week.

THE ALL-INCLUSIVES

A hugely popular option in Jamaica, the all-inclusive resort hotel concept finally has a foothold in The Bahamas. At these resorts, everything is included—sometimes even drinks. You get your room and all meals, plus entertainment and many watersports (although some cost extra). Some people find the cost of this all-inclusive holiday cheaper than if they'd paid individually for each item, and some simply appreciate knowing in advance what their final bill will be.

The first all-inclusive resort hotel in The Bahamas was **Club Med** (© **888/WEB-CLUB;** www.clubmed.com) on Paradise Island. This is not a swinging-singles kind of place; it's popular with everybody, from honeymooners to families with kids along. There's another mammoth Club Med at Governor's Harbour on Eleuthera. Families with kids like it a lot here, and the resort also attracts scuba divers. There's a third branch in San Salvador, in the Southern Bahamas, which has more of a luxurious hideaway atmosphere.

The biggest all-inclusive of them all, **Sandals** (© **888/SANDALS;** www.sandals.com), came to The Bahamas in 1995 on Cable Beach. This Jamaican company is now walking its sandals across the Caribbean, having established firm beachheads in Ocho Rios, Montego Bay, and Negril. The most famous of the all-inclusives (but not necessarily the best) ended its ban against same-sex couples. See chapter 3 for details.

RENTAL VILLAS & VACATION HOMES

You might rent a big villa, a good-size apartment in someone's condo, or even a small beach cottage (more accurately called a cabana).

Private apartments come with or without maid service (ask upfront exactly what to expect). This is more of a no-frills option than the villas and condos. The apartments may not be in buildings with swimming pools, and they may not have a front desk to help you.

Many cottages or cabanas ideally open onto a beach, although others may be clustered around a communal swimming pool. Most of them are fairly simple, containing only a plain bedroom plus a small kitchen and bathroom. In the peak winter season, reservations should be made at least 5 or 6 months in advance.

Hideaways Aficionado (© **877/843-4433** in the U.S., or 603/430-4433; www.hideaways.com) publishes *Hideaways Life,* a 24-page pictorial directory of home rentals throughout the world, with full descriptions so you know what you're renting. Rentals range from cottages to staffed villas, to whole islands! On most rentals, you deal directly with owners. At condos and small resorts, Hideaways offers member discounts. Other services include specialty cruises, yacht charters, airline ticketing, car rentals, and hotel reservations. Annual membership costs $185 (£98).

Sometimes local tourist offices will also advise you on vacation-home rentals if you write or call them directly.

THE BAHAMIAN GUESTHOUSE

Many Bahamians stay at a guesthouse when traveling in their own islands. In The Bahamas, however, the term *guesthouse* can mean anything. Sometimes so-called guesthouses are really like simple motels built around swimming pools. Others are small individual cottages with their own kitchenettes, constructed around a main building in which you'll often find a bar and restaurant serving local food.

SAVING ON YOUR HOTEL ROOM

The **rack rate** is the maximum rate that a hotel charges for a room. Hardly anybody pays this price, however, except in high season or on holidays. To lower the cost of your room:

- **Ask about special rates or other discounts.** You may qualify for corporate, student, military, senior, frequent flier, trade union, or other discounts.

- **Dial direct.** When booking a room in a chain hotel, you'll often get a better deal by calling the individual hotel's reservation desk rather than the chain's main number.

- **Book online.** Many hotels offer Internet-only discounts or supply rooms to Priceline, Hotwire, or Expedia at rates much lower than the ones you can get through the hotel itself.

- **Remember the law of supply and demand.** Resort hotels are most crowded and, therefore, most expensive on weekends, so discounts are usually available for midweek stays. Business hotels in downtown locations are busiest during the week, so you can expect big discounts over the weekend. Many hotels have high-season and low-season prices, and booking even 1 day after high season ends can mean big discounts.

- **Look into group or long-stay discounts.** If you come as part of a large group, you should be able to negotiate a bargain rate. Likewise, if you're planning a long stay (at least 5 days), you might qualify for a discount. As a general rule, expect 1 night free after a 7-night stay.

- **Avoid excess charges and hidden costs.** When you book a room, ask whether the hotel charges for parking. Use your own cellphone, pay phones, or prepaid phone cards instead of dialing direct from hotel phones, which usually have exorbitant rates. And avoid the room's minibar offerings. Finally, ask about local taxes and service charges, which can increase the cost of a room by 15% or more.

- Consider the pros and cons of **all-inclusive** resorts and hotels. The term "all-inclusive" means different things at different hotels. Many all-inclusive hotels will include three meals daily, sports equipment, spa entry, and other amenities; others may include all or most drinks. In general, you'll save money going the "all-inclusive" way—as long as you use the facilities provided. The downside is that your choices are limited and you're stuck eating and playing in one place for the duration of your vacation.

- Carefully consider your hotel's meal plan. If you enjoy eating out and sampling the local cuisine, it makes sense to choose a **Continental Plan (CP),** which includes breakfast only, or a **European Plan (EP),** which doesn't include any meals and allows you maximum flexibility. If you're more interested in saving money, opt for a **Modified American Plan (MAP),** which includes breakfast and one meal, or the **American Plan**

(AP), which includes three meals. If you must choose a MAP, see if you can get a free lunch at your hotel if you decide to do dinner out.

• **Book an efficiency.** A room with a kitchenette allows you to shop for groceries and cook your own meals. This is a big money saver, especially for families on long stays.

FAST FACTS: The Bahamas

American Express Representing American Express in The Bahamas is **Destinatinos,** 303 Shirley St. (between Charlotte and Parliament sts.), Nassau (© **242/ 322-2931**). Hours are 9am to 5pm Monday through Friday. The travel department is also open Saturday 9am to 1pm. If you present a personal check and an Amex card, you can buy traveler's checks here.

Area Code The area code for The Bahamas is **242.**

ATM Networks See "Money & Costs," p. 39.

Business Hours In Nassau, Cable Beach, and Freeport/Lucaya, commercial banking hours are 9:30am to 3pm Monday through Thursday, 9:30am to 5pm on Friday. Hours are likely to vary widely in the Out Islands. Ask at your hotel. Most government offices are open Monday through Friday from 9am to 5pm, and most shops are open Monday through Saturday from 9am to 5pm.

Camera & Film Purchasing film in Nassau/Paradise Island or Freeport/Lucaya is relatively easy, if a little expensive. But stock up if you're going to the Out Islands and need a special kind.

Car Rentals See "Getting Around The Bahamas," p. 55.

Cashpoints See "ATM Networks," above.

Currency See "Money & Costs," p. 39.

Driving Rules See "Getting Around The Bahamas," p. 55.

Drug Laws Importing, possessing, or dealing unlawful drugs, including marijuana, is a serious offense in The Bahamas, with heavy penalties. Customs officers may at their discretion conduct body searches for drugs or other contraband goods.

Drugstores Nassau and Freeport are amply supplied with pharmacies (see individual listings). However, if you're traveling in the Out Islands, it is best to carry your prescribed medication with you, since pharmacies are harder to find.

Electricity Electricity is normally 120 volts, 60 cycles, AC. American appliances are fully compatible; British or European appliances will need both converters and adapters.

Embassies & Consulates The U.S. Embassy is on 42 Queen St., P.O. Box N-8197, Nassau (© **242/322-1181**), and the Canadian consulate is on Shirley Street Shopping Plaza, Nassau (© **242/393-2123**). The British High Commission is located in Kingston, Jamaica, at 28 Trafalgar Rd. (© **876/510-0700**).

Emergencies Throughout most of The Bahamas, the number to call for a medical, dental, or hospital emergency is © **911**. In the Out Islands, the number is © **919**. To report a fire, however, call © **411**.

Holidays Public holidays observed in The Bahamas are New Year's Day, Good Friday, Easter Sunday, Easter Monday, Whitmonday (7 weeks after Easter), Labour Day (the first Fri in June), Independence Day (July 10), Emancipation Day (the first Mon in Aug), Discovery Day (Oct 12), Christmas, and Boxing Day (the day after Christmas). When a holiday falls on Saturday or Sunday, stores and offices are usually closed on the following Monday.

For more information on holidays, see the "Calendar of Events," earlier in this chapter.

Hospitals In Nassau, **Princess Margaret Hospital** (© 242/322-2861), and in Freeport, **Rand Memorial** (© 242/352-6735).

Internet Access Access is limited on the islands, but it can be obtained at **Cybercafe,** in the Mall at Marathon in Nassau (© **242/394-6254**), or in Freeport at **CyberClub** at Seventeen Center (© **242/351-4560**). Web access is increasingly common at hotels in The Bahamas—even in the Out Islands, you can usually access the Web. But if this issue is especially important to you, check with specific accommodations before booking. Also see "Online Traveler's Toolbox" and "Staying Connected," earlier.

Language In The Bahamas, locals speak English, but sometimes with a marked accent that provides the clue to their ancestry African, Irish, or Scottish, for example.

Liquor Laws Liquor is sold in liquor stores and various convenience stores; it's readily available at all hours, though not sold on Sundays. The legal drinking age is 18.

Lost & Found Be sure to tell all of your credit card companies the minute you discover your wallet has been lost or stolen and file a report at the nearest police precinct. Your credit card company or insurer may require a police report number or record of the loss. Most credit card companies have an emergency toll-free number to call if your card is lost or stolen; they may be able to wire you a cash advance immediately or deliver an emergency credit card in a day or two. Visa's U.S. emergency number is © **800/847-2911. American Express** cardholders and traveler's check holders should call © **800/221-7282. Master-Card** holders should call © **800/307-7309.** For other credit cards, call the toll-free number directory at © **800/555-1212.**

If you need emergency cash over the weekend when all banks and American Express offices are closed, you can have money wired to you via **Western Union** (© **800/325-6000;** www.westernunion.com).

Mail You'll need Bahamian (not U.S.) postage stamps to send postcards and letters. Most of the kiosks selling postcards also sell the stamps you'll need to mail them, so you probably won't need to visit the post office. Sending a postcard or an airmail letter (up to ½ oz. in weight) from The Bahamas to anywhere outside its borders (including the U.S., Canada, and the U.K.) costs 65¢ (34p), with another charge for each additional half-ounce of weight.

Mail to and from the Out Islands is sometimes slow. Airmail may go by air to Nassau and by boat to its final destination. If a resort has a U.S. or Nassau address, it is preferable to use it.

Measurements See the chart on the inside front cover of this book for details on converting metric measurements to nonmetric equivalents.

Newspapers & Magazines Three newspapers are circulated in Nassau and Freeport: the *Nassau Guardian* (www.thenassauguardian.com), the *Tribune,* and the *Freeport News.* Circulation in the Out Islands is limited and likely to be slow. You can find such papers as the *New York Times,* the *Wall Street Journal, USA Today,* the *Miami Herald, Times of London,* and *Daily Telegraph* at news-stands in your hotel and elsewhere in Nassau.

Passports Allow plenty of time before your trip to apply for a passport; processing normally takes 3 weeks but can take longer during busy periods (especially spring). And keep in mind that if you need a passport in a hurry, you'll pay a higher processing fee.

For Residents of Australia: You can pick up an application from your local post office or any branch of Passports Australia, but you must schedule an interview at the passport office to present your application materials. Call the **Australian Passport Information Service** at ℂ **131-232,** or visit the government website at www.smartraveller.gov.au.

For Residents of Canada: Passport applications are available at travel agencies throughout Canada or from the central **Passport Office,** Department of Foreign Affairs and International Trade, Ottawa, ON K1A 0G3 (ℂ **800/567-6868;** www.ppt.gc.ca).

For Residents of Ireland: You can apply for a 10-year passport at the **Passport Office,** Setanta Centre, Molesworth Street, Dublin 2 (ℂ **01/671-1633;** www.irlgov.ie/iveagh). Those under age 18 and over 65 must apply for a €12 3-year passport. You can also apply at 1A South Mall, Cork (ℂ **021/494-4700**), or at most main post offices.

For Residents of New Zealand: You can pick up a passport application at any New Zealand Passports Office or download it from their website. Contact the **Passports Office** at ℂ **0800/225-050** in New Zealand or 04/474-8100, or log on to www.passports.govt.nz.

For Residents of the United Kingdom: To pick up an application for a standard 10-year passport (5-year passport for children under 16), visit your nearest passport office, major post office, or travel agency, or contact the **United Kingdom Passport Service** at ℂ **0870/521-0410** or search its website at www.ukpa.gov.uk.

For Residents of the United States: Whether you're applying in person or by mail, you can download passport applications from the U.S. State Department website at **http://travel.state.gov**. To find your regional passport office, either check the U.S. State Department website or call the **National Passport Information Center** toll-free number (ℂ **877/487-2778**) for automated information.

Pets You'll have to get a valid import permit to bring any animal into The Bahamas. Application for such a permit must be made in writing, accompanied by a $10 (£5.30) processing fee and a $5 (£2.65) fax fee, to the **Director of Agriculture,** Department of Agriculture, P.O. Box N-3028, Nassau, The Bahamas (ℂ **242/325-7502**), at least 4 weeks in advance.

Police Dial ℂ **911.** In the Out Islands, the number is ℂ **919.**

Safety See "Health & Safety," earlier in this chapter.

Taxes Departure tax is $15 ($18 from Grand Bahama Island) for visitors ages 7 and up. An 8% tax is imposed on hotel bills; otherwise, there is no sales tax in The Bahamas.

Telephones Although some of the Out Islands are still difficult to reach by phone, direct long-distance dialing is available between North America and Nassau, Grand Bahama, the Abacos, Andros, the Berry Islands, Bimini, Eleuthera, Harbour Island, Spanish Wells, the Exumas, and Stella Maris on Long Island.

To call The Bahamas:

1. Dial the international access code: 011 from the U.S.; 00 from the U.K., Ireland, or New Zealand; or 0011 from Australia.

2. Dial the country code **242.**

3. Dial the seven-digit local number.

To make international calls: To make international calls from The Bahamas, first dial 00 and then the country code (U.S. or Canada 1, U.K. 44, Ireland 353, Australia 61, New Zealand 64). Next you dial the area code and number. For example, if you wanted to call the British Embassy in Washington, D.C., you would dial 00-1-202-588-7800.

For local calls within The Bahamas: Simply dial the seven-digit number. To call from one island to another within The Bahamas, dial 1-242 and then the seven-digit local number.

For directory assistance: Dial ☎ 916 if you're looking for a number inside The Bahamas, and dial 0 for numbers to all other countries.

For operator assistance: To reach an international or domestic operator within The Bahamas, dial **0.** There is no distinction made in The Bahamas between the two types of operators.

Toll-free numbers: Numbers beginning with **881** within The Bahamas are toll-free. However, calling a normally toll-free number within the United States (that is, one beginning with 800, 887, or 888) usually involves a charge within The Bahamas. In fact, it usually costs the same as an overseas call unless the merchant has made arrangements with the local telephone authorities. **Note:** Major airlines generally maintain toll-free 800, 887, or 888 provisions for calls made to them within The Bahamas. If you dial what you think is a toll-free phone number and it ends up costing the long-distance rate, an automated recording will inform you of this fact. In some cases, the recording will suggest a local toll-free alternative—usually one beginning with 881.

To reach the major international services of **AT&T,** dial ☎ **800/CALL-ATT,** or head for any phone with AT&T or USA Direct marked on the side of the booth. Picking up the handset will connect you with an AT&T operator. These phones are often positioned beside cruise-ship docks to help passengers disembarking on shore leave for the day. **MCI** can be reached at ☎ **800/888-8000.**

Note that the old coin-operated phones are still prevalent in The Bahamas and still swallow coins. Each local call costs 25¢ (15p); you can use either Bahamian or U.S. quarters. Those old phones, however, are gradually being replaced by phones that use calling cards (debit cards), similar in appearance to a credit card, that come in denominations of $5, $10, $20, and $50. They can be bought from any office of **BATELCO** (Bahamas Telephone Co.). BATELCO's main branch is on Kennedy Drive, Nassau (© **242/302-7008**), although a popular local branch lies in the heart of Nassau, on East Street off Bay Street.

Time Zone Eastern Standard Time is used throughout The Bahamas, and daylight saving time is observed in the summer.

Tipping Many establishments add a service charge, but it's customary to leave something extra if service has been especially fine. If you're not sure whether service has been included in your bill, don't be shy—ask.

Bellboys and porters, at least in the expensive hotels, expect a tip of $1 (55p) per bag. It's also customary to tip your maid at least $2 (£1.05) per day—more if she or he has performed special services such as getting a shirt or blouse laundered. Most service personnel, including taxi drivers, waiters, and the like, expect 15% (20% in deluxe restaurants).

Useful Phone Numbers Sources of information include:

U.S. Dept. of State Travel Advisory: © 202/647-5225 (manned 24 hr.)

U.S. Passport Agency: © 202/647-0518

U.S. Centers for Disease Control International Traveler's Hotline: © 404/332-4559

Water Technically, tap water is drinkable throughout The Bahamas. But we almost always opt for bottled. Resorts tend to filter and chlorinate tap water more aggressively than other establishments; elsewhere, bottled water is available at stores and supermarkets, and tastes better than that from a tap. On many of the Out Islands, rainfall is the main source of water—drink bottled water there.

Weddings The bride and groom must both be in The Bahamas at the moment they apply for the $100 (£53) wedding license here. If both are single and U.S. citizens, a declaration certifying this fact must be sworn before a consul at the American Embassy in Nassau. The fee is $55 (£29) per person; you'll need to appear in person with ID such as a passport (and, if applicable, proof of divorce). If all of these requirements are met, you can then get married after staying for 24 hours in The Bahamas. No blood test is necessary. Contact the **Registrar General** at P.O. Box N-532, Nassau, The Bahamas (© **242/322-3316**), for more details.

3

New Providence
(Nassau/Cable Beach)

One million visitors a year have cast their vote: They want to visit New Providence Island, setting for Nassau, adjoining Cable Beach, and Paradise Island (which is covered separately in chapter 4). This is the center of all the action: the best shopping, the best entertainment, the most historic attractions—plus some of the best beaches in The Bahamas.

The capital of The Bahamas, the historic city of Nassau is a 35-minute flight from Miami. Despite the development and the modern hotels, a laid-back tropical atmosphere still pervades the city, and it still offers a good dose of colonial charm. The commercial and banking hub of The Bahamas, as well as a mecca for shoppers, Nassau lies on the north side of New Providence, which is 34km (21 miles) long and 11km (6¾ miles) wide at its greatest point.

Cable Beach, a stretch of sand just west of the city, is lined with luxury resorts—in fact, the Nassau/Cable Beach area has the largest tourist infrastructure in The Bahamas, though there's another concentration of luxury hotels on Paradise Island. If you want to stay right on the sands, don't choose a hotel in downtown Nassau itself. Head for Cable Beach or Paradise Island. You can easily reach the beach from a base in Nassau, but it won't be right outside your window.

When you're based in Nassau/Cable Beach, you have an array of watersports, golf, tennis, and plenty of duty-free shopping nearby—not to mention those fine powdery beaches. In addition, the resorts, restaurants, and beaches of Paradise Island, discussed in the next chapter, are just a short distance away. Paradise Island, which lies just opposite Nassau, is connected to New Providence Island by a toll bridge. For northbound traffic (that is, from New Providence Island to Paradise Island), the bridge costs $1 (55p) for cars, $2 (£1.05) for taxis, and is free for pedestrians. Southbound traffic for all vehicles is free. There's also frequent ferry and water-taxi service between Nassau and Paradise Island.

As the sun goes down, Cable Beach and Paradise Island heat up, offering fine dining, glitzy casinos, cabaret shows, moonlight cruises, dance clubs, and romantic evening strolls. (We'd confine the evening stroll to Cable Beach or Paradise Island, and not the streets of downtown Nassau, which can be dangerous at night.)

The shops might draw a lot more business than the museums, but no city in The Bahamas is as rich in history as Nassau. You can take a "royal climb" up the Queen's Staircase to Fort Fincastle. These 66 steps are said to have been cut in the sandstone cliffs by slaves in the 1790s. Other Nassau attractions include Ardastra Gardens, which feature 2 hectares (5 acres) of landscaping and more than 300 exotic birds, mammals, and reptiles. Most popular are the trained pink flamingos that march for audiences daily to their trainer's commands.

It's surprising that Nassau has retained its overlay of British colonial charm despite its proximity to Florida and the massive influx of North American business. It hasn't become completely Americanized, at least not yet; despite new development, traffic, and cruise-ship crowds, Nassau's still a long way from becoming another Miami. Stately old homes and public buildings still stand proudly among the modern high-rises and bland government buildings. Tropical foliage lines streets where horse-drawn surreys still trot by, carrying visitors on leisurely tours. Police officers in white starched jackets and dome-shaped pith helmets still direct traffic on the main streets, as they have long done. It could almost be England—but for the weather, that is, and for the staunch and sometimes defiant presence of a deeply entrenched sense of Bahamian nationalism.

1 Orientation

ARRIVING

BY PLANE   Planes land at Nassau's **Lynden Pindling International Airport** (© 242/377-1759), which lies 13km (8 miles) west of Nassau, in the pine forests beside Lake Killarney.

No bus service goes from the airport to Cable Beach, Nassau, or Paradise Island. Your hotel may provide airport transfers if you've made arrangements in advance; these are often included in package deals. There are also any number of car-rental offices here if you plan to have a car while on New Providence Island (see "Getting Around," below), though we don't really think you need one.

If you don't have a lift arranged, take a taxi to your hotel. From the airport to the center of Nassau, expect to pay around $22 (£12); from the airport to Cable Beach, $15 (£7.95); from the airport to Paradise Island, $28 (£15), a rate which includes the $10 (£5.30) bridge toll for passage between New Providence Island and Paradise Island. Drivers expect to be tipped 15%, and some will remind you should you "forget." You don't need to stop at a currency exchange office before departing the airport: U.S. currency is fine for these (and any other) transactions.

BY CRUISE SHIP   Nassau has spent millions of dollars expanding its port so that a number of cruise ships can come into port at once. Sounds great in theory. Practically speaking, however, facilities in Nassau, Cable Beach, and Paradise Island become extremely overcrowded as soon as the big boats dock. You'll have to stake out your space on the beach, and you will find downtown streets, shops, and attractions overrun with visitors every day you're in port.

Cruise ships dock near Rawson Square, the heart of the city and the shopping area—and the best place to begin a tour of Nassau. Unless you want to go to one of the beach strips along Cable Beach or Paradise Island, you won't need a taxi. You can go on a shopping expedition near where you dock: The Straw Market is nearby, at Market Plaza; Bay Street—the main shopping artery—is also close; and the Nassau International Bazaar is at the intersection of Woodes Rogers Walk and Charlotte Street.

The government has added **"Festival Place"** (© 242/322-7680) to the Prince George dock (where the cruise ships arrive). Designed as a welcome point and service center for cruise ship visitors, Festival Place is a multicolored structure with about 45 shops selling sundries, gift items, duty-free luxury goods, and Bahamian-themed arts, crafts, and souvenirs. It also contains a tourist information booth (© **242/323-3182** or 242/323-3183) and various snack bars and cafes. This mall-like facility is open

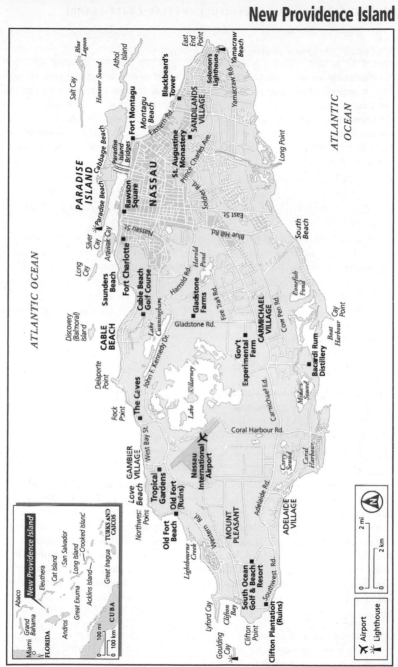

Favorite New Providence Experiences

Listening to the Sounds of Goombay. At some local joint, you can enjoy an intoxicating beat and such island favorites as Andros-born Elon Moxey's "Catch the Crab," and K.B.'s "Civil Servants" (a satire on The Bahamas' sometimes pervasive government bureaucracy). Deeply ingrained in the Bahamian musical psyche is what eventually became a huge international hit, "Funky Nassau." Older, more nostalgic tones include "Goin' Down Burma Road," "Get Involved," and "John B. Sail."

A Ride in a Horse-Drawn Surrey. If you'd like to see Nassau as the Duke of Windsor did when he was governor, consider this archaic but charming form of transportation. It's elegant, romantic, and nostalgic. Surreys await passengers at Rawson Square, in the exact center of Nassau.

A Glass-Bottomed Boat Ride. Right in the middle of Nassau's harbor, numerous boats wait to take you through the colorful sea gardens off New Providence Island. In the teeming reefs offshore, you'll meet all sorts of sea creatures that inhabit this underwater wonderland.

A Day on Blue Lagoon Island. It's like an old Hollywood fantasy of a tropical island. Located off the eastern end of Paradise Island, Blue Lagoon Island has seven sandy beaches. Boats from the Ferryboat Docks on Paradise Island take you there and back.

daily 8am to 8pm, but if cruise ships are in port that day, closing is extended to as late as 10pm. You can lounge and have a daiquiri while you listen to the live calypso entertainment, or even get your hair braided. From a point nearby, you can catch a ride by horse and surrey, or take a water taxi across the channel to Paradise Island. (For more on that, see chapter 4.)

VISITOR INFORMATION

The Bahamas Ministry of Tourism maintains a **tourist information booth** at the Nassau International Airport in the arrivals terminal (© **242/377-6806;** www.bahamas.com). Hours are from 9am to 10pm daily.

Information can also be obtained from the Information Desk at the **Ministry of Tourism's Office,** Bolam House, George Street (© **242/302-2000**), which is open Monday to Friday 9am to 5pm. It's also available from the tourist information booth at Festival Place (© **242/323-3182** or 242/323-3183), where the cruise ships dock. The Festival Place Tourist information kiosk is usually open daily year-round from 7:45am to 6pm.

THE LAY OF THE LAND

Most of the hotels in Nassau are city hotels and are not on the water. If you want to stay right on the sands, choose a hotel in Cable Beach (later in this chapter) or on Paradise Island (see chapter 4).

Rawson Square is the heart of Nassau, positioned just a short walk from **Prince George Wharf,** where the big cruise ships, many of them originating in Florida, berth. Here you'll see the Churchill Building, which contains the offices of the Bahamian prime minister along with other government ministries.

Busy **Bay Street,** the main shopping artery, begins on the south side of Rawson Square. This was the turf of the infamous "Bay Street Boys," a group of rich white Bahamians who once controlled political and economic activity on New Providence.

On the opposite side of Rawson Square is **Parliament Square,** with a statue of a youthful Queen Victoria. Here are more government houses and the House of Assembly. These are Georgian and neo-Georgian buildings, some dating from the late 1700s.

The courthouse is separated by a little square from the **Nassau Public Library and Museum,** which opens onto Bank Lane. It was the former Nassau Gaol (jail). South of the library, across Shirley Street, are the remains of the **Royal Victoria Hotel,** which opened the same year the American Civil War began (1861) and once hosted blockade runners and Confederate spies.

A walk down Parliament Street leads to the post office. Philatelists may want to stop in because some Bahamian stamps are collectors' items.

Going south, moving farther away from the water, Elizabeth Avenue takes you to the **Queen's Staircase.** One of the major landmarks of Nassau, it leads to Bennet's Hill and Fort Fincastle.

If you return to Bay Street, you'll discover the oversized tent which contains the **Straw Market,** a handicrafts emporium where you can buy all sorts of souvenirs.

In Nassau, and especially in the rest of The Bahamas, you will seldom, if ever, find street numbers on hotels or other businesses. In the more remote places, you sometimes won't even find street names. Get directions before heading somewhere in particular. Of course, you can always ask along the way, as most Bahamians are very helpful.

2 Getting Around

BY TAXI

You can easily rely on taxis and skip renting a car. The rates for New Providence, including Nassau, are set by the government. Although working meters are required in all taxis, some of them don't work. Consequently, the government has established a well-defined roster of rates for passage between the airport and various points around the island. When you get in, the fixed rate is $3 (£1.60), plus 40¢ (20p) for each additional quarter-mile. Each passenger over 2 years old pays an extra $3 (£1.60). For sightseeing purposes, taxis can also be hired at the hourly rate of $45 (£24) for a

---

Moments A Surrey with a Fringe on Top

The nostalgic and old-fashioned way to see Nassau is in a horse-drawn surrey—the kind with the fringe on top and a wilted hibiscus stuck in the straw hat shielding the horse from the sun. Before you get in, you should negotiate with the driver and agree on the price. The average charge is between $10 (£5.30) and $15 (£7.95) per person for a 20-minute ride. The maximum load is three adults plus one or two children under the age of 12. The surreys are available daily from 9am to 4:30pm, except when the horses are resting (that's 1–3pm May–Oct, and 1–2pm Nov–Apr). You'll find the surreys at Rawson Square, off Bay Street, close to the Straw Market.

Tips **On Your Own Sturdy Feet**

This is the only way to see Old Nassau, unless you rent a horse and carriage. All the major attractions and the principal stores are within walking distance. You can even walk to Cable Beach or Paradise Island, although it's a hike in the hot sun. Confine your walking to the daytime, and beware of the occasional pickpocket and purse snatcher. In the evening, avoid walking the streets of downtown Nassau, where, from time to time, muggings have been reported.

five-passenger cab. Luggage is carried at a surcharge of $1 (55p) extra per piece, although the first two pieces are transported free. The radio-taxi call number is ✆ **242/323-5111.** It's easy to get a taxi at the airport or at any of the big hotels.

BY CAR

You really don't need to rent a car. It's a lot easier to rely on taxis when you're ready to leave the beach and do a little exploring.

However, if you choose to drive (perhaps for a day of touring the whole island), some of the biggest U.S. car-rental companies maintain branches at the airport, in downtown Nassau, at Cable Beach, and on Paradise Island. **Avis** (✆ **800/331-1212** or 242/326-6380; www.avis.com) operates at the airport and also has branches at the cruise-ship docks at Bay Street and Cumberland Street, across from the British Colonial Hilton (✆ 242/326-6380). **Budget Rent-a-Car** (✆ **800/527-0700** or 242/377-9000; www.budgetrentacar.com) has a branch at the airport and on Shirley Street in downtown Nassau. **Dollar/Thrifty Rent-a-Car** (✆ **800/654-3131** or 242/ 377-8300; www.dollar.com) rents at the airport and also from within a kiosk at the British Colonial Hilton. **Hertz** (✆ **800/654-3131** or 242/377-8684; www.hertz. com) has only one location: at the airport.

Remember: Drive on the left!

BY BUS

The least expensive means of transport is by any of the medium-sized buses (some locals refer to them as "jitneys") that make runs from downtown Nassau to outposts on New Providence. The fare is $1 (55p), and exact change, in coins or with a dollar bill, is required. The jitneys operate daily from 6:30am to 7pm. Buses to the Cable Beach area and points west of that include the much-used #10, the 10A, and the "Western" bus. They depart from the corner of Bay Street and George Street, and stop at various clearly designated spots along Bay Street. Buses headed to the eastern (mostly residential and rarely accessed by short-term visitors) part of New Providence Island depart from the Frederick Street North depot.

BY BOAT

Water taxis operate daily from 9am to 6pm at 20-minute intervals between Paradise Island and Prince George Wharf. An alternative service involves ferryboats, which link the wharves at the end of Casuarina Drive on Paradise Island to Rawson Square, across the channel on New Providence Island. The ferry operates daily from 9:30am to 4:15pm, with departures every half-hour from both sides of the harbor. Both the ferryboats and the water taxis charge the same fixed rate: $3 (£1.60) per person, each way, for passage across the channel.

BY MOPED

Lots of visitors like to rent mopeds to explore the island. Unless you're an experienced moped rider, stay on quiet roads until you feel at ease. (Don't start out in all the congestion on Bay St.) Some hotels maintain rental kiosks on their premises. If yours doesn't, try **Knowles** (© **242/356-0741**), at Festival Place, near the cruise ship dock, which rents mopeds for $50 (£27) per day. Included in the rental price are insurance and mandatory helmets for both drivers and passengers. Mopeds are rented daily between 8am and 5pm.

FAST FACTS: New Providence

American Express The local representative is **Destinations**, 303 Shirley St., between Charlotte and Parliament streets, Nassau (© **242/322-2931**). Hours are Monday to Friday 9am to 5pm.

ATMs Major banks with ATMs in Nassau include the **Royal Bank of Canada** (© **242/322-8700**), **Bank of Nova Scotia** (© **242/356-1517**), and **The First Caribbean Bank** (formerly known as Barclays; © **242/356-8000**). However, some accept cards only in the **Cirrus** network (© **800/424-7787**), while others take only **PLUS** (© **800/843-7587**). ATMs at both the Paradise Island and Cable Beach casinos dispense quick cash. Be alert to the fact that whereas ATM machines within large hotels and casinos tend to dispense U.S. dollars, ATM machines within banks and at the airport dispense Bahamian dollars. Since both U.S. and Bahamian currencies are readily accepted anywhere, it's not a crucial issue, but it's a good idea to read the information on the individual ATM machine before proceeding with your transaction.

Babysitting Hotel staff can help you hire an experienced sitter. Expect to pay around $10 to $15 (£5.30–£7.95) an hour, plus $3 (£1.60) an hour for each additional child.

Climate See "When to Go," in chapter 2.

Dentist Try the dental department of the **Princess Margaret Hospital** on Sands Road (© **242/322-2861**).

Doctor For the best service, use a staff member of the **Princess Margaret Hospital** on Sands Road (© **242/322-2861**).

Drugstores Try **Lowes Pharmacy,** Palm Dale, in downtown Nassau (© **242/322-8594**), open Monday to Saturday 8am to 6:30pm. They also maintain three branches in the Harbour Bay Shopping Center (© **242/393-4813**), open Monday to Saturday 8am to 8:30pm and Sunday 9am to 5pm; in the **Town Center Mall** (© **242/325-6482**), open Monday to Saturday 9:30am to 8pm; and an additional outlet on Soldier Road (© **242/394-6312**), which is open Monday to Saturday 8am to 8pm. Nassau has no late-night pharmacies.

Embassies & Consulates See "Fast Facts: The Bahamas," in chapter 2.

Emergencies For any major emergency, call © either **911** or 919.

Eyeglass Repair The **Optique Shoppe,** 22 Parliament St. at the corner of Shirley Street (© **242/322-3910**), is convenient to the center of Nassau. Hours are Monday to Friday 9am to 5pm and on Saturday 9am to noon.

Hospitals The government-operated **Princess Margaret Hospital** on Sands Road ((℡ **242/322-2861**) is one of the major hospitals in The Bahamas. The privately owned **Doctors Hospital,** 1 Collins Ave. ((℡ **242/322-8411**), is the most modern private health care facility in the region.

Hot Lines For information about help or assistance of any kind, call (℡ **242/326-HELP.**

Information See "Visitor Information," above.

Internet Access Check out **Cyberjack** at the **Mall on Marathon Road** ((℡ **242/394-6254**). Here you can get online from your own laptop or log on to one of their computers. The cost is 15¢ (8p) per minute. Most of the larger hotels also offer guests Internet access for a fee. Payable by credit card, the fee can in some cases be as high as 50¢ (25p) per minute of use, which can add up quickly if you're an addictive web-surfer.

Laundry & Dry Cleaning **Superwash** ((℡ **242/323-4018**), at the corner of Nassau Street and Boyd Road, offers coin-operated machines; it's open 24 hours a day, 7 days a week. Drop-off service is available for a small additional fee. In the same building is the **New Oriental Dry Cleaner** ((℡ **242/323-7249**).

Newspapers & Magazines The *Tribune Daily* and the *Nassau Guardian,* both published in the morning, are the country's two competing daily newspapers. At your hotel and visitor information stations, you can find various helpful magazines, brochures, and booklets.

Photographic Needs The largest camera store in Nassau is **John Bull** ((℡ **242/302-2800**), on Bay Street 3 blocks west of Rawson Square. It maintains four additional branches scattered at heavily visited tourist sites across New Providence and Paradise Island. Each of these outlets also sells perfume, watches, and jewelry.

Police Dial (℡ **911** or 919.

Post Office **The Nassau General Post Office,** at the top of Parliament Street on East Hill Street ((℡ **242/322-3344**), is open Monday to Friday 9am to 5pm and on Saturday 8:30am to 12:30pm. Note that you can buy stamps from most postcard kiosks. A postcard sent airmail to the U.S. or Canada costs 50¢ (25p); a letter to the same destinations costs 65¢ (35p) per half-ounce.

Safety Avoid walking along lonely side streets in downtown Nassau at night, where there are sometimes robberies and muggings. (Because the local government is particularly punitive against crimes against tourists, most visitors from outside The Bahamas are never affected, but it's probably better to be safe than sorry.) Cable Beach and Paradise Island tend to be safer than downtown Nassau after dark.

Taxes There is no sales tax on any purchases made within The Bahamas, though there is a 12% hotel tax. Although it isn't immediately obvious, since the fee is automatically included in the price of any airline or cruise ship ticket, visitors leaving The Bahamas each pay a $20 (£11) departure tax.

3 Where to Stay

In the hotel descriptions that follow, we've listed regular room prices or "rack rates," but these are simply for ease of comparison. They are likely to be accurate for smaller properties, but you can almost always do better at the larger hotels and resorts. *Note:* Read the section "Packages for the Independent Traveler" in chapter 2 before you book a hotel separately from your airfare, and if you do book yourself, always inquire about honeymoon specials, golf packages, summer weeks, and other discounts. In many cases, too, a travel agent can get you a package deal that would be cheaper than these official rates.

Hotels add a 12% "resort levy" tax to your rate. Sometimes this is quoted in advance as part of the net price; at other times, it's added as an unexpected last-minute afterthought to your final bill. When you are quoted a rate, always ask if the tax is included. Many hotels also add a 15% service charge to your bill. Ask about these charges in advance so you won't be shocked when you receive the final tab.

Taxes and service are not included in the rates listed below. We'll lead off with a selection of hotels within the heart of Nassau, followed by accommodations in Cable Beach. Most visitors prefer to stay at Cable Beach since the resorts here are right on the sand. But you can stay in Nassau and commute to the beaches at Cable Beach or Paradise Island; it's cheaper but less convenient. Those who prefer the ambience of Old Nassau's historic district and being near the best shops may decide to stay in town.

NASSAU
EXPENSIVE

British Colonial Hilton 🏨🏨   In the restored British Colonial Hilton, there's a palpable air of the long-ago days when The Bahamas was firmly within the political and social orbit of Britain. This landmark seven-story hotel has seen its share of ups and downs over the years. Plush and glamorous when it was built in 1900, it burned to the ground in 1920 and was rebuilt 3 years later before deteriorating into a flophouse. Between 1996 and 1999, a Canadian entrepreneur poured $68 million into its restoration.

Don't expect the glitz and glitter of Cable Beach or Paradise Island here—the Hilton is after business travelers rather than the casino crowd. It also lacks the aristocratic credentials of Graycliff (see below). Nonetheless, it's a dignified and friendly, but rather sedate, hotel with a discreetly upscale decor (no Disney-style themes or gimmicks). Bedrooms, each renovated sometime during 2006 or 2007, are a bit on the small side but capped with rich crown moldings and accessorized with tile or stone-sheathed bathrooms with tub/showers. The staff, incidentally, is well trained and motivated; we've found them upbeat and hardworking. There's a small beach a few steps away, but it's not very appealing (it's on the narrow channel separating New Providence from Paradise Island, with no wave action at all).

1 Bay St. (P.O. Box N-7148), Nassau, The Bahamas. ⓒ **800/HILTONS** in the U.S. and Canada, or 242/322-3301. Fax 242/302-9009. www.hilton.com. 291 units. Winter $379–$409 (£201–£217) double, $509–$1,400 (£270–£742) suite; off season $299–$369 (£158–£196) double, $429–$1,400 (£227–£742) suite. AE, DC, DISC, MC, V. Bus: 10. **Amenities:** 2 restaurants; 2 bars; outdoor pool; health club; full-service spa; tour desk; business center; secretarial service; room service; babysitting; laundry service; dry cleaning. *In room:* A/C, TV, minibar, coffeemaker, hair dryer, iron, safe, trouser press.

Where to Stay & Dine in Nassau

ACCOMMODATIONS ■

British Colonial Hilton **5**
El Greco Hotel **4**
Graycliff **9**
Nassau Harbour Club Hotel
& Marina **16**
Nassau Palm Resort **3**
Quality Inn Junkanoo Beach
Nassau **2**

DINING ◆

Bahamian Kitchen **10**
Café Matisse **11**
Café Skans **1**
Conch Fritters
Bar & Grill **9**
Double Dragon **13**
East Villa Restaurant
and Lounge **15**

Graycliff **7**
Luciano's of
Chicago **13**
Outback
Steakhouse **14**
Poop Deck **16**
Ristorante Villagio **1**

Shoal Restaurant
and Lounge **6**
Sun and... **17**
Taj Mahal **12**
The White Door **8**

ATLANTIC OCEAN

Pirate Cove

Paradise Beach

PARADISE ISLAND

Cabbage Beach

Arawak Beach

The Atlantis

Paradise Island Golf Club

Paradise Island Golf Course

Paradise Beach St.

Casino Dr.

Nassau Harbour

Potter's Cay

Victoria Beach

Bay St.

Shirley St.

Paradise Island Bridges

Malcolm Park

Nassau Yacht Club

Fort Montagu

Mount Royal Ave.

Shirley Park Ave.

Retirement Rd.

East Bay St.

Montagu Beach

Shirley

Lake Waterloo

Fowler St.

MURPHYVILLE

SHIRLEA ALLENS

St. James Rd.

Kemp Rd.

DUNMORE VILL

Montagu Ave.

Sailing Club

Rosetta St.

Sutton St.

DICKS POINT

Collins Ave.

Sixth Ter. Madeira St.

Shop Centres

Dundas Centre

EASTVILLE

GREEN VILLAGE

Civic Centre

Eastern Rd.

BILNEY

Mackey St.

Supermarket

BROOKLYN

Village Rd.

Commonwealth Rd.

Richmond Rd.

The Hermitage

Wulff Rd.

St. Andrew Dr.

Bristol St.

To East End

ENGLERSTON

Claridge Ave.

CLARIDGEDALE

Soldier Rd.

Bernard Rd.

Johnson Rd.

High Tech Dr.

HIGH VISTA

Balfour Ave.

Pyfrom

Robinson Rd.

Marathon Mall

REGENCY PARK

WINDSOR

Adderley St.

SANDILANDS VILLAGE

Independence Rd.

Old Trail Rd.

Prince Charles Ave.

Windsor St.

Augustines Rd.

Bernard Rd.

Fox Hill Rd.

Soldier Rd.

FOXDALE

N

Nassau International Airport

Lake Killarney

Area of detail

NEW PROVIDENCE ISLAND

0   5 mi

0   5 km

77

Fun Fact **In Suite Double O, a "License to Kill"**

In both the *Thunderball* and *Never Say Never Again* films, James Bond—secret agent 007—was served shaken martinis at the British Colonial. To commemorate that historic event, the Hilton-owned property now has a "Double-O" suite (#417) filled with Bond memorabilia that includes posters, books, CDs, movie stills, and recorded versions of all the best Bond flicks, including *Goldfinger* and *Live and Let Die.* Guests can take a Bond book from the suite, perhaps *Tomorrow Never Dies,* and curl up on a chaise longue at the beach. The suite is a one-bedroom unit with living room and ocean views. When you get tired of the movie Bond, you might be able to stroll over to the next chair and meet the real Bond—Sean Connery is often at his island home on nearby Lyford Cay.

Graycliff ♠ Now in a kind of nostalgic decay, Graycliff remains the grande dame of downtown Nassau hotels even though her tiara is a bit tarnished and her age is showing. In spite of its drawbacks, this place still has its devotees, especially older visitors. Originally an 18th-century private home reflecting Georgian colonial architecture, it's now an intimate inn with old-fashioned atmosphere. Even though the inn isn't on the beach, people who can afford to stay anywhere sometimes choose Graycliff because it epitomizes the old-world style and grace that evokes Nassau back in the days when the Duke and Duchess of Windsor were in residence. Churchill, of course, can no longer be seen paddling around in the swimming pool with a cigar in his mouth, and the Beatles are long gone, but the three-story Graycliff marches onward, without the visiting celebs who today head for Paradise Island. Beach lovers usually go by taxi to either nearby Goodman's Bay or the Western Esplanade Beach, nearly adjacent to Arawak Cay. The bigger British Colonial Hilton is Graycliff's main competitor; they both have a rather staid, deliberately unflashy ambience.

The historic garden rooms in the main house are large and individually decorated with antiques, though the better units are the more modern garden rooms. The Yellow Bird, Hibiscus, and Pool cottages are ideal choices, but the most luxurious accommodation of all is the Mandarino Suite, with Asian decor, a king-size bed, an oversize bathroom, and a private balcony overlooking the swimming pool. Bathrooms are spacious, with tub/showers, deluxe toiletries, and robes.

8–12 W. Hill St. (P.O. Box N-10246), Nassau, The Bahamas. © **242/302-9150** or 242/326-6188. Fax 242/326-6188. www.graycliff.com. 18 units. Winter $325–$370 (£172–£196) double, $450 (£239) cottage; off season $290 (£154) double, $400 (£212) cottage. AE, MC, V. Bus: 10 or 21A. **Amenities:** 2 restaurants; 2 bars; 2 outdoor pools; spa; Jacuzzi; sauna; room service; massage; babysitting; laundry service; dry cleaning. *In room:* A/C, TV, minibar, hair dryer, iron, safe.

MODERATE

Nassau Palm Resort *(Value* A short walk west of downtown Nassau, within a cluster of other cost-conscious hotels that include both the (also-recommended) El Greco and The Quality Inn, this hotel lies across the often-busy West Bay Street from the relatively narrow confines of Junkanoo Beach (which is also known as Lighthouse Beach or the Western Esplanade). Although not as fine or dramatic as Cable Beach, a few miles to the west, it's a safe urban beach with tranquil waters and a lot of shells. This place is a good value for those who don't demand particularly attentive service and who don't want to pay the higher prices charged by the more deluxe and better-accessorized hotels along Cable Beach. Bedrooms are outfitted in a standardized motel style, most with a view of Nassau Harbour, and they come with extras you don't always find in a moderately priced choice, such as alarm clocks, two-line phones, and a working desk. All have relatively well-maintained bathrooms containing tub/showers.

There's a bar and two restaurants within a few steps of the hotel itself, and several others within a 5-minute walk.

W. Bay St. (P.O. Box SS-19055), Nassau, The Bahamas. ℂ 242/356-0000. Fax 242/323-1408. www.nassau-hotels. com. 183 units. Winter $95 (£50) double, $135 (£72) suite; off season $89 (£47) double, $95 (£500) suite. AE, DISC, MC, V. Bus: 10 or 17. **Amenities:** 2 restaurants; 2 bars; 2 outdoor pools; health club; spa; salon; room service; laundry service; dry cleaning; nonsmoking rooms; rooms for those w/limited mobility. *In room:* A/C, TV, fridge, coffeemaker, hair dryer, iron, safe, Wi-Fi.

INEXPENSIVE

El Greco Hotel   This hotel is across the street from Junkanoo Beach/Lighthouse Beach/The Western Esplanade, and a short walk from the sometimes raucous nightlife of Arawak Cay. It's also a quick walk from the shops and restaurants of downtown Nassau. El Greco is a well-managed bargain choice that attracts many European travelers. The Greek owners and staff genuinely seem to care about their guests—in fact, the two-story hotel seems more like a small European B&B than your typical Bahamian hotel.

The midsize rooms aren't that exciting, but they're clean and comfortable, with decent beds and small tile bathrooms, containing tub/showers. Bedrooms have a bright decor—a sort of Mediterranean motif, each with two ceiling fans and carpeted floors. Accommodations are built around a courtyard that contains statues crafted in the Italian baroque style, draped with lots of bougainvillea. A restaurant isn't on-site, but you can walk to many places nearby for meals.

W. Bay St. (P.O. Box N-4187), Nassau, The Bahamas. ℂ 242/325-1121. Fax 242/325 1124. 27 units, Winter $140 (£74) double, $160 $200 (£85–£106) suite; off season $120 (£64) double, $140–$170 (£74–£90) suite. AE, MC, V. Free parking. Bus: 10. **Amenities:** Bar; pool; babysitting. *In room:* A/C, TV.

Nassau Harbour Club Hotel & Marina   Don't expect lush and sprawling gardens or much peace and privacy here—this battered, much-used hotel is in the heart of a busy commercial neighborhood of downtown Nassau that's devoted to boats, boat repair, and the fishing and warehousing industry, even though the more formal showcase neighborhoods of Nassau lie within a 15-minute walk. A compound of two-story pink buildings from the early 1960s arranged like a horseshoe around a concrete terrace, it occupies a bustling strip of land between busy Bay Street and the edge of the channel that separates New Providence from Paradise Island. Rooms offer views of yachts and boats moored at a nearby marina, and easy access to the shops, bars, and restaurants of downtown Nassau and within the Harbour Bay Shopping Centre. Throughout, it's down-to-earth, aggressively unpretentious, and just a bit funky. Bedrooms are simple and compact but comfortable, and equipped with bathrooms with tub/showers. However, they are just a bit beat-up and worn.

E. Bay St. (P.O. Box SS-5755), Nassau, The Bahamas. ℂ 242/393-0771. Fax 242/393-5393. 50 units. Year-round $120 (£64) double; $130 (£69) suite. Extra person $20 (£11) per day. AE, MC, V. Free parking. Bus: 9, 11, or 19. **Amenities:** Restaurant; bar; outdoor pool, babysitting. *In room:* A/C, TV, fridge.

Quality Inn Junkanoo Beach Nassau   This no-nonsense, efficiently designed, green-fronted hotel rises prominently across the sometimes busy traffic of West Bay Street, from the narrow sands known variously as Junkanoo Beach, Lighthouse Beach, Long Wharf, and the Western Esplanade. Partly because of its compact rooms, it's the least desirable, and also the least expensive, of the also-recommended hotels (the Nassau Palm and the El Greco) that lie nearby within this congested neighborhood of downtown Nassau. But during the peak of winter, when other competitors might be more expensive or sold out completely, it offers comfortable, unpretentious lodgings in a six-story venue that might be appealing if you don't expect tons of amenities and superlative service.

W. Bay St. and Nassau St., Nassau, The Bahamas. (℃) 242/322-1515. Fax 242/322-1514. www.choicehotels.com. 63 units. Winter $111–$123 (£59–£65) double; off season $89–$112 (£47–£59) double. AE, DC, MC, V. Bus: 10, 16. Amenities: Bar; outdoor pool; business center; dry-cleaning service; nonsmoking rooms; rooms for those w/limited mobility. In room: A/C, TV, hair dryer, iron, beverage maker.

CABLE BEACH

Cable Beach has always figured high in the consciousness of The Bahamas. Since the development of the more dramatic Atlantis Resort on Paradise Island, it has flourished, and occasionally suffered, in the shadow of its more dramatic counterpart. Cable Beach derived its name from the underwater telephone and telegraph cable that brought directly onto its sands electronic communications from the outside world. For years, it was a rural outpost of New Providence Island, flanked by private homes and a desirable beach that was a destination for local residents. Its first major touristic boost came with the construction of the old Ambassador Beach Hotel, now the site of Breezes Bahamas. In the 1980s, a building boom added the string of condos, timeshares, and hotels that defined the area's appearance for the next 25 years, all designed to serve the holiday needs of sun-seekers and casino-goers. The district boasts a wide variety of restaurants and sports facilities, lots of glitz and glitter, and one of the two biggest casinos (in terms of square footage) in The Bahamas.

In 2005, a consortium of major-league investors, coalescing under the Baha Mar logo, pinpointed Cable Beach as the eventual site of one of the most far-reaching resort developments in the Atlantic. In 2006 and 2007, they inaugurated a plan that will radically alter the present landscape of Cable Beach, adding to the overall competitiveness of Nassau in general and its northern seafront in particular. Expect big changes between 2008 and 2010, when a multitier redevelopment program will alter the status of Cable Beach as the "also-ran" to what might—if all phases of the redevelopment are completed—become one of the most talked-about casino and resort destinations in the world. The project is being run by Baha Mar Resorts Limited, which owns and operates Cable Beach Resorts and Crystal Palace Casino.

In 2007, massive, multimillion-dollar improvements were made to the existing hotel infrastructure, with radical renovations completed within each of the pre-existing accommodations, During most of 2008, look for the destruction of some of the most outmoded of the elements within the Cable Beach landscape and the inauguration of a building program that, by anyone's standards, is awe-inspiring. By 2009, some of the radical redevelopment will be more visible, and by 2010, clients will find an environment that's totally different from the venue as it stands at press time.

We're talking makeovers on an extreme—and hyperexpensive—scale that evoke the labors of the Pharaohs. Major infrastructure changes will include a revised layout of West Bay Street, one of New Providence Island's busiest traffic arteries, to direct traffic away from what will become building sites for as many as four additional name-brand hotels. The overall vision will include dredging new lakes and marinas, creating water traps for a thoroughly redesigned golf course, demolishing some older buildings within the Cable Beach compound, and extensively enlarging the existing casino.

Where to Stay & Dine in Cable Beach

ACCOMMODATIONS ■
Breezes Bahamas **9**
Orange Hill Beach Inn **1**
Sheraton Cable Beach Hotel **7**

Sandals Royal
Bahamian Hotel & Spa **4**
Westwind II **6**
Wyndham Nassau Resort
& Crystal Palace Casino **8**

DINING ◆
Amici's **7**
The Black Angus Grille **8**
Capriccio **5**
Moso **8**

The Poop Deck at Sandy Port **3**
Provence **3**
Sole Mare **8**
Travellers Rest **2**

The project also calls for constructing a new string of resort hotels, all of them members of the Starwood group. Each property will cater to a different resort market. A W hotel, for example, will accent avant-garde design and, it's hoped, attract a youthful, trend-setting clientele. An all-new Saint Regis hotel will offer more conservative—and probably somewhat plusher—comforts geared to the *haute bourgeoisie*. And serious gamblers looking for Las Vegas flash will gravitate toward a new incarnation of a Caesar's Palace hotel, still in the planning stage, but eventually equivalent to the best of big-time Nevada. The makeover melee will also include intelligent reuse of some of the existing structures, including a radical rethinking of the Wyndham and Sheraton properties, which—in their present incarnations—are recommended in "Where to Stay in Cable Beach" (see below).

Even in its current form, Cable Beach has many loyal fans, some of whom think Paradise Island is too expensive, too snobbish, too contrived, too artificial, and too derivative of a Disney-inspired theme park. Come here during the lifetime of this edition for comfortable lodgings, diversion, distraction, and lots of flash. But know in advance that what you see is likely to be remade, reconfigured, replanned, and restructured into something that we predict will become a world-famous tourist sensation beginning in 2010.

WHERE TO STAY IN CABLE BEACH
VERY EXPENSIVE

Breezes Bahamas ⊛   In 1996, SuperClubs, an all-inclusive chain which competes successfully with Sandals (see below), spent $125 million transforming a tired old relic—the Ambassador Beach Hotel—into this all-inclusive resort. Major renovations were completed in 2006, which included an upgrade of most of the plumbing and electrical systems. Today Breezes' biggest competitor is the nearby Sandals Royal Bahamian, which is more imposing, more elegant, more stylish, more expensive, and more upscale. Rowdier and more raucous, and located on a prime 450m (1,476-ft.) beachfront along Cable Beach, Breezes attracts a more middle-of-the-road crowd; it's unpretentious and more affordable (though it isn't exactly cheap, and we think it's a bit overpriced for what it is). This U-shaped beachfront resort has two wings of rooms plus a main clubhouse facing a large, sometimes-overcrowded terrace with a swimming pool that serves as the social centerpiece. Both couples and single travelers are accepted here. Everything is included—the room, meals, snacks, unlimited wine (not the finest) with lunch and dinner, even premium-brand liquor at the bars, plus activities and airport transfers.

The air-conditioned hotel rooms contain pastel-painted furniture with Formica tops. Accommodations are not as luxurious as those at Sandals, but rates are kept deliberately lower. Tiled bathrooms are medium-size, each equipped with a shower and bathtub.

Diners can sample unremarkable international fare at the food court, although the Italian restaurant serves better food. A beachside grill and snacks are available throughout the day. Entertainment includes a high-energy disco, a piano bar, and a nightclub. Karaoke is inevitable, but the professional Junkanoo live shows, which are presented every Saturday night, are more entertaining, and local bands often perform.

P.O. Box CB-13049, Cable Beach, Nassau, The Bahamas. © 800/GO-SUPER or 242/327-5356. Fax 242/327-5155. www.superclubs.com. 391 units. Year-round $144–$219 (£76–£116) per person per night, double occupancy; $234–$269 (£124–£143) per person per night, double occupancy, suite. Rates include all meals, drinks, tips, airport transfers, and most activities. AE, DISC, MC, V. Free parking. Bus: 10. No children under 14 year-round; no one under 18, unless accompanied by an adult 21 or older, Mar–May. **Amenities:** 3 restaurants; 4 bars; 2 outdoor pools; 3 tennis courts; health club; watersports equipment; laundry service; nonsmoking rooms; rooms for those w/limited mobility. *In room:* A/C, TV, coffeemaker, hair dryer, iron, safe.

Moments Junkanoo Festivals

No Bahamian celebration is as raucous as the Junkanoo (which is also the name of the music associated with this festival). The special rituals origi-nated during the colonial days of slavery, when African-born newcomers could legally drink and enjoy themselves only on certain strictly predeter-mined days of the year. In its celebration, Junkanoo closely resembles Car-naval in Rio and Mardi Gras in New Orleans. Its major difference lies in the costumes and the timing (the major Junkanoo celebrations occur the day after Christmas, a legacy of the English celebration of Boxing Day on Dec 26, and New Year's Day). On a more touristy note, a 2-month festival, the **Junkanoo Summer Festival,** takes place in June and July annually.

In the old days, Junkanoo costumes were crafted from crepe paper, often in primary colors, stretched over wire frames. (One sinister offshoot of the celebrations was that Junkanoo costumes and masks were used to conceal the identity of anyone seeking vengeance on a white or on another slave.) Today locals have more money to spend on costumes and Junkanoo festi-vals than they did in the past. The finest costumes can cost up to $15,000 (£7,950) and are sometimes sponsored by local bazaars, lotteries, church groups, and charity auctions. Everyday folks from all walks of Bahamian life also join in, often with homemade costumes that are sensuous or humor-ous. The best time and place to observe Junkanoo is New Year's Day in Nas-sau, when throngs of cavorting, music-making, and costumed figures prance through the streets. Find yourself a good viewing position on Bay Street. Less-elaborate celebrations take place in major towns on the other islands, including Freeport on Grand Bahama Island.

Sandals Royal Bahamian Hotel & Spa ✦✦✦   This all-inclusive property is the most upscale Sandals resort in the world. It's shockingly expensive, though you can often get special promotional rates that make it more reasonable. The property origi-nated as a very posh hotel, the Balmoral Beach, in the 1940s. In 1996, the Jamaica-based Sandals chain poured $20 million into renovating and expanding the resort, and additional renovations have been ongoing ever since. Everywhere, you'll find some of the trappings of Edwardian England in the tropics: manicured gardens, rich cove moldings, neoclassical/Palladian architectural themes, plus hidden courtyards taste-fully accentuated with sculptures. The resort is located on a beach a short walk west of the more glittery megahotels of Cable Beach.

A favorite for honeymoon getaways, Sandals offers well-furnished and often elegant rooms, all classified as suites and positioned within either the resort's core Manor House or the circa-1998 Windsor Building. Others, including some of the most upscale and expensive, occupy outlying villas known collectively as The Royal Village. The villas are preferred because of their rigorously secluded settings and easy access to nearby semiprivate plunge pools. Bedrooms, regardless of their location, have thick cove moldings, formal English furniture, and tub/shower bathrooms loaded with per-fumed soaps and cosmetics. The rooms that face the ocean offer small curved terraces with ornate iron railings and views of an offshore sand spit, Sandals Key.

The Art of the Massage

The Red Lane Spa at Sandals Royal Bahamian Hotel & Spa in Nassau has repeatedly made the top 10 list of spa resorts in the *Condé Nast Traveler* reader's choice survey. The decor features walls and floors of Italian Satumia stone, rich mahogany doors, and a collection of pre-Raphaelite prints in gilded frames. One service offered, Massage Duet, allows couples to learn the art of massage from a professional so they can practice on each other in the comfort of their hotel room.

For a long time, only heterosexual guests were allowed at this resort. But the British and Canadian governments said they wouldn't allow Sandals to advertise its resorts if it continued discriminatory policies against same-sex couples. In 2004, Sandals capitulated and ended the ban. Today self-defined gay couples are accepted as guests, but their numbers since the corporate policy changes haven't been particularly visible.

Bahamian and international fare is offered in generous portions in the property's restaurants. In addition to spectacular buffets, the options include white-glove service and continental dishes in the Baccarat Dining Room. The two latest additions include Kimono's, offering Japanese cuisine, and Casanova, specializing in Italian fare. Other choices include Arizona for Southwestern-style grilled specialties, and Spices for upscale buffets three times a day. The pool here is one of the most appealing on Nassau, with touches of both Vegas and ancient Rome (outdoor murals and replicas of ancient Roman columns jutting skyward above the water). Complimentary shuttle bus service goes to the casino and nightlife options at the nearby Wyndham Crystal Palace complex; concierge service is offered for residents of the resort's higher-priced accommodations.

W. Bay St. (P.O. Box CB-13005), Cable Beach, Nassau, The Bahamas. (© **800/SANDALS** or 242/327-6400. Fax 242/327-6961. www.sandals.com. 403 units. Winter $1,800–$4,000 (£954–£2,120) per couple for 2 days; off season $1,600–$3,800 (£848–£2,014) per couple for 2 days. Rates include all meals, drinks, and activities. AE, DISC, MC, V. Free parking. Bus: 10. Couples only; no children allowed. **Amenities:** 8 restaurants; 9 bars; 6 outdoor pools; 2 tennis courts; health club; full-service spa; watersports equipment; nonsmoking rooms; rooms for those w/limited mobility. *In room:* A/C, TV, coffeemaker, hair dryer, iron, safe.

EXPENSIVE

Sheraton Cable Beach Hotel ⟨ℛ ⟨Kids⟩   Prominently visible in the center of Cable Beach (its best asset) this seven-story high-rise is connected by a shopping arcade to the Crystal Palace Casino. The nearby Wyndham Nassau Resort is glitzier and has better and more exclusive and extensive facilities, but the Sheraton is still one of the most desirable choices for families, as it has the best children's program in the area. Because many of its bedrooms contain two double beds, its accommodations are usually suitable for a family of four. Painted pale coral pink, the property has an Aztec-inspired facade of sharp angles and strongly defined horizontal lines, with prominent balconies. Built in a horseshoe-shaped curve around a landscaped beachfront garden, it's big, brassy, and the beneficiary of an $82-million renovation, half of which had been completed by press time for this edition and the remainder of which was scheduled for completion during the course of 2007 and early 2008. This commitment to a massive outlay of cash was concurrent with the changeover of this property's management contract from Radisson to Sheraton and the Starwood Group.

You'll think of Vegas when you see the rows of fountains in front, the acres of marble sheathing inside, the four-story lobby with towering windows, and the hotel's propensity for hosting large wedding parties, often with groups of participants flown in from the mainland U.S. Big enough to get lost in, but with plenty of intimate nooks, the hotel offers an extensive array of things to do.

Bedrooms are modern and comfortable, reflecting a lighthearted and somewhat whimsical interpretation of "Tommy Bahama" style, replete with dark-stained wood furniture, white walls, and monochromatic, understated colors completely devoid of the floral prints of yesteryear. Big windows open onto views of either the garden or the beach. Units are equipped with one king-size bed or two doubles, along with phones with voice mail. Bathrooms are tiled with tub/showers.

The hotel contains three restaurants, the most glamorous of which is the Amici (recommended separately in "Where to Dine"), serving traditional Italian cuisine in a two-story garden setting. The Outdoor Grill serves Caribbean/continental breakfast and lunch buffets. In the works at press time for this edition was a steak-and-seafood restaurant where guests are seated around a tabletop grill to prepare their own steaks, seafood, or chicken. This older but much-upgraded hotel will function as one of the most important components of a sweeping expansion of the Cable Beach hotel lineup that will be affected during 2009 and 2010. Under the supervision of the Baha Mar Development Corporation, it will be the oldest and most westerly of a massive expansion of the Cable Beach beachfront whose details are laid out in greater detail in other parts of this chapter.

W. Bay St. (P.O. Box N-4914), Cable Beach, Nassau, The Bahamas. ℂ 800/325-3535 or 242/327-6000. Fax 242/327-6987. www.sheraton.com/cablebeach. 694 units. Feb–Apr $249–$389 (£132–£206) double; May–Aug $219–$359 (£116–£190) double; Sept–Jan $189–$329 (£100–£174) double; Christmas/New Year's $369–$489 (£196–£259) double. AE, MC, V. Free parking. Bus: 10. **Amenities:** 3 restaurants; 3 bars; 3 outdoor pools; 2 tennis courts; gym; kid's camp (ages 4–12); shopping arcade; salon; room service; babysitting; laundry service; dry cleaning; rooms for those w/limited mobility. *In room:* A/C, TV, coffeemaker, hair dryer, iron, safe.

Westwind II *(Kids)*   Set on the western edge of Cable Beach's hotel strip, 9.5km (6 miles) from the center of Nassau, the Westwind II is a cluster of two-story buildings that contain two-bedroom, two-bathroom timeshare units, each with a full kitchen (there's a grocery store nearby). The size and facilities of these units make

---

New Hotels in the Making

On New Providence Island, the famous **Compass Point hotel** is reopening in 2008 following a long renovation. It's owned by Chris Blackwell, founder of Island Records, and will offer 18 brightly painted huts, two-story cottages, and cabanas. This is obviously the best place to stay for rock 'n' roll revelers.

In another development announced, the former home of Bob Marley, reggae great, is opening on the island as the **Marley Resort.** Rooms will boast Bose stereos, better to listen to Marley's music. Of course, the reggae star was more famously associated with Jamaica but came to Nassau for a retreat. He and his wife, Rita, escaped here from "the pressures of Jamaica."

The biggest hotel news yet is the announcement by the Ritz-Carlton people that they are going to build an exclusive resort on **Rose Island,** just 4 miles off the coast of Nassau. The deluxe retreat will be set on a 92-hectare (230-acre) enclave that will also include a marina, estate homes, condos, and townhouses.

Family-Friendly Hotels

Both the Sheraton Cable Beach Resort (p. 84) and its immediate neighbor, the Wyndham Nassau Resort (p. 86), provide supervised programs for resident children aged 4 to 12 within their shared facilities, Camp Junkanoo and The Kids Klub, at no additional cost. Activities include swimming, treasure hunts, and nature walks. There's also scavenger hunts, arts and crafts classes, nature explorations, swimming lessons and games, and lessons in such electronic diversions as Nintendo and Xbox. The entire venue is configured as a means of allowing parents to deposit their charges in the morning and pick them up later in the day, secure in the understanding that they'll be fed, watered, amused, and cared for during their short-term separations.

them ideal for traveling families, and the accommodations are available to the public whenever they're not occupied by investors. All the diversions of the megahotels are close by and easily reached, but in the complex itself, you can enjoy a low-key, quiet atmosphere and privacy. (A masonry wall separates the compound from the traffic of W. Bay St. and the hotels and vacant lots that flank it.) Each unit has a pleasant decor that includes white tiled floors, rattan furniture, bathrooms with tub/showers, and either a balcony or a terrace. Since units are identical, price differences are based on whether the units face the beach, the pool, or the garden. The manicured grounds feature palms, flowering hibiscus shrubs, and seasonal flower beds. Don't stay here if you expect any of the luxuries or facilities of the nearby Wyndham Nassau Resort (see above). Westwind II is more for self-sufficient, do-it-yourself types.

W. Bay St. (P.O. Box CB-11006), Cable Beach, Nassau, The Bahamas. © 866/369-5921 or 242/327-7019. Fax 262/327-7529. www.westwind2.com. 54 units. Winter $231–$278 (£122–£147) double; off season $194–$242 (£103–£128) double. MC, V. Bus: 10. **Amenities:** Bar; 2 pools; 2 tennis courts; babysitting; coin-operated laundry; rooms for those w/limited mobility. *In room:* A/C, TV, kitchen, fridge, coffeemaker, iron, Wi-Fi.

Wyndham Nassau Resort & Crystal Palace Casino *(Kids)* This big, flashy

megaresort on the lovely sands of Cable Beach is so vast and all-encompassing that some of its guests never venture into Nassau during their stay on the island. The futuristic-looking complex incorporates five high-rise towers, each painted a shade of pale pink or pale lavender; a futuristic central core illuminated with sunlight streaming through massive greenhouse-style translucent domes; and a cluster of beachfront gazebos—all linked with arcades, covered passageways, and mini pavilions. Guest rooms come in several different price brackets, ranging from standard island view to ocean vista, each with private balconies. Corner suites with lots of space are the way to go, complete with wraparound balconies and king-size beds looking out onto the water through floor-to-ceiling glass. Combination bathrooms (tub/showers) most often come with dressing areas and dual basins.

At press time, management was about three-quarters through a massive $30-million renovation of the interior—which had been sorely needed, in our opinion, because the decor had tended to look a bit too jazzy, a bit too overheated and colorful, and a bit tired. As noted within our introduction to Cable Beach, this hotel will be the carefully planned centerpiece, between 2008 and 2010, of a radical expansion of the hotel lineup along Cable Beach, as envisioned by the Baha Mar Development Corporation. No other hotel on New Providence Island has been through as many changes to its self-image as this one, and thanks to the massive redevelopment of the terrain around it anticipated during the coming 3 years, it's positioning itself to give its biggest competitor, the Atlantis resort on Paradise Island, some fire-breathing competition.

Aside from a massive (and massively upgraded) casino, one of the two largest in The Bahamas, the complex contains a wide array of dining and drinking facilities. Three of its restaurants are among the best-recommended in New Providence. Newest and appealingly experimental, and a personal favorite, is Moso, an enclave of hip that assembles onto one menu the best dishes from around Asia and the Pacific Rim. Even if you're not a guest of the hotel, you might want to avail yourself of the drinking and dining options or the casino action here. As part of a deeply entrenched tradition, the hotel serves as the site for the electoral conventions of the two most powerful political parties in The Bahamas.

W. Bay St. (P.O. Box N-8306), Cable Beach, Nassau, The Bahamas. ℭ 800/222-7466 in the U.S., or 242/327-6200. Fax 954/915-2929. www.wyndhamnassauresort.com. 850 units. Feb–Apr $325–$385 (£172–£204) double; May–Aug $295–$345 (£156–£183) double; Sept–Jan $245–$305 (£130–£1620) double; Christmas/New Year's $465–$525 (£246–£278) double. AE, DC, MC, V. Free self-parking, valet parking $5 (£2.65). Bus: 10. **Amenities:** 6 restaurants; 4 bars; outdoor pool; nearby golf course; health club; Jacuzzi; sauna; children's programs (4–12); business center; massage facilities; room service; babysitting; laundry service; dry cleaning; nonsmoking rooms; rooms for those w/limited mobility. *In room:* A/C, TV, fridge (in some), coffeemaker, hair dryer, iron, safe.

MODERATE

Orange Hill Beach Inn ⭑ *Finds*   This hotel, set on 1.4 landscaped hillside hectares (3½ acres), lies about 13km (8 miles) west of Nassau and 1.5km (1 mile) east of Love Beach, which has great snorkeling. It's perfect for those who want to escape the crowds and stay in a quieter part of New Providence Island; it's easy to catch a cab or jitney to Cable Beach or downtown Nassau. The welcoming owners, Judy and Danny Lowe, an Irish-Bahamian partnership, jokingly refer to their operation as "Fawlty Towers Nassau."

Originally built as a private home in the 1920s, this place became a hotel in 1979 after the Lowes added more rooms and a swimming pool. Rooms and apartments come in a variety of sizes, although most are small. Likewise, the bathrooms are small but well maintained. Each has a balcony or patio, and some of them have kitchenettes. Many of the guests are Europeans, especially in summer. Renovations included updated furniture in the rooms and upgraded bathrooms.

On-site is a bar serving sandwiches and salads throughout the day, and a restaurant that offers simple but good dinners. Diving excursions to the rich marine fauna found along New Providence's southwestern coast are among the most popular activities here. Management maintains free regular jitney service to and from local grocery stores, a fact that's much appreciated by clients who prepare many of their meals within their individual kitchenettes.

W. Bay St., just west of Blake Rd. (P.O. Box N-8583), Nassau, The Bahamas. ℭ 242/327-7157. Fax 242/327-5186. www.orangehill.com. 33 units. Winter $141 (£75) double, $146 (£77) w/kitchenette; off season $123 (£65) double, $126 (£67) w/kitchenette. MC, V. Free parking. Bus: 10. **Amenities:** Restaurant; bar; outdoor pool; laundry service and coin-operated laundry; rooms for those w/limited mobility. *In room:* A/C, TV, kitchenette (in some).

4 Where to Dine

NASSAU

Nassau restaurants open and close often. Even if reservations aren't required, it's a good idea to call first just to see that a place is still functioning. European and American cuisine are relatively easy to find in Nassau. Surprisingly, it used to be difficult to find Bahamian cuisine, but in recent years, more places have begun to offer authentic island fare.

EXPENSIVE

Graycliff ⟨★⟩ CONTINENTAL   Part of the Graycliff hotel, an antiques-filled colonial mansion located in the commercial core of Nassau, opposite Government House, this deeply entrenched, long-enduring restaurant retains a history and an almost palpable sense of nostalgia for the old days of The Bahamas as a colonial outpost of Britain, despite sweeping changes in both the government and the society at large. The chefs use local Bahamian products whenever available and turn them into an old-fashioned cuisine that still appeals to tradition-minded visitors, many of whom return here year after year. Young diners with more contemporary palates might head elsewhere, though, as the food has fallen off a bit of late, and the staff seems chronically overworked and just a wee bit impatient. The chefs, neither completely traditional nor regional, produce such dishes as grouper soup in puff pastry, and plump, juicy pheasant cooked with pineapples grown on Eleuthera. Lobster is another specialty, one half in beurre blanc and the other sided with a sauce prepared with the head of the lobster. Other standard dishes include escargots, foie gras, and *tournedos d'agneau* (lamb). The pricey wine list is usually praised as one of the finest in the country, with more than 180,000 bottles. This hotel and restaurant is managed by the same entrepreneurs who run a cigar-making facility; as such, their collection of Bahama-derived cigars is said to be the most comprehensive and varied in the world.

W. Hill St. ⓒ 242/322-2796. Reservations required. Jacket advised for men. Main courses $22–$32 (£12–£17) lunch, $37–$55 (£20–£29) dinner. AE, MC, V. Mon–Fri noon–3pm; daily 6:30–10pm. Bus: 10, 10A, or 21A.

Ristorante Villagio ⟨★★⟩ TUSCAN/CONTINENTAL   One of the most appealing restaurants on New Providence Island lies 3.2km (2 miles) west of Cable Beach, close enough to the posh and gated residential enclave of Lyford Cay to ensure a steady flow of upscale local residents. Set within an ochre-colored enclave of shopping and office buildings known as Caves Village at Caves Point, it's posh, a bit dilettantish, and charming. There's a cozy dining room with an open-to-view kitchen, elaborate French Empire–style crystal chandeliers, a wall with display cases devoted to a collection of colorful Murano glass, and the kind of thick-legged rustic furniture that you might have pulled out of a farmhouse in Tuscany. Even better is a sprawling covered terrace whose furniture—wrought-iron tables and deep-upholstered sofas and armchairs—seems appropriate for someone's (interior) private library. Menu items are savory and artful. Their lemon-grass-poached lobster salad is fabulous, as are the *trenette* pasta with seafood, the linguini with clams, and the Angus beef with arugula. Veal cutlets Milanese are served with hazelnut sauce. Also delicious: their slices of black sea bass atop a bed of truffle-studded creamed potatoes, bacon-braised organic leeks, and wild mushrooms; and very slow-roasted Norfolk duckling steeped in sherry, onions, and olives, then served over braised cabbage and pancetta ham. Staff here manages to combine some almost cliché-ridden, slightly dotty English supervisors and a rather hip Bahamian and international staff. In 2007, the same administrators established a nearby, somewhat less formal bistro, Mangos, within the same shopping compound, where food is only a bit less expensive, but where service can be excruciatingly slow and serving errors are frequent.

At Caves Point, W. Bay St. at Blake Rd. ⓒ 242/327-0965. Reservations recommended. Main courses $28–$48 (£15–£25). Tues–Sat 6–10pm. Bus: Western.

Sun and . . . ⟨★★⟩ INTERNATIONAL   For nearly 30 years, through good and bad times, this restaurant has been a prominent culinary landmark in Nassau, the best of a core of locally owned restaurants valiantly holding their own against daunting competition from better-funded restaurants within the island's megaresorts. Today, under the hard-working administration of Belgium-born owner and chef Ronny Deryckere and his wife, Esther, it's better and more of an inner sanctum than ever. It occupies the premises of what was originally built in the 1930s as a private residence, Red Mill House, within an upscale, mostly residential neighborhood east of downtown Nassau. You might want a drink within the bar area, which is a distinctly separate entity all its own, before heading into one of several dining rooms, each of them arranged around a central courtyard containing tropical plants, shrubs, and a swimming pool. Some of the dishes emerging from the kitchens of this place are unique on New Providence or Paradise Islands: Examples include sweetbreads, prepared either with white wine and mushroom sauce or with a demiglaze and cognac; the best Roquefort salad in town; an absolutely fabulous version of steak tartare, served with *pommes frites;* and grilled octopus with chopped onions and a tapenade of olives. Of special note is the Bahamian fisher's platter, composed of artfully prepared fish that's entirely caught within local waters. If there's a moment during the dinner when you're not otherwise occupied, check out the photos lining the walls depicting clients of yesterday, who have included Frank Sinatra, Bob Hope, Richard Widmark, and the Duke of Windsor.

Lakeview Rd. at E. Shirley St. (✆ 242/393-1205. Reservations required. Lunch platters $11–$19 (£5.85–£10); dinner main courses $30–$40 (£16–£21). AE, DC, MC, V. Tues–Sun 11:30am–2:30pm and 6:30–9:30pm. Closed Sun June–July and Aug–Sept.

The White Door (✦ INTERNATIONAL   New, hip, and appealingly eccentric, this restaurant enjoys, almost without competition, a setting that's more historic and more closely linked to the British Colonial era than any other restaurant in The Bahamas. Set across the street from the also-recommended Graycliff, in the heart of historic Nassau, it occupies a 250-year-old masonry-and-wood Bahamian house that belonged for many years to Lord Mountbatten, the uncle of Prince Philip. As such, it once housed—within the guest cottage in back—Queen Elizabeth II. The house was acquired a few years ago by Harl Taylor, whose fans describe him as "the leading taste master, or taste maker, in The Bahamas." The product of parents who hail from Georgia (USA) and The Bahamas, with family links to the singer Johnny Mathis, he's known as a crafter of women's handbags and, as such, maintains a boutique of his creations on the building's second floor. Come to this place for an inside view of an old Bahamian house dripping with colonial charm and royal antecedents. Meals here are invariably configured as part of fixed-price menus reflecting very fresh local ingredients and a vague allegiance to someone's conception of Bahamian flair. Although the menu will change by the time of your visit, some recent meals have included organic salads with mango-flavored vinaigrette, grapefruit segments, and kumquats; individual seafood pot pies flavored with sherry and studded with lobster meat and shrimp; mini rack of lamb with red wine reduction, steamed broccoli, and bok choy; and filet mignon with wild portobello mushrooms. Dessert service is configured tapas-style, with several miniature individual confections offered on the same platter: The best examples include guava duff, homemade coconut-mango-chocolate ice cream, and Grand Marnier crepes with coconut-flavored rum sauce.

9 West Hill St. (✆ 242/326-5925. Reservations recommended. Set-price dinners $75 (£40) without wine; set-price Sun brunch $75 (£40) without wine. AE, DC, DISC, MC, V. Thurs–Sat 6–10:30pm (with seatings at 6:30 and 9pm); Sun 11am–3pm (with open seating). Closed Aug. Bus: 10 or 21A.

MODERATE

Café Matisse 🅖 INTERNATIONAL/ITALIAN   Set directly behind Parliament House, in a mustard/beige-colored building that was built a century ago as a private home, this restaurant is on everybody's short list of downtown Nassau favorites. It serves well-prepared Italian and international cuisine to businesspeople, workers from nearby government offices, and all kinds of deal makers. There are dining areas within an enclosed courtyard, as well as on two floors of the interior, which is decorated with colorful Matisse prints. It's run by the sophisticated Bahamian-Italian team of Greg and Gabriella Curry, who prepare menu items that include calamari with spicy chili-flavored jam, served with tomatoes and fresh mozzarella cheese; a mixed grill of seafood; grilled filet of local grouper served with a light tomato and caper sauce; spaghetti with lobster; grilled rack of lamb with gravy; a perfect filet mignon in a green-peppercorn sauce; and a zesty curried shrimp with rice.

Bank Lane at Bay St., just north of Parliament Sq. 🄒 **242/356-7012.** Reservations recommended. Main courses $14–$23 (£7.40–£12) lunch, $19–$40 (£10–£21) dinner. AE, DISC, MC, V. Tues–Sat noon–3pm and 6–10pm. Bus: 17 and 21.

East Villa Restaurant and Lounge CHINESE/CONTINENTAL   You might imagine yourself in Hong Kong during the 1980s in this well-designed modern house across the road from the headquarters of the Nassau Yacht Club, a short drive east from the commercial core of downtown Nassau. It's somewhat upscale and completely devoid of the sense of bureaucracy associated with restaurants within some of the island's larger resorts. It sometimes attracts affluent Florida yachters to its dimly lit precincts, where aquariums bubble in a simple but tasteful contemporary setting. Zesty Szechuan flavors appear on the menu, but there are less spicy Cantonese alternatives, including sweet-and-sour chicken and steamed vegetables with cashews and water chestnuts. Lobster tail in the spicy Chinese style is one of our favorites. Dishes can be ordered mild, medium, or zesty hot.

E. Bay St. 🄒 **242/393-3377.** Reservations required. Main courses $11–$20 (£5.85–£11) lunch, $14–$40 (£7.40–£21) dinner. AE, MC, V. Sun–Fri noon–3pm; daily 6–10pm. Bus: 9A, 9B, 11, or 19.

Luciano's of Chicago 🅖 ITALIAN/SEAFOOD/STEAK   One of Nassau's newer upscale restaurants opened in 2005 within a low-slung, red-painted building that's positioned close to the northbound section of the bridge across the channel that separates New Providence from Paradise Island. The Nassau branch of a successful franchise that originated in Chicago, it emphasizes stiff drinks, two-fisted portions, and a sense of macho charm. Many visitors prefer the terrace that has tables and pergolas positioned for a view of the towers and glittering lights of the Atlantis Resort just across the water. In addition to the terrace (which most diners seem to prefer), there's a smoothly upscale dining room, air-conditioned and outfitted in tones of beige and brown. In addition to a tempting roster of two-fisted steaks, menu items include romaine lettuce topped with basil-and-garlic-marinated sweet peppers; filet mignon Marsala; clay pot–roasted and marinated chicken served with sautéed garlic and kalamata olives; country-style rigatoni with sweet Italian sausage, pancetta ham, and a light tomato-flavored cream sauce; and a succulent Italian stew (*giambotta*) made with chicken, sausage, onion, roasted peppers, garlic, potatoes, white wine, and olive oil. A soup that's particularly successful is made from escarole, white beans, and Italian sausage.

E. Bay St., just before the northbound entrance to the Paradise Island Bridge. 🄒 **242/323-7770.** Reservations recommended. Main courses $12–$30 (£6.35–£16) lunch, $17–$44 (£9–£23) dinner. AE, DC, DISC, MC, V. Mon–Fri 11:30am–3pm; daily 6–10pm. Bus: 10.

Poop Deck BAHAMIAN/SEAFOOD   Raffish and informal, this is the older (and original) version of a restaurant that recently expanded with another branch at Cable Beach. This original is less touristy, hosting a clientele of sailors, yachtspeople, and workers from the nearby marinas and boatyards. Many of them find perches on the second-floor open-air terrace, which overlooks the harbor and Paradise Island. If you like dining with a view, you won't find a better place than this in the heart of Nassau. At lunch, you can order conch chowder (perfectly seasoned) or a juicy beef burger. The waiters are friendly, the crowd is convivial, and the festivities continue into the evening, usually with lots of drinking. Native grouper fingers served with peas 'n' rice is the Bahamian soul food dish on the menu. Two of the best seafood selections are the fresh lobster and the stuffed mushrooms with crabmeat. The creamy linguine with crisp garlic bread is another fine choice.

Nassau Yacht Haven Marina, E. Bay St. (𝄐 242/393-8175. And at Sandy Port, west of Cable Beach, on W. Bay St. (𝄐 242/327-3329. Reservations recommended for dinner, not necessary at lunch. Main courses $10–$25 (£5.30–£13) lunch, $19–$40 (£10–£21) dinner. AE, DC, DISC, MC, V. Daily noon–4:30pm and 5–10:30pm. For the branch at the Nassau Yacht Haven: bus 10, 19, or 23. For the branch on W. Bay St.: bus 10 or the "Western bus."

Shoal Restaurant and Lounge (𝄐 (Value BAHAMIAN   Many of our good friends in Nassau swear that this is one of the best joints for authentic local food. We rank it near the top for a dining venue that's utterly without glamour but which serves sensible down-home food at a locale far removed from the tourist path. After all, where else can you get a good bowl of okra soup these days? This may or may not be your fantasy, but to a Bahamian, it's like pot liquor and turnip greens with corn bread to a Southerner. Many diners follow an inaugural bowl of soup (either split pea or the above-mentioned okra soup) with more conch, either "cracked" or perhaps curried. But you can also order some unusual dishes, such as Bahamian style curried mutton using native spices and herbs, stewed oxtail, or braised short ribs of beef. Peas 'n' rice almost automatically accompanies virtually everything served here.

Nassau St. near its intersection with Poinciana Dr. (𝄐 242/323-4400. Main courses $9.50–$17 (£5–£9). AE, DISC, MC, V. Sun–Thurs 7:30am–11pm. Bus: 16.

Taj Mahal NORTHERN INDIAN   This is the best and most frequently recommended Indian restaurant in Nassau. Within a room lined with Indian art and artifacts, you'll dine on a wide range of savory and zesty Punjabi, tandoori, and curried dishes. Some of the best choices are the lamb selections, although such concessions to local culture as curried or tandoori-style conch have also begun cropping up on the menu. If you don't know what to order, consider a tandoori mixed platter, which might satisfy two of you with a side dish or two. All of the *korma* dishes, which combine lamb, chicken, beef, or vegetables in a creamy curry sauce, are very successful. Takeout meals are also available.

48 Parliament St. at Bay St. (𝄐 242/356-3004. Reservations recommended. Main courses $18–$38 (£9.55–£20). AE, MC, V. Daily noon–3pm and 6:30–11pm. Bus: 10 or 17.

INEXPENSIVE

Bahamian Kitchen (Value (Kids BAHAMIAN/INTERNATIONAL   Located next to Trinity Church, within one of the most congested neighborhoods of downtown Nassau, this is one of the best places for good Bahamian food at modest prices. Solid, unpretentious, and decent, it evokes the kind of restaurant you might find on a remote Bahamian Out Island. Down-home dishes include lobster Bahamian style, fried red snapper, conch salad, stewed fish, curried chicken, okra soup, and pea soup and dumplings. Most dishes are served with peas 'n' rice. You can order such old-fashioned Bahamian fare as stewed fish and corned beef and grits, all served with johnnycake. If you'd like to introduce your kids to Bahamian cuisine, this is an ideal choice. There's takeout service if you're planning a picnic.

Trinity Place, off Market St. ✆ **242/325-0702.** Lunch and dinner main courses $10–$42 (£5.30–£22). AE, MC, V. Mon–Sat 11:30am–10pm. Bus: 10.

Café Skans (Value GREEK/AMERICAN/BAHAMIAN Owned and operated by a hardworking Greek family, this is a straightforward, Formica-clad diner with an open kitchen, offering flavorful food that's served without fanfare in generous portions. Set in the midst of the densest concentration of shops in Nassau, it attracts local residents and office workers from the government buildings nearby. Menu items include Bahamian fried or barbecued chicken; conch chowder; bean soup with dumplings; souvlakia or gyros in pita bread; and burgers, steaks, and various kinds of seafood platters. This is where workaday Nassau comes for breakfast.

Bay St., near the corner of Market St. ✆ **242/322-2486.** Reservations not accepted. Breakfast $4–$9 (£2.10–£4.75); sandwiches $6–$12 (£3.20–£6.35); main-course platters $6–$17 (£3.20–£9). MC, V. Mon–Thurs 8am–5pm; Fri–Sat 8am–6pm; Sun 8am–4pm. Bus: 10 or 17.

Conch Fritters Bar & Grill BAHAMIAN/INTERNATIONAL A true local hangout with real island atmosphere, this light-hearted, family-friendly restaurant changes its focus several times throughout the day. Lunches and dinners are high-volume, high-turnover affairs mitigated only by attentive staff. Guests invariably include older diners and parents with young children in tow. Live music is presented every Thursday to Saturday 7pm until 10pm. Food choices are rather standard but still quite good, including cracked conch, fried shrimp, grilled salmon, blackened rib-eye steak, burgers, sandwiches, and six different versions of chicken, including a combination platter of chicken with barbecued ribs. Specialty drinks from the active bar include a Goombay Smash.

Marlborough St. (across from the British Colonial Hilton). ✆ **242/323-8801.** Burgers, sandwiches, and platters $10–$39 (£5.30–£21). AE, MC, V. Daily 11am–11pm (until midnight Fri–Sat). Bus: 10.

Double Dragon CANTONESE/SZECHUAN The chefs at this unpretentious eatery hail from the province of Canton in mainland China, and that locale inspires most of the food here. You'll find it within an unscenic, raffish-looking waterfront neighborhood a short drive east of the showcase shopping district of downtown Nassau. If you've ever really wondered about the differences between Cantonese and Szechuan cuisine, a quick look at the menu here will highlight them. Lobster, chicken, or beef, for example, can be prepared Cantonese style, with a mild black-bean or ginger sauce; or in spicier Szechuan formats of red peppers, chiles, and garlic. Honey-garlic chicken and orange-flavored shrimp are always popular and succulent. Overall, this place is a fine choice if you're eager for a change from grouper and burgers.

E. Bay St. between Mackey St. and Williams Court. ✆ **242/393-5718.** Main courses $10–$23 (£5.30–£12). AE, DISC, MC, V. Mon–Thurs noon–10pm; Fri noon–11pm; Sat 4–11pm; Sun 5–10pm. Bus: 10, 19.

CABLE BEACH
VERY EXPENSIVE
The Black Angus Grille ✿ STEAKS/SEAFOOD This is a truly excellent steakhouse that's positioned amid a cluster of dining options immediately above Cable Beach's Crystal Palace Casino. Relaxed but macho-looking and undeniably upscale, it's

the most consistently busy restaurant at Cable Beach—a function of its good food and also a function, in the words of its manager, of the predilection of gamblers for juicy, carnivorous steaks after a nerve-jangling session at the gaming tables. Early in 2007, management spent a small fortune upgrading the decor of this place, adding an intricately crafted paneled ceiling and generally improving a dark, slightly overcrowded venue that might have appealed to Frank Sinatra and the Rat Pack from the 1960s.

Steaks are well prepared—succulent, juicy, and cooked to your specifications. There's prime rib, filet mignon, pepper steak, grilled tuna with a white bean salad, blackened conch filet, Caesar salad, different preparations of seafood, and an array of dessert soufflés that include versions with chocolate, praline, and orange. *Hint:* If you're absolutely fixated on steak, this is an excellent choice and indeed a seductive culinary venue. But immediately adjacent to the Black Angus are two other restaurants, the all-Italian Sole Mare, with equivalently priced and, frankly, much more creative food. There's also the less expensive yet highly imaginative nouvelle-Asian Moso, which we also prefer. Note our separate recommendations of these other contenders below.

In the Wyndham Nassau Resort, upstairs from the Crystal Palace Casino, W. Bay St. ℂ 242/327-6200. Reservations recommended. Main courses $27–$48 (£14–£25). AE, DC, DISC, MC, V. Daily 6–11pm. Bus: 10.

Sole Mare ℟℟ NORTHERN ITALIAN   This is our top choice for elegant and stylish dining along Cable Beach, and it also serves the best Northern Italian cuisine on New Providence Island. The chefs are well trained, intuitive, and inventive, as shown by intensely creative dishes that crop up at regular intervals such as lobster macaroni paired on a main-course platter with an herb-infused version of lamb-loin souvlaki, or deep-fried calamari stuffed with a mixture of fresh herbs and feta cheese. The fresh fish of the day is the keynote of many a delectable meal here. Many of the other ingredients have to be imported from the mainland, but the chefs still work their magic with them. A meal might begin with Castilian-style garlic soup, or jumbo shrimp sautéed in ouzo, and reach a high point with either a *piperade* (Basque stew) of lobster or a filet of halibut prepared lyonnaise style with cream, minced onions, and scalloped potatoes. Veal also appears rather delectably sautéed with endive, a dish you might enjoy in an upmarket tavern in northern Italy. The restaurant offers three different flavors of dessert soufflés: The one we prefer is the version prepared with sweet Marsala wine and fresh strawberries.

In the Wyndham Nassau Resort & Crystal Palace Casino, W. Bay St. ℂ 242/327-6200. Reservations required. Main courses $28–$46 (£15–£24). AE, DC, DISC, MC, V. Tues–Wed and Fri–Sun 6–11pm (hours and opening days vary with the season and resort occupancy; call ahead). Bus: 10.

EXPENSIVE

Amici ℟ ITALIAN   Following a radical renovation and upgrade that was completed here during 2007, this well-recommended restaurant works hard to maintain its status as a culinary showcase for the flavorful and savory Italian cuisine that many guests crave after too long an exposure to an all-Bahamian diet. Set within the Sheraton Hotel, directly astride Cable Beach, its includes spinning ceiling fans, a big-windowed view of the beach, and the kind of dark-stained wooden furniture you might expect in a trattoria in Italy. Popular and long-enduring dishes here include scampi cocktails, Caesar salads, fettuccine alfredo, Florentine-style breast of chicken (on a bed of spinach), zesty *gamberelli fra Diavolo* (spicy shrimp), and braised pork shank with olive oil, hot peppers, and angel-hair pasta.

In the Sheraton Cable Beach Resort, W. Bay St. ℂ 242/327-6000. Main courses $23–$45 (£12–£24). AE, DC, DISC, MC, V. Daily 6–10:30pm. Bus: 10.

Capriccio ITALIAN/INTERNATIONAL   Set beside a prominent roundabout, about .5km (¼ mile) west of the megahotels of Cable Beach, this restaurant lies within a much-weathered, faux-baroque Italian building with Corinthian columns and an outdoor terrace. Inside it's a lot less formal, outfitted like an upscale luncheonette, but with lots of exposed granite, busy espresso machines, and kindly Bahamian staff who understand Italian culinary nuance. At lunch you get pretty ordinary fare such as fresh salads, sandwiches, and a few hot platters like cracked conch. But the cooks shine at night, offering dishes such as chicken breast with sage and wine sauce, veal cutlets served Milanese style or with Marsala sauce, spaghetti with pesto and pine nuts, and seafood platters.

W. Bay St. ☎ **242/327-8547.** Reservations recommended. Lunch items $6–$22 (£3.20–£12); dinner main courses $15–$29 (£7.95–£15). MC, V. Mon–Sat 11am–10pm; Sun 5–10pm. Bus: 10 or 17.

Moso 🄌🄌 ASIAN   This is the newest and most experimental restaurant in New Providence, the brainchild of the owner of the rapidly expanding Baha Mar Cable Beach complex. There are many good and intriguing things about it: It deliberately prices meals here several notches below the rates charged by other "signature" restaurants within the same resort. (The more expensive, also-recommended Sole Mare and Angus Grille lie within a few steps of this place, within the same restaurant complex, just above the hotel's megacasino.) You'll quickly get the sense that this is a hipster kind of place serving hipster cuisine—in fact, every dish you've ever liked from every Asian menu you've ever looked at all seem to have found its way onto the menu. Each member of this restaurant's Bahamian waitstaff spent several months studying the preparation and context of Asian food and Asian culture, and they'll guide you through a menu composed of many different small and medium-sized dishes. These you'll compose into combinations that don't necessarily follow Western dining rituals. The best menu items might include aromatic crispy duck; Mongolian-style chicken and beef hot pot; fresh tofu stir-fried with minced pork, garlic, and chili; seared ahi tuna tataki with yazu lemon sauce; and a succulent blend of octopus and local conch with cucumbers in rice vinegar. You can also order meticulously carved portions of chicken breast, shrimp, pork tenderloin, filet mignon, lobster tail, salmon, or mahimahi prepared in any of three different ways: Cantonese, Sichuan dry-rubbed, or teriyaki style.

In the Wyndham Nassau Resort, upstairs from the Crystal Palace Casino, W. Bay St. ☎ **242/327-6200.** Reservations recommended. Small plates $6–$11 (£3.20–£5.85); main courses $14–$30 (£7.40–£16). AE, DC, DISC, MC, V. Thurs–Mon 6–10:30pm (opening days vary according to the season and advance bookings); bar daily 6pm–1am. Bus: 10.

The Poop Deck at Sandy Port INTERNATIONAL/SEAFOOD   This is one of the three most imposing and most desirable restaurants west of Cable Beach, convenient for the owners of the many upscale villas and condos, including Lyford Cay, that occupy New Providence's western edge. It's set within a peach-colored concrete building that's highly visible from West Bay Street. Despite the rosy exterior, it's a bit sterile-looking on the inside. This simple island restaurant evolved from a roughneck bar that occupied this site during the early 1970s. Lunch is usually devoted to well-prepared burgers, pastas, sandwiches, and salads. Dinners are more substantial, featuring filet mignon, surf and turf (seafood and steak combo), cracked conch, and fried shrimp and fresh fish caught off the Bahamian Long Island. The house drink is a Bacardi splish-splash, containing Bacardi Select, Nassau Royal Liqueur, pineapple juice, cream, and sugar cane syrup.

Poop Deck Dr., off W. Bay St. ☎ **242/327-DECK.** Reservations recommended. Main courses $16–$30 (£8.50–£16) lunch, $20–$60 (£11–£32) dinner. AE, DISC, MC, V. Tues–Sat noon–10:30pm; Sun noon–10pm. Bus: 10, or "the Western bus."

Tips **Ingredients for the Island's Best Picnics**

If you're keen on organizing a picnic and want to assemble your provisions in a style that befits owners of some of the island's biggest yachts, consider schlepping about 3km (1¾ miles) west of Cable Beach. Within an ochre-sided office and shopping complex known as the Caves Village Shopping Centre, you'll find **The Gourmet Market** (② 242/327-1067), the most upscale and most impressive deli/grocery on New Providence. Functioning like a magnet for the villa owners within the nearby exclusive gated community of Lyford Cay, it offers fruits, fish, upscale cheeses and wines, gourmet breads and pastries, and some other culinary accessories of the good life, all assembled into a spanking clean, deli-style format. And yes, they'll make sandwiches and even assemble, with or without strong guidance from you, picnic meals to go. If you opt for a visit to this place, you won't be alone: Sean Connery (007 and more) and pop icon Jessica Alba have already preceded you. It's open Monday to Saturday from 9am to 6:30pm, Sunday from 7am to 1:30pm.

Provence ⓕ MEDITERRANEAN   The best dishes in Nassau that feature the sunny cuisine of southern France are showcased within this restaurant that's outfitted in cheerful tones of yellow. Lying near the western terminus of West Bay Street, it's extremely popular with well-heeled local residents (some of whom aren't particularly enchanted with the island's blockbuster casino hotels and their cateries). Decor includes big-windowed views of the sea and oil paintings of landscapes that conjure up the Mediterranean coast. Provence prepares its *cuisine du soleil* with superb simplicity—Atlantic salmon with citrus butter, for example—so as not to mar the natural flavor. Other dishes are heavily spiced, such as the rib-eye steak in a fire-breathing pepper sauce. The chefs also turn out a delightful bouillabaisse evocative of the type served in Marseille. Daily seafood specials are featured—our favorite being the pan-seared sea bass, or else you might order the filet of black grouper. And everybody seems to like the lobster cocktails and the rack of lamb.

Old Town Sandy Port. ② 242/327-0985. Reservations required. Lunch main courses $9–$23 (£4.75–£12); dinner main courses $27–$45 (£14–£24). AE, DISC, MC, V. Mon–Fri 11:30am–3pm and Mon–Sat 6–10:30pm. Bus: 10, or "the Western bus."

WEST OF CABLE BEACH

Travellers Rest ⓕ ⓥalue BAHAMIAN/SEAFOOD   Set in an isolated spot about 2.5km (1½ miles) west of the megahotels of Cable Beach, this restaurant feels far away from it all. Its owners will make you feel like you're dining on a remote Out Island. Travellers Rest is set in a cozy cement-sided house that stands in a grove of sea-grape and palm trees facing the ocean. Because of its location close to the airport, clients whose departing flights are delayed sometimes opt to "chill out" here until the appointed departures of their flights. The restaurant was established by Winnipeg-born Joan Hannah in 1972 and since then has fed ordinary as well as famous folks like Stevie Wonder, Gladys Knight, spy novelist Robert Ludlum, Julio Iglesias, Eric Clapton, and Rosa Parks. You can dine outside, but if it's rainy (highly unlikely), you can go inside the tavern, with its small bar decorated with local paintings. In this laid-back atmosphere, you can feast on well-prepared grouper fingers, barbecued ribs, curried chicken, steamed or cracked conch, or minced crawfish. Finish with guava cake, the best on the island. The conch salad served on the weekends is said to increase virility in men.

W. Bay St., near Gambier (14km/8¾ miles west of the center of Nassau). ℂ 242/327-7633. Main courses $12–$28 (£6.35–£15) lunch, $14–$40 (£7.40–£21) dinner. AE, DISC, MC, V. Daily noon–10pm. Bus: 10, or "the Western bus."

5 Beaches, Watersports & Other Outdoor Pursuits

One of the great sports centers of the world, Nassau and the islands that surround it are marvelous places for swimming, sunning, snorkeling, scuba diving, boating, water-skiing, and deep-sea fishing, as well as playing tennis and golf.

You can learn more about available activities by calling **The Bahamas Sports Tourist Office** (ℂ **800/32-SPORT** or 954/236-9292) from anywhere in the continental United States. Call Monday through Friday from 9am to 5pm, Eastern Standard Time (EST). Or write the center at 1200 South Pine Island Rd., Suite 750, Plantation, FL 33324.

HITTING THE BEACH

In the Bahamas, as in Puerto Rico, the issue about public access to beaches is a hot and controversial subject. Recognizing this, the government has made efforts to intersperse public beaches with easy access between more private beaches where access may be impeded. Although megaresorts discourage nonresidents from easy access to their individual beaches, there are so many public beaches on New Providence Island and Paradise Island that all a beach lover has to do is stop his or her car (or else walk) to many of the unmarked, unnamed beaches that flank these islands.

The average visitor will not have a problem with beaches because most people stay in one of the large beachfront resorts where the ocean meets the sand right outside of their doors. For those hoping to explore more of the coast, here are the "no problem, man" beaches—the ones that are absolutely accessible to the public:

Cable Beach ⟨★★⟩   No particular beach is actually called Cable Beach, yet this is the most popular stretch of sands on New Providence Island. Instead of an actual beach, Cable Beach is the name given to a string of resorts and beaches that lie in the center of New Providence's northern coast, attracting the most visitors. This beachfront offers 6.5km (4 miles) of soft white sand, with many different types of food, restaurants, snack bars, and watersports offered by the hotels lining the waterfront. Calypso music floats to the sand from hotel pool patios where vacationers play musical chairs and see how low they can limbo. Vendors wend their way between sunblock-slathered bodies. Some sell armloads of shell jewelry, T-shirts, beach cover-ups, and fresh coconuts for sipping the sweet "water" straight from the shell. Others offer their hair-braiding services or sign up visitors for water-skiing, jet-skiing, and banana boat rides. Kiosks advertise parasailing, scuba-diving, and snorkeling trips, as well as party cruises to offshore islands. Waters can be rough and reefy, then calm and clear a little farther along the shore. There are no public toilets here because guests of the resorts use their hotel facilities. If you're not a guest of the hotel and not a customer, you are not supposed to use the facilities. Cable Beach resorts begin 4.8km (3 miles) west of downtown Nassau. Even though resorts line much of this long swath of beach, there are various sections where public access is available without crossing through private hotel grounds.

⌐Finds A Beach for Lovers

Continuing west along West Bay Street, you reach **Love Beach,** across from Sea Gardens, a good stretch of sand lying east of Northwest Point. Love Beach, although not big, is a special favorite with lovers. The snorkeling is superb, too. It's technically private, though no one bothers visitors who come, and locals fervently hope it won't ever become overrun like Cable Beach.

Caves Beach   On the north shore, past the Cable Beach hotel properties, Caves Beach is 11km (6¾ miles) southwest of Nassau. It stands near Rock Point, right before the turnoff along Blake Road that leads to the airport. Since visitors often don't know of this place, it's a good spot to escape the hordes. It's also a good beach with soft sands. There are no toilets or changing facilities.

Delaporte Beach   Just west of the busiest section of Cable Beach, Delaporte Beach is a public-access beach where you can also escape the crowds. It opens onto clear waters and boasts white sands, although it has neither facilities nor toilets. Nonetheless, it's an option.

Goodman's Bay   This public beach lies east of Cable Beach on the way toward the center of Nassau. Goodman's Bay and Saunders Beach (see below) often host local fund-raising cookouts, where vendors sell fish, chicken, conch, peas 'n' rice, or macaroni and cheese. People swim and socialize to blaring reggae and calypso music. To find out when one of these beach parties is happening, ask the staff at your hotel or pick up a local newspaper. A playground is here, along with toilet facilities.

Old Fort Beach ⟨   To escape the crowds on weekdays, we often head here, a 15-minute drive west of the Nassau International Airport (take W. Bay St. toward Lyford Cay). This lovely beach opens onto the turquoise waters of Old Fort Bay near the western part of New Providence. The least developed of the island's beaches, it attracts many homeowners from swanky Lyford Cay nearby. In winter, the beach can be quite windy, but in summer it's as calm as the Caribbean Sea.

Saunders Beach   East of Cable Beach, this is where many islanders go on the weekends. To reach it, take West Bay Street from Nassau in the direction of Coral Island. This beach lies across from Fort Charlotte, just west of Arawak Cay. Like Goodman's Bay (see above) it often hosts local fund-raising cookouts open to the public. These can be a lot of fun. There are no public facilities.

Western Esplanade   If you're staying at a hotel in downtown Nassau, such as the British Colonial, this one (also known as Junkanoo Beach) is a good beach to patronize close to town. On this narrow strip of sand convenient to Nassau, you'll find toilets, changing facilities, and a snack bar.

BIKING

A half-day bicycle tour with **Bahamas Outdoors Ltd.** (© 242/362-1574 or 242/457-0329; www.bahamasoutdoors.com) can take you on a 5km (3-mile) bike ride along some scenic forest and shoreline trails in the Coral Harbour area on the southwestern coast of New Providence, under the tutelage and with the ongoing commentary of long-time New Providence resident Carolyn Wardle, an expert in the ecology, bird life, and history of the region. The itinerary follows a series of easy trails, usually hard-packed earth, along seashores and through pink forests. Visited en route are sleepy Adelaide Village (settled by freed slaves in the 1830s) and views, with the naked eye or with binoculars, of local birds. Shorts and a T-shirt are the recommended attire, and tours rarely include more than a half-dozen participants at a time; most are morning events that rarely last for more than 4 hours each. The cost for the tour is around $70 (£37) per person. Some of the major hotels on Paradise Beach and Cable Beach rent bikes to their guests. You can bike along Cable Beach or along the beachfront at Paradise Island, but roads through downtown Nassau are too narrow and traffic is too congested to be genuinely pleasant or even particularly safe.

BOAT CRUISES

Cruises from the harbors around New Providence Island are offered by a number of operators, with trips ranging from daytime voyages for snorkeling, picnicking, sunning, and swimming, to sunset and moonlight cruises.

Barefoot Sailing Cruises, Bay Shore Marina, on East Bay Street (© **242/393-0820;** www.barefootsailingcruises.com), runs the 41-foot *Wind Dance,* which leaves for all-day cruises from this dock, offering many sailing and snorkeling possibilities. This is your best bet if you're seeking a more romantic cruise and don't want 100 people aboard. The cruises usually stop at Rose Island, a charming, picture-perfect spot with an uncrowded beach and palm trees. You can also sail on a ketch, the 56-foot *Riding High.* Cruise options are plentiful, including a half-day of sailing, snorkeling, and exploring for $65 (£34) per person for a half-day and $99 (£52) for a full day. A 2-hour sunset cruise, departing between 5pm and 8pm two to three times a week, depending on the season, the weather forecast, and advance bookings, costs $55 (£29) per person.

Flying Cloud, Paradise Island West Dock (© **242/363-4430**), is a twin-hulled sailing catamaran carrying 50 people on day and sunset trips. It's a good bet for people who want a more intimate cruise and shy away from the heavy volume carried aboard Majestic Tours catamarans (see below). Snorkeling equipment is provided free. Monday to Saturday half-day charters cost $50 (£27) per person; a 2½-hour sunset cruise goes for $60 (£32). Evening bookings are on Monday, Wednesday, and Friday. A 5-hour cruise leaves on Sunday at 10am and costs $75 (£40) per person.

Majestic Tours Ltd., Hillside Manor (© **242/322-2606**), will book 3-hour cruises on two of the biggest catamarans in the Atlantic, offering views of the water, sun, sand, and outlying reefs. This is the biggest and most professionally run of the cruise boats, and it's an affordable option, but we find that there are just too many other passengers aboard. An on-board cash bar keeps the drinks flowing. The *Yellow Bird* is suitable for up to 110 passengers. It departs from Prince George's Dock in downtown Nassau, just behind the tented location of the Straw Market; ask for the exact departure point when you make your reservation. The cost is $25 (£13) per adult, half-price for children under 10 years, and snorkeling equipment is $12 (£6.35) extra. The outfitter has also added another boat, the *Robinson Crusoe,* holding 200 passengers. On Wednesday, Friday, and Sunday, there are cruises from 10am to 4:30pm, costing $50 (£27) for adults and half-price for children 10 and under. Sunset dinner cruises from 7 to 10pm on Tuesday and Friday cost $65 (£35) per adult, again half-price for children.

FISHING

May to August are the best months for the oceanic bonito and the blackfin tuna, June and July for blue marlin, and November through February for the wahoo found in reefy areas.

Arrangements can be made at any of the big hotels, but unfortunately, there's a hefty price tag. With equipment included for parties of between two and six, prices usually begin at around $500 (£265) for a half-day and from $1,000 (£530) for a full day's fishing.

One of the most reliable companies, **Born Free Charters** (© **242/393-4144**) offers a fleet of three vessels, each between 11 and 14m (35–48 ft.) long, that can seat six comfortably; they can be rented for a half-day ($500–$700/£265–£371) or a full day ($1,000–$1,400/£530–£742). Each additional person is charged $50 (£27). Fishing choices are plentiful: You can troll for wahoo, tuna, and marlin in the deep sea, or cast in the shallows for snapper, grouper, and yellowtail. Anchoring and bottom-fishing are calmer options. We recommend this charter because Born Free offers so many types of fishing and gives you a lot of leeway regarding where you want to fish and how much time you want to spend.

Occasionally, boat owners will configure themselves and their boats as businesses for deep-sea fishing. Unless you're dealing with a genuinely experienced guide, your fishing trip may or may not be a success. John Pratt has emerged over the years as one of the most consistently reliable deep-sea fishermen. He maintains a 14m (45-ft.) fishing boat, making it available for full- or half-day deep-sea fishing excursions. It docks every night at the island's largest marina, the 150-slip **Nassau Yacht Haven,** on East Bay Street (© **242/393-8173** or 242/422-0364), where a member of the staff will direct you. Alternatively, you can call © **242/422-0364** to speak to Mr. Pratt directly. It takes about 20 minutes of boat travel to reach an offshore point where dolphin and wahoo may or may not be biting, depending on a raft of complicated seasonable factors. These trips need to be booked several weeks in advance.

GOLF

Some of the best golfing in The Bahamas is found in Nassau and on nearby Paradise Island. Although "dormant," or storm-damaged courses, on the extreme western end of New Providence might one day be rejuvenated, at the time of this writing, the only functioning golf course on New Providence Island that was open to nonmembers was the **Cable Beach Golf Course** ✿✿ on West Bay Street, Cable Beach (© **242/327-1741**). An intricately designed 18-hole, 6,453-yard, par-71 championship golf course, it benefited from a major redesign between 2000 and 2003. The makeover reshaped the fairways, repositioned putting greens, and introduced new hazards and water-lined holes throughout two-thirds of its layout. Better year-round playing conditions were ensured by introducing a salt-tolerant grass known as paspalum that is greener, firmer, and more upright, withstanding the salty breezes and tropical heat while providing a premium putting surface. The golf course's alterations were overseen by veteran designer and consultant Fred M. Settle, Jr., of International Golf Design, Inc.

Many of the players who tee off are guests of hotels on Cable Beach. Between November and April, greens fees cost $145 (£77) for guests of Cable Beach hotels, $180 (£95) for people staying anywhere else. In the off season (May–Oct), residents of the Cable Beach properties pay $95 (£50); people staying at other venues pay $120 (£64). Greens fees include the use of an electric golf cart.

During the lifetime of this edition, the Cable Beach course will gravitate into the orbit of Baha Mar Resorts Limited. As such, it will eventually benefit from massive amounts of capital available for additional improvements and reconfigurations. Along with rebuilding at the Cable Beach megaresort slated for completion in 2010, the golf course might become more Disney-esque and lavish. It's likely that work on the golf course won't begin until late 2008, and it will then remain closed for a full 2 years after that. Transformations will be massive and, in some cases, awe-inspiring. They'll include the addition of dozens of ponds and water traps. Until reconstruction begins, things are likely to remain unchanged from the description as noted here: in other words, a desirable, high-quality golf course that impresses but doesn't necessary blow a golfer's mind.

HORSEBACK RIDING

Windsor Equestrian Centre & Happy Trails Stables, Coral Harbour, on the southwest shore (© **242/362-1820;** www.bahamahorse.com), offers a 90-minute horseback trail ride, which is limited to a maximum of eight riders at a time, for $110 (£58). The price includes free transportation to and from your hotel. Riders must weigh less than 91kg (200 lb.). The stables are signposted from the Nassau International Airport, which is 3km (2 miles) away. Children must be 12 or older, and reservations are required.

SNORKELING, SCUBA DIVING & UNDERWATER WALKS

There's great snorkeling off most of the beaches on New Providence, especially **Love Beach.** Most hotels and resorts will rent or loan guests snorkeling equipment. Several of the companies mentioned above under "Boat Cruises" also offer snorkel trips, as does Bahamas Divers, below. See also "Easy Side Trips to Nearby Islands," later in this chapter, for additional snorkeling excursions.

Our favorite site for snorkeling is **Goulding Cay,** lying off the western tip of New Providence. Underwater you'll find a field of hard corals, especially the elegant elkhorn. The clear waters here and the shallow coral heads make it ideal for filmmakers. In fact, it's been featured in many films, ranging from a number of James Bond movies to *20,000 Leagues Under the Sea.* More elkhorn coral is found to the south at **Southwest Reef,** which also has stunning star coral in water less than 2.4m (8 ft.) deep. To the north is **Fish Hotel,** which is not much on coral but is graced with large schools of fish, especially red snapper, jacks, and grunts.

There are more dive sites around New Providence than you can see in one visit, so we've included a few of our favorites. **Shark Wall** 𝕂𝕂 is the most intriguing, which is a diving excursion 16km (10 miles) off the coast; others include the **Rose Island Reefs,** the **Southwest Reef,** the **Razorback,** and **Booby Rock Reef.** Dive outfitters can also lead you to many old shipwrecks off the coast, along with caves and cliffs. Wrecks include *Mahoney* and *Alcora,* plus the wreck used in the James Bond film *Never Say Never Again.* Divers also explore the airplane propeller used in another Bond film, *Thunderball.* All dive outfitters feature one or more of these sites.

Bahamas Divers, East Bay Street (© **242/393-5644**), has packages that include both a half-day of snorkeling at offshore reefs for $39 (£21) per person and a half-day scuba trip with experienced certified divers, for between $89 (£47) and $109 (£58), depending on the destination. Half-day excursions for certified divers to deeper outlying reefs, drop-offs, and blue holes can be arranged, usually for a fee of $89 (£47) for a two-tank dive and $55 (£29) for a one-tank dive. Novice divers sometimes sign up for a carefully supervised "resort course" which includes instruction with scuba equipment in a swimming pool, followed by a shallow shorefront dive, accompanied with an instructor, for a fee of $89 (£47) per person.

Participants receive free transportation from their hotel to the boats. Children must be 10 or older, and reservations are required, especially during the holiday season.

Voluptuous Vixen as Tourist Attraction

Blonde, busty, and hell-bent on becoming the next Marilyn Monroe, Anna Nicole Smith never came even close to equaling the '50s sex goddess. But one thing she had in common with Marilyn, besides clone looks, is that both beauties died in their 30s. Anna Nicole died in a Florida hotel room in February 2007 but was living in The Bahamas at the time. After a long legal battle, she was buried on New Providence Island next to her 20-year-old son, Daniel, who died from a lethal combination of methadone and two antidepressants in the hospital room where his mother had given birth to Dannielynn, a daughter.

Her gravesite, at least temporarily in 2007, became the number-one tourist attraction in The Bahamas, luring more visitors, especially cruise-ship passengers, than the Paradise Island resort of Atlantis itself. How long this phenomenon will last is anyone's guess.

Her death launched a tourist bonanza for many Bahamians. Even the minister of tourism, Francina Clerke, said that all the worldwide media attention had been positive for the island chain. Mostly the taxi drivers benefited, as hundreds of tourists asked to be taken to sites related to Anna Nicole, including the home where she lived, the church where her funeral was held, but mainly the cemetery where she is buried with her son.

At the funeral, Bahamians sold food and drink to visitors, and one shopkeeper wanted to charge camera crews $5,000 to occupy a lookout spot to broadcast the funeral live. A tattoo shop in Nassau offered Anna Nicole tattoos.

For as long as interest lasts, any tour operator in Nassau will book excursions to Anna Nicole "spots."

Stuart Cove's Dive Bahamas, Southwest Bay Street, South Ocean (© **242/362-4171;** www.stuartcove.com), is about 10 minutes from top dive sites, including the coral reefs, wrecks, and an underwater airplane structure used in filming James Bond thrillers. For the island's most exciting underwater adventure, divers head to the wreck of the *Caribe Breeze,* depicted in the film *Open Water.* Here the staff feeds reef sharks some 15m (49 ft.) below the water; from a position of safety, divers in full scuba gear can witness the show. Steep sea walls and the Porpoise Pen Reefs (named for Flipper) are also on the diving agenda. A two-tank dive in the morning costs $99 (£52); an all-day program goes for $150 (£80). All prices for boat dives include tanks, weights, and belts. An open-water certification course starts at $950 (£504). Bring along two friends, and the price drops to $490 (£260) per person. Three-hour escorted boat snorkeling trips cost $55 (£29); children under 12 are included for $30 (£16) each. A special feature is a series of shark-dive experiences priced from $145 (£77). At Shark Arena, divers kneel while a dive master feeds the toothsome predators off a long pole. On the Shark Buoy dive at about 9m (30 ft.), sharks swim among the divers while the dive master feeds them.

The outfitter has generated much excitement with its introduction of yellow "submarines," actually jet bikes called Scenic Underwater Bubbles. An air-fed bubble covers your head as these self-contained and battery-powered jet bikes propel you through an underwater wonderland. The subs are popular with nondivers, and they're viewed as safe for kids as well (that is, those older than 12). An underwater armada is escorted along to view the reefs, all for a cost of $110 (£58). The whole experience, from pickup at your hotel or cruise ship to return, takes about 3 hours.

6 Seeing the Sights

Most of Nassau can be explored on foot, beginning at Rawson Square in the center. Here is where Bahamian fishers unload a variety of produce and fish—crates of mangoes, oranges, tomatoes, and limes, plus lots of crimson-lipped conch. To experience this slice of Bahamian life, go any morning Monday through Saturday before noon.

The best way to see some of the major public buildings of Nassau is to take our walking tour (see below), which will give you not only an overview of the historic highlights, but also a feel for the city as a whole. Then you can concentrate on specific sights you'd like to take in, notably Ardastra Gardens and Coral Island Bahamas.

THE TOP ATTRACTIONS

Ardastra Gardens ⍟ The main attraction of the Ardastra Gardens, almost 2 hectares (5 acres) of lush tropical planting about 1.5km (1 mile) west of downtown Nassau near Fort Charlotte, is the parading flock of **pink flamingos.** The Caribbean

---

Finds **Hanging Out at Potter's Cay**

One of the liveliest places in Nassau during the day is Potter's Cay, a native market that thrives beneath the Paradise Island Bridge. From the Out Islands, fishing boats and heavily laden sloops arrive early in the morning to unload the day's catch. Spiny lobster is the most expensive seafood, but grouper remains king along with fresh crab, jack, mackerel, and other fish,

If grouper is king, then "sweet, sexy conch," as the locals say, is queen. Conch is arguably the Bahamian's favorite dish. At dozens of stands, you can watch the conch being extracted from its shell. These shells are later dried out (they're really smelly for days) and sold as highly polished souvenirs. Vendors make the freshest conch salad right on the spot here; if you haven't eaten the delicacy before, this is the place to try it.

You'll see chefs eagerly buying the best of the day's catch to inspire their menus for the day. Fish is sold dead or alive and, in some cases, dried or filleted. What we don't like to see are fishmongers chopping up sea turtles, an endangered species. The vendors are not of the politically correct sort, and they're more likely interested in catering to the Bahamian life-long love of turtle flesh than they are in preserving the species for future generations.

Not just fish is sold here. Sloops from the Out Islands also bring in cartons of freshly harvested vegetables, including the fiery hot peppers so beloved by locals, along with paw-paws (papaya), stalks of bananas, fresh herbs, various root vegetables, tomatoes, and squash along with an array of luscious exotic fruits. *Here's a tip:* Many of these vendors have a wicked sense of humor and will offer you a taste of the tamarind fruit, claiming it's the "sweetest taste on God's earth." Invariably, tricked visitors spit it out. The taste is horrendously offensive.

You can also see mail boats leaving and coming to this quay. Watching the frenetic departure or arrival of a mail boat is one of the more amusing scenes to be viewed on New Providence.

Area of detail

NEW PROVIDENCE ISLAND

Nassau International Airport

Lake Killarney

5 mi
5 km

SILVER CAY

ARAWAK CAY

PARADISE ISLAND

Cabbage Beach

Pirate Cove

Paradise Beach

Colonial Beach

Nassau Harbour

Paradise Lake

Lake Waterloo

Casuarina Dr.

Casino Dr.
Paradise Island Dr.
Bayview Dr.
Ridge Rd.
Harbour Rd.
Paradise Rd.
Paradise Beach Dr.
Paradise Island Bridges

Prince George Wharf

Western Esplanade

East Bay St.
Fowler St.
Essex St.
St. James Rd.
Sutton St.
Montagu Ave.
Village Rd.
Jerome Ave.
Arawak Ave.
Retirement Rd.
Mackey St.
Shirley Park Ave
Rosetta St.
Madeira St.
Montrose Ave.
Mount Royal Ave.
Collins Ave.
Shirley St.
Bay St.
Elizabeth Ave.
North St.
East St.
Gibbs Corner
Ross Corner
Market St.
Cumberland St.
West Hill St.
West St.
East Hill St.
Meeting St.
Delancy St.
Nassau St.
Cambridge St.
Meadow Rd.
Boyd Rd.
Bethel Dr.
Marcus
Providence Ave.
Columbus Ave.
Chippingham Rd.
West Bay St.
St. Alban's Dr.

Beach
Cruise Ship Dock

0   1/4 mi
0   0.25 km

Ardastra Gardens **2**
Balcony House **7**
Blackbeard's Tower **6**
Cable Beach **1**
Central Bank of the Bahamas **8**
Fort Charlotte **3**

Fort Fincastle/ Queen's Staircase **12**
Fort Montagu **14**
Junkanoo Expo **9**
National Art Gallery of the Bahamas **4**

Pirates of Nassau **5**
Potter's Cay **13**
Rawson Square **10**
Seaworld Explorer **11**

Finds **The Secret Garden**

The Retreat, Village Road (© **242/393-1317**), on the southern outskirts of downtown Nassau, is the home of the Bahamas National Trust. A clapboard-sided green-and-white building, it was originally conceived as the homestead of the Langlois family and purchased from them by the National Trust in 1925. Whereas there's nothing of particular interest inside the house (it contains mostly rather workaday offices), its gardens are worth a visit. They consist of 4.4 hectares (11 acres) of the most unspoiled gardens on New Providence, home to about 200 species of exotic palm trees. The grounds, which are, for the most part, flat, can be navigated with a map available on-site. A gift shop sells books and memorabilia that's approved and associated with the National Trust. The grounds can be visited Monday to Friday from 9am to 5pm for a $2 (£1.05) admission for adults and $1 (55p) for children and students.

flamingo, national bird of The Bahamas, had almost disappeared by the early 1940s but was brought back to significant numbers through the efforts of the National Trust. They now flourish in the rookery on Great Inagua. A flock of these exotic feathered creatures has been trained to march in drill formation, responding to the drillmaster's commands with long-legged precision and discipline. The flamingos perform daily at 10:30am, 2:10pm, and 4:10pm.

Other exotic wildlife at the gardens include boa constrictors (very tame), macaws, kinkajous (honey bears) from Central and South America, peacocks and peahens, capuchin monkeys, iguanas, ring-tailed lemurs, red-ruff lemurs, margays, brown-headed tamarins (monkeys), and a crocodile. There are also numerous waterfowl to be seen in Swan Lake, including black swans from Australia and several species of wild ducks. Parrot feedings take place at 11am, 1:30pm, and 3:30pm.

You can get a good look at Ardastra's flora by walking along the signposted paths. Many of the more interesting and exotic trees bear plaques with their names.

Chippingham Rd. © **242/323-5806.** www.ardastra.com. Admission $12 (£6.35) adults, $6 (£3.20) children 4–12, under 4 free. Daily 9am–4:30pm. Bus: 10.

National Art Gallery of The Bahamas 🐦   At long last, this archipelago nation has a showcase to display its talented artists. In a restored 18th-century building in the center of Nassau, the gallery features Bahamian art, which as an entity has existed for only 50 years. Museum curators claim that the present collection is only the nucleus of a long-range strategy to beef up the present number of works. Most of the paintings on exhibit are divided into a historical and a contemporary collection. Pioneering Bahamian artists are honored, as are younger and more modern painters. Among island artists, Amos Ferguson is one of the most acclaimed. See his somewhat naive yet sophisticated technique at its best in the painting *Snowbirds*. He used house paint on cardboard to create a remarkable portrait. Maxwell Taylor and Antonius Roberts are two other heavily featured Bahamian painters.

Villa Doyle, W. Hill St. in downtown Nassau. © **242/328-5800.** www.nagb.org.bs. Admission $5 (£2.65) adults, $3 (£1.60) seniors and students, free for children 12 and under. Tues–Sat 10am–4pm. Bus: 10.

Seaworld Explorer 🐦   If you are curious about life below the waves but aren't a strong swimmer, hop aboard this submarine that holds about 45 passengers. Tours last

Meet the Bahamians

The People-To-People Program, established by The Ministry of Tourism, provides an opportunity for visitors to learn more about the culture of The Bahamas by interacting with the Bahamians themselves. The program "matches" visitors, often entire families, with more than 1,500 Bahamian volunteers of similar ages and interests for a day or evening activity, which could include boating, fishing, shopping at the local outdoor market, enjoying a "back-street tour," or, more often, visiting Bahamians in their home for a traditional meal of peas 'n' rice, fried fish, and guava duff. The People-To-People encounters also have resulted in lasting friendships between visitors and locals. Philip Archer, a program volunteer for more than 18 years, has received hundreds of invitations to visit families from different countries through his participation in People-To-People. Celebrating its thirtieth anniversary in 2007, The People-To-People Program has expanded beyond Nassau to Abaco, Bimini, Eleuthera, Grand Bahama Island, and San Salvador. To participate in People-To-People in Nassau/Paradise Island and The Out islands, e-mail peopletopeople@ bahamas.com. To participate in the program on Grand Bahama Island, email peopletopeople@gbmot.com.

90 minutes and include 45 to 55 minutes of actual underwater travel at depths of about 3.5m (11 ft.) below the waves. Big windows allow big views of a protected ecology zone offshore from the Paradise Island Airport. About 20 minutes are devoted to an above-water tour of landmarks on either side of the channel that separates Nassau from Paradise Island.

W. Bay St. at Elizabeth Ave. (✆) 242/356-2548. Reservations required. Tours $45 (£24) adults, $23 (£12) children 2–12. Tours Tues, Wed, Fri, and Sat at 11:30am year-round; additional departure at 1:30pm Dec–June. Bus: 10.

MORE ATTRACTIONS

Balcony House   The original design of this landmark house transplants late-18th-century Southeast American architecture. The pink two-story structure is named for its overhanging and much-photographed balcony. Restored in the 1990s, the House has been returned to its original design, recapturing a historic period. The mahogany staircase inside was thought to have been salvaged from a wrecked ship in the 1800s. At press time for this edition, the house was closed for renovations but might, by the time of your visit, have reopened. Call in advance before you go.

Trinity Place and Market St. (✆) 242/302-2621. Free admission, but donation advised. Mon–Wed and Fri 10am–4:30pm; Thurs 10am–1pm. Bus: 10.

Blackbeard's Tower   These crumbling remains of a watchtower are said to have been used by the infamous pirate Edward Teach in the 17th century. The ruins are only mildly interesting—there isn't much trace of buccaneering. What's interesting is the view: With a little imagination, you can see Blackbeard peering out from here at unsuspecting ships. Blackbeard also purportedly lived here, but this is hardly well documented.

Yamacraw Hill Rd. (8km/5 miles east of Fort Montagu). No phone. Free admission. Daily 24 hr. Reachable by jitney.

Central Bank of The Bahamas   The nerve center that governs the archipelago's financial transactions is also the venue for a year-round cycle of temporary exhibitions of paintings that represent the nation's multifaceted artistic talent. The cornerstone of the building was laid by Prince Charles on July 9, 1973, when the country became independent from Britain. Queen Elizabeth II officially inaugurated the bank in February 1975.

Trinity Place and Frederick St. ⓒ 242/322-2193. Free admission. Mon–Fri 9:30am–4:30pm. Bus: 10.

Fort Charlotte   Begun in 1787, Fort Charlotte is the largest of Nassau's three major defenses, built with plenty of dungeons. It used to command the western harbor. Named after King George III's consort, it was built by Gov. Lord Dunmore, who was also the last royal governor of New York and Virginia. Its 42 cannons never fired a shot—at least, not at an invader (only seven cannons remain on-site). Within the complex are underground passages, which can be viewed on free tours. Tours at the fort are free, but guides are very happy to accept a tip.

Off W. Bay St. on Chippingham Rd. No phone. Admission $5 (£2.65). Daily 8am–4pm. Bus: 10.

Fort Fincastle   Reached by climbing the Queen's Staircase, this fort was constructed in 1793 by Lord Dunmore, the royal governor. You can take an elevator ride to the top and walk on the observation floor (a 38m-high/125-ft. water tower and lighthouse) for a panoramic view of the harbor. The tower is the highest point on New Providence. The so-called bow of this fort is patterned like a paddle-wheel steamer used on the Mississippi; it was built to defend Nassau against a possible invasion, though no shot was ever fired.

   Although the ruins of the fort hardly compete with the view, you can walk around on your own. Be wary, however, of the very persistent young men who will try to show you the way here. They'll try to hustle you, but you really don't need a guide to see some old cannons on your own.

Elizabeth Ave. No phone. Free admission. Mon–Sat 8am–5pm. Bus: 10 or 17.

Fort Montagu   Built in 1741, this fort—the oldest one on the island—stands guard at the eastern entrance to the harbor of Nassau. The Americans captured it in 1776 during the Revolutionary War. Less interesting than Fort Charlotte and Fort Fincastle, the ruins of this place are mainly for fort buffs. Regrettably, this fort can be visited only from the outside, but many visitors find the nearby park, with well-maintained lawns and plenty of shade, more interesting than the fort itself. Vendors often peddle local handicrafts in this park, so you can combine a look at the fort with a shopping expedition, if you like.

Eastern Rd. No regular hours. Bus: 10 or 17.

Junkanoo Expo   This museum is dedicated to Junkanoo—the colorful, musical, and surreal festival that takes place on December 26 when Nassau explodes into sounds, festivities, celebrations, and masks. It is the Bahamian equivalent of the famous Mardi Gras in New Orleans. If you can't visit Nassau for Junkanoo, this exhibition is the next best thing. You can see the lavish costumes and floats that the revelers use during this annual celebration. The bright colors and costume designs are impressive, if for no other reason than the sheer size of the costumes themselves. Some of the costumes are nearly as big as one of the small parade floats, but they are worn and carried by one person. The Expo has been installed in an old customs warehouse at the entrance to the Nassau wharf. The Expo also includes a souvenir boutique with Junkanoo paintings and a variety of Junkanoo handicrafts.

Prince George Wharf, Festival Place. ⓒ 242/323-3182. Admission $1 (55p). Mon–Sat 9am–4:30pm. Bus: 10.

(Finds) Going Over-the-Hill

Few visitors make the trip anymore, but it used to be a tradition to go "Over-the-Hill" to Nassau's most colorful area. "Over-the-Hill" is the actual name of this poor residential district, where the descendants of former slaves built compact, rainbow-hued houses, leaving the most desirable lands around the harbor to the rich folks. This, not the historic core of Nassau around Rawson Square, is truly the heart of Bahamian-African culture.

The thump of the Junkanoo-Goombay drum can be heard here almost any time of the day or night. The area never sleeps, or so it is said. Certainly not on Sunday morning, when you can drive by the churches and hear hell and damnation promised to all sinners and backsliders.

This fascinating part of Nassau begins .5km (¼ mile) south of Blue Hill Road, which starts at the exclusive Graycliff hotel. But once you're "Over-the-Hill," you're a long way from the vintage wine and expensive Cuban cigars of Graycliff. Some people usually savvy store owners from abroad—come here to buy local handicrafts from individual vendors. The area can be explored on foot (during the day *only*), but many visitors prefer to drive. *Note:* This area is well worth a visit, but keep your eyes open; most criminal incidents in Nassau take place in this part of town.

Pirates of Nassau *(Kids)* This museum, which opened in 2003, celebrates the dubious "golden age of piracy" (1690–1720). Nassau was once a bustling and robust town where buccaneers grew rich from gold and other goods plundered at sea. Known as a paradise for pirates, it attracted various rogues and the wild women who flooded into the port to entertain them—for a price, of course. The museum re-creates those bawdy, lusty days in exhibits illustrating pirate lore. You can walk through the belly of a pirate ship (the *Revenge*) as you hear "pirates" plan their next attack. You can smell the dampness of a dungeon, and you'll even hear the final prayer of an ill-fated victim before he walks the gangplank. It's fairly cheesy but fun for kids. Exhibits also tell the saga of Capt. Woodes Rogers, who was sent by the English crown to suppress pirates in The Bahamas and the Caribbean.

Marlborough and George sts. (© 242/356-3759. Admission $12 (£6.35) adults, $6 (£3.20) children 3–17, free for children 2 and under (1 child gets in free). Mon–Sat 9am–6pm; Sun 9am–12:30pm. Bus: 10.

WALKING TOUR · HISTORIC NASSAU

Start:	Rawson Square.
Finish:	Prince George Wharf.
Time:	2 hours.
Best Times:	Monday through Saturday between 10am and 4pm.
Worst Times:	Sunday, when many places are closed and a day when lots of cruise ships are in port.

Begin your tour at:

❶ Rawson Square

The center of Nassau, Rawson Square lies directly inland from Prince George Wharf, where many of the big cruise ships dock. Everyone seems to pass through this crossroads, from the prime minister to bankers and local attorneys, to cruise-ship passengers, to shoppers from Paradise Island, to Junkanoo bands. On the square is the Churchill Building, used by the prime minister and some government ministries. Look for the statue of Sir Milo Butler, a former shopkeeper who became the first governor of The Bahamas after Britain granted independence in 1973.

Across Rawson Square is:

❷ Parliament Square

A statue of a youthful Queen Victoria dominates the square. To the right of the statue stand more Bahamian government office buildings, and to the left is the House of Assembly, the oldest governing body in continuous session in the New World. In the building behind the statue, the Senate meets; this is a less influential body than the House of Assembly. Some of these Georgian-style buildings date from the late 1700s and early 1800s. Immediately south of Parliament Square, in a Georgian-inspired building between Parliament Street and Bank Lane, is the Supreme Court. The bewigged and begowned judges here, looking very British, interpret Bahamian law and dispense justice at the highest authority.

TAKE A BREAK
If you'd like to relax, try **Café Matisse**, Bank Lane and Bay Street, behind Parliament Square (⏂ **242/356-7012**). The house specialty is pizza topped with fresh local seafood. Lunch is served Tuesday to Sunday noon to 3pm.

The Supreme Court building stands next to the:

❸ Nassau Public Library and Museum

This 1797 building was once the Nassau Gaol (jail) and became the public library in 1873. Chances are, you will have seen greater libraries. But what's amusing here is that the small prison cells are now lined with books. Another item of interest is the library's collection of historic prints and old documents dating from colonial days. If you want to pop in here for a look, you can do so Monday through Thursday from 10am to 8pm, Friday from 10am to 5pm, and Saturday from 10am to 4pm.

Across from the library on Shirley Street is the:

❹ Former Site of the Royal Victoria Hotel

The hotel that once occupied this site was the haunt of Confederate spies, royalty, smugglers of all sorts, and ladies and gentlemen. The American journalist Horace Greeley pronounced it "the largest and most commodious hotel ever built in the Tropics," and many agreed with him. The Royal Victoria Hotel experienced its heyday during the American Civil War. At the Blockade Runners' Ball, some 300 guests reportedly consumed 350 magnums of champagne. Former guests have included two British prime ministers, Neville Chamberlain and his successor, Winston Churchill. Prince Albert, consort of Queen Victoria, also stayed here once. The hotel closed in 1971. After it was destroyed by fire, it was demolished and razed to the ground. Today the locale accommodates one of Nassau's showcase parking lots. Ironically, the parking lot seems to be such a source of pride to the city that it is unlikely the Royal Victoria will ever be rebuilt, at least in that spot.

Walking Tour: Historic Nassau

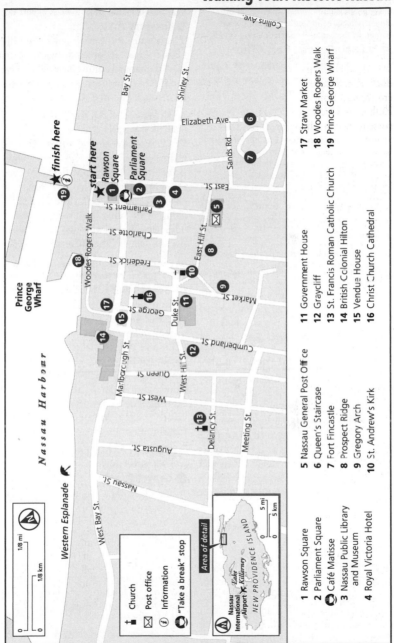

1 Rawson Square
2 Parliament Square
3 Café Matisse
4 Nassau Public Library and Museum
5 Royal Victoria Hotel

5 Nassau General Post Office
6 Queen's Staircase
7 Fort Fincastle
8 Prospect Ridge
9 Gregory Arch
10 St. Andrew's Kirk

11 Government House
12 Graycliff
13 St. Francis Roman Catholic Church
14 British Colonial Hilton
15 Vendue House
16 Christ Church Cathedral

17 Straw Market
18 Woodes Rogers Walk
19 Prince George Wharf

After imagining the former splendor of the Royal Victoria, head south along Parliament Street. At the end of Parliament Street stands:

❺ Nassau General Post Office

If you're a collector, you may want to purchase Bahamian stamps, which might be valuable in future years. You can also mail letters and packages here.

Armed with the colorful stamps you've purchased, walk east (right) on East Hill Street and turn left onto East Street, then right onto Shirley Street, and head straight on Elizabeth Avenue. This will take you to the landmark:

❻ Queen's Staircase

The stairway leads to Bennet's Hill. In 1793, slaves cut these 66 steps out of sandstone cliffs.

These stairs provided (and still provide) access from the center of Old Nassau to:

❼ Fort Fincastle

Lord Dunmore built this fort in 1793. Designed in the shape of a paddle-wheel steamer, the fort was a place to look out for marauders who never came. It was eventually converted into a lighthouse because it occupied the highest point on the island. The tower is more than 60m (197 ft.) above the sea, providing a panoramic view of Nassau and its harbor.

A small footpath leads down from the fort to Sands Road. Once you reach it, head west (left) until you approach East Street again, then bear right. When you come to East Hill Street (again), go left because you will have returned to the post office.

Continue your westward trek along East Hill Street, which is the foothill of:

❽ Prospect Ridge

This was the old dividing line between Nassau's rich and poor. The rich people lived along the waterfront, often in beautiful mansions. Black Bahamians went "Over-the-Hill" to work in these rich homes during the day but returned to Prospect Ridge to their own homes (most often shanties) at night.

Near the end of East Hill Street, you come to:

❾ Gregory Arch

This tunnel was cut through the hill in 1850. After it opened, working-class black Bahamians didn't have to go "Over-the-Hill"—and steep it was—but could go through the arch to return home.

At the intersection with Market Street, turn right. On your right rises:

❿ St. Andrew's Kirk (Presbyterian)

Called simply "the Kirk," the church dates from 1810 but has seen many changes over the years. In 1864, it was enlarged, and a bell tower was added along with other architectural features. This church had the first non-Anglican parishioners in The Bahamas.

On a steep hill, rising to the west of Market Street, you see on your left:

⓫ Government House

This house is the official residence of the governor-general of the archipelago, the queen's representative to The Bahamas. (The post today is largely ceremonial, as an elected prime minister does the actual governing.) This pink-and-white neoclassical mansion dates from the early 19th century. Poised on its front steps is a rather jaunty statue of Christopher Columbus.

Opposite the road from Government House on West Hill Street rises:

⓬ Graycliff

A Georgian-style hotel and restaurant, this stamping ground of the rich and famous was constructed by Capt. John Howard Graysmith in the 1720s. In the 1920s, it achieved notoriety when it was run by Polly Leach, a pal of gangster Al Capone. Later, under royal ownership, it attracted such famous guests as the Duke and Duchess of Windsor and Winston Churchill.

Upon leaving Graycliff, you will see a plaque embedded in a hill. The plaque claims that this site is the spot where the oldest church in Nassau once stood.

On the corner of West Hill Street and West Street is Villa Doyle, former home of William Henry Doyle, chief justice of the Bahamian Supreme Court in the 1860s and 1870s.

Opposite it stands:

⑬ St. Francis Roman Catholic Church

Constructed between 1885 and 1886, it was the first Catholic church in The Bahamas. The Archdiocese of New York raised the funds to construct it.

Continue along West Street until you reach Marlborough. Walk the short block that leads to Queen Street and turn right, passing the front of the American embassy. At the corner of Queen Street and Marlborough rises the:

⑭ British Colonial Hilton

Built in 1923, the most famous hotel in The Bahamas was once run by Sir Harry Oakes, who was at the time the most powerful man on the islands and a friend of the Duke of Windsor. Oakes's murder in 1943, still unsolved, was called "the crime of the century." A set for several James Bond thrillers, this historic location was also the site of Fort Nassau. In the summer of 1999, it became a Hilton hotel.

One part of the hotel fronts George Street, where you'll find:

⑮ Vendue House

One of the oldest buildings in Nassau, Vendue House was once called the Bourse (Stock Exchange) and was the site of many slave auctions. It is now a museum.

Not far from Vendue House on George Street is:

⑯ Christ Church Cathedral

Dating from 1837, this Gothic Episcopal cathedral is the venue of many important state ceremonies, including the opening of the Supreme Court: a procession of bewigged, robed judges followed by barristers, accompanied by music from the police band.

Continue north on George Street to the intersection with Bay Street.

⑰ Straw Market

The market—largely destroyed by a fire in the fall of 2001, and still not rebuilt by the Bahamian government—is now housed within a tentlike temporary structure that opens onto Bay Street at George Street. It has long been a favorite of cruise-ship passengers. You'll find not only straw products, but all sorts of souvenirs and gifts as well. Bahamian women at the market have traditionally woven baskets and braided visiting women's hair with beads. Due to the fire's destruction of its building, the market is temporarily housed in a tent, about 2 blocks from its original premises. Hours of the Straw Market are daily from 7am to around 8pm, although each individual vendor (there are around 200 of them) sets his or her own hours.

Continue north toward the water until you reach:

⑱ Woodes Rogers Walk

The walk was named for a former governor of the colony who was thrown into debtors' prison in London before coming back to Nassau as the royal governor. Head east along this walk for a panoramic view of the harbor, with its colorful mail and sponge boats. Markets sell vegetables, fish, and lots of conch.

The walk leads to:

⑲ Prince George Wharf

The wharf was constructed in the 1920s, the heyday of American Prohibition, to provide harbor space for hundreds of bootlegging craft defying the American blockade against liquor. The yacht of Queen Elizabeth II, the HMS *Britannia,* has been a frequent visitor over the years. Cruise ships also dock here.

Moments   **Journeys into the Wilds**

You can take a day off from the beach and join one of the wildlife tours offered by **Bahamas Outdoors,** P.O. Box CB12564 (*©* **242/362-1574** or 242/457-0329; www.bahamasoutdoors.com). We highly recommend Carolyn Wardle, president of Bahamas Outdoors, for insight into the best of the island's remaining wildlife habitats. Born in Surrey, England, and a resident of New Providence for at least 42 years, Ms. Wardle, a passionate conservationist, is a well-known figure to residents of New Providence's more isolated regions. Armed with sturdy shoes, a Bahamas Outdoors T-shirt, sunglasses, a hat, and binoculars, she knows the island's wildlife habitats (forest, seashore, and freshwater ponds) better than anyone on the island. Consider signing on for a half-day tour, priced at $59 (£31) per person, or a full-day tour, at $99 (£52) per person. Tours rarely include more than a half-dozen participants and can be conducted either within a vehicle (with frequent stops along the way for closer observation) or on an all-terrain bike. Depending on what you communicate in advance, the focus of your island tour could include birds, native flora and fauna, butterflies, national parks, historic sites, or—best of all—a combination of all of them. Access to binoculars and a battered collection of field guides are included as part of the price of any tour. The full-day tours also include a picnic lunch.

Advance reservations at least a day in advance are advised. Most tours begin in front of the tour participants' hotel at whatever time was prearranged. Bird-watching tours tend to begin earlier (around 7am) than biking and/or historic and nature tours, which begin just a bit later. Ms. Wardle, incidentally, is a director of the Society for the Conservation and Study of Caribbean Birds (SCSCB).

ORGANIZED TOURS

There's a lot to see in Nassau. Many tour options can suit your taste and take you through the colorful historic city and outlying sights of interest.

Walking tours, arranged by the Ministry of Tourism, leave from the Tourist Information Booth at Festival Place every day intermittently, depending on demand, at 10am. Tours last an hour each and include descriptions of some of the city's most venerable buildings, with commentaries on Nassau's history, customs, and traditions. The cost is $10 (£5.30) per person for all ages. Call *©* **242/395-8382** to confirm that tours are scheduled. Advance reservations are "helpful but not essential," according to a Ministry spokesperson.

Majestic Tours, Hillside Manor, Cumberland Street, Nassau (*©* **242/322-2606**), offers a number of trips, both night and day. A 2½-hour city-and-country tour leaves daily at 2pm, visiting major points of interest in Nassau, including the forts, the Queen's Staircase, the water tower, and the former site of the Straw Market (passing but not entering it). The tour costs $40 (£21) per person. An extended city-and-country tour also leaves daily at 2pm and includes the Ardastra Gardens. The charge is $50 (£27) per person, half-price for children 12 and under. Combination tours depart Tuesday, Wednesday, and Thursday at 10am and combine all the sights you see on the first tour listed above, plus the Retreat Gardens and lunch. They cost $60 (£32) per person, half-price for children. Many hotels have a Majestic Tours Hospitality Desk in the lobby, for information about these tours, as well as for reservations and tickets. Other hotels can supply brochures and tell you where to sign up.

EASY SIDE TRIPS TO NEARBY ISLANDS

Remote **Rose Island** is a sliver of land poking out of the sea northeast of the Prince George waterfront docks of Nassau. Shelling is one of the lures of this little islet. If you want to escape the crowds of Nassau, you can take a boat, the *Robinson Crusoe,* which leaves Wednesday, Friday, and Sunday at 10am from Nassau and returns at 4:30pm. The cost is $50 (£27) for adults, $25 (£13) for children ages 2 through 11, and free for kids under 5. You can relax in a hammock, snorkel among the coral reefs, and enjoy the white-sand beach before and after your sizzling barbecue lunch with unlimited white wine (included in the price). Bookings for this island retreat trip are available through **Majestic Tours** (© **242/322-2606;** www.majesticholidays.com).

If you want to see the Exuma island chain on a daylong excursion, try the **Fantastic Exuma Powerboat Adventure.** The name may sound silly, but the trip provides an excellent overview of the area. The boat departs Nassau Harbour at 9am and arrives in the Exuma Cays about an hour later. There are several stops, with snorkeling at a private cay (Ship Channel), visiting the iguanas on Allan's Cay, feeding stingrays along the shore, and enjoying a barbecue lunch. A full bar is available all day, and the drinks are free. The cost is $190 (£101) per adult and $120 (£64) for children 2 through 12. Transportation from a participant's hotel to the port of embarkation is included in the price. The experience comes to a conclusion around 5pm. For more information and prices, contact **Powerboat Adventures** (© **242/363-1466;** www.powerboat adventures.com)

7 Shopping

Today Nassau shopping is more upscale than in decades past. Swanky jewelers and a burgeoning fashion scene have appeared. There are still plenty of T-shirts claiming that "It's Better in The Bahamas," but in contrast, you can also find platinum watches and diamond jewelry.

The range of goods is staggering; in the midst of all the junk souvenirs, you'll find an increasing array of china, crystal, watches, and clothing from such names as Bally, Herend, Lalique, Baccarat, and Ferragamo.

But can you really save money compared to what you would pay stateside? The answer is "yes" on some items, "no" on others. To figure out what's a bargain and what's not, you've got to know the price of everything back in your hometown, turning yourself into a sort of human calculator about prices.

Don't try to bargain with the salespeople in Nassau stores as you would do with merchants at the local market. The price asked in the shops is the price you must pay, but you won't be pressed to make a purchase. The salespeople here are courteous and helpful in most cases.

There are no import duties on 11 categories of luxury goods, including china, crystal, fine linens, jewelry, leather goods, photographic equipment, watches, fragrances, and other merchandise. Antiques, of course, are exempt from import duty worldwide. But even though prices are "duty-free," you can still end up spending more on an item in The Bahamas than you would back in your hometown. It's a tricky situation.

> *Fun Fact* **The "Pirate" of The Bahamas**
>
> You might see expat actor Johnny Depp, star of *Pirates of the Caribbean*, shopping and walking around the streets of Nassau. He hasn't moved here, but he's purchased Little Halls Pond Cay, 96km (60 miles) south of Nassau, for $3.6 million. Nassau is his refueling stop. The private island for this reclusive star is not open for tours and is accessible only by helicopter, seaplane, or private boat, plus an invitation. When not in The Bahamas and when not on location, Depp spends most of his time in Paris with singer/actress Vanessa Paradis.

If you're contemplating a major purchase, such as a good Swiss watch or some expensive perfume, it's best to do some research in your local discount outlets or online before making a serious purchase in The Bahamas. While the alleged 30% to 50% discount off stateside prices might apply in some cases, it's not true in others. Certain cameras and electronic equipment, we have discovered, are listed in The Bahamas at, say, 20% or more below the manufacturer's "suggested retail price." That sounds good, except the manufacturer's suggested price might be a lot higher than what you'd pay back home. You aren't getting the discount you think you are. Some shoppers even take along department-store catalogs from the States or print out online buying guides to determine if they are indeed getting a bargain.

A lot of price-fixing seems to be going on in Nassau. For example, a bottle of Chanel is likely to sell for pretty much the same price, regardless of the store.

How much you can take back home depends on your country of origin. For more details, plus Customs requirements for some other countries, refer to "Entry Requirements & Customs," in chapter 2.

The principal shopping areas are **Bay Street** and its side streets downtown, as well as the shops in the arcades of hotels. Not many street numbers are used along Bay Street; just look for store signs.

BRASS & COPPER
Brass and Leather Shop With two branches on Charlotte Street, this shop offers English brass, handbags, luggage, briefcases, attachés, and personal accessories. Shop no. 2 has handbags, belts, scarves, ties, and small leather goods from such designers as Furla, Tumi, HCL, and others. If you look and select carefully, you can find some good buys here. 12 Charlotte St., between Bay and Shirley sts. ℂ 242/322-3806.

CIGARS
Remember, U.S. citizens are prohibited from bringing Cuban cigars back home because of the trade embargo. If you buy them, you're supposed to enjoy them in The Bahamas.

COINS & STAMPS
Bahamas Post Office Philatelic Bureau Here you'll find beautiful Bahamian stamps slated to become collector's items. One of the most sought-after stamps has a seashell motif. *Insider's tip:* If you don't want to take the trouble to go to the main office, try the smaller philatelic bureau at the Welcome Center, Festival Place, Prince

George Dock, open Monday to Saturday 9am to 1pm. In the General Post Office, at the top of Parliament St. on E. Hill St. ☎ 242/322-1112.

Coin of the Realm   This family-run shop is in a lovely building that was hewn out of solid limestone more than 200 years ago. The shop offers not only fine jewelry, but also Bahamian and British postage stamps, mint and used, and rare (and not-so-rare) Bahamian silver and gold coins. It also sells old and modern paper Bahamian currency. Bahama pennies that were minted in 1806 and 1807 are now rare and expensive items. Charlotte St., just off Bay St. ☎ 242/322-4497.

CRYSTAL, CHINA & GEMS

Solomon's Mines   Evoking the title of a 1950s MGM flick, this is one grand shopping adventure. This flagship store, with many branches, is one of the largest duty-free retailers in either The Bahamas or the Caribbean, a tradition since 1908. Entering the store is like making a shopping trip to London or Paris. The amount of merchandise is staggering, from a $50,000 Patek Philippe watch to one of the largest collections of Herend china in the West. Most retail price tags on watches, china, jewelry, crystal, Herend, Baccarat, Ferragamo, Bally, Lalique, and other names are discounted 15% to 30%—and some of the merchandise and oddities here are not available in the States, such as their stunning collection of African diamonds. The selections of Italian, French, and American fragrances and skin-care products are the best in the archipelago. Bay St. ☎ 242/356-6920. Charlotte and Bay sts. ☎ 242/325-7554.

FASHION

Barry's Limited   One of Nassau's more formal and elegant clothing stores, this shop sells garments made from lamb's wool and English cashmere. Elegant sportswear (including Korean-made guayabera shirts) and blazers are sold here. Most of the clothes are for men, but women often stop in for the stylish cuff links, studs, and other accessories. Bay and George sts. ☎ 242/322-3118.

Bonneville Bones   The name alone will intrigue, but it hardly describes what's inside. This is the best men's store we've found in Nassau. You can find everything here, from standard T-shirts and designer jeans to elegant casual clothing, including suits. Bay St. ☎ 242/328-0804.

Cole's of Nassau   This boutique offers the most extensive selection of designer fashions in Nassau. Women can find everything from swimwear to formal gowns, from sportswear to hosiery. Cole's also sells gift items, sterling-silver designer and costume jewelry, hats, shoes, bags, scarves, and belts. Parliament St. ☎ 242/322-8393.

Finds Going Up in Smoke

What do Pierce Brosnan, Ben Kingsley, Michael Jordan, and Salma Hayek have in common? They are aficionados of a Graycliff Cigar. The owner of Nassau's fabled and venerable **Graycliff** (p. 78), Enrico Garzaroli, operates the **Graycliff Cigar Company** on the grounds of his hotel at 12 W. Hill St. (☎ 242/302-9150). This is the only cigar factory in The Bahamas. If you call for an appointment, you can see the old-fashioned way that Cuban cigars were created—from breeding to planting and leaf selection, right up to the final hand-rolling and shaping in the factory itself.

Fendi   This is Nassau's only outlet for the well-crafted Italian-inspired accessories endorsed by this famous leather-goods company. With handbags, luggage, shoes, watches, wallets, and portfolios to choose from, the selection may well solve some of your gift-giving quandaries. Charlotte St. at Bay St. ☎ 242/322-6300.

HANDBAGS

The Harl Taylor Bag Collection   Housed on the second floor of the same richly historic home that contains the (also-recommended) White Door restaurant (see "Where to Dine") this boutique showcases the artfully stylish, and sometimes painfully stylish, handbags of a man who's sometimes referred to as "The Bahamas' leading tastemaker," Harl Taylor. Handbags come as part of two distinctly separate lines: The Beachware Collection, where mostly straw, Bahama-made bags cost from $45 (£24) to $125 (£66) each; and the haute Collection, which focuses on bags (priced at $300–$3,000/£159–£1,590 each) like you've never ever seen carried around by the Queen of England. Open Monday to Saturday 9am to 6pm. 9 West Hill St. ☎ 242/326-5925.

HANDICRAFTS

Sea Grape Boutique   This is one of the genuinely fine gift shops on New Providence, with an inventory of exotic decorative items that you'll probably find fascinating. It includes jewelry crafted from fossilized coral, sometimes with sharks' teeth embedded inside, and clothing, some of it made from BatikArts.com that's well suited to the sometimes-steamy climate of The Bahamas. There's a second branch of this outfit, Sea Grape Too, in the Radisson Hotel's Mall, on Cable Beach (☎ 242/327-5113). W. Bay St. (next to Travellers Restaurant). ☎ 242/327-1308.

JEWELRY

Colombian Emeralds   Famous around the Caribbean, this international outlet is not limited to emeralds, although its selection of that stone is the best in The Bahamas. You'll find an impressive display of diamonds, as well as other precious gems. The gold jewelry here sells for about half the price it does Stateside, and many of the gems are discounted 20% to 30%. Ask about their "cybershopping" program. Bay St. ☎ 242/326-1661.

(Finds) Goin' Local—Coconut Gin & a Fish Fry

The most raffish-looking and densest concentration of low-end bars and eateries on New Providence rises in boxy, brightly colored rectangles from the sand and rock of **Arawak Cay.** Known as "Fish Fry" to many locals, it lies in the heart of Nassau, across West Bay Street (from the Botanical Gardens, walk back along Chippingham Rd.). Early in the day, you'll be able to buy fresh conch; vendors will crack the mollusk before your eyes (this cracking and cleaning process isn't everybody's favorite attraction). They'll give you some hot sauce and tell you to chow down. Beginning around noon, you'll find at least a half-dozen simple bars and kiosks dispensing cracked conch, fried fish, and grits garnished with either spicy corned beef or tuna salad. With it, you can sample a favorite drink of the islands, coconut milk laced with gin (an acquired taste, to say the least, but you'll feel like a real Bahamian). It's at its most crowded and popular every Sunday night, beginning around 5pm until around midnight, when hundreds of Bahamians gather together next to bonfires to gossip, flirt, raise hell, and hang out.

John Bull   The jewelry department here offers classic selections from Tiffany & Co.; cultured pearls from Mikimoto; the creations of David Yurman, Carrera y Carrera; Greek and Roman coin jewelry; and Spanish gold and silver pieces. It's the best name in the business. The store also features a wide selection of watches, cameras, perfumes, cosmetics, leather goods, and accessories. It is one of the best places in The Bahamas to buy a Gucci or Cartier watch. Bay St. ✆ **242/322-4253.**

LEATHER

In addition to the stores mentioned below, another good store for leather goods is the **Brass and Leather Shop,** described under "Brass & Copper," above.

Gucci   This shop, opposite Rawson Square, is the best place to buy leather goods in Nassau. The wide selection includes handbags, wallets, luggage, briefcases, gift items, scarves, ties, evening wear for men and women, umbrellas, shoes, sandals, watches, and perfume, all by Gucci of Italy. Saffrey Sq., Bay St., corner of Bank Lane. ✆ **242/325-0561.**

Leather Masters   This well-known retail outlet carries an internationally known collection of leather bags, luggage, and accessories by Ted Lapidus, Lanvin, and Lancel of Paris; Etienne Aigner of Germany; and i Santi of Italy. Leather Masters also carries luggage by Piel and Travel Pro; leather wallets by Bosca; and pens, cigarette lighters, and watches by Colibri. Silk scarves, neckties, and cigar accessories are also featured. 8 Parliament St. ✆ **242/322-7597.**

LINENS

The Linen Shop   This is the best outlet for linens in Nassau. It sells beautifully embroidered bed linens, Irish handkerchiefs, and tablecloths. Look also for the most exquisite children's clothing and christening gowns in town. In the Ironmongery Building, Bay St., near Charlotte St. ✆ 242/322-4266.

MAPS

Balmain Antiques   This place offers a wide and varied assortment of 19th-century etchings, engravings, and maps, many of them antique and all reasonably priced. Other outlets have minor displays of these collectibles, but this outlet has the finest. Some items are 400 years old. It's usually best to discuss your interests with Mr. Ramsey, the owner, so he can direct you to the proper drawers. His specialties include The Bahamas, America during the Civil War, and Black history. He also has a collection of military historical items. The shop now features Haitian primitive art. You'll find the shop on the second floor, three doors east of Charlotte Street. In the Mason's Building, Bay St., near Charlotte St. ✆ **242/323-7421.**

MARKETS

The **Nassau International Bazaar** consists of some 30 shops selling international goods in a new arcade. A pleasant place for browsing, the $1.8-million complex sells goods from around the globe. The bazaar runs from Bay Street down to the waterfront (near the Prince George Wharf). With cobbled alleyways and garreted storefronts, the area looks like a European village.

   Prince George Plaza, Bay Street, is popular with cruise-ship passengers. Many fine shops (Gucci, for example) are found here. When you get tired of shopping, you can dine at the open-air rooftop restaurant that overlooks Bay Street.

What Happened to the Straw Market?

A tremendous fire on September 4, 2001, destroyed virtually all of the merchandise and most of the infrastructure of the permanent home of **Nassau's Straw Market,** a concrete shell a few steps from the administration of the Bahamian Tourist Board, at the corner of Bay and Market streets. Since then, the Straw Market has occupied a tent on Bay Street, opposite the intersection of Bay Street with George Street, about 2 blocks from its original premises. Merchandise is what it's always been: hats, weavings, baskets, valises—all woven from reeds, straw, and grasses. Hours of the Straw Market are daily from 7am to around 8pm, although each individual vendor (there are around 200 of them) sets his or her own schedule.

PERFUMES & COSMETICS

Nassau has several good perfume outlets, notably **John Bull** and **Little Switzerland,** which also stock a lot of nonperfume merchandise.

The Beauty Spot   The largest cosmetic shop in The Bahamas, this outlet sells duty-free cosmetics by Lancôme, Chanel, YSL, Elizabeth Arden, Estée Lauder, Clinique, Christian Dior, and Biotherm, among others. It also operates facial salons. Bay and Frederick sts. © 242/322-5930.

The Perfume Bar   This little gem has exclusive rights to market Boucheron, and it also stocks the Clarins line (though not exclusively). Bay St. © 242/322-7216.

The Perfume Shop   In the heart of Nassau, within walking distance of the cruise ships, the Perfume Shop offers duty-free savings on world-famous perfumes. Women can treat themselves to a flacon of Eternity or Chanel. For men, the selection includes Drakkar Noir, Polo, and Obsession. Corner of Bay and Frederick sts. © 242/322-2375.

8 New Providence After Dark

Gone are the days when tuxedo-clad gentlemen and elegantly gowned ladies drank and danced the night away at such famous nightclubs as the Yellow Bird and the Big Bamboo. You can still find dancing, along with limbo and calypso, but for most visitors, the major attraction is gambling.

Cultural entertainment in Nassau is limited, however. The chief center for this is the **Dundas Center for the Performing Arts,** which sometimes stages ballets, plays, or musicals. Call © 242/393-3728 to see if a production is planned during your visit.

ROLLING THE DICE

As another option, you can easily head over to Paradise Island and drop into the massive, spectacular casino in the Atlantis resort. See chapter 4.

Wyndham Nassau Resort & Crystal Palace Casino   This dazzling casino, radically upgraded and refined during 2007, is the only one on New Providence Island and is now run by the Wyndham Nassau Resort. During the lifetime of this edition, the gaming establishment will fall under the orbit of the new Baha Mar development group, which plans big and imaginative things for it through 2008. Thanks to constant and ongoing improvements, and the willingness of its management to restock it with some of the world's most up-to-date casino games and slot machines, it stacks up well against the major casinos of the Caribbean. Incorporating more than 3,252 sq. m (35,004 sq. ft.) into its flashy-looking premises, it's animated, bustling, and filled with the serious business of people having fun with their money and their temptations. The gaming room features hundreds of slot machines—only a few of which resemble the low-tech one-armed bandits that were in vogue 20 years ago. You'll also find blackjack tables, roulette wheels, craps tables, a baccarat table, and a hypersophisticated electronic link to Las Vegas that provides gaming odds on most of the major sporting events in the world. There's also a serious commitment to poker, which management here defines as one of the fastest-growing and most passionate gaming sports of the millennium. W. Bay St., Cable Beach. ℂ 242/327-6200.

THE CLUB & MUSIC SCENE

Club Fluid   Set within a two-story building in downtown Nassau, this basement-level nightclub features a baby-blue-and-white interior, dozens of mirrors that are much appreciated by narcissists, two bars, and a dance floor. It attracts an animated crowd of local residents, most of them between 20 and 45, who appreciate the reggae, soca, hip-hop, and R&B music. It's open Wednesday to Saturday from 9pm to 2am. W. Bay St., near the corner of Frederick St. ℂ 242/356-4691. Cover $12–$20 (£6.35–£11).

Rain Forest Theater   Accessible directly from the Crystal Palace Casino on Cable Beach, this 800-seat theater is a major nightlife attraction. Revues tend to be small-scale, relatively restrained, and very definitely on the safe and "family-friendly" side of the great cultural divide. Fake palm trees on each side and touches of glitter set the scene for the on-stage entertainment. Hours vary with the season, the act, and the number of guests in the hotel at the time. Billboards located prominently throughout the hotel will hawk whoever is headlining at the moment. At press time for this edition, it was Jambalaya, a Caribbean/West African dance troupe, which showed tremendous verve and style. In the Crystal Palace Casino, W. Bay St., Cable Beach. ℂ 242/327-6200. Entrance $30–$35 (£16–£19) per person. Drinks are extra.

THE BAR SCENE

Charlie's on the Beach/Cocktails 7 Dreams   The focus within this sparsely decorated club is local gossip, calypso and reggae music, and stiff drinks, all of which translates to a high-energy night out in Nassau. The setting is a simple warehouselike structure a few blocks west of the British Colonial Hilton, though management warns that during some particularly active weekends (including spring break), the entire venue might move, short term, to a larger and as yet undetermined location. Open only Wednesday and Friday to Sunday 9pm to 4am. W. Bay St. near Long Wharf Beach. ℂ 242/328-3745. Cover $10–$20 (£5.30–£11).

Señor Frog's   How can you hate a bar that manages to satirize itself as richly as this one does? The interior is deliberately and somewhat claustrophobically overcrowded with frogs, faux palm trees, and battered wooden tables. Choices range from midday salsa and chips to "Let's sample all of the margaritas available on this menu" contests conducted informally among heavy-drinking cruise-ship drop-ins. Expect merengue music (especially on weekends, when tables are pushed aside to form an ersatz dance floor) and a menu loaded with burgers, fajitas, and tacos. W. Bay St., near the British Colonial Hilton. Snacks and platters $5–$15 (£2.65–£7.95). ℂ 242/323-1777.

4

Paradise Island

Located just 180m (590 ft.) off the north shore of Nassau, Paradise Island is a favorite vacation spot for East Coast Americans who flee their icy winters for the stunning white sands of Paradise Beach. In addition to its gorgeous strands, the island boasts beautiful foliage, including brilliant red hibiscus and a grove of casuarina trees sweeping down to form a tropical arcade.

Now the priciest piece of real estate in The Bahamas, this island once served as a farm for Nassau and was known as Hog Island. Purchased for $294 by William Sayle in the 17th century, it cost A&P grocery-chain heir Huntington Hartford $11 million in 1960. He decided to rename the 6.5km-long (4-mile) sliver of land Paradise before selling out his interests. Long a retreat for millionaires, the island experienced a massive building boom in the 1980s. Its old Bahamian charm is now gone forever, lost to the high-rises, condos, second homes of the wintering wealthy, and gambling casino that have taken over. The centerpiece of Paradise Island is the mammoth Atlantis Paradise Island Resort & Casino, which has become a nightlife mecca and a sightseeing attraction in its own right.

For those who want top hotels, casino action, Vegas-type revues, fabulous beaches, and a posh address, Paradise Island is the place. It's now sleeker and more upscale than Cable Beach, its closest rival, and Freeport/Lucaya. True, Paradise Island is overbuilt and overly commercialized, but its natural beauty still makes it a choice vacation spot, perfect for a quick 3- or 4-day getaway.

Paradise Island is treated as a separate entity in this guide, but it is actually part of New Providence, connected by a bridge. You can travel between the two on foot, by boat, or by car. It's easy to stay in Nassau or Cable Beach and come over to enjoy the beaches, restaurants, attractions, and casino on Paradise Island. You can also stay on Paradise Island and head over into Nassau for a day of sightseeing and shopping. So view this section as a companion to chapter 3. Refer to chapter 3 for transportation details, nearby sights, and a wider array of sports and recreation choices.

1 Orientation

ARRIVING

Most visitors to Paradise Island arrive in Nassau and commute to Paradise Island by ground transport.

When you arrive at the Lynden Pindling International Airport (also known as the **Nassau International Airport;** see chapter 3 for information on flying into Nassau), you won't find bus service to take you to Paradise Island. Many package deals will provide hotel transfers from the airport. Otherwise, if you're not renting a car, you'll need to take a taxi. Taxis in Nassau are metered and take cash only, no credit cards. It will usually cost you $30 (£16) to go by cab from the airport to your hotel. The driver will

A hotel can close for all kinds of reasons.
Our Guarantee ensures that if your hotel's undergoing construction, we'll let you know in advance. In fact, we cover your entire travel experience. See www.travelocity.com/guarantee for details.

You'll never roam alone.

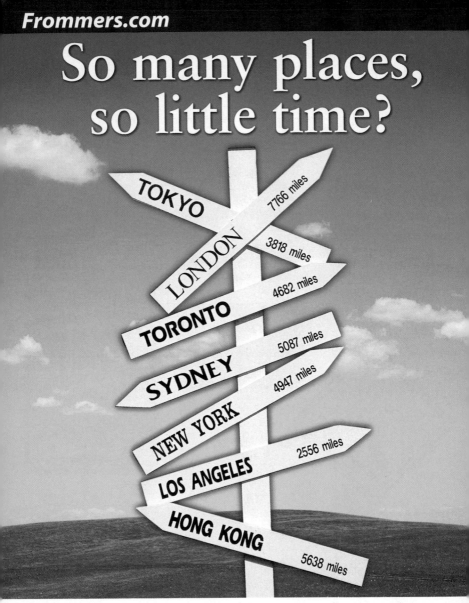

also ask you to pay the northbound one-way $1 (55p) bridge toll (this charge will be added onto your metered fare at the end).

VISITOR INFORMATION

Paradise Island does not have a tourist office, so refer to the tourist facilities in downtown Nassau (see "Orientation," at the beginning of chapter 3). The concierge or the guest services staff at your hotel can also give you information about the local attractions.

ISLAND LAYOUT

Paradise Island's finest beaches lie on the Atlantic (northern) coastline; the docks, wharves, and marinas are located on the southern side. Most of the island's largest and glossiest hotels and restaurants, as well as the casino and a lagoon with landscaped borders, lie west and north of the roundabout. The area east of the roundabout is less congested, with only a handful of smaller hotels, a golf course, the Versailles Gardens, the cloister, the airport, and many of the island's privately owned villas.

2 Getting Around

You don't need to rent a car. Most visitors walk around Paradise Island's most densely developed sections and hire a taxi for the occasional longer haul. For information on renting a car, refer to "By Rental Car," on p. 56 in chapter 2.

The most popular way to reach nearby Nassau is to **walk across the toll bridge.** There is no charge for pedestrians.

If you want to tour Paradise Island or New Providence by **taxi,** you can make arrangements with either the taxi driver or the hotel reception desk. Taxis wait at the entrances to all the major hotels. The hourly rate is about $60 (£32) in cars or small vans.

If you are without a car and don't want to take a taxi or walk, you can take a **ferry to Nassau.** The ferry to Nassau leaves from the dock on Casino Drive every half-hour, and the 10-minute ride costs $3 (£1.60) one-way. Quicker and easier than a taxi, the ferry deposits you right at Prince George Wharf, in downtown Nassau Bay Street. Daily service is from 9am to 6pm.

Water taxis also operate between Paradise Island and Prince George Wharf in Nassau. They depart daily from 8:30am to 6pm at 20-minute intervals. Round-trip fare is $6 (£3.20) per person.

If you are a guest at one of the properties associated with Atlantis Paradise Island Resort & Casino, you can hop aboard one of the complimentary shuttle buses for drop-offs at any of the hotel accommodations within the Atlantis Resort. They depart from the Lynden Pindling International Airport at 30-minute intervals every day between 7am and 11pm, costing $6 (£3.20) per person round-trip. Atlantis guests can also take a complimentary tour of the island, leaving daily at noon.

Unlike New Providence, no public buses are allowed on Paradise Island.

3 Where to Stay

In the off season (mid-Apr to mid-Dec), prices are slashed by at least 20%—and perhaps a lot more, though the weather isn't as ideal. But because Paradise Island's summer business has increased dramatically, you'll never see some of the 60% reductions that you might find at a cheaper property in the Greater Nassau area. Paradise Island doesn't have to lower its rates to attract summer business. For inexpensive accommodations, refer to

Where to Stay & Dine in Paradise Island

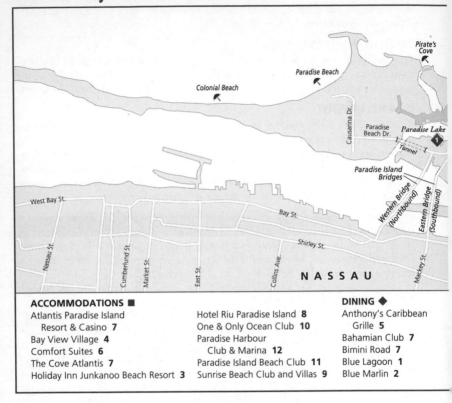

Pirate's Cove

Paradise Beach

Colonial Beach

Causarina Dr.

Paradise Beach Dr.

Paradise Lake

Tunnel

Paradise Island Bridges

West Bay St.

Bay St.

Western Bridge (Northbound)

Eastern Bridge (Southbound)

Shirley St.

Nassau St.

Cumberland St.

Market St.

East St.

Collins Ave.

Mackey St.

NASSAU

ACCOMMODATIONS ■
Atlantis Paradise Island
   Resort & Casino **7**
Bay View Village **4**
Comfort Suites **6**
The Cove Atlantis **7**
Holiday Inn Junkanoo Beach Resort **3**

Hotel Riu Paradise Island **8**
One & Only Ocean Club **10**
Paradise Harbour
   Club & Marina **12**
Paradise Island Beach Club **11**
Sunrise Beach Club and Villas **9**

DINING ◆
Anthony's Caribbean
   Grille **5**
Bahamian Club **7**
Bimini Road **7**
Blue Lagoon **1**
Blue Marlin **2**

the recommendations on New Providence Island (see chapter 3). Paradise Island isn't cheap!

VERY EXPENSIVE

Atlantis Paradise Island Resort & Casino 🏨🏨🏨 (Kids)   This creatively designed megaresort, the biggest in The Bahamas, functions as a vacation destination and theme park in its own right. A blockbuster in every sense of the word, it contains the most creative interiors, the most intriguing aesthetics, and the most elaborate waterscapes of any hotel in the country. It's the most recent incarnation of a resort that originated early in the days of Paradise Island tourism, passing through rocky and sometimes less glamorous days before reaching its startling newest incarnation as a destination that appeals to adults (its gambling facilities are the largest in The Bahamas) and to ecologists (its focus on the protection of marine life adds a welcome dose of "save the planet" to an otherwise relentlessly consumerist theme). And it exerts a potent lure for children, and the child that remains within many of us, thanks to its evocation of a "Lost Continent" whose replicated ruins evoke—you guessed it—Atlantis.

But whereas the newest of its buildings manage to conjure thoughts of both science fiction and ancient mythology at the same time (no easy feat), its older buildings still retain a whiff of the old Resorts International and Merv Griffin days of the 1980s. But thanks to skillful landscaping and the presence on-site of miles of canals whose currents

Café at the Great Hall of Waters **7**	Dune **10**	
Café Martinique **7**	Fathoms **7**	
Carmine's **7**	Mama Loo's **7**	
Casa d'Angelo **7**	Marketplace **7**	
The Cave Grill **7**	News Café **2**	
Columbus Tavern **12**	Seagrapes Restaurant **7**	
	The Water's Edge **7**	

carry swimmers with flotation devices on meandering runs down mythical rivers, no one seems to notice. The entire sprawling compound opens onto a long stretch of white-sand beach with a sheltered marina. Think Vegas in the Tropics, with a mythological theme and an interconnected series of lagoons, lakes, rivers, waterfalls, and water tubes thrown in, and you'll get the picture. One advantage to the place is that there's a lot of visual distraction and high-energy, upbeat stimulation; the downside is that it's sprawling, impersonal, and at times downright bureaucratic, and the service from the sometimes bored staff just can't keep up with the number of guests here.

Overall, however, it's an appropriate choice for a (rather expensive) family vacation, since the price of the resort includes direct access to endless numbers of watery gimmicks. Children's programs are widely comprehensive and well choreographed, and many parents simply turn their kids loose for a day onto the extensive grounds and the dozens of inland canals and water tunnels crisscrossing the flat and sand terrain on which the resorts sits, with the understanding that a battalion of lifeguards and supervisors keep the show rolling and the safety levels up to par. Singles and young couples who want a lot of razzle-dazzle appreciate the place, too, though some people find it over-the-top, too expensive, and too firmly mired in the limitations of its own "lost continent" theme.

Much of the look of the place derives from its ownership by Kerzner International, a global investment company that originated in South Africa. Atlantis offers so many sports, dining, and entertainment options that many guests never venture off the property during their entire vacation. It's expensive, but for your money, you'll find yourself neck-deep amid many of the diversions you might have otherwise expected from a theme park. And if you opt for accommodations in one of the resort's less plush accommodations, especially within the Beach Tower of the Atlantis's main core, the cost bite won't seem quite as severe. Accommodations within The Atlantis Resort retain distinctly different levels of opulence, for the most part based on where they're located. The most opulent and most expensive accommodations lie in semisecluded annexes whose facilities are not open to the general hotel population of Atlantis. They include The One&Only Ocean Club and The Cove, a 600-unit, all-suite hotel-within-the-hotel, which opened in 2007. Both of those pockets of heightened posh were conceived and designed as separate and semi-independent components within the Greater Atlantis, and each is described in separate recommendations below.

As this resort has expanded, accommodations within the central core of the Atlantis megacompound are emerging as the less expensive accommodations within the resort. And of those accommodations, the most plush lie within the Royal Towers—the tallest and most imaginative building in The Bahamas. You'll get the feeling that an army of designers labored long and hard over the interior decors, replete as they are with decorative replicas of sea horses, winged dragons, and megasize conch shells sprouting from cornices and rooflines. (Rooms in the Royal Towers' Imperial Club have a personal concierge and upgraded amenities.) The most deluxe accommodation anywhere within the Atlantis fiefdom is the Bridge Suite, an architectural oddity that links, several stories above ground level, the two spires of the Royal Towers. It rents for $25,000 (£13,250) a day and during its celebrated history was occupied by Michael Jordan during his involvement with tournaments at the on-site golf course.

The casino and entertainment complex lie in an area over the watery depths of a lagoon. Less posh and less plush are rooms within the Coral Tower, and least expensive of the entire lot are accommodations within the still-serviceable but older Beach Tower, with a floor plan shaped like an airplane propeller, from the dimly remembered 1980s. But even in the older, least expensive sections, accommodations are comfortable and well accessorized, and available with the full understanding that occupants get full access to the sprawling water parks that are otherwise accessible only on a limited basis to nonresidents. Most units sport a balcony or terrace with water views, individually controlled air-conditioning, in-room movies, and voice mail and modem access, plus roomy bathrooms with tubs and showers.

Any old hotel might sport tropical gardens, but the Atlantis goes one better by featuring the world's largest collection of outdoor open-air marine habitats, each of them aesthetically stunning. A few of these were conceived for snorkelers and swimmers, but most were designed so guests could observe the marine life from catwalks above and from glassed-in underwater viewing tunnels. Even folks who don't stay here, including thousands of cruise-ship passengers, can take part in orchestrated tours. These jaunts include 11 different exhibition lagoons, containing millions of gallons of water and at least 200 species of tropical fish. On-site marine habitats include a separate lagoon for sharks, for dolphins, and for stingrays, respectively, and individual habitats for lobsters, piranhas, and underwater exotica. Swimmers can meander along an underwater snorkeling trail (Paradise Lagoon) and explore a five-story replica of an ancient ziggurat-shaped Mayan temple. The temple's sides incorporate a waterslide with slippery, wet, and wild runs that feature an 18m (59-ft.) nearly vertical drop.

Tips **Coming Attractions**

During the lifetime of this edition, Atlantis will begin a new phase of development that will continue to enlarge and, to some extent, redefine the megaresort's present layout. Individual elements (only some of which will be completed in time for 2009) include the opening of a 400-unit condominium complex whose units will be rented to hotel guests according to the whims and priorities of each individual owner. There will almost certainly be an ongoing configuration of some of the resort's dining and drinking options, and the fine-tuning of features added new in 2007, including the dolphin encounter known as Dolphin Cay, which was still in its infancy at press time for this edition but which showed strong commitment to eventually housing up to 75 trained dolphins; and a sprawling (4,645-sq.-m/49,998-sq.-ft.) new cluster of additional meeting and convention facilities.

But for us, at least, the ultimate proof of Atlantis's wildly innovative and creative style lies in plans for the creation of an Atlantis megaresort, sometime during 2010 or 2011, in Dubai. We've seen the architectural renderings of this Aladdin's Lamb/Arabian Nights fantasy. The scale and scope of the place evokes the labors of the Pharaohs, and the sense of fantasy and imagination does nothing but inspire awe for both the Kerzner Group and the growth that's happening in Dubai. Since gambling is illegal in the Muslim context of Dubai, the place is being planned without a casino, but with a nod to principles of the Koran; inspiration from some of the great mosques of Turkey, Persia, the Magreb, and the Arab Emirates; and a water park that's even bigger than the one on Paradise Island. All we can say to Kerzner's involvement in this new venture is "Wow" and "*Inshallah.*"

Participants emerge from the sculpted mouths of giant Mayan gods like human sacrifices as they race giddily down the course of the waterslide.

In 2007, additional water features known collectively as Aquaventure were added to the layout, bringing the number of hectares devoted to water features at Atlantis to 39 (97 acres). The most visible monument within Aquaventure is a mythical-looking building, the Power Tower, site of another set of waterslides more imaginative even than those within the above-noted Mayan temple, each skillfully landscaped into the surrounding vegetation. Aquaventure, its labyrinth of meandering streams and waterfalls, is accessible, without charge, for residents of any of the accommodations within the Atlantis complex but otherwise is strictly off-limits to the general public.

One major entertainment venue within the Paradise Island layout includes the Marina Village. It was inspired by an old Bahamian harborfront in "the good old days" with a string of clapboard-sided houses (think historic Key West, Florida, but with a lot more money). Flanking a marina that draws some of the most spectacular yachts in the world, it's a self-enclosed venue, within the orbit of Atlantis, for dozens of shops, bars, and restaurants, replete with gazebos and live musicians. Along with the casino and an arcade of shops, it is one of the areas open to the general public: The water park and many of the grounds surrounding this place are strictly reserved only for hotel guests of the resort.

Tips Wandering Through "The Lost Continent"

Regrettably for casual walk-through visitors, the marine habitats, gardens, and other attractions here are open only to guests at the Atlantis Resort, or to nonguests who sign up for a guided tour of the resort. The cost of this "Discover Atlantis" tour is $29 (£15) per person, with children under 12 getting in for half-price. Even if you sign up for it, know in advance that some of the most intriguing areas of the 39 hectares (97 acres) of waterscape within the resort remain off-limits to everyone except registered guests. Despite that, there's a lot to see on one of these guided tours. But in the end, it's a tour, and a rather tightly choreographed one at that. It doesn't allow free time for participants to float down the lazy rivers of the resort on a rubber raft. If anything, it will pique your interest in Atlantis, hopefully as an incentive for you to return one day as a registered guest. For information on participating in one of these guided tours, call the Atlantis Resort (© 242/363-3000). Tours last about an hour each and feature a brisk, well-rehearsed overview of the marine habitats and all other areas of the resort as well, with the exception of the beaches, the swimming pools, the waterslides, and large areas of the waterscapes.

Note that if you want to visit Atlantis on your own, not as part of a guided tour, the general public has unrestricted access to the casino, the nightclubs, the shopping arcade, and the shops and restaurants of Marina Village. But access to Aquaventure, the waterslides, and most of the waterscapes is strictly off-limits to nonresidents.

The focal point of this extravagance is the massive **Paradise Island Casino,** the best-designed and—at the time of this writing—most imaginatively conceived casino in The Bahamas. The casino alone contains four separate bars and two separate restaurants. Within the diverse and scattered elements of this extended resort, you'll find around 38 separate food and beverage outlets, some of which open, close, and are reconfigured at occasionally dizzying rates. (For detailed descriptions of the most intriguing, see "Where to Dine" and "Paradise Island After Dark," later in this chapter.) None of them comes cheap: You should expect to pay a lot to dine or drink in most of them.

Casino Dr. (P.O. Box N-4777), Paradise Island, The Bahamas. © 800/ATLANTIS in the U.S., or 242/363-3000. Fax 242/363-6300. www.atlantis.com. 2,900 units. Winter $420–$785 (£223–£416) double; from $940 (£498) suite. Off-season $380–$715 (£201–£379) double; from $715 (£379) suite. Package deals available. AE, DC, DISC, MC, V. Self-parking $12 (£6.35) per day, valet parking $14 (£7.40) per day. **Amenities:** 20 restaurants within the Atlantis subsection of the resort; 18 lounges and clubs; 17 outdoor pools interspersed with 39 hectares/97 acres of waterscape; golf course; 5 tennis courts; health club; spa; sauna; watersports equipment/rentals; children's programs (ages 4–12); salon; room service; massage; babysitting; laundry service; dry cleaning; nonsmoking rooms; rooms for those w/limited mobility. *In room:* A/C, TV, minibar, hair dryer, iron, safe, in-room fridge available for $15 per day.

The Cove Atlantis 𝒜𝒜𝒜   Housed within a handsome, newly built turquoise-and-coral-colored tower whose fanciful detailing matches the mythical theme of the other showcase designs of the Atlantis Resort, this hotel was configured as a semiprivate hideaway. Don't expect anything conventional about this place: It contains only suites and an adult-oriented venue that takes pains to dilute a growing perception that The Atlantis has placed too heavy an emphasis on family fun, hordes of short-term cruise-ship passengers, and the ongoing daycare and amusement of teeny-boppers from the

North American mainland. Inaugurated in the spring of 2007, it boasts an avant-garde design that's a combination of the best of minimalist Japan and ultra-high-end postmodern Florida. Every accommodation is luxurious, some of presidential proportions (including a duplex with a total of more than 372 sq. m/4,000 sq. ft.), with personal butlers and every imaginable electronic and service-related amenity. Most of the units, however, are spacious but not obscenely oversized, ranging in square footage from 62 to 158 sq. m (672–1,700 sq. ft.); and each manages to be opulent, postmodern, summery, and tasteful. The social centerpiece of the hotel is a 2,700m (9,000-ft.) rectangular "ultrapool" which is strictly off-limits to anyone under 18. It is ringed with 22 private cabanas, which can be rented by the day for sybaritic adults seeking seclusion from the family-with-children crowds. On the premises is the Mandara Spa, whose design was inspired by the architecture of Bali, with rampant use of stone, bamboo, and tropical hardwoods. Although it hadn't opened before press time for this edition, a branch of Bobby Flay's Mesa Grill had carved out space for itself on the ground floor of this hotel-within-a hotel.

Casino Dr. (P.O. Box N-4777), Paradise Island, The Bahamas. ℂ 800/ATLANTIS in the U.S., or 242/363-3000. Fax 242/363-6300. www.atlantis.com. 600 suites. Winter $735–$1,510 (£390–£800) suite; off-season $625–$1,415 (£331–£750) suite. **Amenities:** 2 restaurants; 2 bars; 3 pools; access to an 18-hole golf course; access to 5 tennis courts; health club; spa; steam room; shuttle to the One&Only Ocean Club; access to the Atlantis casino; room service; babysitting; laundry service; dry cleaning; nonsmoking rooms. *In room:* A/C, TV, minibar, hair dryer, iron, safe, butler service.

One&Only Ocean Club 𝓡𝓡𝓡 Tranquil, secluded, and intimate, this is the most exclusive address on Paradise Island, with sky-high prices that match the refined ambience and pampering service (the best in The Bahamas). Although it's owned by the same entity that controls the much larger Atlantis Resort nearby, huge efforts are expended to separate it from the clients at the less personalized, more family-friendly, theme-oriented Atlantis. In fact, although the facilities of the Atlantis are open and available to the residents of the One&Only Ocean Club, that same privilege does not extend in the opposite direction. As such, you'll find a boutique-style hotel with a highly visible security force that, to a large degree, is cloistered from the larger and much splashier "upscale mass market" venue nearby. This is one of the best-developed tennis resorts in The Bahamas, and the white-sand beach adjacent to the hotel is the finest in the Nassau/Paradise Island area.

The spacious and elegantly furnished rooms are plushly comfortable, with king-size beds, gilt-framed mirrors, and dark-wood armoires. The marble bathrooms in the suites are massive, and each contains a bidet, twin basins, and both a tub and a shower.

The real heart and soul of the resort lies in the surrounding gardens, which were designed by the island's former owner, Huntington Hartford II, heir to the A&P grocery fortune. This resort, in fact, was once the site of his private home. Formal gardens surround a rebuilt medieval French cloister set on 14 hectares (35 acres) of manicured lawns. (Bought by newspaper mogul William Randolph Hearst during one of his trips through France and later sold to Huntington Hartford, it was disassembled and rebuilt on this site as part of a major drama that's more fully explained later within this chapter.) The graceful 12th-century arcades of the cloister are visible at the crest of a hill, across a stretch of terraced waterfalls, fountains, a stone gazebo, and rose gardens. Larger-than-life statues dot the vine-covered niches on either side of the gardens. Begin your tour of the gardens at the large swimming pool, which feeds a series of reflecting pools that stretch out toward the cloister. A new addition is the child-friendly family pool, replete with aqua toys and a waterfall.

Arguably the best dining on Paradise Island can be found at the resort's Dune restaurant, creation of culinary legend Jean-Georges Vongerichten. See "Where to Dine," later in this chapter, for a review.

Ocean Club Dr. (P.O. Box N-4777), Paradise Island, The Bahamas. © **800/321-3000** in the U.S., or 242/363-2501. Fax 242/363-2424. www.oneandonlyresorts.com. 106 units, 3 private villas. Winter $750–$1,250 (£398–£663) double; from $1,330 (£705) suite; from $7,500 (£3,975) villa. Off-season $490–$1,190 (£260–£631) double; from $805 (£427) suite; from $7,000 (£3,710) villa. AE, MC, V. Free parking. **Amenities:** 2 restaurants; 3 bars; 2 pools; 18-hole golf course; 6 tennis courts; health club; spa; steam room; shuttle to Atlantis casino; room service; babysitting; laundry service; dry cleaning; nonsmoking rooms. *In room:* A/C, TV, kitchenette (in some), minibar, hair dryer, iron, safe, butler service.

EXPENSIVE

Holiday Inn Junkanoo Beach Resort ℜ *Kids*   This older 12-floor property adjacent to the waters of Nassau Harbour opens onto a marina with very little beach but a good-size swimming pool. It was rescued from oblivion in the late 1990s when a Florida-based investment group, Driftwood Ventures, renovated it. This group turned it into an all-inclusive resort, which lies just a short stroll away from the popular Atlantis and all its attractions. Bedrooms are midsize with twin or king-size beds, plus well-maintained bathrooms with tub/showers. The decor is comfortable, airy, and sunny, and outfitted with tropically inspired colors and upholstery. All third-floor rooms and select units on the fourth floor are designated for nonsmokers only. The food served at the restaurants is palatable but needs much improvement, and service is very slow, so be duly warned. However, there are nightly live shows to spice up the lackluster meal offerings, including fire dancing and Bahamian bands.

Harbour Dr. (P.O. Box SS-6249), Paradise Island, The Bahamas. © **800/HOLIDAY** in the U.S., or 242/363-2561. Fax 242/363-3803. www.paradiseislandbahama.com. 246 units. Winter $303–$413 (£161–£219) double, $520 (£276) suite; off season $238–$388 (£126–£206) double, $470 (£249) suite. Rates are all-inclusive. AE, DC, DISC, MC, V. **Amenities:** 3 restaurants; 2 bars; pool; 2 tennis courts; health club; Jacuzzi; watersports equipment/rentals; children's programs; car rental; massage; nonsmoking rooms; rooms for those w/limited mobility. *In room:* A/C, TV, fridge, beverage maker, hair dryer, iron, safe.

Hotel Riu Paradise Island ℜ *Kids*   Opening onto a 5km (3-mile) stretch of beach, this is the newest addition to the beachfront. In December 2004, the Riu Hotels chain refurbished the old Sheraton Grand here into an all-inclusive megaresort. Renovations included enlarging the pool, adding a restaurant, and generally enhancing rooms. This 14-story ecru-colored high-rise offers some of the most comfortably appointed bedrooms on Paradise Island. It's more understated than the Atlantis, a lot cheaper, and more user-friendly and manageable in terms of size and layout. Your kids would be happier with all the spectacular events at the Atlantis, but the Riu is a viable runner-up for the family trade. Guests can leave the shelter of the poolside terrace and settle almost immediately onto one of the waterside chaise longues at the beach. The hotel is within walking distance of the casino, restaurants, and nightlife facilities of the Atlantis Paradise Island Resort & Casino properties.

Welcoming drinks are served while you relax on comfortable chairs in the lobby bar amid palm trees and tropical foliage. All the spacious accommodations here are deluxe and tastefully decorated, and equipped with medium-size bathrooms containing tub/showers. Many have spacious balconies that afford sweeping water views or luxurious terraces.

For an extra charge, you can skip the all-inclusive dinner fare and dine at Tengoku, a Japanese-themed restaurant. Other choices available to jaded buffet-goers include

Atlantic Restaurant, serving some of Paradise Island's finest steaks and featuring a nonsmoking section, plus a terrace; and Sir Alexander, which is Riu's gourmet a la carte restaurant, featuring highly refined, mainly continental gourmet cuisine with first-rate ingredients. Live entertainment is available 6 nights a week.

6307 Casino Dr. (P.O. Box SS-6307), Paradise Island, The Bahamas. © **888/666-8816** in the U.S., or 242/363-3500. Fax 242/363-3900. www.riu.com. 379 units. Winter $438–$454 (£232–£241) double, from $522 (£277) suite; off season $424–$444 (£225–£235) double, from $484 (£257) suite. Rates are all-inclusive. AE, MC, V. **Amenities:** 3 restaurants; 2 bars; pool; 4 tennis courts; gym; spa; Jacuzzi; sauna; kids' club; watersports equipment; salon; room service; massage; babysitting; laundry service; dry cleaning; nonsmoking rooms; rooms for those w/limited mobility. *In room:* A/C, TV, minibar, hair dryer, safe, ceiling fan.

Paradise Island Beach Club *☆*

This two- and three-story timeshare complex is set near the eastern tip of Paradise Island, adjacent to a relatively isolated strip of spectacular beachfront. Managed by Marriott, it's more of a self-catering condo complex than a full-fledged resort. Many guests cook at least some meals in their own kitchens and head elsewhere, often to bigger hotels, for restaurants, watersports, gambling, and entertainment. Views from the bedrooms are usually ocean panoramas; overall, the setting is comfortable and, at its best, even cozy. You'll feel like you have your own Florida apartment, with easy access to the beach. Accommodations have two bedrooms (a maximum of six persons), with wicker and rattan furnishings, and nice touches that include double basins in each bathroom, plus a tub and shower.

On the premises are both a round and a triangular swimming pool, one with a simple snack bar that's open only at lunchtime, except on Monday and Wednesday, when there's a Bahamian buffet. The entertainment and casino facilities of the more densely developed sections of Paradise Island are just a short walk away. The major drawback here is the service, which is very laissez-faire.

Ocean Ridge Dr. (P.O. Box N-10600), Paradise Island, The Bahamas. © **242/363-2523.** Fax 242/363-2130. www.pibc -bahamas.com. 44 units. Winter $534 (£283) 2-bedroom apt; off season $422 (£224) 2-bedroom apt. AE, MC, V. **Amenities:** Pool bar; 2 pools; exercise room; salon; massage; coin-operated laundry service; limited mobility rooms. *In room:* A/C, TV, kitchen, hair dryer, iron, safe.

Sunrise Beach Club and Villas *☆* *Kids*

This cluster of Spanish-inspired low-rise town houses occupies one of the most desirable stretches of beachfront on Paradise Island. Midway between the Riu Hotel and the One&Only Ocean Club, it's a short walk from the casino and a variety of sports and dining options. Accommodations are clustered within five separate groupings of red-roofed town houses, each with access to the resort's two swimming pools (one of which has a waterfall) and a simple snack bar. The hotel is usually full of Germans, Swiss, and Austrians, many of whom stay for several weeks. Guests can prepare most of their own meals because units have kitchens. Expect pastel colors, summery-looking furniture, and a private patio or veranda, plus king-size beds and floor-to-ceiling mirrored headboards, as well as average-size bathrooms with tub and shower. The best units are the three-bedroom apartments, situated directly on the beach. This is a good bet for "quieter" families who want a more subdued and relaxed vacation, and who want to avoid the circus at the Atlantis.

P.O. Box SS-6519, Paradise Island, The Bahamas. © **800/451-6078** or 242/363-2234. Fax 242/363-2308. www.sunrise beachclub.com. 100 units. Winter $315–$350 (£167–£186) 1-bedroom unit, $551–$612 (£292–£324) 2-bedroom unit; off season $210–$243 (£111–£129) double, $441 (£234) 2-bedroom unit. AE, MC, V. **Amenities:** Restaurant; bar; 2 pools; babysitting; coin-operated laundry; nonsmoking rooms; rooms for those w/limited mobility. *In room:* A/C, TV, kitchen, hair dryer, iron, safe, beverage maker.

MODERATE

Bay View Village ✦ More than 20 kinds of hibiscus and many varieties of bougainvillea beautify this 1.6-hectare (4-acre) condo complex. The accommodations here are near the geographic center of Paradise Island and also only a 10-minute walk to either the harbor or Cabbage Beach (the complex has no beach of its own). The restaurants, nightlife, and casino of Atlantis are only a few minutes away, although the modest Terrace restaurant here is nothing to be ashamed of.

We particularly recommend rooms near the center of the resort because they are closest to the three swimming pools and laundry facilities. Each accommodation has its own kitchen with dishwasher, plus a patio or balcony and daily maid service. A shopping center is only 3 minutes away. Some units open onto views of the harbor. A full-time personal cook can be arranged on request. The units come in a wide variety of sizes; the largest can hold up to six. Rates are slightly less for weekly rentals. Penthouse suites contain roof gardens with views of the harbor. Bedrooms come with king-, queen-, or twin-size beds. Bathrooms are medium in size, well maintained, and equipped with tub/showers.

Bayview Dr. (P.O. Box SS-6308), Paradise Island, The Bahamas. ✆ **242/363-2555.** Fax 242/363-2370. 75 units. www.bwbayviewsuites.com. Winter $248 (£131) 1-bedroom suite, $385 (£204) town house (for 4 persons), from $405 (£215) villa; off season $187 (£99) 1-bedroom suite, $290 (£154) town house (for 4 persons), from $300 (£159) villa. AE, DC, MC, V. **Amenities:** Restaurant; bar; 3 pools; tennis court; babysitting; coin-operated laundry; nonsmoking rooms; rooms for those w/limited mobility. *In room:* A/C, TV, kitchen, coffeemaker, hair dryer, iron, safe.

Comfort Suites (Value A favorite with honeymooners and a good value, this three-story all-suite hotel is across the street from the Atlantis. If the mammoth Atlantis seems too overpowering, Comfort Suites is a nice alternative. You get the splash and wonder of the Atlantis, but you don't have to stay there all night or when the cruise-ship crowds descend. Although Comfort Suites has its own pool bar and restaurant, guests are also granted signing privileges at the nearby Atlantis for its drinking-and-dining spots, as well as the pool, beach, and sports facilities. Accommodations are priced by their views: over the island, the pool, or the garden. The medium-size bathrooms have beach towels and ample vanities. Bedrooms are standard motel size, with two double beds or one king.

Paradise Island Dr. (P.O. Box SS-6202), Paradise Island, The Bahamas. ✆ **877/424-6423** in the U.S. or Canada, or 242/363-3680. Fax 242/363-2588. www.comfortsuites.com. 227 units. Winter $195–$315 (£103–£167) double; off season $264–$314 (£140–£166) double. Rates include continental breakfast. AE, DISC, MC, V. **Amenities:** Restaurant; bar; pool; tennis court; health club; babysitting; laundry service and coin-operated laundry; nonsmoking rooms; rooms for those w/limited mobility. *In room:* A/C, TV, fridge, hair dryer, iron, safe (in some), beverage maker.

INEXPENSIVE

Paradise Harbour Club & Marina The noteworthy thing about this place is its sense of isolation, despite being on heavily developed Paradise Island. Built in 1991 near the island's extreme eastern tip, it's just a few steps from the also-recommended Columbus Tavern (see review below). It's pale pink, with rambling upper hallways; terra-cotta tile floors; and clean, well-organized bedrooms with tub/showers in the bathrooms. If available, opt for one of the top-floor accommodations so you can enjoy the view. Some of its quaint amenities, all free, include a water taxi to downtown Nassau, a beach shuttle (albeit in a golf cart), snorkeling gear, and bikes.

Paradise Island Dr. (P.O. Box SS-5804), Paradise Island, The Bahamas. ✆ **242/363-2992.** Fax 242/363-2840. www.phc-bahamas.com. 23 units. Winter $150 (£80) double, $210 (£111) junior suite, $275 (£146) 1-bedroom unit; off season $120 (£64) double, $180 (£95) junior suite, $250 (£133) 1-bedroom unit. MC, V. **Amenities:** Restaurant; bar; pool;

exercise room; Jacuzzi; watersports equipment/rentals; golf cart shuttle to the beach; room service; babysitting; coin-operated laundry; rooms for those w/limited mobility. *In room:* A/C, TV, kitchen (in some), minibar, coffeemaker, hair dryer, iron, safe (in some).

4 Where to Dine

Paradise Island offers an array of the most dazzling, and the most expensive, restaurants in The Bahamas. If you're on a strict budget, cross over the bridge into downtown Nassau, which has far more reasonably priced places to eat. Meals on Paradise Island are often expensive but unimaginative. (Surf and turf appears on many a menu.) Unfortunately, you may not get what you pay for.

The greatest concentration of restaurants, all near the casino, is owned by Kerzner International. There are other good places outside this complex, however, including Dune at the One&Only Ocean Club, which is that hotel's showcase restaurant.

EXPENSIVE

Bahamian Club ✦✦ STEAKS   With an upscale British colonial–era feel and an aura that's like that of a posh, elegant, and somewhat macho-looking country club, this is a big but civilized and clubby spot, with spacious vistas, mirrors, gleaming mahogany, and forest-green walls. The excellent food is served in two-fisted portions. Meat is king here, all those old favorites from roasted prime rib to Cornish hen, plus the island's best T-bone, along with a selection of veal and lamb chops. The retro menu also features the inevitable Dover sole, lobster thermidor, and grilled salmon. All of these dishes are prepared with top-quality ingredients from the mainland. Appetizers also hearken back to the good old days, with fresh jumbo shrimp cocktail, baby spinach salad with a blue-cheese dressing, and onion soup. Try the Bahamian conch chowder for some local flavor. Side dishes are excellent here, especially the penne with fresh tomato sauce and the roasted shiitake mushrooms. Proper attire required—no jeans or sneakers.

In the Atlantis Paradise Island Resort's Coral Towers, Casino Dr. ☎ 242/363-3000. Reservations required. Main courses $38–$50 (£20–£27). AE, DC, DISC, MC, V. Wed–Mon 6–11pm.

Blue Lagoon ✦ SEAFOOD   Views of the harbor and Paradise Lake, along with music from a one-man band, complement your candlelight meal here—a nice escape from the casino's glitter and glitz. Many of the fish dishes, including stone crab claws and the Nassau conch chowder, are excellent. The chef even whips up a good Caesar salad for two. The ubiquitous broiled grouper almondine is on the menu, as are dishes such as steak au poivre with a brandy sauce and duck à l'orange. Yes, you've probably had better versions of these dishes elsewhere, but they are competently prepared and served here, even though the meats are shipped in frozen.

Tips Hopping, Skipping & Jumping with Dining Hours

Restaurants, especially in hotels on Paradise Island, are not known for keeping fixed dining hours. Hours of operation can vary with the season and the occupancy levels of a hotel. Dining rooms—again, mainly in hotels—can open and close with no reason that's immediately obvious. If you're planning on going to a particular restaurant, it's always good to call in advance even if reservations aren't required.

In the Club Land'or, Paradise Dr. © 242/363-2400. Reservations required. Main courses $29–$75 (£15–£40). AE, DISC, MC, V. Mon–Sat 5–10pm.

Café at the Great Hall of Waters ℛ *Kids* INTERNATIONAL   Speaking to us confidentially, a staff member of the Atlantis said that this was probably its most underappreciated dining spot. After a close second look, we've upgraded our evaluation of the place, recommending it highly to anyone except agoraphobics, who might be frightened by its soaring ceiling and relative lack of intimacy. If you prefer to dine in a monumental setting ringed with the most "marine habitats" of any restaurant in the world, the place might be for you. You actually feel like an underwater diver as rainbow-hued fish float past the huge plate-glass windows and the illuminated underwater "ruins" of Atlantis, while rows of lobsters parade through the sand. With a ceiling that seems miles above you, the Café's dining areas are located on the lower floor of the Royal Towers. There's a kids' menu, and little ones love taking walks along the edges of the marine habitats between courses. In such a watery setting, the food becomes almost secondary, although it's quite good. The chef imports top-quality ingredients for such dishes as rack of lamb with an arugula pesto. Lobster is a specialty, and you can also order well-prepared versions of smoked salmon with lemon grass and jumbo lump Andros crab cakes. Desserts are uniformly delicious.

Royal Towers, Atlantis Paradise Island Resort, Casino Dr. © 242/363-3000. Reservations required. Main courses $30–$50 (£16–£27). AE, DC, MC, V. Thurs–Mon 7–11am, 11:30am–2:30pm, and 6–10pm.

Café Martinique ℛℛℛ FRENCH   The most elegant and upscale restaurant on Paradise Island lies within the Marina Village restaurant and shopping compound that's associated with the Atlantis Paradise Island. It occupies a replica of the kind of town house that might belong to a billionaire who happened to live, say, in Martinique and happened to have imported art and antiques from Belle Epoque Paris. This mixture of haute Paris with a French Colonial twist is enormously appealing and especially visible, for example, within the wrought-iron "bird cage" elevator that brings you and your party upstairs to the dining room. We propose that you begin your meal in the supremely comfortable bar area—the kind of place where Charles de Gaulle might have been feted during one of his official visits to his *departements d'outre-mer*. The carved mahogany antiques are pure French Caribbean, the upholsteries scream "upscale Paris," and the food items communicate "luxe." In the tastefully posh dining area, masses of flowers, cheese and dessert trolleys, and the cuisine of superchef Jean-Georges Vongerichten await your pleasure. This is one of the very few dining areas at Atlantis where men are asked to wear jackets, but in consideration of the upscale nature of the place and the air-conditioned environment, no one seems to object. Begin with such delectable items as foie gras or caviar, perhaps smoked salmon. The main courses are limited, but each dish is sublime, especially the lobster thermidor and the Dover sole meunière. The chefs are known for their grills, everything from prime rib for two to a succulent veal chop.

In the Marina Village at the Atlantis Paradise Island, Casino Dr. © 242/363-3000. Reservations required. Main courses $31–$75 (£16–£40). AE, DC, DISC, MC, V. Daily 6–11pm.

Casa d'Angelo ℛ ITALIAN   Posh, plush, richly upholstered, and lined with art and art objects reflecting the tastes of Old World Italy, Paradise Island's premier Italian restaurant offers classic dishes prepared with skill, served with flair, and evocative of the kind of elegant manicured food you'd expect from a topnotch Italian restaurant in Florida. Some of the best main courses include sautéed "Fra Diavolo–style" calamari and clams served over crostini bread; carpaccio of tuna with spinach, olives, and artichoke hearts with orange sauce; risotto with porcini mushrooms, truffle oil, goat cheese, and thyme; wood oven–roasted free-range chicken with roasted garlic and Tuscan potatoes; and grilled swordfish steak with garlic, white wine, tomatoes, capers, black olives, onions, and fresh oregano.

In the Coral Tower at the Atlantis Paradise Island Resort, Casino Dr. © **242/363-3000**. Reservations required. Main courses $32–$60 (£17–£32). AE, DC, MC, V. Daily 6–10pm.

Dune 🍴🍴🍴 INTERNATIONAL   One of the most sophisticated and cutting-edge restaurants on Paradise Island is in the west wing of the lobby level of the One&Only Ocean Club. It has a charcoal gray and black decor that looks like it was plucked from a chic enclave in Milan, a sweeping view of the ocean, a teakwood floor that evokes that aboard a yacht, and very attentive service. Near the restaurant's entrance is a thriving herb garden from which many of the culinary flavorings are derived. The chefs here invariably select the very finest ingredients, which are then handled with a razor-sharp technique. Every dish has a special something, especially shrimp dusted with orange powder and served with artichokes and arugula. A splendid choice is tuna spring rolls with soybean salsa. Also charming to the palate is a chicken and coconut-milk soup served with shiitake cakes. The goat cheese and watermelon salad is an unexpected delight. Filet of grouper—that standard throughout The Bahamas—is at its savory best here when served with a zesty tomato sauce.

In the One&Only Ocean Club, Ocean Club Dr. © **242/363-2501**, ext. 64739. Reservations required. Main courses $22–$40 (£12–£21) lunch, $42–$60 (£22–£32) dinner. AE, DC, DISC, MC, V. Daily 7–11am, noon–3pm, and 6–10:30pm.

Fathoms 🍴 SEAFOOD   You'll feel as if you're dining under the sea in this very dark seafood palace. The grotto-themed decor, depending on your tastes, might be either mystical or a bit spooky. Illuminating its glossy, metallic interior and four enormous plate-glass windows, sunlight filters through the watery marine habitats that surround the Dig, Atlantis's re-creation of an archaeological excavation of the underwater ruins of the Lost Continent.

At first you'll think the best appetizer is a selection of raw seafood in season. But then you're tempted by the blackened sashimi flavored with red ginger as it passes by. The lobster gazpacho is terrific, and you can also dig into a bowl of steamy black mussels flavored with chardonnay, garlic, and tomato. The wood-grilled yellowtail appears perfectly cooked with a wasabi potato mash and caviar, and the grilled Atlantic salmon becomes extra inviting with its side dish of Parmesan garlic fries, a first for many diners. The meat devotee will find a wide selection here. Save room for dessert, and make it a light, feathery soufflé—a different one is served every night.

In the Royal Towers of the Atlantis Paradise Island, Casino Dr. © **242/363-3000**. Reservations recommended. Main courses $27–$50 (£14–£27). AE, DC, MC, V. Daily 5:30–10pm.

Mama Loo's 🍴 ASIAN   Many people come here just to hang out in the bar of this engaging and stylish restaurant. But if you're in the mood for a good Chinese meal, you'll be ushered to a table in a circular dining room with a ceiling draped with peach-colored fabric that evokes a plushly decorated tent. Sophisticated and with a decor that seems to encourage both your sense of humor and your sense of camp, it suggests Shanghai during the British colonial age. The menu includes dishes from the Szechuan, Cantonese, Polynesian, and Caribbean repertoire. The best dish on the menu is Mama Loo's Shanghai lobster broiled with Asian spices and served with broccoli flavored with ginger. Two specialties we also like are shrimp in spicy chile sauce with a peanut sauce on the side, and deep-fried chicken filets with honey-garlic sauce. Even their spicy conch salad puts an Asian twist on an otherwise local Bahamian staple.

In the Coral Tower, Atlantis Paradise Island, Casino Dr. © **242/363-3000**. Reservations recommended. Main courses $26–$45 (£14–£24). AE, DC, DISC, MC, V. Tues–Sat 6–10pm.

Marketplace ℛ *Value* BUFFETS/INTERNATIONAL Unless you're hopelessly jaded or blasé, you won't leave here without feeling amazement at how abundant and elaborate the buffets at a casino-themed resort can really be. Decorated with old vases and terra-cotta tiles, it evokes a sprawling market where all the food just happens to be beautifully prepared, elegantly displayed, and showcased in breathtaking variety and quantity—the best buffet on Paradise Island. Before you start loading things onto your plate, browse your way past the various cooking stations and do some strategic planning. From fresh fruit to made-as-you-watch omelets, you can make breakfast as light or as heavy as you want. At lunch and dinner, you'll find everything from fresh seafood and made-to-order pastas to freshly carved roast beef and lamb. No intimate affair, this place seats some 400 diners. Sit inside or on the patio overlooking a lagoon.

In the Royal Towers, Atlantis Paradise Island Resort, Casino Dr. © **242/363-3000**. Reservations not needed. Breakfast buffets $25 (£13) per person; lunch buffets $28 (£15) per person; dinner buffets $53 (£28) per person. AE, DC, MC, V. Daily 7–11am, noon–3pm, and 5:30–10pm.

Nobu ℛℛℛ JAPANESE/ASIAN In its way, it's the most talked-about, hip, and sought-after restaurant within the Atlantis resort, thanks to massive publicity, stylish and avant-garde Asian food, and an association with an ongoing round of celebrities. It's the culinary statement of Japanese chef Nobu Matsushisa, whose branch in New York City caused a sensation among the glitterati there when it opened in the '90s. Don't expect a conventional meal here, as dishes appeal as much to the intellect as they do to the stomach. The kitchen staff here is as finely tuned as their New York or London counterparts. Some diners prefer to start with Nobu's special cold dishes, including lobster ceviche. But since conch is queen in The Bahamas, you might opt instead for conch ceviche. The best appetizer we've sampled in this array is the yellowtail sashimi with jalapeño. If you prefer your dishes hot, try the rock shrimp tempura with a creamy spicy sauce or else Chilean sea bass with black bean sauce. Many of the dishes, such as a whole fish, emerge from a wood-fired oven. The tempura selection is vast, ranging from pumpkin to shiitake. Most patrons order pieces of sushi or sashimi, and the selection here is wide, including some exotica such as "live" conch, sea urchins, or freshwater eel. Of course, you can also order well-prepared standards which include tuna, octopus, and salmon, as well as snow crab or king crab. A wide selection of sushi rolls is also offered, including a lobster roll. If you want the most lavish and exotic menu on Paradise Island, you can request the chef's signature fixed-price meal, which he calls "Chef's Choice Omakase Menu."

In the Atlantis Paradise Island Resort's Royal Towers, Casino Dr. © **242/363-3000**. Reservations required. Main courses $15–$70 (£7.95–£37); sushi or sashimi $4–$15 (£2.10–£7.95); sushi or sashimi dinner $49 (£26); chef's special menu $150 (£80). AE, DC, DISC, MC, V. Daily 6–11pm.

Water's Edge ℛ BUFFETS/SEAFOOD Frankly, we prefer the buffet station at the also-recommended Marketplace, but if you're looking for a buffet venue where ongoing displays of seafood are the main appeal, this fits the bill. Three 4.5m (15-ft.) waterfalls splash into an artificial lagoon just outside the dining room's windows. Huge chandeliers illuminate the room, which has views of an open kitchen where a battalion of chefs create a nightly seafood buffet. And if you're in the mood for pasta and pizza, they're here, but for the most part garnished with (guess what?) seafood. Depending on the night, some of the dishes are better than others, but almost universally, the lavish displays of fresh shellfish from the raw bar will include 6-ounce lobster tails, stone crab claws, more shrimp than you can cope with, and, when they're in season, fresh raw oysters. The main problem here is that the food has a hard time competing with the ambience. If you've already sampled the Marketplace, you might have already had enough buffets, at least for a while.

In the Coral Towers at the Atlantis Paradise Island, Casino Dr. ℂ 242/363-3000. Reservations recommended. Seafood buffet $45 (£24). AE, DC, DISC, MC, V. Daily 5:30–10pm.

MODERATE

Bimini Road ⋇ BAHAMIAN/INTERNATIONAL   The name Bimini Road refers to a mysterious underwater rock formation off the coast of Bimini that resembles a ruined triumphal boulevard that might have been designed by the ancient Romans or, more appropriately, the ancient Atlanteans. Partly because of its relatively reasonable prices and partly because it showcases the cuisine of The Bahamas more proudly than any other restaurant at the Atlantis Paradise Island, this eatery is among the most consistently popular and crowded dining spots on Paradise Island. Some aspects of the place, especially the red leatherette banquettes and Formica tables, evoke a Goombay version of a brightly painted diner somewhere in the Out Islands. Yet a second glance will reveal a sophisticated-looking and hysterically busy open kitchen (entertainment in its own right), and walls covered with tropical murals, some of them influenced by the Junkanoo festival. The kitchen constantly chugs out food items that include lobster and beef rib-eye. You might start with such specialties as a scorched conch salad or else Rum Bay boiled fish in a citrus broth. Other island favorites include the catch of the day, which can be grilled, blackened, or fried island style. A tasty dish is chicken mojo—boneless breast with spices and a lime mojo sauce that is charcoal-roasted and served over native rice. The only problem with this place involves an inconvenient crowd of expectant diners who cluster, somewhat uncomfortably, near the entrance waiting for an empty table. A phone call in advance for information about wait times might help you avoid this inconvenience.

In the Marina Village at the Atlantis Paradise Island, Casino Dr. ℂ 242/363-3000. Reservations accepted only for parties of 6 or more. Main courses $24–$40 (£13–£21). AE, DISC, MC, V. Daily noon–3pm and 6–11pm.

Blue Marlin ⋇ *Finds* BAHAMIAN/SEAFOOD   With a name like Blue Marlin, you expect and get fish and seafood dishes, although there are other choices as well. The catch always tastes fresh, and it's well prepared. If you've never had cracked conch, this place provides a good introduction to that famous Bahamian dish (it's like breaded veal cutlet). Lobster thermidor is a popular choice here, and the chef always fashions a linguine studded with morsels of fresh seafood. For the poultry or meat fancier, choices include Eleuthera coconut chicken and tender spare ribs basted with guava. Some nights at 7:30pm, a limbo show is presented along with a slightly gruesome live glass-eating act. You have a choice of dining inside or out.

Hurricane Hole Plaza. ℂ 242/363-2660. Reservations recommended. Main courses $12–$25 (£6.35–£13). AE, DISC, MC, V. Daily 5–10pm.

Carmine's ITALIAN   A lot of the signals that emanate from this place communicate "family." Here we're talking about a large, loud, and in-your-face Italian family who work out their emotional conflicts with gusto, verve, and platters piled high with an amazing amount of food. Set at the most distant point of the Marina Village from the casino, this is the local branch of a restaurant that will always be associated with the Little Italy or the outer boroughs of New York City.

Even though it was custom-built, you'll get the idea that a team of decorators gentrified this boathouse, with its installation of many square yards of mahogany bar tops, terra-cotta tiles, and monumental wine racks. This place prides itself on serving portions that could feed a party of four to six diners. As such, it's at its best when family members or friends gather together and order several platters for consumption by the entire table. If you're a single diner or a couple, head instead for other dining haunts such as the Café Martinique or Bahamian Club.

In the Marina Village at the Atlantis Paradise Island, Casino Dr. ℂ 242/363-3000. Reservations accepted only for parties of 6 or more. Main courses $30–$36 (£16–£19). AE, DC, DISC, MC, V. Daily 6–11pm.

Columbus Tavern *(R) (finds* CONTINENTAL/BAHAMIAN   Far removed from the glitz and glamour of the casinos, the tavern seems relatively little known, even though Freddie Lightbourne of the Poop Deck restaurant has been running it for years now. It deserves to be discovered because it serves good food at reasonable (for Paradise Island) prices. The tavern has the typical nautical decor (don't come here for the setting), with tables placed both inside and outside overlooking the harbor. The bar is worth a visit in itself, with its long list of tropical drinks. You can go local by starting off with the conch chowder, or opt for cheese-stuffed mushrooms with foie gras. Even though it's imported frozen, the rack of lamb is flawless. You can also order tamarind chicken and a quite good filet of grouper with a tantalizing lobster and shrimp sauce.

In the Paradise Harbour Club Resort, Paradise Island Dr. ℂ 242/363-5923. Reservations required for dinner. Main courses $11–$26 (£5.85–£14) lunch, $20–$48 (£11–£25) dinner. AE, MC, V. Daily 9am–10:30pm.

INEXPENSIVE

Anthony's Caribbean Grill AMERICAN/CARIBBEAN   Its owners think of this place as an upscale version of Bennigan's or TGI Fridays. But the decor is thoroughly Caribbean, thanks to psychedelic tropical colors, underwater sea themes, and jaunty maritime decorative touches. A bar dispenses everything from conventional mai tais to embarrassingly oversize 48-ounce "sparklers"—with a combination of rum, amaretto, vodka, and fruit punch that is about all most serious drinkers can handle. Menu items include burgers, pizzas capped with everything from lobster to jerk chicken, barbecued or fried chicken, ribs with Caribbean barbecue sauce, and several meal-size salads.

In the Paradise Island Shopping Center, at the junction of Paradise and Casino drives. ℂ 242/363-3152. Lunch $10–$15 (£5.30–£7.95); dinner $10–$39 (£5.30–£21). AE, DISC, MC, V. Daily 7:30am–11pm.

News Café DELI   Low-key and untouristy, this spot has a Formica-clad decor that's a far cry (and, to some people, a welcome change from) the unrelenting glossiness of other parts of Paradise Island. This is where you'll find most of the island's construction workers, groundskeepers, and hotel staff having breakfast and lunch. The eatery maintains a stack of the day's newspapers, so you can have something to read as you sip your morning cappuccino or latte. You can also stock up here on sandwiches for your beach picnic.

In the Hurricane Hole Plaza, Paradise Island. ℂ 242/363-4684. Reservations not accepted. Breakfast, lunch sandwiches, and platters $7–$12 (£3.70–£6.35); assorted coffees $2–$4 (£1.05–£2.10). AE, DC, DISC, MC, V. Daily 24 hr.

Seagrapes Restaurant *(kids* BUFFET/INTERNATIONAL   Buffet lunches and dinners are the specialty of this pleasantly decorated tropical restaurant. This is the most affordable and family-oriented choice in the Atlantis Paradise Island, offering Cuban, Caribbean, and Cajun dishes. It's pretty straightforward fare, but you get a lot of food for not a lot of money—a rarity on pricey Paradise Island. The restaurant, which can seat 200 to 300 diners at a time, overlooks the lagoon and has a marketplace look, with buffet offerings displayed in little stalls and stations. Every Thursday, Friday, and Saturday between 6 and 9pm, the place goes absolutely gaga over children. During those hours, a battalion of clowns, jugglers, and magicians transform the place into a circuslike venue replete with cotton candy and popcorn stands (bad for appetites), and a face-painting station. Depending on how family-centered you like your dining to be, you'll be either charmed or annoyed by this—just know in advance.

In the Atlantis Paradise Island, Casino Dr. ℭ 242/363-3000. Breakfast and lunch buffet $19 (£10); dinner buffet $32 (£17). AE, DC, DISC, MC, V. Daily 7–11am, noon–2:30pm, and 5:30–10pm.

5 Beaches, Watersports & Other Outdoor Pursuits

Visitors interested in something more than lazing on the beaches have only to ask hotel personnel to make the necessary arrangements. Guests at the **Atlantis Paradise Island** (ℭ 242/363-3000), for example, can have access to a surprising number of diversions without so much as leaving the hotel property. They can splash in private pools; play tennis, Ping-Pong, and shuffleboard; ride the waves; snorkel; or rent Sunfish, Sailfish, jet skis, banana boats, and catamarans from contractors located in kiosks.

HITTING THE BEACH

On Paradise Island, **Cabbage Beach** 𝒜𝒜 (also known in some circles as **West Beach**) is the real showcase. Its broad white sands stretch for at least 3km (2 miles). Casuarinas, palms, and sea grapes border it. It's likely to be crowded in winter, but you can find a little more elbowroom by walking to the northwestern stretch of the beach. You can reach Paradise Island from downtown Nassau by walking over the bridge, taking a taxi, or boarding a ferryboat at Prince George Dock. Cabbage Beach does not have public facilities, but you can patronize one of the handful of bars and restaurants nearby and use their facilities. Technically, to use the facilities, you should be a customer—even if that means buying only a drink. Note that during the construction of the Atlantis Paradise Island's new waterfront hotel and timeshare accommodations, access to some sections of Cabbage/West Beach might be off-limits.

Our other favorite beach in this area is the white-sand **Paradise Beach** 𝒜𝒜. The beach is used mainly by guests of The Cove Atlantis (p. 126), as it lies at the far western tip of the island. (Sunsets viewed from its sands are particularly beautiful.) If you're not a resident, access is difficult. If you're staying at a hotel in Nassau and want to come to Paradise Island for a day at the beach, it's better to go to Cabbage Beach (see above).

FISHING

Anglers can fish close to shore for grouper, dolphin fish, red snapper, crabs, even lobster. Farther out, in first-class fishing boats fitted with outriggers and fighting chairs, they troll for billfish or giant marlin.

The best way to pursue this pastime is to go to the activities desk of your hotel. All hotels have contacts with local charter operators who take their passengers out for a half-day or full day of fishing. For other possibilities, refer to "Beaches, Watersports & Other Outdoor Pursuits," in chapter 3.

Favorite Paradise Island Experiences

Sunset at the Cloister. Here, amid the reassembled remains of a 12th-century French stone monastery once owned by William Randolph Hearst, you can enjoy one of the most beautiful pink and mauve sunsets in all The Bahamas.

A Night at the Casino. The Atlantis Paradise Island Casino—the only one on Paradise Island—is one of the most impressive and imaginatively decorated casinos in the world. Many visitors arrive on the island just to test their luck in this 4,645-sq.-m (49,998-sq.-ft.) casino. Once you're here, make it a point to check out the huge clusters of hand-blown glass arranged into amazing sculptures, conceived by American glass-blowing master Dale Chihuly. This casino contains at least four of his sculptures, each one massive, hyperfragile, and awe-inspiring, and giving the impression that it emanates light all on its own. Looking for a dining venue? The echoing interior passageway that interconnects the various parts of this far-flung resort is home to a medley of shops and restaurants, some of them among the finest in The Bahamas.

GOLF

Ocean Club Golf Club ✸✸, on Paradise Island Drive (② **242/363-3000;** www.one andonlyresorts.com), at the east end of the island, is an 18-hole championship golf course designed by Tom Weiskopf that overlooks both the Atlantic Ocean and Nassau Harbour. Attracting every caliber of golfer, the par-72 course is known for its hole 17, which plays entirely along the scenic Snorkelers Cove. Greens fees include use of a golf cart. They range from $190 to $260 (£101–£138) per player, without reductions for guests at any individual hotels. Rental clubs and shoes are available.

Golfers who want more variety will find one other course on New Providence Island (see "Beaches, Watersports & Other Outdoor Pursuits," in chapter 3).

SNORKELING & SCUBA DIVING

For more scuba sites in the area, see "Snorkeling, Scuba Diving & Underwater Walks," in chapter 3.

Bahamas Divers, in the Yachthaven Marina, on East Bay Street (② **242/393-5644;** www.bahamadivers.com), is the best all-around center for watersports on the island, specializing in scuba diving and snorkeling. A two-tank morning dive goes for $89 to $109 (£47–£58), whereas a single-tank afternoon dive costs $55 (£29). A half-day snorkeling trip is only $39 (£21), and dive packages are also offered.

Finds Spa Serenity

The 2,323-sq.-m (25,005-sq.-ft.) **Mandara Spa** at the **Atlantis** (p. 122) is a Zen-inspired enclave of calm and serenity (and some not necessarily serene prices) designed to make guests feel like gods and goddesses. Services include exotic body scrubs and wrap treatments with names like Caribbean Coffee Scrub, Tropical Coconut Scrub, and Sunburn Cooler. Spa guests also get to take a dip in Poseidon's Thalassotherapy Pool, a beautiful open-air natural seawater pool.

TENNIS

No other hotel in The Bahamas pays as much attention to tennis as **One&Only Ocean Club,** Ocean Club Drive (© **242/363-2501**). It's the site of six Har-Tru courts, which go a long way toward evoking the days when Paradise Island was a lot more British-looking than it is today and when tennis was a lot more widely played. Guests booked into the cabanas and villas of the club can practically roll out of bed onto the courts. The courts are often filled with first-class competitors, although beginners and inter-mediate players are welcome. Tennis is free for guests of the One&Only Ocean Club; access to the courts is forbidden to virtually everyone else. Guests of the Ocean Club can play with the resident tennis pro for $70 (£37) per hour.

Other hotels with courts include the **Atlantis** ✺ (© **242/363-3000**), with five hard-surface clay courts. Residents of the Atlantis pay $20 (£11) per hour for access to the courts and can play with the organization's resident pro for another $70 (£37) per hour. Ball rentals go for $9.50 (£5.05) per hour, tennis racquets for an additional $10 (£5.30) per hour. At least two major tennis championships a year are held at the Atlantis courts, drawing players from around Europe and the Americas.

6 Seeing the Sights

Most of the big hotels here maintain activity-packed calendars, especially for that occasional windy, rainy day that comes in winter. Similar to life aboard a large-scale cruise ship, the resorts offer activities (some of them age-specific) that include water-volleyball games, bingo, fish-feeding demonstrations, and movie screenings. And that doesn't include the disco parties for teens and preteens that tend to be scheduled for late afternoon or very early evenings. To an increasing degree, hotels such as the Atlantis have configured themselves as destinations in their own right.

Atlantis Paradise Island Resort & Casino ✺✺ Regardless of where you're stay-ing—even if it's at the most remote hotel on New Providence—you'll want to visit this lavish theme park, hotel, restaurant complex, casino, and entertainment center. It's Paradise Island's biggest attraction. You could spend all day here—and all night, too—wandering through the shopping arcades; sampling the international cuisine of the varied restaurants; or gambling at the roulette wheels, slot machines, poker tables, and blackjack tables. And once you're here, don't even think about leaving without a walk along the Marina or a visit to The Dig, a theme-driven marine attraction that cele-brates the eerie and tragic legend of the lost continent of Atlantis. During the day, you can wear casual clothes, but at night you should dress up a bit, especially if you want to try one of the better restaurants.

The most crowded time to visit Atlantis is between 9am and 5pm on days when cruise ships are berthed in the nearby harbor. (That's usually every Tues, Fri, and Sat from 9am to around 5pm.) The most crowded time to visit the casino is between 8 and 11pm any night of the week. There is no cover to enter: You pay just for what you gamble away (and that could be considerable), eat, and drink. Ironically, it's illegal for Bahamian citizens or residents to gamble. That restriction, however, most definitely does not apply to visitors from offshore. Except for the price of the liquor, entertainment within the bars is free. That usually includes live salsa, Goombay, and calypso music provided by local bands.

Casino Dr. © 242/363-3000. Free admission. Daily 24 hr.

The Cloister ✺ Located in the Versailles Gardens of the One&Only Ocean Club, this 12th-century cloister built by Augustinian monks in southwestern France was

---

Moments A Special Place of Beauty

If you head up Paradise Island Drive, you'll reach Ocean Club Drive and a garden of tranquillity known as the **Versailles Gardens at the Ocean Club.** This is the loveliest spot on Paradise Island, far removed from the glitz and faux-glamour of the casinos. Its seven terraces frequently host weddings. Statues of some of A&P heir Huntington Hartford's favorite people are found in the gardens, including Mephistopheles, Franklin D. Roosevelt, Napoleon, and the British-born explorer of Africa, Doctor Livingstone. The gardens are open any time, day or night—and admission is free. Note that the higher you climb within the terraces of the gardens and approach the boundaries of The One&Only Ocean Club, the greater the chances are that you'll be barred by a security guard.

---

reassembled here stone by stone. Huntington Hartford, the A&P heir, purchased the cloister from the estate of William Randolph Hearst at San Simeon in California. Regrettably, after the newspaper czar originally bought the cloister, it was hastily dismantled in France for shipment to America. However, the parts had not been numbered—they all arrived unlabeled on Paradise Island. The reassembly of the complicated monument baffled most conventional methods of construction until artist and sculptor Jean Castre-Manne set about to reassemble it piece by piece. It took him 2 years, and what you see today presumably bears some similarity to the original. The gardens, which extend over the rise to Nassau Harbour, are filled with tropical flowers and classic statues. Although the monument retains a timeless beauty, recent buildings have encroached on either side, marring Huntington Hartford's original vision.

In the gardens of the One&Only Ocean Club, Ocean Club Dr. ℂ **242/363-2501.** Free admission. Daily 24 hr.

7 Shopping

For serious shopping, you'll want to cross over the Paradise Island Bridge into Nassau (see chapter 3). However, many of Nassau's major stores also have shopping outlets on Paradise Island.

The Shops at the Atlantis, in the Atlantis Paradise Island Resort (ℂ **242/363-3000**), is the largest concentration of shops and boutiques on Paradise Island, rivaling anything else in The Bahamas in terms of size, selection, and style. The boutiques are subdivided into two different sections that include the well-appointed Crystal Court Arcade corridor that meanders between the Royal Tower and the Coral Tower, and that encompasses 3,252 sq. m (35,004 sq. ft.) of prime high-traffic retail space. Newer, and usually with entrances that open directly to the outside air, are boutiques within the resort's waterfront **Marina Village.** An additional handful of emporiums is scattered randomly throughout other sections of the resort, as noted below. It's all about flagrantly conspicuous consumption that's sometimes fueled by the gaming frenzy in the nearby casino. So if you want to do more than browse, bring your platinum card and remain alert that in a high-ticket venue like this, maxing out your credit cards might be easier, and happen sooner, than you might ever have believed.

The resort contains two separate branches of **Colombian Emeralds** (one in the Marina Village, another within the Atlantis Paradise Island's Beach Tower), where the colored gemstones far outnumber the relatively limited selection of diamonds. Individual purveyors on-site include **Lalique,** the France-based purveyor of fine crystal and fashion accessories for men and women; **Cartier; Versace,** the late designer to the stars (this boutique also has a particularly charming housewares division); **Façonnable,** a youthful, sporty designer for young and beautiful club-hoppers; **Bulgari,** purveyor of the most enviable jewels in the world, as well as watches, giftware, and perfumes; and **Gucci** and **Ferragamo,** in case you forgot your dancing shoes. And if you want a bathing suit, **Coles of Nassau** sells swimwear by Gottex, Pucci, and Fernando Sanchez. Finally, **John Bull,** known for its Bay Street store in Nassau and as a pioneer seller of watches throughout The Bahamas, also has an interesting assortment of watches, jewelry, and designer accessories at this outlet.

One of our favorite shops, **Doongalik Studios** (📞 242/394-1886), in the Marina Village compound, doesn't sell the predictably upscale roster of gemstones and fashion that you might have had your fill of by now. At the time of this writing, it's the only art gallery within Marina Village. Owned and operated by the architect and art connoisseur who designed Marina Village itself (Jackson Burnside), it positions itself as a bastion of Bahamian culture within the glittering row of shops otherwise devoted to luxury goods. Come here for insight into who is creating contemporary art in The Bahamas. Oil paintings by locally famous artists (including John Cox, John Paul, Jessica Colebrooke, and Eddie Minnis) range from $800 to $2,000 (£424–£1,060) each; prints—sometimes of works by the same artists—go for between $15 and $100 (£7.95–£53) each. Sculptures can be especially interesting, with some crafted from gnarled driftwood.

8 Paradise Island After Dark

Paradise Island has the best nightlife in The Bahamas, and most of it centers on the Atlantis.

The Atlantis Paradise Island Resort's Casino and Discothèque   There's no other spot in The Bahamas, with the possible exception of the Crystal Palace complex on Cable Beach, with such a wide variety of after-dark attractions, and absolutely nothing that approaches its inspired brand of razzle-dazzle. Even if you stay in Nassau or Cable Beach, you'll want to drop into this artfully decorated self-contained temple to decadence, even if gambling isn't really your passion. Love it or hate it, this place is simply a jaw-dropper.

The casino is the most lavishly planned, most artfully "themed" casino this side of Vegas. The only casino in the world built above a body of water, it was designed in homage to the lost continent of Atlantis, and it appears to have risen directly from the waters of the lagoon. The gaming area is centered on buildings representing a Temple of the Sun and a Temple of the Moon, with a painted replica of the zodiac overhead. Rising from key locations are four of the most elaborate sculptures in the world. Massive and complex, they were crafted by teams of artisans spearheaded by Dale Chihuly, the American-born resident of Venice whose glass-blowing skills are the most celebrated in the world. Other than the decor, the casino's gaming tables, open daily from 10am to 4am, are the main attraction in this enormous place, and about a thousand whirring and clanging slot machines operate 24 hours a day.

Recent additions to this blockbuster casino include a lineup of poker tables and the **Pegasus Race and Sports Book,** with an illuminated and computerized display that lists the odds for many of the world's upcoming sporting events. Thanks to instantaneous communications with a centralized betting facility in Las Vegas, the staff here will make odds on a staggering number of sports events, both professional and college, as well as horseracing and greyhound racing. This facility also contains a mini amphitheater with plush armchairs and views over a battery of TV screens, each displaying one of the sporting and/or racing events for which odds are being calculated and money is changing hands. One side of the casino contains **Aura,** a club that manages to attract a few local hipsters as well as guests of the Atlantis. Come here anytime during casino hours for a drink. A sweaty, flirty crowd parties all night on the dance floor. Often you can catch some of the best live music in The Bahamas, as bands take to the stage that's cantilevered above the dance floor. The club gets going around 9pm nightly, with a cover charge of $30 (£16) required from all nonguests of the Atlantis. (Note that the entrance charge is usually waived for women.) Ringing the casino are at least 3,252 sq. m (35,004 sq. ft.) of retail shopping space, with even more located nearby in the Marina Village (see "Shopping," above) and an impressive cluster of hideaway bars and restaurants.

Also in the same Atlantis complex, **Joker's Wild** (✆ 242/363-3000) is the only real comedy club in The Bahamas, with a talented company of funny people who work hard to make you laugh. Show times are Tuesday through Sunday at 9:30pm. At least two comedians will appear on any given night, most of them hailing from The Bahamas, with occasional appearances of performers from London and New York. Midway between the Beach Tower and the Coral Tower, Casino Dr. ✆ 242/363-3000. No cover charge for casino, but a cover charge of $20–$25 (£11–£13) applies for entrance to individual clubs and discos, depending on the night of the week, the season, and occupancy levels at the resort. Cover charges apply to both guests and nonguests.

THE BAR SCENE

Bimini Road   The joint is always jumping at the Marina Village at the Atlantis. This bar and restaurant are imbued with a junkanoo theme with wall-sized murals. At many bars at this sprawling resort, the bartenders seem to ignore you. Not here. They are a lively bunch, slinging drinks with names like the Fountain of Youth. A specialty is a sour-apple-flavored mixture known as Gussie Mae. The place is especially popular with yachties, who tie up at the nearby marina. A costumed dance troupe performs 4 nights a week (times vary), and live bands pump out island music for most of the night. Even patrons get in on the act with conga lines. The restaurant serves food daily from 11am to 10pm, including conch fritters and cracked lobster tail. The bar itself is open from 11am to 1:30pm daily. Marina Village, Atlantis Resort, Casino Dr. ✆ 242/363-3000.

Dune Bar   This luxe dining room is also the setting for the island's most elegant and sophisticated lounge; it's becoming increasingly popular as a plush and appealing meeting spot for singles. The action centers around a translucent white marble bar skillfully illuminated from behind, and its outdoor terrace can be undeniably romantic. At the One&Only Ocean Club, Ocean Club Dr. ✆ 242/363-2501. Call for open hours, which can vary.

Plato's Lounge   This is the most popular bar at the Atlantis Paradise Island, a sensual spot where you can escape the din of the slot machines and relax within an upscale environment that's flanked with replicas of Greek-language texts that might have been hand-lettered in ancient times by Plato himself. (Presumably, the framed ancient Greek papyrus texts on the wall are copies of what Plato wrote about Atlantis.) Sofas are deep and plushly comfortable, a pianist sets the mood during cocktail hour and early evening, and you'll invariably get the sense here that you're right in the heart of everything. In the morning, the site doubles as a cafe, serving pastries and snacks from 6am until 4pm. It's open around the clock daily. On the lobby level of the Royal Towers, Atlantis Resort, Casino Dr. ✆ 242/363-3000.

5

Grand Bahama (Freeport/Lucaya)

Fabulous beaches and relatively affordable prices continue to make Grand Bahama Island a year-round destination. Weather also enhances its continued popularity. Even though the island sits in the Atlantic Ocean, the forever-warm waters of the Gulf Stream make the beaches, particularly at the western tip, desirable even in winter. The Little Bahama Bank protects the island from the storms that roar in from the northeast. Grand Bahama Island is also convenient to reach, lying only 81km (50 miles) east of Palm Beach, Florida.

Despite some cutting-edge architectural development in the late 1990s near Lucaya Beach, the island may never return to its high-roller days with the gloss and glitz of the '60s. In that era, everybody from Howard Hughes to Frank Sinatra and the Rat Packers showed up to feud, play, act out, maneuver, manipulate, and overindulge. However, recent improvements in Port Lucaya and massive redevelopment on the island's West End have brought a smile back to its face, which had grown wrinkled and tired over the latter part of the 20th century. But downtown Freeport is "blighted" by the closure, and continuing decay, of a megaresort that once flourished as its centerpiece, the Crowne Plaza. That scar has, regrettably, extended into the island's once-largest and once-fabled shopping mall, the International Bazaar. Due to the lack of business and "the morgue" (that is, the sprawling, storm-damaged corpse of the nearby Crowne Plaza Resort), the shopping area remains in a lackluster state of decay and decline.

The second-most-popular tourist destination in The Bahamas (Nassau/Cable Beach/Paradise Island ranks first), Grand Bahama lies just 81km (50 miles) and less than 30 minutes by air off the Florida coast. The island is the northernmost and fourth-largest landmass in The Bahamas (118km/73 miles long and 6.5–13km/4–8 miles wide).

Freeport/Lucaya was once just a dream. Wallace Groves, a Virginia-born financier, saw the prospect of developing the island into a miniature Miami Beach. Almost overnight in the 1950s, the low-lying pine forest turned into one of the world's major resorts. Today, although the island's center of gravity has firmly shifted from Freeport to Lucaya, Groves's dream has at least been partially realized.

The Lucaya district was developed 8 years after Freeport, as a resort center along the coast. It has evolved into a blend of residential and tourist facilities. As the two communities grew, their identities became almost indistinguishable. But elements of their original purposes still exist today. Freeport is the downtown area and attracts visitors with its commerce, industry, and own resorts. Meanwhile, Lucaya is called the "Garden City" and pleases residents and vacationers alike with its fine beaches.

Grand Bahama is more than an Atlantic City clone, however. If you don't care for gambling in the island's only casinos or if shopping and fun-in-the-sun is not your scene, try one of the alternatives. Because the island is so big, most of it remains relatively unspoiled. You can commune with nature at plenty of quiet places, including the Rand Nature Centre. Lucayan National Park—with its underwater caves, forest trails, and secluded beach—is another major attraction. Just kilometers from Freeport/Lucaya are serene places where you can wander in a world of casuarina, palmetto, and pine trees. During the day, you can enjoy long stretches of beach, broken by inlets and fishing villages.

The reviews of Grand Bahama Island are definitely mixed. Some discerning travelers who could live anywhere have built homes here; others vow never to set foot on the island again, finding it, with the exception of Port Lucaya, "tacky" or "uninspired." Judge for yourself.

1 Orientation

For a general discussion on traveling to The Bahamas, refer to chapter 2.

ARRIVING

A number of airlines fly to Grand Bahama International Airport from the continental United States, including **American Airlines** (© **800/433-7300;** www.aa.com) and **Bahamasair** (© **242/377-3218;** www.bahamasair.com), both with daily flights from Miami. **Gulfstream Continental Connection** (© **800/231-0856;** www.gulfstream air.com) flies to Freeport from Miami and West Palm Beach once daily, and from Fort Lauderdale five times daily. **US Airways** (© **800/428-4322;** www.usairways.com) flies once daily from Charlotte, North Carolina.

Other competing airlines include **AirTran** (© **800/247-8726;** www.airtran.com), flying nonstop from Atlanta (daily) as well as Baltimore (Thurs–Mon). **Delta Connection** (© **800/221-1212**) flies daily from Atlanta.

Many visitors arrive in Nassau and then hop on one of the five daily Bahamasair flights to Freeport. These 30-minute hops run $135 to $200 (£72–£106) round-trip.

No buses run from the airport to the major hotel zones. But many hotels will provide airport transfers, especially if you've bought a package deal. If yours does not, no problem; taxis meet arriving flights and will take you from the airport to one of the hotels in Freeport or Lucaya for about $12 to $22 (£6.35–£12). The ride shouldn't take more than about 10 minutes.

Discovery Cruise Lines (© **800/937-4477** or 242/351-1339; www.discovery cruiseline.com) offers daily passage between the Fort Lauderdale Seaport and Grand Bahama Island. Frankly, the Discovery vessels making this 89km (55-mile) jaunt haven't been the newest or glitziest cruise ships sailing in the past 3 or 4 decades, but they are shipshape and fit the bill. The trip over from Florida takes about 5 hours, and they have the required pool deck and bar, along with a casino, bar show lounge, and dining facilities. They do feed passengers very well. A round-trip fare runs $180 to $200 (£95–£106) per person, and you can make reservations online.

VISITOR INFORMATION

Assistance and information are available at the **Grand Bahama Tourism Board,** International Bazaar in Freeport (© **242/352-6909;** www.grand-bahama.com). Two other information booths are located at the **Freeport International Airport** (© **242/352-2052**) and at the Port Lucaya Marketplace (© **242/373-8988**). Hours for all three branches are 9am to 5pm Monday to Saturday, and the branches at the airport and at the Port Lucaya Marketplace are also open on Sunday 9am to 5pm.

Grand Bahama Island

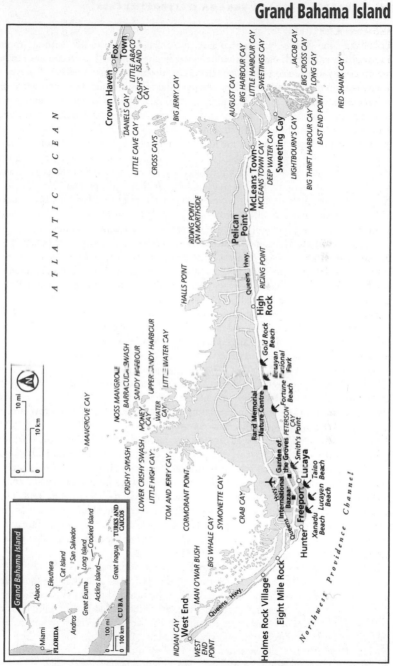

ISLAND LAYOUT

Other than the perhaps unexpected novelty of driving on the left, getting around Freeport/Lucaya is fairly easy because of its flat terrain. Although Freeport and Lucaya are frequently mentioned in the same breath, newcomers should note that Freeport is a landlocked collection of hotels and shops rising from the island's center, while the better-maintained and more appealing Lucaya, about 4km (2½ miles) away, is a bustling waterfront section of hotels, shops, and restaurants clustered next to a saltwater pond on the island's southern shoreline.

Freeport lies midway between the northern and southern shores of Grand Bahama Island. Bisected by some of the island's largest roads, it was originally conceived as the site of the biggest hotels and what until a few years ago was one of the most-visited attractions in the country, the International Bazaar shopping complex. Now in a dismaying state of disrepair, it's a theme-oriented retail mall that has seen better days, now a depressing remnant of its former glory. Immediately adjacent is the local straw market, where you can buy inexpensive souvenirs and Bahamian handicrafts.

To reach **Port Lucaya** from Freeport, head east from the International Bazaar along East Sunrise Highway, then turn south at the intersection with Seahorse Road. The intersection—actually an oversize roundabout—is marked with a prominent stone marker saying PORT LUCAYA. From that roundabout, less than a mile later, you'll find yourself within the heart of the Lucaya complex. Know in advance that the shops and restaurants on the marina side of Seahorse Road are identified as being within the "Port Lucaya" subdivision of the Lucaya Complex. Conversely, the Westin and the Sheraton hotels, their restaurants and shops, and the Isle of Capri Casino, all of which are clustered on the landward side of Seahorse Road, are identified as the "Our Lucaya" subdivision of the Lucaya complex.

The architectural centerpiece of Port Lucaya is **Count Basie Square,** named for the great entertainer who used to have a home on the island. A short walk east or west of the square, most of the hotels in the Lucaya Complex rise above the narrow strip of sand that separates the sea from a saltwater pond.

Life on Grand Bahama Island doesn't get more glamorous after you leave the Lucaya Complex. To the west of Freeport and Lucaya, the West Sunrise Highway passes grim and impersonal-looking industrial complexes that include The Bahamas Oil Refining Company. Once you pass the built-up waterfront sprawl of Freeport's western end, you can take Queen's Highway northwest all the way to **West End,** a distance of some 45km (28 miles) from the center of Freeport. Along the way you pass the unpicturesque wharves of Freeport Harbour, where cruise ships dock. Just to the east lies Hawksbill Creek, a not-particularly-interesting-looking village that houses some of the workers at the nearby port facilities.

Much less explored is the isolated **East End** of Grand Bahama. Its most distant tip lies about 72km (45 miles) from the center of Freeport and is reached via the Grand Bahama Highway. Despite its name, the route is bumpy and potholed in some spaces and—along extensive stretches of its central area—either is blocked by piles of sand, rock, and fallen trees or is not-as-yet-completed. For access to the most distant reaches of the East End from Freeport or Lucaya, allow about 2 hours of driving time. First you pass the **Rand Nature Centre,** about 5km (3 miles) east of Freeport. About 11km (6¾ miles) on is **Lucaya National Park,** and 8km (5 miles) farther lies the hamlet of **Free Town;** east of Free Town is **High Rock,** known for its Emmanuel Baptist Church. From here, the road becomes considerably rougher until it ends in **MacLean's Town,** which celebrates Columbus Day with an annual conch-cracking contest. From here, it's possible to take a water taxi across Runners Creek to the exclusive Deep Water Cay club, catering to serious anglers.

In Freeport/Lucaya, but especially on the rest of Grand Bahama Island, you will almost never find a street number on a hotel or a store. Sometimes in the more remote places, including underpopulated areas on the outskirts of Lucaya itself, you won't even find signs identifying the names of the streets. In lieu of numbers, locate places by their relation to nearby hotels, beaches, or landmarks.

2 Getting Around

BY TAXI

The government sets the taxi rates, and the cabs are metered (or should be). Metered rates are $3 (£1.60) for the first .3km (quarter-mile) and 40¢ each additional 1.6km (1 mile). Additional passengers over the age of 2 are $3 each. If there's no meter, agree on the price with the driver in advance. You can call for a taxi, although most taxis wait at the major hotels or the cruise-ship dock to pick up passengers. One major taxi company is **Freeport Taxi Company,** Logwood Road (© 242/352-6666), open 24 hours. Another is **Grand Bahama Taxi Union,** at the Freeport International Airport, Old Airport Road (© 242/352-7101), also open 24 hours. *Note:* Typical taxi rates are as follows. From the Cruise Ship Harbour to: Xanadu Beach Hotel, $17 (£9); Port Lucaya Marketplace, $24 (£13); Flamingo Beach Resort/The Ritz, $24 (£13); Viva Fortuna Beach, $29 (£15). From the airport to: anywhere in Port Lucaya or Our Lucaya, $19 (£10); Viva Fortuna, $20 (£11); Royal Oasis, $11 (£5.85); Xanadu $14 (£7.40).

BY BUS

Public bus service runs from the International Bazaar and downtown Freeport to the Lucaya area. The typical fare is $1 (55p) for adults, 50¢ (25p) for children. Check with the tourist office (see "Visitor Information," above) for bus schedules. There is no number to call for information.

BY CAR

If you plan to confine your exploration to the center of Freeport with its International Bazaar and Lucaya with its beaches, you can rely on public transportation. However, if you'd like to branch out and explore the rest of the island (perhaps finding a more secluded beach), a rental car is the way to go. Terrain throughout Grand Bahama Island is universally flat, a fact that's appreciated by drivers trying to conserve gasoline. Try **Avis** (© 800/331-1212 or 242/332-4062; www.avis.com) or **Hertz** (© 800/654-3131 or 242/352-9250; www.hertz.com). Both of these companies maintain offices in small bungalows near the Freeport International Airport. From inside the terminal, an employee of either company will contact a colleague, who will direct you to the curb outside the luggage pickup point. There someone from the rental car company will arrive in a car or van to drive you to their pickup location.

One of the best companies is **Dollar Rent-a-Car,** Old Airport Road (© 242/352-9325; www.dollar.com), which rents everything from a new-style Kia Sportage to a VW Jetta. Rates range from $60 (£32) per day manual or from $49 (£26) for an automatic, with unlimited mileage, plus another $12 (£6.35) per day for a CDW (Collision Damage Waiver; $500/£265 deductible). Gas costs around $6.50 (£3.45) per gallon. Remember to drive on the left as British rules apply.

BY SCOOTER

A scooter is a fun way to get around, as most of Grand Bahamas is flat with well-paved roads. Scooters can be rented at most hotels or, for cruise-ship passengers, in the Freeport Harbour area. Helmets are required and provided by the outfitter. You can find dozens of stands along the road in Freeport and Lucaya, and also in the major parking lots, charging rates ranging from $40 to $55 (£21–£29) per day.

ON FOOT

You can explore the center of Freeport or Lucaya on foot, but if you want to venture into the East End or West End, you'll need to rent a car, hire a taxi, or try Grand Bahama's erratic public transportation.

FAST FACTS: Grand Bahama

Banks In Freeport/Lucaya, banks are open from 9:30am to 3pm Monday to Thursday, and 9:30am to 4:30pm on Friday. Most banks here have ATMs that accept Visa, MasterCard, American Express, and any other bank or credit card on the Cirrus, Honor, Novus, and PLUS networks.

Climate See "When to Go," in chapter 2.

Currency Exchange Americans need not bother to exchange their dollars into Bahamian dollars because the currencies are on par. However, Canadians and Brits will need to convert their money, which can be done at local banks or sometimes at a hotel, though hotels tend to offer less favorable rates.

Doctors For the fastest and best service, head to Rand Memorial Hospital (see "Hospitals," below).

Drugstores For prescriptions and other pharmaceutical needs, go to Mini Mall, 1 West Mall, Explorer's Way, where you'll find **L.M.R. Drugs** (✆ 242/352-7327), next door to Burger King. Hours are Monday to Saturday 8am to 8pm and Sunday 8am to 3pm.

Embassies & Consulates See "Fast Facts: The Bahamas," in chapter 2.

Emergencies For all emergencies, call ✆ 911, or dial 0 for the operator.

Eyeglass Repair The biggest specialist in eyeglasses and contact lenses is the **Optique Shoppe,** 7 Regent Centre, downtown Freeport (✆ 242/352-9073).

Hospitals If you have a medical emergency, contact the government-operated, 90-bed **Rand Memorial Hospital,** East Atlantic Drive (✆ **242/352-6735** or 242/352-2689 for ambulance emergency).

Internet Access Visit the **Cybercafe at the Port Lucaya Marketplace** (✆ 242/559-0111), open Monday to Saturday 9am to 8pm.

Information See "Visitor Information," earlier in this chapter.

Laundry & Dry Cleaning Try **Jiffy Cleaners Number 3,** West Mall at Pioneer's Way (✆ 242/352-7079), open Monday 8am to 1pm, Tuesday to Saturday 8am to 6pm.

Newspapers & Magazines The *Freeport News* is a morning newspaper published Monday through Saturday except holidays. The two dailies published in Nassau, the *Tribune* and the *Nassau Guardian,* are also available here, as are some New York and Miami papers, especially the *Miami Herald*, usually on the date of publication. American news magazines, such as *Time* and *Newsweek*, are flown in on the day of publication.

Police In an emergency, dial ☎ **911**.

Post Office The main post office is on Explorer's Way in Freeport (☎ **242/ 352-9371**).

Safety Avoid walking or jogging along lonely roads. There are no particular danger zones, but stay alert: Grand Bahama is no stranger to drugs and crime.

Taxes All visitors leaving The Bahamas from Freeport must pay a departure tax, but because it's factored into the cost of your airline or cruise ship ticket, very few visitors even realize that it's even being charged. Hotel bills are saddled with a 12% tax regardless of the category of room you occupy. But other than that, as an encouragement to shoppers, no other sales taxes are charged.

Taxis See "Getting Around," earlier in this chapter.

Weather Grand Bahama, in the north of The Bahamas, has temperatures in winter that vary from about 60°F to 75°F (16°C–24°C) daily. Summer variations range from 78°F to the high 80s (26°C to the low 30s Celsius). In Freeport/ Lucaya, phone ☎ **915** for weather information.

3 Where to Stay

Your choices are the Freeport area (near the Bahamia Casino and the International Bazaar) or Lucaya (closer to the beach).

Remember: In most cases, a resort levy of 8% and a 15% service charge will be added to your final bill. Be prepared, and ask if it's already included in the initial price you're quoted.

FREEPORT
EXPENSIVE

Island Seas Resort A three-story timeshare property that's open to nonmembers and painted a tone of peach, this resort opens onto a secluded beach positioned midway between downtown Freeport and Port Lucaya. The resort also offers its own water fun with its pool, hot tub, and waterfall. Also on-site is a tiki-hut restaurant and bar. The location is convenient for the Port Lucaya Market and the Lucaya Golf and Country Club. Depending on their individual owners, each condo is furnished with a decor that's different from that of its immediate neighbor. Floor plans include both one- and two-bedroom suites. Each contains a full bathroom with tub/shower, plus a full kitchen and balcony. Although technically they're not associated with the hotel in any way, many watersports outfitters are located right on the beach.

William's Town (P.O. Box F-44735), Freeport, Grand Bahamas, The Bahamas. ☎ **242/373-1271.** Fax 242/373-1275. www.islandseas.com. 197 units Year-round $109–$129 (£58–£68) double; $129–$149 (£68–£79) 2-bedroom suite. AE, DISC, MC, V. **Amenities:** Restaurant; bar; pool; tennis court; gym/exercise facilities; bike rentals; on-site car-rental kiosk; massage. *In room:* A/C, TV, fully equipped kitchen, iron, safe.

INEXPENSIVE
Best Western Castaways Resort & Suites *(Kids)* Castaways is a modest and unassuming hotel that's almost immediately adjacent to the International Bazaar in downtown

Where to Stay & Dine in Freeport/Lucaya

ACCOMMODATIONS ■

Bell Channel Inn **15**
Best Western Castaways
  Resort & Suites **4**
Flamingo Bay Yacht Club
  & Marina Hotel **21**
Island Palm Resort **2**
Island Seas Resort **9**
Old Bahama Bay **3**
Pelican Bay at Lucaya **17**
Port Lucaya Resort & Yacht Club **13**

Ritz Beach Resort **20**
Royal Islander **4**
Royal Palm Hotel & Resort **1**
Viva Wyndham Fortuna Beach **23**
Westin Grand Bahama Island
  at Our Lucaya Resort & Sheraton
  Grand Bahama Island at Our
  Lucaya Resort **16**
Xanadu Beach Resort & Marina **8**

← Freeport Int'l
Airport
Grand Bahamian Hwy.

Settlers Way

REGENCY
PARK

FREEPORT

Explorers Way

Santa Maria Ave.

Pioneers Way

Cadwallader Dr.

Nansen Ave.

Ellis Lightfoot Ave.

Frobisher Drive

Pioneers Way East

Bahamia Princess
Ruby Golf Course

West Atlantic Drive

West Mall Drive

East Mall Drive

Adventurers Way

SUNRISE
PARK

Coral Rd.

West Sunrise Hwy.

Princess
Casino

International
Bazaar

Poinciana St.

Ranfurly
Circus

Tamarind St.

Gambier St.

Santa Maria Ave.

Bahamia Princess
Emerald Golf Course

Hydroflora
Gardens

East Sunrise Hwy.

Pinetree
Stables

Pinta Ave.

The Mall South

Drumfish St.

Glover St.

E. Beach St.

CARAVEL
BEACH

Beachway Dr.

Tahiti St.

ROYAL
BAHAMIAN
ESTATES

Pinta Ave.

Lunar Blvd.

BAHAMAS
TERRACE

Bahama Reef

Xanadu
Beach

JOHN
JACK PT.

Port-of-Call St.

WILLIAMS
TOWN

Silver Pt. Dr.

Northwest Providence Channel

MADIOCA PT.

East Palm
Beach

SILVER PT.

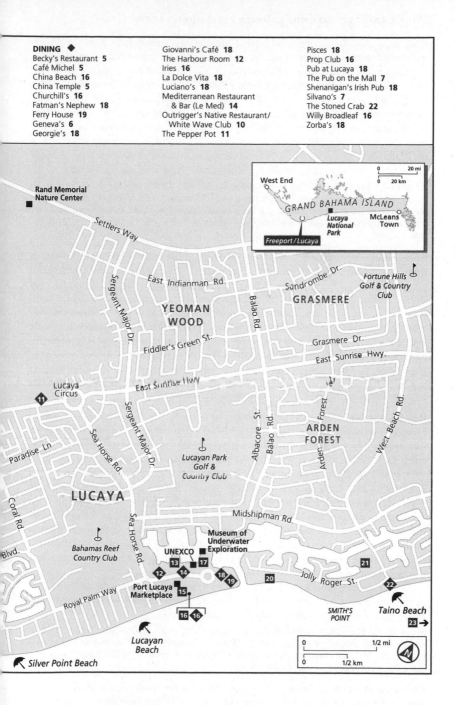

Rand Memorial
Nature Center

West End

GRAND BAHAMA ISLAND

Lucaya
National
Park

McLeans
Town

Freeport/Lucaya

0   20 mi
0   20 km

Settlers Way

East Indianman Rd.

Sandrombe Dr.

Fortune Hills
Golf & Country
Club

YEOMAN
WOOD

GRASMERE

Balao Rd.

Fiddler's Green St.

Sergeant Major Dr.

Grasmere Dr.

East Sunrise Hwy.

Lucaya
Circus

East Sunrise Hwy

Albacore St.

Balao Rd.

Arden Forest

ARDEN
FOREST

West Beach Rd.

Paradise Ln.

Sea Horse Rd.

Sergeant Major Dr.

Lucayan Park
Golf &
Country Club

LUCAYA

Coral Rd.

Midshipman Rd.

Blvd.

Bahamas Reef
Country Club

Museum of
Underwater
Exploration

UNEXCO

Sea Horse Rd.

13 **17**

12 **14** **18** **19**

Port Lucaya
Marketplace **15**

20

Jolly Roger St.

21

22

Royal Palm Way

16 **16**

SMITH'S
POINT

Taino Beach

23 →

Lucayan
Beach

Silver Point Beach

0   1/2 mi
0   1/2 km

Freeport. A mix of vacationers and business travelers stay here because of its clean, well-maintained motel-style rooms and its moderate prices. Pink-walled, green-shuttered rooms surround a quartet of landscaped courtyards, creating shelter from the traffic outside. It's not on the water, but a free shuttle will take you to nearby Williams Town Beach. Surrounded by gardens, the four-story hotel has an indoor/outdoor garden lobby with a gift shop and on-site kiosks selling island tours and watersports venues. Cheerful bedrooms are outfitted in your basic motel/tropical resort style. The Flamingo Restaurant features Bahamian and American dishes daily from 7:30am to 10pm; it also serves one of the island's best breakfasts. There's a swimming pool area with a wide terrace and a pool bar serving sandwiches and cool drinks. A children's playground adjoins the pool.

E. Mall Dr. (P.O. Box F-42629), Freeport, Grand Bahama, The Bahamas. ✆ **800/780-7234** or 242/352-6682. Fax 242/352-5087. www.bestwestern.com. 118 units. Winter $155 (£82) double, $180 (£95) suite; off season $130 (£69) double, $165 (£87) suite. Children under 12 stay free in parent's room. AE, MC, V. **Amenities:** Restaurant; 2 bars; pool; babysitting; self-service laundry; nonsmoking rooms; rooms for those w/limited mobility. *In room:* A/C, TV, hair dryer, iron, safe.

Island Palm Resort *(Value* Set within the commercial heart of Freeport, this simple three-story motel consists of four buildings separated by parking lots and greenery. An easy walk to virtually everything in town and 2km (1¼ miles) from the International Bazaar, it offers good value in no-frills, eminently serviceable rooms with well-kept bathrooms equipped with tubs/showers. Complimentary shuttle-bus service ferries anybody who's interested to nearby Williams Town Beach (also called Island Seas Beach), where you can use the seaside facilities (including jet skis and snorkeling equipment) of its sibling resort, a timeshare unit known as Island Seas.

E. Mall Dr. (P.O. Box F-44881), Freeport, Grand Bahama, The Bahamas. ✆ **242/352-6648.** Fax 242/352-6640. 143 units. Winter $89 (£47) double; off season $79 (£42) double. Extra person $15 (£7.95). AE, DISC, MC, V. **Amenities:** Bar; pool; nonsmoking rooms; rooms for those w/limited mobility. *In room:* A/C, TV.

Royal Islander This hotel was built during an unfortunate Disney-style period in Freeport's expansion during the early 1980s. Its improbable-looking pyramidal roofs inspired by a trio of Mayan pyramids were rendered somewhat less obvious in 2004 when they were resheathed with dark gray metal. Inside it's tasteful and hospitable, with rooms arranged around a verdant courtyard that seems far removed from the busy traffic and sterile-looking landscape outside. Rooms on the street level have white-tile floors, while those upstairs have wall-to-wall carpeting. Bathrooms are a bit on the small side, with sinks and tub/showers. Throughout, the motif is Florida/tropical, with some pizzazz and rates that tend to be cheaper than at the Best Western across the street. There's a family link between the owners of this place and the owners of the more opulent and famous Xanadu (see separate recommendation). A bus shuttles about every hour between this hotel and Xanadu beach.

There's a coffee-shop-style snack bar and a small restaurant on the premises, but other than that, you'll have to wander a short distance, perhaps to the International Bazaar just across the street, to find diversions and dining.

E. Mall Dr. (P.O. Box F-42549), Freeport, Grand Bahama, The Bahamas. ✆ **242/351-6000.** Fax 242/351-3546. www.bahamasvacationguide.com/royalislander.html. 100 units. Year-round $90 (£48). Children under 14 stay free in parent's room. AE, MC, V. **Amenities:** Restaurant; snack bar; bar; pool; Jacuzzi; self-service laundry; nonsmoking rooms; children's playground. *In room:* A/C, TV, safe.

Royal Palm Hotel & Resort Don't confuse this hotel with some of its competitors, whose names and amenities are roughly equivalent. The staff here commented to us about how often a taxi will arrive with passengers whose reservations are at other

hotels with similar names that included the Royal Islander, the Island Palm, and the relatively more expensive Island Seas. This particular choice is a well-maintained, cost-effective motel that's the closest property to the airport on Grand Bahama Island. It's set behind a hot-pink two-story facade. Though inland from the beach, it provides an oasis of resort-style living, with its wings wrapping around a swimming pool. A radical renovation was completed during the winter of 2005. Without any extra charge, rooms are suitable for up to four occupants each. Each is outfitted like you'd expect at a motel-style tropical resort—with tile floors, simple but tasteful furniture, and flower-patterned upholsteries. Although it's usually a bit more expensive than either the Royal Islander or the Island Palm, its repeat clientele—about 50% of whom are on-island for business reasons—don't seem to mind.

East Mall at Settlers' Way (P.O. Box F-44900), Freeport, The Bahamas. (C) 242/352-3462. Fax 242/352-5759. www.royalpalmsuites.com. 48 units. $129–$149 (£68–£79) double. AE, DC, MC, V. **Amenities:** Restaurant; Internet cafe; poolside bar (Conch Juice Corner); tennis court; gift shop; shuttles approximately every hour to Xanadu Beach; children's playground. *In room:* A/C, TV, kitchenette, fridge, coffeemaker, hair dryer, microwave.

LUCAYA
EXPENSIVE
Westin Grand Bahama Island at Our Lucaya Resort & Sheraton Grand Bahama Island at Our Lucaya Resort 𝒦𝒦 *Kids*   This massive $400-million resort is one of the largest in The Bahamas—and by far, it's the finest, most appealing, and best-accessorized property on Grand Bahama Island. The resort is set beside one of the best white strands in The Bahamas—Lucaya Beach. Although the area had been losing tourist business to Paradise Island, it got a big boost in 1999 when this sprawling metropolis opened its doors.

Guests of any of the subdivisions of this resort usually get more than they bargained for. The first of the three sections was completed late in 1998 as the **Sheraton Grand Bahama Island at Our Lucaya Resort.** With a vague South Beach Art Deco design, it's laid out like a massive open-sided, stone-trimmed hexagon. About half of the rooms face the beach and the swimming pool, the other half look toward the gardens. The 513-room resort is contemporary but relaxed; the developers have created a young vibe that draws a high number of families. Bedrooms are whimsical and fun, thanks to fabric designs you'd expect on a loud Hawaiian shirt from the Elvis era and maple-veneered furniture, all put together with artful simplicity.

In 2000, two newer, more upscale, and more cutting-edge subdivisions of Our Lucaya opened immediately next door. The smaller and somewhat more private of the two is **Westin Lighthouse Pointe,** a 322-unit low-rise condo and timeshare complex that focuses on an adult clientele. Its larger counterpart—and, frankly, the one we find the most appealing and intriguing—is the 536-unit **Westin Breakers Cay.** This grand 10-story, white-sided tower has edges that bend in a postmodern S-curve beside the beach. Each of this complex's three subsections stretches like pearls in a necklace along a narrow strip of beachfront, allowing guests to drop into any of the bars, restaurants, and gardens that flank its edges. Also on-site, in a two-story compound flanking the sea, The Lanai is composed of just 23 sprawling two-bedroom suites. Each is richly furnished, melding Colonial Caribbean style with 21st-century decor.

A complex this big contains an impressive array of restaurants, each designed with a different theme and ambience. The most interesting of the resort's dining venues will be reviewed under "Where to Dine," later in this chapter. And consistent with the broad themes, each of the subdivisions has a dramatic and/or unconventional swimming pool.

For example, the Sheraton at Our Lucaya's pool seems to flow around a replica of a 19th-century sugar mill, complete with an aqueduct that might be worthy of the ancient Romans. And the Westin at Our Lucaya is separated from the powder-white sands of Lucaya Beach by a trio of lap pools, each 15m (49 ft.) long and 1.2m (4 ft.) deep, with edges that replicate the sinuous S-shape of the hotel's footprint. Lap swimmers especially appreciate these spans of water, each of which has a subtly different temperature. The pools culminate in a watery crescent whose "invisible edge" seems to merge directly into the waters of the Atlantic. In particular, the swim-up bar and hot tubs seem perfect for wedding celebrations after the ceremony.

A spa and fitness center, a quartet of tennis courts, a convention center, a state-of-the-art casino (The Isle of Capri—at press time, the only functioning casino on Grand Bahama Island), and an upscale shopping mall have all also been added in recent years. There's also an increasing emphasis on golf, thanks to the opening of the spectacular Reef Course (p. 171). An innovative feature for tennis players is the Fast Grand Slam of Tennis, which features replicas of the world's best-known court surfaces—red clay at the French Open, manicured grass at Wimbledon, Rebound Ace at the Australian Open, and DecoTurf at the U.S. Open.

Children aged 2 to 12 can be amused and entertained throughout daylight hours every day at The Bahamas' best-run children's venue, Camp Lucaya.

Royal Palm Way (P.O. Box F-42500), Lucaya, Grand Bahama, The Bahamas. ✆ 877/OUR-LUCAYA in the U.S., or 242/373-1333. Sheraton fax 242/373-8804; Westin fax 242/350-5060. www.ourlucaya.com. 1,260 units. Sheraton year-round $149–$220 (£79–£117) double; from $480 (£254) suite; $30 (£16) extra per day for 3rd and 4th occupants. Westin Lighthouse Pointe or Breakers Cay year-round $210–$279 (£111–£148) double; from $730 (£387) suite; $30 (£16) extra per day for 3rd and 4th occupants. 2-bedroom Lanai suites $1,600–$3,000 (£848–£1,590) per night year-round for up to 6 occupants. AE, DC, DISC, MC, V. **Amenities:** 10 restaurants; 10 bars; 5 pools; 2 18-hole golf courses; 4 tennis courts; health club; spa; watersports equipment/rentals; kids' camp and children's programs; business center; salon; room service; babysitting; laundry service; dry cleaning; nonsmoking rooms; rooms for those w/limited mobility. *In room:* A/C, TV, kitchenette (in suites), minibar, iron, safe.

MODERATE

Pelican Bay at Lucaya 🐚🐚   Here's a good choice for travelers with champagne tastes and beer budgets, a hotel with more architectural charm than any other small property on Grand Bahama. It's built on a peninsula jutting into a labyrinth of inland waterways, with moored yachts on several sides. Pelican Bay evokes a Danish or Dutch seaside village with rows of "town houses," each painted a different color and sporting whimsical trim, and each overlooking the harbor. The hotel opened in the fall of 1996 and later expanded with another wing in 1999, and refurbished in 2005 into the kind of venue you might expect from an upscale decorating magazine. Its location couldn't be better, immediately adjacent to Port Lucaya Marketplace, where restaurants and entertainment spots abound. Lucaya Beach, one of the best stretches of white sand on the island, lies within a 5-minute walk. Taíno Beach, with equally good sands, lies immediately to the east of the hotel, on the opposite side of a saltwater channel with hourly ferryboat service. UNEXSO, which provides some of the best dive facilities in The Bahamas, is next door. If that's not enough, the extensive amenities of Our Lucaya (see previous listing) are available for use.

Accommodations—especially the suites—are about as stylish and high-fashion as you'll find on Grand Bahama Island, rivaled only by the Westin/Sheraton compound at Our Lucaya, located a very short walk away. Each has either a veranda or a balcony, usually with water views, and floors of buffed, tinted concrete with a scattering of rustic art objects and handicrafts from all over the world. The hotel has one main restaurant, the

Ferry House, which specializes in imaginative international cuisine and serves lunch Monday to Saturday and dinner daily. The Yellow Tail Pool Bar offers drinks, salads, and sandwiches throughout the day.

Seahorse Rd. (P.O. Box F-42654), Lucaya, Grand Bahama, The Bahamas. ℂ 800/600-9192 in the U.S., or 242/373-9550. Fax 242/373-9551. www.pelicanbayhotel.com. 183 units. Winter $259–$319 (£137–£169) double, $379 (£201) suite; off season $159–$229 (£84–£121) double, $319 (£169) suite. Rates include breakfast. AE, MC, V. Amenities: Restaurant; bar; 3 pools; Jacuzzi; business center; babysitting; nonsmoking rooms. In room: A/C, TV, minibar (in suites), minifridge, coffeemaker, hair dryer, iron, safe.

Port Lucaya Resort & Yacht Club ☆   Comfortable, cost-conscious, unpretentious, and convenient, this resort opened in 1993 in the heart of the Port Lucaya restaurant, hotel, and nightlife complex. Many guests are drawn to the nautical atmosphere of the resort and its proximity to Port Lucaya Marketplace. It was designed as a compound of pastel-colored two-story structures that guests reach either on foot or (if they're transporting luggage) via golf cart after checking in. They're scattered in rows that wind around a horseshoe-shaped courtyard, very close to a marina and within a very short walk from the restaurants, bars, shops, and nightlife options of the marketplace at Port Lucaya. The wings of guest rooms separate the piers—home for some very expensive marine hardware—from a verdant central green space with a gazebo-style bar and a swimming pool. Although set inland on a waterway (Lucayan Harbour), this resort lies within a few minutes' walk of Lucaya Beach, one of the island's finest, and is also close to Taíno Beach. Even though it's not right on the beach, it's such an easy walk that no one seems to complain.

The medium-size rooms have tile floors and are attractively and comfortably furnished with rattan pieces and big wall mirrors. The rooms are divided into various categories, ranging from standard to deluxe, and open onto the marina (preferred by yachting guests), the Olympic-size swimming pool, or the well-landscaped garden. (If you don't want to hear the sounds coming from the lively marketplace, request units 1–6, which are more tranquil and distanced from the noise.) Bathrooms are tidy but not overly large, with tub/showers and a layout like what you might get at a middle-bracket motel in south Florida.

Bell Channel Bay Rd. (P.O. Box F-42452), Lucaya, Grand Bahama, The Bahamas. ℂ 800/LUCAYA-1 or 242/373-6618. Fax 242/373 6652. www.portlucayaresort.com. 160 units. Winter $112–$162 (£59–£86) double, $196–$280 (£104–£148) suite; off season $90–$134 (£48–£71) double, $214–$224 (£113–£119) suite. Extra person $28 (£15) per day. Children 12 and under stay free in parent's room. AE, DISC, MC, V. Amenities: 2 bars; pool; Jacuzzi; babysitting; nonsmoking rooms. In room: A/C, TV, hair dryer, iron, fridge available for $10 (£5.30) extra per day.

INEXPENSIVE

Bell Channel Inn   This is the best resort choice for scuba divers, lying as it does near the Port Lucaya and close to the ocean. Much of it looks like a moderately priced motel in Florida, opening onto a solar-heated pool. The inn offers its own full-service dive shop and a private boat. You don't come here for luxurious bedrooms, but each unit is spacious, well furnished, and comfortable. Most of them contain small refrigerators as well, and each comes with a private balcony with a view over the channel and Port Lucaya. The hotel maintains its own free shuttle to the beach. If you're a diver, ask about the various dive packages available when booking a room; some of the best dive sites lie only a 5- to 10-minute boat ride from the dive center. The on-site Seafood Restaurant & Bar specializes in the fresh catch of the day.

Kings Rd., Lucaya, Grand Bahama Island, The Bahamas. ℂ 242/373-1053. Fax 242/373-2886. www.bellchannel inn.com. 32 units. $85 (£45) double; $107 (£57) triple; $129 (£68) quad. AE, MC, V. Amenities: Restaurant; bar; outdoor pool; laundry service; babysitting; nonsmoking rooms; dive shop; Wi-Fi in lobby. *In room:* A/C, TV, hair dryer, coffeemaker, fridge (in some).

TAÍNO BEACH
MODERATE

Ritz Beach Resort 🏊 (Kids) Not associated in any way with the Ritz Hotels in London or Paris, this hotel lies across a saltwater canal from the grounds of the Westin & Sheraton at Our Lucaya. It's also located adjacent to Taíno Beach, the "sister beach" of the better-known Lucaya Beach. Enveloped by semitropical gardens, but without the posh and cutting-edge glamour of the Westin and Sheraton hotels, it dates back to 1995, when construction began on what eventually evolved into a three-phase construction program. All the bedrooms are in concrete buildings, each painted a shade of coral. Units start with efficiencies, studios, and one-bedroom suites, and go on up to elaborate villa and penthouse accommodations. The bedrooms are spacious, well furnished, and handsomely maintained, with a tub/shower in the efficiency rooms and a walk-in shower in the studios.

The quality and size of your accommodation and amenities depends on how much you want to pay. Penthouses (on the fourth floor) include a multilevel studio with its own sun deck and private pool. On the premises, two separate restaurants serve international cuisine; there's a scattering of bars whose number (a maximum of five) varies with the occupancy level of the hotel and the season. Although the scale of this compound was diminished after the 2004 hurricanes (one of the hotels next door, Taíno Beach, is still closed from the storms of that year), it's still a worthwhile hotel for a holiday on the beach. The hotel maintains a ferry service that makes frequent trips across the canal to a dock associated with the Westin & Sheraton at Our Lucaya ($2.50/£1.30 per person each way, free for infants under 2). From the Westin's dock, the restaurants, shops, and bars of the Port Lucaya Marketplace and access to Grand Bahama's only casino, the Isle of Capri, lie within a 10-minute walk.

Jolly Roger Dr. (P.O. Box F-43819), Taíno Beach, Lucaya, Grand Bahama Island, The Bahamas. (℃ **888/311-7945** or 242/373-9354. Fax 242/373-4421. www.timetravelcorp.com. 110 units. Year-round $220 (£117) efficiency; $320 (£170) studio; $535 (£284) penthouse. Children 12 and under stay free in parent's room. AE, MC, V. **Amenities:** Restaurant; pool bar; pool; tennis court; babysitting; laundry service; nonsmoking rooms (all); rooms for those w/limited mobility. *In room:* A/C, TV, hair dryer, iron, beverage maker.

INEXPENSIVE

Flamingo Bay Yacht Club & Marina Hotel Unlike the Ritz Beach Resort (its nearby sibling resort), which sits directly astride Taíno Beach, this hotel is set back from the water, about a 5-minute walk from a highly appealing length of white sand. Built of painted concrete, with three stories, it offers midsize, unpretentious, and uncomplicated bedrooms that are comfortable and attractively furnished in a Caribbean motif. Each has a well-maintained bathroom with tub/shower, and either two double beds or a king-size bed. Each comes with such extras as a microwave and toaster. From a nearby 20-slip marina, a water taxi runs hourly across a narrow saltwater canal to a pier operated by the Westin hotel. From here, it's a short walk to the Isle of Capri casino and the center of the Lucaya district, with its multiple bars, shops, restaurants, and entertainment options. (The fee for transportation either way is $2.50/£1.30 per person, free for infants under 2.) Although amenities are sparse, customers are permitted to use the plentiful options at the Ritz Beach Resort.

Jolly Roger Dr., Taíno Beach, Lucaya, Grand Bahama Island, The Bahamas. (℃ **800/824-6623** or 242/373-4677. Fax 242/373-4421. www.timetravelcorp.com. 58 units. Year-round $100–$130 (£53–£69) double. Children 12 and under

(Kids) **Especially Fun Places for Kids**

The Westin & Sheraton at Our Lucaya resorts (p. 153)   Camp Lucaya (also known as the Westin Children's Camp) is the best-run, most-amenities-packed children's camp in The Bahamas, a full-service child-minding facility available for infants to 12-year-olds. The camp is open only to children of guests at either the Sheraton or the Westin at Our Lucaya. Open daily year-round from 9am to 5pm, it includes a supervised children's pool and classes about Bahamian culture (politics, arts, ecosystems, and crafts). A day's involvement might include learning native dances, creating island-inspired arts and crafts, coconut bowling, or exploring a garden whose access is reserved just for kids. The Marine Explorer's Club, co-sponsored with the Underwater Explorer's Society (UNEXSO), offers ocean and marine experiences to youngsters, including an opportunity to go nose-to-nose with dolphins. For infants aged 2 and under, the staff imposes a 2-hour time limit for babysitting services. Children aged 3 to 12, however, can remain within the camp premises throughout the day, without charge, though supervisors advise parents to check on their children periodically, just to see that their vacation is progressing smoothly.

Viva Wyndham Fortuna Beach (p. 158)   This all-inclusive beachfront hotel, a 10-minute drive east of Port Lucaya (but still the most easterly resort on Grand Bahama Island), maintains its Kids Club exclusively for children aged 2 to 11. It provides sports, games, and lessons throughout the day, under the supervision of trained staff members who know when to get parents involved and when to let them slip away for pursuits of their own

stay free in parent's room. AE, DISC, MC, V. **Amenities:** Coin-operated laundry; nonsmoking rooms. *In room:* A/C, cable-connected TV, kitchenette, beverage maker.

AT XANADU BEACH

Xanadu Beach Resort and Marina 𝔸   Permeated with one of the most quirky and idiosyncratic histories of any hotel in The Bahamas, and now painted a cheerful shade of yellow, this hotel is radically different from the way it was when it housed the reclusive billionaire Howard Hughes. Despite storm damages in 2004 and 2005, and all kinds of setbacks, Xanadu is back, soaring triumphantly above a scrub-dotted landscape that's crisscrossed with canals, mysteriously upscale villas, and reminders of the hurricane damages of the past several years. You'll get the sense here of a brave and valiant hotel that has struggled to provide service and comfort to visitors, despite negative fortunes and a hotel scene that has shifted to an increasing degree away from Freeport and toward Port Lucaya. Much of the allure of Xanadu today is the result of the hard work and devotion of the Donato family. It benefited in 2005 from a big influx of cash that reconfigured the lobby area into a Spanish baroque fantasy. Macho-looking and elegant, it evokes a private club where billionaires of the stature of Hughes himself might feel at home. Regrettably, however, there's a sense that this place is still barely clinging to economic viability. Damaged rooflines and some of the balustrades remain in need of repair. Nevertheless, bedrooms are comfortable and the nearby beach is still alluring, even though many of the shoreline structures need rebuilding.

Is the ghost of Howard Hughes still lurking in the penthouse? Perhaps. Members of the staff, particularly the ultracharming and very capable general manager, Ms. Toni Donato, have a lot to say about that, if you're able to pin them down.

P.O. Box F-42438, Freeport, Grand Bahama Island, The Bahamas. © 242/352-6783. Fax 242/352-6299. www. xanadubeachhotel.com. 186 units, plus 3 1-bedroom waterfront villas. Year-round $145 (£77) double; $245–$400 (£130–£212) suites; $450 (£239) villas per day for up to 4 occupants. AE, DC, MC, V. **Amenities:** Pool; 2 tennis courts; gym; gift shop; babysitting; full-service PADI dive shop; watersports concessions. *In room:* A/C, TV, minibar.

ON GRAND BAHAMA ISLAND'S WEST END
EXPENSIVE
Old Bahama Bay 🌟🌟   One of the most dramatic real estate developments in The Bahamas is unfolding at this outpost on the island's extreme western tip. Here descendents of local residents of the West End, each educated and trained in the U.S., are organizing and repairing, after the 2005 hurricanes, one of the most ambitious and upscale development projects in the country. Built on a site that in the early 1980s was the setting for an unsuccessful Jack Tar Village, the project centers around a cluster of upscale hotel units, a state-of-the-art 72-slip marina, and a palm-flanked beach. It's also the venue for some ambitious development plans for the very near future, including a radical reconfiguration of the coastline through the dredging of all-new saltwater lagoons and a redesign of the (man-made) docking facilities and harborfront.

Don't expect to find any evidence of former developments on this site. Virtually everything that had been here previously was demolished to make way for the new construction. The core of the resort consists of nine two-story beach houses, each with between four and six living units inside. Spacious and breezy living quarters, they're outfitted in a Caribbean colonial/tropical country club style. Bathrooms are sheathed in marble, and each contains a shower/whirlpool tub combination and deluxe toiletries. A pair of restaurants—the Dockside Grille and Aqua—serve well-prepared Bahamian and international dishes on a rotating basis.

Though the hotel is appealing, it's the homesites and plans for new marinas to be dredged out of the low-lying scrubland that have the real estate community buzzing. During the lifetime of this edition, we expect interesting big-scale development on this 89-hectare (220-acre) site that's ready and able to catch the real estate boom as it spills over from the Florida mainland. This resort encompasses much more than just hotel accommodations. Its owners envision it as an entire village-in-the-making, relentlessly upscale and dotted with celebrity references. There's even an airplane landing strip within a quarter-mile of this resort. Plans call for the expansion of the marina and an improvement of the beachfronts. Building sites range in price from $400,000 to $1 million each; most are already sold, we were told. Investors have included John Travolta, who presently owns four of the beachfront hotel units. Celebrity sightings include *Sex and the City* star Chris Noth, Geraldo Rivera, and Jack Nicklaus.

West End (P.O. Box F-42546), Grand Bahama Island, The Bahamas. © 800/444-9469 in the U.S. or 242/350-3500. Fax 242/346-6546. www.oldbahamabay.com. 73 units. Winter $330–$575 (£175–£305) suite, from $790 (£419) 2-bedroom suite; off season $235–$395 (£125–£209) suite, from $560 (£297) 2-bedroom suite. Breakfast and dinner $115 (£61) per person extra per day. AE, MC, V. **Amenities:** 2 restaurants; 2 bars; pool; 2 tennis courts; fitness center; watersports equipment/rentals; room service; massage; babysitting; laundry service; nonsmoking rooms (all). *In room:* A/C, TV, kitchenette, minifridge, hair dryer, iron, safe, beverage maker.

Viva Wyndham Fortuna Beach 🌟 (Kids)   While Grand Bahama Island has sprawling, undeveloped tracts of land to the east of this property, this is the easternmost resort on the island. Some visitors argue that the beachfront here is even better than the more extensively developed strands at Port Lucaya. The swimming pool, however, packs a lot less drama than those associated with the Westin & Sheraton at Our Lucaya. This place has made a name for itself by surviving more than one destructive hurricane. During the midsummer months, the staff welcomes an almost exclusively Italian clientele, the result of an exclusive arrangement with a tour operator. Because of that arrangement, you might have difficulty getting a room here between May and September. Throughout the rest of the year, a mostly North American clientele vacations here, and the property is promoted as an all-inclusive venue where all meals, drinks, lodgings, and most watersports are included as part of one price.

The setting is a sprawling compound of 10 hectares (25 acres) of remote and breezy beachfront property, loaded with sports activities that are covered by the price. Established in 1993, Viva Fortuna lies 9.5km (6 miles) east of the International Bazaar along the southern coast of Grand Bahama Island, amid an isolated landscape of casuarinas and scrubland. Comfortably furnished, stylish, and midsize bedrooms lie in a colorful group of two-story outbuildings, some of which are technically classified as timeshares but which are added to the resort's rental pool whenever they're not occupied. About three-quarters have ocean views; the others overlook the surrounding scrublands. Most have a private balcony and two queen-size beds; a small bathroom offers a shower stall but no tub in almost every unit. Singles are charged 40% more than the per-person double-occupancy rate.

All meals, which are included in the rates, are served buffet-style in any of three separate restaurants. In addition to an ongoing series of buffets, you'll find an Italian restaurant and an Asian restaurant, the latter centered around an appealing statue of Buddha. Know in advance that if you stay here, you'll find yourself far from Port Lucaya and its bustle (although a shuttle bus brings guests to the International Bazaar in downtown Freeport twice per day). For clients who appreciate the all-inclusive format where there's not a lot of incentive for straying very far from the property, it's a worthwhile choice.

1 Dubloon Rd. (P.O. Box F-42398), Freeport, Grand Bahama, The Bahamas. ☎ 800/898-9968 or 242/373-4000. Fax 242/373-5555. www.wyndham.com. 276 units. Winter $140 (£74) per person double occupancy, $65 (£34) extra person; off season $251 (£133) per person double occupancy, $78 (£41) extra person. Rates are all-inclusive. AE, DC, MC, V. **Amenities:** 4 restaurants; 4 bars; disco; pool; 2 tennis courts; gym; sauna; Jacuzzi; watersports equipment/rentals; kids' club; babysitting; nonsmoking rooms; rooms for those w/limited mobility. *In room:* A/C, TV, fridge, coffeemaker, hair dryer, iron, safe.

4 Where to Dine

Foodies will find that the cuisine on Grand Bahama Island doesn't match the more refined fare served at dozens of places on New Providence (Nassau/Paradise Island). However, a few places in Grand Bahama specialize in fine dining; others get by with rather standard fare. The good news is that the dining scene is more affordable here.

FREEPORT
MODERATE

Silvano's ✿ ITALIAN   This 80-seat restaurant with its Mediterranean decor serves a worthy but not exceptional cuisine. A competently prepared repertoire inspired by the culinary favorites of Italy is presented here with quality ingredients, most of them shipped in from the United States. Service is polite and helpful. The grilled veal steak is one of the genuinely commendable dishes, along with the homemade pastas served with a variety of freshly made sauces. The chef also works his magic with fish and fresh shrimp. Other traditional Italian dishes round out the menu.

Ranfurley Circle. ℂ **242/352-5111.** Reservations recommended. Lunch specials $7–$14 (£3.70–£7.40); main courses $16–$42 (£8.50–£22). AE, DISC, MC, V. Daily noon–3pm and 5–11pm.

INEXPENSIVE

Beckey's Restaurant BAHAMIAN/AMERICAN   Set near a busy landlocked traffic artery midway between Port Lucaya and downtown Freeport, this unpretentious yellow-and-white restaurant offers authentic Bahamian cuisine prepared in the time-tested style of the Out Islands. The place offers a welcome dose of down-to-earth non-casino reality to local Bahamians and to off-island visitors who appreciate local, nonglittery lifestyles. Breakfasts are either all-American or Bahamian and are available all day. Also popular are minced lobster, curried mutton, fish platters, baked or curried chicken, and conch salads. Stick to the local specialties instead of the lackluster American dishes.

E. Sunrise Hwy. and E. Beach Dr. ℂ **242/352-5247.** Breakfast $5–$11 (£2.65–£5.85); main courses $9–$25 (£4.70–£13). AE, MC, V. Daily 7am to between 8pm and 10pm, depending on the season and on business.

Geneva's BAHAMIAN/SEAFOOD   If you want to eat where the locals eat, head for this unpretentious local venue, where food is made the old-fashioned way. This restaurant is one of the best places to sample conch, which has fed and nourished Bahamians for centuries. The Monroe family will prepare it for you stewed, cracked, or fried, or as part of a savory conch chowder that makes an excellent starter. Grouper also appears, prepared in every imaginable way. The bartender will get you into the mood with a rum-laced Bahama Mama.

Kipling Lane and E. Mall, at W. Sunrise Hwy. ℂ **242/352-5085.** Lunch sandwiches and platters $6–$12 (£3.20–£6.35); dinner main courses $9–$27 (£4.75–£14). DISC, MC, V. Daily 7am–11pm.

The Pepper Pot BAHAMIAN   This might be the only place on Grand Bahama that focuses exclusively on takeout food in the Bahamian style. It's popular throughout the day and evening, but it's especially mobbed on weekends after midnight, when nightclubbers descend upon it for after-bar, after-disco munchies. (It's the only 24-hr. eatery we know of on Grand Bahama Island.) Don't expect glamour, as it's set in a cramped and very ordinary-looking modern building that's within a shopping center that's a 5-minute drive east of the International Bazaar, beside the road leading to Port Lucaya. You can order takeout portions of the island's best guava duff (a dessert specialty of The Bahamas that resembles a jelly roll), as well as pork chops; fish dishes, usually deep-fried and served as part of "fish and chips"; chicken souse (an acquired taste); sandwiches and hamburgers; and an array of daily specials.

E. Sunrise Hwy. (at Coral Rd.). ℂ **242/373-7655.** Breakfast $3–$6 (£1.60–£3.20); main courses $11–$15 (£5.85–£7.95); vegetarian plates $5–$6 (£2.65–£3.20). No credit cards. Daily 24 hr.

The Pub on the Mall INTERNATIONAL   Located on the same floor of the same building and under the same management, three distinctive eating areas lie across the boulevard from the International Bazaar and attract many locals. The **Prince of Wales** serves such Olde English staples as shepherd's pie, fish and chips, platters of roast beef or fish, and real English ale. One end of the room is devoted to the **Red Dog Sports Bar**, with a boisterous atmosphere and at least four TV screens (including one that's a whopping 96 in. wide) blasting away for dedicated fans. **Silvano's** (see above) is an Italian restaurant serving lots of pasta, usually with verve, as well as veal, chicken, beefsteaks, seafood, and such desserts as tiramisu. A final venue that may or may not be open, depending on the plans of its staff, is Bahamian-themed **Islander's Roost,** which has a bright tropical decor and a balcony overlooking the bazaar. Throughout this place, food is good if not great; the main platters are a good value, usually very filling and satisfying.

Ranfurley Circle, Sunrise Hwy. $\textcircled{C}$ 242/352-5110. Reservations recommended. Main courses $7–$36 (£3.70–£19). AE, DISC, MC, V. Prince of Wales and Red Dog daily noon–midnight; Silvano's daily noon–3pm and 5–11pm; Islanders' Roost usually, depending on business, Mon–Sat 5–11pm.

IN THE INTERNATIONAL BAZAAR
INEXPENSIVE
Café Michel BAHAMIAN/AMERICAN   The name implies that you've found an authentic French bistro amid the bustle of the International Bazaar. In reality, this place is rather akin to a tropical, vaguely Rastafarian version of a coffee shop and bar. Nonetheless (and the place has declined, like the rest of the International Bazaar, in recent years), it provides a funky and sometimes amusing option for refueling when you're shopping the cracked and dusty byways of the bazaar. Beneath a once bright, now faded red awning (inspired, one suspects, by Maxim's in Paris) are clusters of somewhat claustrophobic cafe tables, displays loaded with conch shell souvenirs, and chalkboards listing the food available that day. Local shopkeepers know to come here for coffee, platters, salads, and sandwiches throughout the day, or perhaps a drink after cruise ship passengers have gone for the day. Both American and Bahamian dishes are served, including seafood platters, steaks, and, of course, grouper.

International Bazaar. $\textcircled{C}$ 242/352-2191. Reservations recommended for dinner. Main courses $7–$42 (£3.70–£22). AE, MC, V. Mon–Sat 9am–5pm. Closed Sept.

China Temple CHINESE   This battered looking Chinese joint—and don't expect more than just that—also does takeout. Over the years it's proved to be the dining bargain of the bazaar, surviving in a venue that hasn't been profitable for many of its (now-defunct) competitors. The menu is familiar, standard, and a bit shopworn: chop suey, chow mein, and sweet-and-sour chicken. It's certainly not gourmet Asian fare, but it's cheap, and it might hit the spot when you're craving something different.

International Bazaar. $\textcircled{C}$ 242/352-5610. Lunch $7–$9 (£3.70–£4.80); main courses $10–$14 (£5.30–£7.40). AE, MC, V. Mon–Sat 10:30am–10pm.

AT OUR LUCAYA AND TAÍNO BEACH
EXPENSIVE
China Beach ⊛ ASIAN FUSION   Within its own separate stone-and-stucco building on the seafronting grounds of the Westin & Sheraton at Our Lucaya, this restaurant offers a culinary passport to the Pacific Rim. Exotic delights include the spicy hot cuisines of Vietnam and Thailand, with calls at Korea, Indonesia, and Malaysia. The menu changes every month, but some dishes appear with regularity. Our favorites among these are a savory Hong Kong roast duckling and a zesty Thai chicken. The beef marinated in soy sauce is served with fresh spring onion, and the grouper filet appears with fresh ginger and scallions. Other Far East specialties include a seafood teppanyaki and stir-fry conch. The decor of this place is particularly imaginative, with scarlet parasols doubling as ceiling chandeliers, and an architecture that seems to float above one of the resort's serpentine-shaped swimming pools.

At the Westin & Sheraton at Our Lucaya resorts, Royal Palm Way. $\textcircled{C}$ 242/373-1444. Reservations recommended. Main courses $21–$36 (£11–£19). AE, DC, DISC, MC, V. Tues–Sat 6–11pm, with occasional variations in hours based on occupancy of the surrounding resort.

Churchill's 🍴🍴 AMERICAN   One of the island's most elegant and formal restaurants, it's imbued with a sense of the faded grandeur of what used to be known as the British Empire. Surpassed only, we believe, by the Ferry House and Luciano's, both of which are recommended below, Churchill's lures diners from other parts of Grand Bahama Island to a dining room that opens onto the lobby of the Westin Hotel at Our Lucaya. The venue includes a British-colonial bar with dark-wood floor and trim, potted plants, ceiling fans, a grand piano, and big-windowed views over the sea. The island's best chophouse, it features both succulent steaks flown over from the mainland and locally caught seafood. The manor house setting is an appropriate foil for the finely honed service and top-quality ingredients, deftly prepared. Regrettably, it's open less frequently than we'd like, sometimes operating only on weekends during low and shoulder season.

At the Westin & Sheraton at Our Lucaya resorts, Royal Palm Way. 📞 242/373-1444. Reservations required. Main courses $27–$65 (£14–£34). AE, DC, DISC, MC, V. Usually Mon–Sat 6–11pm, but during off season, hours vary according to occupancy levels of the hotel.

Iries 🍴 CARIBBEAN   This is one of the newest restaurants at the Westin & Sheraton at Our Lucaya. As such, a team of food and beverage experts threw tons of money and research into developing the appropriate blend of Caribbean tradition and postmodern sales and marketing. The result will remind you of the dining room of a massive colonial Caribbean (probably Jamaican) manor house. Decor is replete with replicas of pineapples (the region's traditional symbol of hospitality), Rastafarian-inspired paintings, and elaborately carved mahogany furniture similar to what might have graced the home of a 19th-century Caribbean planter. You'll get a sense of spaciousness and old-fashioned dignity and restraint. Menu items include cracked conch with spicy Pick-a-Pepper sauce and sweet potato wedges, grilled sirloin steak with cumin and thyme, blackened grouper with fire-roasted peppers and pineapple sauce, and tamarind-glazed hen. On your way in, check out the Bahamian Junkanoo costume, which hangs like a permanent exhibition in a museum. Replete with sequins and mystical references, it's one of the most elaborate, most outrageous, and most costly examples of its kind.

The Westin & Sheraton at Our Lucaya resorts, Royal Palm Way. 📞 242/373-1444. Main courses $27–$50 (£14–£27). AE, MC, V. Sat–Wed 6–11pm, but hours vary according to the season and occupancy levels of the hotel which contains it.

The Stoned Crab 🍴 SEAFOOD   Tired of frozen seafood shipped in from the mainland? Come to this independent (that is, not associated with any hotel) restaurant for sweet stone crab claws and the lobster, both caught in Bahamian waters. There's none better on the island. You can't miss this place—a triple pyramid (ca. 1968) whose isolated, four-story, wood-and-steel framework is strong enough to withstand any hurricane. Swiss-born Livio Peronino is the manager and chef, preparing a seafood platter with everything on it, including grouper, conch fritters, and varied shellfish. The best pasta on the menu is linguine al pesto with lobster and shrimp. For starters, try the zesty conch chowder. Have a lobster salad with your meal and finish with Irish coffee.

At Taíno Beach, Lucaya. 📞 242/373-1442. Reservations recommended. Main courses $8–$18 (£4.25–£9.55) lunch, $22–$34 (£12–£18) dinner. AE, MC, V. Tues–Sun 11am–3pm; daily 5–10pm.

MODERATE
Prop Club AMERICAN/INTERNATIONAL   This is one of our favorite informal restaurants in the Our Lucaya/Port Lucaya compound. Set within its own low-slung

building on the grounds of the Westin & Sheraton at Our Lucaya, it's the kind of place that raffish-looking crew members from charter yachts moored nearby search out during their time in port. Despite its location on the grounds of the most upscale resort on Grand Bahama Island, it manages to remain fun, funky, laid-back, and with a bemused humor at its own Rastafarian references. Looking for a bar, a cafe, a restaurant, a dance hall, or a pickup joint? This place can be (and has been) all things to all kinds of people. It evokes a battered airplane hangar where mail planes might have been repaired during World War II. Many of the industrial parts hanging from the ceiling, including semiantique airplane propellers and ship hulls, evoke a low-tech age when an airplane engine might actually have been repaired by a pilot wielding a monkey wrench, some grease, and some copper wire. When the weather's right, which it is most of the time, large doors open to bring the outdoors inside, and the party overflows onto the beach. The all-Bahamian staff is good-looking, the drinks are stiff, the music is fine, and the place can be a lot of fun. Dig into a "mountain of ribs," or else savor the blackened grouper. Ever had a grilled margarita chicken sandwich? You can order juicy oversize burgers, fajitas, spicy conch chowder, and the like. Many dishes are at the lower end of the price scale, making it an affordable choice.

At the Westin & Sheraton at Our Lucaya resorts, Royal Palm Way. © 242/373-1444. Main courses $14–$32 (£7.40–£17). AE, DC, MC, V. Restaurant daily 11:30am–10pm; bar Sun–Thurs 11:30am–1am; Fri–Sat noon–2am.

INEXPENSIVE

Willy Broadleaf *Finds* INTERNATIONAL   Set on the street level of the Westin at Our Lucaya, facing one of its S-curved swimming pools, this imaginatively decorated restaurant focuses on one of the most lavish buffet breakfasts we've ever seen in The Bahamas. The decor fits the cuisine, with various sections evoking a courtyard in Mexico, a marketplace in old Cairo, the dining hall of an Indian maharajah (including tables that are partially concealed from neighbors with yards of translucent fabric), and even an African village. There are food stations here for both cold and hot breakfast foods, lavish buffet spreads, and separate chefs preparing omelets, eggs, pancakes, and French toast (the best version of which is laced with coconut) at state-of-the-art cook stations.

The Westin & Sheraton at Our Lucaya resorts, Royal Palm Way. © 242/373-1444. Breakfast buffets $12 (£6.35) for cold foods, $20 (£11) for both hot and cold foods. AE, DC, DISC, MC, V. Daily 6:30–11am and 6–11pm.

AT PORT LUCAYA MARKETPLACE
EXPENSIVE

Ferry House *Finds* CAJUN/SEAFOOD   This restaurant serves the most celebrated, the most elaborate, and the most "fussed-over" cuisine on Grand Bahama Island. Much of its excellence derives from the hard work and talent of its Iceland-born owner. Designed to look like the mostly brown interior of a wood-trimmed ferryboat, it faces the ocean, just at the edge of Bell Channel, the waterway that funnels boats from the open sea into the sheltered confines of the Port Lucaya Marina. Lunches are relatively simple affairs, consisting of pastas, catch of the day, and meal-size salads. Dinner might feature a seafood platter laden with calamari, fish, and shrimp; a delectable filet mignon with potatoes and vegetables; fresh salmon with hollandaise sauce; and savory grilled rack of New Zealand lamb. But our favorite meal here is the seared yellow-fin tuna steak with vegetable couscous. Many of the herbs used here are grown in the restaurant's own garden. Dessert might include a melt-in-your-mouth version of chocolate cake, one of the best we've ever tasted. Since they're baked to order, make your request 15 minutes in advance.

Beside Bell Channel, Port Lucaya. ℂ **242/373-1595**. Reservations recommended for dinner. Lunch platters $10–$19 (£5.30–£10); set-price lunch $25 (£13); dinner main courses $33–$40 (£18–£21). AE, MC, V. Mon–Fri noon–2:30pm; Tues–Sun 6–9pm.

Luciano's 👁 FRENCH/CONTINENTAL   With its tables usually occupied by local government officials and deal makers, Luciano's is the grande dame of Freeport restaurants, with a very European atmosphere. It's the only restaurant in Port Lucaya offering caviar, foie gras, and oysters Rockefeller, all served with a flourish by a formally dressed waitstaff (who, fortunately, have a very definite sense of charm and humor). There's a bar inside and elegantly decorated tables set in the kind of socially correct dining rooms you might find in Paris. Additional seating on a breezy upstairs veranda overlooks the marina. Lightly smoked and thinly sliced salmon makes a good opener, as does a seafood crepe or snails in garlic butter. Fresh fish and shellfish are regularly featured and delicately prepared, allowing their natural flavors to shine through without heavy, overwhelming sauces. A good example includes local grouper topped with toasted almonds and a lemon-flavored butter sauce, or broiled Bahamian lobster tail. Steak Diane is one of Luciano's classics, along with an especially delectable veal medallion sautéed with shrimp and chunks of lobster.

Port Lucaya Marketplace. ℂ **242/373-9100**. www.portlucaya.com/lucianos. Reservations required in winter. Main courses $25–$44 (£13–£23). AE, MC, V. Daily 5:30–9:45pm (last order).

MODERATE

Fatman's Nephew 👁 BAHAMIAN   In another location, "Fatman" became a legend on Grand Bahama Island. Although he's no longer with us, the Fatman must have left his recipes and cooking skills to another generation of cooks. Today the place, which used to cater mainly to locals, has gone touristy, but much of the same traditional fare is still served with the same unflagging allegiance to Bahamian ways. The restaurant overlooks the marina at Port Lucaya from an eagle's-nest position on the second floor. You can enjoy drinks or meals inside, but we like to head out to an outdoor covered deck to watch the action below. At least 10 different kinds of game fish—including both wahoo and Cajun blackened kingfish—plus curried chicken, mutton, turtle steak (lightly breaded and pan-fried), or beef are usually offered. Bahamian-style shark soup, made from the flesh of either nurse sharks (they're especially flavorful because they feed primarily on lobsters) or hammerheads ("little tender ones," according to the chef), is sometimes featured on the menu. Most dishes, except for expensive shellfish, fall at the lower end of the price scale. Beware, as the local staff can be flighty.

Port Lucaya Marketplace. ℂ **242/373-8520**. Main courses $10–$40 (£5.30–£21). AE, DISC, MC, V. Mon–Sat 11am–10pm.

Giovanni's Cafe 👁 ITALIAN/SEAFOOD   Tucked into one of the pedestrian thoroughfares of Port Lucaya Marketplace, this cream-colored clapboard house provides the setting for a charming 38-seat Italian trattoria. The chefs (including head chef Giovanni Colo) serve Italian-influenced preparations of local seafood, highlighted by seafood pasta (usually prepared only for two diners) and a lobster special. Giovanni stamps each dish with his Italian verve and flavor, whether it be Bahamian conch, local seafood, or scampi. Dishes show off his precision and rock-solid technique, exemplified by sirloin steak with fresh mushrooms, delectable shrimp scampi, and fattening but extremely good spaghetti carbonara.

Port Lucaya Marketplace. ℂ **242/373-9107**. Reservations recommended. Main courses lunch $9.50–$15 (£5–£7.95), dinner $15–$38 (£7.95–£20). AE, MC, V. Mon–Sat 8:30am–10pm; Sun 5–10pm.

The Harbour Room *GG Kids* EUROPEAN/CARIBBEAN The only member of the prestigious *Chaîne des Rotisseurs* on Grand Bahama Island, this is one of the best restaurants in Port Lucaya. It offers a definite continental flair; a creative kitchen; a polite, hardworking staff; and a sense of *Gemütlichkeit* in the tropics. Tucked away into one corner, its bar area is the most lavish part, with esoteric liquors and liqueurs, and an upscale and stylish decor that recalls a chic hideaway in Berlin. The dining room is simpler. Designed as a counterpart for the cuisine, and not an architectural statement in its own right, it's outfitted with dark-wood trim and a nautical decor that's especially charming when the Atlantic winds outside blow hard and cold. Its owners are not shy about publicizing their culinary ambitions. They serve one of the few white (that is, New England–style) conch chowders we've seen in The Bahamas. Jumbo cheeseburgers are appropriately juicy, but more appealing might be the Delmonico steaks, veal chops with Provençal herbs, and shrimp Alfredo with marinara-flavored pasta. Chilean sea bass poached in Irish butter and chardonnay sauce is a specialty, as is "lobster St. Jacques," wherein chunks of lobster are spooned over a bed of garlic-flavored mashed potatoes, covered with cheese, and broiled.

In the Port Lucaya Marketplace. **©** 242/374-4466. Reservations recommended. Main courses $16–$34 (£8.50–£18); children's platters $5–$9 (£2.65–£4.80). AE, MC, V. Wed–Sun 5–11pm; Sun brunch 11am–4:30pm.

La Dolce Vita *G* ITALIAN Next to the Pub at Lucaya (see listing below), this small upscale Italian trattoria has a modern decor and traditional food. Enjoy freshly made pastas on a patio overlooking the marina or in the 44-seat dining room. Start with portobello mushrooms, fresh mozzarella with tomatoes, and a vinaigrette, or else carpaccio with arugula and spices. Homemade ravioli appears with fillings such as cheese, lobster, or spinach. An excellent risotto flavored with black squid ink is served, or else you can order roast pork tenderloin or a crisp and aromatic rack of lamb.

Port Lucaya Marketplace. **©** 242/373-8652. Reservations recommended. Main courses $21–$38 (£11–£20). AE, MC, V. Daily 5–11pm. Closed Sept.

Mediterranean Restaurant & Bar (Le Med) *G Value* FRENCH/GREEK/ BAHAMIAN This is a simpler and more cost-effective version of the also-recommended Luciano's, with which it shares the same management and similar location (on the second floor of a building almost immediately next door). The decor includes a hard-working, almost indestructible combination of sand-colored floor tiles and refrigerated display cases loaded with pastries and salads. Devoid of linen, tables are so simple and angular-looking that they might have appeared within a coffee shop/diner. Don't let this simplicity fool you: The place serves well-flavored and surprisingly sophisticated food that attracted many of the actors filming the sequel to *Pirates of the Caribbean,* as well as rock star Jon Bon Jovi and a gaggle of hangers-on. The place is crowded during the breakfast hour, when omelets (including a feta cheese and spinach–laden version of a Greek omelet), eggs and bacon, and Bahamian stewed fish and steamed conch are crowd-pleasers. Lunch and dinner feature assorted Greek and Turkish-style mezes and Iberian-style tapas that include both marinated octopus and grilled calamari. Crepes, priced at $8 to $10 (£4.25–£5.30) each, come in both sweet and savory versions. Other tempters include a seafood combo piled high with lobster, shrimp, conch, fish, and mussels; Delmonico-style steaks; *shashlik* (marinated kabobs redolent with herbs); and braised lamb shank cooked in red wine.

Port Lucaya Marketplace. **©** 242/374-2804. Breakfast $6–$10 (£3.20–£5.30); main courses $15–$25 (£7.95–£13). AE, DC, MC, V. Daily 8am–11:30pm

Pisces ✿ INTERNATIONAL   This ranks high among our favorites among the many restaurants in the Port Lucaya Marketplace, and we're seconded by the locals and sailors who pack the place every weekend. The place is outfitted with a quirky mixture of nautical accessories and dark-varnished wood, with a prominent bar where more and more gossip is exchanged as the evening progresses. Tabletops contain laminated samples of seashells, fake gold coins, and sand. The place has a charming all-Bahamian staff outfitted in black and white. Pizzas are available and come in 27 different varieties, including a version with conch, lobster, shrimp, and chicken, as well as one with Alfredo sauce. Dinners are more elaborate, with a choice of curries; all kinds of fish and shellfish; and several kinds of pasta.

Port Lucaya Marketplace. ℂ **242/373-5192.** Reservations recommended. Pizzas $12–$28 (£6.35–£15); dinner main courses $9–$30 (£4.75–£16). AE, DISC, MC, V. Mon–Sat 5pm–1:30am.

Pub at Lucaya ENGLISH/BAHAMIAN   Opening onto Count Basie Square, and reminiscent of the days when the Royal Navy might have hauled some of its sailors out to The Bahamas from a home base in, say, Liverpool, this restaurant and bar lies near the center of the Port Lucaya Marketplace. Returning visitors might remember the joint when it was called Pusser's Pub, named after that popular brand of rum.

Many patrons visit just for the drinks, especially rum-laced Pusser's Painkillers. You can order predictable pub grub such as shepherd's pie or steak-and-ale pie. Juicy American-style burgers are another lure. There's also a scattering of more substantial Bahamian fare, especially Bahamian lobster tail, cracked conch, chicken breast with herbs, or the fresh grilled catch of the day. The tables outside overlooking the water are preferred, or else you can retreat inside under a wooden beamed ceiling, where the rustic pinewood tables are lit by faux Tiffany-style lamps.

Port Lucaya Marketplace. ℂ **242/373-8450.** Sandwiches and burgers $8–$11 (£4.25–£5.85); main courses $13–$40 (£6.90–£21). AE, MC, V. Daily 11am–11pm (bar until 1am).

Shenanigan's Irish Pub IRISH/INTERNATIONAL   Dark and beer-stained from the thousands of pints of Guinness, Harp, and Killian's that have been served and spilled here, this pub and restaurant is the premier Irish or Boston-Irish hangout on Grand Bahama Island. Many visitors come just to drink, sometimes for hours at a time, soaking up the suds and perhaps remembering to eventually order some food. If you do get hungry, the menu here recently took a noticeable swing toward the more upscale. They still serve steak-and-kidney pie, burgers, and surf and turf, but newer items include French-style rack of lamb for two, seafood Newburg, and "chicken Connemara" drenched in whiskey sauce

Port Lucaya Marketplace. ℂ **242/373-4734.** Main courses $10–$49 (£5.30–£26). AE, DISC, MC, V. Mon–Thurs 5pm–midnight; Fri–Sat 5pm–2am (last order at 9:45pm).

INEXPENSIVE

Georgie's BAHAMIAN/AMERICAN   This laid-back, informal restaurant provides a harborside perch at Port Lucaya for breakfast, lunch, or dinner. It gets particularly busy at late afternoon happy hour, when prices on drinks are reduced. Service shows more effort than polish, but dishes do arrive and they are quite flavorful time-tested recipes, a repertoire of old favorites like cracked conch (similar to breaded veal cutlet) served with tasty coleslaw. The catch of the day is usually pan-fried grouper or snapper served with peas 'n' rice. The chef almost daily prepares hot roast beef, serving it with mashed potatoes and mixed vegetables; for lunch, try one of the island's better chef's salads, loaded with turkey, ham, fresh tomatoes, cheese, and other good things. Other favorites include lobster, conch fritters, and barbecue chicken.

Port Lucaya Marketplace. © 242/373-8513. Breakfast $5–$7 (£2.65–£3.70); main courses lunch $8–$11 (£4.25–£5.85), dinner $9–$23 (£4.75–£12). DC, MC, V. Thurs, Fri, Mon–Tues 10am–8pm; Sat–Sun 8am–9pm.

Outrigger's Native Restaurant/White Wave Club BAHAMIAN   Cement-sided and simple, with a large deck extending out toward the sea, this restaurant was here long before construction of the Port Lucayan Marketplace, which lies only 4 blocks away. The restaurant is the domain of Gretchen Wilson, whose kitchens produce a rotating series of lip-smacking dishes such as lobster tails, minced lobster, steamed or cracked conch, pork chops, chicken, fish, and shrimp, usually served with peas 'n' rice and macaroni. Every Wednesday night, from 5pm to 2am, the restaurant is the venue for Outrigger's Famous Wednesday Night Fish Fry, when as many as a thousand diners will line up for platters of fried or steamed fish ($10–$15/£5.30–£7.95 each) which are accompanied by a DJ and dancers. Almost as well attended are the establishment's Bonfire Nights, where set-price all-you-can-eat barbecued dinners, in addition to the a la carte offerings, go for $30 (£16) per person every Tuesday and Thursday evening. If you pay for the Bonfire night at Outrigger's, the price for the bonfire is $30 (£16); however, booking through your hotel may cost you an extra $20 (£11). Drinks are served within the restaurant, but you might consider stepping into the nearby ramshackle bar, the White Wave Club, which serves only drinks.

Smith's Point. © 242/373-4811. Main courses $10–$16 (£5.30–£8.50). No credit cards. Sun–Fri 4–10pm; Sat 1–9pm.

Zorba's *Value* BAHAMIAN/GREEK   If you've ever been captivated by "the Greek experience," this place might bring back happy memories, as well as providing some of the best food value at the Port Lucaya Marketplace. There's a narrow outside veranda with a relatively uninteresting view over the all-pedestrian alleyway outside, and a pale-blue-and-white Formica-clad interior that might remind you of a diner, with a TV set blasting out a Greek-language news broadcast. Big photos of Alan Bates and Anthony Quinn (playing Zorba, get it?) dancing on a beach add a touch of nostalgia for *ouzo* and *retsina*. The cuisine is a quirky and idiosyncratic mixture of Greek and Bahamian, and if you don't remember exactly what *taramasalata* or baklava is, the good-looking Bahamian staff will rattle off the ingredients like Peloponnesian pros. First thing in the morning, you'll see locals standing in line for the Bahamian breakfasts served at Zorba's, with dishes that include chicken souse, corned beef and grits, and an array of pancakes, waffles, and omelets. Lunch could be a fat gyro, burgers and salads, or a souvlakia. Dinner can begin with a Greek salad and then move on to moussaka, grilled chicken on a bed of spinach, or any of several different pasta dishes, and end with baklava (honey and nut-studded pastries) for a sweet finish. We won't pretend the food here is a substitute for a trip to the Greek isles, but it's satisfying and filling.

Port Lucaya Marketplace. © 242/373-6137. Main courses lunch $4–$17 (£2.10–£9), dinner $16–$28 (£8.50–£15). AE, DISC, MC, V. Daily 7am–10:30pm.

OUTSIDE FREEPORT/LUCAYA

Bishop's Restaurant *Finds* BAHAMIAN   This eatery, known mainly to East End locals, is patronized for its real down-home cooking. Just over 50km (31 miles) east of Lucaya, the restaurant opens onto views of the sea. Far from the high-rise hotels, and set within a small residential community that's utterly devoid of casino-inspired glitz, this little restaurant and lounge look the way they did in The Bahamas of the 1920s and 1930s. Some of the best cracked conch we've sampled on Grand Bahama Island is served here, rolled in a light batter and fried in piping hot oil so that its crust is slightly crunchy. Another favorite, always on the menu, is fried grouper with classic peas 'n' rice. Or, for a savory dish, order the chicken barbecued in zesty sauce. Frankly, don't set out on a trek to the East End with this place envisioned as your final destination without making a phone call in advance, since opening hours have been erratic since the hurricanes of 2005.

High Rock. © 242/353-4515. Main courses $10–$15 (£5.30–£7.95). MC, V. Daily 9am–7pm.

5 Beaches, Watersports & Other Outdoor Pursuits

HITTING THE BEACH

Grand Bahama Island has enough beaches for everyone. The best ones open onto Northwest Providence Channel at Freeport and sweep east for some 97km (60 miles) to encompass Xanadu Beach, Lucaya Beach, Taíno Beach, and others, eventually ending at such remote eastern outposts as Rocky Creek and McLean's Town. Once you leave the Freeport/Lucaya area, you can virtually have your pick of white sandy beaches all the way east. Once you're past the resort hotels, you'll see a series of secluded beaches used mainly by locals. If you like people, a lot of organized watersports, and easy access to hotel bars and rest rooms, stick to Xanadu, Taíno, and Lucayan beaches.

Though there's fine snorkeling offshore, you should book a snorkeling cruise aboard one of the catamarans to see the most stunning reefs.

Xanadu Beach 🎣🎣 is one of our favorites, immediately east of Freeport and the site of the famed Xanadu Beach Resort. The 1.6km-long (1-mile) beach may be crowded at times in winter, but that's because of those gorgeous, soft, powdery white sands, which open onto tranquil waters. The beach is set against a backdrop of coconut palms and Australian pines. In theory, at least, you can hook up here with an assortment of watersports, including snorkeling, boating, jet-skiing, and parasailing. But many of the beachfront concessions were damaged by hurricanes during the autumn of 2005, so it's a good idea to phone the Xanadu Resort in advance of your arrival to find out which purveyors have returned after the storm devastation.

Immediately east of Xanadu is **Silver Point Beach,** a little beach, site of a timeshare complex where guests are out riding the waves on water bikes or playing volleyball on the beach. You'll see horseback riders from Pinetree Stables (see below) taking beach rides along the sands.

Despite the allure of other beaches on Grand Bahama Island, most visitors will be found at **Lucaya Beach,** right off Royal Palm Way and immediately east of Silver Point Beach. This is one of the best strands in The Bahamas, with long stretches of white sand. In the vicinity of the Westin and Sheraton hotels, you'll also encounter a worthy scattering of beach bars. At any of the hotel resorts along this beach, you can hook up with an array of watersports or get a frosty drink from a hotel bar. It's not for those seeking seclusion, but it's a fun beach-party scene.

Immediately to the east of Lucaya Beach, and separated from it with a saltwater canal, **Taíno Beach** is a family favorite and a good place for watersports. This, too, is a fine wide beach of white sands, opening onto generally tranquil waters.

Another choice not too far east is **Gold Rock Beach,** a favorite picnic spot with locals on weekends, although you'll usually have this beach to yourself on weekdays. Gold Rock Beach is a 19km (12-mile) drive from Lucaya. At Gold Rock you are at

---

Moments **Private White Sands for You Alone**

Once you head east from Port Lucaya and Taíno, you'll discover so many splendid beaches that you'll lose count. Although these beaches have names, you'll
never really know what beach you're on, unless you ask a local, because they
are unmarked. If you like seclusion and don't mind the lack of any facilities,
you'll find a string of local favorites. Directly east of Taíno is **Churchill's Beach,**
followed by **Smith's Point, Fortune Beach,** and **Barbary Beach.** Fortune Beach is
a special gem because of its beautiful waters and white sands.

---

the doorstep to the **Lucayan National Park** (see below), a 16-hectare (40-acre) park
filled with some of the longest, widest, and most fabulous secluded beaches on the
island.

BIKING

A guided bike trip is an ideal way to see parts of Grand Bahama that most visitors
miss. Starting at **Barbary Beach,** you can pedal a mountain bike along the southern
coast parallel to the beach. Stop for a snack, lunch, and a dip. Finally, you reach
Lucayan National Park, some 19km (12 miles) away. Explore the cave where the
Indians buried their dead in the days when Grand Bahama was theirs, centuries before
the coming of Columbus. Crabs here have occasionally come up through holes in the
ground carrying bits of bowls once used by the Lucayans. Grand Bahama Nature
Tours (also known as **Kayak Nature Tours;** (C) 242/373-2485; www.grandbahama
naturetours.com) runs these trips and transports you home to your hotel by van, so
you don't have to exhaust yourself in the heat cycling back. The same company offers
variations on this itinerary, with more time spent on kayaking and snorkeling and less
time on bicycling. All versions of the tour last about 5 hours and cost $79 (£42) for
adults, half-price for children under 12. All equipment, sustenance, and round-trip
transportation from your hotel is included.

BOAT CRUISES

Ocean Wonder, Port Lucaya Dock ((C) **242/373-5880**), run by Reef Tours, is a gar-
gantuan 18m (59-ft.) Defender glass-bottom boat. Any tour agent can arrange for you
to go out on this vessel. You'll get a panoramic view of the beautiful underwater life
off the coast of Grand Bahama. Cruises depart from Port Lucaya behind the Straw
Market on the bay side at 9:30am, 11:15am, 1:15pm, and 3:15pm, except Friday,
when only two tours leave at 9:30 and 11:15am. The tour lasts 1½ hours, costs $25
(£13) for adults and $15 (£7.95) for children 6 to 12, and is free for children 5 and
under. During high season (that is, midwinter), arrange for reservations a day or two
in advance, as the boat does fill up quickly.

  Superior Watersports (P.O. Box F-40837, Freeport; (C) **242/373-7863;** www.
superiorwatersports.com) offers trips on its *Bahama Mama,* a two-deck, 22m (72-ft.)
catamaran. Its Robinson Crusoe Beach Party is offered four times a week and costs
$59 (£31) per adult and $39 (£21) for children under 12. Schedules vary with the seasons: from 11am to 4pm from October through March, but from noon to 5pm from
April through September. There's also a shorter sunset booze cruise that goes for $45
(£24). (Apr–Sept, these cruises are on Tues, Thurs, and Sat night 6:30–8:30pm, and

Oct–Mar the same nights, but 6–8pm.) Call for information about how to hook up with this outfitter.

For an underwater cruise, try the company's quasi-submarine, the *Seaworld Explorer*. The sub itself does not descend; instead, you walk down into the hull of the boat and watch the sea life glide by. The "semisub" departs daily at 9:30am, 11:30am, and 1:30pm, and the 2-hour ride costs $39 (£21) for adults and $25 (£13) for children age 2 to 12.

THE DOLPHIN EXPERIENCE

A pod of bottle-nosed dolphins is involved in a unique dolphin/human familiarization program at Dolphin Experience, located at **Underwater Explorers Society (UNEXSO),** next to Port Lucaya, opposite the entrance to the Westin & Sheraton at Our Lucaya (✆ **800/992-DIVE** or 242/373-1244; www.unexso.com). This "close encounter" program allows participants to observe these intelligent and friendly animals and hear an interesting talk by a member of the animal-care staff. At the world's largest dolphin facility, the conditions aren't cramped. In addition, dolphins can swim out to sea, passing through an underwater "sea gate" that prevents their natural predators from entering the lagoon; the dolphins later return of their own free will to the relative safety of their protected marine habitat. After a 25-minute ferryboat ride from Port Lucaya, you'll step onto a shallow wading platform and interact with the dolphins. At press time, the dolphin colony had 17 members. The experience costs $75 (£40) and is an educational, fun adventure for all ages. Children under 3 participate free, while it costs $38 (£20) for those aged 4 to 12. If you like to document your life's unusual experiences, you'll want to bring your camera. For certified divers, UNEXSO offers a "dolphin dive," wherein a school of dolphins swim out from their marine habitat in Sanctuary Bay for a closely supervised diver-to-dolphin encounter. The cost is $169 (£90). If business warrants, the dolphin dive is offered daily.

Swimming with dolphins has its supporters as well as its highly vocal critics. For an insight into the various points of view surrounding this issue, you may want to visit the Whale and Dolphins Conservation Society's website at www.wdcs.org. For more information about responsible travel in general, check out this website: the International Ecotourism Society (www.ecotourism.org).

FISHING

In the waters off Grand Bahama, you can fish for barracuda, snapper, grouper, yellowtail, wahoo, and kingfish, along with other denizens of the deep.

Moments Land & Sea Eco-Tours

If you're a nature lover, escape from the casinos and take one of the **East End Adventures** (✆ **242/373-6662;** www.bahamasecotours.com) bush and sea safaris. You're taken through dense pine forests and along deserted beaches, going inland on hikes to such sites as blue holes, mangrove swamps, and underground caverns. You may even learn how to crack conch. A native lunch is served on a serene beach in Lightbourne's Cay, a remote islet in the East End. Most of the tour is laid-back, as you can snorkel in blue holes or shell hunt. These "Island Hopping Safaris" are conducted Sunday to Friday between 9:30am and 5pm; the cost is $120 (£64) for adults and $65 (£34) for kids ages 2 to 12.

Reef Tours, Ltd., Port Lucaya Dock (© **242/373-5880** or 242/373-5891; www. bahamasvg.com/reeftours), offers one of the least expensive ways to go deep-sea fishing around Grand Bahama Island. Adults pay $110 (£58) if they fish, $50 (£27) if they go along only to watch. Four to six people can charter the entire 13m (43-ft.) craft for $650 (£345) per half-day or $1,250 (£663) per whole day. The 9.6m (31-ft.) boat can be chartered for $425 (£225) for a half-day and $825 (£437) for a full day. Departures for the 4-hour half-day excursions are daily at 8:30am and 1pm, while the 8-hour full-day excursions leave daily at 8:30am. Bait, tackle, and ice are included in the cost.

GOLF

Since the closing of two of the island's older courses (The Ruby and The Emerald) after the hurricane damages of the early millennium, Grand Bahama Island is not as richly accessorized with golf courses as it was before. But golf on the island recently experienced a resurgence, thanks to the improvement of the golf layouts described below. Each of them is open to the public year-round, and clubs can be rented from their respective pro shops.

Fortune Hills Golf & Country Club, Richmond Park, Lucaya (© **242/373-2222**), was originally intended to be an 18-hole course, but the back 9 were never completed. You can replay the front 9 for 18 holes and a total of 6,916 yards from the blue tees. Par is 72. Greens fees cost $47 (£25) for 9 holes, $61 (£32) for 18. Carts are included in greens fees. Club rental costs $18 (£9.55) for 18 holes and $14 (£7.40) for 9 holes.

The best kept and most manicured course on Grand Bahama is the **Lucayan Golf Course,** Lucaya Beach at Our Lucaya (© **242/373-1333**). Made over after Hurricane Jeanne of 2004, this beautiful course is a traditional golf layout with rows of pine trees separating the fairways. Greens are fast, with a couple of par 5s more than 500 yards long, totaling 6,824 yards from the blue tees and 6,488 from the whites. Par is 72. Greens fees are $120 (£64) for 18 holes, including a mandatory shared golf cart.

Its sibling golf course, with an entirely separate clubhouse and staff, is the slightly older **The Reef Course** ⚘⚘, Royal Palm Way, at Our Lucaya (© **242/373-1333**). Designed by Robert Trent Jones, Jr. (who called it "a bit like a Scottish course but a lot warmer"), the course boasts 6,920 yards of links-style playing grounds. It features a wide-open layout without rows of trees to separate its fairways and lots of water traps—you'll find water on 13 of the 18 holes and various types of long grass swaying in the trade winds. Play requires patience and precise shot-making to avoid the numerous lakes.

At either of the above-mentioned golf courses, guests at either the Westin or Sheraton hotels, with which the courses are associated, pay between $90 and $140 (£48–£74), depending on the season, for 18 holes. Nonguests are charged between $110 and $160 (£58–£85) for 18 holes. Rates include use of an electric-powered golf cart.

HORSEBACK RIDING

Pinetree Stables, North Beachway Drive, Freeport (© **242/373-3600** or 305/433-4809; www.pinetree-stables.com), are the best and—with a boarded inventory of more than 50 horses—biggest riding stables in The Bahamas, superior to rivals on New Providence Island (Nassau). Pinetree offers trail rides to the beach Tuesday through Sunday year-round at 9 and 11:30am. The cost is $75 (£40) per person for a

Finds **The Ultimate in Relaxation**

The ideal place to relieve the stresses of everyday life can be found at the **Westin & Sheraton at Our Lucaya's Senses Spa** (p. 153). The spa boasts an exercise facility with health checks, personal trainers, and yoga classes. A cafe serves fresh natural food and elixirs. During one of their signature treatments, the Total Senses Massage, two massage therapists work in sync to relieve your tension. Throughout the Salt Glo body polish treatment, a therapist buffs away dead skin cells and polishes your body with natural elements from The Bahamas. Note that residents of either the Westin or the Sheraton can use the health and exercise facilities without charge, but spa, health, massage, and beauty treatments must be scheduled in advance and require payment of additional fees.

trail ride lasting 2 hours. No children under 8 are allowed. As a means of protecting the horses, the weight limit for riders is 200 pounds.

SEA KAYAKING
If you'd like to explore the waters off the island's north shore, call **Grand Bahama Nature Tours** (© 866/440-4542 or 242/373-2485; www.grandbahamanaturetours. com), who'll take you on kayak excursions through the mangroves, where you can see wildlife as you paddle along. The cost is $79 (£42) per person (children 11 and under pay half-price), with lunch included. Double kayaks are used on these jaunts, and children must be at least 3 years of age. For the same price, you can take a 30-minute trip by kayak to an offshore island, with 1½ hours of snorkeling included along with lunch. Call ahead for reservations for either of these tours. A van will pick you up at your hotel between 9am and 10am and deliver you back at the end of the tour, usually sometime between 3 and 4pm. A popular variation on this tour, which operates during the same hours and at the same prices, includes more time devoted to snorkeling above a series of shallow offshore reefs and slightly less time allocated to kayaking.

SNORKELING & SCUBA DIVING
Serious divers are attracted to such Grand Bahama sites as the Wall, the Caves (one of the most interesting of which is Ben's Cavern), Theo's Wreck, and Treasure Reef. **Theo's Wreck** 𝄞𝄞 is the most evocative site; it was a freighter that was deliberately sunk off Freeport to attract marine life. Today it teems with everything from horse-eyed jacks to moray eels. Other top locales include Spit City, Ben Blue Hole, Pygmy Caves, Gold Rock, Silver Point Reef, and the Rose Garden.

　　Underwater Explorers Society (UNEXSO) 𝄞𝄞𝄞 (© 800/992-DIVE or 242/373-1250; www.unexso.com), one of the premier dive outfitters in The Bahamas and the Caribbean, offers seven dive trips daily, including reef trips, shark dives, wreck dives, and night dives. Divers can even dive with dolphins in the open ocean here—a rare experience offered by very few facilities in the world (see "The Dolphin Experience," above).

　　A popular 3-hour learn-to-dive course, the "Mini-B Pool and Reef Adventure," is offered daily. Over UNEXSO's 30-year history, more than 50,000 people have successfully completed either this course or its similar predecessors. For $85 (£45), students learn the basics in UNEXSO's training pools and dive the beautiful shallow reef with their instructor.

A nearby competitor, **Reef Tours** (© **242/373-5880**; www.bahamasvacation guide.com/reeftours), offers well-recommended snorkeling tours. Lasting just under 2 hours each, they depart from Port Lucaya three times a day. Tours are priced at $35 (£19) each for adults and at $18 (£9.55) for children aged 6 to 12, with all equipment included. A variation on that program is a 3-hour "sail and snorkel tour." Departing daily at 9:30am and 1:30pm, it's priced at $45 (£24) for adults and at $25 (£13) for children aged 6 to 12.

TENNIS

The island's best tennis facilities are part of the **Ace Tennis Center** at the Westin & Sheraton at Our Lucaya resorts, Royal Palm Way (© **242/373-1333**), where four separate tennis courts feature different playing surfaces. They include a grass court that's often favored by players from the U.K. (which rents for $100/£53 an hour), a clay surface (which rents for $50/£27 an hour), an "Ace Rebound" surface made from Nike rubber that's equivalent to the norm at the Australian Open (renting for $35/£19 an hour), and a hard decoturf (renting for $25/£13 an hour) that's similar to what's used at the U.S. Open. Advance reservations are necessary, and there is no discount of any kind for residents of the Westin & Sheraton at Our Lucaya. A resident pro on-site offers individual 1-hour tennis lessons for $90 (£48) each, and group tennis lessons for $50 (£27) per person.

WATERSPORTS IN GENERAL

Ocean Motion Water Sports Ltd., Sea Horse Lane, Lucaya Beach (© **242/ 374-2425**; www.oceanmotionbahamas.com), is one of the largest watersports companies on Grand Bahama. It offers a wide variety of activities daily from 9am to 5pm, weather permitting, including snorkeling, parasailing, Hobie Cats, banana boats, water-skiing, jet skis, windsurfing, and other activities. Parasailing, for example, costs $60 (£32) per person for 5 to 7 minutes in the air. Snorkeling trips cost $35 (£19; $18/£9.55 for kids under 12) for 1½ hours; water-skiing, $40 (£21) per 3.2km (2-mile) pull, $60 (£32) for a 30-minute lesson; Hobie Cats, $50 (£27) for the 4.2m (14 ft.), $75 (£40) for the 4.8m (16-ft.), $20 (£11) for a lesson; windsurfing, $30 (£16) per hour, $100 (£53) for a 2-hour lesson; kayaking, $20 (£11) for a single kayak, $25 (£13) for a double; water trampoline, $20 (£11) full day, $10 (£5.30) half-day; and banana boating, $15 (£7.95) per person for a 3.2km (2-mile) ride along a white-sandy beach. Call for reservations, especially for windsurfing.

Lucaya Watersports, Taíno Beach (© **242/373-6375**), also offers options for fun in the surf, including WaveRunners rented at $65 (£34) per 30 minutes and double kayaks costing $25 (£13) per hour for two passengers. The outfitter also offers double paddle boats, holding four people, for $25 (£13) per hour. The sunset cruises—a 2-hour sailboat ride offered every Wednesday between 5 and 7pm—are especially popular and cost $45 (£24) per person.

6 Seeing the Sights

Several informative tours of Grand Bahama Island are offered. One reliable company is **H. Forbes Charter Services Ltd.,** the Mall at West Sunrise Highway, Freeport (© **242/ 352-9311**; www.forbescharter.com). From headquarters in the International Bazaar, this company offers half- and full-day bus tours. The most popular option is the half-day Super Combination Tour, priced at $35 (£19) per adult and $25 (£13) per child age 5 to 12. It includes drive-through tours of residential areas and the island's commercial center, stops at the island's deep-water harbor, shopping, and a visit to a wholesale liquor store. Departures are Monday through Saturday at 9am and 1pm; the tour lasts 3½ hours. Full-day tours, conducted whenever business warrants, last from 9am to 3:30pm. In addition to everything included in the half-day tours, they bring participants in a bus or van, with guided commentary, all the way to The Caves, near Grand Bahama Island's easternmost tip, for a price of $50 (£27) per adult, $35 (£19) per child.

See also "Beaches, Watersports & Other Outdoor Pursuits," above, for details on UNEXSO's Dolphin Experience, and "Shopping," below, for coverage of the International Bazaar and the Port Lucaya Marketplace.

Lucayan National Park   This 16-hectare (40-acre) park is filled with mangrove, pine, and palm trees. It also contains one of the loveliest, most secluded beaches on Grand Bahama, a long, wide, dune-covered stretch of sandy beach reached by following a wooden path winding through the trees. Bring your snorkeling gear so you can glimpse the colorful creatures living beneath the turquoise waters of a coral reef offshore. As you wander through the park, you'll cross Gold Rock Creek, fed by a spring from what is said to be the world's largest underground freshwater cavern system. There are 36,000 entrances to the caves—some only a few feet deep. Two of the caves can be seen because they were exposed when a portion of ground collapsed. The pools in the caves are composed of 2m (6½ ft.) of fresh water atop a heavier layer of salt water. Spiral wooden steps have been built down to the pools.

The freshwater springs once lured native Lucayans, those Arawak-connected tribes who lived on the island and depended on fishing for their livelihood. They would come inland to get fresh water for their habitats on the beach. Lucayan bones and artifacts, such as pottery, have been found in the caves, as well as on the beaches.

Settlers Way, eastern end of East Sunrise Hwy. © 242/352-5438. Admission $3 (£1.60); tickets available only at the Rand Nature Centre (see below). Daily 9am–5pm. Drive east along Midshipman Rd., passing Sharp Rock Point and Gold Rock.

Rand Nature Centre   This 40-hectare (99-acre) pineland sanctuary, located 3km (2 miles) east of the center of Freeport, is the regional headquarters of The Bahamas National Trust, a nonprofit conservation organization. Nature trails highlight native flora and "bush medicine," and provide opportunities for bird-watching. As you stroll,

---

Finds **A Sudsy Look at Grand Bahama**

You don't think of Freeport as brewery country, but the island is known for its Hammerhead Ale, a favorite of connoisseurs. The **Grand Bahama Brewing Co.,** Logwood Road, Freeport (© **242/351-5191**), a 10-minute drive northwest of Port Lucaya, near the airport, offers loosely scheduled 25-minute tours of its brewing facilities every Monday to Friday beginning at 10am, with the absolute last departure of the day at 4:40pm. The enterprise manufactures beer under two separate labels, Hammerhead and Lucayan, ranging from light lagers to stouts. Tours cost $5 (£2.65), but the fee is credited to any lager or ale purchases you might make.

keep your eyes peeled for the lush blooms of tropical orchids or the brilliant flash of green and red feathers in the trees—wild birds abound at the park. You can join a bird-watching tour on the first Saturday of every month at 8am. Other features of the nature center include native animal displays, an education center, and a gift shop selling nature books and souvenirs.

E. Settlers Way. ✆ 242/352-5438. Admission $5 (£2.65) adults, $3 (£1.60) children 5–12, free for children under 5. Mon–Fri 9am–5pm.

7 Shopping

Shopping hours in Freeport/Lucaya are generally Monday to Saturday 9am to 6pm. However, in the International Bazaar, hours vary widely, with shops usually closing a bit earlier. Most places are open Monday through Saturday. Some begin business daily at 9:30am; others don't open until 10am, and closing time ranges from 5:30 to 6pm.

PORT LUCAYA MARKETPLACE

Port Lucaya and its Marketplace supplanted the International Bazaar (see below) in the mid-1990s, when it became clear that the future of merchandising on Grand Bahama Island had moved. Today Port Lucaya Marketplace on Seahorse Road rocks and rolls with a spankingly well-maintained physical plant that's set within a shopping, dining, and marina complex on 2.4 hectares (6 acres) of low-lying, seafronting land. Regular bouts of free entertainment, such as steel-drum bands and strolling musicians, as well as recorded music that plays throughout the evening hours, add to a festival atmosphere.

The complex emulates the 19th-century clapboard-sided construction style of the Old Bahamas, all within a short walk of the most cutting-edge and desirable hotel accommodations on Grand Bahama Island, including the Westin & Sheraton at Our Lucaya. It's also within a minute's walk of the island's only casino, the Isle of Capri. The development rose on the site of a former Bahamian straw market. Today, in addition to dozens of restaurants and upscale shops, the Market incorporates rows of brightly painted clapboard-sided huts out of which local merchants sell handicrafts and souvenirs.

The waterfront location is a distinct advantage. Lots of the business that fuels this place derives from the expensive yachts and motor craft that tie up at the marina here. Most of those watercraft are owned by residents of nearby Florida. You might get the sense that many of them just arrived from the U.S. mainland, disgorging their passengers out onto the docks that immediately flank the Marketplace.

Androsia   This is the Port Lucaya outlet of the famous house that produces handmade fabrics on Andros Island. Designs and colors capture the spirit of The Bahamas. The store sells quality, 100%-cotton resort wear, including simple skirts, tops, jackets, and shorts for women, and it also offers a colorful line of children's wear. Port Lucaya Marketplace. ✆ 242/373-8387.

Animale   Trendy fashionistas, who know a lot about this sort of thing, would define this as a hot boutique with the kind of clingy sophisticated tropical fashion that makes any reasonably shaped woman look good. Come here for long cotton dresses that make the female form look more-than-usually provocative, and the kind of fashion accessories—oversize straw hats, chunky necklaces, animal-print scarves—that emphasize the feline, the *animale,* and perhaps, the seductress. In the Port Lucaya Marketplace. ✆ 242/374-2066.

Bandolera The staff can be rather haughty here, but despite its drawbacks, the store carries a collection of chic women's clothing that's many cuts above the T-shirts and tank tops that are the norm for many of its competitors. Port Lucaya Marketplace. ℂ 242/373-7691.

Colombian Emeralds International This branch of the world's foremost emerald jeweler offers a wide array of precious gemstone jewelry and one of the island's best watch collections. Careful shoppers will find significant savings over U.S. prices. The outlet offers certified appraisals and free 90-day insurance. Port Lucaya Marketplace. ℂ 242/373-8400.

Corporate Casual Boutique Positioned close to Giovanni's Restaurant, this women's clothing store is owned and operated by a sophisticated Bahamian press and public relations agent (Ms. Earnestine Moxyz) who's deeply familiar with dressing for success. Well acquainted with the corporate climates of Nassau, London, and New York, she's made it a point to inventory the kinds of clothing that a female executive would need on her climb up the corporate ladder. All of this is done with flair and an undeniable sense of style. Popular colors, at least during the lifetime of this edition, included hot pink, white, aquamarine, and creative combinations of black and gold. Sizes on hand (they include sizes 2–24) could, at least in theory, dress virtually anyone. Port Lucaya, Building 9. ℂ 242/373-5626. There's another, even larger, branch of this enterprise in downtown Freeport, at #2 Millennium Mall on West Atlantic Dr. ℂ 242/351-5620.

Flovin Gallery II This branch of the art gallery located in the International Bazaar sells a collection of oil paintings (both Bahamian and international), along with lithographs and posters. In its limited field, it's the best in the business. It also features a number of gift items, such as handmade Bahamian dolls, decorated corals, and Christmas ornaments. Port Lucaya Marketplace. ℂ 242/373-8388.

Les Parisiennes This outlet offers a wide range of fine jewelry and watches. It also sells crystal, Versace wear, and perfumes, including the latest from Paris. Port Lucaya Marketplace. ℂ 242/373-2974.

UNEXSO Dive Shop This premier dive shop of The Bahamas sells everything related to the water—swimsuits, wetsuits, underwater cameras, video equipment, shades, hats, souvenirs, and state-of-the-art divers' equipment. Port Lucaya Marketplace. ℂ 800/992-3483 or 242/373-1244. www.unexso.com.

THE INTERNATIONAL BAZAAR

The older and less glamorous of Grand Bahama Island's two main shopping venues, the International Bazaar has steadily declined since the collapse of the megaresort Crowne Plaza Hotel, immediately next door. Originally conceived as a warren of alleyways loaded with upscale, tax-free boutiques, and still plugging away valiantly at its location at East Mall Drive and East Sunrise Highway, it encompasses 4 hectares (10 acres) in the heart of Freeport. Frankly, today it's a pale shadow of what it was during its peak in the mid-1980s, when it boasted 130 purveyors of luxury goods, when the Marketplace at Port Lucaya was still a dream, and when busloads of cruise ship passengers would be unloaded in front of its gates at regular intervals. Today it's a bit tarnished and gives off a sense of dusty redolence in the streaming sunlight, with many shops permanently closed and with cracks in its masonry. Its aggressively touted role as an "international" venue seems a bit theme-driven and tired. Even worse, its rising competitor, the Port Lucaya Marketplace, is looking better every day.

Buses at the entrance of the complex aren't numbered, but those marked INTERNA-
TIONAL BAZAAR will take you right to the gateway at the Torii Gate on West Sunrise
Highway. The fare is $1 (55p). Visitors walk through this much-photographed gate,
a Japanese symbol of welcome, into a miniature World's Fair setting (think of it as a
kitschy and somewhat run-down version of Epcot). The bazaar blends architecture
and cultures from some 25 countries, each re-created with cobblestones, narrow alleys,
and a layout that evokes a theme-driven, somewhat dusty casbah in North Africa. In
the approximately 34 shops that remain in business today, you might find something
that is both unique and a bargain. You'll see African handicrafts, Chinese jade, British
china, Swiss watches, Irish linens, and Colombian emeralds. Many of the enterprises
represented here also maintain branches within the Port Lucaya Marketplace. Various
sections evoke the architecture of the Ginza in Tokyo, with merchandise—electronic
goods, art objects, and luxury products—from Asia. Other subdivisions evoke the Left
Bank of Paris, various regions of India and Africa, Latin America, and Spain.

Some merchants claim their prices are 40% less than comparable costs in the
United States, but don't count on that. If you're contemplating a big purchase, it's best
to compare prices before you leave home. Most of the merchants can ship your purchases back home at relatively reasonable rates.

A **straw market** next door to the International Bazaar contains items with a special
Bahamian touch—colorful baskets, hats, handbags, and place mats, and an endless
array of T-shirts—some of which make worthwhile gifts or souvenirs from your trip.
(Be aware that some items sold here are actually made in Asia, and expect goodly
amounts of the tacky and tasteless as well.)

Here's a description of the best shops that remain in the bazaar.

ART
Flovin Gallery   This gallery sells original Bahamian and international art, frames,
lithographs, posters, and Bahamian-made Christmas ornaments and decorated coral.
It also offers handmade Bahamian dolls, coral jewelry, and other gift items. Another
branch is at the Port Lucaya Marketplace (see above). In the Arcade section of the International Bazaar. © 242/352-7564.

FASHION
Cleo's Boutique   This shop offers everything from eveningwear to lingerie. A warm
and inviting destination, Cleo's prides itself on capturing the Caribbean woman in all
of her moods. You can also find a wide array of costume jewelry beginning at $25 per
piece. International Bazaar. © 242/352-3340.

Paris in The Bahamas   This shop contains the biggest selection of luxury goods
under one roof in the International Bazaar. The staff wears couture black dresses like
you might expect in Paris, and everywhere there's a sense of French glamour and conspicuous consumption. You can find both Gucci and Versace leather goods for men
and women; crystal from Lalique, Baccarat, Daum, and Kosta Boda; and a huge collection of cosmetics and perfumes. International Bazaar. © 242/352-5380.

Unusual Centre   Where else can you get an array of items made of walrus skin or
peacock feathers? There's another branch at the Port Lucaya Marketplace (© 242/373-
7333). International Bazaar. © 242/352-3994.

PERFUMES & FRAGRANCES

The Perfume Factory Fragrance of The Bahamas   This is the top fragrance producer in The Bahamas. The shop is housed in a re-creation of an 1800s mansion, in which visitors are invited to hear a 5-minute commentary and to see the mixing of fragrant oils. There's even a "mixology" department where you can create your own fragrance from a selection of oils. The shop's well-known products include Island Promises, Goombay, Paradise, and Pink Pearl (with conch pearls in the bottle). The shop also sells Guanahani, created to commemorate the 500th anniversary of Columbus's first landfall, and Sand, the leading Bahamian-made men's fragrance. At the rear of the International Bazaar. © 242/352-9391. www.perfumefactory.com.

8 Grand Bahama After Dark

Many resort hotels stage their own entertainment at night, and these shows are open to the general public.

ROLLING THE DICE

At press time, Grand Bahama maintained only one casino, the **Isle of Capri,** at Our Lucaya. Set within its own free-standing building on the grounds of the Westin & Sheraton at Our Lucaya, this is the big draw for anyone looking to gamble on Grand Bahama Island. Outfitted in a neutrally modern, not-particularly ostentatious design, it contains a crescent-shaped bar, a restaurant, and games that include baccarat, Caribbean stud poker, blackjack, roulette, and aisles loaded with some 400 slot machines. It's open daily from 10am to 2am or later, and entrance is free. The Westin & Sheraton at Our Lucaya resorts, Royal Palm Way. © 242/373-1333.

THE CLUB & BAR SCENE

Located in the center of the **Port Lucaya Marketplace** waterfront restaurant and shopping complex, **Count Basie Square** contains a vine-covered bandstand where the best live music on the island is performed several nights a week, usually beginning around 7:30 or 8pm. And it's free! The square honors the "Count," who used to have a grand home on Grand Bahama. Steel bands, small Junkanoo groups, and even gospel singers from a local church are likely to be heard performing here, their voices or music wafting across the marina and the nearby boardwalk and wharves. You can sip a beer or a tropical rum concoction at one of the bars in the complex. (See "Where to Dine," earlier in this chapter, for details on a few of these, including **Fatman's Nephew** and **Shenanigan's Irish Pub.**)

Finds **Bahamian Theater**

Instead of one of those Las Vegas leggy showgirl revues, you can call the 450-seat **Regency Theater,** West Sunrise Highway (© 242/352-5533), and ask what performance is scheduled. This is the home of two nonprofit companies, The Freeport Players' Guild and Grand Bahama Players. The season runs from September to June, and you are likely to see reprises of such Broadway and West End (London) blockbusters as *Mamma Mia!,* as well as contemporary works by Bahamian and Caribbean playwrights. Some really intriguing shows are likely to be staged every year by both groups, which are equally talented. Tickets cost from $10 to $20 (£5.30–£11).

Club Amnesia   This is one of the most popular discos and pickup joints on Grand Bahama Island, a local spot that seems a world away from the somewhat sanitized version of nightlife at the island's tourist hotels. Positioned across the street from the Best Western Castaways Hotel, it features an interior outfitted with big mirrors, strobe lights, and Junkanoo colors that are psychedelic. Recorded music grooves and grinds, and live bands are often imported either from the mainland of Florida or from nearby Caribbean islands. Crowds range in age from 18 to 35, and the cover charge, depending on who's playing that night, costs from $10 to $20 (£5.30–£11) per person (concerts cost up to $50/£27 per ticket). Open nights vary with the season, but it's a good bet that the place is operating Thursday to Saturday from 8:30pm till around 2am. East Mall Dr. ⓒ 242/351-2582.

Margaritavilla Sand Bar   Arguably the hottest bar on island is this lively "jump-up" place opening onto an isolated stretch of Mather Town Beach, about a 15-minute drive southeast of Lucaya. It's really a one-room sand-floor shack, but a lot of fun. Before the opening of this bar, this part of Grand Bahama used to be relatively sleepy—no more. A weekly bonfire cookout is staged Tuesdays from 6:30 to 9:30pm, with fish or steak on the grill along with a DJ. Main courses cost $15 (£7.95) and up if you'd like to stick around to eat. The place rocks on Wednesday night with younger Bahamians, although Sunday is for an older crowd that prefers sing-alongs. The bar swings open at 11am. As for closing times, the owner Jinx Knowles says it "might be 7 at night if it's quiet or 7 in the morning if it's jumpin'." Millionaire's Row, Mather Town Beach. ⓒ 242/373-4525.

Prop Club   Previously recommended in "Where to Dine," this sports bar and dance club flourishes as a singles bar that rocks at high intensity, fueled by high-octane cocktails. A lot of things seem to happen here, including occasional bouts of karaoke, cultural showcasing of emerging Bahamian and Caribbean bands, and both Junkanoo and retro-disco revival nights, depending on the season. You can also expect a "get down with the DJ" night on Sundays and game nights on slow Mondays. The DJ arrives at 10pm every night. The Westin & Sheraton at Our Lucaya resorts, Royal Palm Way. ⓒ 242/373-1333.

9 A Side Trip to West End

If you crave a refreshing escape from the plush hotels and casinos of Freeport/Lucaya, head to West End, 45km (28 miles) from Freeport. At this old fishing village, and along the scrub-flanked coastal road that leads to it, you'll get glimpses of how things used to be before package-tour groups began descending on Grand Bahama.

To reach West End, you head north along Queen's Highway, going through Eight Mile Rock, to the northernmost point of the island.

A lot of the old village buildings had become seriously dilapidated even before the destructive hurricanes of 2004 and 2005, but those that remain hint at long-ago legends and charm. Old-timers remember when rum boats were busy and the docks buzzed with activity day and night. This was from about 1920 to 1933, when Prohibition rather unsuccessfully held the United States in its grip. West End was (and is) so close to the U.S. mainland that rumrunning became a lucrative business, with booze flowing out of West End into Florida at night. Al Capone was reputed to have been a frequent visitor.

Villages along the way to West End have colorful names, such as **Hawksbill Creek.** For a glimpse of local life, try to visit the fish market along the harbor here. You'll pass some thriving harbor areas, too, but the vessels you'll see will be oil tankers, not rum-runners. Don't expect too much in terms of historic buildings en route.

Eight Mile Rock is a hamlet of mostly ramshackle houses that stretches along both sides of the road. At **West End,** you come to an abrupt stop. By far the most compelling developments here are associated with Old Bahama Bay (see separate write-up in "Where to Stay"), a good spot for a meal, a drink, and a look at what might one day become one of the most important real estate developments in The Bahamas.

6

Bimini, the Berry Islands & Andros

In this chapter, we begin a journey through the Out Islands—a very different place from the major tourist developments of Nassau, Cable Beach, Paradise Island, and Freeport/Lucaya.

Bimini, the Berry Islands, and Andros are each unique. Bimini is famous and overrun with tourists, particularly in summer, but visitors will have the Berry Islands practically to themselves. These two island chains to the north and west of Nassau could be called the "westerly islands" because they, along with Grand Bahama, lie at the northwestern fringe of The Bahamas. They are the closest islands to the Florida coastline.

In contrast, much larger Andros is located southwest of Nassau. In many ways, Andros is the most fascinating part of The Bahamas. The story goes that mysterious creatures once inhabited this series of islands laced with creeks and dense forests.

Each of the three island chains attracts a different type of visitor. **Bimini,** just 81km (50 miles) off the east coast of Florida (and the setting for Hemingway's *Islands in the Stream*), lures the big-game fisher, the yachter from Miami, and even the drug dealer from south Florida. (The proximity to the Florida mainland helps make drug smuggling big business here.) Bimini is home to world-famous sportfishing, excellent yachting and cruising, and some good scuba diving. Anglers will find seas swarming with tuna, dolphinfish, amberjack, white and blue marlin,

swordfish, barracuda, and shark, along with many other varieties. Bonefish are also plentiful around the flats off the coast of Alice Town, the capital, but the blue marlin is the prize. (Bahamians think so highly of this fish that they even put it on their $100 bill.) Scuba divers can see black coral trees over the Bimini Wall and reefs off Victory Cay.

The **Berry Islands** might attract the weary Bill Gates or Steve Forbes types. It also draws fishermen, but this string of islands, which has only 700 residents, is mainly for escapists—*rich* escapists. The islands' very limited accommodations (some of which used to be private clubs) lie near the Tongue of the Ocean, home of the big-game fish.

Andros, the largest island in the nation, is mainly uninhabited. If The Bahamas still has an unexplored wilderness, this is it. The island's forest and mangrove swamps are home to a wide variety of birds and animals, including the nonpoisonous Bahamian boa constrictor and the 2m-long (6½-ft.) iguana. The Bahamian national bird, the West Indian flamingo, can also be spotted during migration in late spring and summer. The waters off Andros are home to a wondrous barrier reef, the third largest in the world and a diver's dream. The reef plunges 167km (104 miles) to a narrow drop-off known as the Tongue of the Ocean. Andros's mysterious blue holes, another diver's delight, are formed when subterranean caves fill with seawater, causing the ceiling to collapse and expose clear, deep pools. Few come here anymore looking for Sir Henry Morgan's pirate treasure, said to be buried in one of the caves off Morgan's Bluff on the north tip of the island. But Andros does attract anglers, mostly because it is known for its world-class fishing for marlin and the bluefin tuna, and its bonefishing is perhaps the best in the world.

1 Bimini ⟨★

Bimini is still known as the big-game fishing capital of the world, and fishermen come here throughout the year to fish in flats, on the reefs, and in the streams. Ernest Hemingway came to write and fish. Here he wrote much of *To Have and Have Not,* and his novel *Islands in the Stream* put Bimini on the map. Regrettably, fishing isn't what it used to be in Papa's day, and such species as marlin, swordfish, and tuna have been dangerously overfished by commercial longline boats.

Located 81km (50 miles) east of Miami, Bimini consists of a number of islands, islets, and cays, including North and South Bimini, the main tourist areas. You'll most often encounter the word "Bimini," but it might be more proper to say "The Biminis," since North Bimini and South Bimini are two distinct islands, separated by a narrow ocean passage. Ferry-service shuttles between the two. The major development is on North Bimini, mostly in Alice Town. The western side of North Bimini is a long stretch of lovely beachfront.

Off North Bimini, in 9m (30 ft.) of water, are some large hewn-stone formations that some people say came from the lost continent of Atlantis. Divers find the reefs laced with conch, lobster, coral, and many tropical fish.

Bimini's location off the Florida coastline is at a point where the Gulf Stream meets the Bahama Banks. This fact has made Bimini a favorite cruising ground for America's yachting set, who follow the channel between North and South Bimini into a spacious, sheltered harbor, where they can stock up on food, drink, fuel, and supplies at well-equipped marinas. From here they can set off to cruise the cays that begin south of South Bimini. Each has its own special appeal, beginning with Turtle Rocks and stretching to South Cat Cay (the latter of which is uninhabited). Along the way, you'll pass Holm Cay, Gun Cay, and North Cat Cay.

Hook-shaped North Bimini is 12km (7½ miles) long, and combined with South Bimini, it makes up a landmass of only 23 sq. km (9 sq. miles). That's why Alice Town looks so crowded. Another reason is that a large part of Bimini is privately owned; despite pressure from the Bahamian government, the landholders have not sold their acreage, and Bimini can't "spread out" until they do. At Alice Town, the land is so narrow that you can walk "from sea to shining sea" in just a short time. Most of Bimini's population of some 1,600 people lives in Alice Town; other hamlets include Bailey Town and Porgy Bay.

Although winter is usually high season in The Bahamas, visitors flock to Bimini's calmer summer waters, which are better for fishing. Winter, especially from mid-December to mid-March, is quieter, and Bimini has never tried to develop a resort structure that would attract more winter visitors. If you go to Bimini, you'll hear a lot of people mention **Cat Cay** (not to be confused with Cat Island, in the Southern Bahamas). You can stay overnight at Cat Cay's marina, which lies 13km (8 miles) off South Bimini. Transient slips are available to mariners. The island is the domain of **Cat Cay Yacht Club** (© **242/347-3565;** www.catcayclub.com), whose initiation fee is a cool $25,000. This privately owned island—attracting titans of industry and famous families—is for the exclusive use of Cat Cay Club members and their guests. At their leisure, they can enjoy the golf course, tennis, a large marina, white-sand beaches, and club facilities such as restaurants and bars. Many wealthy Americans have homes on the island, which has a private airstrip.

GETTING THERE

Note: A passport or an original birth certificate or a voter's registration card with a government-issued picture ID is required of *everyone* for entry to Bimini (bring your passport, to be on the safe side), and an outbound (return) ticket also must be presented to Bahamian Customs before you will be allowed entry. Starting January 1, 2008, a passport will be required for all U.S. citizens. A departure tax is included in all airfares.

BY PLANE   The island's only airstrip is at the southern tip of South Bimini, a time-consuming transfer and ferryboat ride away from Alice Town on North Bimini, site of most of the archipelago's hotels and yacht facilities.

The best way to avoid this transfer is to fly for 20 to 30 minutes via the small **Chalk's Ocean Airways** (© **877/924-2557;** www.flychalks.com). The airline has a fleet of 17-passenger amphibious aircraft that depart from the runway at Ft. Lauderdale/Hollywood International Airport and land in the waters near Alice Town. The baggage allowance per passenger is 30 pounds; if you're carrying heavy travel or fishing gear, you'll be hit with overweight charges. *Note:* Chalk's doesn't allow any hand luggage on board—every piece of your luggage must be weighed and checked in.

Also, **Island Air** (© **800/444-9904** or 954/359-9942; www.islandaircharters.com) flies four times a week from Fort Lauderdale to South Bimini. Finally, **Western Air** (© **242/347-4100;** www.westernairbahamas.com) wings in from Nassau's domestic air terminal to South Bimini.

BY BOAT In the old days, the way to get from Nassau to Bimini was by a slow-moving boat; you can still do it, and it'll take you 12 hours. You can go by sea on the MV *Bimini Mack,* which leaves from Potter's Cay Dock in Nassau and stops at Cat Cay and Bimini. The vessel leaves Nassau Thursdays at 2pm. For details about departure, call the dock master at **Potter's Cay Dock** in Nassau (© **242/393-1064**).

GETTING AROUND

If you've taken our advice and traveled lightly to Bimini, you can walk to your hotel from the point where the seaplanes land in Alice Town. If not, a small minibus will transport you for $2 (£1.05) per person. If you arrive at the small airport on South Bimini, you'll need to pay for a $5 (£2.65) taxi and ferry ride to Alice Town.

You won't need a car on Bimini—and in fact, you won't find a car-rental agency here. Most people walk to where they want to go (though your hotel may be able to arrange a minibus tour or rent you a bike or golf cart). The walk runs up and down King's Highway, which has no sidewalks. It's so narrow that two automobiles have a tough time squeezing by. Be careful walking along this highway, especially at night, when drivers might not see you.

This highway, lined with low-rise buildings, splits Alice Town on North Bimini. If you're the beachcombing type, stick to the side bordering the Gulf Stream. It's here that you'll find the best beaches. The harborside contains a handful of inns (most of which are reviewed below), along with marinas and docks where supplies are unloaded. You'll see many Floridians arriving on yachts.

FAST FACTS: Bimini

Banks **The Royal Bank of Canada** has a branch office in Alice Town (© **242/347-3031**) with an **ATM**, open Monday to Thursday 9:30am to 3pm, Friday 9:30am to 4:30pm.

Clothing If you're going to Bimini in the winter months, take along a windbreaker for those occasional chilly nights.

Customs & Immigration The Chalk's flight from Miami stops right near the Alice Town office of **Customs and Immigration** (© **242/347-3100** for Customs; **242/347-3446** for Immigration) for The Bahamas. There's only one Immigration officer, plus another Customs official.

In Miami you will have been handed a Bahamian Immigration Card to fill out, and you must carry a passport.

Drugs The rumrunners of the Prohibition era have now given way to those smuggling illegal drugs into the United States from The Bahamas. Because of its proximity to the U.S. mainland, Bimini, as is no secret to anyone, is now a major drop-off point for drugs, many on the way from Colombia. If not inter-cepted by the U.S. Coast Guard, these drugs find their way to Florida and even-tually to the rest of the United States.

Buying and/or selling illegal drugs, such as cocaine and marijuana, is an extremely risky business in The Bahamas. You may be approached by dealers on Bimini, some of whom are actually undercover agents. If caught with illegal drugs, you face immediate imprisonment.

Emergencies To call the police or report a fire, dial © **919**.

Medical Care Nurses, a doctor, and a dentist are on the island, as is the **North Bimini Medical Clinic** (© **242/347-2210**). However, for a serious medical emer-gency, patients are usually airlifted to either Miami or Nassau. Helicopters can land in the well-lit baseball field on North Bimini.

Visitor Information There's a branch of **The Bahamas Ministry of Tourism** in Bimini, located in the Government Building, Queens Highway, Alice Town (© **242/347-3529**). It's open Monday to Friday 9am to 5pm.

WHERE TO STAY

Accommodations in Bimini are extremely limited, and it's almost impossible to get a room during one of the big fishing tournaments unless you've reserved way in advance. Inns are cozy and simple; many are family-owned and -operated (chances are, your innkeeper's name will be Brown). Furnishings are often timeworn, the paint chipped. No one puts on airs here; the dress code, even in the evening, is very simple and relaxed. From wherever you're staying in Alice Town, it's usually easy to walk to another hotel for dinner or drinks.

Bimini Big Game Resort & Marina 𝒦𝒦   The chosen "watering hole" of big-game fishermen since the 1950s, this resort is better than ever following multimillion-dol-lar renovations. Its 81-slip marina often makes it a favorite stopover with the yachting crowd from Florida's east coast. The resort's restoration has been called a rebirth, and its patrons—mainly boaters, divers, eco-adventurers, and the deep-sea and bonefish-ing elite—have remained loyal. Both the resort and marina facilities have been improved. The guest rooms and the dining and drinking facilities were completely overhauled. Accommodations are now well furnished, both the guest units in the main building and those in surrounding cottages. All rooms have patios or porches opening onto the marina and the club's swimming pool; the ground-floor cottages are more spacious than the standard bedrooms and have tiny kitchenettes and refrigera-tors. The small bathrooms are well maintained and come with shower stalls.

If you want to charcoal-broil your catch at the end of the day (hotel staff can arrange all sorts of fishing charters), you can use one of the outdoor grills. This hotel is also the best place for food and entertainment on the island (see "Where to Dine" and "Bimini After Dark," later in this chapter).

King's Hwy. (P.O. Box 699), Alice Town, Bimini, The Bahamas. © **800/737-1007** in the U.S. or 242/347-3391. Fax 242/347-3392. www.biminibiggame.com. 47 units (12 cottages, 35 rooms). Year-round $135–$185 (£72–£98) dou-ble; $175–$225 (£93–£119) cottage. Extra person $25 (£13). AE, MC, V. **Amenities:** Restaurant; 3 bars; pool; all non-smoking rooms. *In room:* A/C, TV, kitchenette (in some), minibar (in some), fridge (in some), hair dryer, no phone.

Island in the Stream

Nevil Norton Stuart, a Bahamian, came to Bimini in the late 1920s and purchased the Fountain of Youth, a Prohibition-era bar, renaming it the **Bimini Big Game Resort & Marina**. In 1940, Stuart reclaimed land in Bimini Harbor, constructed a marina, and added several cottages along with a desalination plant. Thus began the legend of one of the most highly publicized sportfishing meccas in the world.

Film stars, including Judy Garland and Sir Anthony Hopkins, among others, have lodged at the club, and Martin Luther King, Jr., visited twice. Of course, no one immortalized the island as much as Hemingway, who called it "My Island in the Stream."

Today the complex has grown to more than 50 rooms, including cottages and penthouses, and it's owned by the rum maker Bacardi International. In the 100-slip marina, you'll find enormous sportfishing boats, costing more than several million dollars, proudly standing alongside simple outboard-powered runabouts.

Bimini Blue Water Resort Ltd. 🞳 *Finds*   This is essentially a resort complex for sportfishermen, with complete dockside services and 32 modern slips—one of the finest places of its kind in The Bahamas. The main building is a white-frame waterfront Bahamian guesthouse, the Anchorage, where Michael Lerner, the noted fisherman, used to live. It's at the top of the hill, with a dining room and bar from which you can look out to the ocean (see "Where to Dine," below). The midsize bedrooms contain double beds, wood-paneled walls, white furniture, and picture-window doors that lead to private balconies. Bathrooms are small with showers.

The Marlin Cottage, although much altered, was one of Hemingway's retreats in the 1930s. He used it as a main setting in *Islands in the Stream*. It has three bedrooms, three bathrooms, a large living room, and two porches.

King's Hwy. (P.O. Box 601), Alice Town, Bimini, The Bahamas. ✆ 242/347-3166. Fax 242/347-3293. 14 units. Year-round $90 (£48) double; $190 (£101) suite; $285 (£151) cottage. MC, V. **Amenities:** Restaurant; bar; pool; babysitting. *In room:* A/C, TV, fridge, iron, no phone.

Sea Crest Hotel and Marina *Kids*   Built in 1981 and upgraded every year since, this hotel lies right on the main highway and was the first place to give the Bimini Big Game Resort & Marina some real competition. It's still not as good as that traditional leader, but the price is right. Rooms in this three-story hotel, which looks like a motel, are at their best on the third floor due to the better ocean or bay views there. Rooms don't have phones, and many are small, with rather cramped bathrooms, each with a shower stall, but they're comfortably furnished in a simple, traditional way. Accommodations open onto small balconies. Much better, larger, and more comfortable are the units lying in a new building set directly beside the marina. Since the location is right in the heart of Alice Town, you can generally walk where you want to go. The Sea Crest is a family favorite, and children under 12 stay free. There's an on-site restaurant, Captain Bob's, which is independently operated and serves good seafood. The hotel is also a favorite of the boating crowd because it offers a small 18-berth marina.

King's Hwy. (P.O. Box 654), Alice Town, Bimini, The Bahamas. © **242/347-3071.** Fax 242/347-3495. www.seacrest bimini.com. 14 units. Year-round $99–$130 (£52–£69) double; $230 (£122) 2-bedroom suite; $320 (£170) 3-bedroom suite. Extra person $15 (£7.95). MC, V. **Amenities:** Marina. *In room:* A/C, TV, no phone.

WHERE TO DINE

Anchorage Dining Room SEAFOOD/BAHAMIAN/AMERICAN   This dining room overlooks the harbor of Alice Town; you can see the ocean through picture windows. The modern, paneled room is filled with captain's chairs and Formica tables. You might begin your dinner with conch chowder and then follow with one of the tempting seafood dishes, including spiny broiled lobster or perhaps a cracked conch. They also do a good fried Bahamian chicken and a tender New York sirloin. The cooking is straightforward and reliable, and never pretends to be more than just that.

In the Blue Water Resort, King's Hwy., Alice Town. © **242/347-3166.** Main courses $14–$27 (£7.40–£14). AE, MC, V. Wed–Mon 6–10pm.

Red Lion Pub BAHAMIAN   This centrally located restaurant is far larger than its simple facade would indicate. With a relaxed, friendly atmosphere, it's one of the best places on the island to retreat to after a day of fishing and sailing. It's one of the few nonsmoking restaurants in the Out Islands. The dining room is in a large extension of the original pub and overlooks the marina in back. The well-prepared meals are local home cooking: the local fish of the day, cracked conch, barbecued ribs, baked grouper in foil, followed by either Key lime pie or banana cream pie. Portions are large and come accompanied by peas 'n' rice, so you don't need to order appetizers or even dessert unless you're ravenous.

King's Hwy., Alice Town. © **242/347-3259.** Main courses $16–$30 (£8.50–£16). No credit cards. Tues–Sun 6–10pm; pub Tues–Sun until 10:30pm.

The Tackle Box BAHAMIAN/INTERNATIONAL   Set in the annex of the Bimini Big Game Resort & Marina (p. 185), this restaurant is the one most likely to be open at the time of your visit. Expect fine views, as it's located directly adjacent to the marina with dozens of world-class fishing boats. Don't expect grand or even particularly esoteric cuisine, as the menu might remind you of what's available at a bar and grill in neighboring Florida. Lunches are simpler than dinners, with salads, simple grills, burgers, chicken fingers, soups, and stews. Lunches are leisurely; dinners are even more so, but with a wider choice of steaks, grills, lobster dishes, pastas, and fresh fish, especially wahoo, mahimahi, swordfish, and tuna. Bear in mind that the offerings here might (or might not, depending on a seemingly whimsical collection of factors) be supplemented with a slightly more expensive on-site restaurant, The Clubhouse, which lies in a building of its own a few paces away.

In the Bimini Big Game Resort & Marina, King's Hwy., Alice Town. © **242/347-3391.** Reservations recommended. Main courses lunch $4.75–$9 (£2.50–£4.75), dinner $19–$30 (£10–£16). AE, MC, V. Sun–Thurs 7am–10pm, Fri–Sat 7am–1am.

WATERSPORTS & OTHER OUTDOOR ACTIVITIES
BEACHES
The beaches on Bimini are all clearly marked and signposted from the highways.

The beach that's closest to Alice Town is **Radio Beach,** the only one on Bimini with toilets, vendors, and snack bars. It's set adjacent to the piers and wharves of Alice Town, and, consequently, it's the most popular and crowded beach on the island.

About 3km (2 miles) north of Alice Town, facing west, is **Spook Hill Beach.** Both it and its cousin, **Bimini Bay Beach,** about 4km (2½ miles) north of Alice Town, offer fewer crowds, good snorkeling, and lots of sunshine. Both are sandy bottomed and comfortable on your feet. Above all, many local residents prefer **Bimini Bay Beach,** which is wider than any other on the island.

On South Bimini, the two favorites are the west-facing **Bimini Sands Beach,** a sandy-bottomed stretch that's immediately south of the channel separating North from South Bimini; and the **Bimini Reef Club Beach,** south of the airport, where off-shore snorkeling is especially worthwhile, thanks to very clear waters.

FISHING

Ernest Hemingway made fishing here famous. But Zane Grey came this way, too, as did Howard Hughes. Richard Nixon used to fish here aboard the posh cruiser of his friend Bebe Rebozo. In the trail of Hemingway, fishermen still flock to cast lines in the Gulf Stream and the Bahama Banks.

Of course, everyone's still after the big one, and a lot of world records have been set in this area for marlin, sailfish, swordfish, wahoo, grouper, and tuna. But these fish are becoming evasive, and their dwindling numbers are edging them close to extinction. Fishing folk can spin cast for panfish and boat snapper, yellowtail, and kingfish. Many experts consider stalking bonefish, long a pursuit of baseball great Ted Williams, to be the toughest challenge in the sport.

Five charter boats are available in Bimini for big-game and little-game fishing, with some center-console boats rented for both bottom and reef angling. At least eight bonefishing guides are available, and experienced anglers who have made repeated visits to Bimini know the particular skills of each of these men who will take you for a half- or full day of "fishing in the flats." Most skiffs hold two anglers, and part of the fun in hiring a local guide is to hear his fish tales and other island lore. If a guide tells you that 16-pound bonefish have turned up, he may not be exaggerating—catches that large have really been documented.

Reef and bottom-fishing on Bimini are easier than bonefishing and can be more productive. Numerous species of snapper and grouper can be found, as well as amberjack. This is the simplest and least expensive boat fishing because you need only a local guide, a little boat, tackle, and a lot of bait. Sometimes you can negotiate to go out bottom-fishing with a Bahamian, but chances are, he'll ask you to pay for the boat fuel for his trouble. That night, back at your Bimini inn, the cook will serve you the red snapper or grouper you caught that day.

Most hotel owners will tell you to bring your own fishing gear to Bimini. A couple of small shops sell some items, but you'd better bring major equipment with you if you're really serious. Bait, of course, can be purchased locally.

Finds Ruins of the Roaring Twenties

A major attraction for both snorkelers and divers, not to mention rainbow-hued fish, is the *Sapona,* lying hard aground in 4.5m (15 ft.) of water between South Bimini and Cat Cay ever since it was blown here by a hurricane in 1929. In the heyday of the Roaring Twenties, the ship, which was built by Henry Ford, served as a private club and speakeasy. You'll have to take a boat to reach the wreck site. Spearfishermen are attracted to the ruins, looking for the giant grouper, and dive operators on Bimini include the site in their repertoire. It's shallow enough that even snorkelers can see it.

Fire Guts Hemingway's Favorite Bar

A fire in January 2006 destroyed the Ernest Hemingway Museum and the Compleat Angler Bar, Bimini's number-one tourist attraction. The early-morning blaze leveled the wood structure in Alice Town and destroyed photographs and other Papa memorabilia. Hemingway made the Compleat Angler his headquarters on and off from 1935 to 1937 when he was fishing for marlin. He penned parts of *To Have and Have Not* on the site.

At the **Bimini Big Game Resort & Marina,** King's Highway, Alice Town (℗ 242/347-3391), you can charter a 10m (34-ft.) Hatteras at $1,100 (£583) for a full day of fishing, or $600 (£318) for a half-day. Although this outfitter is your best bet, you can also pick up a list of locals whose boats are available for charter at **Bimini Blue Water Marina,** King's Highway, Alice Town (℗ 242/347-3166). Rates for bonefishing are $300 (£159) per half-day. For deep-sea fishing, charges range from $500 to $600 (£265–£318) for a half-day.

SCUBA DIVING & SNORKELING

Explore the black coral gardens and reefs here, plus wrecks, blue holes, and a mysterious stone formation on the bottom of the sea that some people claim is part of the lost continent of Atlantis (it's 457m/1,499 ft. offshore at Bimini Bay, under about 6m/20 ft. of water). Bimini waters are known for a breathtaking drop-off at the rim of the continental shelf, an underwater mountain that plunges 600m (1,968 ft.) down.

The finest and most experienced outfitter is **Bimini Undersea,** King's Highway, Alice Town (℗ 242/347-3089; www.biminiundersea.com). The people to see here are Bill and Nowdla Keefe. Scuba divers pay $59 (£31) for a one-tank dive or $99 (£52) for a two-tank dive. Snorkelers are charged $39 (£21) for a single trip, including complimentary use of mask and fins. All-inclusive dive packages are also available. For further information or reservations, the Keefes can be reached at ℗ 800/348-4644 or 305/653-5572.

You can also swim with dolphins in the wild two or three times a week, depending on demand. Most excursions take from 3 to 4 hours and cost $119 (£63) for ages 13 and up or $99 (£52) for ages 8 to 12. Swimming with dolphins has its critics and supporters. You may want to visit the Whale and Dolphins Conservation Society's website at www.wdcs.org. For more information about responsible travel in general, check out these websites: Tread Lightly (www.treadlightly.org) and the International Ecotourism Society (www.ecotourism.org).

TRACING THE FOOTSTEPS OF PONCE DE LEON & PAPA

At the southern tip of North Bimini, ramshackle **Alice Town** is all that many visitors ever see of the islands, since the major hotels are found here. You can see the whole town in an hour or two. The **Bimini Big Game Resort & Marina,** King's Highway, has some of the best duty-free liquor buys in town. If you're a souvenir collector, ask at the front office for T-shirts, sunglasses, coffee mugs, and Big Game hats.

As you're exploring the island, you may want to stop off at the **Bimini Straw Market,** located next door to the Bahamas Customs Building. You'll usually find two dozen vendors here. Strike up a conversation with some islanders, and perhaps pick up a souvenir.

Fun Fact **Myths of Bimini**

These islands have long been shrouded in myths, none more far-fetched than the one claiming that the lost continent of **Atlantis** lies off the shores of North Bimini. This legend grew because of the weirdly shaped rock formations that lie submerged in about 6m (20 ft.) of water near the shoreline. Pilots flying over North Bimini have reported what they envision as a "lost highway" under the sea. This myth continues, and many scuba divers are attracted to North Bimini to explore these rocks.

Ponce de León came to South Bimini looking for that celebrated **Fountain of Youth.** He never found it, but people still come to South Bimini in search of it. Near the end of the 19th century, a religious sect reportedly came here to "take the waters"—supposedly a bubbling fountain or spring. If you arrive on South Bimini and seem interested enough, a local guide (for a fee) will be happy to show you "the exact spot" where the Fountain of Youth once bubbled.

If you're curious, drop into the little **Bimini Museum** (© 242/347-3038) on King's Highway, a sort of grab bag of mementos left behind by visiting celebrities. The museum owns the 1964 immigration card of Martin Luther King, Jr., a domino set left by frequent visitor Adam Clayton Powell (the former congressman from New York), and Ernest Hemingway's fishing log and vintage fishing films. Other island artifacts such as rum kegs are also exhibited. The location in a two-story 1920s house is a 4-minute walk from the seaplane ramp. Charging $2 (£1.05), the museum is open Monday to Saturday 9am to 9pm, Sunday noon to 9pm. Elementary-school-age children are admitted free.

The **Queen's Highway** runs up the western side of North Bimini, and as you head north along it, you'll find it lined with beautiful beachfront. **King's Highway** runs through the town and continues north. It's bordered by houses painted gold, lime, buttercup yellow, and pink that gleam in the bright sunshine.

At some point, you may notice the ruins of Bimini's first hotel, the **Bimini Bay Rod and Gun Club,** sitting unfinished on its own beach. Built in the early 1920s, it did a flourishing business until a hurricane wiped it out later in that decade. It was never rebuilt, though developers once made a never-finished attempt.

If you want to visit **South Bimini,** you can hire a taxi for about $18 (£9.55) to see the island's limited attractions, which, at least to our knowledge, do not include Ponce de León's legendary Fountain of Youth. There's not a lot to see, but you are likely to hear tall tales worth the cab fare. You can also stop off at some lovely, uncrowded beaches.

BIMINI AFTER DARK

You can dance to a Goombay drum beat or try to find some disco music. Most people have a leisurely dinner, drink a lot in one of the local watering holes, and go back to their hotel rooms by midnight so they can get up early to continue pursuing the elusive "big one" the next morning. Every bar in Alice Town is likely to claim that it was Hemingway's favorite. He did hit quite a few of them, in fact. There's rarely a cover charge anywhere unless some special entertainment is being offered.

Moments **A Drink at the End of the World**

Everybody eventually makes his or her way to the **End of the World Bar** (no phone) on King's Highway in Alice Town. When you get here, you may think you're in the wrong place—it's just a waterfront shack with sawdust or sand on the floor and graffiti everywhere. The late New York congressman Adam Clayton Powell put this bar on the map in the 1960s. Between stints in Washington battling Congress and preaching at the Abyssinian Baptist Church in Harlem, the controversial congressman could be found sitting at a table here. While the bar doesn't attract the media attention it did in Powell's heyday, it's still a local favorite. Open daily from 9am to 3am.

Beginning at midmorning and lasting until midnight at least, the bars at the **Bimini Big Game Resort & Marina,** King's Highway, Alice Town (© **242/347-3391**), are the place to hang out. Tall fish tales of the big one that got away fill the air. **The Tackle Box** (p. 187) starts serving its famed conch pizza at noon. You can play a hand of cards here or tune in to one of the TV sets positioned for your favorite sports program; it's the best place to entertain yourself during a lazy day in Bimini. The poolside **Barefoot Bar,** open from midmorning to late afternoon, serves favorite island drinks and ice-cold beer. Off the main dining room is the **Clubhouse,** featuring live bands on occasion.

2 The Berry Islands ☀

A dangling chain of cays and islets on the eastern edge of the Great Bahama Bank, the unspoiled and serene Berry Islands begin 56km (35 miles) northwest of New Providence (Nassau), 242km (150 miles) east of Miami. This 30-island archipelago is known to sailors, fishermen, yachtspeople, Jack Nicklaus, and a Rockefeller or two, as well as to the beachcombers who love its pristine sands.

As a center of fishing, the Berry Islands are second only to Bimini. At the tip of the Tongue of the Ocean, aka TOTO, world-record-setting big-game fish are found, along with endless flats (the shallow bodies of water near the shore where bonefish congregate). In the "Berries," you can find your own tropical paradise islet and enjoy—sans wardrobe—totally isolated white-sand beaches and palm-fringed shores. Some of the best shell collecting in The Bahamas is found on the beaches of the Berry Islands and in their shallow-water flats.

The main islands are, beginning in the north, Great Stirrup Cay, Cistern Cay, Great Harbour Cay, Anderson Cay, Haines Cay, Hoffmans Cay, Bond's Cay, Sandy Cay, Whale Cay, and Chub Cay. One of the very small cays, lying north of Frazev's Hog Cay and Whale Cay, has, in our opinion, the most unappetizing name in the Bahamian archipelago: Cockroach Cay.

The largest island within the Berry Islands is **Great Harbour Cay,** which sprawls over 1,520 hectares (3,754 acres) of sand, rock, and scrub. Development here received a great deal of publicity when Douglas Fairbanks, Jr., was connected with its investors. It became a multimillion-dollar resort for jet-setters who occupied waterfront town houses and villas overlooking the golf course or marina. Cary Grant, Brigitte Bardot, and other stars have all romped on the 12km (7½ miles) of almost-solitary beachfront you can still find here.

Bond's Cay, a bird sanctuary in the south, and tiny Frazer's Hog Cay (stock is still raised here) are both privately owned. An English company used to operate a coconut and sisal plantation on Whale Cay, also near the southern tip. Sponge fishermen and their families inhabit some of the islands.

BERRY ISLANDS ESSENTIALS

GETTING THERE   Great Harbour Cay is an official point of entry for The Bahamas if you're flying from a foreign territory such as the United States.

You can get here only via charter flights from South Florida, making these some of the most inconvenient islands to reach in all The Bahamas. **Tropical Diversions** (© **954/921-9084**) flies from Fort Lauderdale to Great Harbour Cay, usually in a small twin-engine Aztec Cessna 402, and **Island Express** (© **954/359-0380**) also operates charters from Fort Lauderdale, winging in to Chub Cay Airport.

If you're contemplating the **mail-boat** sea-voyage route, the **MV *Captain Gurthdean*** leaves Potter's Cay Dock in Nassau once a week on Tuesday at 7pm, heading for the Berry Islands. Inquire at the **Potter's Cay Dock** for an up-to-the-minute report (contact the dock master at © **242/393-1064**).

FAST FACTS   The **Great Harbour Cay Medical Clinic** is located at Bullock's Harbour on Great Harbour Cay (© **242/367-8400**). The **police station** is also at Bullock's Harbour (© **242/367-8344** and 242/367-8104).

GREAT HARBOUR CAY

An estimated 700 residents live on Great Harbour Cay, making it the most populated island of the Berry chain. Its main settlement is **Bullock's Harbour,** which might be called the "capital of the Berry Islands." The cay is about 2.5km (1½ miles) wide and some 13km (8 miles) long. A grocery store and some restaurants are about all you'll find in town. Most visitors arrive to stay at the **Great Harbour Cay Yacht Club & Marina,** which for 2006 is being turned into a posh and much bigger resort. Check its status before coming here.

Great Harbour Cay lies between Grand Bahama Island and New Providence (Nassau). It's 97km (60 miles) northwest of Nassau and 242km (150 miles) east of Miami, about an hour away from Miami by plane or half a day by powerboat. Unlike most islands in The Bahamas, the island isn't flat, but contains rolling hills.

Deep-sea fishing possibilities abound here, including billfish, dolphinfish, king mackerel, and wahoo. Light-tackle bottom-fishing is also good. You can net yellowtail, snapper, barracuda, triggerfish, and plenty of grouper. Bonefishing here is among the best in the world. The Great Harbour Cay marina is an excellent facility, with some 80 slips and all the amenities. Some of Florida's fanciest yachts pull in here.

When you tire of fishing, you can relax on 13km (8 miles) of gorgeous beaches, play the 9-hole golf course designed by Joe Lee, or try your backhand on one of the four clay tennis courts.

CHUB CAY

Named after a species of fish that thrives in nearby waters, Chub Cay is well known to sportfishing enthusiasts. A self-contained hideaway with a devoted clientele, it's the southernmost of the Berry Islands, separating the mainland of South Florida from the commercial frenzy of Nassau.

Chub Cay's development began in the late 1950s as the strictly private (and rather spartan) enclave of a group of Texas-based anglers and investors. It was originally uninhabited, but over the years a staff was imported, dormitory-style housing was built, and the island's most famous man-made feature (its state-of-the-art 90-slip marina) was constructed in the 392-hectare (968-acre) island's sheltered lagoon.

Chub Cay is today a tranquil, scrub-covered sand spit with awesome amounts of marine hardware, a dozen posh private homes, the marina, and a complex of buildings devoted to the **Chub Cay Resort & Marina** (see below). Today membership in the club begins at around $2,500 (£1,325) per year and grants reduced rates for marina slip rental, boat repairs, and hotel-room and villa rental. Nonmembers, however, are welcome to use the facilities and rent rooms at the rates listed below.

A liquor store and a yachties' commissary are on the island, as well as an outlet for the sale of marine supplies and a concrete runway for landing anything up to and including a 737. Most visitors reach Chub Cay by private yacht from the Florida mainland, but if you prefer to charter your fishing craft on Chub Cay, you'll find a miniarmada of suitable craft at your disposal. **Island Express Airlines** (© **954/359-0380**) flies charter flights to Chub Cay from Fort Lauderdale. Charter flights can be arranged with the help of the Chub Cay Resort & Marina's desk staff. If you opt to fly here, travel light; no more than 40 pounds of baggage is allowed per passenger.

The water temperature around Chub Cay averages a warm 80°F to 85°F (27°C–29°C) year-round, even at relatively deep depths. There's only a small tidal change and, under normal conditions, no swell or noticeable current in offshore waters. The waters are incredibly clear, making for great snorkeling.

WHERE TO STAY & DINE

Chub Cay Resort & Marina *(Finds)*   Breezy and comfortable, these air-conditioned accommodations are the only option on all of Chub Cay. Their opening is slated for sometime in late 2007. (Although there was a former resort here, the new one is so vastly altered it could be called "new" instead of an expansion.) Get a construction update before booking here. The place prides itself on its marina, freshwater swimming pools, and many nearby sandy beaches. Throughout the resort, there's a nautical, laid-back kind of feeling and a clubby atmosphere. The decor consists of modern wicker with firm beds, plus small, well-organized bathrooms with tub/showers. The remote feeling here is a welcome relief to many guests.

There's a restaurant, the Harbour House, with its own bar, and the Hilltop Bar on the island's highest elevation. The latter offers a TV for sports broadcasts and pool tables.

Chub Cay, Berry Islands, The Bahamas (mailing address: Chub Cay Resort & Marina, P.O. CB-13746, Nassau, The Bahamas). © **877/234-CHUB** or 242/325-1490. Fax 242/322-5199. www.chubcay.com. 44 units (subject to change). Prices to be determined at the time of the club's opening; call for the latest rates and information. AE, MC, V. **Amenities:** Restaurant; 3 bars; 2 pools; 2 tennis courts; babysitting; laundry service. *In room:* A/C, TV, kitchenette (in some), hair dryer, iron (in some), beverage maker (in some), no phone.

3 Andros ★★

The largest island in The Bahamas, Andros is an excellent budget destination. One of the biggest unexplored tracts of land in the Western Hemisphere, it's still quite mysterious. Mostly flat, its 5,957 sq. km (2,323 sq. miles) are riddled with lakes and creeks, and most of the local residents—who still indulge in fire dances and go on wild boar hunts on occasion—live along the shore.

Andros is 161km (100 miles) long and 64km (40 miles) wide. Its interior consists of a dense tropical forest, really rugged bush, and mangrove country. The marshy and relatively uninhabited west coast is called the "Mud," and the east coast is paralleled for 193km (120 miles) by the third-largest underwater barrier reef in the world. The reef drops more than 167km (104 miles) into the Tongue of the Ocean, or TOTO. On the eastern shore, this "tongue" is 229km (142 miles) long and 1,000 fathoms (2.9km/ 2 miles) deep.

Lying 274km (170 miles) southeast of Miami and 48km (30 miles) west of Nassau, Andros is actually three major land areas: North Andros, Middle Andros, and South Andros. In spite of its size, Andros is very thinly populated (its residents number only around 5,000), although the tourist population swells it a bit. The temperature range here averages from 72°F to 85°F (22°C–29°C).

You won't find the western side of Andros written about much in yachting guides because tricky shoals render it almost unapproachable by boat. The east coast, however, has kilometers of unspoiled beaches and is studded with little villages. Hotels that range from simple guest cottages to dive resorts, to fishing camps have been built here. "Creeks" (we'd call them rivers) intersect the island at its midpoint. Also called *bights*, they range in length from 8 to 40km (5–25 miles), and they are dotted with tiny cays and islets.

The fishing at Andros is famous, establishing records for blue marlin caught offshore. Divers and snorkelers find that the coral reefs are among the most beautiful in the world, and everyone loves the pristine beaches.

Warning: Be sure to bring along plenty of mosquito repellent.

ANDROS ESSENTIALS

GETTING THERE   Reaching Andros is not that difficult. **Western Air** (© 242/ 377-2222 in the U.S.; www.westernairbahamas.com) has twice-daily 15-minute flights from Nassau to the airport at Andros Town in Central Andros (© 242/368-2759). Airports are also at San Andros in the north (© 242/329-4000), at Mangrove Cay (© 242/369-0003), and at Congo Town in South Andros (© 242/369-2222 or 954/772-9808). **Lynx Air International** (© **888/596-9247;** www.lynxair.com) flies from Fort Lauderdale to Congo Town three times a week.

Make sure you know where you're going in Andros. For example, if you land at Congo Town on South Andros and you've booked a hotel in Nicholl's Town, you'll find connections nearly impossible at times (involving both ferryboats and a rough haul across a bad highway).

Andros's few available taxis know when the planes from Nassau are going to land, and they drive out to the airports, hoping to drum up some business. Taxis are most often shared. A typical fare from Andros Town Airport to Small Hope Bay Lodge is about $30 (£16).

Many locals, along with a few adventurous visitors, use **mail boats** to get to Andros; the trip takes 5 to 7 hours across some beautiful waters. North Andros is serviced by the **MV** *Lisa J. II,* a mail boat that departs Potter's Cay Dock in Nassau heading for Morgan's Bluff, Mastic Point, and Nicholl's Town. It departs Nassau on Wednesday, returning to Nassau on Tuesday. The **MV** *Captain Moxey* departs Nassau on Monday, calling at Long Bay Cays, Kemps Bay, and the Bluff on South Andros. It heads back to Nassau on Wednesday. The **MV** *Mangrove Cay Express* departs Nassau Wednesday night for Lisbon Creek, the trip taking 5½ hours. It sails back to Nassau on Monday afternoon. Finally, **MV** *Lady D* departs Nassau on Wednesday for Fresh Creek, stopping at Spaniard Creek, Blanket Sound, and Browne Sound. The trip takes

Andros

To the Bimini Islands

Morgan's
Bluff

To the Berry Islands

Lowe
Sound

Nicholl's Town

San Andros

Mastic Point

Tongue of the Ocean

BARRIER REEF

Staniard Creek

Coakley Town
(or Fresh Creek)

Andros
Town

Williams
Island

A N D R O S

Cargill Creek

Behring Point

North Bight

Moxey Town

Middle Bight

Mangrove
Cay

Driggs
Hill

South Bight

*Alcorine
Cay*

Congo
Town

Scuba Diving
Shipwreck
Reef
Airport

| 0 | 10 mi |
| 0 | 10 km |

N

Miami
FLORIDA

Grand
Bahama
Nassau

Abaco

New Providence Island

Eleuthera

Cat Island

Andros

San Salvador

Great Exuma

Long Island

Crooked Island

Acklins Island

| 0 | 100 mi |
| 0 | 100 km |

CUBA

Great Inagua

TURKS AND
CAICOS

195

5½ hours. The return voyage to Nassau is on Sunday. For details about sailing and costs, contact the dock master at **Potter's Cay Dock** in Nassau (© **242/393-1064**).

A far more luxurious way to go over the waters is aboard *Sea Link* or *Sea Wind* (© **242/323-2166;** fax 242/393-7451; www.bahamasferries.com). The *Sea Link* carries 250 passengers, and the *Sea Wind* seats 180, with another 100 seats available on the open-air decks of both vessels. Depending on where you dock on Andros, trip time from Nassau to Fresh Creek takes 1 hour and 45 minutes. From Nassau to Driggs Hill on Andros, however, takes 2 hours and 30 minutes.

ORIENTATION   Chances are, your hotel will be in **North Andros,** in either Andros Town or Nicholl's Town. North Andros is the most developed of the three major Andros islands. **Nicholl's Town** is a colorful old settlement with some 600 people and several places serving local foods. Most visitors come to Nicholl's Town to buy supplies at a shopping complex. Directly to the south is **Mastic Point,** which was founded in 1781. If you ask around, you'll be shown to a couple of concrete-sided dives that offer spareribs and Goombay music. To the north of Nicholl's Town is **Morgan's Bluff,** namesake of Sir Henry Morgan, a pirate later knighted by the British monarch. **Andros Town,** with its abandoned docks, is another village, about 47km (29 miles) south of Nicholl's Town. Most visitors come to Andros Town to stay at the **Small Hope Bay Lodge** (p. 199) or to avail themselves of its facilities. The biggest retail industry, Androsia batik, is in the area, too. The scuba diving—minutes away on the barrier reef—is what lures much of the world to this tiny place; others come here just for the shelling. On the opposite side of the water is **Coakley Town.** If you're driving, before you get to Andros Town, you may want to stop and spend some restful hours on the beach at **Staniard Creek,** another old settlement on Andros that feels like it drifted from the South Seas.

Moving south to the second major landmass, **Central Andros** is smaller than either North or South Andros. The least developed of the three, the island is studded with hundreds upon hundreds of palm trees. The Queen's Highway runs along the eastern coastline, but the only thing about this road that's regal is its name. In some 7km (4¼ miles), you can travel practically the whole island. It's truly sleepy, and for that very reason, many people come here to get away from it all. You won't find much in the way of accommodations, but you'll find some.

The third and last major land area, **South Andros** is the home of the wonderfully named **Congo Town,** where life proceeds at a snail's pace. The Queen's Highway, lined in part with pink-and-white conch shells, runs for about 40km (25 miles) or so. The island, as yet undiscovered, has some of the best beaches in The Bahamas, and you can enjoy them almost by yourself.

Another tiny island, undeveloped **Mangrove Cay,** is an escapist's dream, attracting naturalists and anglers, as well as a few divers. It's separated from the northern and southern sections of Andros by bights. The settlements here got electricity and a paved road only in 1989. The best place for snorkeling and diving on Mangrove Cay is **Victoria Point Blue Hole** (any local can point you there if you're interested). Another village (don't blink as you pass through, or you'll miss it) is **Moxey Town,** where you are likely to see fishermen unloading conch from the fishing boats. Ferries, operated free by the Bahamian government, ply back and forth over the waters separating Mangrove Cay from South Andros. At the end of the road in North Andros, private arrangements can be made to have a boat take you over to Mangrove Cay.

GETTING AROUND   Transportation can be a big problem on Andros. If you have to go somewhere, try to use one of the local taxi drivers, though this can be a pricey undertaking.

The few rental cars available are in North Andros. These are scarce, owing to the high costs of shipping cars to Andros. The weather also takes a great toll on the cars that are brought in (the salt in the air erodes metal), so no U.S. car-rental agencies are represented. Your best bet is to ask at your hotel to see what's available. It's not really recommended that you drive on Andros because roads are mainly unpaved and in bad condition, and gasoline stations are hard to find. Outlets for car rentals come and go faster here than anybody can count. Renting a car is less formal, and less organized, than you might be used to, and you won't find organized links to any toll-free company stateside. The concierge at Andros's most upscale hotel, Kamaleme Cay, will arrange a cab or a rental car for you, but frankly, it's all word of mouth and terribly unlicensed and informal, with no options for purchase of additional insurance. Taxi drivers and owners of a handful of battered cars that can be rented will be at the airport in time for the landing of most flights from the U.S. mainland or from Nassau. You can negotiate a car rental on-site or—perhaps more safely and conveniently—you can hire one of the local taxis for access to wherever you want to go. Rates go for between $85 and $100 (£45–£53) a day, plus gas. Be warned that signpostings and road conditions are horrible, but it's hard to get lost because the only road is the north-south much-rutted thoroughfare known as Queen's Highway.

You may want to rent a bike, but you'll experience the same bad roads you would in a rental car. Guests of the Small Hope Bay Lodge, Chickcharnie, and Mangrove Cay Inn can rent bikes at their hotels.

VISITOR INFORMATION   The **Ministry of Tourism** is located in Andros Town ((*C* **242/368-2286**). It is open Monday to Friday 9am to 5pm.

FAST FACTS   Banks are rare on Andros. There's one, **ScotiaBank** (*C* **242/329-2700**), in Nicoll's Town, with an **ATM,** open Monday to Thursday 9:30am to 3pm, and Friday 9:30am to 4:30pm.

The island's post office is in Nicholl's Town on North Andros (*C* **242/329-2034**). Hours are Monday through Friday from 9am to 4:30pm. Hotel desks will also sell you Bahamian stamps. Make sure you mark cards and letters as airmail; otherwise, you'll return home before they do. Each little village on Andros has a store that serves as the post office.

Government-run clinics are found at Nicholl's Town on **North Andros** (*C* **242/329-2055**), at Mangrove Cay on **Central Andros** (*C* **242/369-0089**), and at Kemp's Bay in **South Andros** (*C* **242/369-4849**). To reach the **police,** call *C* 919 in North Andros, *C* 242/368-2626 in Central Andros, and *C* 242/369-4733 in South Andros.

WHERE TO STAY

At the hotels listed below with no phone in room, phone service is available only at the front desks.

IN STANIARD CREEK

Kamalame Cay *★★★ Finds*   In 1995, a group of international investors created one of the most exclusive resorts in the Out Islands from the scrub-covered 38-hectare (94-acre) landscape of a private cay off the east coast of Andros Island. Since then, it has discreetly and quietly attracted a clientele of banking moguls and financial wizards from Europe and North America, all of whom come for the superb service, escapist charm, 5km (3 miles) of beaches, and a series of waterborne adventures that are among the best of their kind in The Bahamas. A staff of 30 to 50, some of whom were brought in from other parts of The Bahamas, includes six full-time gardeners, an army of chambermaids and cooks, and a sporting-adventure staff that's ready, willing, and able to bring groups of urban refugees out for scuba, windsurfing, snorkeling, plus deep-sea and bonefishing excursions above one of the largest barrier reefs in the world.

Accommodations include a few smaller rooms, tasteful and very comfortable, located next to the marina. More opulent are the cottages and suites, all of which lie adjacent to the beach; these are mainly crafted from local coral stone, cedar shingles, tropical-wood timbers, tile, and, in some cases, thatch. Each is outfitted in a breezy but stylish tropical motif that evokes a decorator's journal. Food is superb, focusing on fresh fish, lobster, local soups, homemade breads, and surprisingly good wines.

Staniard Creek, Andros, The Bahamas. © 242/368-6281 or 242/236-6279. www.kamalame.com. Winter $840–$1,190 (£445–£631) double, $1,380 (£731) suite, from $1,480 (£784) 1-bedroom villa; off season $840–$950 (£445–£504) double, $1,100 (£583) suite, from $1,180 (£625) 1-bedroom villa. Rates all-inclusive, including a boat ride from Kamalame Cay. Discounts of up to 20% June–Oct. MC, V. **Amenities:** Restaurant; bar; pool; tennis court; watersports equipment/rentals; room service (upon request); babysitting; laundry service. *In room:* A/C, minibar, hair dryer, iron, safe, beverage maker, no phone.

IN ANDROS TOWN

Andros Lighthouse Yacht Club & Marina   At the mouth of Fresh Creek with an 18-slip marina, this complex is a favorite of the yachting crowd. The hotel rents comfortably furnished villas, each with a certain flair enhanced by Caribbean fabrics and ceiling fans. Accommodations open onto private patios and come with well-maintained private bathrooms with shower units. Scuba divers, snorkelers, and fishermen make ample use of the beach and the offshore waters because the hotel lies near one of the world's largest barrier reefs and the deep Tongue of the Ocean.

The hotel has a good restaurant serving Bahamian and American dishes. Fishing charters are readily available, and scuba diving and snorkeling can easily be arranged through the hotel. The package rates offered by the hotel, in addition to room and meals, include airport pickup.

Andros Town, Andros, The Bahamas. © 242/368-2305 or 242/368-2306. Fax 242/368-2300. www.androslighthouse. com. 20 units. Winter $120–$145 (£64–£77) double, from $150 (£80) villa; off season $115–$130 (£61–£69) double, from $145 (£77) villa. MAP (breakfast and dinner) $40 (£21) per person. Ask about dive packages. AE, DISC, MC, V. **Amenities:** Restaurant; 2 bars; pool; 2 tennis courts; limited room service; coin-operated laundry; nonsmoking room; rooms for those w/limited mobility. *In room:* A/C, TV, kitchenette, fridge, hair dryer, iron, safe.

IN CARGILL CREEK

Andros Island Bonefishing Club ⊕ (Finds)   If Hemingway were around today and wanted to go bonefishing, we'd invite him here. This rustic lodge lies at the confluence of Cargill Creek, the Atlantic Ocean, and the eastern end of North Bight. It fronts a small protected creek, a short distance from a wadeable flat, and fishing boats can dock directly in front of the lodge. Constructed in 1988, this is a modern but rather bare-bones facility that draws more repeat guests than any other hostelry in The Bahamas. The Bonefishing Club recently merged with the nearby Creekside Lodge, adding 18 more rooms to the complex. More than two dozen fishermen can stay here at any time in accommodations with queen-size beds, ample dresser and closet space, bathrooms equipped with tub/showers, and ceiling fans. The club is the domain of Captain Rupert Leadon, who knows more fishing stories than anybody else in Andros.

Hearty and plentiful food, with an emphasis on fresh seafood, including Bahamian lobster and conch, is served at communal tables.

Cargill Creek, Andros, The Bahamas. © 242/368-5167. Fax 242/368-5397. www.androsbonefishing.com. 30 units. Year-round $1,235 (£655) per person for 3 nights and 2 days of fishing. Rates include tax, all meals, all-day fishing with boat and guide, and transportation to and from Andros Town. Room only, $205 (£109) per person. MC, V. **Amenities:** Restaurant; bar; pool; babysitting; laundry service; rooms for those w/limited mobility. *In room:* A/C, fridge, ceiling fan.

IN FRESH CREEK

Small Hope Bay Lodge 𝘒𝘒 *Kids*   This is the premier diving and fishing resort of Andros, and one of the best in the entire Bahamas, with a beach right at its doorstep. It's an intimate and cozy beachside cottage colony, where tall coconut palms line a lovely beach and a laid-back atmosphere always prevails. And because this place is all-inclusive, the price you pay includes all accommodations, meals, drinks, taxes, service charges, airport taxi transfers, and even the use of kayaks, windsurfers, and other boats, as well as bicycles and scuba lessons.

Its name comes from a prediction (so far, accurate) from pirate Henry Morgan, who claimed there was "small hope" of anyone finding the treasure he'd buried on Andros. For conversations and meals, guests congregate in a spacious living and dining room. Andros Town Airport is a 10-minute taxi ride from the lodge. Large cabins, cooled by ceiling fans, are made of coral rock and Andros pine, and are decorated with Androsia batik fabrics. Honeymooners like to order breakfast served in (their water) bed.

For groups of three or more, the resort has a limited number of family cottages, featuring two separate rooms connected by a single bathroom. Single travelers have a choice of staying in a family cottage with private accommodations (which is the same as per-person double occupancy) or staying in a regular cottage with private bathroom. All bathrooms are neatly kept.

The bar is an old boat, dubbed the *Panacea*. The food is wholesome, plentiful, and good—including favorites such as conch chowder, lobster, and hot johnnycake. The chef will even cook your catch for you or make up a picnic lunch. Lunch is a buffet; dinner, a choice of seafood and meat every night. Children under 10 dine in the game room. Drinks are offered on a rambling patio built out over the sea. Nightlife is spontaneous—with dancing in the lounge or on the patio, and water slides. Definitely do not wear a tie at dinner.

Diving is the lodge's specialty. The owners have been diving for more than 3 decades, and their well-respected dive shop has sufficient equipment, boats, and flexibility to give guests any diving experience they want, including a resort course for beginners. If you'd rather fish, the lodge can hook you up with an expert guide, especially for bonefishing.

Fresh Creek, Andros, The Bahamas (mailing address: P.O. Box CB11817, Nassau, Bahamas). © 800/223-6961 in the U.S. and Canada, or 242/368-2014. Fax 242/368-2015. 21 units. www.smallhope.com. Winter $229 (£121) per person adult; off season $209 (£111) per person adult; year-round $95 (£50) ages 2–12. Dive packages available. Rates include tax, all meals, drinks, tips, airport transfers, and most activities. AE, MC, V. **Amenities:** Restaurant; bar; Jacuzzi; kayak; children's programs; massage; babysitting; laundry service; nonsmoking rooms. *In room:* Ceiling fan, no phone.

IN NICHOLL'S TOWN

Green Windows Inn   Kenny Robinson and her husband, Patrick, run this small, laid-back hotel set in a landscape of fruit trees and palms, where guests like to take their after-meal walks. The small rooms are over the restaurant and bar on the second floor of the two-story inn. One recent improvement at the inn is the installation of

tiny private bathrooms with tub/showers in every bedroom, along with both ceiling fans and air-conditioning. The restaurant caters only to hotel guests, with mainly seafood and local food cooked to order. The beach is a 10-minute walk from the inn, and the Robinsons can arrange bonefishing and snorkeling trips.

Rawfon St. (P.O. Box 23076), Nicholl's Town, Andros, The Bahamas. © 242/329-2515. Fax 242/329-2016. 10 units. Year-round $100 (£53) double. No credit cards. **Amenities:** Restaurant; bar; nonsmoking room. *In room:* A/C, TV, iron, beverage maker, no phone.

ON SOUTH BIGHT

Tiamo Lodge *(Finds)*   One of the most ecologically aware places in the entire Bahamas, this lodge was built in stages between 1999 and 2003. It's nestled on 4.8 hectares (12 acres) of land that's studded with unusually large trees, directly beside the bight (inland waterway) that runs along the midsection of Andros. About 30% of the guests here come for the fishing, and if that's your interest, a boat rental (without fishing equipment included) goes for $400 (£212) a day. Accommodations are within wood-framed, plank-sided bungalows, each with a screened-in wraparound porch, a sense of privacy, and a handful of "rustically elegant" amenities that are limited by the eco-sensitive nature of the resort. This lack of plush hugely appeals to the nature-loving clients who come here. Days are spent reading, swimming off the white-sand beach that flanks one side of the resort, and generally reflecting on life. It's strongly advised that you bring your own company to this place, since many of the activities are engineered for couples.

Drigg's Hill, South Bight, Andros Island. © 242/357-2489. Fax 305/768-7707. www.tiamoresorts.com. 11 units. Winter $345 (£183) per person based on double occupancy; off season $285–$295 (£151–£156) per person based on double occupancy. Rates include meals, airport transfers, and almost all activities. AE, DISC, MC, V. **Amenities:** Restaurant; bar; laundry service; kayaking; snorkeling; hiking. *In room:* No phone.

ON MANGROVE CAY

The Mangrove Cay Inn   This pleasant, well-managed inn belongs to a native son, Elliott Greene, who returned with his wife, Pat, after years of cold-weather life in Syracuse, New York, to establish this breezy motel. It's located a short walk from the center of Grants, the third-largest village on Mangrove Cay (Moxey Town and Burnt Rock, though tiny, are still larger). Positioned amid scrubland, in the geographic center of the 14km-long (8¾-mile) island, the hotel was built in the early 1990s, 2 years after the inn was established as an easygoing and affable restaurant.

Separated from Grant's Beach by a brackish lake that's stocked with fish, the inn has a mysterious blue hole positioned beside the path connecting the hotel to the beach. Accommodations have cozy but completely unpretentious furnishings. Each unit contains a small bathroom with a tub/shower. How do guests spend their time here? Sitting on a veranda that runs the length of the building and overlooks the water, riding on one of the bicycles that the hotel rents for around $10 (£5.30) a day, snorkeling with the hotel's equipment on the outlying reef (waters offshore are particularly rich in natural sponges and spiny Caribbean lobster), hiking, hill climbing, and looking for chickcharnies (mythical red-eyed, three-toed, birdlike creatures). And if you're interested in fishing excursions, the Greenes can hire a local fishing guide for a full-day outing (about $300/£159 a day for up to four).

The wing that contains the bedrooms is attached to a restaurant that serves a combination of Bahamian and American food with specialties of cracked conch, grilled grouper and snapper, burgers, and steaks.

c/o General Post Office, Grants, Mangrove Cay, Andros, The Bahamas. ✆ 242/369-0069. Fax 242/369-0014. www.mangrovecayinn.net. 14 units. Year-round $125 (£66) double; $175 (£93) 1-bedroom cottage; $300 (£159) 3-bedroom cottage. No credit cards. **Amenities:** Restaurant; bar; bike rentals; limited room service; laundry service; nonsmoking rooms; rooms for those w/limited mobility. *In room:* A/C, TV (in some), kitchens (in some), hair dryer, iron, ceiling fan, beverage maker (in some), no phone.

Seascape Inn 🕭 *Finds* Joan and Mickey McGowan are some of the most welcoming innkeepers in the Andros chain of islands. They took several cottages with private decks opening onto the ocean and turned them into secluded retreats for discerning guests. The cabins here are handsomely furnished with handmade mahogany pieces along with original Bahamian art. Each cottage is spacious and well maintained, with neat shower-only bathrooms. Included in the price is one of the best breakfasts you'll get on Andros: Mrs. McGowan is an excellent baker, turning out such early-morning delights as banana bread. Fellow guests meet in the elevated dining room to dine on excellent American and Bahamian cuisine. The McGowans will also help arrange scuba diving and snorkeling trips, if you wish.

Mangrove Cay, Andros, The Bahamas. ✆/fax 242/369-0342. www.seascapeinn.com. 5 cottages. Year-round $140–$150 (£74–£80) double. Rates include breakfast and use of kayaks and bikes. AE, MC, V. **Amenities:** Restaurant; bar; bikes; kayaks; watersports equipment/rentals; laundry service; all nonsmoking rooms. *In room:* Ceiling fan, no phone.

SOUTH ANDROS

Emerald Palms Resort 🕭 Lodging at this laid-back place, 3km (2 miles) from the Congo Town airport, is like staying at a beachside ranch. The accommodations are set on 8km (5 miles) of beachfront on an island that contains 10,000 palm trees. The hotel is casual—a place to get away from urban life and rest your jangled nerves on a lovely beach. Guests are treated like members of the family.

The rooms are large and comfortable, with well-laid-out bathrooms with adequate shelf space and shower stalls. All in all, it's a relaxed, tropical ambience.

Scattered over the palm-studded property are hammocks and a freshwater swimming pool. The dining room features Bahamian seafood, and outdoor steak barbecues and seafood buffets are sometimes held. South Bight marina is 2.5km (1½ miles) away, serving as a yacht anchorage for anyone who arrives by boat. The hotel will also rent you a car or bike if you need one.

Driggs Hill (P.O. Box 800), South Andros, The Bahamas. ✆ 800/504-1794 or 242/357-2873. Fax 242/369-2711. www.emerald-palms.com. 42 units. Winter $155–$295 (£82–£156) double, $245–$495 (£130–£262) 1-bedroom villa, $445–$695 (£236–£368) 2-bedroom villa; off season $105–$245 (£56–£130) double, $195–$395 (£103–£209) 1-bedroom villa, $395–$595 (£209–£315) 2-bedroom villa. AE, MC, V. **Amenities:** Restaurant; 2 bars; pool; Jacuzzi; car-rental desk; limited room service; nonsmoking rooms; rooms for those w/limited mobility. *In room:* A/C, TV, mini-bar, kitchenette (in some), hair dryer, safe, beverage maker.

WHERE TO DINE

Andros follows the rest of The Bahamas in its cuisine. Conch, in all its many variations, is the staple of most diets, along with heaping portions of peas 'n' rice, johnny-cake, and pig or chicken souse.

Emerald Palms Resort, outside Congo Town (✆ 242/369-2661), is the best place to dine in South Andros. Eating here is pay-as-you-go rather than inclusive. Guests are usually out touring at lunchtime. However, nonguests can also visit this hotel for dinner, paying from $25 to $45 (£13–£24) per person.

If you're touring the island during the day, you'll find some local spots that serve food. If business has been slow at some of these little places, however, you might find nothing on the stove. You take your chances. On Mangrove Cay, try **Dianne Cash's Total Experience,** Main Road (© **242/369-0430**), where you can sample Dianne's version of baked crab backs served with peas 'n' rice. Don't plan on dropping by this place without some kind of advance notification, though.

BEACHES, WATERSPORTS & OTHER OUTDOOR PURSUITS

Golf and tennis fans should go elsewhere, but if you want some of the best bonefishing and scuba diving in The Bahamas, head to Andros.

HITTING THE BEACH

The eastern shore of Andros, stretching for some 161km (100 miles), is an almost uninterrupted palm grove opening onto beaches of white or beige sand. Several dozen access points lead to the beach along the eastern shore. The roads are unmarked but clearly visible. The clear warm waters offshore are great for snorkeling.

FISHING

Andros ✦✦✦ is called the "Bonefish Capital of the World." The epicenter is Lowe Sound Settlement, a tiny hamlet with only one road, 6.5km (4 miles) north of Nicholl's Town. Anglers come here to hire bonefish guides. **Cargill Creek** is one of the best places for bonefishing on the island; nearby, anglers explore the flats in and around the bights of Andros (some excellent flats, where you can wade in your boots, lie only 68–113m/223–371 ft. offshore).

Whether you're staying in North, Central, or South Andros, someone at your hotel can arrange a fishing expedition with one of the many local guides or charter companies. In particular, the **Small Hope Bay Lodge,** in Andros Town on North Andros (© **242/368-2014**), is known for arranging fishing expeditions for both guests and nonguests; a guide will take you out for superb bonefishing. They also offer fly-, reef-, and deep-sea fishing, and provide tackle and bait.

SCUBA DIVING & SNORKELING

Divers from all over the world come to explore the **Andros barrier reef** ✦✦✦, which runs parallel to the eastern shore of the island. It's one of the largest reefs in the world. Unlike Australia's Great Barrier Reef, which is kilometers off the coast, the barrier reef of Andros is easily accessible, beginning a few hundred yards offshore.

Tips Saving Andros for Future Generations

The **Andros Conservancy and Trust** might be called the guardian angel of Andros. This nongovernmental organization was created to preserve and enhance the island's natural assets. In 2002 The Bahamas National Trust began to deal with their concerns. Today nearly 120,000 hectares (300,000 acres) of Andros have been preserved as wetlands, reefs, and marine replenishment zones—doubling the size of the country's national park system.

All this development falls under the general authority of the **Central Andros National Park** ✦✦✦. A great deal of self-policing is involved in this massive landmass, with bonefishermen keeping watch over the flats, crabbers protecting local breeding grounds, and divers helping preserve the reefs.

This park is only emerging. At the moment, there are no organized tours, no guides, no nature walks. It is a national park in the making.

Fun Fact **The Bahamian Loch Ness Monster**

When the Atlantic Undersea Testing and Evaluation Centre (AUTEC) first opened, Androsians predicted that the naval researchers would turn up **"Lusca."** Like the Loch Ness Monster, Lusca reportedly had been sighted by dozens of locals. The sea serpent was accused of sucking both sailors and their vessels into the dangerous blue holes around the island's coastline. No one has captured Lusca yet.

One side of the reef is a peaceful haven for snorkelers and novice scuba divers, who report that the fish are tame (often a grouper will eat from your hand, but don't try it with a moray eel). The water here is from 2.5 to 4.5m (8¼–15 ft.) deep.

On the other side of the reef, it's a different story. The water plunges to a depth of 167km (104 miles) into the awesome **TOTO (Tongue of the Ocean)** 𝕏𝕏𝕏. One diver reported that, as an adventure, diving in the ocean's "tongue" was tantamount to a flight to the moon.

Myriad multicolored marine life thrives on the reef, and it attracts nature lovers from all over the world. The weirdly shaped coral formations alone are worth the trip. This is a living, breathing garden of the sea, and its caves feel like cathedrals.

For many years, the U.S. Navy has conducted research at a station on the edge of TOTO. The research center—devoted to oceanographic, underwater weapons, and antisubmarine research—is at Andros Town. Called **AUTEC** (Atlantic Undersea Testing and Evaluation Centre), this is a joint U.S. and British undertaking.

Among other claims to fame, Andros is known for its **"blue holes,"** which drop into the brine. Essentially, these are narrow circular pits that plunge as much as 60m (197 ft.) straight down through rock and coral into murky, difficult-to-explore depths. Most of them begin under the level of the sea, although others appear unexpectedly—and dangerously—in the center of the island, usually with warning signs placed around the perimeter. Scattered at various points along the coast, they can be reached either in rented boats or as part of a guided trip. The most celebrated blue hole is Uncle Charlie's Blue Hole, mysterious and fathomless, and once publicized by Jacques Cousteau. The other blue holes are almost as incredible.

One of these blue holes, called **Benjamin's Blue Hole** 𝕏, is named after its discoverer, George Benjamin. In 1967, he found stalactites and stalagmites 360m (1,181 ft.) below sea level. What was remarkable about this discovery is that stalactites and stalagmites are not created underwater. This has led to much speculation that The Bahamas are actually mountaintops, and all that remains of a mysterious continent that sank beneath the sea (perhaps Atlantis?). Although Cousteau made a film—making the Blue Holes of Andros internationally famous—most of the blue holes, like most of the surface of the island itself, remain unexplored. Tour boats leaving from Small Hope Bay Lodge will take you to these holes.

As for snorkeling, you might head a few kilometers north of Nicholl's Town, where you'll find a crescent-shaped beach, along with a headland, **Morgan's Bluff,** honoring the notorious old pirate himself. If you're not a diver and can't go out to the Andros Barrier Reef off the shorefront at Fresh Creek and Andros Town, you can do the second-best thing and snorkel near a series of reefs known as The Three Sisters. Sometimes, if the waters haven't turned suddenly murky, you can see all the way to the sandy bottom. The stands of elkhorn coral are especially dramatic.

Since **Mangrove Cay** is very underdeveloped, rely on the snorkeling advice and gear rentals you'll get from the dive shop at the **Seascape Inn** (✆ **242/369-0342;** www. seascapeinn.com). A two-tank dive costs $125 (£66) for guests of the hotel. Nonguests are not accepted.

Small Hope Bay Lodge, Fresh Creek, Andros Town, Central Andros (✆ **800/ 223-6961** in the U.S. and Canada, or 242/368-2014; www.smallhope.com), lies a short distance from the barrier reef, with its still-unexplored caves and ledges. A staff of trained dive instructors at the lodge caters to beginners and experienced divers alike. Snorkeling expeditions can be arranged, as well as scuba outings (visibility underwater exceeds 30m/98 ft. on most days, with water temperatures ranging 72°F–84°F/ 22°C–29°C). You can also rent gear here. To stay at the hotel for 7 nights and 8 days, all-inclusive (meals, tips, taxes, airport transfers, and three dives per day), costs adults $1,943 to $2,083 (£1,030–£1,104). (For children aged 10–17, the cost is $1,260/ £668.) All guests are allowed access to the beachside hot-tub whirlpool, as well as to all facilities, such as free use of sailboats, windsurfers, and bicycles.

EXPLORING THE ISLAND

Andros is largely unexplored, and with good reason—getting around takes some effort. With the exception of the main arteries, the few roads that exist are badly maintained and full of potholes. Sometimes you're a long way between villages or settlements. If your car breaks down, all you can do is wait and hope that someone comes along to give you a ride to the next place, where you'll hope to find a skilled mechanic. If you're striking out on your own, make sure you have a full tank because service stations are few and far between.

At present, not all of Andros can be explored by car. We hope that as Andros develops, roads will be constructed so that it will be easier to get around. Most of the driving and exploring is currently confined to North Andros; even there, roads go only along the eastern sector past Nicholl's Town, Morgan's Bluff, and San Andros.

If you're driving on Central or South Andros, you must stay on the rough **Queen's Highway.** The road in the south is paved and better than the one in Central Andros, which should be traveled only in an emergency or by a local.

Near Small Hope Bay at Andros Town, you can visit the workshop where **Androsia batik** is made (the same Androsia batik sold in the shops of Nassau and other towns). Androsia's artisans create their designs using hot wax on fine cotton and silk fabrics. The fabrics are then made into island-style wear, including blouses, skirts, caftans, shirts, and accessories. All hand-painted and hand-signed, the resort wear comes in dazzling red, blue, purple, green, and earth tones. You can visit the factory in Andros Town (✆ **242/368-2080;** www.androsia.com) Monday to Friday from 8am to 5pm, and Saturday 9am to 2pm.

Morgan's Bluff, at the tip of North Andros, lures men and women hoping to strike it rich. The pirate Sir Henry Morgan is supposed to have buried a vast treasure here, but it has eluded discovery to this day, although many have searched for it.

Bird-watchers are attracted to Andros for its varied **bird population.** In the dense forests, in trees such as lignum vitae, mahogany, Madeira, "horseflesh," and pine, live many parrots, doves, marsh hens, and whistling ducks.

(Moments What Would Tennessee Have Thought?

One custom in Andros is reminiscent of the Tennessee Williams drama *Suddenly, Last Summer*: catching **land crabs,** which leave their burrows and march relentlessly to the sea to lay their eggs. The annual ritual occurs between May and September. However, many of the hapless crabs will never have offspring; both visitors and Androsians walk along the beach with baskets and catch the crustaceans before they reach the sea. Later they clean them, stuff them, and bake them for dinner.

Botanists are lured by the **wildflowers** of Andros. Some 40 to 50 species of wild orchids are said to thrive here, some of which can be found nowhere else. New discoveries are always being made, as more and more botanists study the rich vegetation of Andros.

Red Bay Village is the type of discovery that continues to make Andros seem mysterious. Just a quarter of a century ago, an ancient tribe, headed by a chief and devotedly following old rituals, was found living here. The passage of time has made little difference to these people, who still practice their customs of fishing. Now the world comes to their door, and changes are inevitable. The village is believed to have been settled sometime in the 1840s by Seminoles and blacks fleeing slavery in Florida. Located off the northwestern coast of Andros, it's connected by a causeway to the mainland, and tourists can visit. You can reach Red Bay Village by road from Nicholl's Town and San Andros. You should be polite and ask permission before indiscriminately photographing the residents

7

The Abacos

Called the "top of The Bahamas," the Abacos comprise the northernmost portion of the nation. This boomerang-shaped mini-archipelago is 209km (130 miles) long and consists of Great Abaco and Little Abaco, as well as a sprinkling of cays. The islands are about 322km (200 miles) east of Miami and 121km (75 miles) north of Nassau.

People come here mainly to explore the outdoors. The **sailing** ✸✸ and **fishing** ✸✸ are spectacular, and the diving is excellent, too. There are also many lovely, uncrowded beaches. The Abacos are definitely a world apart from the glitzy pleasures of Freeport/Lucaya, Nassau, or Paradise Island.

Many residents of the Abacos descend from Loyalists who left New England after the American Revolution. Against a backdrop of sugar-white beaches and turquoise water, their pastel-colored clapboard houses and white-picket fences retain the Cape Cod architectural style of the first settlements on Abacos. One brightly painted sign in Hope Town says it all: SLOW DOWN. YOU'RE IN HOPE TOWN. The same could be said for all the Abacos.

The weather is about 10 degrees warmer here than in southern Florida, but if you visit in January or February, remember that you're not guaranteed beach weather every day (Miami and Fort Lauderdale, even Key West, can get chilly at times). When winter squalls hit, temperatures can drop to the high 40s (high single digits Celsius) in severe cases. Spring in the Abacos, however, is one of the most glorious and balmy seasons in all the islands. In summer, it gets very hot around noon, but if you act as the islanders do and find a shady spot to escape the broiling sun, the trade winds will cool you off.

Some yachters call the Abacos the world's most beautiful cruising grounds. Excellent marine facilities, with fishing guides and boat rentals, are available here; in fact, Marsh Harbour is the bareboat-charter center of the northern Bahamas. There you can rent a small boat, pack a picnic, and head for one of many uninhabited cays just big enough for two.

Anglers from all over the world come to test their skill against blue marlin, kingfish, dolphinfish, yellowfin tuna, sailfish, wahoo, amberjack, and grouper. Like fishing tournaments? They abound at Walker's Cay.

Finally, scuba divers can plumb the depths and discover caverns, inland "blue holes," and coral reefs and gardens, along with marine preserves and wrecks. Some scuba centers feature night dives.

ABACOS ESSENTIALS
GETTING THERE
BY PLANE   Three airports are found in the Abacos: **Marsh Harbour** (the major one, on Great Abaco Island), **Treasure Cay,** and **Walker's Cay.** The official points of entry by water are at Marsh Harbour, Treasure Cay, Walker's Cay, and Green Turtle

Legend:
- ✈ Airport
- 🤿 Scuba Diving
- ⚓ Shipwreck

Cay (New Plymouth). Green Turtle Cay doesn't have an airstrip, but many members of the yachting crowd clear Customs and Immigration there.

Many visitors arrive from Nassau or Miami on **Bahamasair** (© 800/222-4262 or 242/377-8451; www.bahamasair.com). Flight schedules change frequently in The Bahamas, but you can usually get two to three flights out of Nassau on Fridays and Sundays, going first to Marsh Harbour and then on to Treasure Cay. From West Palm Beach, you can often take a direct morning flight to Marsh Harbour and Treasure Cay.

Other connections include **American Eagle** (© 800/433-7300 or 242/367-2231; www.aa.com), with flights from Miami to Marsh Harbour once daily; and **Continental Connection** (© 800/231-0856 or 242/367-3415 in Marsh Harbour, 242/365-8615 in Treasure Cay; www.continental.com), which flies to Marsh Harbour and Treasure Cay two to three times daily from several Florida locales. A smaller carrier is **Twin Air** (© 954/359-8266; www.flytwinair.com), flying from Fort Lauderdale to Treasure Cay on Mondays, Wednesdays, and Fridays.

BY BOAT The mail boat **MV _Legacy_** sails on Tuesday from Nassau to Hope Town, Marsh Harbour, Turtle Cay, and Green Turtle Cay. It returns to Nassau on Friday. Trip time is 12 hours. The **MV _Legacy_** leaves Nassau on Tuesday, with stops at Green Turtle Cay, Hope Town, Marsh Harbour, and Turtle Cay, going back to Nassau on Thursday. Each trip takes 12 hours. For details on sailings (subject to change) and costs, contact the dock master at **Potter's Cay Dock** in Nassau (© 242/393-1064).

Bahamas Ferries (www.bahamasferries.com) operates a direct service from Nassau aboard the _Sea Wind._ A round-trip passage costs $110 (£58) for adults and $70 (£37) per child. For more information and for bookings, call © 242/323-2166. The trip from Nassau to Sandy Point in the Abacos takes 1 hour and 50 minutes.

GETTING AROUND
BY TAXI Unmetered taxis, which you often have to share with other passengers, meet all arriving flights. They will take you to your hotel if it's on the Abaco "mainland"; otherwise, they will deposit you at a dock where you can hop aboard a water taxi to one of the neighboring offshore islands, such as Green Turtle Cay or Elbow Cay. Most visitors use a combination taxi and water-taxi ride to reach the most popular hotels. From Marsh Harbour Airport to Hope Town on Elbow Cay, the cost is about $13 (£6.90) for the transfer. From the Treasure Cay Airport to Green Turtle Cay, the charge is about $15 (£7.95). Elbow Cay costs about $12 (£6.35) for the transfer.

It's also possible to make arrangements for a taxi tour of Great or Little Abaco. These, however, are expensive, and you don't really see much.

BY FERRY Mostly, you'll get around with **Albury's Ferry Service** (© 242/367-3147; www.albursyferry.com), which provides several ferry connections between Marsh Harbour and both Elbow Cay (Hope Town) and Man-O-War Cay, a 20-minute trip to either destination. The one-way fare is $15 (£7.95) adults, $7.50 (£3.95) for children 11 and younger. (Ferries also go to Guana Cay.) The ferry docks are not far from the Marsh Harbour Airport; it's about a 10-minute, $13 to $14 (£6.90–£7.40) cab ride for two passengers (plus $3/£1.60 for each additional passenger).

For car-ferry service to Green Turtle Cay, see the section, "Green Turtle Cay (New Plymouth)," later in this chapter. Ferries go from Great Abaco Island to Green Turtle Cay, but those docks are a 35-minute, $70 (£37) cab ride for up to four passengers from the Marsh Harbour Airport. It's better to fly to Treasure Cay than Marsh Harbour to do this, and then take a taxi to the ferry docks.

1 Marsh Harbour (Great Abaco Island)

The largest town in the Abacos, and the third largest in The Bahamas, Marsh Harbour lies on Great Abaco Island and is the major gateway to this island group.

Marsh Harbour is also a shipbuilding center, but tourism accounts for most of its revenues. A number of good inns are located here. Although the town doesn't have the quaint New England charm of either New Plymouth or Hope Town, it does have a shopping center and various other facilities not found in many Out Island settlements. Good water-taxi connections, too, make this a popular place from which to explore offshore cays, including Man-O-War and Elbow. Several hotels will also rent you a bike if you want to pedal around town.

MARSH HARBOUR ESSENTIALS

GETTING THERE See "Abacos Essentials," above. Marsh Harbour is the most easily accessible point in the Abacos from the U.S. mainland, served by daily flights from Florida.

GETTING AROUND You won't need a car to get around the town itself, but if you want to explore the rest of the island on your own, you can rent a car for $75 (£40) a day or $350 (£186) per week (be prepared for bad roads, though). In Marsh Harbour, call **A&P Rentals** at © 242/367-2655 to see if any vehicles are available.

Rental Wheels of Abaco at Marsh Harbour (© 242/367-4643) will rent bikes at $10 (£5.30) a day or $45 (£24) a week, and also mopeds at $45 (£24) per day or $200 (£106) a week.

VISITOR INFORMATION The **Abaco Tourist Office** is at Queen Elizabeth Drive in the commercial heart of town (© 242/367-3067). It's open Monday to Friday 9am to 5pm.

FAST FACTS There's a **First Caribbean International Bank** on Don MacKay Boulevard (© 242/367-2152), plus several other banks and a **post office** (© 242/367-2571).

For medication, go to the **Chemist Shop Pharmacy,** Don MacKay Boulevard (© 242/367-3106), open Monday to Saturday 8:30am to 5:30pm.

Dial **911** if you need the **police.**

SPECIAL EVENTS In July, Marsh Harbour hosts **Regatta Week,** the premier yachting event in the Abacos, attracting sailboats and their crews from around the world. It's held sometime around the U.S. and Bahamian Independence Days (July 4 and July 10). Many of the yachters participating in this event stay at the Green Turtle Club (p. 229). For registration forms and more information, write to **Regatta Time in Abaco,** P.O. Box AB20551, Marsh Harbour, Abaco, The Bahamas, or call David Ralph at © 242/367-2677.

WHERE TO STAY

Abaco Beach Resort & Boat Harbour ✵ This beachfront resort—the biggest and best in Marsh Harbour—is a good choice, especially if you're serious about diving or fishing. Extending over a sprawling acreage at the edge of town and fronting a small but lovely beach, it's a business with several different faces: the hotel, with handsomely furnished rooms that overlook the Sea of Abaco; the well-managed restaurant and bar; the Boat Harbour Marina, which has slips for 180 boats and full docking facilities; and a full-fledged dive shop.

Angler's Restaurant is one of Marsh Harbour's best (see listing under "Where to Dine," below). There's a swim-up bar and a beachfront bar serving light snacks and grog. To reach the resort from Marsh Harbour Airport, take a taxi ($15/£7.95, but be sure to agree on the price first with the driver; 6.5km/4 miles).

P.O. Box AB20669, Marsh Harbour, Abaco, The Bahamas. © **800/468-4799** in the U.S., or 242/367-2158. Fax 242/367-4154. www.abacoresort.com. 82 units. Year-round $250–$390 (£133–£207) double; from $510 (£270) suite. AE, DISC, MC, V. **Amenities:** Restaurant; 2 bars; 2 pools; 2 tennis courts; fitness room; bike rentals; free use of water-sports equipment; boat rentals; dive shop; gift shop; massage; coin-operated laundry; nonsmoking rooms; rooms for those w/limited mobility. *In room:* A/C, TV, kitchen (in some), minibar, hair dryer, iron, safe, beverage maker.

Conch Inn Marina & Hotel   Set at the southeastern edge of the harbor, this is a casual one-story hotel leased on a long-term basis by one of the world's largest yacht-chartering companies, The Moorings. A number of small sandy beaches are within walking distance. Its motel-style, midsize bedrooms are small, each with two double beds (rollaways are available for extra occupants). Bathrooms are small but neatly kept with tub/showers. All units overlook the yachts bobbing in the nearby marina.

On the premises are an open-air swimming pool fringed with palm trees, and a nearby branch of the Dive Abaco scuba facility. The on-site restaurant and bar (Curly Tails Restaurant & Bar) is under independent management.

E. Bay St. (P.O. Box AB20469), Marsh Harbour, Abaco, The Bahamas. © **242/367-4000.** Fax 242/367-4004. www.conchinn.com. 9 units. Feb–July $160 (£85) double; Aug–Jan $120 (£64) double. Extra person $20 (£11) per day. AE, MC, V. **Amenities:** Restaurant; bar; pool; nonsmoking rooms. *In room:* A/C, TV, fridge, iron.

Lofty Fig Villas   This family-owned bungalow colony across from the Conch Inn overlooks the harbor. It doesn't have the services of a full-fledged resort, but it's good for families and self-sufficient types. Built in 1970, it stands in a tropical landscape with a freshwater pool and a gazebo where you can barbecue. Rooms have one queen-size bed and a queen-size hide-a-bed sofa, a fully tiled bathroom with shower, a din-ing area, a kitchen, and a private screened-in porch. Maid service is provided Monday through Saturday.

You're about a 10-minute walk from a supermarket and shops, and restaurants and bars lie just across the street. Marinas, a dive shop, and boat rentals are also close at hand. From the Lofty Fig, walk, bike, or drive 1.5km (1 mile) east to a point near the Marsh Harbour ferryboat docks for access to a sandy beach and a snorkeling site (many visitors opt to go to Guana Cay for their day at the beach, via ferryboat).

P.O. Box AB20437, Marsh Harbour, Abaco, The Bahamas. ©/fax **242/367-2681.** http://go-abacos.com/theabs/ marsh/mh_fig.html. 6 villas. Dec 15–Sept 15 $135 (£72) double, $850 (£450) weekly, extra person $20 (£11) per day; Sept 16–Dec 14 $115 (£61) double, $690 (£366) weekly, extra person $10 (£5.30) per day. MC, V. **Amenities:** Out-door pool. *In room:* A/C, kitchen, beverage maker, no phone.

WHERE TO DINE

If you'd like to go really casual, try **Island Bakery,** Don McKay Boulevard (© **242/ 367-2129**), which has the best Bahamian bread and cinnamon rolls on the island, often emerging fresh from the oven. You might even pick up the makings for a picnic.

The best pizzas are sold at **Sapodilly's Bar & Grill,** Bay Street (© **242/367-3498**); see below.

Angler's Restaurant ✿ BAHAMIAN/INTERNATIONAL   At the Boat Harbour, overlooking the Sea of Abaco, this is the main restaurant of the town's major resort. The interior features a nautical theme and Bahamian decor. Within a few steps of your seat, dock pilings rise from the water, yachts and fishing boats come and go, and the

place is open and airy. The menu changes daily, but fresh seafood, which the chef prepares with finesse, is always featured, along with a well-chosen selection of meat and
poultry dishes. Begin with crab cakes served with a Caribbean salsa and garnished
with mesclun greens, or perhaps the sesame seed–encrusted tuna steak accompanied
with sweet soy sauce. Main dishes dance with flavor, notably the island cracked conch
marinated in a coconut-lime sauce, grilled veal with tomato basil spatzle, and freshly
caught grouper with a red or white cream sauce.

In the Abaco Beach Resort & Boat Harbour, Marsh Harbour. © 242/367-2158. Reservations recommended for dinner. Main courses $6–$29 (£3.20–£15). AE, DISC, MC, V. Daily 6am–2:30pm and 6–10pm.

Curly Tails Restaurant & Bar BAHAMIAN   Adjacent to the Conch Inn and the
facilities of the Moorings, the eatery attracts a lot of yachties and visiting professional
athletes. The cooks use local ingredients, such as freshly caught grouper and snapper,
whenever they can. They also know every conceivable way to prepare conch. The reg-
ulars don't even have to consult the menu; they just ask, "What's good?" Fish and
seafood are always on the menu. Diners also look for daily specials, such as curried
chicken or steamed chicken. If you're frittering away a few hours, drop in for a Conch
Crawl, a rum-based drink with secret ingredients. The bar, set beneath an octagon
gazebo near the piers, is a fine place to meet people.

At the Conch Inn (The Moorings), Bay St. © 242/367-4444. Reservations not required. Main courses $22–$50
(£12–£27). MC, V. Daily 7am–10pm.

The Jib Room BAHAMIAN/AMERICAN   This funky restaurant/bar is a hangout
for local residents and boat owners who savor its welcoming spirit. If you want the
house-special cocktail, a Bilge Burner, get ready for a head-spinning combination of
apricot brandy, rum, coconut juice, and Kahlúa. Saturday night brings Jib's steak barbecue, when as many as 300 1-pound New York strip steaks are served. The only other
night dinner is served is Wednesday, when grilled baby back ribs might be the featured
dish of the day. Other choices include a seafood platter, grilled chicken, and broiled
lobster—and yes, you've probably had it all before in better versions, but the dishes
are well prepared. Go for the convivial atmosphere rather than the food.

Marsh Harbour Marina, Pelican Shores. © 242/367-2700. Reservations required for dinner. Lunch platters
$8.50–$14 (£4.50–£7.40); fixed-price dinners $20–$25 (£11–£13). MC, V. Wed–Sat 11:30am–2:30pm; dinner Wed
and Sat 7–11pm.

Mangoes Restaurant BAHAMIAN/INTERNATIONAL   Near the harbor in
one of the town's most distinctive buildings, Mangoes is the best, and certainly the
most popular, restaurant on the island, attracting both yachties and locals. It boasts a
cedar-topped bar and a cathedral ceiling that soars above a deck jutting over the water.
Somehow the chefs seem to try a little harder here, offering a typical menu along with
a hint of island spirit. Our faithful friend, grilled grouper, is dressed up a bit with
mango and tomatoes, and cracked conch makes an appearance as well. Your best bet,
as in nearly all Bahamian restaurants, is usually the fresh catch of the day. At lunch
you can sample its locally famous "conch burger."

Front St. © 242/367-2957. Reservations recommended. Main courses lunch $13–$17 (£6.90–£9), dinner $14–$33
(£7.40–£17). MC, V. Mon–Sat 11:30am–2:30pm; daily 6pm–midnight.

Sapodilly's Bar & Grill BAHAMIAN   This restaurant occupies an open-air pavilion
across the road from the harborfront, in an area of town known as "the tourist strip."
Even if you eventually head into the high-raftered interior dining room, take time out

for a drink or two on the covered open-air deck, surrounded by vibrant Junkanoo colors and a crowd of local hipsters, yacht owners, marina workers, and businessmen visiting from other parts of The Bahamas. Lunch might consist of grilled fish sandwiches, burgers, salads, and quiche. Dinners are more elaborate, with 12-ounce New York strip steak, a flavor-filled shrimp kabob in teriyaki sauce, and zesty curried filets of grouper. There's a happy hour with live music every Friday from 5:30 to 7:30pm.

E. Bay St. (*c* 242/367-3498. Reservations recommended. Lunch platters and sandwiches $8–$13 (£4.25–£6.90); dinner main courses $20–$27 (£11–£14). MC, V. Daily 11:30am–3pm and 6–10pm.

Wally's BAHAMIAN/INTERNATIONAL   Across the street from the water, this eatery occupies a tidy pink colonial villa on a lawn dotted with hibiscus. You'll find here an outdoor terrace, a boutique, and an indoor bar and dining area filled with Haitian paintings. The special drink of the house is a Wally's Special, containing four kinds of rum and a medley of fruit juices. The chef prepares the best Bahamian cracked conch at Marsh Harbour, as well as tender filet mignon, lamb chops, tarragon chicken, and an excellent version of smothered grouper. Main dishes come with a generous house salad and vegetables. The place really shines at lunchtime, when things tend to get very busy as hungry diners devour dolphinfish burgers, several kinds of chicken platters, and some well-stuffed sandwiches. Part of the style here comes courtesy of sisters Barbara and Maureen Smith, who head to Paris every fall and bring culinary discoveries back to their enterprise in Marsh Harbour. Live music performances take place on Wednesday and Saturday nights.

E. Bay St. (*c* 242/367-2074. Reservations recommended for dinner. Lunch sandwiches and platters $9–$15 (£4.75–£7.95); dinner main courses $27–$34 (£14–£18). AE, DISC, MC, V. Tues–Sat 11:30am–3pm and 6–9pm. Closed 6 weeks Sept–Oct.

BEACHES, WATERSPORTS & OTHER OUTDOOR PURSUITS

Whatever sport you want to pursue—whether snorkeling or a full-day's fishing charter—the innkeepers at Marsh Harbour can set you up with the right people or equipment. For variety, you can also take the ferry over to Hope Town and check out the facilities and outfitters there.

Of the major towns of the Out Islands, Marsh Harbour has some of the least appealing beaches. You can try one of three private beaches, but none is very enticing, and none really wants outsiders. The easiest to get into is the one at the Abaco Beach Resort, but it's small, not really fabulous, and, again, private. Buy a drink for a local at the hotel bar, and you're in, but that, at best, is a somewhat uncomfortable arrangement.

To compensate, beachgoers get into their cars and head south of Marsh Harbour. Once south of Little Harbour after 15 to 20 minutes of driving, lots of good beaches begin to appear. The beaches near the hamlet of **Casuarina Point** benefit from some battered, all-Bahamian restaurants in the vicinity.

Some swimmers heading south from Marsh Harbour make it a point to go eastward from the main highway whenever an offshoot road appears, usually at points near Little Harbour or at points south of Little Harbour. Other times, they simply stop their cars wherever they feel like it.

None of the beaches on Great Abaco Island has facilities or lifeguards. Guard your valuables and stay alert to be safe.

BOAT CHARTERS

If you'd like to try bareboating in The Bahamas—seagoing without captain or crew— **Abaco Bahamas Charters,** Hopetown, Abaco (*c* **800/626-5690;** fax or local phone

242/366-0151; www.abacocharters.com), can set you up; weekly charters with a choice of eight boats begin at $1,625 (£861; and can go as high as $4,450/£2,359 during winter), with a $1,500 (£795) deposit required. Only experienced sailors can rent.

The Moorings (© 888/952-8420 or 242/367-4000; www.moorings.com) is one of the leading charter sailboat outfitters in the world. It operates from an eagle's nest perch behind the Conch Inn Resort and Marina, overlooking intersecting piers and wharves—at least 80 berths, with more on the way—where hundreds of upscale watercraft are tied up (many of them are for rent). With one of its vessels, you can enjoy short sails between the islands, stopping at white-sandy beaches and snug anchorages. Yacht rentals generally range from $500 to $1,300 (£265–£689) a day, with a skipper costing another $150 (£80) per day, and an onboard cook (if you want one) priced at an additional $140 (£74) per day.

For the more casual boater, **Sea Horse Boat Rentals,** at the Abaco Beach Resort (© 242/367-2513), offers some of the best rentals. A 4.5m (15-ft.) Boston Whaler rents for $145 (£77) per day, and you can also book a 5.4m (18-ft.) Privateer for $165 (£87) per day. Other vessels are for rent, too, and all boats are equipped with a Bimini top, coolers, a compass, and a swimming platform, along with life jackets, a paddle, docking lines, and other equipment. Sea Horse is open daily from 8am to 5pm.

SNORKELING & SCUBA DIVING

The strangest dive site of all is the **Abacos Train Wreck,** which can be explored in 4.5 to 6m (15–20 ft.) of water. This unusual wreck consists of two locomotives lying on their sides. During the U.S. Civil War, the locomotives were reportedly part of a Union train, captured by Confederate troops, which had been sold to Cuba. The wooden barge transporting the train ran aground on the reef during a storm in 1865. Enough of the train still exists to make it an interesting shore dive. Yet another wreck nearby, *Adirondack,* lies in shallow water some 3 to 7.5m (10–25 ft.) deep. Many divers also come here to explore the government-protected **Sea Preserve and Fowl Cay Land,** which teems with multicolored sea life in shallow reefs.

The best place to snorkel is **Mermaid Reef and Beach,** with its colorful reef, moray eels, and plethora of beautiful rainbow-hued fish. The reef and beach lie on Pelican Shores, the northernmost edge of the Marsh Harbour waterfront directly west of the Marsh Harbour Marina. From the center of Marsh Harbour at East Bay Street, walk east along the harbor and then head northwest until you reach the marina. Once at the marina, continue to walk west to Pelican Shores across the stretch of scrub and sand until you reach Mermaid Reef and Beach, where you can enjoy the beach or else go snorkeling in the clear waters. **Sea Horse Boat Rentals** at the Abaco Beach Resort & Boat Harbour marina (© 242/367-2513) rents snorkel gear.

Scuba divers might want to check out the nearby **Pelican Cays Land and Sea Park** ✦. You won't find any organized excursions here, but Dive Abaco (see below) is the best source of information and might arrange a trip. You can also drive down to the park by following the road immediately south of Marsh Harbour and then turning east at the sign leading toward the park. Several small beaches are suitable for swimming. The easiest jumping-off point is at Pelican Harbour.

Dive Abaco, Marsh Harbour (© 800/247-5338 in the U.S., or 242/367-2787; www.diveabaco.com), rents snorkel gear and offers dive trips to tunnels and caverns along the world's third-longest barrier reef. Resort courses for uncertified novice divers are all-inclusive for $155 (£82). Two-tank dives, including tanks and weights for certified divers, cost $90 (£48) and depart daily at 9:30am; afternoon trips are dictated by demand. Shop hours are daily from 8:30am to 5pm; ask for owner-operator Keith Rogers.

ATTRACTIONS ON LAND

Marsh Harbour is the best center for exploring the nature-created attractions of both Great Abaco and Little Abaco.

A fully graded and tarred main highway links all the settlements on the "mainland," with such colorfully named hamlets as Fire Road, Mango Hill, Coopers Town, Joe Creek, Red Bays, Snake Cay, Little Harbour, Sandy Point, Cherokee Sound, and, our favorite, Hole-in-the-Wall, which lies at the "bottom" of Great Abaco.

Driving south for 40km (25 miles) from Marsh Harbour along the Great Abaco Highway, you come first to **Cherokee Sound,** set at the end of a peninsula jutting out into Cherokee Sound. The 150 residents are descended from Loyalists who fled mainland U.S. in 1783 and remained faithful to the British Crown. These people faced an inhospitable land and for 2 centuries have tried to make a living as best they can. The men dive for lobsters or go out at night "sharking." The jaws of the sharks are sold in Marsh Harbour. They also hunt down tiniki crabs, as well as pigeon and wild boar in the remote pinelands of the Abacos.

The unhurried routine around here is in the process of major change. Entrepreneur Peter de Savary has opened the most exclusive club in The Bahamas. Called the **Abaco Club on Winding Bay** (© **800/303-2765** or 242/367-0077; www.theabacoclub. com), it is deluxe living personified, but is only for the super rich. The first time you stay, a cabana suite costs between $650 and $800 (£345–£424) a night; two- to four-bedroom units range from $1,200 to $3,500 (£636–£1,855) a night. If you return for a visit, you'll have to pay a membership cost of $85,000 (£45,050).

Forty-eight kilometers (30 miles) south of Marsh Harbour takes you to **Little Harbor,** a cay shaped like a circle with a white-sandy beach running along most of its waterfront. The location is to the immediate east of Cherokee Sound. At Little Harbour, you can visit **Pete Johnston's Foundry** (© **242/366-3503**), the only bronze foundry in The Bahamas. Settling here in 1951, the Johnston family achieved international fame as artists and sculptors. They use an old "lost-wax" method in the casting of their bronze sculptures, many of which are sold in prestigious art galleries in America, although you can also buy them directly from the foundry itself. Mrs. Johnston creates porcelain figurines of island life such as birds, fish, boats, and even fishermen. The Johnstons welcome visitors at their studio daily from 10 to 11am and 2 to 3pm. You can also purchase a remarkable book here, *Artist on His Island,* detailing the true-life adventures of Randolph and Margot Johnston, who lived a Swiss Family Robinson adventure when they first arrived at Little Harbour with their three sons. Sailing in an old Bahamian schooner, the *Langosta,* they stayed in one of the local caves until they eventually erected a thatched dwelling for themselves.

After a visit to the foundry, you can stop in for a drink at the laid-back **Pete's Pub and Gallery** nearby (© **242/477-5487;** www.petespubandgallery.com). At the pub, you'll think you've arrived in *Gilligan's Island* (remember the old TV sitcom?). The beer is cold and the art on the walls is for sale. The pub was constructed in part from the timbers of the *Langosta.* You can also order lunch here daily, costing from $20 (£11). Fresh seafood such as mango-glazed grouper or lemon-pepper dolphin is served along with burgers. A wild boar roast is offered every Saturday from April to July. In the evening, Pete Johnston might sing a medley of sea chanteys, accompanying himself on his guitar. The pub is open daily from 11am "until everyone leaves at night." It is closed September and October.

After leaving Cherokee and Little Harbour, you can return to the Great Abaco Highway, heading south once again to reach the little fishing village of **Casuarina Point** west of Cherokee Sound. Here you'll find a lovely stretch of sand and some jade-colored boneflats (low water areas where bonefish are caught). If you keep going south, you come to **Crossing Rocks,** a little fishing village 64km (40 miles) to the south of Marsh Harbour, noted for its kilometer-long beach of golden sand. The hamlet where locals barely eke out a living takes its name from the isthmus where Great Abaco Island narrows to its thinnest point.

From here, if you continue traveling south, you come to a fork in the road, the southern road going to the **Abaco National Park** (also called Bahamas National Trust Sanctuary; ☎ 242/393-1317) and the aptly named **Hole-in-the-Wall.** A poor little hamlet with a few settlers, Hole-in-the-Wall marks the end of the line for drives along the Abacos.

Protected by the government, the 8,296-hectare (20,491-acre) Abaco National Park, established in 1994, sprawls across the southeastern portion of Grand Abaco Island. Some 2,023 hectare (4,997 acres) of it is pine forest, with a lot of wetlands that are home to native bird life, including the endangered Bahama parrot. Hardwood forests, sand dunes, and mangrove flats fill the area. Rangers, under the sponsorship of the Bahamas National Trust, operate occasional tours of the sanctuary and protect the area.

SHOPPING

Bahama Dawn, Engar Gottlieb Boulevard, next to the public library (☎ 242/367-4648), carries Androsia batik clothing, along with some local crafts. For souvenir items, try **Iggy Biggy,** Main Street, across from Conch Inn (☎ 242/367-3596).

MARSH HARBOUR AFTER DARK

The **Sand Bar,** opening onto the Sea of Abaco at the Abaco Beach Resort & Boat Harbour (☎ 242/367-2158), is the most popular gathering spot in town. The yachting crowd, often from Miami, hangs out here, swapping tall tales of the sea while downing strong rum punches. Another good hangout is **Wally's,** East Bay Street (☎ 242/367-2074). You can enjoy the special punch on an outdoor terrace or inside a cozy bar. On Wednesday and Saturday, live entertainment is often presented. **Sapodilly's Bar & Grill,** East Bay Street (☎ 242/367-3498), attracts a blend of locals and visitors, some of whom play at its pool table, others preferring to mix and mingle at the bar.

2 Elbow Cay (Hope Town) ★

Elbow Cay is known for its spectacular beaches. One of The Bahamas's best, **Tahiti Beach** lies in splendid isolation at the far end of Elbow Cay, with sparkling waters and powdery white sands. Access is possible only on foot, by riding a rented bicycle across sand and gravel paths from Hope Town, or by private boat.

The cay's largest settlement is **Hope Town,** a little village with a candy-striped 36m (118-ft.) lighthouse—the most photographed attraction in the Out Islands. Hope Town seems frozen in time. Like other offshore cays of the Abacos, it was settled by Loyalists who left the new United States and came to The Bahamas to remain subjects of the British Crown. Its clapboard, saltbox cottages are weathered to a silver gray or painted in pastel colors, with white picket fences setting them off. The buildings may remind you of New England, but this palm-fringed island has South Seas flavor.

The island is almost free of cars. In exploring Hope Town, you can take one of two roads: "Up Along" or "Down Along," which both run along the water.

ELBOW CAY ESSENTIALS

GETTING THERE You can reach Elbow Cay in about 20 minutes via regularly scheduled ferry service from Marsh Harbour on Great Abaco. A one-way fare is $10 (£5.30), same-day round-trip is $15 (£7.95), and service is three times daily. For details, call **Albury's Ferry Service** at © 242/365-6010 or visit www.alburysferry.com.

GETTING AROUND Many visitors rent boats to get around the island, explore nearby cays, and go fishing and snorkeling. But if you're not interested in playing sea captain, you can still move easily around Elbow Cay. The quiet, narrow streets of Hope Town are reserved for pedestrians, and you can walk to many other parts of tiny Elbow Cay. You can't rent a car on Elbow Cay, but it isn't a problem. Hope Town, the scenic seaside village, bans all motor vehicles. If you'd like a golf cart delivered to your hotel, call **Island Cart Rental** (© 242/366-0448 in U.S.; www.islandcartrentals.com); these gas or electric carts cost $45 (£24) a day or $270 (£143) per week. Hotels provide shuttle vans to and from town. Some dining rooms offer pick-up and drop-off service at dinnertime if you call ahead. Bicycles—often free for hotel guests—are available at or near most accommodations. Taxis meet incoming flights at the Marsh Harbour airport, and they greet arriving ferries as well. During your stay, the staff at your hotel can call one for you when you need it.

FAST FACTS If you're in need of medical attention, you must go to Marsh Harbour. A local **post office** (© 242/366-0098) is at the head of the upper public dock, but expect mail sent from here to take a long time. Hours are Monday to Friday from 9am to noon and from 1 to 5pm.

WHERE TO STAY

Elbow Cay's long and secluded white-sand shores, some backed by dunes, are some of The Bahamas' most stunning locales. Although accommodations are on or near beaches, the strands remain virtually vacant because the hotels are small and few in number.

Abaco Inn (R) (Finds) A sophisticated little hideaway about 3km (2 miles) south of Hope Town, the Abaco Inn faces a lovely sandy beach on White Sound. Compared to its main rival, Club Soleil Resort, Abaco Inn is actually more of a resort. An informal barefoot elegance and a welcoming spirit prevail here on the narrowest section of Elbow Cay, between the crashing surf of the jagged eastern coast and the sheltered waters of White Sound and the Sea of Abaco to the west. From the cedar-capped gazebo, you can gaze out over the rocky tidal flats of the Atlantic. Excellent snorkeling is close.

The midsize accommodations are arranged in a crescent facing the beach. They're set amid palms and sea grapes, and each has its own hammock placed conveniently nearby for quiet afternoons of reading or sleeping. Each comfortable unit has a ceiling fan, a bathroom with a tub/shower, white-tile floors, sliding-glass doors, and traditional furniture.

A modern, rambling clubhouse with a fireplace is both the social center and the most appealing restaurant/bar on the island (see "Where to Dine," below). Shuttle service is available from the airport. Boating and fishing can be arranged through the hotel.

White Sound, Hope Town, Elbow Cay, Abaco, The Bahamas. ℂ 800/468-8799 in the U.S., or 242/366-0133. Fax 242/366-0113. www.abacoinn.com. 22 units. Year-round $126–$165 (£67–£87) double. Extra person $50 (£27) per day. AE, DISC, MC, V. **Amenities:** Restaurant; bar; pool; bike rentals; babysitting; laundry service; nonsmoking rooms; rooms for those w/limited mobility. *In room:* A/C, hair dryer, iron, beverage maker, no phone.

Club Soleil Resort

Abaco Inn (see listing above) may have better accommodations, but nothing surpasses the tranquillity of this inn. Because of its isolated position near the lighthouse on the western edge of Hope Town's harbor, the only way to get to this Spanish-style resort is by boat. Once there, you're just a short walk from some lovely beaches. If you bring your own boat, you can moor it at this hotel's marina, but if you just happen to have left your boat at home, call the owners. They will arrange a free waterborne transfer from any nearby coastline you designate. Mid-size rooms with shower units are set in a two-story, Mediterranean-inspired annex, and they overlook a swimming pool and the boats in the harbor. Each room contains two double beds and a clean and tasteful decor.

Western Harbourfront, Hope Town, Elbow Cay, The Bahamas. ℂ 888/291-5428 or 242/366-0003. Fax 242/366-0254. www.clubsoleil.com. 7 units. Year-round $130–$150 (£69–£80) double; $149 (£79) triple; $150 (£80) quad; $160 (£85) 2-bedroom apt. AE, MC, V. Closed Sept. **Amenities:** Restaurant; bar; pool; laundry service; all non-smoking rooms. *In room:* A/C, TV, kitchen (in apt), minibar, coffeemaker, hair dryer, no phone.

Hope Town Harbour Lodge 🕊🕊

This much-expanded former private home lies in Hope Town near the beach and harbor. It was the home of Brigadier Thomas Robbins, a retired British army officer, who constructed the original core as his retirement house in 1948. After hurricane damage from Floyd in 1999, the property lay dormant for a while until its recent renovation. Hurricane-strength windows and doors were added, along with new furnishings. Possibly the best addition was the installation of private balconies in all the rooms in the main building, each opening onto a water view. Boardwalks and artful landscaping added other grace notes. Permission was granted for the construction of independent cottages scattered across the ground, each with terra-cotta tile floors. French doors open onto private decks overlooking the grounds. The best way to stay here is to rent the luxurious century-old Butterfly House. In addition to six cottages, the hotel offers six cabanas.

Upper Rd., Hope Town, Elbow Cay, The Bahamas. ℂ 242/366-0095. Fax 242/366-0286. www.hopetownlodge.com. 25 units. Year-round $155–$200 (£82–£106) double; $190–$195 (£101–£103) cabanas; $255–$275 (£135–£146) cottages; $425 (£225) for 4 or $550 (£292) for 6 in Butterfly House. DC, MC, V. **Amenities:** 2 restaurants; 2 bars; outdoor pool; laundry service; nonsmoking rooms. *In room:* A/C, TV in Butterfly House only, minibar, hair dryer, iron, kitchenette (in some), Wi-Fi, no phone.

Hope Town Hideaways

Staying here is like living in your own "second home" in The Bahamas. Five gingerbread-trimmed villas lie across the harbor from where the ferryboats arrive from Marsh Harbour. Located on 4.5 hectares (11 acres) of grounds and reached by boat, this hideaway lives up to its name. The accommodations are part of a larger complex of privately owned homes, surrounded by grounds handsomely landscaped with orange trees, mangoes, and flamboyant bougainvillea. One or two couples—the maximum is six guests—can sleep comfortably in the units, each of which includes a large kitchen, a dining room, a living area with two single daybeds, and two bedrooms. Furnishings are custom built, and each private bathroom comes with a tub/shower. You're not on the beach, but you can enjoy the freshwater pool here. Hideaways is also a management company featuring more than 75 privately owned cottages and villas to rent on the island.

1 Purple Porpoise Plaza, Hope Town, Elbow Cay, Abaco, The Bahamas. (℮ 242/366-0224. Fax 242/366-0434. www.hopetown.com. 5 villas. Year-round from $1,000 (£530) per week cottage for up to 4 guests. DISC, MC, V. Amenities: Freshwater pool. In room: A/C, kitchen, no phone.

Sea Spray Resort and Villas ℛ

On 2.4 hectares (6 acres) of landscaped grounds, 5.5km (3½ miles) south of Hope Town and near the southernmost tip of Elbow Cay, these beachfront villas are owned and operated by Ruth Albury, who runs them in a welcoming, personal way. Rented villas include full kitchens and decks that overlook the water. Accommodations are spacious and comfortably furnished, each with a small bathroom containing a tub/shower. The Alburys and their hardworking staff are happy to share their vast experience of what to see and do on Elbow Cay and in the Abacos: You can bike, sail, go deep-sea fishing, snorkel, go bonefishing, or explore nearby deserted islands.

Sea Spray also operates a restaurant serving well-prepared food at all three meals, while diners enjoy a view of the crashing surf and a weathered gazebo. Nonguests are welcome, too; if you phone in advance for a reservation, management will send a van to collect you from Hope Town.

White Sound, Elbow Cay, Abaco, The Bahamas. (℮ 242/366-0065. Fax 242/366-0383. www.seasprayresort.com. 5 units. Year-round $180–$260 (£95–£138) 1-bedroom unit; $350 (£186) 2-bedroom unit; $430 (£228) 3-bedroom unit. AE, MC, V. Amenities: Restaurant; bar; pool; watersports equipment/rentals. In room: A/C, TV, kitchen, no phone.

Turtle Hill Vacation Villas ℛ

On the outskirts of Hope Town, a trio of luxury villas lies just steps from a vast secluded beach where sea turtles return to nest. Fruit trees and other tropical foliage make this a secluded getaway. Each house sleeps six persons comfortably in two large bedrooms, with a queen-size sleeper sofa in the living room, a full bathroom, a well-equipped kitchen, a spacious living and dining area, and both central air-conditioning and ceiling fans. Linens are provided, and a Caribbean-style cabana bar serves drinks and finger foods daily.

Between Abaco Sea and Hope Town, Hope Town, Abaco, The Bahamas. (℮ 800/339-2124 in the U.S., or 242/366-0557. Fax 242/366-0557. www.turtlehill.com. 6 units. Winter $380 (£201) daily for 4 guests, $420 (£223) for 5–6 guests; off season $270 (£143) daily for 4 guests, $310 (£164) for 5–6 guests. AE, MC, V. Amenities: Restaurant; bar; 2 pools; babysitting; laundry service; dry cleaning; nonsmoking rooms. In room: A/C, TV, kitchen, hair dryer (in some), iron, ceiling fans, beverage maker, no phone.

WHERE TO DINE

Abaco Inn ℛ BAHAMIAN/INTERNATIONAL

Flavorful food is served in a breezy, almost elegant waterfront setting. The chef prepares lunch dishes such as conch chowder, pasta primavera, and salads with delectable homemade dressings featuring tarragon and other herbs. The dinner menu changes frequently but usually offers seafood, vegetarian, and meat dishes, each expertly seasoned and well prepared. Typical meals are likely to begin with seafood bisque or vichyssoise, followed by coconut grouper (a house specialty), spinach fettuccine Alfredo, roasted lamb with herbs and mint sauce, or, our favorite, broiled red snapper with a light salsa. The crème brûlée and Key lime, coconut, and chocolate silk pies are delectable. The inn will send a minivan to pick you up from other parts of the island if you phone in advance.

About 4km (2½ miles) south of Hope Town. (℮ 242/366-0133. Reservations required for dinner. Lunch sandwiches, salads, and platters $8–$12 (£4.25–£6.35); dinner main courses $15–$34 (£7.95–£18). AE, DISC, MC, V. Daily 8–10:30am, noon–3pm, and 6:30–9:30pm.

Cap'n Jacks BAHAMIAN

Depending on when you come, you may find turtle burgers or crawfish on the menu at this casual alfresco dining spot at the edge of the harbor. Any time of year, the grouper and conch are well prepared and the freshest food on the menu. Landlubbers gravitate toward the more routine fried chicken and burgers. The Key lime and chocolate silk pies are justifiably popular dessert choices. Try Cap'n Jacks' version of the omnipresent Goombay Smash. Come on Wednesday or Friday for live local music in the evening between 8 and 11pm.

On the harbor in Hope Town. ✆ 242/366-0247. Main courses $9–$22 (£4.75–£12). MC, V. Mon–Sat 8am–9pm.

Harbour's Edge ✪ BAHAMIAN   Hope Town's best and most popular restaurant is set on piers above the water in a clapboard house. It's the island's lighthearted social center. The bar has an adjacent waterside deck where you can moor if you arrive by boat, as many visitors do. Here and in the dining room as well, the crackle of VHF radio is always audible—boat owners and local residents often reserve tables on short-wave radio, channel 16.

Lunch includes such typical yet flavor-filled dishes as conch fritters, conch chowder, hamburgers, sandwiches, and conch platters. In the evening, dinners are also well prepared—generous portions of chicken in white wine with potatoes, Greek or Caesar salad, pan-fried pork chops, chargrilled grouper, New York strip steak, fish in coconut milk, and more.

Hope Town, next to the post office. ✆ 242/366-0087. Reservations recommended. Main courses lunch $10–$18 (£5.30–£9.55), dinner $15–$40 (£7.95–£21). MC, V. Wed–Mon 11:30am–11pm; bar Wed–Mon 10am–2am. Closed mid-Sept to mid-Oct.

Hope Town Harbour Lodge ✪ BAHAMIAN   One of the first lodges or inns ever built in Hope Town, this restaurant is still winning new friends. At night, romantic couples opt for a table on the cozy terrace with views of the harbor and the lights from the yachts. Begin the evening with a rum punch in Wrecker's Bar, overlooking the water. The menu here is hardly inventive, but it's good, featuring the usual array of chicken, steak, and pork chops. Occasionally, a fisherman will bring in a big marlin that the chef grills to perfection. Bahamian lobster appears delightfully in a creamy fettuccine and the local grouper is fashioned into Chinese-style spring rolls served with a mustard-laced chutney sauce. In the main dining area are picture windows, rattan chairs, and nautical prints. During lunch, diners gravitate to the Reef Bar and Grill fronting the water.

Don't overlook the lodge as a possibility for rooms. It rents 20 comfortably furnished and air-conditioned doubles, with prices going from $150 to $195 (£80–£103) all year. Accommodations lie on any of three floors, each with a patio or balcony, sliding glass doors, a small bathroom with shower stall, and wicker furnishings.

Hope Town. ✆ 242/366-0095. Reservations recommended for dinner. Main courses lunch $7–$12 (£3.70–£6.35), dinner $20–$38 (£11–£20). MC, V. Daily 11:30am–3pm; Tues–Sun 6:30–8pm.

BEACHES, WATERSPORTS & OTHER OUTDOOR PURSUITS

In Hope Town, you'll find sandy beaches right at your doorstep, and more beaches in the south are only about a 15-minute ride away. **Garbanzo Beach,** near Sea Spray Resort, lures many surfers. Isolated **Tahiti Beach** ✪✪, at the southern end of the island (a little more than .6km/1 mile from Sea Spray), got its name from the thick wall of palms there. At low tide, the shelling can be excellent along this gorgeous curve of sand, and the shallow waters make for good bonefishing, too. Across the way, you can see uninhabited **Tilloo Cay** and the Atlantic's crashing waves in the distance.

Tahiti Beach is about a 10-minute bike ride from Sea Spray and about 20 minutes from Abaco Inn, both in the White Sound area. To get here, you have to walk your bike up and down a few small but rocky rises.

Finds   Exploring the Abacos by Boat

The ideal way to explore the Abacos is by boat. **Island Marine,** Parrot Cay in Hope Town (℃ **242/366-0282;** fax 242/366-0281), will set you up with one of its rental boats. You can then cruise to the boat-building settlement of Man-O-War Cay, to artist Pete Johnson's bronze foundry/gallery/pub in Little Harbour (see section 1, "Marsh Harbour [Great Abaco Island]," earlier in this chapter), and to many uninhabited cays and deserted beaches where you can go shelling, exploring, and picnicking in peace.

Small-boat rentals range from a 5.1m (17-ft.) Boston Whaler to 7m (23-ft.) Man-O-War boats. Prices run from $125 to $250 (£66–£133) per day or $625 to $1,100 (£331–£583) per week.

Traveling along, you'll pass sea-grape trees, fluffy long-needled pines, and other varied roadside vegetation. Turn left when you come to the first major left (by the white house on the bluff). Turn right when you see two stone pillars. Go downhill and turn left at the end of the road at the wire fences. Take this path to the end. Walk along the dense palm grove to the beach. Because you're heading for the shore, which is public, ignore the PRIVATE—NO TRESPASSING signs.

Irresistible deserted beaches lie to the south of Elbow Cay on pencil-thin **Tilloo Cay** (see above) and the tiny **Pelican Cays.** They make excellent targets for a day's sail. The waters around Tilloo Cay, packed with grouper and conch, are particularly good for both fishing and swimming. In the Pelican Cays Land and Sea Park, **Sandy Cay Reef** is one of the most colorful dive sites around. Line fishing, spear fishing, and shelling, however, are all taboo in this protected area.

The waves and breezes at **Garbanzo Beach,** in the **White Sound** area, make it prime hang-ten territory. If you don't bring your own surfboard, the staff at nearby **Sea Spray Resort** (℃ 242/366-0065) can help you get one.

The waters off the coast of Elbow Cay are a popular spot for boating and fishing. Head to the marina to join the fun.

Set about 20 steps south of Hope Town's post office, **Froggie's Out Island Adventures,** Harbour Road (℃ 242/366-0431; www.froggiesabaco.com), is the largest dive outfitter in the Abacos, with three boats (ranging 9–17m/30–55 ft. in length) that owner Theresa Albury uses to take divers to local dive sites. A certified diver with gear provided is charged $95 (£50); full-day snorkeling excursions are also arranged for $55 (£29) for adults and $40 (£21) for children.

The company also organizes tours, from snorkel cruises to dolphin-watching trips. A full-day cruise out to Great Guana Cay costs $45 (£24) per person (passengers only). An equivalent tour to Little Harbour, near the southernmost point of the Abacos, including visits to selected restaurants, bars, and an art gallery, also costs $45 (£24) per person.

LAND ATTRACTIONS

No cars are allowed in the heart of **Hope Town,** so bikers and pedestrians have the narrow paved streets, with names like Lovers' Lane, to themselves. As you wander through the town, you see harbor-side restaurants and pastel-painted saltbox cottages with purple and orange bougainvillea tumbling over stone and picket fences. Amid the usual island fare at the handful of souvenir shops is resort wear made from Androsia, the fabric produced on the Bahamian island of Andros. See "Shopping," below.

To find out why Malone is such a common surname, stop by the **Wyannie Malone Museum** (officially open most days from 10am–noon, but unofficially open "whenever"). This small collection of island lore is in tribute to the South Carolinian widow and mother of four who founded Hope Town around 1783.

Before **Hope Town's red-and-white striped lighthouse** was erected in 1838, many of Hope Town's residents made a good living luring ships toward shore to be wrecked on the treacherous reefs and rocks, and then turning the salvaged cargoes into cash. To protect this livelihood, some people tried in vain to destroy the beacon while it was being built. Today you can climb to the top of the 36m (118-ft.) tower for panoramic views of the harbor and town. Most weekdays between 10am and 4pm, the lighthouse keeper will be happy to give you a peek. The lighthouse is within walking distance of **Club Soleil** and **Hope Town Hideaways.** If you're staying elsewhere, you can make arrangements through your hotel for a visit.

SHOPPING

Of course, no one comes to Hope Town just to shop, but once you're here, you might want to pick up a souvenir. The **Ebb Tide Gift Shop** (© 242/366-0088), the best-stocked gift shop in town, lies in a white clapboard house with aqua trim 1 block from the harbor. Inside you'll find many treasures, including Androsia batiks made on Andros, costume jewelry, T-shirts, original watercolors, and fabrics sold by the yard. It's open 9am to 5pm Monday to Saturday.

ELBOW CAY AFTER DARK

On Saturday nights, a young party crowd gathers at **Harbour's Edge** (© 242/366-0087), a Hope Town bar and restaurant with the island's only pool table. On Monday night, Bahamian barbecues draw many people to **Sea Spray Resort** (© 242/366-0065), about 4.8km (3 miles) from Hope Town. The food is good, considering the low prices, and you can hear live music. Other evenings, people hang out at the bars of hotels and restaurants—or they turn in early to rest up for yet another day of exploring.

3 Man-O-War Cay

Visiting here is like going back in time. The island has lovely beaches, and many visitors come here to enjoy them—but it's best to leave more daring swimwear at home. The people who reside on this island are deeply religious and conservative. You won't find any crime—unless you bring it with you. No alcoholic beverages are sold on the island, although you can bring your own supply.

Like New Plymouth on Green Turtle Cay or Hope Town on Elbow Cay, Man-O-War is a Loyalist village, with similarities to a traditional New England town. The pastel clapboard houses, built by ships' carpenters and trimmed in gingerbread, are set off by freshly painted white picket fences intertwined with bougainvillea.

The people here are shy, but they do welcome outsiders to their isolated island. They are proud of their heritage, which includes a long boat-building tradition, and many, especially the old-timers, have known plenty of hard times. Many of them are related to the "conchs" of Key West and, like them, are a tough, insular people who have exhibited a proud independence for many years.

Tourism has only just begun to infiltrate Man-O-War Cay. Because of the relative lack of hotels and restaurants, many visitors come over just for the day, often in groups from Marsh Harbour. If you do stay for a while, stop by the Man-O-War Marina to arrange your boat rentals and watersports; there's also a dive shop there.

GETTING THERE & GETTING AROUND

To reach Man-O-War Cay, you must cross the water from Marsh Harbour. **Albury's Ferry Service** (© **242/367-3147** in Marsh Harbour or 242/365-6010 in Man-O-War; www.alburysferry.com) leaves from a dock near the Abaco Beach Resort. The round-trip same-day fare is $20 (£11) for adults and $10 (£5.30) for children ages 6 to 12. The ride takes about 20 minutes.

Except for a few service vehicles, Man-O-War Cay has almost no cars. If you want to explore farther than your own two feet will carry you, ask around and see if one of the locals will rent you a golf cart.

WHERE TO STAY

Schooner's Landing   Set in isolation on Man-O-War Cay's northeastern edge, this four-unit apartment complex is the only officially designated place to stay on the island. A seawall separates its lawns and hibiscus shrubs from the crashing surf, so swimmers and snorkelers meander a short distance down to the sands of a nearby beach. Each two-story unit contains a kitchen, ceiling fans, two private bathrooms, a TV, and a summery decor of wicker and rattan furniture. Each comes with a small, tidily kept bathroom with a tub/shower. There's no bar or restaurant, but either of two grocery stores on the island will deliver; most visitors opt to cook in, anyway.

Man-O-War Cay, Abaco, The Bahamas. © 242/367-4469 or 242/365-6072. Fax 242/365-6285. www.schooners landing.com. Year-round $275 (£146) daily; $1,850 (£981) weekly. MC, V. **Amenities:** Pool; laundry service; nonsmoking rooms; rooms for those w/limited mobility. *In room:* A/C, TV, kitchen, iron, ceiling fan, microwave, barbecue grill, beverage maker.

WHERE TO DINE

Man-O-War Marina Pavilion 🅖 *finds* AMERICAN/BAHAMIAN   The sides of this wooden pavilion are open to the breezes and a view of the boats bobbing at the nearby harbor. A crowd of loyal boat owners and local residents is always here, enjoying the simple but savory cuisine of Marjorie Eldon. Monday to Thursday, the focus is on such time-favored staples as roasted chicken fingers, grilled fish, burgers, fried conch with peas 'n' rice, and steaks. On Friday and Saturday nights, however, many locals arrive for grilled lamb, fish, steaks, or chicken, and the place is practically transformed into a neighborhood block party. Though liquor isn't served, you can BYOB.

Man-O-War Marina, Man-O-War Cay. © 242/365-6185. Main courses lunch $4–$12 (£2.10–£6.35), dinner $15–$32 (£7.95–£17). No credit cards. Mon–Thurs 11am–2pm; Fri–Sat 5:30–9pm. Closed Aug 15–Sept 30.

SHOPPING

The most unusual store and studio on the island, **Albury's Sail Shop,** located at the Man-O-War marina (© **242/365-6014**), occupies a house overlooking the water at the eastern end. The floor space is devoted to the manufacture and display of an inventory of brightly colored canvas garments and accessories. The 8-ounce cotton duck fabric once served as sailcloth for the community's boats. When synthetic sails came into vogue, four generations of Albury women put the cloth and their talents to use. Don't stop without chatting with them. Hours are Monday through Saturday from 7am to 5pm.

4 Great Guana Cay ⟨★⟩

The longest of the Abaco cays, Great Guana, on the east side of the chain, stretches 11km (6¾ miles) from tip to tip and lies between Green Turtle Cay and Man-O-War Cay. The beachfront running the length of the cay is spectacular, one of the loveliest in The Bahamas. The reef fishing is superb, and bonefish are plentiful in the shallow bays.

The settlement stretches along the beach at the head of the palm-fringed Kidd's Cove, named after the pirate. Ruins of an old sisal mill near the western end of the island make for an interesting detour. The island has about 150 residents, most of them descendants of Loyalists who left Virginia and the Carolinas to settle in this remote place, often called the "last spot of land before Africa."

As in similar settlements in New Plymouth and Man-O-War Cay, houses here resemble those of old New England. Over the years, the traditional pursuits of the islanders have been boat-building, carpentry, farming, and fishing. It won't take you long to explore the village; it has only two small stores, a one-room schoolhouse, and an Anglican church—and that's about it.

GETTING THERE & GETTING AROUND

Albury's Ferry Service, Marsh Harbour (© 242/365-6010; www.alburysferry.com), runs a four-times-a-day service to Great Guana Cay. A round-trip ticket costs $20 (£11) for adults, $10 (£5.30) for children under 11.

Instead of driving on the island, most people get around in small boats. Boats are available to charter for a half-day or a full day (or a month, for that matter). For example, a 7m (23-ft.) sailboat, fully equipped for living and cruising, is available for charter, and deep-sea fishing trips can be arranged. Try **Island Marine Boat Rentals** (© 242/366-0282; www.islandmarine.com), which rents 5m (16-ft.) Boston Whalers at $125 (£66) per day, $100 (£53) per day for 3 days, or $625 (£331) per week. **Sea Horse Boat Rentals** (© 242/367-2513; www.sea-horse.com) rents 5.4m (18-ft.) Privateers at $165 (£87) per day (for rentals of 7 days or more, the cost is $105/£56 per day or $735/£390 for the week). Both establishments are open Monday to Saturday 8am to 5pm. Island Marine is also open on Sunday 8am to noon.

WHERE TO STAY

Dolphin Beach Resort ⟨★⟩   Set directly astride one of the best beaches in The Bahamas, a 15-minute walk north of Guana Cay's largest settlement (Guana Village), with miles of powder-soft sand in front of you, this resort offers informal but very comfortable lodgings. Four of the units are in the main house and have queen-size beds and ceiling fans, TVs, small refrigerators, and microwaves; three of them have private screened-in decks with teakwood furniture. The oceanfront cottages (nine in all) also have queen-size beds, ceiling fans, air-conditioning, and full-size kitchenettes with stoves and charcoal grills. Cottages can accommodate between two and four guests, depending on their size. The showers are placed outside, but are secluded and screened off by island flora. The place is private, intimate, and laid-back.

There's a restaurant on the premises, Bluewater Grill, with a "conch crawl," a Bahamian take on a lobster tank. Nippers, a beachfront bar and grill, is within a 5-minute walk.

Great Guana Cay, Abaco, The Bahamas (Mailing address: General Delivery, Great Guana Cay, Abaco, Bahamas). ℂ 800/222-2646 or 242/365-5137. www.dolphinbeachresort.com. 13 units. Winter $200–$290 (£106–£154) double, $350–$400 (£186–£212) 2-bedroom unit, $360–$440 (£191–£233) 3-bedroom unit; off season $135–$205 (£72–£109) double, $290–$325 (£154–£172) 2-bedroom unit, $300–$330 (£159–£175) 3-bedroom unit. MC, V. **Amenities:** Restaurant; bar; pool; watersports equipment/rentals; limited room service. *In room:* A/C, TV, kitchen, hair dryer, microwave, beverage maker, no phone. Closed Sept to mid-Oct.

WHERE TO DINE

For fun on the beach, head for **Nippers Beach Bar & Grill,** Great Guana Cay (ℂ **242/365-5143;** www.nippersbar.com), a dive where visitors hang out with the locals. Right on the sands, you sit in split-level gazebos and take in the surf, the most stunning seascape in the Abacos, with a snorkeling reef just 11m (36 ft.) offshore. Burgers and well-stuffed sandwiches satisfy your hunger at lunch. But the best time to go is on a Sunday afternoon, for a pig roast with 900 to 1,000 people who gather for food, drinks, and dancing on the beach. One guest is said to have consumed five "Nipper Trippers"—and lived to tell about it. This is the bartender's specialty, a mix of five different rums along with tropical juices. It's lethal. The Sunday pig roast is from 12:30 to 4:30pm and costs $20 (£11); other menu items range in price from $9 to $16 (£4.75–£8). The grill is open daily 11:30am to 10pm, the bar 7am to 10pm. American Express, MasterCard, and Visa are accepted.

5 Treasure Cay ✦

Treasure Cay now contains one of the most popular and elaborate resorts in the Out Islands. On the east coast of Great Abaco, it boasts not only 5.5km (3½ miles) of spectacular sandy beach, widely recognized as one of the top 10 beaches in The Bahamas, but also one of the finest marinas in the Commonwealth, with complete docking and charter facilities.

Before the tourist complex opened, the cay was virtually unsettled. As a result, the resort has become the "city," providing its thousands of visitors with everything they need, including medical supplies, grocery-store items (liquor, naturally), and even bank services. But don't count on these services when you need them. There are no ATMs on the island, and the bank is open only Tuesday and Thursday (and Thurs is payday on the island, so it's impossibly overcrowded). Medical supplies, even solutions for contact lenses, aren't available on the weekends. The real-estate office peddles condos, and the builders predict that they will one day reach a capacity of 5,000 guests. They're hoping that many visitors will like Treasure Cay enough to buy into it.

See "Getting There" under "Abacos Essentials," at the beginning of this chapter, for details on flying to Treasure Cay. Some direct service is available to the island from Florida. You could also fly into Marsh Harbour (see section 1, "Marsh Harbour [Great Abaco Island]," earlier in this chapter) and take a 32km (20-mile) taxi ride north along the paved but bumpy Sherben A. Boothe Highway.

Treasure Cay also hosts one of the most popular fishing tournaments in The Bahamas: the **Treasure Cay Billfish Championship** in May.

GETTING AROUND

Renting a car isn't necessary. To get where you're going, you can walk, bike, take a golf cart, or take a taxi. Some restaurants outside the resort will even send a shuttle to pick you up from your hotel. Except for moving between the airport or ferry dock and your hotel, you won't need a cab. For details about taxi fares, call the **Treasure Cay Airport Taxi Stand** (ℂ **242/365-8661**). For a special occasion when you need airport pickups or a trip to dinner in style, call **Elegante Limo Service** (© 242/365-8248 or 242/365-8053; $120/£64 an hour for up to 10 passengers); this company also rents golf carts.

The only real reason to rent a car is for the 35-minute drive to **Marsh Harbour** to catch the ferries to **Elbow Cay** and **Man-O-War Cay,** two offshore islands (see above). If you decide you want to do so, you can rent a car for about $75 (£40) a day at the **Cornish Car Rental** (© 242/365-8623 at the Treasure Cay Airport).

Through **Wendell's Bicycle Rentals** (© 242/365-8687), across from the bank in the Treasure Cay shopping center, you can rent beach cruisers (single-gear bikes with wide wheels) or mountain bikes (wide-wheeled bikes with multiple gears) for $8 (£4.25) a day or $43 (£23) a week. Four-seater electric golf carts go for $40 (£21) a day or $245 (£130) a week through Wendell's or **Claridge Golf Carts** (© 242/365-8248 or 242/365-8053), just outside town.

WHERE TO STAY

Rooms can be scarce in May, when the place is packed with anglers trying to achieve fame in the Treasure Cay Billfish Championship.

In addition to the cay's two main hotels, you can arrange condo rentals. The best agency for this service is **Bahama Beach Club** (© 800/284-0382 in the U.S. or Canada). A 3-night minimum stay is required, and prices are $350 (£186) per night for a two-bedroom unit, $400 (£212) a night for a three-bedroom unit, and $500 (£265) a night for a four-bedroom unit.

Treasure Cay Hotel Resort & Marina ⊕   One of the biggest of the Out Island resorts, this property attracts boaters, golfers, fishermen, and divers, as well as yachties and escapists seeking a remote yet rather luxurious retreat. The foundation for this resort was laid in 1962, when a group of international investors recognized the potential of the property. The vast majority of the peninsula, as well as the marina facility, all of the villas, 80 privately owned condominiums, the tennis courts, and several blocks of other housing, remains under the ownership of the original investors. Guests can rent electric golf carts (around $35/£19 a day) or bicycles to explore the far-flung palm and casuarina groves of the sprawling compound.

Along with architecture that looks like it jumped off the pages of *House and Garden,* the setting here includes tropical plantings, a spectacular beachfront, an excellent golf course, and marina facilities. Simply furnished in conservatively modern tropical motifs, most accommodations overlook the dozens of sailing craft moored in the marina. The renovated rentals are very attractive, with full kitchens, two bedrooms, and washer/dryers, plus a midsize bathroom with a tub/shower.

The restaurant, the Spinnaker, serves standard fare, and two bars dispense tropical drinks.

Treasure Cay, Abaco, The Bahamas. © 800/327-1584 or 954/525-7711. Fax 954/525-1699. (Reservations: Treasure Cay Services, Inc., 2301 S. Federal Hwy., Fort Lauderdale, FL 33316; © 954/525-7711.) www.treasurecay.com. 96 units. Jan–Feb and Aug–Dec $140–$240 (£74–£127) double, $240–$290 (£127–£154) 2-bedroom suite; $340 (£180) 3-bedroom suite; Mar–July $160–$280 (£85–£148) double, $330 (£175) 2-bedroom suite, $380 (£201) 3-bedroom suite. Full board $60 (£32) per person per day. $20 (£11) extra person per day. AE, DISC, MC, V. **Amenities:** Restaurant; 2 bars; pool; golf course; 6 tennis courts; watersports equipment/rentals; nonsmoking rooms; rooms for those w/limited mobility. *In room:* A/C, TV, kitchenette, hair dryer, iron, beverage maker.

WHERE TO DINE

Many vacationers stay in accommodations with kitchens or kitchenettes. However, if you know you're never going to feel like cooking, consider purchasing your hotel's meal plan or dine at nearby local restaurants, some of which provide transportation.

Platters of food cost $4 to $8 (£2.10–£4.25). Another eatery worth checking out is the roadside **Coconut's** on Queen's Highway ((©) **242/365-8885**), which serves typically Bahamian fare, such as grouper and conch, along with a few Italian specialties. Main courses range from $12 to $25 (£6.35–£13), and it's open daily from 6 to 9:30pm.

The Spinnaker Restaurant AMERICAN/BAHAMIAN   Serving reliable seafood, steak, pasta, and Bahamian specialties, this resort restaurant at the Treasure Cay Marina has a prime waterside spot. For lunch, the cracked conch makes a good choice. At night, the portions of meat and potatoes or fresh fish (prepared in a variety of ways, from steamed to blackened) are generous. Guests of the Banyan Beach Club, about a half-mile away, usually arrive by golf cart.

On the water in Treasure Cay Marina. (©) **242/365-8469**. Reservations suggested for dinner. Main courses $17–$32 (£9–£17). MC, V. Daily 7am–10pm. Limited hours in autumn and early winter.

BEACHES, WATERSPORTS & OTHER OUTDOOR PURSUITS

The beaches here are blissfully tranquil. Watersports in Treasure Cay are lots of fun, especially highlighted during the Treasure Cay Billfish Championship each spring. And although this area is far less developed than the more popular islands, golfers don't have to head to Nassau or Freeport for a great game. The course here is a big draw.

If you desire a beach with some of the softest, whitest sand you can imagine and water in some of the most amazing shades of blue and green, then **Treasure Cay Beach** 𝒢𝒢 is it. What's especially alluring about this beach is that—unlike eye-catching stretches on busier, more built-up islands—this 5.5km (3½ miles) shore is never crowded.

Treasure Cay Golf Club ((©) **242/365-8535**), designed by Dick Wilson, offers 6,985 yards of fairways, though it's hardly the best course this famed golf architect ever designed. Greens fees for hotel guests are $45 (£24) for 9 holes and $65 (£34) for 18 holes; for nonguests, it costs $60 (£32) for 9 holes and $95 (£50) for 18 holes. This is the only golf course in the Abacos, and it lies 1km (⅔ mile) from the center of the resort.

Treasure Cay Marina ((©) **242/365-8250**) offers full-service facilities for a variety of watersports. Fishing boats with experienced skippers will guide anglers to tuna, marlin, wahoo, dolphinfish, barracuda, grouper, yellowtail, and snapper. You can also arrange to rent a sailboat, a Hobie Cat, windsurfing boards, and snorkeling gear. The marina has showers, fish-cleaning facilities, daily laundry service, and water and electricity hookups.

Deep-sea fishing is set up through the reception desk of the **Treasure Cay Hotel Resort & Marina** ((©) **242/365-8535**), which will also arrange for you to hire a bone-fishing guide. The same resort has six of the best tennis courts in the Abacos, four of which are lit for night games. Fees are $18 (£9.55) hourly for the hard courts and $20 (£11) hourly for the clay courts.

Treasure Cay Hotel Resort & Marina ((©) **242/365-8801**) also offers six tennis courts—three clay surfaces ($16/£8.50 an hour) and three hard surfaces ($14/£7.40) an hour)—all lit for night play. Check with the hotel to make arrangements to play.

The best diving is provided by **J.I.C. Boat Rentals & Treasure Divers** ((©) **242/ 365-8582**), which rents equipment and takes scuba divers to some of the best sites in the Abacos with spectacular marine life in all its rainbow-hued glory. Guana Cay, Whale Cay, and No Name Cay are some of the best sites for viewing Bahamian marine life. Divers can also visit the 1865 wreck of *San Jacinto,* a steamship freighter that went down. The cost for any dive is $83 (£44).

TREASURE CAY AFTER DARK

Fishermen, yachties, and hotel guests head nightly to the **Tipsy Seagull Bar,** Treasure Cay (© **242/365-8535**), which presents live music sometime after 8pm in winter (off season on Fri–Sat nights only). The setting is an A-frame and the decor is nautical memorabilia. When there's a fishing tournament on island, this bar is jam-packed. Bar patrons who want to hang out can order such treats as pizza and lobster from the resort's adjoining Spinnaker restaurant, which can then be eaten at the bar here. Happy hour is nightly from 5 to 7pm. It's closed in autumn and early winter.

6 Green Turtle Cay (New Plymouth) *★*/*★*

Five kilometers (3 miles) off the east coast of Great Abaco, Green Turtle Cay is the jewel of the archipelago, a little island with an uneven coastline, deep bays, sounds, and good beaches, one of which stretches for 1,080m (3,542 ft.). You can roam through green forests, gentle hills, and secluded inlets. The island is 5.5km (3½ miles) long and 1km (⅔ mile) across, lying some 274km (170 miles) due east of Palm Beach, Florida.

Water depths seldom exceed 4.5 to 6m (15–20 ft.) inside the string of cays that trace the outer edge of the Bahama Bank. Coral gardens teem with colorful sea life, making for fabulous snorkeling. Shelling on the lovely beaches and offshore sandbars is among the finest in The Bahamas. If you have a boat, you can explore such deserted islands as Fiddle Cay to the north, and No Name Cay and Pelican Cay to the south of Green Turtle Cay.

New Plymouth, at the southern tip of the cay, is an 18th century settlement that has the flavor of an old New England sailing port. Much of the original masonry was made from lime that was produced when conch shells were broken up, burned, and sifted for cement (records say that the alkali content was so high that it would burn the hands of the masons who used it). Clapboard houses with gingerbread trim line the narrow streets of the little town, which once had a population of 1,800 people, now shrunk to 400. Green Turtle Cay became known for the skill of its shipbuilders, although the industry, like many others in the area, failed after slaves were totally emancipated in The Bahamas in 1838.

Parliament is the village's main street, and you can walk its length in just 10 minutes, passing only by a few clucking hens. Many of the houses have front porches, where locals sit in the evening enjoying the breezes.

GREEN TURTLE CAY ESSENTIALS

GETTING THERE   Fly to **Treasure Cay Airport,** where a taxi will take you to the ferry dock for departures to Green Turtle Cay (New Plymouth). At the dock, you may have to wait a while for the ferry. From the dock, the crossing takes about 15 to 20 minutes to Green Turtle Cay. The ferry will take you directly to the Green Turtle Club, if you're staying there, or to New Plymouth. This land-and-sea transfer costs $16 (£8.50) per person round-trip.

GETTING AROUND   Although you can walk to many parts of Green Turtle Cay, water is the most common mode of transportation. Many vacationers rent boats, but if you'd rather not, you have other choices for getting around. Some hotels provide water transport to town or to weekly hotel parties. Most of the island is accessible by foot. The virtually car-free streets of New Plymouth, the quiet 18th-century village by the sea, are prime walking territory. On Green Turtle Cay, golf carts stand in for rental cars. **D & P Rentals** (© 242/365-4655) at the Green Turtle Club marina rents theirs for $45 (£24) for 8 hours or $55 (£29) for 24 hours. You can bike all over the island, and pedaling is especially scenic in historic New Plymouth.

FAST FACTS   First Caribbean International Bank operates a branch (© 242/ 365-4144) open only from 10am to 2pm on Tuesday and Thursday. There is an **ATM** here.

If you need medical attention on **Green Turtle Cay,** visit the government clinic (© 242/365-4028), run by a nurse.

You enter Green Turtle Cay's **post office** (© 242/365-4242) through a pink door on Parliament Street. It has a public telephone. Hours are Monday to Friday from 9am to 5pm.

As for safety, there's no crime in New Plymouth, unless you import it yourself. The little stone jail here makes visitors chuckle. No one can remember when, if ever, it held a prisoner.

SPECIAL EVENTS   One event that draws visitors in droves is the **Green Turtle Club Fishing Tournament,** held in May. In 1984, the winner hooked a 226kg (498-lb.) blue marlin; it was so heavy that the competing participants from other boats generously climbed aboard the winning craft to bring the fish in. For more information, contact one of the Bahamian Tourist Offices or the **Green Turtle Club Hotel** (© 242/365-4271), which is more or less the official headquarters when the tournament is held.

WHERE TO STAY

The Bluff House Beach Hotel 🏆🏆   One of the most famous and legendary hotels in the Out Islands, Bluff House originated in the 1950s when it was the private home of C. Pearce Cody III and his wife, Kitty. When friends of their friends asked if they could pay for a few days' stay, the Codys reinvented their home as the first hotel in the Out Islands. They've welcomed some extremely famous guests in the intervening years, including a well-heeled "same time next year" group. Bluff House occupies one of the most desirable pieces of real estate in The Bahamas: 4 hectares (10 acres) on the highest point in the Abacos with panoramic views. The property fronts the Sea of Abaco on one side and the sheltered harbor of White Sound on the other. A romantic spot, it has a lovely nautical charm with British colonial overtones. Against a backdrop of palm, oak, and pine–forested jogging trails, it lies within a 5-minute boat ride from the village of New Plymouth.

The hotel offers villas and hotel rooms in a variety of configurations and sizes, either set beside the beach or cantilevered into the steep hillside facing the sheltered harbor; all have lovely views and some have kitchens. The best accommodations are the spacious colonial-style suites, with cathedral ceilings and balconies that overlook the Sea of Abaco. Inside, decor includes floral bed covers and tropical furniture.

Breakfast and dinner are served in the main Club House (p. 230), where drinks and fresh hors d'oeuvres are offered before a candlelit dinner that features local conch, grouper, snapper, and lobster, as well as roast duck à l'orange. The bar/lounge in the hotel's main building is one of our favorite rooms in The Bahamas, with vistas sweeping across Green Turtle Cay. The blue-and-white cypress-paneled interior is cozy and comfortable, with simple good taste. Peace and prosperity prevail among nautical memorabilia and a flickering fire within an iron stove as slow-whirling tropical fans, wicker furnishings, and polished wooden floors create an upscale and highly appealing ambience. The bar and grill, the Jolly Roger Bistro, specializes in light meals. Dinner is served as part of an elaborate beachfront barbecue that's accompanied by music from a live local band (Tues nights only).

Green Turtle Cay, Abaco, The Bahamas. ℭ **800/745-4911** or 242/365-4247. Fax 242/365-4248. www.bluffhouse. com. 30 units. Year-round $160–$215 (£85–£114) double; $150–$265 (£80–£140) suite; $235–$565 (£125–£299) villa; from $500 (£265) cottage. MAP (breakfast and dinner) $20 (£11) per person. AE, MC, V. **Amenities:** 2 restaurants; 2 bars; pool; tennis court; nonsmoking rooms. *In room:* A/C, hair dryer, beverage maker, no phone.

Coco Bay Cottages

On the north end of Green Turtle Cay, at a point where 150m (492 ft.) of land separate the Atlantic from the Sea of Abaco, this cottage complex opens onto a beach on the Atlantic side of the island and another sandy beach on the more tranquil bay. It's ideal for those who'd like to anchor in for a while. In fact, lots of folks arrive by private boat, which you can moor here free. Otherwise, guests arrive directly by water taxi from the airport dock. The cottages enjoy a 70% repeat clientele. Set on 2 hectares (5 acres) dotted with some 50 tropical fruit trees, the cottages feature Caribbean furnishings and refreshing pastel colors. The smallest accommodation, the honeymoon cottage, sleeps only two in one bedroom. The largest lodging is a two-bedroom, two-bathroom unit, which can sleep five comfortably. It offers a living room, dining room, and fully equipped kitchen with microwave.

The spacious cottages have improved over the years. Linens and kitchen utensils are provided (you can stock up on food and beverages at one of the three grocery shops in New Plymouth), and air-conditioning, ceiling fans, and trade winds cool the rooms. A 1-week minimum stay is required.

P.O. Box AB22795, Green Turtle Cay, Abaco, The Bahamas. ℭ **800/752-0166** or 242/365-5464. Fax 242/365-5465. www.cocobaycottages.com. 6 cottages. Year-round $350–$550 (£186–£292) daily cottage for 6 guests, or $2,200–$3,600 (£1,166–£1,908) weekly; $275–$400 (£146–£212) daily cottage for 2 guests, or $1,700–$2,700 (£901–£1,431) weekly. MC, V. **Amenities:** Exercise equipment; laundry service; nonsmoking rooms. *In room:* A/C, kitchen, hair dryer, beverage maker, no phone.

Green Turtle Club 🐢🐢

An outstanding place for laid-back luxury, this resort attracts honeymooners and snorkelers. The excellent full-service marina and the dive shop on its premises draw serious anglers, boaters, and divers as well. The waters around the resort are shallow enough to spot schools of fish from the shore—and sometimes you'll even see a green turtle paddling above the sandbanks. Spread across 32 hectares (79 acres) of low-lying scrubland, the inn's ambience is very much that of a clubhouse, lodge, and country club. The courteous staff offers assistance yet doesn't intrude on anyone's peace and privacy.

The Green Turtle Yacht Club, host of the prestigious Bahama Cup Around the Island Race, has its base here. It's associated with the Palm Beach Yacht Club and with the Birdham Yacht Club, one of the oldest in England. Members have their own villas right on the water, often with private docks, although temporary guests will be lodged in spacious bungalows (usually two accommodations to a building) set within a gently sloping, carefully landscaped garden. Rooms are among the most upscale and luxurious in the Out Islands. Think England in the Tropics, for the bedrooms boast Sheraton-style mahogany furniture, four-poster beds, French-inspired draperies, oak floors, terra-cotta-tiled patios, and wicker or rattan furniture. Each comes with an immaculate midsize bathroom, and almost all contain tub/showers plus generous shelf space.

The flag-festooned bar is the social center of the resort, where there's occasionally live music. There's an unmistakable British tone to evenings here, beginning with predinner cocktails beside a roaring fire in the bar's iron stove (in chilly weather only, of course) before everyone adjourns to the pine-paneled dining room for well-prepared dinners. Breakfast and lunch are usually served on the veranda.

Green Turtle Cay, Abaco, The Bahamas. (€) 242/365-4271. Fax 242/365-4272. www.greenturtleclub.com. 34 units. Year-round $180–$295 (£95–£156) double; $395 (£209) 2-bedroom unit; $495 (£262) 3-bedroom unit. Children under 12 stay free in parent's room. Extra person $20 (£11) per day. MAP (breakfast and dinner) $41 (£22) per adult, $26 (£14) for children under 12. AE, MC, V. Take a taxi from Treasure Cay Airport to the ferry dock, transfer to a water taxi to the club for a fee of about $11 (£5.85) each way. **Amenities:** Restaurant; 2 bars; pool; watersports equipment/rentals; bike rentals; babysitting; coin-operated laundry; nonsmoking rooms; Internet access. *In room:* A/C, TV, fridge, hair dryer, iron, beverage maker, no phone.

WHERE TO DINE

The previously recommended hotels have the best food on the island, but consider one of these local spots as well.

The Club House Restaurant ⸙ INTERNATIONAL   You can drop in here at midday for a burger, sandwich, or salad, but dinner has an elegant note. Start an evening meal off with the cocktail hour at the bar, which we think is one of the most beautiful and appealing in the Out Islands. Lined with limed cypress, trimmed in cerulean blue, and beautifully proportioned, it includes sweeping views out over two shorefronts from the highest point in the Abacos. Dinner is served within a Queen Anne–style dining room. It's always a set menu, with items that change every night, but the cuisine is invariably excellent. You might start with something like Waldorf salad or smoked salmon, followed by grilled and mango-flavored chicken breast, or lobster tail that's simply broiled with lemon and butter. Triple chocolate cheesecake or Key lime pie makes a soothing dessert.

At the Bluff House Club Beach Hotel, Green Turtle Cay. (€) 242/365-4247. Reservations required. Lunch platters $10–$24 (£5.30–£13); fixed-price dinners $35 (£19) per person. AE, MC, V. Daily 11:30am–2:30pm; hors d'oeuvre service (included in the dinner price) begins at 6:30pm, dinner begins at 7:30pm.

Laura's Kitchen BAHAMIAN/AMERICAN   On the main street of town, across from the Albert Lowe Museum, this family-owned spot occupies a well-converted white Bahamian cottage. Laura Sawyer serves up lunch and dinner in a simple, homey decor. The menu changes nightly, depending on what's at the market, but she always serves the old reliables her family has eaten for generations: fried grouper, fried chicken, and a tasty cracked conch. The eatery is mainly known for its burgers: fish burgers, conch burgers, hamburgers, cheeseburgers, and bacon-and-cheese burgers.

King St. (€) 242/365-4287. Reservations recommended for dinner. Lunch $4–$12 (£2.10–£6.35); dinner $15–$25 (£7.95–£13). MC, V. Mon–Sat 11am–3pm and 6–9pm; Sun 5:30–8pm. Closed Sept and Christmas Day.

Plymouth Rock Liquors & Café BAHAMIAN/AMERICAN   This place has the best selection of wines and liquors for sale in New Plymouth, including at least 70 kinds of rum; it also carries Cuban cigars. Part of its space is set aside for a pleasant and attractive luncheonette run by hardworking co-owners Kathleen and David Bethell. They serve up tasty sandwiches, split-pea soup, beef souse, and cracked conch with cucumber slices and potato salad. There's also an art gallery on the premises, featuring works by about 50 artists, many of whom specialize in local themes.

Parliament St. (€) 242/365-4234. Sandwiches and platters $4–$10 (£2.10–£5.30). DISC, MC, V. Cafe Mon–Sat 9am–3:30pm; liquor store Mon–Thurs 9am–6pm, Fri–Sat 9am–7pm.

Rooster's Rest Pub & Restaurant BAHAMIAN   This local dive just beyond the edge of town serves good Bahamian food, including lobster, conch, and your best bet, fresh fish. It's casual through and through, the way The Bahamas used to be; nouvelle cuisine hasn't washed up on these shores yet. All main courses in the evening are served with peas 'n' rice, coleslaw, and potato salad. The cook also prepares some tasty ribs. Live music is offered at least 2 nights a week.

Gilliam's Bay Rd. ℂ **242/365-4066.** Reservations recommended for dinner. Lunch burgers and snacks $8–$12 (£4.25–£6.35); main courses $10–$20 (£5.30–£11). MC, V. Mon–Sat 11:30am–9:30pm.

The Wrecking Tree Bar & Restaurant BAHAMIAN   This funky place is recognized by its coral and terra-cotta colors, and by the much-mangled casuarinas tree that grows next to its foundation. The hearty menu is as simple as can be, featuring mostly peas 'n' rice, conch, grouper fingers, chicken souse, and burgers. Come here for a simple lunch, a midday beer, and a view over the boats in the nearby harbor.

The Harbourfront. ℂ **242/365-4263.** Main courses $13–$15 (£6.90–£7.95). No credit cards. Mon–Sat 11am–9pm.

BEACHES, WATERSPORTS & OTHER OUTDOOR PURSUITS

Along with sampling Green Turtle Cay's aquatic diversions, you can visit a museum and wander the streets of New Plymouth, the historic waterfront village.

About a 10-minute walk from **Bluff House** and 5 minutes from the **Green Turtle Club, Coco Bay** 𝒢𝒢 is one of the most beautiful crescents in The Bahamas. Shaded by casuarina pine trees and lapped by lazy waves, this long beach is often empty. The rougher **Ocean Beach,** about a 10-minute stroll from either Bluff House or the Green Turtle Club, is another stunner. Frothy waves thrash the stark white sand, set off by the intense blue of the Atlantic.

You can take a boat trip to one of the nearby uninhabited islands that are ringed with even more pristine beaches. On **Manjack Cay,** for example, the expanse of sugar-white sand seems to go on forever, and the shallow, clear water is a brilliant shade of turquoise. There's no regular service from the ferry dock; negotiate with one of the local boatmen. The staff at your hotel will be helpful in this regard.

With one of the world's largest barrier reefs, **the Abacos** offers some of The Bahamas' most varied and least crowded (also known as best) snorkeling and diving sites. You can get an eyeful at reefs starting in depths of just 1.5m (5 ft.) and ranging to 18m (59 ft.) and more. Like sheets on a clothesline, sprawling schools of fish billow by coral caverns, huge tube and barrel sponges, and fields of elk and staghorn coral. Sea turtles and large groupers are common sights. In fact, the waters are so clear that you can often see farther than 30m (98 ft.).

Scuba divers can poke around the wreck of the *San Jacinto.* At this American steamship that was built in 1847 and sank 2 decades ago, you can feed the resident bright-green moray eel. Rates run about $140 (£74) for a scuba resort course, $500 (£265) for full certification, $60 (£32) for a one-tank dive, and $80 (£42) for a two-tank dive.

If you like small groups and big fun, try **Brendal's Dive Center** (ℂ **242/365-4411;** www.brendal.com) at the **Green Turtle Club Marina.** Whether you're an experienced diver or snorkeler or you're just getting your feet wet, the personal attention makes the difference here. Originally from **Acklins,** a small Bahamian island to the south, Brendal has more than 2 decades of underwater experience. A special treat for snorkelers is the wild dolphin encounter trip ($75/£40 per person), which includes stops at undisturbed islands. This company also rents kayaks ($10/£5.30 per hour for singles, $12/£6.35 per hour for doubles, or $190/£101 a week for the single,

$250/£133 for the double). You can also hook up with this activity at **Green Turtle Divers** (© **242/365-4271**), which has a full-service dive shop right at the hotel. Both divers and snorkelers get a 15% discount if registered at the hotel.

Call Lincoln Jones at © **242/365-4223**, and he'll arrange a snorkeling adventure for you—probably on some deserted beach that only he knows about. Prices are to be negotiated, of course, but a lunch of fresh conch or lobster is a fine addition to any day.

If you've had enough of sitting on the beach and relaxing, you can explore the ocean. From boat rentals to fishing expeditions, Green Turtle Cay offers an array of things to do.

Based at the Green Turtle Club marina, **Brendal's Dive Center** (© **242/365-4411**) can take you on a group sunset cruise (complete with rum punch) on an 8.8m (29-ft.) sailboat for $60 (£32) per person (up to eight passengers). To see the coral without getting wet, Brendal's hosts glass-bottom boat trips for $50 (£27) per person.

Contact **Donny's Boat Rentals** (© **242/365-4119**) in **Black Sound** for speedboats. This company rents Whalers and Makos (types of motorboats) starting at $70 (£37) a day for a 4.2m (14-ft.) boat. Or try **Reef Rentals** (© **242/365-4145**), directly across from the ferry dock in **New Plymouth.** This fleet includes a sleek motorboat made on **Man-O-War Cay,** the nearby island long known for its excellent boat building. Rentals start at $265 (£140) for 3 days for a 5.7m (19-ft.) Wellcraft.

Reserving a boat when you make your hotel and airline reservations is a good idea, particularly during the busy spring and summer.

Fishermen from all over the world visit Green Turtle Cay, seeking yellowfin, dolphin (not the mammal), and big game wahoo, among other catches. If you want to go deep-sea fishing, check with the two cousins in the Sawyer family. Referrals are usually made through the **Green Turtle Club** (© **242/365-4070**), or you can call directly at © **242/365-2461.**

The annual **Green Turtle Club Fishing Tournament** (© **800/688-4752** or 242/365-4271) was on hold at press time, but call for information to see whether it's on when you're visiting in May. There's a tennis court at **Bluff House** (© **242/365-4247**), where guests play free.

EXPLORING THE ISLAND: A JOURNEY TO THE 18TH CENTURY

New Plymouth celebrated its bicentennial in 1984 by establishing a memorial that honors American Loyalists and also some of their notable descendants, including Albert Lowe, a pioneer boat-builder and historian.

Across from New Plymouth Inn on Parliament Street, the **Memorial Sculpture Garden** honors residents of the Abacos, both living and dead. What blooms at this garden are busts of island notables on stone pedestals. Read about some of the American Loyalists who came to The Bahamas from New England and the Carolinas. Statues are also dedicated to their descendants and to those people who were enslaved in these islands. You can see everyone from Albert Lowe (see below)—whose forebears were among New Plymouth's original European-American settlers—to African-Bahamian Jeanne I. Thompson, the second woman to practice law in The Bahamas. This garden is laid out in the pattern of the Union Jack flag.

There isn't much shopping here, but consider a visit to the **Ocean Blue Gallery,** adjoining the Plymouth Rock Café on Parliament Street (© **242/365-4234**). This two-room outlet has one of the best collections of local artwork in the Abacos, including some original sculptures and paintings.

Albert Lowe Museum 🏛️🏛️   More than anything else we've seen in The Bahamas, this museum—set in a beautifully restored Loyalist home—conveys the rawboned and sometimes difficult history of the Out Islands. You can easily spend a couple of hours reading the fine print of the dozens of photographs that show the hardship and the valor of citizens who changed industries as often as the economic circumstances of their era dictated.

The caretaker will give you a guided tour of the stone kitchen, which occupants of the house used as a shelter when a hurricane devastated much of New Plymouth in 1932. Inside the house, a narrow stairway leads to three bedrooms that reveal the simplicity of 18th-century life on Green Turtle Cay. Amid antique settees, irreplaceable photographs, and island artifacts, you'll see a number of handsome ship models, the work of Albert Lowe, for whom the museum was named.

The paintings of Alton Lowe, son of the former boat-builder and founder of the museum, are also on display. Cherub-faced and red-haired, Alton is—and has been for a while—one of the best-known painters in The Bahamas. His works hang in collections all over the world; some appears on Bahamian postage stamps, blowups of which are displayed here. Your tour guide might open the basement of the house, where some of Alton's paintings are for sale alongside work by other local artists. There's also a garden in the back of the house.

Parliament St. ⓒ 242/365-4094. Admission $5 (£2.65) adults, $2.50 (£1.30) students, free for children 5 and under. Mon–Sat 9–11:45am and 1–4pm.

GREEN TURTLE CAY AFTER DARK

Ask at your hotel if the local Junkanoo band, the **Gully Roosters,** are playing their reggae- and calypso-inspired sounds. They're the best in the Abacos and often appear at various spots on the island. Also make sure to visit **Miss Emily's Blue Bee Bar** (described below). You might catch a live band, and you'll certainly enjoy a wonderful setting for a drink in the bars at the **Bluff House** and the **Green Turtle Club** (see

---

Finds **Miss Emily's Blue Bee Bar**

Our favorite bar in the Out Islands is **Miss Emily's Blue Bee Bar,** on Victoria Street in New Plymouth (ⓒ **242/365-4181**). This simple bar is likely to be the scene of the liveliest party in the Out Islands at any time of day; even normally buttoned-up types find themselves flirting or dancing before long. You never know what will be going on here. Until rising waters from the 1999 hurricanes washed some of them away, most of its walls were covered with the business cards of past guests and celebrities. Stop by and see how many replacements have been plastered up. The Goombay Smash, a specialty here, has been called "Abaco's answer to atomic fission." Its recipe includes secret proportions of coconut rum, "dirty" rum, apricot brandy, and pineapple juice. Miss Emily (Mrs. Emily Cooper) was a legend in these parts. She's gone now, but her memory lives on: Her daughter, Violet Smith, knows her secret recipe for the Goombay Smash and makes a potent rum punch. Tips at the bar go to St. Peter's Anglican Church. No food is ever served here, but the bar is open Monday to Saturday from 11am until late.

"Where to Stay," above). **Rooster's Rest Pub & Restaurant** (see "Where to Dine," above) is yet another option.

A much more upscale bar than Miss Emily's is the **Yacht Club Pub** (© 242/365-4271), at the Green Turtle Club. Along with sailors and fisherman, some of the captains (and the owners) of the world's most expensive yachts stop off here to enjoy the lively atmosphere and the bartender's special, a Tipsy Turtle, made by the gallon (orange juice, pineapple juice, vodka, coconut rum, banana rum, and grenadine). Appetizers are served nightly from 6:30 to 7:30pm. Live bands are featured on Monday, Wednesday, and Friday nights.

7 Spanish Cay

Set 19km (12 miles) northwest of Green Turtle Cay, this island was named after a pair of Spanish galleons that sank offshore during the 17th century. Originally owned by Queen Elizabeth II, the island was purchased in the 1960s by Texas-based investor (and former owner of the Dallas Cowboys) Clint Murchinson. After his death in the early 1980s, two successive Florida conglomerates poured time, money, and landscaping efforts into developing the island as a site for upscale private homes. Today guests of the inn (see below) and local residents putter along the island's paved roads in electric-powered golf carts.

Most visitors arrive by private boat or chartered aircraft from Fort Lauderdale. You can also fly to Treasure Cay from West Palm Beach on **Bahamasair** (© 242/377-8451; fax 242/377-7409; www.bahamasair.com) and have the inn arrange water transportation. Two daily flights arrive here from Nassau.

WHERE TO STAY & DINE

The Spanish Cay Resort & Marina ✦   Renovations and improved transportation have made this property better and more accessible than ever. Bedrooms have been improved and completely refurbished to accommodate more than two guests per room. All the suites are roomy and spacious, with a double bed, a foldout sofa bed, and a small refrigerator, plus a tidy bathroom with a shower stall. The apartments are even more spacious, with both king-size beds and twins in their two bedrooms, plus a full kitchen, living room, dining room, and deck overlooking the marina. A one-bedroom apartment can sleep up to four people; a two-bedroom accommodates six.

Two on-site restaurants (Point House, open daily, and Wrecker's Bar, open in high season) serve conch, chicken, fresh fish, steak, and occasionally lobster. Dinners are reasonably priced. You can also get food and drinks at the poolside Tiki Bar.

Cooper's Town, Abaco, The Bahamas. © 242/365-0083. Fax 242/365-0453. www.spanishcay.com. 22 units. Sept 16–Mar 14 $165–$195 (£87–£103) double, $295 (£156) 1-bedroom unit, $370 (£196) 2-bedroom unit, $775 (£411) 4-bedroom unit; Mar 15–Sept 15 $215–$255 (£114–£135) double, $375 (£199) 1-bedroom unit, $455 (£241) 2-bedroom unit, $875 (£464) 4-bedroom unit. MC, V. **Amenities:** 2 restaurants; bar; 4 tennis courts; freshwater pool; spa; watersports equipment/rentals. *In room:* A/C, TV, fridge, no phone.

8 Walker's Cay

Lying at the edge of the Bahama Bank, this is the northernmost, the outermost, and one of the smallest islands in the Abaco chain. Coral reefs surround this island, dropping off to depths of some 300m (984 ft.). It's known around the world as one of the best deep-sea fishing resorts. The cay produces its own fresh water and electricity.

Ponce de León reportedly stopped here in 1513 in search of fresh water—just 6 days before he "discovered" Florida. From the 17th century, this was a place known to pirates, who stored their booty here. It became a bastion for blockade-runners during the American Civil War, and later it was a hide-out for rumrunners in the days of U.S. Prohibition.

To get here, prospective guests should call the Walker's Cay Hotel and Marina at ℂ **800/WALKERS** and make arrangements for a flight from Fort Lauderdale.

WHERE TO STAY & DINE

Walker's Cay Hotel & Marina ℛ   Established in the 1930s and a legend among sportfishermen ever since, this resort occupies all 41 hectares (101 acres) of a private island that contains the largest and most elaborate full-service marina in the Abacos. Each year, it runs at least two of the country's biggest deep-sea fishing tournaments. Come here for the fishing, for the marina and its charter boats, and for the way that sports permeate the air, but not necessarily for the luxury of the accommodations. Although they benefited from a renovation, these are rather standard motel-style units. Each accommodation contains a small bathroom with a shower stall. Meals are generally adequate, served in the Lobster Trap and Conch Pearl restaurants; both have bars and offer American/Bahamian fare, chiefly steak and fresh fish.

Walker's Cay, Abaco, The Bahamas (Mailing address: 2101 S. Andrews Ave., #201, Fort Lauderdale, FL 33316). ℂ **800/WALKERS** in the U.S. and Canada, or 954/763-6025 or 242/353-1252. Fax 954/462-4100. www.walkerscay. com. Year-round $130–$170 (£69–£90) double; from $425 (£225) villa. MAP (breakfast and dinner) $40 (£21) per person. AE, MC, V. **Amenities:** 2 restaurants; 2 bars; tennis court; babysitting. *In room:* A/C, no phone.

8

Eleuthera

A sort of Bahamian Plymouth Rock, Eleuthera Island (pronounced Ah-*leu*thra) was the first permanent settlement in The Bahamas, founded in 1648. A search for religious freedom drew the Eleutherian Adventurers from Bermuda here, to the "birthplace of The Bahamas." The long narrow island they discovered and colonized still bears the name Eleuthera—Greek for "freedom." The locals call it Cigatoo.

These adventurers found an island of white- and pink-sand beaches framed by casuarina trees; high, rolling green hills; sea-to-sea views; dramatic cliffs; and sheltered coves—and they're still here, unspoiled, waiting for you to discover today. More than 161km (100 miles) long but merely 3km (2 miles) wide (guaranteeing that you're never far from the beach), Eleuthera is about 113km (70 miles) east of Nassau (a 30-min. flight). The population of 10,000 is largely made up of farmers, shopkeepers, and fishermen who live in old villages of pastel-washed cottages. The resorts here are built around excellent harbors, and roads run along the coastline, though some of them are inadequately paved.

Eleuthera and its satellite islands, **Spanish Wells** and **Harbour Island,** offer superb snorkeling and diving amid coral gardens, reefs, drop-offs, and wrecks. Anglers come to Eleuthera for bottom-, bone-, and deep-sea fishing, testing their skill against the dolphinfish, the wahoo, the blue and the white marlin, the Allison tuna, and the amberjack. Charter boats are available at Powell Point, Rock Sound, Spanish Wells, and Harbour Island. You can also rent Sunfish, sailboats, and Boston Whalers for reef fishing.

Eleuthera rivals the Abacos in popularity among foreign visitors, although boaters are more drawn to the Abacos and the Exumas. Along with the Abacos, Eleuthera has the largest concentration of resort hotels outside of the major developments of Nassau/Paradise Island and Freeport/Lucaya.

We love gorgeous **Harbour Island,** with its charming Dunmore Town, even more than New Plymouth or Hope Town in the Abacos; it's almost a Cape Cod in the Tropics. Of the 10 destinations recommended in this chapter, Harbour Island gets our vote as the number-one choice.

Spanish Wells is another small island just off the north end of Eleuthera. Spanish galleons put sailors ashore to fill the ships' casks with fresh water after long sea voyages—hence the present-day name of the island.

ELEUTHERA ESSENTIALS
GETTING THERE
BY PLANE   Eleuthera has two main airports. **North Eleuthera Airport** (© 242/ 335-1068), obviously, serves the north along with the two major offshore cays, Harbour Island and Spanish Wells. **Governor's Harbour Airport** (© 242/332-2321) serves the center of the island.

Eleuthera

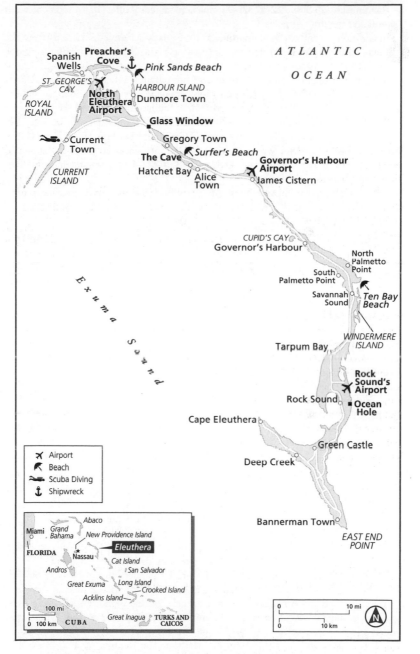

ATLANTIC OCEAN

Spanish Wells
Preacher's Cove
Pink Sands Beach
ST. GEORGE'S CAY
ROYAL ISLAND
North Eleuthera Airport
HARBOUR ISLAND
Dunmore Town
Current Town
CURRENT ISLAND
Glass Window
Gregory Town
Surfer's Beach
The Cave
Hatchet Bay
Alice Town
Governor's Harbour Airport
James Cistern

Exuma Sound

CUPID'S CAY
Governor's Harbour
North Palmetto Point
South Palmetto Point
Savannah Sound
Ten Bay Beach
WINDERMERE ISLAND
Tarpum Bay
Rock Sound's Airport
Rock Sound
Ocean Hole
Cape Eleuthera
Green Castle
Deep Creek
Bannerman Town
EAST END POINT

✈ Airport
🏖 Beach
🤿 Scuba Diving
⚓ Shipwreck

Abaco
Miami
Grand Bahama
New Providence Island
FLORIDA
Nassau
Eleuthera
Andros
Cat Island
San Salvador
Great Exuma
Long Island
Crooked Island
Acklins Island
CUBA
Great Inagua
TURKS AND CAICOS

0   100 mi
0   100 km

0   10 mi
0   10 km

Bahamasair (© **800/222-4262;** www.bahamasair.com) offers daily flights between Nassau and the three airports.

In addition, several commuter airlines with regularly scheduled service fly from the Florida mainland with either nonstop or one-stop flights. Many private flights use the North Eleuthera Airport, with its 1,350m (4,428-ft.) paved runway. It is an official Bahamian port of entry, and a Customs and Immigration official is on hand. **USAir Express** (© **800/428-4322;** www.usairways.com) operates one of the most popular ways of reaching two of Eleuthera's airports from the Florida mainland. Flights depart once a day from Miami flying nonstop to North Eleuthera and then continue on, after briefly unloading passengers and baggage, to Governor's Harbour. **Continental Airlines** (© **800/525-0280;** www.continental.com) flies once daily from Miami and twice daily from Fort Lauderdale. **Delta** (© **800/221-1212;** www.delta.com) flies three times a week from Atlanta.

Other small carriers include **Twin Air** (© **954/359-8266;** www.flytwinair.com), flying from Fort Lauderdale three times a week to Rock Sound and Governor's Harbour, and Thursday to Tuesday to North Eleuthera.

BY FERRY   An interisland link, **Bahamas Fast Ferries** (© **242/323-2166;** www.bahamasferries.com) originates in Potter's Cay, beneath the Paradise Island Bridge, and fans out at regular intervals to Harbour Island, North Eleuthera, and Governor's Harbour. Round-trip fares are $110 (£58) for adults, $70 (£37) for children under 12.

BY MAIL BOAT   Several mail boats visit Eleuthera from Nassau, leaving from Potter's Cay Dock. Weather conditions often cause their schedules to change. For details about sailings, consult the dock master at **Potter's Cay Dock** in Nassau (© **242/393-1064**).

The **MV** *Current Pride* goes from Nassau to Current Island, serving lower and upper Bogue. It departs Nassau every Thursday and returns on Tuesday.

The *Bahamas Daybreak III* departs on Monday for South Eleuthera, stops at Rock Sound, and returns to Nassau on Tuesday. It then leaves from Nassau on Thursday for the Bluff and Harbour Island, with a Sunday return scheduled. The *Eleuthera Express* sails from Nassau to Spanish Wells and Governor's Harbour on Monday and Thursday, and returns to Nassau on Sunday and Tuesday.

GETTING AROUND

It's virtually impossible to get lost on Eleuthera—there's only one road that meanders along the entire length of its snake-shaped form, and you'll stray from it only very rarely. Most visitors take a taxi only when they arrive at one of the local airports or when they have to return to that airport to go home. Taxis meet all incoming flights and are also available at ferry docks. Because cabbies are independent operators on Eleuthera, you can't call one central number. If you need to call a taxi, your hotel staff can summon one for you, but you may have to wait a while, so plan ahead.

You can easily traverse all the settlements—really, hamlets, in most cases—on foot. With little traffic on the island, walking is an enjoyable experience here.

You don't find any American car-rental agencies on the island. Usually, your hotel staff can arrange for a car rental (prices are $80–$100/£42–£53 a day). Often we've ended up with someone's private car. The best bet for car rentals on the island is **Highway Service Station** (© **242/332-2077**) or **Hilton's Car Rentals** (© **242/335-6241**).

1 Rock Sound

Located in South Eleuthera, Rock Sound is a small, shady village, the island's main town and once its most exclusive enclave. The closing of two old-time landmark resorts, the Cotton Bay Club and the Windermere Club, has, at least for now, halted the flow of famous visitors, who once included everybody from the late Princess Diana to a parade of CEOs. No reopenings are yet in sight, but at least that means that you can have many of South Eleuthera's best beaches practically to yourself.

Rock Sound opens onto Exuma Sound and is located to the south of Tarpum Bay. The town is at least 2 centuries old, and it has many old-fashioned homes with picket fences out front. Once notorious for wreckers who lured ships ashore with false beacons, it used to be known as "Wreck Sound."

After leaving Rock Sound, head south, bypassing the Cotton Bay Club, and continue through the villages of Green Castle and Deep Creek. At this point, you take a sharp turn northwest along the only road leading to **Cape Eleuthera.** Locals call this Cape Eleuthera Road, though you won't find any markings other than a sign pointing the way. If you continue to follow this road northwest, you'll reach the end of the island chain, jutting out into Exuma Sound.

Now relatively deserted, Cape Eleuthera was once home to a chic resort and yacht club that drew some of the movers and shakers from America's East Coast, including President Richard Nixon. Some of the top golfers in America played its Bruce Devlin–Bob van Haage 18-hole course, which winds its way along the water. They're all gone now, but the **white-sand beaches**—three of them—remain splendid, and locals claim the deep-sea fishing is as fine as it ever was.

ROCK SOUND ESSENTIALS

Rock Sound itself boasts a shopping center and a bank—with an ATM—in addition to its airport, but not a lot else. Many residents who live in South Eleuthera come here to stock up on groceries and supplies.

A doctor and four resident nurses form the staff of the **Rock Sound Medical Clinic** (© 242/334-2226). Office hours are Monday to Friday from 9am to 4pm; after that, the doctor is always available to handle emergency cases.

If you need the police, call © 242/334-2244.

OUTDOOR ACTIVITIES

The only place to play golf in Eleuthera is at the **Cotton Bay Golf Course** designed by Robert Trent Jones, Jr., on the site of the now defunct Cotton Bay Club, Rock Sound (© 242/334-6156; www.eleu.net/golf.html). This 18-hole, 7,000-yard, par-72 course has attracted some of the most famous players in the world. Even though the Cotton Bay Club itself is closed, many Americans who maintain second homes at

---

Fun Fact **A "Hole" in the Ocean**

The **Ocean Hole,** which is about 2km (1¼ miles) east of the heart of Rock Sound, is said to be bottomless. This saltwater lake that eventually meets the sea is one of the most attractive spots on Eleuthera. You can walk right to the edge of the water. Many tropical fish can be seen here; they seem to like to be photographed—but only if you feed them first.

Eleuthera, the Comeback Kid

In the heyday of Pan American Airlines and its founder, Juan Trippe, the Cotton Bay Club in Eleuthera was the chicest enclave in The Bahamas. (Once a household word in America, Trippe was a relatively forgotten figure until his character appeared in *The Aviator*, Martin Scorsese's film about Howard Hughes.) The Cotton Bay Club was hailed as the place where the Who's Who of America went barefoot in the sand. But it folded and has been a ghost of itself, in spite of its picture-perfect white- and pink-sand beaches. The good news is that change is on the way. Expect some small luxury hotels to be launched up and down the length of Eleuthera. Some openings are set for 2008, including Starwood's 600-hectare (1,482-acre) Cotton Bay Villas. Stay tuned.

Rock Sound still use the course. Regrettably, golf course maintenance isn't what is used to be in the heyday of the resort. Many fairways aren't marked properly, and the restaurant and clubhouse are long gone. The club still has caddies but no more golf carts. The greens fees are $70 (£37) for 9 holes and $100 (£53) for 18 holes. Reservations are necessary.

WHERE TO STAY & DINE

Sammy's Place BAHAMIAN   Hot gossip and cheap, juicy burgers make Sammy's the most popular hangout in Rock Sound—come here for a slice of local life. Sammy's is on the northeastern approach to the settlement, in a neighborhood that even the owner refers to as "the back side of town." Sammy Culmer (who's assisted by Margarita, his daughter) will serve you drinks (including Bahama Mamas and rum punches), conch fritters, Creole-style grouper, breaded scallops, pork chops, and lobster. If you drop in before 11am, you might be tempted by the selection of egg dishes or omelets.

This is primarily a restaurant and bar, but Sammy does rent four rooms with air-conditioning and cable TV, plus two efficiency cottages containing two bedrooms with a kitchen. The double-occupancy accommodations can be yours for $66 (£35) per night; cottages cost $100 (£53) per night.

Albury's Lane, Rock Sound. (C) 242/334-2121. Breakfast $5–$12 (£2.65–£6.35); lunch $6–$14 (£3.20–£7.40); main courses $10–$25 (£5.30–£13). No credit cards. Daily 7:30am–10pm.

2 Tarpum Bay

If you're looking for an affordable vacation on high-priced Eleuthera, head here. This charming waterfront village, some 15km (9¼ miles) north of Rock Sound, is good for fishing and has a number of simple, inexpensive guesthouses. This tiny settlement with its many pastel-washed, gingerbread-trimmed houses is a favorite of artists, who have established a small colony here with galleries and studios.

Gaulding's Cay, north of town, has a lovely beach with great snorkeling.

WHERE TO STAY

Cartwright's Ocean Front Cottages   Cartwright's is a cluster of simple cottages right by the sea, with fishing, snorkeling, and swimming at your door. This is one of the few places where you can sit on your patio and watch the sunset. The small cottages are fully furnished, with utensils, stove, refrigerator, pots and pans, and maid service provided. Each unit comes with a small bathroom containing a shower stall. You'll be within walking distance of stores and local eateries.

Bay St., Tarpum Bay, Eleuthera, The Bahamas. (© 242/334-4215. 3 units. Year-round $120 (£64) 1-bedroom cottage; $150 (£80) 2-bedroom cottage; $180 (£95) 3-bedroom cottage. No credit cards. **Amenities:** Babysitting; laundry service. *In room:* A/C, TV, kitchenette, coffeemaker, iron, no phone.

3 Windermere Island

Windermere is a very tiny island, connected by ferry to "mainland" Eleuthera. It is midway between the settlements of Governor's Harbour and Rock Sound.

This island couldn't be more discreet. "We like to keep it quiet around here," one of the staff at the presently closed Windermere Island Club once told us. Regrettably, that wasn't always possible for this once-deluxe and snobbish citadel. When Prince Charles first took a pregnant Princess Diana here in the 1980s, she was photographed by paparazzi in her swimsuit. Much to the horror of the club, the picture gained worldwide notoriety.

Even without its posh hotel, Windermere Island is worth a day trip. Major construction may soon be launched, so this once-sleepy place should start waking up by 2008. **Savannah Sound,** with its sandy sheltered beaches and outstanding snorkeling, is particularly appealing (bring your own gear). The beaches here are excellent for shelling and picnicking, and offer good bonefishing, with some catches more than 10 pounds.

West Beach, a good place for sunning and swimming (great for children), is about a 10-minute walk from the shut-down Windermere Island Club. The beach is on Savannah Sound, the body of calm, protected water separating Windermere from the main island of Eleuthera.

Visitors can enjoy a number of activities, from bonefishing to windsurfing. The dock master at West Beach is well qualified to guide and advise about bonefishing, or perhaps you'd like to go deep-sea fishing for white marlin, dolphinfish, grouper, wahoo, Allison tuna, and amberjack. Since there is no permanent outfitter, you have to ask around locally about who can take you out.

4 Palmetto Point

On the east side of Queen's Highway, south of Governor's Harbour, North Palmetto Point is a little village where visitors rarely venture (although you can get a meal there). This laid-back town will suit you if you want peace and quiet off the beaten track.

Ten Bay Beach ⊘⊘ is one of the best beaches in The Bahamas, with its sparkling turquoise water and wide expanse of soft white sand. The beach lies a 10-minute drive south of Palmetto Point and just north of Savannah Sound. There are no facilities, only idyllic isolation.

WHERE TO STAY

Unique Village   Located on a steep rise above the Atlantic coast of Eleuthera, this hotel is the creative statement of a Palmetto Point businessman who also owns the local hardware store (Unique Hardware). Built in 1992, the hotel offers accommodations in several configurations (everything from conventional single or double rooms to a one-bedroom apartment with a kitchenette, to two-bedroom villas with full kitchens). Each comes with a small bathroom with a tub/shower. A flight of wooden steps will bring you to the beach, where a reef breaks up the Atlantic surf and creates calm waters on this sandy cove. There's a bar and restaurant, also called Unique

Village Restaurant & Lounge, on-site (see "Where to Dine," below), but few other luxuries. Although you won't find sailing, scuba, or tennis on-site, the staff can direct you to other facilities that lie within a reasonable drive (you'll probably want a car here).

N. Palmetto Point, The Bahamas. ✆ 888/820-8471 or 242/332-1830. Fax 242/332-1838. www.uniquevillage.com. 15 units. Winter $120–$130 (£64–£81) double, $140 (£74) minisuite, $160 (£85) 1-bedroom apt, $190 (£101) 2-bedroom apt; off season $90–$100 (£48–£53) double, $110 (£58) minisuite, $130 (£81) 1-bedroom apt, $160 (£85) 2-bedroom apt. MAP (breakfast and dinner) $35 (£19) per person. FAP $50 (£27) per person. MC, V. **Amenities:** Restaurant; bar; free snorkeling equipment; laundry service. *In room:* A/C, TV, kitchenette, coffeemaker, iron.

WHERE TO DINE

Mate & Jenny's Pizza Restaurant & Bar BAHAMIAN/AMERICAN This restaurant, known for its conch pizza, has a jukebox and a pool table. It's the most popular local joint, completely modest and unassuming. In addition to pizza, the Bethel family will prepare pan-fried grouper, cracked conch, or light meals, including snacks and sandwiches. Lots of folks come here just to drink. Try their Goombay Smash, Rumrunner, a piña colada, or just a Bahamian Kalik beer.

S. Palmetto Point, right off Queen's Hwy. ✆ 242/332-1504. Pizza $8–$29 (£4.25–£15); main courses $5–$28 (£2.65–£15). MC, V. Mon and Thurs–Sat 11am–9pm; Sun 5:30–9pm.

Muriel's Bakery ℛ *Finds* BAHAMIAN Muriel Cooper's operation runs a bakery and a takeout food emporium. Her rich and moist pineapple and coconut cakes and tarts, as well as her lemon pies, are some of the best in the Out Islands.

N. Palmetto Point. ✆ 242/332-1583. No credit cards. Mon–Sat 10am–6pm.

Unique Village Restaurant & Lounge BAHAMIAN/AMERICAN This is the best place for food in the area, offering the widest selection. You can drop in for a Bahamian breakfast of boiled or stewed fish served with johnnycake, or steamed corned beef and grits ("regular" breakfasts, including hearty omelets, are also available). Lunch offerings include zesty conch chowder and an array of salads. Burgers are served, along with what the kitchen calls "Bahamian belly pleasers," including the steamed catch of the day. At night the choices grow, and you'll find the best New York sirloin available in mid-Eleuthera, ranging in size from 8 to 16 ounces. Cracked conch fried in a light beer batter is one of the better renderings of this dish on the island.

In the Unique Village, N. Palmetto Point. ✆ 242/332-1830. Main courses $15–$36 (£7.95–£19). MC, V. Daily 7:30–11am, 11:30am–5pm, and 6–9pm.

5 Governor's Harbour

At some 300 years old, Governor's Harbour is the island's oldest settlement, reportedly the landing place of the Eleutherian Adventurers. The largest town on Eleuthera after Rock Sound, it lies midway along the 161km-long (100-mile) island; its airport is likely to be your gateway to the island.

The town today has a population of about 1,500, with some bloodlines going back to the original settlers, the Eleutherian Adventurers, and to the Loyalists who followed some 135 years later. Many old homes line the streets amid the bougainvillea and casuarina trees.

GOVERNOR'S HARBOUR ESSENTIALS

GETTING THERE See "Eleuthera Essentials: Getting There," at the beginning of this chapter, for details. The town airport is one of the island's major gateways, with daily flights arriving from Nassau and Florida.

VISITOR INFORMATION The **Eleuthera Tourist Office** is on Queens Highway (© **242/332-2142**); it's generally open Monday to Friday 9am to 5pm.

FAST FACTS If you're staying outside the town in a cottage or an apartment, you can find services and supplies in Governor's Harbour or at nearby Palmetto Point.

Governor's Harbour has a branch of **First Caribbean International Bank** on Queen's Highway (© **242/332-2300**) with an **ATM.** Hours are Monday to Thursday 9:30am to 3pm and Friday 9:30am to 4:30pm.

The Governor Harbour's Medical Clinic (© **242/332-2774**), located on Queen's Highway, is open Monday to Friday from 9am to 5:30pm. The clinic is also the site of a dentist's office. The dentist is here from 9am to 1pm Monday, Tuesday, and Friday. Call for an appointment before going. The Governor Harbour's Medical Clinic also fills prescriptions.

Check with your hotel for Internet access. An Internet cafe is located on the second floor of the Haynes Library (© **242/332-2877**) at Governor's Harbour. The charge is $5(£2.65) per hour, and the library is open Monday to Friday 9am to 5pm, Saturday 10am to 4pm.

If you need the police, call © **242/332-2111** for the Queen's Highway, Governor's Harbor police station.

There's a **post office** on Haynes Avenue (© **242/332-2060**); hours are Monday to Friday 9am to 4:30pm.

WHERE TO STAY

Cocodimama Charming Resort 𝄞 *(Finds* This charmingly named and private hideaway is set by the water 9.5km (6 miles) north of Governor's Harbour. Built in a modern Bahamian style with verandas, the property opens onto a beach where you can enjoy such sports as kayaking, Hobie Catting, snorkeling, and windsurfing. Scuba-diving trips and deep-sea fishing can also be arranged. The spacious and handsomely furnished bedrooms are spread over a trio of pastel-painted cottages in a tropical garden. Opening onto views, the accommodations are furnished with teak from Bali and Italian ceramics. Each unit is a suite unto itself with a hammock-hung patio. Some of the bedrooms have a comfortable sofa that can be used as a third bed. The owners of the hotel are expatriates from Italy, and the menu reflects their origin, along with many Bahamian dishes.

Alabaster Bay (P.O. Box 122), Governor's Harbour, Eleuthera, The Bahamas. © **242/332-3150.** Fax 242/332-3155. www.cocodimama.com. 12 units. Year-round $185–$230 (£98–£122) double. MAP (breakfast and dinner) $65 (£34) per person, free for children under 9. MC, V. Closed Sept 2–Dec 15. **Amenities:** Restaurant; bar; watersports equipment/rentals; limited room service; rooms for those w/limited mobility. *In room:* A/C, TV, kitchenette, coffeemaker, hair dryer, iron.

Duck Inn and Orchid Gardens 𝄞 *(Finds* The accommodations you'll rent here are larger, plusher, more historic, and more charming than what you'd expect in a conventional hotel. All come with kitchenettes. The complex consists of three clapboard-sided houses, each built between 80 and 175 years ago, and each almost adjacent to another, midway up a hillside overlooking the sea. The finest of these is Floris Cottage, with four bedrooms which can sleep eight comfortably. Nassau-born John (J. J.) Duckworth and his Michigan-born wife, Katie, along with their son John Lucas, are your hosts. Much of their time is spent nurturing a sprawling collection of beautiful orchids being cultivated for export to Europe and the U.S. Their collection of orchids, some 4,000 strong, is one of the largest in North America.

Queen's Hwy., Governor's Harbour, Eleuthera, The Bahamas. © 242/332-2608. Fax 242/332-2106. www.duckinn cottages.com. 3 units. Winter $150 (£80) double; off season $125 (£66) double. Year-round $300 (£159) for Floris Cottage. AE, DISC, MC, V. **Amenities:** Babysitting; nonsmoking rooms. *In room:* A/C, TV, kitchenette, coffeemaker, iron, no phone.

Pineapple Fields &&& *Finds*   Right on a good sandy beach, this is an idyllic retreat—our favorite on "mainland" Eleuthera. Built on the grounds of the once-fabled and very exclusive Potlatch Club, it occupies a lush 32-hectare (79-acre) site on the Atlantic just minutes from the center of Governor's Harbour. Rooms open onto 305m (1,000 ft.) of beachfront along a 3.2km (2-mile) stretch of "sugar sand," as locals call it. From the property there are panoramic views of the beach and the Atlantic. Bedrooms are spacious and well furnished, with both one- and two-bedroom units offered. There are also outdoor showers, if you're coming in from the beach. Tippy's is the on-site bistro, serving one of the best cuisines in the area. A menu featured on a blackboard cites the daily specials, such as pecan-encrusted grouper or lobster pizza with caramelized onions.

Banks Rd., Governor's Harbour, Eleuthera, The Bahamas. © 242/332-2221. Fax 242/332-2203. www.pineapple fields.com. 32 condo units. Winter $240–$270 (£127–£143) 1-bedroom unit, $315–$345 (£167–£183) 2-bedroom unit; off season $170–$200 (£90–£106) 1-bedroom unit, $255–$285 (£135–£151) 2-bedroom unit. AE, MC, V. **Amenities:** Restaurant; bar; outdoor pool. *In room:* A/C, TV, kitchen, safe.

Quality Inn Cigatoo *Value*   This is an older hotel with a faded sense of style, evoking the kind of motel you might find in a quiet small town somewhere in Florida. It's set on the crest of a steep hill overlooking the rest of town, a downhill 7-minute walk to the beach. The hotel is small scale and unpretentious, consisting of one two-story central core, site of the in-house restaurant, and three one-story buildings, each painted white, with doors to each room a different, bright primary color. Each of the buildings is clustered around a swimming pool, the resort's focal point. Management is a bit blasé but cordial.

Governor's Harbour, Queen's Hwy., Eleuthera, The Bahamas. © 242/332-3060. Fax 242/332-3061. www.choicehotels. com. 22 units. $99–$129 (£52–£68) double. MC, V. **Amenities:** Restaurant; bar; outdoor pool; tennis court; room service (7am–10pm); babysitting; self-service laundry. *In room:* A/C, TV, dataport, hair dryer, iron, safe.

WHERE TO DINE

Cigatoo Restaurant BAHAMIAN   Set beside the swimming pool within the also-recommended hotel, this is one of the more reliable and substantial dining areas within a town that isn't known for a wide variety of choices. Expect a mixture of Bahamian food with what you'd expect from a steakhouse in the U.S., with a choice of sandwiches, salads, and platters focusing on meats and catch of the day.

In the Quality Inn Cigatoo, Queen's Hwy. © 242/332-3060. Reservations not necessary. Sandwiches and salads $8–$15 (£4.25–£7.95); main courses $17–$28 (£9–£15). MC, V. Daily 7am–10pm.

Pammy's BAHAMIAN   Tile-floored and Formica-clad, this is just a little cubby-hole with a few tables. Lunchtime brings sandwiches or platters of cracked conch, pork chops, and either broiled or fried grouper. Don't expect anything fancy because this definitely isn't. It's a true local joint serving up generous portions of flavor-filled food.

Queen's Hwy. at Gospel Chapel Rd. © 242/332-2843. Reservations accepted only for dinner. Breakfast $3.50–$7 (£1.85–£3.70); light lunch $5–$10 (£2.65–£5.30); main courses $14–$20 (£7.40–£11). No credit cards. Mon–Sat 8am–5pm.

HITTING THE BEACH

Near the center of town are two beaches known locally as the **Buccaneer Public Beaches;** they're adjacent to the Buccaneer Club, on the sheltered western edge of the island, facing Exuma Sound. Snorkeling is good here—it's best at the point where the pale turquoise waters near the coast deepen to a dark blue. Underwater rocks shelter lots of marine flora and fauna. The waves at these beaches are relatively calm.

On Eleuthera's Atlantic (eastern) side, about 1km (⅔ mile) from Governor's Harbour, is a much longer stretch of mostly pale pink sand, similar to what you'll find in Harbour Island. Known locally as the **Club Med Public Beach,** it's good for bodysurfing and, on days when storms are surging in the Atlantic, even conventional surfing.

Don't expect any touristy kiosks selling drinks, snacks, or souvenirs at any of these beaches because everything is very pristine and undeveloped.

GOVERNOR'S HARBOUR AFTER DARK

Ronnie's Smoke Shop & Sports Bar, Cupid's Cay (© 242/332-2307), is the most happening nightspot in central Eleuthera, drawing folks from miles away. You'll find it adjacent to the cargo depot of Cupid's Cay, in a connected cluster of simple buildings painted in combinations of black with vivid Junkanoo colors. Most folks come here just to drink Kalik beer and talk at either of the two bars. But if you want to dance, there's an all-black room just for disco music on Friday and Saturday nights. There's also the only walk-in cigar humidor on Eleuthera. If you get hungry, order up a plate of barbecue, a pizza, chicken wings, or popcorn. The place is open Monday to Friday 10am until midnight. On weekends it often stays open until about 2am.

6 Hatchet Bay

Forty kilometers (25 miles) north of Governor's Harbour, Hatchet Bay was once known for a British-owned plantation that had 500 head of dairy cattle and thousands of chickens. Today that plantation is gone, and this is now one of the sleepiest villages on Eleuthera, as you can see if you veer off Queen's Highway onto one of the town's ghostly main streets, Lazy Shore Road or Ocean Drive.

WHERE TO STAY & DINE

Rainbow Inn ⟨★⟩   Three kilometers (2 miles) south of Alice Town, and near a sandy beach, the Rainbow Inn is a venerable survivor in an area where many competitors have failed. Quirky and appealing to guests who return for quiet getaways again and again, it's an isolated collection of seven cedar-sided octagonal bungalows. The accommodations are simple but comfortable, spacious, and tidy; each has a kitchenette, lots of exposed wood, a ceiling fan, a small bathroom with a shower unit, and a porch. A sandy beach is just steps away.

One of the most appealing things about the place is its bar and restaurant, a destination for residents far up and down the length of Eleuthera. It's an octagon with a high-beamed ceiling and a thick-topped woodsy-looking bar where guests down daiquiris and piña coladas amid nautical trappings. It has live Bahamian music twice a week and one of the most extensive menus on Eleuthera. The owners take pride in the fact that the menu hasn't changed much in 20 years, a fact that suits its loyal fans just fine. Local Bahamian food includes fish, conch chowder, fried conch, fresh fish, and Bahamian lobster. International dishes feature French onion soup, escargot, and steaks, followed by Key lime pie for dessert. Table no. 2, crafted from a triangular teakwood prow of a motor yacht that was wrecked off the coast of Eleuthera in the 1970s, is a perpetual favorite.

(P.O. Box EL25053) Governor's Harbour, Eleuthera, The Bahamas. © 800/688-0047 in the U.S. or 242/335-0294. Fax 242/335-0294. www.rainbowinn.com. 5 units. Winter $140 (£74) double; off season $115 (£61) double. Year-round $200 (£106) for 2-bedroom villa; $225 (£119) for 3-bedroom villa. MAP (breakfast and dinner) $45 (£24) per person. MC, V. **Amenities:** Restaurant; bar; pool; tennis court; watersports equipment/rentals; car-rental desk; babysitting; laundry service. *In room:* A/C, kitchenette, fridge, coffeemaker.

7 Gregory Town

Gregory Town stands in the center of Eleuthera against a backdrop of hills, which break the usual flat monotony of the landscape. A village of clapboard cottages, it was once famed for growing pineapples. Though the industry isn't as strong as it was in the past, the locals make good pineapple rum out of the fruit, and you can visit the Gregory Town Plantation and Distillery, where it's produced. You're allowed to sample it, and we can almost guarantee you'll want to take a bottle home with you.

WHERE TO STAY

The Cove Eleuthera 🐟🐟   On a pink-sandy cove 2.5km (1½ miles) northwest of Gregory Town and 5km (3 miles) southeast of the Glass Window, this year-round resort is set on 11 hectares (27 acres) partially planted with pineapples; it consists of a main clubhouse and eight tropical-style bungalows, each containing four units, nestled on the oceanside. All the rooms were recently upgraded and imbued with island charm. Each one has tile floors and a porch, with no TVs or phones to distract you. All accommodations, each with a spacious living area, are equipped with a bathroom that includes a shower stall.

The restaurant (see listing below) serves three meals a day, and the lounge and poolside patio are open daily for drinks and informal meals. Kayaks, bicycles, two tennis courts, and a small freshwater pool compete with hammocks for your time. There's fabulous snorkeling right off the sands here, with colorful fish darting in and out of the offshore reefs.

Queen's Hwy. (P.O. Box GT1548), Gregory Town, Eleuthera, The Bahamas. © 800/552-5960 in the U.S. and Canada or 242/335-5142. Fax 242/335-5338. www.thecoveeleuthera.com. 26 units. Year-round $235–$285 (£125–£151) double; $395 (£209) 1-bedroom suite; $450 (£239) 2-bedroom suite; $995 (£527) Point House. MC, V. **Amenities:** Restaurant; bar; outdoor hilltop pool; 2 tennis courts; watersports equipment/rentals; laundry service; nonsmoking rooms. *In room:* A/C, hair dryer, kitchenettes (in some), no phone.

Finds For a Drop-Dead Pineapple Tart

Follow the smell of fresh-baked goods to **Thompson's Bakery,** Johnson Street (© 242/335-5053), which is open Monday to Saturday 8:30am to 6pm. Run by two local sisters, Monica and Daisy Thompson, this simple bakery occupies a wooden lime-green building near the highest point in town. Although it churns out lots of bread—including raisin, whole wheat, and coconut—every day, the best reason to stop by are the fresh pineapple tarts, priced at $1 (55p) each, which are among the best we've ever tasted. You might also find fresh-baked doughnuts and cinnamon rolls.

WHERE TO DINE

Cambridge Villas BAHAMIAN   One of the few choices in town, it occupies a cement-sided room on the ground floor of a battered hotel (the accommodations aren't as appealing as the restaurant). Harcourt and Sylvia Cambridge, the owners, serve conch burgers, conch chowder, and sandwiches, usually prepared by Sylvia herself. It's just a simple spot, where you might be entertained by the continually running soap operas broadcast from a TV over the bar.

Main St. ☎ 242/335-5080. Reservations not required. Sandwiches and platters $3.50–$9 (£1.85–£4.75). MC, V. Mon–Sat 8am–9pm; Sun 10am–9pm.

The Cove 𝒢𝒢 BAHAMIAN/CONTINENTAL   In the previously recommended hotel 2.5km (1½ miles) north of Gregory Town, this spacious dining room is your best bet in the area, featuring a gourmet continental cuisine with local delights as well. The restaurant is decorated in a light, tropical style. Lunch begins with the inevitable conch chowder. We recommend you follow it with a conch burger, a generous patty of ground seafood blended with green pepper, onion, and spices. Conch also appears several times in the evening, and we think this is the best cracked conch in town, tenderized, dipped in a special batter, and fried to a golden perfection. The kitchen serves the best fried chicken in the area, too.

Queen's Hwy. ☎ 242/335-5142. Breakfast $8–$14 (£4.25–£7.40); lunch $8–$16 (£4.25–£8.50); main courses $28–$34 (£15–£18). MC, V. Daily 8–10:30am, 11:30am–2:30pm, and 6–8:30pm.

EXPLORING THE AREA: THE GLASS WINDOW & BEYOND

Behind a colorful facade on Queen's Highway in the heart of town, the **Island Made Gift Shop** (☎ 242/335-5369) carries an outstanding inventory that owes its quality to the artistic eye and good taste of owner Pamela Thompson. Look for one-of-a-kind paintings on driftwood or crafted on the soles of discarded shoes, handmade quilts from Androsian fabrics, Abaco ceramics, and jewelry made from pieces of glass found on the beach. There are extraordinary woven baskets from the descendants of Seminole Indians and escaped slaves living in remote districts of Andros Island. Especially charming are bowls crafted from half-sections of conch shells.

Dedicated surfers have come here from as far away as California and Australia to test their skills at **Surfers Beach,** 4km (2½ miles) south of town on the Atlantic side. The waves are at their highest in winter and spring; even if you're not brave enough to get out there, it's fun to watch.

South of town on the way to Hatchet Bay are several caverns worth visiting, the largest of which is called simply **the Cave.** It has a big fig tree out front, which the people of Gregory Town claim was planted long ago by area pirates who wanted to conceal the cave because they had hidden treasure in it.

Local guides (you have to ask around in Gregory Town or Hatchet Bay) will take you into the interior of the cave, where the resident bats are harmless (even though they must resent the intrusion of tourists with flashlights). At one point, the drop is so steep—about 3.5m (11 ft.)—you have to use a ladder to climb down. Eventually, you reach a cavern studded with stalactites and stalagmites. At this point, a maze of passageways leads off through the rocky underground recesses. The cave comes to an abrupt end at the edge of a cliff, where the thundering sea is some 27m (89 ft.) below.

After leaving Gregory Town and driving north, you come to the famed **Glass Window,** Eleuthera's chief sight and narrowest point. Once a natural rock arch bridged the

Note: Crash Pad for Surfers

A short walk from Surfers Beach, the **Surfers Beach Manor** (℃ 242/335-5300; www.surfersmanor.com) is a restored, laid-back inn offering 11 newly refurbished and air-conditioned bedrooms, either with twin or queen-size beds. In winter, doubles range in price from $89 to $109 (£47–£58), with summer rates lowered to $79 to $99 (£42–£52). A rental car can also be arranged for $50 (£27) a day. There is a restaurant and a lounge on-site serving Bahamian cuisine. Swimming, surfing (but of course), and doing nothing are the pastimes here. MasterCard and Visa are accepted.

land, but it's gone now, replaced by an artificially constructed bridge. As you drive across it, you can see the contrast between the deep blue ocean and the emerald green shoal waters of the sound. The rocks rise to a height of 21m (69 ft.). Often, as ships in the Atlantic are being tossed about, the crew looks across the narrow point to see a ship resting quietly on the other side, hence the name Glass Window. Artist Winslow Homer was so captivated by this spot that he once captured it on canvas.

FISHING TRIPS

Your best bet is **Capt. Z Fishing and Dive Charters,** located at the Cove House (see above) in Gregory Town. Both half- and full-day fishing trips are offered aboard their custom-built boats. Some of the best spear-fishing in either The Bahamas or the Caribbean are offered by this charter outfit. Phone ℃ **242/335-5185** for details or bookings.

GREGORY TOWN AFTER DARK

The place to be in Gregory Town, especially on a Saturday night, is **Elvina,** on Main Street (℃ **242/335-5032**). Owners Ed and Elvina Watkins make you feel right at home and practically greet you at the door with a cold beer. Surfers and locals alike flock here to chow down on burgers, Bahamian dishes, and Cajun grub, served daily from 10am to "whenever we close." Elvina's husband, "Chicken Ed," is from Louisiana and makes great jambalaya. Live music is played on Tuesday and Friday nights.

8 The Current

The inhabitants of the Current, a settlement in North Eleuthera, are believed to have descended from a tribe of Native Americans. A narrow strait separates the village from Current Island, where most of the locals make their living from the sea or from plaiting straw goods.

This is a small community where the people often welcome visitors. You won't find crowds or artificial attractions. Everything focuses on the sea, a source of pleasure for the visiting tourists, but a way to sustain life for the local people.

From the Current, you can explore some interesting sights in North Eleuthera, including **Preacher's Cave,** where the Eleutherian Adventurers found shelter in the mid–17th century when they were shipwrecked with no provisions. (Note that your taxi driver may balk at being asked to drive there; the road is hard on his expensive tires.) If you do reach it, you'll find a cave that seems like an amphitheater. The very devout Eleutherian Adventurers held religious services inside the cave, which is pierced by holes in the roof, allowing light to intrude. The cave is not far from the airport, in a northeasterly direction. Another sight is **Boiling Hole,** which is in a shallow bank that seems to boil at changing tides.

WHERE TO STAY

Sandcastle Apartments   For escapists seeking a location far removed from the usual tourist circuit, this utterly plain but airy accommodation is a good bet. The on-site kitchen, the easy access to a simple grocery store within a 5-minute walk, and the self-contained nature of this extremely modest accommodation often appeal to families. Each bedroom has a double bed, a queen-size pullout bed in the living room, and a view over shallow offshore waters, where children can wade safely for a surprisingly long distance offshore. The accommodations each have a small bathroom with a shower stall and lie just across the road from the sea; if you want to explore, bicycles are available for $5(£2.65) per day.

The Current, Eleuthera, The Bahamas. ℂ 242/335-3244. Fax 242/393-0440. 2 units. Year-round $85–$90 (£45–£48) double. No credit cards. **Amenities:** Nonsmoking rooms. *In room:* A/C, coffeemaker.

9 Harbour Island ⋆⋆⋆

One of the oldest settlements in The Bahamas, founded before the United States was a nation, Harbour Island lies off the northern end of Eleuthera, some 322km (200 miles) from Miami. It is 5km (3 miles) long and 1km (⅔ mile) wide. The media have hailed this pink-sand island as the new St. Bart's, a reference to how chic it has become. If you're jogging along the beach, you might trip over a movie star.

Affectionately called by its original name, "Briland," Harbour Island is studded with good resorts. The spectacular **Pink Sands Beach** ⋆⋆⋆ runs the whole length of the island on its eastern side. The famous beach is protected from the ocean breakers by an outlying coral reef, which makes for some of the safest swimming in The Bahamas. Except for unseasonably cold days, you can swim and enjoy watersports year-round. The climate averages 72°F (22°C) in winter, 77°F (25°C) in spring and fall, and 82°F (28°C) in summer. Occasionally, evenings are cool, with a low of about 65°F (18°C) from November to February.

HARBOUR ISLAND ESSENTIALS

GETTING THERE   To reach Harbour Island, take a flight to the **North Eleuthera airstrip,** which is only a 1½-hour flight from Fort Lauderdale or Miami, and a 30-minute flight from Nassau (see "Eleuthera Essentials," at the beginning of this chapter, for details on which airlines provide service). From there, it's a 1.5km (1-mile) taxi ride to the ferry dock. The taxi costs about $4 (£2.10) per person if you share the expense with other passengers. From the dock, you'll take a 3km (2-mile) motorboat ride to Harbour Island. There's usually no waiting because a flotilla of high-powered motorboats makes the crossing whenever at least two customers show up, at a cost of around $5 (£2.65) per person. (If you're traveling alone and are willing to pay the $8/£4.25 one-way fare, the boat will depart immediately, without waiting for a second passenger.)

Another way you can get to Harbour Island is to board a speedy 177-passenger catamaran in Nassau. Contact **Bahamas Fast Ferries** (ℂ 242/323-2166; www.bahamas ferries.com). You can begin this 2-hour trip at **Potter's Cay Dock,** which is under the bridge leading from Paradise Island to downtown Nassau. The fare for one of these daily excursions is $110 (£58) round-trip or $65 (£34) one-way for adults, and $70 (£37) round-trip or $45 (£24) one-way for children ages 2 to 11. This ferry pulls up to Harbour Island's Government Dock, where taxis wait to take you to your hotel.

GETTING AROUND   Once they reach Harbour Island, most people don't need transportation. They walk to where they're going, rent a bicycle (check your equipment carefully before you rent it because some bicycles rented to tourists on Harbour Island are way past their prime), or putt-putt around the island on an electric golf cart. Most hotels offer these for rent or at least will arrange for a cart or bicycle; usually, they'll be delivered directly to your hotel.

Michael's Cycles, on Colebrook Street (© **242/333-2384**), is the best place to go if you want some mobility other than your own two feet. The shop is open daily from 8am to 6pm. Bikes rent for $12 (£6.35) per day, and you can also rent two-seater motorbikes for $30 (£16) a day, or even a four-seater golf cart for $48 (£25) per day. You can also rent kayaks for $40 (£21) per day, paddle boats for $40 (£21) per day (or $10/£5.30 per hour), and jet skis for $85 (£45) per hour.

VISITOR INFORMATION   The **Harbour Island Tourist Office** is on Dunmore Street (© **242/333-2621**); it's generally open Monday to Friday 9am to 5pm.

FAST FACTS   The **Royal Bank of Canada** is on Dunmore Street (© **242/333-2250**). Hours are Monday to Thursday 9:30am to 3pm and Friday 9:30am to 4:30pm.

The **Harbour Island Health Centre,** South Street, Dunmore Town (© **242/333-2225**), handles routine medical problems. Hours are Monday to Friday 9am to 5pm. The on-call doctor can be reached at © **242/333-2822.**

Resorts usually have Internet access. Arthur's Bakery, located in the center of town, also offers it. You can use the computer there or bring your own laptop. Hours are Monday to Saturday 8am to 2pm, costing $10 (£5.30) for 15 minutes.

You can get prescriptions filled at **Briland's Pharmacy** (© **242/333-3427**), located at Johnson's Plaza, Dunmore Street. Hours are Monday to Saturday 9am to 5pm.

The post office (© **242/333-2215**) is on Gaol Alley, and it's open Monday to Friday 9am to 5:30pm.

The police can be reached at either © **919** or © **242/333-2111.**

WHERE TO STAY
VERY EXPENSIVE
Dunmore Beach Club *𝒻*   This formal and exclusive colony of cottages is the quintessentially elegant hideaway, with 3.2 hectares (8 acres) of well-manicured grounds along the island's legendary 5km (3-mile) pink-sand beach. It's not as elaborate or sleek as its nearest rival, Pink Sands, but it's cozier, although in a bit of decline. Renovations brought some of the units up to standard with huge showers and whirlpool tubs. The Bahamian-style bungalows attractively combine traditional furnishings and tropical accessories, with no phones or TVs to distract you. The Dunmore's heyday may have come and gone, but the feeling here is still dignified, comfortable, and pleasant.

Breakfast is offered on a garden terrace under pine trees with a view of the beach. Dinner is served at one sitting at 8pm; men must wear jackets (ties are optional). Bahamian and international cuisine is served formally in a dining room with a beamed ceiling, louvered doors, expensive china, and windows with views over the blue Atlantic. A clubhouse is the focal point for socializing; a living room with a library and fireplace provides additional cozy nooks, as does an oceanview bar.

Colebrook Lane (P.O. Box EL27122), Harbour Island, The Bahamas. ℂ 877/891-3100 or 242/333-2200. Fax 242/333-2429. www.dunmorebeach.com. 15 units. Nov–Apr $499–$599 (£264–£317) double, $669–$789 (£355–£418) suite for 2; May–Aug $265–$300 (£140–£159) double, $350–$420 (£186–£223) suite. Rates include all meals. MC, V. Closed Sept–Oct. **Amenities:** Restaurant; bar; tennis court; bike rentals; babysitting; laundry service; nonsmoking rooms; rooms for those w/limited mobility. *In room:* A/C, minibar, hair dryer, safe, no phone.

Pink Sands 🏵🏵🏵 Posh and sophisticated, this hideaway is just the place to sneak away to with that special (wealthy) someone, located adjacent to a 5km (3-mile) stretch of pink-sand beach sheltered by a barrier reef. Yes, that was Julia Roberts in a bikini we spotted leaving the cottage next door. The elegant, relaxed retreat occupies an 11-hectare (27-acre) beachfront estate. Although it feels a bit like a pricey private club, it's less snobbish and a lot more hip than the Dunmore Beach Club. The owner is Chris Blackwell, founder of Island Records. Increasingly known as a hotel entrepreneur, he spared no expense here. The resort's outrageous clubhouse is the most beautifully and imaginatively decorated room in the Out Islands.

The airy, spacious bedrooms have either an ocean or a garden view. Smaller units contain Art Deco touches straight out of Miami's South Beach; larger, more expensive units have Indonesian (especially Balinese) furnishings and art, and huge decks. All rooms have kitchenettes or kitchens, central air-conditioning, pressurized water systems, walk-in closets, satellite TVs, CD players and a CD selection, wet bars, private patios with teak furnishings, and beautifully tiled bathrooms with tubs and showers. The interior design features marble floors with area rugs, oversize Adirondack furnishings, local artwork, and batik fabrics. The rooms have dataports, and fax machines and cellular phones can be supplied if you need them.

Hotel guests get some of the best meals on the island, an "A-B-C" fusion of Asian, Bahamian, and Caribbean cuisine. Dinner is an elegant four-course nightly affair. Lunches are much less formal, served in the Blue Bar, a postmodern pavilion beside the beach.

Chapel St., Harbour Island, The Bahamas. ℂ 800/OUTPOST or 242/333-2030. Fax 242/333-2060. www.pinksands resort.com. 25 units. Winter $800–$900 (£424–£477) double, from $1,400 (£742) 2-bedroom unit; off season $650–$750 (£345–£398) double, from $1,200 (£636) 2-bedroom unit. Rates include MAP (breakfast and dinner). AE, MC, V. **Amenities:** 2 restaurants; 2 bars; pool; 3 tennis courts; health club; limited room service; babysitting; laundry service; nonsmoking rooms. *In room:* A/C, TV, dataport, kitchenette or kitchen, minibar, wet bar, coffeemaker, hair dryer, iron, safe, CD player (and CDs).

EXPENSIVE

Coral Sands 🏵🏵 *Kids* The hotel, whose exterior is painted a soft coral pink, stands on 3.6 hilly hectares (9 acres) overlooking the beach and within walking distance of the center of Dunmore Town, which is in a British Colonial style. This is one of the most consistently reliable hotels on the island, avoiding the glitter of some of the more volatile properties. It also opens onto one of the best beach locations and is a favorite of families, whereas some of the more posh resorts don't really cater to children. Coral Sands is a longtime favorite that does a big business with happy repeat visitors. Originally built with an airy design that featured big-windowed loggias and arcades, it opens directly onto the 5km (3-mile) pink-coral-sand beach for which the town is famous. Casual elegance, with ample doses of personal charm and friendliness, permeates every aspect of this hotel. Improvements have revitalized the property and freshened up the decor. Many rooms have private verandas or terraces, all are eminently comfortable, and all allow you to fall asleep to the soothing sounds of waves breaking on the shore. Bathrooms are midsize and well kept, mostly with tub/showers. The latest series of restored rooms are on the second floor of the complex in the Caribe building. They have been converted into luxury one-bedroom deluxe oceanview suites, some with two bathrooms, others with one bathroom. All of these suites have a bedroom facing the ocean, plus a separate living room with sofa.

The hotel's Terrace restaurant offers fine cuisine. Simpler, less elaborate food is also offered at the beachfront Commander's Beach Bar & Restaurant, which is dramatically cantilevered high above the pale-pink sands.

Chapel St., Harbour Island, The Bahamas. © **800/468-2799** in the U.S. and Canada or 242/333-2350. Fax 242/333-2368. www.coralsands.com. 39 units. Dec–Sept $305–$385 (£162–£204) double, from $575 (£305) suite for 4 persons; Oct 19–Dec 15 $280–$360 (£148–£191) double, from $380 (£201) suite for 4 persons. 3-night minimum stay. Closed Sept 5–Oct 18. AE, MC, V. **Amenities:** Restaurant; bar; pool; tennis court; watersports equipment/rentals; babysitting; laundry service; nonsmoking rooms; rooms for those w/limited mobility. *In room:* A/C, TV (in some), kitchen, coffeemaker, hair dryer, safe.

Rock House Hotel 🏝🏝🏝 *(Finds)*   This hotel (originally an unpretentious B&B) recently reopened in a lavishly augmented format that thrust it into the spotlight as one of Harbour Island's most glamorous and stylish inns. The forces behind the restoration were two partners who included J. Wallace Tutt, a building contractor who had designed buildings for clients such as Cher and Versace.

Painted a pale shade of yellow, the hotel sits on a low bluff above the harbor in the center of Harbour Island's only village. The property combines the original 1940s-era B&B with an adjoining site that had functioned for several decades as a Catholic schoolhouse. Today the complex reflects the aesthetics you might encounter in a hip enclave of Miami and incorporates a stylish (and separately recommended) restaurant. Nine of the most whimsical accommodations on Harbour Island are found here. Each is outfitted with a name and a decorative style that's unique to each of its neighbors. Examples include the Reef Room, the Palm Room, the Asian Room, the Nautilus Room, the Pineapple Room, and the Parrot Room. Social life centers on the bar and the lavishly landscaped swimming pool, which is lined with the kind of tentlike cabanas that you might expect along the coast of Sardinia.

Bay and Hill sts., Harbour Island, Eleuthera, The Bahamas. © **242/333-2053**. Fax 242/333-3173. www.rockhouse bahamas.com. 10 units. Year-round $380–$495 (£201–£262) double; $575 (£305) junior suite; $725 (£384) 2-bedroom unit. AE, MC, V. No children under 18 accepted. **Amenities:** 2 restaurants; 2 bars; pool; gym/exercise room; room service; laundry service; all nonsmoking rooms. *In room:* A/C, TV, minibar, safe.

Romora Bay Club & Resort 🏝🏝   After several upheavals in management, this cluster of cottages on the island's bay side is up and running, and welcoming visitors to its restored premises. Although it's not on Pink Beach, it's just a short golf-cart ride away. The inn was originally developed as a private club for reclusive millionaires, but today is open to all. Built on a sloping hillside, these clusters of cottages are scattered about the landscaped grounds. Rooms have tiled floors and are cozily furnished with feather beds and plush pillows, each with a private patio. The junior suites and water-view rooms are the most desirable, opening onto panoramic vistas of the bay.

You can take a dip in the hotel's infinity pool or else enjoy a cabana at the hotel's own beach. The inn offers the best-stocked library on the island, with dozens of films, CDs, and even books; and there is also a pool deck with views of the bay. The food is among the best on island, with the steaks flown in from Chicago and the fish caught in local waters. This is a great spot for sunset-watching even if you're not a guest. An international tapas menu is featured nightly at sundown.

Dunmore St., Dunmore Town, Harbour Island, Eleuthera, The Bahamas. ℂ 800/333-2325 or 242/333-2325. Fax 242/333-2500. www.romorabay.com. 19 units. Winter $333–$450 (£176–£239) double, $450 (£239) suite; off-season $215–$295 (£114–£156) double, $295 (£156) suite. AE, DC, MC, V. **Amenities:** 2 restaurants; 2 bars; pool; tennis court; gym; watersports; library; Internet; dock. *In room:* A/C, TV, hair dryer.

Runaway Hill Club   Small and intimate, this conservative, comfortable hotel overlooks acres of pink-sandy beachfront. It has a huge lawn and is separated from Colebrook Street by a wall. Built in the 1940s, the building retains its English colonial–style dormers and many other original features. In winter, a crackling fire is sometimes built in the hearth near the entrance. The social center is a cheerfully decorated lounge/dining room/bar/reception area painted in joyful island colors with a sense of Bahamian whimsy. Each of the bedrooms is different, giving the impression that you are lodging in a private home—as indeed this used to be. Only two of the rooms at this place are in the original house, and these are accessible via the building's original 18th-century staircase. The others are within comfortable annexes built during the '70s and '80s. Bathrooms are small but well maintained, and seven contain tub/showers, the rest showers.

Dinners are served on the breeze-filled rear porch overlooking the swimming pool, and nonguests are welcome (see "Where to Dine," below).

Colebrook St. (P.O. Box EL27031), Harbour Island, The Bahamas. ℂ 242/333-2150. Fax 242/333-2420. www. runawayhill.com. 10 units. Year-round $375–$425 (£199–£225) double; $450 (£239) villa. MAP (breakfast and dinner) $99 (£52) per person. MC, V. Closed Sept 5–Nov 15. **Amenities:** Restaurant; bar; pool; watersports equipment/rentals; bike rentals; laundry service. *In room:* A/C, hair dryer, safe, no phone.

MODERATE

The Landing 🎟🎟   This intimate inn is understated, tasteful, and lovely. Virtually destroyed by a hurricane in 1999, it was well restored by its owners. India Hicks, the daughter of the famed London decorator David Hicks, has taken over, drawing much of England to Harbour Island. She is the granddaughter of Lord Mountbatten of Burma (grandson of Queen Victoria) and was a bridesmaid to the Princess of Wales at her wedding to Charles. The first doctor on Harbour Island built the house in the 1850s as his private residence. It's set within a pair of stone- and clapboard-sided buildings constructed in the early 1800s, located close to the piers where ferryboats arrive from Eleuthera. A veranda looks out over the harbor. Accommodations are breezy, airy, and high-ceilinged, and they open onto wraparound verandas, which seem to expand the living space within. Expect bold, cheerful island colors and design touches that evoke the seafaring days of old Harbour Island. The bathrooms are large and tiled, with tubs and showers.

Bay St. (P.O. Box 190), Harbour Island, The Bahamas. ℂ 242/333-2707. Fax 242/333-2650. www.harbourisland landing.com. 8 units. Winter $265–$375 (£140–£199) double, $330 (£175) 2-bedroom unit; off season $240–$330 (£127–£175) double, $330 (£175) 2-bedroom unit. Rates include breakfast. MC, V. **Amenities:** Restaurant; bar; babysitting; nonsmoking rooms. *In room:* A/C, hair dryer, no phone.

INEXPENSIVE

Bahama House Inn 🎟 *Finds*   This is the only authentic B&B, with the owners living on-site, on Harbour Island. The setting is a pink-sided clapboard house that was built between 1798 and 1800 by the island's first justice of the peace, Dr. Johnson. In 1999, Denver-born owners John and Joni Hersh bought a 1950s-era house next door for future expansions. Midsize rooms are artfully old-fashioned, low-key, and comfortable, and they are usually accessible via gracious verandas that wrap around the upper and lower floors. Bathrooms are tiled and beautifully maintained, and come with shower stalls. Everything shows a personal touch here, including the beautiful gardens. The beach is a 5-minute walk away, and the house's living room has satellite TV.

At the corner of Dunmore and Hill sts., Harbour Island, The Bahamas. ℂ 242/333-2201. Fax 242/333-2850. www.bahamahouseinn.com. 7 units. Winter $150–$195 (£80–£103) double; off season $135–$180 (£72–£95) double. Rates include breakfast. MC, V. Closed Aug–Sept. Children under 12 not accepted. **Amenities:** Restaurant; bar; laundry service; rooms for those w/limited mobility. *In room:* A/C, hair dryer, safe, no phone.

Tingum Village   This is a simple, no-frills choice, but it does the trick at bargain prices and draws a loyal repeat business. It lies just off the main street, a 3-minute walk to the beach. Set in a steamy tropical garden, Tingum Village offers basic accommodations in small cement-sided bungalows. Each of the rooms has air-conditioning, ceiling fans, and a patio with plastic furniture, plus a small bathroom with a shower stall. Rooms aren't the most comfortable, and you'll really wish they'd improve the wattage in the reading lamps and that the ceiling fans wouldn't squeak. But it has its charming aspects as well. The cottage is meant for six to eight people, though it can hold up to 10 (but that would be very cramped).

The hotel's restaurant, Ma Ruby's, overlooks the garden and offers standard Bahamian and American food (see box below).

Colebrook St. (P.O. Box 61), Harbour Island, Eleuthera, The Bahamas. ℂ 242/333-2161. Fax 242/333-2161. 19 units. Year-round $135 (£72) double; $140 (£74) triple; $150–$200 (£80–£106) suite; $300 (£159) 2-bedroom suite or cottage. MC, V. **Amenities:** Restaurant; bar; limited room service; babysitting; laundry service; nonsmoking rooms; rooms for those w/limited mobility. *In room:* A/C, kitchenettes, coffeemaker (in some), hair dryer (in some), no phone.

WHERE TO DINE

If you don't want to dress up for lunch, you can head for **Seaview Takeaway** (ℂ 242/333-2542), at the foot of the ferry dock. Here you can feast on all that good stuff: pig's feet, sheep-tongue souse, and, most definitely, cracked conch. Everything tastes better with peas 'n' rice. Daily specials range from $3 to $9 (£1.60–£4.75), and service is Monday to Saturday 8am to 5pm. Another casual drop-in spot for both visitors and locals is **Arthur's Bakery and Café,** Dunmore St. (ℂ 242/333-2644), owned by Robert Arthur, the screenwriter for *M*A*S*H*. Artists, writers, media people, and what Arthur calls "international lollygaggers" hang out here. There are only a few tables, and they fill up quickly with those catching up on the local gossip. Arthur's Trinidadian wife, Anna, bakes the best Key lime tart on the island and is also noted for her croissants and banana bread. At lunch you can drop in for freshly made salads and sandwiches. Many guests come here to use the Internet.

EXPENSIVE

The Landing ✸ INTERNATIONAL   This restaurant occupies the ground floor and most of the garden of the previously recommended hotel, a stately looking building set to the right of the dock as your ferryboat pulls into Harbour Island. Built with a combination of thick stone walls and clapboards in 1800, with an annex that's only 20 years younger, it's the domain of India Hicks (see listing above).

The menu changes with the availability of fresh ingredients. You might begin with an arugula salad with shaved Parmesan cheese, or else steamed stone crab and shrimp wrapped in a lettuce leaf with a tamarind-flavored broth. Among the more delectable main courses are pan-fried mahimahi, or else tuna with a salad of soba noodles. A spicy Thai-inspired green chicken curry is served with jasmine-scented rice.

Bay St. ℂ 242/333-2707. www.harbourislandlanding.com. Reservations recommended. Main courses dinner $36–$42 (£19–£22). AE, MC, V. Sun 8am–11pm; Mon–Tues and Thurs–Sat 6:30–10:30pm.

Finds Ma Ruby's Conch Burger

If you'd like to sample some real local fare, head to **Ma Ruby's** on Colebrook Street (ⓒ **242/333-2161**). Some islanders claim you will get the best meal in Eleuthera if Ma Ruby (the cook and owner) is in the kitchen herself. Her conch burger is certainly worthy of an award. She's been stewing chicken, baking grouper, and serving hearty meals in a trellised courtyard for a long time, and she's got a lot of devoted fans. The place is well known for its cheeseburgers, which the manager says were ranked as one of the 10 best in the world by "Mr. Cheeseburger in Paradise" himself, Jimmy Buffett. The prices range from $5 to $15 (£2.65–£7.95) for the a la carte menu; a four-course fixed-price Bahamian dinner costs $26 to $40 (£14–£21). The restaurant is open daily 8am to midnight.

Rock House Restaurant ⓡⓡ INTERNATIONAL   Set on a covered terrace that overlooks boats bobbing at anchor in the harbor, this restaurant is the showpiece of Harbour Island's newest and perhaps most stylish hotel, which was previously recommended. Inside there's a feeling of a hip bodega in Miami, with decor that features lots of varnished mahogany, pale yellow walls, and ceiling fans. In addition to the tables for two and four diners, the restaurant offers a large "chef's table" with 16 chairs, reputed to have been among the furnishings in Washington, D.C.'s White House before a long-ago redecoration. Although lunches are charming, they are gastronomically simple affairs, with dishes that include burgers, rock lobster salad sandwiches, and conch chowders. Dinners are more elaborate and more of a showcase for the chef. The best menu items include curried Colorado lamb chops with toasted couscous salad; seared yellow-fin tuna steak with orange segments, cucumber, sesame seeds, and wasabi cream; roasted lobster tail with green basil butter; and vegetarian arugula pesto pasta. Especially flavorful is a crispy pan-fried "almost deboned" chicken breast with a citrus-flavored herb sauce.

In the Rock House Hotel, Bay and Hill sts. ⓒ 242/333-2053. www.rockhousebahamas.com. Reservations recommended. Main courses lunch $15–$24 (£7.95–£13), dinner $36–$55 (£19–£29); Fri night buffet $35 (£19). AE, MC, V. Daily 6–11pm.

Runaway Hill Club ⓡ BAHAMIAN/AMERICAN/INTERNATIONAL   The dining room here enjoys a sweeping view over the beachfront. Inside, the decor is brightly painted in strong, whimsical colors, with wicker and rattan furniture and a fine collection of watercolors the owner has spent years collecting. The kitchen is known for such well-prepared dishes as rack of veal with a sherry-flavored caper sauce and noodles, conch marinara, crabmeat soup with scotch, scallops in sherry sauce, spicy lobster bisque, beef tenderloin, and many versions of local fish.

Colebrook St. ⓒ 242/333-2150. www.runawayhill.com. Reservations required. Fixed-price dinner from $78 (£41). AE, MC, V. Mon–Sat dinner at 8pm. Closed Sept 5–Nov 15.

MODERATE
The Harbour Lounge INTERNATIONAL   This old clapboard-sided building dating to the early 1800s is the first place you're likely to see as you step off the ferryboat arriving from the "mainland" of Eleuthera. Today it's one of the most satisfying and authentic restaurants on the island. Sometimes eating here feels like attending an island dinner party. The menu has included such items as marinated blackened

grouper, soft-shell or stone crabs, lobster tail, different preparations of conch, and a combination of feta cheese and shrimp marinara. Overall, it's a charming place, and the veranda will give you a front-row seat for all the goings-on of Harbour Island.

Bay St. ⓒ **242/333-2031.** Reservations recommended for dinner. Lunch salads, sandwiches, platters $10–$22 (£5.30–£12); dinner main courses $12–$38 (£6.35–£20). MC, V. Tues–Sun 11:30am–3pm and 6–9:15pm.

Restaurant Sip Sip ⓕ *Finds* BAHAMIAN/INTERNATIONAL   The only problem with this restaurant is that it's closed every evening (except for large parties), preferring to focus on lunch instead. Set on a dune, close to both the Ocean View Guest House and the Dunmore Beach Club, it was built in 2003 in a traditional, green-painted clapboard-sided design evocative of Harbour Island buildings that are a lot older. Inside, the cuisine is the product of the Bahamian/American couple Jim Black and Julie Lightbourne, who met in Africa while Jim was working in the safari business. Within a brightly painted blue and mostly green interior, with mahogany doors, windows, and bar tops, you'll find a changing menu that, depending on the whim of the owners, might highlight Bahamian, Italian, French, Thai, or Pacific Rim cuisine. The menu might include hummus with grilled pita bread; conch chili (a welcome variation on conch chowder); fresh salads made with tomatoes and buffalo mozzarella; baba ghanouj, the eggplant specialty that originated in Lebanon; quesadillas, including a version stuffed with lobster, shrimp, and tropical fruit salsa; and a flavorful curried chicken salad studded with chunks of apple and served with mango chutney. Grouper filets, prepared in at least two different ways, are usually available as well. The restaurant's name, incidentally, translates from local patois as "gossip."

Court St. ⓒ **242/333-3316.** Reservations not necessary. Main courses $15–$30 (£7.95–£16). MC, V. Wed–Mon 11:30am–4pm. Closed Wed June–Nov.

INEXPENSIVE

Avery's Restaurant & Grill BAHAMIAN/AMERICAN   From the moment you enter, you get the sense that this is a simple, friendly, family-run restaurant. It occupies a tiny wooden house, painted in tones of orange and yellow, near Tingum Village. Inside you'll find a clean, white-tiled room with no more than four tables, and a deck with three more. Mariah Campbell and her daughter, Murieta, are the owners. Their breakfasts provide nourishment to city employees around town. The rest of the day, an unending stream of sandwiches and steaming platters of seafood and steaks emerge from the kitchens.

Colebrook St. ⓒ **242/333-3126.** Reservations not accepted. Breakfast and lunch platters $7–$18 (£3.70–£9.55); dinner main courses $25–$32 (£13–£17). No credit cards. Daily 6:30am–3pm and 6–10pm.

BEACHES, WATERSPORTS & OTHER OUTDOOR PURSUITS

Pink Sands Beach ⓕⓕⓕ is our favorite strand in all The Bahamas; its sands stretch for 5 uninterrupted kilometers (3 miles). Although the beach is set against a backdrop of low-rise hotels and villas, it still feels tranquil and pristine. The sun is best in the morning (afternoons start to become shadowy), and waves are generally gentle, owing to an offshore reef that breaks waves coming in from the Atlantic. Many places are good for snorkeling, and this beach is also the best place on the island for a long, leisurely morning stroll.

The **diving** in this part of The Bahamas is among the most diverse in the region. The most spectacular site, judged among the 10 top dives in the world, is **Current Cut Dive** ⓕⓕⓕ. One of the fastest (9 knots) drift dives in the world, it involves descending into the water flow racing between the rock walls that form the underwater chasm between Eleuthera and Current Island. Swept up in the currents with schools of stingrays, mako sharks, and reef fish, divers are propelled along 1km (⅔ mile) of underwater distance in less than 10 minutes. The dive may be one of the highlights of your whole life.

Valentine's Dive Center, Harbourfront (© **242/333-2080;** www.valentinesdive. com), maintains a full range of dive activities. The dive center is in a wooden building near the entrance to Valentine's Marina. Lessons in snorkeling and scuba diving for beginners are given daily at 10am. Snorkeling trips cost $45 (£24) per half-day, including equipment. A two-tank dive goes for $75 (£40), with night dives costing $85 (£45).

Lil' Shan's Watersports, Bay Street (© **242/422-9343;** www.lswatersports.com), offers everything from scuba diving to boat rentals and fishing trips. A two-stop snorkeling jaunt goes for $45 (£24) per person, including gear. The staff here also offers special kids' programs.

You can rent a motorboat through **Michael's Cycles** (© **242/333-2384** or 242/464-0994), on Colebrook Street near Seagrapes nightclub. Plan to spend about $75 (£40) for a full day on a 4m (13-ft.) boat, and $100 (£53) for a half-day or $150 (£80) for a full day on a 5m (16-ft.) boat (rates do not include gas charge). Kayaks go for $40 (£21) a day.

You can make arrangements for fishing guides and charters through your hotel or by contacting **Valentine's Dive Center** (© **242/333-2080;** www.valentinesdive. com), on the harbor side of the island in Dunmore Town.

EXPLORING THE ISLAND

Dunmore Town, located on the harbor side of Harbour Island, was named for the 18th-century royal governor of The Bahamas who had a summer home here. You can walk around the narrow, virtually car-free lanes here in less than 20 minutes, or stroll slowly to savor the sight of the old gingerbread cottages that line the waterfront. Overhung with orange, purple, and pink bougainvillea, white picket fences enclose wooden houses painted pastel blue, green, and lilac. Wind chimes tinkle in front of shuttered windows. Coconut palms and wispy casuarina pines shade grassy yards.

Americans and Canadians own some of these houses, which have whimsical names such as Up Yonder and Beside the Point, instead of house numbers. One of the oldest, **Loyalist Cottage,** was built in 1797. It survives from the days when the original settlers, loyal to the British Crown, left the American colonies after the Revolutionary War. The porches along the harbor make for prime sunset-watching. Lucky for you, some porches aren't connected to private homes. The terrace at Harbour Lounge Bar and Restaurant is an idyllic perch. Just across the road from Loyalist Cottage, you can browse through straw goods, T-shirts, and fruits and vegetables at the vendors' stalls.

On Sundays, dressed-up residents socialize in clusters outside churches before and after services. Two of The Bahamas' first churches are found in Dunmore Town and are still going strong: **St. John's,** The Bahamas' oldest Anglican church, established in 1768, and **Wesley Methodist Church,** built in 1846.

Spend some time wandering the streets—some hilly, some flat—away from the heart of town. You can see roosters doing their jerky marches through front yards and horses grazing in small fields. You'll find unassuming but perfectly good Bahamian restaurants, bars, and nightclubs in this locals' area.

SHOPPING

Miss Mae's, Dunmore Street (℗ 242/333-2002), lives up to its billing as one of the island's finest clothing boutiques.

Briland's Androsia, King Street (℗ 242/333-2342), sells the best selection of bathing suits, with bright batik fabrics printed on the island of North Andros.

Blue Rooster, in the center of town (℗ 242/333-2240), along with the Shop at the Landing (see below), offers what might be the most upscale and stylish collection of men's and women's clothing and (casual) eveningwear on the island. Come here for something sporty and trim-looking to wear into a posh hotel's dining room, especially if the New Englandish button-down look appeals to you. The **Shop at the Landing,** at the Landing Resort (℗ 242/333-2707), usually wins as the most fashionable clothing store on the island. It focuses on chic and wearable sportswear and things you might wear to a casual island cocktail party, a posh brunch, or a buffet dinner aboard a yacht.

Finally, check out **Princess Street Gallery** (℗ 242/333-2788), where Charles Carey has restored an ancestral home and uses it as a showcase to display works by local artists.

HARBOUR ISLAND AFTER DARK

Unpretentious **Gusty's,** Coconut Grove Avenue (℗ 242/333-2165), boasts sweeping sea and sunset views. Inside you'll find a sand-covered floor, while the outdoor veranda is sometimes the scene of fashion shows of local dressmakers. Live music by a DJ is featured every night.

Seagrapes, Colebrook Street (no phone), is another favorite place of the locals, where you can boogie down to the sounds of disco or catch a live band. Expect to be jostled and crowded on a Saturday night because everyone on the island comes here for a wild Bahamian hoedown.

Vic-Hum Club, Barracks Street (℗ 242/333-2161), established in 1955, is the quintessential Harbour Island dive. Walls have been layered with the covers of hundreds of record albums and sports posters that music-industry and basketball buffs find fascinating. The Vic-Hum is open 24 hours a day, catering to breakfasting construction workers in the morning, and locals meeting friends for a beer all afternoon. Some of them play basketball on an indoor court that's transformed later in the evening into a dance floor (music begins at 10pm every Fri and Sat).

Locals call the **Vic-Hum Club,** Barracks Street (℗ 242/333-2161), a "rum-rockin' shack." Originally opened in 1955, the boozery is a local dive founded by two musician brothers, Humphrey and Victor Percentie. Today it is run by Humphrey Jr., who welcomes the likes of Mick Jagger, Tyra Banks, and Drew Barrymore to his dance floor. Humphrey Jr. goes by the nickname of both Poison Snake and Crooked Dog. While other joints on island close at midnight, Vic-Hum Club just starts rocking then, often nightly until 3am.

10 Spanish Wells

Called a "quiet corner of The Bahamas," Spanish Wells is a colorful cluster of houses on St. George's Cay, 1km (⅔ mile) off the coast of northwest Eleuthera. Here you'll find sparkling bays and white beaches, sleepy lagoons, excellent diving, and a fine fishing colony.

You can walk or bicycle through the village, looking at the houses, some more than 200 years old, which have New England saltbox styling but bright tropical coloring. You can see handmade quilts in many colors, following patterns handed down from generations of English ancestors. Homeowners display these quilts on their front porches or out their windows, and they are for sale. No one locks doors or removes ignition keys from cars.

GETTING THERE

To reach the island, you can fly to the **airstrip on North Eleuthera,** from which taxis will deliver you to the ferry dock. Regardless of the time of day you arrive, a ferryboat will be either waiting for passengers or about to arrive with a load of them.

A ferry (© **242/554-6268**) runs between Gene's Bay in North Eleuthera to the main pier at Spanish Wells. The ferries depart whenever passengers show up, and the cost is $10 (£5.30) per person round-trip.

WHERE TO STAY

The Adventurer's Resort   This is your only choice for lodging in Spanish Wells. It occupies a two-story, pale lavender building in a well-tended garden about .5km (⅓ mile) west of the town center. A staff member will direct you to the beach, which lies about 1km (⅔ mile) away. The small bedrooms have simple, durable furniture with tropical upholstery; six of the units are apartments with kitchenettes. Each comes with a tub/shower. Maid service is provided when you rent the regular double room, but not the apartments.

Harbourfront (P.O. Box EI 27498), Spanish Wells, The Bahamas. © 242/333-4883. Fax 242/333-5073. www.bahamas vg.com/adventurers.html. 22 units. Year-round $96 (£51) double; $137 (£73) 1-bedroom apt; $200 (£106) 2-bedroom apt. MC, V. **Amenities:** Watersports arrangements; room service; coin-operated laundry; nonsmoking rooms. *In room:* A/C, TV, kitchenette, coffeemaker, iron, no phone.

WHERE TO DINE

Anchorage BAHAMIAN   Although you won't find Spanish Wells written up in any gourmet books, you can dine well here if you stick to locally caught fish and the like. Decent, unpretentious, and well scrubbed, this little eatery serves such home-cooked Bahamian-style items as cracked conch and grouper fish fingers. The island is known for its *langoustes* (small Bahamian lobsters), and this is what you should order if featured on the menu. Locals also grow their own tomatoes, onions, and pineapples. For dessert, try one of the cook's mud pies.

Along the waterfront at the port in Spanish Wells. © 242/333-4023. Reservations required Sat–Sun. Main courses $12–$24 (£6.35–£13). No credit cards. Mon–Sat 9am–1:30pm; daily 5–10pm.

9

The Exumas

The Exumas are some of the prettiest islands in The Bahamas. Shades of jade, aquamarine, and amethyst in deeper waters turn to transparent opal near sandy shores: The water and the land appear almost inseparable. Sailors and their crews like to stake out their own private beaches and tropical hideaways, and several vacation retreats have been built by wealthy Europeans, Canadians, and Americans.

A spiny, sandy chain of islands, the Exumas begin just 56km (35 miles) southeast of Nassau and stretch more than 161km (100 miles) from Beacon Cay in the north to Hog Cay and Sandy Cay in the south. These islands have not been developed like the Abacos and Eleuthera, so they are relatively inexpensive. But they still have much to offer, with crystal-clear waters on the west around the Great Bahama Bank, the 1,500m-deep (4,920-ft.) Exuma Sound on the east, uninhabited cays ideal for picnics, rolling hills, ruins of once-great plantations, and coral formations of great beauty. Although they're crossed by the Tropic of Cancer, the islands have average temperatures ranging from the mid-70s to the mid-80s (mid- to upper 20s Celsius).

Most of our resort recommendations are in and around George Town, the pretty pink capital of the Exumas, on Great Exuma. A community of some 900 residents, it was once considered a possible site for the capital of The Bahamas because of its excellent **Elizabeth Harbour** (see "Exploring George Town," later).

Nearly all the other cays are uninhabited or sparsely populated. Over the years, remote accommodations have come and gone on these islands. Today the only resort hotels, which attract mostly the yachting set, are found at Staniel Cay and Sampson Cay.

The cruising grounds around the Exumas, which are scattered over an ocean area of 233 sq. km (91 sq. miles), are among the finest to be found in the Western Hemisphere, if not in the world, for both sail- and powerboats. The **sailing** rivals both those of the Grenadines in the Caribbean and the Abacos in The Bahamas. Which yachters prefer depends on personal taste; each is paradise if you're a boater. If you don't come in your own craft, you can rent one here, from a simple little Daysailer to a fishing runabout, with or without a guide. The annual regatta in April in Elizabeth Harbour has attracted such notables as Prince Philip and the ex-king of Greece, Constantine. The Exumas are often referred to by yachting people as "where you go when you die if you've been good."

Snorkeling and scuba-diving opportunities draw aficionados from around the world to the vast underwater preserve of **Exuma Cays National Land and Sea Park** ✿✿✿ and to the island group's other exotic limestone and coral reefs, blue holes, drop-offs, caves, and night dives. Dive centers in George Town and Staniel Cay provide air fills and diving equipment.

Fishing is superb here, and the "flats" on the west side of Great Exuma are

The Exumas

ATLANTIC OCEAN

ELEUTHERA ISLAND

SHIP CHANNEL CAY

NORMAN'S CAY

HAWKSBILL CAY

Exuma Cays Land and Sea Park

CAT ISLAND

E x u m a   S o u n d

SAMPSON CAY

STANIEL CAY

Black Point

GREAT GUANA CAY

BRIGANTINE CAYS

Barraterre

Rolleville

Steventon

Richmond Hill

The Bluff

Mosstown

George Town

STOCKING ISLAND

LITTLE EXUMA ISLAND

Exuma Bank

GREAT EXUMA ISLAND

Elizabeth Harbour

Tropic of Cancer

Rolle Town

Williamstown

HOG CAY

Abaco

Miami

Grand Bahama

New Providence Island

Nassau

FLORIDA

Eleuthera

Cat Island

San Salvador

Andros

Long Island

The Exumas

Crooked Island

Acklins Island

Great Inagua

TURKS AND CAICOS

0   100 mi

0   100 km

CUBA

Scuba Diving

Airport

0   30 mi

0   30 km

N

Finds Saddle Cay: The Perfect Beach

For years boaters have known of a special beach, **Saddle Cay,** whose horseshoe-shaped curve lies near the northern tip of the small archipelago. The only way to reach it is by private boat; there are no organized excursions or tours (the Exumas are much too laid-back for that). However, if you own a boat, head for Saddle Cay, and you won't be disappointed when you see this totally unspoiled beach of white sands and tranquil waters. The cay is perfect for beachcombers, bird-watchers, and snorkelers—but don't expect facilities.

famous for bonefishing. You can find (if you're lucky) blue marlin on both sides of Exuma Sound, as well as sailfish, wahoo, and white marlin, plus others.

The Exumas are among the friendliest islands in The Bahamas; the people are warmhearted and not (yet) spoiled by tourism. They seem genuinely delighted to receive and welcome visitors to their shores. They grow a lot of their own food, including cassava, onions, cabbages, and pigeon peas, on the acres their ancestors worked as slaves. Many fruits grow on the cays, including guavas, mangoes, and avocados. At Government Wharf in George Town, you can watch these fruits being loaded for shipment to Nassau. The sponge industry is being revived locally; this product of the sea is found in shallow waters and creeks to the south side of the Exumas.

EXUMAS ESSENTIALS
GETTING THERE

BY PLANE   The Exumas' major commercial airport—the **Exuma International Airport**—is 16km (10 miles) from George Town, the capital. The most popular way to visit the Exumas is to fly there aboard **Bahamasair** (© **800/222-4262;** www. bahamasair.com), which has twice-daily service from Nassau to George Town. The first flight usually leaves Nassau in the morning sometime around 6:20am, depending on the day. The second flight is at 4pm. Be sure and call ahead because flight schedules are subject to change.

American Eagle (© **800/433-7300;** www.aa.com) serves Exuma from Miami three times a day. **Delta** (© **800/221-1212;** www.delta.com) has also recently begun service to George Town, flying from Atlanta four times a week.

Other minor carriers servicing the archipelago include **Lynx Air International** (© **888/596-9247;** www.lynxair.com), on Thursday, Friday, and Sunday, with air links from Fort Lauderdale.

For flights to the private airstrip at Staniel Cay, see section 3 of this chapter.

BY BOAT   There is now a motorized catamaran making the 8-hour transit from Nassau. It arrives in George Town every Monday and Wednesday at 7:30pm. It departs George Town on Tuesday and Thursday. The cost of a round-trip fare is $95 (£50) per person. Technically designed for the transport of building supplies and freight, it nonetheless allows passengers as well, many of whom stretch out on the deck in sleeping bags. There are no sleeping compartments on board. For information, call **Bahamas Fast Ferry** at © **242/323-2166** or check www.bahamasferries.com.

Several **mail boats** leave from Potter's Cay Dock in Nassau, stopping at various points along the Exumas.

Two separate mail steamers, the **MV** *Grand Master* and the *Captain C,* sail from Nassau several days a week, stopping at Big Farmer's Cay, Staniel Cay, Black Point, George Town, and Barraterre. Stopovers including George Town last no more than a few hours. Passengers as well as small amounts of freight are allowed on board. It usually takes about 21 hours for either of the ships to make the full-circuit itinerary described above.

Since hours and sailing schedules are subject to change because of weather conditions, it's best to check with the dock master at **Potter's Cay Dock** in Nassau (© **242/393-1064**).

GETTING AROUND

After arriving at the George Town airport, chances are, you'll meet Kermit Rolle. Kermit, who runs things up in Rolleville, knows as much about the Exumas as anyone else (maybe more). You can stop in at **Kermit's Airport Lounge,** from 7am to 5:30pm, Exuma International Airport (© **242/345-0002**), which is just across from the airport terminal building. If you're lucky, Kermit will be free and you can negotiate a deal with him to take you in his car for a tour.

BY TAXI   If your hotel is in George Town, it will cost about $25 (£13) to get there in a taxi from the airport. Rides often are shared. If you're going on to **Stocking Island,** an islet in Elizabeth Harbour, make prior arrangements with your hotel for boat transfers. The island has only a few taxis, and most of them wait at the airport. Hotels can usually get you a taxi if you need to go somewhere and don't have a car. Otherwise, for a taxi, call **Leslie Dames** at © **242/357-0015.**

BY CAR   It's also possible to rent a car during your stay, though the major North American companies aren't represented here. Try **Exuma Transport,** Main Street, George Town (© **242/336-2101**). They have cars to rent for $60 (£32) per day and up or $325 (£172) per week. A $200 (£106) deposit is required. Your hotel can also usually arrange a rental car for you through a local firm.

The George Town area has two gas stations: one near Exuma International Airport and the other in Farmers Hill. They're generally open Monday to Saturday 8am to 5pm, Sunday 8am to noon, and on holidays 8 to 10am.

BY BOAT   For ferries between George Town and the beaches on Stocking Island, call **Club Peace & Plenty** at © **242/336-2551.** With departures twice a day, the ferries are complimentary to Club Peace & Plenty guests. If you're not staying at that hotel, the cost is $10 (£5.30) round-trip and free for children under age 10.

BY FOOT   George Town is designed for strolling, but don't expect sights that scream "tourist attraction." This is a handsome little waterfront village where browsing at the tree-shaded straw market, sampling fresh conch salad at the dock, and mingling with residents and fellow vacationers over drinks and home-style meals are the big draws. The most idyllic walk is around **Lake Victoria.**

Shuttle service is provided to town from **Peace & Plenty Beach Inn,** or you can walk the scenic mile. If you don't succumb to wheels, you can enjoy leisurely glimpses of the turquoise and neon blue water through the wispy casuarina pines and bushy coconut palms lining **Queen's Highway.** "Highway" is a serious overstatement, so walking here is fine, as traffic is sparse.

1 George Town

The Tropic of Cancer runs directly through George Town, the capital and principal settlement of the Exumas, located on the island of Great Exuma. This tranquil seaport village opens onto a 24km-long (15-mile) harbor. George Town, partly in the Tropics and partly in the temperate zone, is a favorite port of call for the yachting crowd.

If you need to stock up on supplies, George Town is the place to go, as it has more stores and services than any other spot in the Exumas. There are dive centers, marinas, markets, a doctor, and a clinic. The town often doesn't bother with street names, but everything's easy to find.

GEORGE TOWN ESSENTIALS

GETTING THERE   Flights from Nassau and Miami come into nearby Exuma International Airport, 16km (10 miles) away. See the beginning of this chapter for details on airlines and taxis.

FAST FACTS   A branch of the **Bank of Nova Scotia,** Queen's Highway (② 242/336-2651), is open Monday to Thursday 9:30am to 3pm, on Friday 9:30am to 4:30pm. It has an ATM.

For information about the Exumas, go to the Ministry of Tourism Office in Exuma (② 242/336-2457), on Queens Highway, across from the Exuma Market. It is open Monday to Friday 9am to 5pm.

If you come to the Exumas aboard your own boat, **Exuma Docking Services,** Main Street, George Town (② 242/336-2578), has slips for 52 boats, with water and electricity hookups. There's a restaurant on the premises, and you can replenish your liquor stock from the store here. They also have a laundromat, a fuel dock, fuel pumps, and a store with supplies for boats and people.

The government-operated **medical clinic** can be reached by phone at ② 242/336-2088. Go here to have a prescription filled. To call the **police** in George Town, dial ② 242/336-2666, but only for an emergency or special services.

The **post office** lies in the Government Building in George Town and is open Monday to Friday 9am to 4:30pm. For **Internet access,** check with your hotel. You can also go to the **ABC Exuma Internet Café** at the Exuma International Airport (② 242/345-6038).

SPECIAL EVENTS   In April, the **Family Island Regatta** (② 954/475-8315 for more information) draws a yachting crowd from all over the world to Elizabeth Harbour. It's a rollicking week of fun, song, and serious racing when the island sloops go

Malaria Risk Reported

In the summer of 2006 newspaper headlines announced a malaria outbreak on Great Exuma Island, with at least 60 people, mostly locals, testing positive for the potentially fatal disease. Immediately the government responded with intense surveillance and mosquito-control measures, including repeated spraying of the airport area. The **Centers for Disease Control and Prevention** (www.cdc.gov/travel) issued recommendations that potential visitors take prophylactic chloroquine, an antimalarial medication, as a preventive measure. Just to be on the safe side, check for an update on this disease by logging onto this website. No cases of malaria have been reported beyond Great Exuma.

all out to win. It's said that some determined skippers bring along extra crewmen to serve as live ballast on windward tacks, and then drop them over the side to lighten the ship for the downwind run to the finish. The event, a tradition since 1954, comes at the end of the crawfish season.

WHERE TO STAY
VERY EXPENSIVE
Four Seasons Resort Great Exuma at Emerald Bay ★★★ *(Kids)*   The quiet Exumas emerged from a sleep of centuries with the official opening of this resort in the winter of 2004. Its sweeping ocean vistas and tropical beauty frame an experience unique in this part of the world; the Out Islands have seen nothing like this in their history, and the resort is expected to change the entire character of the archipelago.

All accommodations here open onto private terraces and balconies with scenic views of the bay. You're given a choice of rooms, from generously proportioned garden-view units to oceanview rooms opening directly onto the bay. For the big spender, the resort also offers a series of executive suites and beachfront properties of one and two bedrooms.

So much goes on at this resort that you may never get around to exploring the surrounding islands. The most spectacular feature is a championship 18-hole golf course designed by Greg Norman. The full-service spa and health club is the finest in The Bahamas, and you can swim either at the hotel's crescent-shaped white-sand beach or in one of two pools. The best marina in the Southern Bahamas operates here. And the cuisine is among the best in the Out Islands, with both indoor and outdoor dining options and a selection of Italian, Caribbean, Bahamian, and international dishes. Since its "soft" opening, the hotel has worked out its kinks and is running smoothly, with an improvement in food and service. The restaurant, Il Cielo, is perhaps the finest in the Southern Bahamas, and it's accentuated by floor-to-ceiling panels and screens. Seating 180 diners, it opens onto landscaped gardens or the stars overlooking Emerald Bay. A wide selection of Italian dishes is offered, including locally caught seafood, everything backed up by an impressive wine cellar. A children's menu is also available.

Emerald Bay, Great Exuma, The Bahamas. ℂ **800/819-5053** in the U.S. and Canada, or 242/366-6800. Fax 242/336-6801. www.fourseasons.com. 183 units. Winter $495–$995 (£262–£527) double; off season $375–$795 (£199–£421) double; year-round from $995 (£527) suite. AE, DC, DISC, MC, V. **Amenities:** Restaurant; bar; 2 pools; golf course; 6 tennis courts; gym; spa; sauna; watersports equipment/rentals; children's programs; business center; salon; room service; babysitting; laundry service; dry cleaning; nonsmoking rooms; rooms for those w/limited mobility. *In room:* A/C, TV, minibar, coffeemaker, hair dryer, iron, safe.

Hotel Higgins Landing ★   The beach at this resort is a major attraction. It is one of the first eco-resorts in The Bahamas and still the only hotel on undeveloped Stocking Island. Higgins Landing takes great care to preserve the natural beauty of its surroundings on this gorgeous island. It's bordered by Elizabeth Harbour and the Atlantic on one side, the crystal blue waters of Turtle Lagoon and its colorful reefs on the other. This solar-powered hideaway is one of the self-billed great escapes of The Bahamas.

Cottages are exquisitely decorated with antiques, mirrors, and Higgins family heirlooms. Accommodations are furnished with queen-size beds, and each unit is given an island accent with cool tile floors and ceiling fans, plus a well-maintained private bathroom with shower stalls. The landscaped grounds are as colorful as your imagination, attracting many types of wildlife, ranging from herons and hummingbirds to green sea turtles. The island is reached by hotel ferry service from George Town.

Finds Life on a Houseboat

The most offbeat way to live in the Exumas is on a brightly decorated floating houseboat. Each boat is like a hotel suite that can be used to explore Elizabeth Harbour and the coast of the Exumas. In between moving your houseboat from anchorage to anchorage, you can go fishing, snorkeling, scuba diving, or beachcombing. Each houseboat is fully equipped, sleeping six to eight, with air-conditioning, hot and cold running water, a marine radio, an inflatable dinghy, a fully equipped galley, all linens, purified water, and a propane barbecue grill. Boats range from a one-bedroom 11m (36 ft.) to a two-bedroom 13m (43 ft.). It doesn't take a special license or even much experience to operate one of these boats. For reservations, contact **Bahamas Houseboats** (P.O. Box EX29031, George Town, Exuma, The Bahamas; ℭ **242/336-BOAT**; fax 242/336-2629; www.bahamahouseboats. com). Daily rentals (3-day minimum) range from $385 to $520 (£204–£276). A $500 (£265) deposit is required. American Express, MasterCard, and Visa are accepted.

Rates include a full breakfast and a candlelit first-rate dinner (nonguests are welcome, too, with advance reservations). The open-air bar overlooks the water.

Stocking Island (P.O. Box EX29146), George Town, Great Exuma, The Bahamas. ℭ **242/357-0008.** Fax 866/289-0919. www.higginslanding.com. 5 units. Year-round $385 (£204) 1-bedroom cottage; $670 (£355) 2-bedroom cottage. Rates include dinner and transportation from Georgetown. Minimum stay of 4 nights required; 50% deposit required to secure reservation. MC, V. No children under 6. Closed Aug 1–Nov 25. **Amenities:** Restaurant; bar; watersports equipment/rentals; laundry service; nonsmoking rooms. *In room:* Kitchenette (in some), coffeemaker, hair dryer, no phone.

EXPENSIVE

Palm Bay Beach Club 𝔊 *Finds*   This is one of the most tranquil accommodations in the archipelago. Overlooking the waters of Elizabeth Harbour, this attractive resort offers beachfront villas featuring either a studio, a one-bedroom unit, or a more luxurious and spacious two-bedroom accommodation. The cottages are beautifully appointed, mostly with kitchenettes, cable TV, and Internet available. Each villa is individually decorated featuring queen- or king-size beds, ceramic tile flooring, and comfortable tropical style furniture. There is a shuttle bus carrying visitors to and from George Town. Kayaks and paddle boats are available.

Elizabeth Harbour, George Town, Great Exuma, The Bahamas. ℭ **242/336-2787.** www.palmbaybeachclub.com. 38 units. Winter $189–$325 (£100–£172) double, $280–$440 (£148–£233) 2-bedroom unit; off season $160–$240 (£85–£127) double, $270–$380 (£143–£201) 2-bedroom unit. AE, MC, V. **Amenities:** Beach bar; outdoor pool. *In room:* A/C, TV, kitchenette (in some), ceiling fan.

Peace & Plenty Bonefish Lodge 𝔊   South of George Town, this is one of three Peace & Plenty properties in the Exumas—and the poshest of them all. It caters almost exclusively to fishermen and their companions. In a setting of young palms, the two-story inn is built of concrete and stone, and lies on a peninsula enveloped by crystal-clear waters and sandy flats. This is the most elegant bonefishing inn in The Bahamas; you can fish all day and come back to be pampered in luxury.

The lobby is inviting, with tile floors and rattan pieces. From many of the midsize rooms opening onto the wraparound balcony, you'll have a great view of the turquoise waters, or perhaps you'd rather doze in a hammock. Accommodations are furnished in bright floral spreads and prints, with air-conditioning and ceiling fans, along with spacious, immaculate bathrooms and tub/showers. You don't have to be an angler to stay here—but it helps. If you don't fish, you may be left out of the conversation at night.

The food served in the clubby dining room is excellent, with a well-trained chef who not only knows how to grill your steak to perfection, but can whip up a vegetarian platter, too. Of course, the finest way to dine here is on fish caught that day by the chef or one of the guests. After cleaning the fish, he tosses scraps to the resident sharks in the adjoining waters. This is the chief evening entertainment, although there's an honor bar and a lobby lounge upstairs with TV and VCR.

Queen's Hwy. (P.O. Box EX29173), George Town, Great Exuma, The Bahamas. © 242/345-5555. Fax 242/345-5556. www.ppbonefishlodge.net. 8 units. Year-round $846 (£448) per person for 3 nights/4 days. Rates include all meals, drinks, tips, airport transfers, and most activities. MC, V. **Amenities:** Restaurant; 2 bars; pool; watersports equipment/rentals; laundry service; nonsmoking rooms; rooms for those w/limited mobility. *In room:* A/C, hair dryer, no phone.

MODERATE

Club Peace & Plenty   This attractive, historic waterside inn is a classic island hotel in the heart of George Town. Once a sponge warehouse and later the home of a prominent family, it was converted into a hotel in the late 1940s, making it the oldest in the Exumas. The two-story pink-and-white hotel has dormers and balconies opening onto a water view. The grounds are planted with palms, crotons, and bougainvillea. Peace & Plenty fronts Elizabeth Harbour, making it a favorite of the yachting set, including former visitor Prince Philip.

The midsize units are all tastefully furnished, although there is still a lingering 1950s vibe. A refurbishment has freshened things up a bit with bright print spreads and draperies, and furnishings in white wicker or rattan. All rooms have queen, double, or twin beds, and a tiled bathroom with a tub/shower. Many also contain balconies opening onto harbor views; oceanfront rooms are the most desirable.

You can dine either indoors or outside, with calypso music on the terrace (see "Where to Dine," below). There are also two cocktail lounges, one of which was converted from an old slave kitchen and is now filled with nautical gear including lanterns, rudders, and anchors. The hotel faces Stocking Island and maintains a private beach club there, offering food and bar service, as well as kilometers of sandy dunes. A boat, free for hotel guests ($8/£4.25 round-trip for nonguests), makes the run.

Queen's Hwy. (P.O. Box EX29055), George Town, Great Exuma, The Bahamas. © 800/525-2210 in the U.S. and Canada or 242/336-2551. Fax 242/336-2093. www.peaceandplenty.com. 32 units. Winter $172–$250 (£91–£133) double, $192–$350 (£102–£186) suite; off season $148–$215 (£78–£114) double, $162–$320 (£86–£170) suite. MAP (breakfast and dinner) $36 (£19) per person. Ask about bonefishing packages. AE, DC, MC, V. **Amenities:** Restaurant; 2 bars; pool; laundry service; nonsmoking rooms; rooms for those w/limited mobility. *In room:* A/C, TV, fridge, hair dryer, safe, ceiling fan, no phone.

Coconut Cove Hotel   Set about 1.6km (1 mile) west of George Town—on a seafronting plot of land that's dotted with groves of coconut palms and palmettos and host to a brackish saltwater pond favored by bird life—this is the most recent, much-renovated incarnation of a hotel that has stood here for at least 20 years. Designed with three wings that radiate out from a central core, much like the shape of an airplane propeller, it offers simple but well-cared-for rooms, a bar where the rum-based

Coconut Cove Specials are appropriately pink and heady, and a restaurant (see listing below) whose cuisine is praised as among the best on the island. The staff can arrange access to island tours and watersports options.

George Town, Great Exuma, The Bahamas. (C) **242/336-2659**. Fax 242/336-2658. www.exumabahamas.com/coconutcove.html. 11 units. Winter $152–$262 (£81–£139) double; off season $132–$242 (£70–£128) double. Add $30 (£16) for extra person. AE, MC, V. **Amenities:** Restaurant; bar; pool; babysitting; laundry service; nonsmoking rooms; rooms for those w/limited mobility. *In room:* A/C, TV, fridge, ceiling fan.

Peace & Plenty Beach Inn   This tranquil inn is a world-class bonefishing resort, opening onto 90m (295 ft.) of white-sand beach. Its sibling, the Peace & Plenty Bonefish Lodge, is more posh, but the price tag here compensates. This is also a favorite resort for snorkelers, offering a special Jean-Michel Cousteau snorkeling program. The inn contains first-class, well-furnished double rooms, plus small bathrooms with tub/showers. The bedrooms have Italian tile floors, as well as balconies overlooking Bonefish Bay and Elizabeth Harbour. For some action, and additional activities and facilities, you can go over to the Club Peace & Plenty (there are shuttles between all the Peace & Plenty properties).

An adjacent structure housing the attractive bar and restaurant was designed to reflect the colonial flavor of George Town. Very good meals are served here.

Harbourfront (P.O. Box EX29055), George Town, Great Exuma, The Bahamas. (C) **800/525-2210** in the U.S. and Canada, or 242/336-2250. Fax 242/336-2253. www.peaceandplenty.com. 16 units. Winter $178–$198 (£94–£105) double, $218–$238 (£116–£126) triple, $258–$278 (£137–£147) quad; off season $158–$173 (£84–£92) double, $198–$213 (£105–£113) triple, $238–$255 (£126–£135) quad. Up to 2 children under 12 stay free in parent's room. AE, MC, V. **Amenities:** Restaurant; bar; pool; watersports equipment/rentals. *In room:* A/C, fridge, hair dryer, ceiling fan, no phone.

Regatta Point 𝒦 𝒦𝒾𝒹𝓈   This inn lies on a small cay just across the causeway from George Town, opening onto a small sandy beach. The cay used to be known as Kidd Cay, named after the notorious pirate. Overlooking Elizabeth Harbour, the present complex consists of six apartments, each with a full kitchen, which are not air-conditioned, although the cross-ventilation is good. Ceiling fans help, too. Each of the pleasantly furnished, summery units has its own kitchen and maid service, plus a small bathroom containing tub/showers. The kitchens make this a good choice for families. Those who don't wish to cook can have dinner at one of the previously mentioned hotels in town or at a local restaurant. Nearby grocery stores are fairly well stocked if you feel like cooking. Bicycles are available at no extra charge. This colony hums in April during the Family Island Regatta.

Regatta Point (P.O. Box 6), Kidd Cove, George Town, Great Exuma, The Bahamas. (C) **800/688-0309** or 242/336-2206. www.regattapointbahamas.com. 6 units. Winter $184–$204 (£98–£108) double; $258 (£137) 2-bedroom suite; off season $148–$176 (£78–£93) double; $258 (£137) 2-bedroom suite. Extra person $20 (£11) per day. No credit cards. **Amenities:** Laundry service. *In room:* Kitchen, ceiling fans, games and books, no phone.

WHERE TO DINE

With a few exceptions, the best places to take meals in George Town are in the main hotels reviewed above.

There are several casual joints in George Town where you can grab a quick meal. **Towne Cafe,** in the Marshall Complex ((C) **242/336-2194**), serves one of the best breakfasts in George Town. It's really the town bakery. Drop in any day but Sunday for a lunch of local Exumian specialties such as stewed grouper or chicken souse or a sandwich.

A former school bus was recycled and turned into **Jean's Dog House** 𝒦 ((C) **242/345-5055**), along Queen's Highway in George Town. Here you'll find the island's best

---

Finds **Fresh, Sexy Conch**

The best conch salad is found at **Big D's Conch Spot No. 2,** Government Dock (*© 242/358-0059*). "Fresh, sexy conch," as it's called here, is served daily. They'll make it right in front of you, so you know what's going into your salad. They're open Tuesday to Sunday noon to midnight. Reservations are required only for large parties.

---

lobster burger in a cramped but spotless kitchen on wheels. Instead of eating in the hotel dining room, we like to go here for breakfast and order the "MacJean," a robust sandwich with sausage or bacon, plus cheese, on freshly baked bread. Of course, she's also noted for her "dogs," or frankfurters. The owner is a well-loved personality known only as Jean. Visit only from 7am to 3pm, and don't bother bringing your credit card.

MODERATE

Club Peace & Plenty Restaurant CONTINENTAL/BAHAMIAN/AMERICAN Come here for the finest island dining, with plentiful, good home-cooking that leaves everyone satisfied. You might begin with conch salad or one of the salads made with hearts of palm or artichoke hearts, then follow with local lobster. Bahamian steamed grouper regularly appears on the menu (of course), simmered with onions, sweet pepper, tomatoes, and thyme. But you can also order such special dishes as an herb-flavored Cornish game hen that is juicy and perfectly roasted and flavored. Lunch options include homemade soups, conch burgers, a chef's salad, or deep-fried grouper. Breakfast offerings range from traditional French toast or scrambled eggs and sausage to the truly Bahamian boiled fish and grits.

You sit under ceiling fans, looking out over the harbor. Windows on three sides and candlelight make it particularly nice in the evening. And who knows who will be at the next table? It may be a celeb or two, or a crowd of yachters providing conversation and amusement.

In the Club Peace & Plenty, Queen's Hwy. *©* **242/336-2551.** Reservations recommended for dinner. Breakfast $9.25 (£4.90); lunch $8–$10 (£4.25–£5.30); dinner main courses $18–$30 (£9.55–£16). AE, DISC, MC, V. Daily 7:30–10:30am, noon–2:30pm, and 6:30–9:30pm.

Coconut Cove ITALIAN   Set on the premises of the previously recommended hotel, this dining room sits close to the sea, within a glassed-in, blue, white, and coral–colored dining room whose mahogany-and-glass doors slide open for maximum exposure to the breeze. American-born Pamela Chimento, in cooperation with her Bahama-born assistant, Shelia, churns out well-flavored versions of Italian and Mediterranean-inspired food that's far removed from the usual Bahamian fare you might have expected. Starters include breaded calamari with oregano and parsley sauce, linguini marinara, jalapeño peppers, breaded mozzarella sticks, onion soup, and seafood salads. Main courses feature stone crabs, different preparations of shrimp, crayfish, poached salmon served with a tropical fruit salsa, and "cowboy steaks." There's also a choice of pizzas from a "pizza bar" on-site. Most dishes, except for lobster, are priced at the low end of the scale.

In the Coconut Cove Hotel, George Town. *©* **242/336-2659.** Reservations recommended. Main courses $25–$54 (£13–£29); pizzas $12–$30 (£6.35–£16). AE, DISC, MC, V. Wed–Sun 6–9pm.

Fisherman's Inn *Finds* BAHAMIAN   This is the most isolated restaurant in the Exumas, a ramshackle, wood-sided hideaway that's set on a low ridge above the sea on the island of Barraterre, a 40- to 60-minute drive from George Town. Connected with two separate causeways to the "mainland" of Great Exuma Island, it's literally at the end of the line for motorists looking for a lonely, sun-bleached, and wind-blasted excursion from George Town. Don't come here with the assurance that there will be anything in the larder at the time of your arrival. If the season is slow, or if the supplies "didn't make it in that week," you might be faced with a smile and perhaps a somewhat erratic dialogue from the owner, and nary a crust of bread. The best plan is to call ahead, survey the gastronomic lay of the land, and then discuss with the staff what may, or may not, be available that day. Expect a roster of fish, chicken, beefsteaks, soups, salads, and stews; lots of local color; and a genuine sense of the degree to which parts of The Bahamas archipelago are isolated from the rest of the world.

Barraterre. © 242/355-5016. Reservations required. Main courses lunch $9–$15 (£4.75–£7.95), dinner $20–$25 (£11–£13). No credit cards. Hours vary, but in theory it's daily from 7am until around midnight.

Sam's Place BAHAMIAN/INTERNATIONAL   If Bogie were alive today, he'd surely head for this laid-back second-floor restaurant and bar overlooking the harbor in George Town. Sam Gray, the owner, offers breakfasts to catch the early boating crowd. Lunches could include everything from freshly made conch chowder to curry chicken. You'll also be able to order an array of sandwiches throughout the day. The dinner menu changes daily, but you're likely to find such well-prepared main courses as Exuma lobster tail, roast lamb, and Bahamian pan-fried grouper. At dinner, the talk here is of one of everybody's dreams—owning a private utopia, one of those uninhabited cays still remaining in the Exuma chain.

Main St. © 242/336-2579. Breakfast and lunch $7–$10 (£3.70–£5.30); dinner main courses $15–$35 (£7.95–£19). MC, V. Daily 8am–9pm.

INEXPENSIVE
Kermit's Airport Lounge BAHAMIAN   Owned by one of the island's most entrepreneurial taxi drivers, Kermit Rolle, this simple but appealing place lies across the road from the entrance to the airport. It's the semiofficial waiting room for most of the island's flights, and it might make your wait more convenient and fun. You can usually find Kermit hanging out here. The cook will fry you some fish, and there's always beans and rice around. Johnnycake and sandwiches are also available, along with burgers and an array of tropical drinks. Until an airplane flies you to a better restaurant, this place can come in handy.

Exuma International Airport. © 242/345-0002. Beer $4.25 (£2.25); cheeseburgers $6–$9 (£3.20–£4.75); platters from $8.50 (£4.50). No credit cards. Daily 6:30am–5pm.

BEACHES, WATERSPORTS & OTHER OUTDOOR PURSUITS
BEACHES
Stocking Island *F*, which lies in Elizabeth Harbour, faces the town across the bay, less than 1.6km (1 mile) away. This long, thin barrier island has some of the most gorgeous beaches in The Bahamas. Snorkelers and scuba divers come here to explore the blue holes, and it is also ringed with undersea caves and coral gardens. Boat trips leave daily from Elizabeth Harbour heading for Stocking Island at 10am and 1pm. The cost is $8 (£4.25) per person round-trip. However, guests of Club Peace & Plenty ride free.

If you'd like to go shelling, walk the beach that runs along the Atlantic side of Stocking Island.

The island has its own activities center run by **Exuma Scuba Adventures** (✆ 242/ 336-2893). Stocking Island used to be a private enclave for guests at Club Peace & Plenty, but now all visitors use it. Visibility is great in these waters, and there are many rainbow-hued fish to see. For a 3-hour trip, snorkeling, including all equipment, costs $65 (£34). A one-tank dive goes for $75 (£40), going up to $125 (£66) for a two-tank dive.

Yachting types and others visiting the island like to drop in at Kenneth Bowe's **Chat & Chill** 🐠 (no phone), a laid-back place that somehow manages to be both upmarket and a kind of local dive. Many of the dishes such as fresh fish are grilled over an open fire, and the Sunday pig roasts are an island event. The conch burgers are the best in the Exumas. But the seasonings? They're a secret.

BOATING

Landlocked **Lake Victoria** covers about .8 hectares (2 acres) in the heart of George Town. It has a narrow exit to the harbor and functions as a diving-and-boating headquarters.

If you come to the Exumas aboard your own boat, **Exuma Docking Services,** Main Street, George Town (✆ 242/336-2578), has slips for 52 boats, with water and electricity hookups. You can also stock up on supplies here, get fuel, and do laundry.

Through the **Starfish Activity Center** (✆ 242/336-3033; www.kayakbahamas. com), you can rent Hobie Waves, high-performance sailboats that are easy to use. These stable, lightweight-yet-durable, 4.5m (15-ft.) catamarans are ideal for families, as they are simple to maneuver. Sailboat rentals, including Hobie Waves, cost $60 (£32) per half-day or $325 (£172) weekly. One-hour sailboat lessons cost $60 (£32) for one to three participants.

If motor boats are more your speed, **Minns Water Sports** (✆ 242/336-3483 or 242/336-2604), based out of George Town, rents boats ranging from 4.5 to 6.6m (15–22 ft.) for $85 to $195 (£45–£1030) per day. **Exuma Dive Center** (✆ 242/336-2390), where boat rentals start at $80 (£42) per day, also offers more economical rates when you keep a boat for a week or longer. With your boat, you can set out to sail the most stunning waters in The Bahamas, rivaled only by the Abacos. The best territory for recreational boating is the government-protected **Exumas Cays Land and Sea Park,** stretching south from Wax Cay to Conch Cay, with magnificent sea gardens and coral reefs.

FISHING

Many visitors come to the Exumas just to go bonefishing. Arrangements for outings can be made at **Club Peace & Plenty,** Queen's Highway (✆ 800/525-2210 or 242/336-2551), or at **Peace & Plenty Bonefish Lodge,** Queen's Highway (✆ 242/ 345-5555). The Exumas offer miles of wadeable flats (shallow bodies of water), where trained guides will accompany you. Fly-fishing instruction and equipment are also offered.

GOLF

The **Four Seasons Resort Emerald Bay Golf Club** 🐠🐠🐠, Emerald Bay (✆ 242/ 366-6800 or 358-4185), is one of the great oceanfront courses in either The Bahamas or the Caribbean. The Greg Norman design features six oceanfront holes. The par-72 course stretches a challenging 7,001 yards, yet was laid out to accommodate golfers of various skill levels. The course uses environmentally friendly seashore paspalum grass and finishes on a rocky peninsula with a panoramic view of the sea. There's also a pro shop. Greens fees are a steep $95 to $145 (£50–£77) for 18 holes ($145–$175/£77–£93 for nonguests), and reservations are required.

KAYAKING

You can best appreciate some of the Exumas' most dramatic scenery from the peaceful perch of a sea kayak. In fact, many areas—including mangrove lakes, rivers, manta ray gathering spots, and bonefish flats—are too shallow for other boats to enter. Don't worry if you haven't hit the gym lately. Anyone in at least average physical condition—from children to seniors—can kayak with a smile. The **Starfish Activity Center** (© 242/336-3033) rents sit-on-top kayaks for singles and doubles. Singles are $30 (£16) per half-day, $45 (£24) a day, and $160 (£85) a week. Doubles run $45 (£24) per half-day, $55 (£29) a day, and $180 (£95) a week.

For more adventure, book one of Starfish's guided kayak trips, which are offered daily. You don't have to spend the whole time paddling your kayak. During half- and full-day excursions, lunch and beverages are served, and the price covers all gear, including snorkeling equipment. You may find yourself watching a blizzard of fish swarm a shipwreck, searching for sand dollars on a deserted beach, snorkeling into a sea cave, or finding out about bush medicine while you hike along a nature trail. Guided trips begin at $35 (£19) an hour for adults and $25 (£13) for children.

Another good outfitter is **Ecosummer Expeditions** (© 800/465-8884). Ecosummer is especially skilled in exploring **Exuma Cays National Land and Sea Park** (© 242/357-8344), a government-protected natural preserve with excellent wildlife-viewing opportunities.

SCUBA DIVING

Surrounding the Exumas, fields of massive coral heads, eerie blue holes, and exciting walls covered with marine life attract scuba divers. Many excellent reefs are just 20 or 25 minutes away from the George Town area, so long boat rides don't cut into your underwater time.

For scuba divers, the great attraction here is the **Exuma Cays National Land and Sea Park,** which is 35km (22 miles) long and 13km (8 miles) wide. It draws scuba divers to its 453 sq. km (177 sq. miles) of sea gardens, with their magnificent coral reefs, flora, and fauna. The park, which was inaugurated in 1958, lies some 35km (22 miles) northeast of **Staniel Cay.** Call your hotel to ask whether it offers a hotel/dive package, or try **Exuma Scuba Adventures** (© 242/336-2893) at Peace & Plenty Beach Inn for information about scuba-diving excursions. A one-tank morning boat dive goes for $75 (£40); a two-tank dive costs $125 (£66). You can also take an afternoon one-tank boat dive for $65 (£34) or a one-tank night dive for $65 (£34). A reef boat trip for snorkeling costs $25 (£13).

SNORKELING

The best bet for snorkeling is found in the magnificent waters off the coast of **Stocking Island** (see above). Boat trips from George Town depart for the island twice a day. You can also rent snorkeling equipment for $10 (£5.30) a day at **Minns Water Sports** in George Town (© 242/336-3483).

If you want to snorkel around some of the Exumas' most well-preserved reefs, call **Exuma Scuba Adventures** (© 242/336-2893; www.dive-exuma.com). Its 3-hour-plus excursions cost $65 (£34) per adult, $30 (£16) for children under 12.

SHOPPING

In George Town shopping is a very casual event, especially at the **Exuma Straw Market,** open Monday to Saturday 7am to 5pm. Here in the shade of a large Indian fig tree, some local Bahamian women spend their day making straw baskets, colorful handbags, dolls, and other keepsakes. Bargaining is allowed, and prices go from $25 (£13) for a hat to $100 (£53) for an intricate basket.

EXPLORING GEORGE TOWN

There isn't much to see here in the way of architecture except the confectionery-pink-and-white **Government Building,** which was "inspired" by the Government House architecture in Nassau. Under an old ficus tree in the center of town, there's a **straw market** where you can talk to the friendly Exumian women and perhaps purchase some of their handicrafts.

George Town has a colorful history, despite the fact that it appears so sleepy today. (With so little traffic, it doesn't even need a traffic light.) Pirates used its deep-water harbor in the 17th century, and those called the "plantation aristocracy," mainly from Virginia and the Carolinas, settled here in the 18th century. In the next 100 years, **Elizabeth Harbour,** the focal point of the town, became a refitting base for British man-of-war vessels, and the U.S. Navy used the port again during World War II.

There's not too much shopping, but there are a few places where you can purchase souvenirs and gifts. **Exuma Liquor and Gifts,** Queen's Highway (© 242/336-2101), is the place to stock up on liquor, wine, and beer. The **Peace & Plenty Boutique,** Queen's Highway (© 242/336-2761), stands next to the Sandpiper and across the street from the previously recommended Club Peace & Plenty, which owns it. Its main draw is a selection of Androsia batiks for women, and Androsia cloth is sold by the yard. You can also find such practical items as film and suntan lotion. The boutique stocks a large selection of men and women's sportswear as well.

The Sandpiper, Queen's Highway (© 242/336-2084), stands across from Club Peace & Plenty. Its highlights are the original serigraphs by Diane Minns, but it also offers a good selection of Bahamian arts and crafts, along with such items as Bahamian straw baskets and other handcrafted works, sponges, ceramics, watches, baskets, jewelry, books, and postcards. Diane designs and silk-screens T-shirts here in the shop, and she welcomes anyone to watch her at work.

One of the offshore sights in Elizabeth Harbour is tiny **Crab Cay,** which can be reached by boat. This was believed to have been a rest camp for British seamen in the 18th century.

GEORGE TOWN AFTER DARK

The best place to head for some after-dark diversion is **Club Peace & Plenty** (© 800/525-2210 or 242/336-2093), located in George Town. Although summer nights are slow, something is usually happening here in winter, ranging from weekly poolside bashes to live bands that keep both locals and visitors jumping up on the dance floor.

EXPLORING FARTHER AFIELD

Queen's Highway, which is still referred to as the "slave route," runs the length of Great Exuma, and you can travel it in either a taxi or a rented car to take in the sights in and around George Town.

Forty-five kilometers (28 miles) north of George Town, **Rolleville,** named after Lord Rolle, is still inhabited by descendants of his freed slaves. It is claimed that his will left them the land. This land is not sold but is passed along from one generation to the next.

As you travel along the highway, you'll see ruins of plantations. This land is called **"generation estates,"** and the major ones are **Steventon, Mount Thompson,** and **Ramsey.** You pass such settlements as Mosstown (which has working farms), Ramsey, the Forest, Farmer's Hill, and Roker's Point. Steventon is the last settlement before you reach Rolleville, which is the largest of the plantation estates. There are several beautiful beaches along the way, especially the ones at **Tarr Bay** and **Jimmie Hill.**

Some visitors may want to head south of George Town, passing Flamingo Bay and Pirate's Point. In the 18th century, Captain Kidd is said to have anchored at **Kidd Cay.** You, however, can stay at the previously recommended Regatta Point.

Flamingo Bay, the site of a hotel and villa development, begins just 1km (⅔ mile) from George Town. It's a favorite rendezvous of the yachting set and bonefishers.

WHERE TO DINE

Iva Bowe's Central Highway Inn Restaurant & Bar BAHAMIAN   This roadside tavern, operated by Gottfried B. Bowe, specializes in very tender cracked conch. The conch is marinated in lime, pounded to make it tender, and then fried with Iva's own special seasonings. It's the best in the Exumas. You might also try the lobster linguini or shrimp scampi. This is good Bahamian cookery.

Queen's Hwy. (.5km/⅓ mile from the entrance to the International Airport and about 9.5km/6 miles northwest of George Town). ☎ 242/345-7014. Lunch $12–$15 (£6.35–£7.95); dinner main courses $15–$27 (£7.95–£14). No credit cards. Mon–Sat 8am–11pm.

2 Little Exuma ★

This is a faraway retreat, the southernmost of the Exuma Cays. Despite the fact that it's in the Tropics, it has a subtropical climate and lovely white-sand beaches. The waters are so crystal clear in some places that you can spot the colorful tropical fish more than 18m (59 ft.) down. The island, about 31 sq. km (12 sq. miles) in area, is connected to Great Exuma by a 182m-long (597-ft.) bridge. It's about a 16km (10-mile) trip from the George Town airport.

Less than a kilometer (⅔ mile) offshore is **Pigeon Cay,** which is uninhabited. Visitors often come here for the day and are later picked up by a boat that takes them back to Little Exuma. You can go snorkeling and visit the remains of a 200-year-old wreck, right offshore in about 2m (6½ ft.) of water.

On one of the highest hills of Little Exuma are the remains of an old pirate fort. Several cannons are located nearby, but documentation is lacking as to when it was built or by whom. (Pirates didn't leave too much data lying around.)

Coming from Great Exuma, the first community you reach on Little Exuma is called **Ferry,** so named because the two islands were linked by a ferry service before the bridge was built. Ask around about visiting the private chapel of an Irish family, the Fitzgeralds, erected generations ago.

Along the way, you can take in **Pretty Molly Bay,** site of the now-shuttered Sand Dollar Beach Club. Pretty Molly was a slave who committed suicide by walking into the water one night. The natives claim that her ghost can still be seen stalking the beach every night.

Fun Fact **A Romantic Legend & a Movie Star**

On the road to Little Exuma, you come to the hamlet of **Rolle Town**. It was once, like Rolleville in the north, owned by Lord Rolle. It is populated today with the descendants of his former slaves. This sleepy town has some 100-year-old houses.

In an abandoned field, where goats frolic, you can visit the Rolle Town Tombs, burial ground of the McKay family. Capt. Alexander McKay, a Scot, came to Great Exuma in 1789 after he was granted 161 hectares (398 acres) for a plantation. His wife joined him in 1791, and soon after, they had a child. However, tragedy struck in 1792 when Anne McKay, who was only 26, died along with her child. Perhaps grief-stricken, her husband died the following year. Their story is one of the romantic legends of the island.

The village also claims a more contemporary famous daughter: the actress Esther Rolle. Her parents were born here (though they came to the United States before she was born). Rolle is best remembered for her role as the strong-willed mother on the '70s sitcom *Good Times*. She won an Emmy playing a maid in *Summer of My German Soldier;* Rolle's other film credits included *Driving Miss Daisy, Rosewood,* and *How to Make an American Quilt.* She died at the age of 78 in 1998.

Many visitors come to Little Exuma to visit the **Hermitage,** a plantation constructed by Loyalist settlers. It is the last surviving example of the many that once stood in the Exumas. It was originally built by the Kendall family, who came to Little Exuma in 1784. The family established their plantation at **Williamstown** and, with their slaves, set about growing cotton. But they encountered so many difficulties having the cotton shipped to Nassau that in 1806 they advertised the plantation for sale. The ad promised "970 acres more or less," along with "160 hands" (referring to the slaves). Chances are, you'll be approached by a local guide who, for a fee, will show you around. Also ask to be shown the several old tombs in the area.

At Williamstown (look for the seaside marker), you can visit the remains of the **Great Salt Pond.**

If you really have to see everything, you may be able to get a local to take you over to **Hog Cay,** the end of the line for the Exumas. This is really just a spit of land, and there are no glorious beaches here. It's visited mainly by those who like to add obscure islets at the very end of the road to their list of explorations. Hog Cay is privately owned, and it is farmed. The owner seems friendly to visitors. His house lies in the center of the island.

3 Staniel Cay ★

Staniel Cay lies 129km (80 miles) southeast of Nassau at the southern end of the little Pipe Creek archipelago, which is part of the Exuma Cays. It's a 13km (8-mile) chain of mostly uninhabited islets, sandy beaches, coral reefs, and bonefish flats. There are many places for snug anchorages, making this a favorite yachting stopover in the

Tips **An Insider's Guide for Sailors & Beach Buffs**

If you want a beach to yourself, one of the uninhabited islands surrounding Staniel Cay could be yours for the day. In the unlikely event that another yachting party has arrived, just sail on to another island nearby, and, chances are, it'll be deserted. The local map given out by Staniel Cay Yacht Club pinpoints the location of **Thunderball Grotto** 🔦, where part of the James Bond film *Thunderball* was filmed. This is one of the best places for snorkeling in the Exumas. To the north of Thunderball Grotto lies the curiously named **"Major Spot."** Believe it or not, **swimming pigs** will surround your boat here. They are harmless but expect to be treated to food. At another point on your nautical map, about 6.4km (4 miles) beyond Major Spot, you'll come across shallow waters where tame (at least, we hope so) nurse sharks like their pictures taken. Food makes them even less camera shy.

mid-Exumas. Staniel Cay, known for years as "Stanyard," has no golf course or tennis courts, but it's the perfect island for "the great escape." It's home to just 80 full-time residents.

An annual bonefishing festival is sponsored here on August 5, during the celebration of Bahamian Independence Day. The **Happy People Marina** (✆ **242/355-2008**) arranges guided sportfishing trips, as well as snorkeling trips. There's a **straw market** where you can buy crafts, hats, and handbags.

The **Staniel Cay Yacht Club** (see below) arranges charter flights from Fort Lauderdale, costing $250 (£133) per person one-way. Flight time is only 3 hours.

WHERE TO STAY & DINE

Staniel Cay Yacht Club   Staniel Cay is a great getaway, and the Staniel Cay Yacht Club—only a 5-minute golf-cart ride from the airstrip—is the place to get away to. Although once famous in yachting circles, drawing celebrities like the late Malcolm Forbes, the property became rundown and lost its chic clientele for several years. Now it has bounced back. Fully restored and improved, it again welcomes the yachting world to its location near a white sandy beach. Guest cottages, each with a small shower unit, have been completely remodeled and refurbished, and are quite charming. Each cottage is painted a different color with different decorative features. The cottages also have west-facing balconies, which make for unimpeded views of the sun setting over the water. This is one of the few guarantees each day on Staniel Cay. Since the island is only a kilometer (⅔ mile) wide, you can easily walk to the local village, which has a grocery store, straw market, church, and post office. A Boston Whaler is docked outside each accommodation, and guests are given a map of local waters and invited to sail on their own. There are many deserted islands surrounding Staniel Cay.

An on-site clubhouse offers American/Bahamian cuisine for breakfast, lunch, and dinner, with a menu featuring steaks and seafood, nothing too foreign or experimental. The club can rent you boats for activities, from a 4m (13-ft.) Boston Whaler including fuel for $110 (£580) and a 5.1m (17-ft.) boat for $235 (£125) per day, to something smaller, plus scuba and snorkeling gear.

Staniel Cay, the Exumas, The Bahamas. (For information, write to: 2233 S. Andrews Ave., Fort Lauderdale, FL 33316.) ✆ 954/467-8920 in the U.S., or 242/355-2024. Fax 242/355-2044. www.stanielcay.com. 9 units. Nov 20–Sept 9

$165 (£87) double, from $195 (£103) suite; off season $145 (£77) double, from $175 (£93) suite. Breakfast and dinner $35 (£19) per person extra. MC, V. **Amenities:** Restaurant; bar; outdoor pool; laundry service; nonsmoking rooms; marina; airstrip. *In room:* A/C, fridge, coffeemaker, hair dryer, no phone.

4 Sampson Cay

Tiny Sampson Cay, directly northwest of Staniel Cay and just to the southeast of the Exuma Cays National Land and Sea Park, has a certain charm. It has a full-service marina, as well as a small dive operation. Other than Staniel Cay, Sampson Cay has the only marina in the Central Exumas; thus, most visitors here arrive in their own boats, and local guides taking out sportfishers for the day provide the chief entertainment. Sampson Cay is 67 nautical miles southeast of Nassau and one of the safest anchorages in the Exumas—it's a natural "hurricane hole" (in other words, a fully protected anchorage with land all around). The cay lies near the end of Pipe Creek, which has been called a "tropical Shangri-La."

WHERE TO STAY & DINE
Sampson's Cay Club ⭐   This is a rather remote outpost, but a honey once you get here. The resort has been considerably improved in recent years and is now better than ever. The bedrooms are comfortable, well furnished, and generally spacious. The bedrooms are found in two houses, and five of them are singles. Two of these have king-size beds; the others have queen-size beds. Two of the units are right on the beach, and all of the accommodations have private bathrooms with showers. Both houses are also

Norman's Cay

Throughout the Exumas, you'll see islands with NO TRESPASSING signs posted. In the early 1980s, on Norman's Cay, these signs were extremely serious: You could have been killed if you had gone ashore. Fortunately, the drug smuggling that used to occur here has been cleaned up and the area is safe for travelers. However, private NO TRESPASSING signs should still be obeyed. Even without drug activity, privacy of individual property owners has to be respected, of course.

Once upon a time, you might have run into Ted Kennedy, Walter Cronkite, or William F. Buckley, Jr., enjoying the island's pleasures. The remote outpost enjoyed great popularity with the Harvard/Boston clique. During the 1980s, however, all this changed when German-Colombian Carlos Lehder Rivas purchased most of the island. Experts say it soon became the major distribution point for drug exportation to the United States. Millions of dollars' worth of cocaine was flown from Colombia to Norman's Cay before being smuggled onward to the United States.

Eventually, the U.S. applied strong pressure on the Bahamian government to clean up the island. Lehder fled for Colombia, where he was captured and extradited to the United States. He is now in prison. Norman's Cay may one day realize its tourist potential once again, but for now it remains relatively quiet, visited only by stray yachting parties and occasional cruise vessels.

equipped with outdoor showers and have their own dinghy docks. Community life here revolves around the grocery store and commissary, the fuel and dockage facilities of the full-service marina, and a bar and restaurant favored by visiting yachters. The restaurant and bar serve drinks and sandwiches any time of day to anyone who shows up, but reservations are required before 4pm for the single-seating dinner, which is served nightly at 7:30pm. The staff will rent you a 3.9m (13-ft.) or 5.1m (17-ft.) whaler, as well as Hobie cats and Aqua fins. From the hotel, the staff will also point to walking trails that will link you up to one of seven beaches.

Sampson Cay, the Exumas, The Bahamas. © 877/633-0305 or 242/355-2034. Fax 242/355-2034. www.sampson cayclub.com. 10 units. Year-round $250 (£133) double; $350 (£186) villa. MC, V. **Amenities:** Restaurant; bar; coin-operated laundry service; nonsmoking rooms; rooms for those w/limited mobility. *In room:* A/C, kitchenette, fridge, coffeemaker, no phone.

10

The Southern Bahamas

This cluster of islands on the southern fringe of The Bahamas is one of the last frontier outposts that can be reached relatively quickly from the U.S. mainland. Their remoteness is one of the most compelling reasons to visit them—that, and a chance to see life in The Bahamas the way it used to be. Some of the islands are proud to proclaim that "we are as we were when Columbus first landed here," an exaggeration, of course, but one that certainly contains a kernel of the truth.

The Southern Bahamas have a colorful history. In the 18th century, Loyalists from the Carolinas and Virginia came here with slave labor and settled many of the islands. For about 20 years they had thriving cotton plantations until blight struck, killing crops and destroying the industry. In 1834, the United Kingdom Emancipation Act freed slaves throughout the British Empire. When the Loyalists moved on to more fertile ground,

they often left behind the emancipated blacks, who then had to eke out a living as best they could.

With some notable exceptions, such as Long Island, tourism developers have stayed clear of these islands. However the isles have enormous potential, as most of them have excellent beaches, good fishing, and fine dive sites.

If you consider visiting any of these islands, be forewarned that transportation is inconvenient, and except for two or three resorts, accommodations are limited. For these and other reasons, the boating and yachting crowd composes the majority of visitors.

Many changes are in the wind for the Southern Bahamas. Right now, however, there's almost no traffic, no banks, no lawyers. There are, however, mosquitoes. Plan to bring a good insect repellent and a long-sleeved shirt for protection.

1 Cat Island ★ ★

Untainted by tourism, lovely Cat Island is the sixth-largest island in The Bahamas. The fishhook-shaped island—some 77km (48 miles) long and 1 to 6.5km (²⁄₃–4 miles) wide—lies about 209km (130 miles) southeast of Nassau and 523km (324 miles) southeast of Miami. (Don't confuse Cat Island with Cat Cay, a smallish private island near Bimini.)

Cat Island, named after the pirate Arthur Catt (and not wild packs of marauding cats), is located near the Tropic of Cancer, between Eleuthera and Long Island. It has one of the most pleasant climates in The Bahamas, with temperatures in the high 60s (low 20s Celsius) during the short winters, rising to the mid-80s (low 30s Celsius) in summer, with trade winds making the place even more comfortable. It is also home to some 2,000 residents, among the friendliest in all of The Bahamas.

With its pristine virgin **beaches,** the island is beautiful to see, yet little-visited enough that it remains relatively inexpensive and undiscovered.

Many local historians claim that Cat Island residents were the first to see Columbus. The great explorer himself was believed by some to have been welcomed here by the peaceful Arawaks. Regardless of whether Columbus stopped here, the island has a rich history of adventurers, slaves, buccaneers, farmers, and visionaries of many nationalities. Cat Island remains mysterious to some even now. It's known as a stronghold of such strange practices as obeah (West Indian witchcraft) and of miraculously healing bush medicines.

A straight asphalt road (in terrible shape) leads from the north to the south of the island. Along the way you can select your own beach—and chances are, you'll have complete privacy. These beaches offer an array of watersports, and visitors can go swimming or snorkeling at several places. **Fernandez Bay** is a picture-postcard, white-sand beach set against a turquoise blue sea and lined with casuarina trees. The island's north side is wild, untamed shoreline. Boating and diving are among the main reasons to go to Cat Island, and diving lessons are available for novices.

Arthur's Town, in the north, is the major town and the boyhood home of actor Sidney Poitier. (He has many relatives still living on the island, including a few amazing look-alikes.) Poitier shares memories of his childhood home in his book *This Life.*

CAT ISLAND ESSENTIALS

GETTING THERE   A commercial flight on **Bahamasair** (© 800/222-4262 in the U.S.; www.bahamasair.com) leaves Nassau for Arthur's Town on Friday and Sunday at 10:30am. There is also an airport near **New Bight,** the most scenic village on the island. Flying to New Bight from Fort Lauderdale is **Lynx Air International** (© 888/596-9247; www.lynxair.com), which has service between Fort Lauderdale and Cat Island three times a week.

Cat Island is also serviced by **mail boat.** The **MV *Worth Cat Island Special*** (© 242/393-1064) departs Potter's Cay Dock in Nassau weekly, heading for Bennett's Harbour and Arthur's Town. It leaves on Tuesday at 1pm and returns to Nassau on Thursday. Another vessel, the **MV *Lady Emerald*** (© 242/393-1064), departs Potter's Cay in Nassau on Tuesday at 3pm, going to Old and New Bight, and returns on Sunday.

GETTING AROUND   Limited, but quite adequate, taxi service is available on Cat Island. Hotel owners, if notified of your arrival time, will have someone drive to the airport to pick you up. You can, however, rent a car from **Bridge Inn Car Rentals,** Bridge Inn, New Bight (© 242/342-3014), to go exploring on your own. Prices begin at $70 (£37) daily, with unlimited mileage. Hours are daily from 6:30am to 7:30pm.

FAST FACTS   There are three medical clinics, each of which is among the simplest in The Bahamas. They are found in the settlements of Arthur's Town, Old Bight, and Smiths Bay, and they're not always open. In case of an emergency, notify your hotel staff immediately. Someone will try to get in touch with a medical person. Serious cases are flown to Nassau. If you're not in good health and might require medical assistance on vacation, Cat Island is not the island to choose. There is no central number to call for help.

SPECIAL EVENTS   The island's annual **Three-Day Regatta** takes place every summer, usually at the end of July. It attracts the largest collection of visitors to Cat Island; the inns prove inadequate to receive them. Call your local Bahamas Tourist Office (see chapter 2) for more information.

Arthur's Town

CAT ISLAND

Arthur's
Town Airport

Moss Town

Cockburn Town

CONCEPTION
ISLAND

SAN
SALVADOR

Exuma Sound

ATLANTIC
OCEAN

RUM CAY

Stella Maris
Airport

Port Nelson

Simms

Tropic of Cancer

LITTLE EXUMA
ISLAND

LONG ISLAND

Deadman's Cay
Airport

Clarence
Town

Samana Cay

JUMENTO
CAYS

Crooked Island Passage

Colonel
Hill

CROOKED ISLAND

Landrail
Point

Chesters Bay

ACKLINS
ISLAND

Pirates
Well

FORTUNE
ISLAND

The Bight
of
Acklins

Snug Corner

Windward Passage

Duncan Town

RAGGED ISLAND

Spring Point

MAYAGUANA
ISLAND

Caicos Passage

CASTLE
ISLAND

Hogsty Reef

LITTLE
INAGUA

Scuba Diving

Airport

GREAT INAGUA

Inagua
National
Park

Matthew Town

0   50 mi

0   50 km

N

CUBA

Area of detail (inset)

Miami

Grand
Bahama

Abaco

New Providence Island

Eleuthera

FLORIDA

Nassau

Cat Island

San Salvador

Andros

Great Exuma

Long Island

Crooked Island

Acklins Island

0   100 mi

0   100 km

CUBA

Great
Inagua

TURKS AND
CAICOS

Area of detail

WHERE TO STAY & DINE

Bridge Inn   Lying 274m (899 ft.) from a beach, the relaxed and casual Bridge Inn is owned by Cat Islander Allan Russell, who is ably assisted by a group of family members. The inn offers babysitting services (at an extra charge) so that parents can play tennis or go diving, sailboarding, snorkeling, jogging, bicycling, fishing, or just sightseeing with the knowledge their youngsters are being carefully tended. Bedrooms are modest, motel-style affairs, but each unit can house three to four guests. Each of the high-ceilinged rooms does come with a private bathroom containing a shower stall.

On the premises you'll find a full bar and a restaurant that serves a rather simple Bahamian and international cuisine.

New Bight, Cat Island, The Bahamas. © 242/342-3013. Fax 242/342-3041. www.catislandbridgeinn.com. 15 units. Year-round $140 (£74) double; $190 (£101) villa. MC, V. Rates include breakfast. **Amenities:** Restaurant; bar; limited room service; laundry service. *In room:* A/C, TV, kitchenettes (in some), iron.

Fernandez Bay Village *(Finds)*   Opening onto Fernandez Bay, this is the island's best resort. Although rustic, it has a certain charm, mainly because of its position on a curvy beach set against casuarinas blowing in the trade winds. The beach (or anywhere else, for that matter) is never crowded, so come here only if you *really* want to get away from it all; this place is far too laid-back for full hotel service. Things get done, but it takes time—and no one's in a hurry.

Fernandez Bay Village has been in the Armbrister family since it was originally established on a plantation in 1870. Its rusticity and seclusion are part of its charm, and yet, if you wish, you can get acquainted with other guests with similar interests. Yachters, who moor in the water offshore—there are no marina facilities—often visit the resort to take advantage of the general store's fresh supplies. (Nearby Smith's Bay is one of the best storm shelters in the region—even the government mail boats take refuge here during hurricanes.)

The "village" consists of full housekeeping villas, each of which sleeps up to six people, as well as five double-occupancy cottages, all built of stone, driftwood, and glass. Each unit comes with a private garden bathroom with a shower stall.

Meals are served in a clubhouse decorated with antiques and Haitian art. This clubhouse, which opens onto a view of the beach and sea, also features a sitting library area, a stone fireplace, and overhead fans. Dinners are served on a beach terrace adjacent to a thatched-roof tiki bar that runs on the honor system. On many nights, guests gather around a blazing bonfire near the water to hear island music.

1.6km (1 mile) north of New Bight, Cat Island, The Bahamas. © 800/940-1905, 242/342-2018, or 954/474-4821. Fax 242/342-3051 or 954/474-4864. www.fernandezbayvillage.com. 16 units. Nov–May $350–$395 (£186–£209) villa, $240–$290 (£127–£154) cottage; June–Aug $305–$335 (£162–£178) villa, $205–$230 (£109–£1220) cottage. AE, MC, V. Closed Sept–Oct. **Amenities:** Restaurant; bar; watersports equipment/rentals; bike rentals; car-rental desk; babysitting; laundry service. *In room:* Kitchen, fridge, coffeemaker, iron, no phone.

Greenwood Beach Resort & Dive Center *(*)*   The location on a 13km (8-mile) stretch of the Atlantic, bordered by pink sands, is always idyllic, and there's good snorkeling right off shore. Since 1992, a German family has run this beach resort and dive center, constantly making improvements. This group of modern buildings on the most isolated section of the island has a private beach and a freshwater pool. It's better run and equipped than the Bridge Inn, and it attracts mostly divers. The small oceanview double rooms are all equipped with showers and their own terraces. There is an all-purpose bar and a dining room.

The hotel's dive center is the best on the island. The inn has a 7.5m (25-ft.) and a 11m (36-ft.) motorboat for diving excursions, and its Cat Island Dive Center has complete equipment for 20 divers at a time. A two-tank dive costs $95 (£50) per diver. A half-day snorkeling trip costs $35 (£19), including equipment. The resort also has two fishing boats available for bonefishing. The staff greets each arriving Bahamasair flight.

Port Howe, Cat Island, The Bahamas. ⓒ 242/342-3053. Fax 242/342-3053. www.greenwoodbeachresort.net. 22 units. Year-round $99–$130 (£52–£69) double. Breakfast and dinner $48 (£25) per person. AE, MC, V. **Amenities:** Restaurant; bar; pool; watersports equipment/rentals; business center; babysitting. In room: A/C (in some), ceiling fan (in some), no phone.

Hawk's Nest Resort & Marina

This remote getaway lies on the southwestern side of Cat Island, fronting a long beach and containing its own runway for charter flights and private planes, plus a 28-slip full-service marina attracting yachters. This intimate resort is set near the village of Devil's Point, lying some 16km (10 miles) west of Columbus Point close to the ruins of two once-flourishing but now-abandoned plantations, Richman Hill and Newfield. Bedrooms, with either two queen-size beds or a king-size bed, are well furnished and brightly decorated, each with a shower unit. Each room features a patio for those late-afternoon toddies overlooking the sunset. If you bring the family, you may want to look at the two-bedroom house on the beach, separate from the other structures. The clubhouse, the rooms, and the main house are spacious and inviting.

They serve full breakfasts (cooked to order), sandwiches for lunch, and a buffet-style dinner, with the unannounced fare changing nightly. A one-tank dive costs $60 (£32), a two-tank dive $80 (£42).

Devil's Point, Cat Island, The Bahamas. ⓒ 800/688-4752 or 242/342-7050. Fax 242/342-7051. www.hawksnest.com. 10 units. Year-round $204 (£108) double; $455 (£241) house. MAP (breakfast and dinner) $50 (£27) per person. MC, V. **Amenities:** Restaurant; bar; pool; tennis court; marina, watersports equipment/rentals; bike rentals; laundry service; nonsmoking rooms. In room: A/C, TV, coffeemaker, hair dryer.

Pigeon Cay Beach Club

This B&B fronts a tranquil bay at the north end of the island, about a 15-minute ride from the airport. The main building consists of a trio of separate but attached units, a small store, and the check-in office. Each accommodation comes with a fully equipped kitchen. In addition, the property has some light and airy cottages built of stucco and coral stone, with beamed ceilings and Mexican tile floors. Ranging in size from one to three bedrooms, each unit comes with a shower stall.

North End, Cat Island, The Bahamas. ⓒ/fax 242/354-5084. www.pigeoncay-bahamas.com. 11 units. Year-round $140–$180 (£74–£95) 1-bedroom unit; $225–$250 (£119–£133) 2-bedroom unit; $375 (£199) 3-bedroom unit. AE, MC, V. **Amenities:** Limited room service; babysitting; laundry service; nonsmoking rooms. In room: Kitchen, coffeemaker, hair dryer, iron, ceiling fan, no phone.

EXPLORING THE ISLAND: PLANTATIONS, PEAKS & A HERMITAGE

There's an interesting Arawak cave at Columbus Point on the southern tip of the island. In addition, you can see the ruins of many once-flourishing plantations that saw their heyday during the island's short-lived cotton boom. Early planters, many of them Loyalists, marked their property boundaries with stone mounds—some of which are now nearly 200 years old. The ruined plantations include the Deveaux Mansion, built by Col. Andrew Deveaux of the fledgling U.S. Navy (who recaptured Nassau from the Spanish in 1783), and the Armbrister Plantation, which lies in ruins near Port Howe.

You can also hike along the nature paths through native villages and past exotic plants. Finally, you reach the peak of Mount Alvernia, the highest point in The ahamas, at 62m (203 ft.) above sea level, where you will be rewarded with a spectac-ular view. The mount is capped by the **Hermitage,** a religious retreat built entirely by hand by the late Father Jerome, the former "father confessor" of the island, who was once a mule skinner in Canada. Curiously, the building was scaled to fit his short stature (he was a very, very short man). Formerly an Anglican, this Roman Catholic hermit priest became a legend on Cat Island. He died in 1956 at the age of 80, but his memory is kept very much alive here.

The **Cat Island Dive Center** at the Greenwood Beach Resort (© 242/342-3053) will take you out on diving or snorkeling excursions, or rent you snorkeling gear and other water toys. Our favorite spot for diving is along the west coast, where **Dry Heads** is the finest reef. It gets its name because at low tide a blanket of purple sea fans stands high and dry. The drop here is 7.6m (25 ft.), and as you plunge below you'll meet butterflyfish and queen angels swimming over the coral heads.

2 San Salvador ✯

This may be where the New World began. For some years, it has been believed that Christopher Columbus left his first footprints in the Western Hemisphere here, although some scholars strongly dispute this. The easternmost island in the Bahamian archipelago, San Salvador lies 322km (200 miles) southeast of Nassau. Much of its 163 sq. km (64 sq. miles) in total area is occupied by water. There are 28 landlocked lakes on the island, the largest of which is 19km (12 miles) long and serves as the prin-cipal route of transportation for most of the island's population of 1,200. A badly maintained 64km (40-mile) road circles the perimeter of San Salvador.

The tiny island keeps a lonely vigil in the Atlantic. **The Dixon Hill Lighthouse** at South West Point, about 50m (164 ft.) tall, can be seen from 145km (90 miles) away. The light is a hand-operated beacon fueled by kerosene. Built in the 1850s, it is the last lighthouse of its type in The Bahamas. The highest point on the island is **Mount Kerr,** at 41m (134 ft.).

Except for the odd historian or two, very few people ever used to visit San Salvador. Then **Club Med–Columbus Isle** opened, and the joint's been jumping ever since—at least, at the Club Med property. Away from here, San Salvador is as sleepy as it ever was, although it's been known for years as one of the best dive sites in The Bahamas. The snorkeling, fishing, and lovely beaches are equally good.

SAN SALVADOR ESSENTIALS

GETTING THERE   Club Med (see listing below) solves transportation problems for its guests by flying them in on weekly charter planes from Miami. In winter there are also charter flights from New York once a week. You can also rely on public trans-portation by land or sea, but if you do, you'll have to wait a long time before getting off the island.

Bahamasair (© 800/222-4262; www.bahamasair.com) has flights 6 days a week to the island from Nassau. Departure times constantly change, so check with the airline for a schedule.

From Nassau, the mail boat **MV *Lady Francis*** leaves Tuesday heading for San Sal-vador and Rum Cay. The trip takes 12 hours under uncomfortable conditions. For details about sailing, contact the dock master at **Potter's Cay Dock** in Nassau (© 242/393-1064).

GETTING AROUND

If you want to tour the island, ask your hotel staff to help you with arrangements and taxi service. If you have the staff at **Club Med** (© **242/331-2000**) arrange an island tour for you, the cost is around $25 (£13) per person for a half-day ramble.

Fun Fact **The Columbus Mystery**

In 1492, a small group of peaceful Lucayan natives (Arawaks) were going about their business on a little island they called Guanahani, where they and their forebears had lived for at least 500 years. Little did they know how profoundly their lives would change when they greeted the arrival of three small, strange-looking ships bearing Christopher Columbus and his crew of pale, bearded, oddly costumed men. It is said that when he came ashore, Columbus knelt and prayed—and claimed the land for Spain.

Unfortunately, the event was not so propitious for the reportedly handsome natives. Columbus later wrote to Queen Isabella that they would make ideal captives—perfect servants, in other words. It wasn't long before the Spanish conquistadors cleared the island, as well as most of The Bahamas, of Lucayans, sending them into slavery and early death in the mines of Hispaniola (Haiti) in order to feed the Spanish lust for gold from the New World.

But is the island now known as San Salvador the actual site of Columbus's landing? Columbus placed no lasting marker on the sandy, sun-drenched island of his landfall. The result has been much study and discussion during the past century or so as to just where he actually landed.

In the 17th century, an English pirate captain, George Watling, took over the island and built a mansion to serve as his safe haven. The island was listed on maps for about 250 years as Watling's (or Watling) Island.

In 1926 the Bahamian legislature formally changed the name of the island to San Salvador, feeling that enough evidence had been brought forth to support the belief that this was the site of Columbus's landing. Then in 1983, artifacts of European origin (beads, buckles, and metal spikes) were found here together with Arawak pottery and beads and a shard of Spanish pottery. Although the actual date of these artifacts cannot be pinned down, they are probably from 1490 to 1560. The beads and buckles fit the description of goods recorded in Columbus's log.

National Geographic published a meticulously researched article in 1986 written by its senior associate editor, Joseph Judge, with a companion piece by the former chief of the magazine's foreign editorial staff, Luis Marden. The articles set forth the belief that Samana Cay, some 105km (65 miles) to the southeast of the present San Salvador, was actually Guanahani, the island Columbus named San Salvador when he first landed in the New World. The question may never be resolved, and there will doubtless be years and years of controversy about it. Nevertheless, history buffs still flock here hoping to follow in the footsteps of the explorer.

On San Salvador, you don't need to rent a car unless you want to explore far-flung places on your own. If that's the case, you can rent a car through **Riding Rock Inn Resort and Marina** (© 242/331-2631; www.ridingrock.com) for about $85 (£45) a day.

Club Med guests have use of bikes for cycling around the property and for guided tours around the island.

FAST FACTS   The San Salvador Medical Clinic, a 5-minute drive north of Club Med (© 242/331-2105), serves island residents, but serious cases are flown to Nassau. The clinic, which also fills prescriptions, is open Monday to Friday 8:30am to 4:30pm; only emergencies are handled on Saturday and Sunday.

To call the police, dial © 919. (Phones are rare on the island, but the front desk at Riding Rock Inn will place calls for you.)

WHERE TO STAY

Club Med–Columbus Isle 🏖🏖   This is one of the most ecologically conscious, and one of the most luxurious, Club Meds in the Western Hemisphere. Set at the edge of one of the most pristine beaches in the archipelago, about 3km (2 miles) north of Cockburn Town, this is the splashiest resort in the Southern Bahamas. Its promoters estimate that more than 30% of the island's population works at the club.

Most of the prefabricated buildings here were barged to the site in 1991. The resort is built around a large free-form swimming pool. The public rooms are some of the most lavish and cosmopolitan in the country, with art and art objects imported from Asia, Africa, the Americas, and Europe, and assembled by a battalion of designers. Bedrooms each contain a private balcony or patio, furniture that was custom-made in Thailand or the Philippines, sliding glass doors, and feathered wall hangings crafted in the Brazilian rainforest by members of the Xingu tribe. Rooms are large (among the most spacious in the entire chain). Most have twin beds, but you might be able to snag one of the units with a double or a king-size bed, if you're lucky. Each comes with a midsize bathroom with shower stall. Dozens of multilingual GOs (guest relations organizers, or *gentils organisateurs*) are on hand to help initiate newcomers into the resort's many diversions. Unlike many other Club Meds, this one does not encourage children and deliberately offers no particular facilities for their entertainment.

The main dining room, where meals are an ongoing series of buffets, lies in the resort's center. Two specialty restaurants offer Italian and grilled food, respectively. Nonfat, low-calorie, and vegetarian dishes are also featured. Nightly entertainment is presented in a covered open-air theater and dance floor behind one of the bars.

3km (2 miles) north of Cockburn Town, San Salvador, The Bahamas. © 800/CLUB-MED or 242/331-2000. Fax 242/331-2458. www.clubmed.com. 240 units. Winter $1,450–$2,100 (£769–£1,113) weekly per person double occupancy; off season $1,350–$1,900 (£716–£1,007) weekly per person double occupancy. Weekly rates include all meals, drinks during meals, and most sports activities. AE, DISC, MC, V. Not recommended for children under 12. **Amenities:** 3 restaurants; 2 bars; disco; pool; 10 tennis courts; health club; watersports equipment/rentals; laundry service or coin-operated laundry; nonsmoking rooms. *In room:* A/C, TV, fridge, beverage maker, hair dryer, iron, safe.

Riding Rock Inn Resort & Marina   San Salvador's second resort is the motel-style Riding Rock Inn, catering largely to divers. Its simple ambience is a far cry from the extravagant Club Med. Each accommodation faces either a pool or the open sea. The most recent improvement to the inn is an 18-room oceanfront building. Here bedrooms are decorated in a tropical decor with two double beds, satellite TV, a refrigerator, a telephone, ceiling fans, and air-conditioning. Each unit is equipped with a midsize bathroom with a tub/shower.

Many different dive packages are available—check with the hotel. The resort specializes in weeklong trips that include three dives a day, all meals, and accommodations. Packages begin and end on Saturday. Although most guests are already experienced and certified divers, beginners can take a $150 (£80) resort course for the first day of their visit and afterward participate in most of the community's daily dives. Full PADI certification can also be arranged for another supplement of $450 (£239).

An island tour is included in the rates, but after that, most folks rent a bike or scooter from the hotel. On the premises, a restaurant serves routine Bahamian specialties, and a bar features a seating area that juts above the water on a pier.

Cockburn Town, San Salvador, The Bahamas. ☎ 800/272-1492 in the U.S., 954/359-8353 in Florida, or 242/331-2631 in The Bahamas. Fax 242/331-2020. www.ridingrock.com. 42 units. Year-round $120–$145 (£64–£77) double; $135–$160 (£72–£85) triple; $170 (£90) quad. Children 11 or younger stay free in parent's room. MC, V. **Amenities:** Restaurant; bar; pool; tennis court; watersports equipment/rentals. *In room:* A/C, TV, fridge, hair dryer.

WHERE TO DINE

Rock Inn Restaurant BAHAMIAN/AMERICAN   Sit on the deck overlooking the water or eat inside; either way, you can dine on hearty portions of comfort food. Pancakes make a good choice for breakfast, and sandwiches are on the menu for lunch. The fixed-price dinners include soup, salad, main course, dessert, wine, and soft, just-baked Bahamian bread. Launch your meal with the well-seasoned conch chowder or okra soup, and follow it up with steak, prime rib, veal, chicken, or fresh fish. The Wednesday-night barbecues, featuring reggae music, are popular social events.

Cockburn Town. ☎ 242/331-2631. Reservations recommended. Breakfast $13 (£6.90); lunch $15 (£7.95); dinner $28 (£15). MC, V. Daily 7:30–9am, 12:30–2pm, and 6:30–9pm.

BEACHES, WATERSPORTS & OTHER OUTDOOR PURSUITS

If you prefer finding a stretch of sand where the only footprints on it are your own, rent a car or a bike at **Riding Rock Inn Resort & Marina** or call a taxi. Empty beaches are everywhere. Just remember to take plenty of water and, of course, sunblock. You won't find much shade. Along the way, you can look for the island's various monuments to Christopher Columbus.

On the northeast coast, **East Beach** stretches for some 10km (6 miles). Crushed coral and shells turned the shore a rosy pink. The deep turquoise patches in the clear waters are coral heads, but the beach isn't good for snorkeling because people have spotted sharks here. Tall sea wheat or sea grass sprouts up from the sand. Off mile marker number 24 on the main road, you can pick your way to the **Chicago Herald Columbus Monument** (see below).

Scuba divers flock to this remote island—a major dive destination with some **40 dive sites** that lie no more than 45 minutes by boat from either of the two resorts. A major attraction here is *wall diving*—diving where the sloping shoreline suddenly drops off and plummets to the ocean depths.

Associated with the Riding Rock Inn (see above), **Guanahani Dive Ltd.** (☎ 242/ 331-2631) offers dive packages, as well as snorkeling, fishing, and boating trips. Divers can book a getaway package year-round for 5 days and 4 nights that costs from $875 to $925 (£464–£490) per diver, including meals, transportation, diving, and rental gear. Prices are based on double occupancy.

Club Med–Columbus Isle, just north of Cockburn Town, should really be called an *almost*-all-inclusive resort because scuba diving is not covered by its rates. Resort courses run around $180 (£95), and certification courses are $445 (£236). A one-tank dive costs $50 (£27) and a two-tank $90 (£48).

With so many unspoiled and unpopulated kilometers of beaches, this area is ideal for swimming, shelling, and, of course, snorkeling. If you stay here a week, you've only begun to explore the possibilities. Places such as **Bamboo Point, Fernandez Bay,** and **Long Bay** all lie within a few miles of the main settlement of Cockburn Town on the more tranquil western side of the island. At the southern tip of San Salvador are some of our favorite places for snorkeling: **Sandy Point** and nearby **Grotto Bay,** with fine elkhorn coral reefs. Another wonderful spot for snorkeling is the wreck of the SS *Frascate,* which ran aground on January 1, 1902. Filled with such marine life as moray eels and grouper, it ranks, we think, as the best shallow wreck for snorkeling in the area. It lies on the west coast, directly north of the previously recommended Riding Rock Inn.

Club Med–Columbus Isle offers 10 tennis courts (3 lit for night play); courts are open for nonguests who buy a day pass. Riding Rock Inn Resort & Marina has one (often empty) court. Fishermen test their skill against blue marlin, yellowfin tuna, and wahoo on fishing trips, which you can arrange through Riding Rock Inn Resort & Marina (© 242/331-2631). The trips run around $400 (£212) for a half-day and $600 (£318) for a full day. Bone fishermen enjoy **Pigeon Creek,** and some record catches have been chalked up here. Rent a boat from a local or get your hotel to help set you up.

EXPLORING THE ISLAND: COMMEMORATING COLUMBUS

For such a small island, San Salvador offers a great deal of history as well as some sights that merit a look.

Rent a bike, hire a taxi, or start walking, and see how many of the **Christopher Columbus monuments** you can hit. All these monuments are supposed to mark the place where Columbus and his crew anchored the *Nina, Pinta,* and *Santa Maria* early that morning in 1492.

Just south of Cockburn Town, the **Tappan Monument,** a small four-sided stone pillar, stands on the beach at **Fernandez Bay** (mile marker number 5 on the main road). The Tappan gas company embedded this monument here on February 25, 1951, in honor of Columbus.

The Chicago Herald Monument is located at mile marker number 24, on the east coast. To reach it, turn off the main road and drive 1.6 km (1 mile) to **East Beach.** Unless you meet a resident who can give you a ride in a four-wheel-drive car, you have to get out and walk. Turn right and hike 3km (2 miles) parallel to the beach until the sandy road ends. You'll see a cave to the left, at the water's edge. Follow the path to the right. Cupped by vegetation, a stone structure lies on the slice of land between the ocean and the bay. Although many historians dispute the claim, the marble plaque boasts, "On this spot Christopher Columbus first set foot upon the soil of the New World, erected by the *Chicago Herald,* June 1891." The only problem with the monument's claim is that the treacherous reefs here make this a dangerous—and highly unlikely—landing spot.

At Long Bay, the **Olympic Games Memorial** to Columbus, located 5km (3 miles) south of Cockburn Town, was erected in 1968 to commemorate the games in Mexico. Runners carrying an Olympic torch circled the island before coming to rest at the monument and lighting the torch there. The torch was then taken to Mexico on a warship for the games. Another marker is underwater, supposedly where Columbus dropped anchor on his *Santa Maria.*

Just north of the Olympic Games Memorial stands the **Columbus Monument.** On December 25, 1956, Ruth Durlacher Wolper Malvin—a leading U.S. expert on Columbus research—established a simple monument commemorating the explorer's landfall in the New World. Unlike the spot marked by the *Chicago Herald* monument, this is actually supposed to be the place where Columbus and his men landed.

Among the settlements on San Salvador are Sugar Loaf, Pigeon Creek, Old Place, Holiday Track, and Fortune Hill. United Estates, which has the largest population, is a village in the northwest corner near the Dixon Hill Lighthouse. The U.S. Coast Guard has a station at the northern tip of the island.

Except for the party people at Club Med, San Salvador is mainly visited by the boating set that lives aboard their craft. If you're exploring for the day, you'll find one or two local cafes that serve seafood.

In the northeastern portion of the island, the **Dixon Hill Lighthouse,** built in 1856, sends out an intense beam two times every 25 seconds. This signal is visible for 31km (19 miles). The oil-using lighthouse rises 49m (161 ft.) into the sky, and the lighthouse keeper still operates it by hand. For permission to climb to the top, just knock on the door of the lighthouse keeper, who's almost always in the neighboring house.

After huffing and puffing your way up, you'll be surprised when you see how tiny the source of light actually is. From the top of the lighthouse, you can take in a panoramic view of San Salvador's inland lakes, a distant Crab Cay, and the surrounding islets. Ask the lighthouse keeper to show you the **inspector's log,** with signatures that date back to Queen Victoria's reign. Be sure to leave at least a $1 (55p) donation when you sign the guest book on your way out. The lighthouse lies about a 30-minute taxi ride from Riding Rock Inn Resort & Marina or Club Med.

At French Bay, **Watling's Castle,** also known as Sandy Point Estate, has substantial ruins that are about 26m (85 ft.) above sea level. The area is located some 4km (2½ miles) from the "Great Lake," on the southwestern tip of the island. Local "experts" will tell you all about the castle and its history. The only problem is that each "expert" we've listened to (three in all, at different times) has told us a different story about the place. Ask around and perhaps you'll get yet another version; they're entertaining, at least. One of the most common legends involves a famous pirate who made his living either by salvaging the wreckage from foundered ships or by attacking ships for their spoils.

Once plantations—all doomed to failure—were scattered about the island. The most impressive ruins of this former life are **Farquharson's Plantation,** west of Queen's Highway, near South Victoria Hill. In the early part of the 19th century, some Loyalist families moved from the newly established United States to this island, hoping to get rich from farmland tended by slave labor. That plan collapsed when the United Kingdom Emancipation Act freed the slaves in 1834. The plantation owners moved on, but the former slaves stayed behind.

A relic of those times, Farquharson's Plantation is the best-known ruin on the island. People locally call it "Blackbeard's Castle," but it's a remnant of slavery, not piracy. You can see the foundation of a great house, a kitchen, and what is believed to have been a jail.

COCKBURN TOWN

San Salvador's capital, Cockburn (pronounced "Coburn") Town, is a harbor village that takes its name from George Cockburn, said to have been the first royal governor of The Bahamas to visit this remote island, stopping by in 1823.

Look for the town's landmark: a giant almond tree. Major events in San Salvador, like the Columbus Day parade held every October 12, generally take place here.

Holy Saviour Roman Catholic Church   The very first Christian worship service in the New World was Catholic. It thus seems fitting that the Roman Catholic Diocese of

The Bahamas in 1992, on the eve of the 500th anniversary of the Columbus landfall, dedicated a new church on San Salvador.

Cockburn Town. Free admission. Services Sun 10am.

New World Museum   This museum, located 5.5km (3½ miles) north of Riding Rock Inn, has relics dating from Indian times, but you'll have to ask until you find someone with a key if you want to go inside. The museum lies just past Bonefish Bay in the little village of North Victoria Hill. Part of a large estate called Polaris-by-the-Sea, it's owned by Ruth Durlacher Wolper Malvin.

North Victoria Hill. No phone. Free admission. Open anytime during the day.

SAN SALVADOR AFTER DARK

Club Med (℃ 242/331-2000), just north of Cockburn Town, keeps its guests entertained every night, with musical revues and shows starring vacationers themselves. At **Riding Rock Inn Resort & Marina** (℃ 242/331-2631), also north of Cockburn Town, the Wednesday-night barbecue features reggae music, and many locals come to party. The hotel's **Driftwood Bar** is also hot on Friday nights (℃ 242/331-2631). If you're still game for some fun after the lodgings' festivities, head to the **Harlem Square Bar** (℃ 242/331-2777) in Cockburn Town. This friendly place is open daily 7am "until food runs out."

SIDE TRIPS: DISCOVERING RUM CAY & CONCEPTION ISLAND

"Where on earth is Rum Cay?" Even many Bahamians have never heard of it. Located between San Salvador and Long Island, this is another cay, like Fortune Island (see "The Ghost Island of Fortune," later in this chapter), that time forgot.

That wasn't always the case, though. The very name conjures up images of swashbucklers and rumrunners. Doubtless, it was at least a port of call for those dubious seafarers, as it was for ships that took on supplies of salt, fresh water, and food before crossing the Atlantic or going south to Latin America. The cay's name is supposed to have derived from a rum-laden sailing ship that wrecked upon its shores.

Like many other Bahamian islands, Rum Cay once attracted British Loyalists fleeing the new United States of America. They hoped to establish themselves here as farmers and plantation overlords, but even those brave and homeless immigrants abandoned the island as unproductive. Salt mines were the mainstay of the island's economy before they were wiped out by a hurricane at the turn of the 19th century. After that, most of the inhabitants migrated to Nassau; by the 1970s, the population of Rum Cay stood at "80 souls."

Today most of Rum Cay's 100 inhabitants live at Port Nelson, the island's capital. The well-known underwater cinematographer Stan Waterman once described Rum Cay as the "unspoiled diving jewel of The Bahamas." For that reason, a diving club was opened here in 1983, but it closed, regrettably, in 1990.

Some maintain that Rum Cay was the next island where Columbus landed after he found and named San Salvador. He dubbed that second spot Santa María de la Concepción. However, many students of history and navigation believe that Columbus made this second landfall at the island today called Conception, which lies northwest of Rum Cay and about the same distance northeast of Long Island. You'll have to travel here in a private boat.

Joseph Judge, a writer whose articles have appeared in *National Geographic,* believes that neither Rum Cay nor Conception was Columbus' second stop. He holds that, based on modern computer science and knowledge of oceanography, the island the discoverer named Santa María de la Concepción has to be Crooked Island.

The uninhabited Conception Island is under the protection of The Bahamas National Trust, which preserves it as a sea and land park. It's a sanctuary for migratory birds. The most esoteric divers find excellent scuba sites here, and endangered green turtles use the beaches as egg-laying sites. Park rules are strict about littering, or removing any plant or animal life.

With the demise of the Rum Cay Club, tourist traffic to the island came to a halt except for the odd yachting party or two. It's gaining renewed interest, however, and at present, you can arrange for boaters on San Salvador to take you to see Rum Cay and Conception, which remain frozen in time.

3 Long Island

The Tropic of Cancer runs through this long, thin sliver of land, located 242km (150 miles) southeast of Nassau. The island stretches north to south for some 97km (60 miles). It's 2.5km (1½ miles) wide on average, and only 5km (3 miles) wide at its broadest point. Only recently has the island emerged as a minor tourist resort.

Long Island is characterized by high cliffs in the north, wide and shallow sand beaches, historic plantation ruins, native caves, and Spanish churches. The famed **diving sites** *☞* are offshore, including the Arawak "green" hole, a "bottomless" blue hole of stunning magnitude. The best beach bets include **Deal's Beach, Cape Santa Maria Beach, Salt Pond Beach, Turtle Cove Beach,** and the **South End beaches,** the latter offering kilometers of waterfront with powdery white or pink sands.

Most historians agree that Long Island was the third island Columbus sailed to during his first voyage of discovery.

LONG ISLAND ESSENTIALS

GETTING THERE There are two airstrips here, connected by a road. The **Stella Maris strip** is in the north, and the other, called **Deadman's Cay,** is in the south, north of Clarence Town (it's highly unlikely that you'll land here, and this one is a very expensive cab ride from most of the island's accommodations). **Bahamasair** (*☎* **800/222-4262** in the U.S.; www.bahamasair.com) flies direct once a day (a 45-min. trip) from Fort Lauderdale, landing at the Stella Maris airport, which is near most of the hotels.

From Nassau, the **MV** *Mia Dean* sails weekly to Clarence Town, leaving on Tuesday. Mail boat trips take a grueling 10 hours. For information contact the dock master at **Potter's Cay Dock,** Nassau (*☎* **242/393-1064**).

GETTING AROUND The **Stella Maris Resort Club** (*☎* **242/338-2051;** www.stellamarisresort.com) can make arrangements to have you picked up at the airport upon arrival and can also arrange for a rental car.

FAST FACTS The **police** can be reached by calling *☎* **242/337-0999** or 242/337-0444.

The **Scotia Bank** (*☎* **242/338-2000**) has an **ATM** and operates a small currency-exchange facility at the Stella Maris Resort. Hours are Monday to Thursday 9am to 1pm, Friday 9:30am to 3pm.

SPECIAL EVENTS In June, Long Island sailors participate in the big event of the year, the 4-day **Long Island Regatta,** an annual event held at Salt Pond since 1967. In addition to the highly competitive sailboat races, Long Island takes on a festive air with calypso music and reggae and lots of drinking and partying. Many expatriate Long Islanders come home at this time, usually from Nassau, New York, or Miami, to enjoy not only the regatta, but rake 'n' scrape music. Call your local Bahamas Tourist Office (see chapter 2) for more information.

WHERE TO STAY

Cape Santa Maria Beach Resort ⚡ *(Kids*   This cozy nest has become the most luxurious resort on the island, taking over the position long held by the Stella Maris Resort Club. Cottages with two rooms are centered around a clubhouse, and the entire complex opens onto a stunning 6.5km (4-mile) strip of white sand. All units are only 18m (59 ft.) from the beach, which offers great snorkeling. Although the accommodations don't have phones or TVs, each room is air-conditioned and also has ceiling fans, plus a small bathroom with a tub/shower. Bedrooms have a light, tropical, and airy feeling, with marble floors and tasteful rattan furniture. As part of a multimillion-dollar development, the resort in 2006 added eight beachfront villas, each with luxury appointments such as jetted tubs and an Internet service. There's also a screened-in porch with ceiling fans so you can enjoy the outdoors without the mosquitoes, the curse of the Southern Bahamas. The place is ideal for families, and several accommodations are configured so that children will have a separate room. The hotel's 65-seat restaurant is also good, serving a tasty Bahamian, North American, and seafood cuisine.

Cape Santa Maria, off Queen's Hwy., Long Island, The Bahamas. ℂ **800/663-7090** or 242/338-5273. Fax 242/338-6013. www.capesantamaria.com. 29 units. Winter $325 (£172) double, $795 (£421) 2-bedroom villa; off season $235 (£125) double, $595 (£315) 2-bedroom villa. Breakfast and dinner $65 (£34) per person extra. AE, MC, V. Closed Sept–Oct. **Amenities:** Restaurant; bar; health club; watersports equipment/rentals; bike rentals; car-rental desk; babysitting; laundry service; nonsmoking rooms. *In room:* A/C, fridge (in some), coffeemaker, hair dryer, iron, safe (in some), ceiling fan, no phone.

Chez Pierre ⚡ *(Finds*   Just south of the Tropic of Cancer, Montreal expats Pierre and Anne Laurence found their little bit of heaven on 3.2 hectares (8 acres) of land opening onto a wide crescent beach. Here they built and attractively furnished a cluster of bungalows overlooking the sea, each with a screened-in porch. All the units come with private bathrooms with showers. This is the most eco-sensitive resort in the Southern Bahamas, as Chez Pierre is powered by alternative energy; the sun and the wind keep it running.

A few steps from the beach cottages, an oceanfront restaurant serves the best food on the island. Dishes blend French, Italian, and Caribbean cuisines, using island-grown fresh produce along with fresh fish and seafood from local waters. The location is halfway between Stella Maris and Deadman's Cay.

Simms, Long Island, The Bahamas. ℂ 242/338-8809. www.chezpierrebahamas.com. 6 units. Year-round $140 (£74) double. Rates include breakfast and dinner. AE, MC, V. **Amenities:** Restaurant; bar; bikes; babysitting; fishing; kayaking; reef fishing; saltwater fly-fishing; snorkeling; island tours. *In room:* Fans, no phone.

Lochabar Beach Lodge   One of the most remote retreats listed in this guide, this lodge offers escapist studios for those fleeing from the civilized world. You step from your studio to a pristine beach 23m (75 ft.) away, surrounding a "blue hole" in a natural cove. The only acceptable lodgings in the southern part of Long Island, these guest studios measure 56 or 111 sq. m (603 or 1,195 sq. ft.) each. In lieu of ceiling fans, the studios were built to take advantage of the trade winds. Guests keep their Bahama shutters and double screen doors open to capture those breezes. Each studio comes with a small bathroom containing a shower stall. Studios have kitchenettes, and a member of the staff will drive you to a nearby store to stock up on provisions.

Big Blue Hole, 1.6km (1 mile) south of Clarence Town, Long Island, The Bahamas. (© **242/337-3123**. Fax 242/337-6556. www.bahamasvacationguide.com/lochabarbeachlodge. 3 units. Year-round $138–$180 (£73–£95) double. Extra person $20 (£11) per day. MC, V. **Amenities:** Watersports equipment/rentals; car-rental desk; nonsmoking rooms; room for those w/limited mobility. In room: A/C, TV, kitchenette, fridge, coffeemaker, iron.

Stella Maris Resort Club ☞ Situated on a ridge overlooking the Atlantic, the Stella Maris Resort Club stands in a palm grove on the grounds of the old Adderley's Plantation. Although you can swim here, the beach isn't the best, so the hotel maintains a cabana at Cape Santa Maria, a gorgeous beach directly north, and offers shuttle service for its guests.

Accommodations vary widely—rooms, studios, apartments, and cottages with one to four bedrooms. Each accommodation has its own walk-in closet and fully equipped bathroom. Some are directly on the water. All of the buildings, including the cottages and bungalows, are set around a central clubhouse and a trio of pools. The resort makes a great honeymoon destination; everything is relaxed and informal.

The inn serves a good Bahamian cuisine, as well as continental specialties. There are rum-punch parties, cave parties, barbecue dinners, Saturday dinners, and dancing. Numerous watersports include complete diving facilities. Divers and snorkelers can choose from coral head, reef, and drop-off sites along the protected west coast of the island, at the north, and all along the east coast, as well as around Conception Island and Rum Cay. Water-skiing and bottom- and reef fishing are also offered; there are three good bonefishing bays close by. Their 3.5m (11-ft.) Scorpion and Sunfish sailboats are free to hotel guests.

Ocean View Dr. (P.O. Box LI30105), Long Island, The Bahamas. (© **800/426-0466** or 242/338-2051; 954/359-8238 for the Fort Lauderdale booking office. Fax 242/338-2052. www.stellamarisresort.com. 47 units. Winter $175 (£93) double, $200 (£106) 1-bedroom cottage, $330 (£175) 2-bedroom bungalow, $315 (£167) 2-bedroom villa; off season $155 (£82) double, $180 (£95) 1-bedroom cottage, $280 (£148) 2-bedroom bungalow, $265 (£140) 2-bedroom villa. AE, MC, V. **Amenities:** Restaurant; bar; 3 pools; watersports equipment/rentals; laundry service; nonsmoking rooms; rooms for those w/limited mobility. In room: A/C, fridge, hair dryer, no phone.

WHERE TO DINE

All the inns above serve food, but you should call for a reservation. In addition, you can try local joints, such as the **Forest,** Queen's Highway, Miley's (© **242/337-3287**), lying south of Clarence Town. Its cracked conch is the island's finest, and you can also order the standard grouper fingers or barbecued chicken. The bar is made of seashells. On Friday nights, a live band plays for dancing, and the Forest becomes an island hot spot.

One of our favorite stopovers here is at a little roadside dive called **Max's Conch Grill,** Deadman's Cay (© **242/337-0056**), which also serves some of the best conch on the island. Daily specials are also posted.

FISHING, SCUBA DIVING & SNORKELING

A lot of savvy anglers come to Long Island to **fish,** eschewing more famous places such as Andros and Bimini. The secret of good fishing here: the major North Equatorial Current, which originates in the Canary Islands and washes the shores of Long Island. The current transports huge schools of blue marlin, white marlin, sailfish, rainbow runners, yellowfin tuna, blackfin tuna, wahoo, and dolphinfish. Wahoo is best hunted from September through November. Catches weigh from 4.5 to 41kg (10–90 lb.), and some yellowfin have weighed up to 68kg (150 lb.). The small blackfin tuna (July–Dec) weigh from 4.5 to 14kg (10–31 lb.). In addition, there are kilometers and kilometers of reef fishing, with hundreds of species, including snapper or grouper that have been known to weigh 45kg (99 lb.). A jewfish caught here weighed 226kg (498 lb.). In-shore fishing for bonefish is also possible. These fish can be caught from an anchored boat, from the beach, or while wading in foot-deep water.

Although there are no watersports outfitters on Long Island, the two major resorts, the **Stella Maris Resort Club** and the **Cape Santa Maria Beach Resort** (see above), fill the void and offer more watersports than you can do in a week. Both offer bone-fishing at a rate of $400 (£212) per day for up to two people; reef fishing is from $400 (£212) per day for up to six people; deep-sea fishing is $800 (£424) per day for up to six people. **Snorkeling** ✸ off the beach is complimentary at both resorts. However, boat excursions can be as little as $15 (£7.95) per hour at Cape Santa Maria; on Wednesday and Saturday, these excursions are complimentary at the Stella Maris. Both resorts offer scuba diving ranging from $45 to $75 (£24–£40) per person per day, with equipment rentals ranging from $10 to $50 (£5.30–£27). Both also offer kayaks, wind-surfers, and bicycles. The Cape Santa Maria also offers Hobie Cats and boogie boards.

EXPLORING THE ISLAND

At **Wild Tamarind** (© 242/337-0262)—1km (⅔ mile) east of Queen's Highway at the hamlet of Petty's—Denis Knight makes the best ceramics on the island. You might want to carry off one of his ceramic sculptures, or at least a bowl or vase.

Most of the islanders live at the unattractively named **Deadman's Cay.** Other set-tlements have equally colorful names: Roses, Newfound Harbour, Burnt Ground, Indian Head Point, and, at the northern tip of the island, Cape Santa Maria, gener-ally believed to be the place where Columbus landed and from where he looked on the Exumas (islands that he did not visit). Our favorite name, however, is **Hard Bar-gain,** located 16km (10 miles) south of Clarence Town. No one seems to know how this hamlet (now a shrimp-breeding farm) got its name.

Try to visit **Clarence Town** ✸, 16km (10 miles) south of Deadman's Cay along the eastern coastline. It was here that Father Jerome, the priest who became known as the "father confessor" of the islands, built two churches before his death in 1956: **St. Paul's,** an Anglican house of worship, and **St. Peter's,** a Roman Catholic church. The "hermit" of Cat Island (you can visit his Hermitage there, see earlier in this chapter) was inter-ested in Gothic architecture. He must also have been somewhat ecumenical because he started his ministry as an Anglican but embraced Roman Catholicism along the way.

Many ruins recall the days when local plantation owners figured their wealth in slaves and cotton. The remains of **Dunmore's Plantation** at Deadman's Cay stand on a hill surrounded by the sea on three sides. There are six gateposts (four outer and two inner), as well as a house with two fireplaces and wall drawings of ships. At the base of the ruins is evidence that a mill wheel was once used. The property was part of the estate of Lord Dunmore, for whom Dunmore Town on Harbour Island was named.

In the village of Grays stand the ruins of **Gray's Plantation,** where you'll see the remnants of at least three houses, one with two chimneys. One is very large, and another seems to have been a one-story structure with a cellar.

Adderley's Plantation, off Cape Santa Maria, originally occupied all the land now known as Stella Maris. The ruins at this cotton plantation consist of three structures that are partially intact but roofless.

Two underground sites that can be visited on Deadman's Cay are **Dunmore's Caves** and **Deadman's Cay Cave.** You'll need to hire a local guide to explore these. Dunmore's Caves are believed to have been inhabited by Lucayans and later to have served as a hideaway for buccaneers. The cave at Deadman's Cay, one of two that lead to the ocean, has never been fully explored. There are two native drawings on the cavern wall.

4 Acklins Island & Crooked Island

These little tropical islands, approximately 386km (239 miles) southeast of Nassau, make up an undiscovered Bahamian frontier outpost. Columbus came this way looking for gold. Much later, Acklins Island, Crooked Island, and their surrounding cays became hide-outs for pirates who attacked vessels in the Crooked Island Passage (the narrow waterway Columbus sailed), which separates the two islands. Today a well-known landmark, the **Crooked Island Passage Light,** built in 1876, guides ships to a safe voyage through the slot. Also known as the Bird Rock Lighthouse, it is a popular nesting spot for ospreys, and the light still lures pilots and sailors to the **Pittstown Point Landing Resort.** A barrier reef begins near the lighthouse, stretching down off Acklins Island for about 40km (25 miles) to the southeast.

Although Acklins Island and Crooked Island are separate, they are usually mentioned as a unit because of their proximity to one another. Together the two islands form the shape of a boomerang. Crooked Island, the northern one, is 181 sq. km (71 sq. miles) in area, whereas Acklins Island, to the south, occupies 311 sq. km (121 sq. miles). Both islands, which have good white-sand beaches and offer fishing and scuba diving, are inhabited mainly by fishermen and farmers.

In his controversial article in *National Geographic* in 1986, Joseph Judge identified Crooked Island as the site of Columbus's second island landing, the one he named Santa María de la Concepción.

Estimates say that by the end of the 18th century, more than three dozen working plantations were on these islands, begun by Loyalists fleeing mainland North America in the wake of the Revolutionary War. At the peak plantation period, there could have been as many as 1,200 slaves laboring in the 3,000 "doomed" acres of cotton fields (which were later wiped out by a blight). The people who remained on the island survived not only by fishing and farming, but also, beginning in the mid–18th century, by stripping the Croton cascarilla shrub of its bark to produce the flavoring for Campari liquor.

ACKLINS ISLAND & CROOKED ISLAND ESSENTIALS

GETTING THERE   There's an airport at Colonel Hill on Crooked Island and another airstrip at **Spring Point** on Acklins Island.

Bahamasair (© 800/222-4262 in the U.S.; www.bahamasair.com) has two flights a week from Nassau, on Wednesday and Saturday, to Crooked Island and Acklins Island, with returns to Nassau scheduled on the same day.

Mail-boat service, with the **MV *United Star,*** leaves Potter's Cay Dock in Nassau and heads for Acklins Island, Crooked Island, Fortune Island (Long Cay), and Mayaguana Island each week. Check the schedule and costs with the dock master at **Potter's Cay Dock** in Nassau (© 242/393-1064).

A government-owned **ferry** service connects the two islands; it operates daily from 9am to 4pm. It links Lovely Bay on Acklins Island with Browns on Crooked Island. The one-way fare is $4 (£2.10).

Once you arrive at Crooked Island, a **taxi** service is available, but it's wise to advise your hotel in advance of your arrival—they'll probably send a van to meet you.

FAST FACTS   There are several government-operated clinics. Phones are scarce on the islands, but your hotel desk can reach one of these clinics by going through the local operator. The clinic on Acklins Island is at Spring Point (© 242/344-3172). On Crooked Island, the clinic is at Landrail Point (© 242/344-2166).

The **police** station on Crooked Island can be reached by dialing © 242/344-2599.

WHERE TO STAY & DINE

Out Island Inn at Pittstown Point Landing *(Finds)*   Located on a beach at the extreme northwestern tip of Crooked Island, this hotel is so isolated you'll forget all about the world outside. For most of the early years of its life, it was a well-guarded secret shared mostly by the owners of private planes who flew in from the mainland of Florida for off-the-record weekends. Even today, about 70% of the clients arrive by one- or two-engine aircraft that they fly themselves as part of island-hopping jaunts around The Bahamas. The island maintains its own 690m (2,263-ft.) hard-surface landing strip, which is completely independent from the one used for the flights from Nassau on Bahamasair.

Surrounded by scrub-covered landscape at the edge of a turquoise sea, it lies 4km (2½ miles) north of the hamlet of Landrail Point (pop. 50) on a sandy peninsula. Within easy access are some of the weirdest historic sites in The Bahamas, including the sun-baked ruins of a salt farm (Marine Farms Fortress) that was sacked by American-based pirates in 1812.

Spartan accommodations with tub/shower bathrooms occupy three low-slung, cement-sided buildings. They lie directly on the beach, usually with verandas facing the sea. Because of the constant trade winds, not all bedrooms have air-conditioning, but do contain paddle-shaped ceiling fans. The entire resort shares only one telephone/fax, which is reserved for emergency calls.

Meals are served in a stone-sided building that was originally erected late in the 1600s as a barracks for the British West Indies Naval Squadron and later was the region's post office. The restaurant serves seafood, as well as North American and Bahamian specialties. Guests always take the meal plan here. You'll also usually find a scattering of yacht owners or aviators who drop in spontaneously for drinks and dinner.

Landrail Point, Crooked Island, The Bahamas. (For reservations and information, contact Pittstown Point Landing, 9274 SE Hawks Nest Court, Hobe Sound, FL 33455.) © 242/344-2507. www.pittstownpointlandings.com. 12 units. Year-round $190 (£101) double. Rates include all meals (AP). AE, MC, V. **Amenities:** Restaurant; bar; laundry service; nonsmoking rooms. *In room:* A/C (in some), no phone.

A PIRATE HIDE-OUT & MORE

Crooked Island opens onto the **Windward Passage,** the dividing point between the Caribbean Sea and The Bahamas. Whatever else he may have named it, when Columbus landed at what is now Pittstown Point, he supposedly called it Fragrant Island because of the aroma of its many herbs. One scent was cascarilla bark, used to flavor Campari liquor as well as the native Cascarilla Liqueur, which is exported. For the best view of the island, climb **Colonel Hill** *(★)*—unless you arrived at the Crooked Island Airport (also known as the Colonel Hill Airport), which has the same vantage.

Guarding the north end of this island is the **Marine Farms Fortress,** an abandoned British fortification that saw action in the War of 1812. It looks out over Crooked Island Passage and can be visited (ask your hotel to make arrangements for you).

Hope Great House is also on the island, with orchards and gardens that date from the time of George V of England.

Other sights include **French Wells Bay,** a swampy delta leading to an extensive mangrove swamp rich in bird life, and the **Bird Rock Lighthouse,** built a century ago.

At the southern end of Acklins Island lies **Castle Island,** a low bit of land where an 1867 lighthouse stands. Pirates used it as a hide-out, sailing forth to attack ships in the nearby passage.

Finds **The Ghost Island of Fortune**

Lying off the coast of Crooked Island, **Fortune Island** is truly a place that time forgot. Your hotel can put you in touch with a boater on Crooked Island who will take you here. Experts believe, based on research done for *National Geographic,* that Fortune Island (sometimes confusingly called Long Cay) is the one Columbus chose to name Isabella, in honor of the queen who funded his expedition. Its only real settlement is Albert Town, which is classified as a ghost town but officially isn't—some hardy souls still live here. Fortune Hill, visible from 19km (12 miles) away at sea, is the local landmark. Hundreds of Bahamians came here in the 2 decades before World War I and would wait to be picked up by oceangoing freighters, which would take them to seek their fortunes as laborers in Central America—hence, the name Fortune Hill.

Acklins Island has many interestingly named villages—Binnacle Hill, Delectable Bay, Golden Grove, Goodwill, Hard Hill, Snug Corner, and Lovely Bay. Some Crooked Island sites have more ominous names, such as Gun Point and Cripple Hill.

5 Mayaguana Island

The least-visited of the Bahamian islands, sleepy Mayaguana seems to float adrift in the tropical sun at the remote extremities of the southeastern edge of The Bahamas, 564km (350 miles) southeast of Nassau. It occupies 285 sq. km (111 sq. miles) and has a population of about 400. It's a long, long way from the development of Nassau and Paradise Island.

Standing in the Windward Passage, Mayaguana is just northwest of the Turks and Caicos Islands. It's separated from the British Crown Colony by the Caicos Passage. Around the time of the American Civil War, inhabitants of Turks Island began to settle in Mayaguana, which before then had dozed undisturbed for centuries.

Acklins Island and Crooked Island lie across the Mayaguana Passage. Mayaguana is only 9.5km (6 miles) across at its widest point, and about 39km (24 miles) long. Its beaches are enticing, but you'll rarely see a tourist on them, other than the occasional German. A few developers have flown in to check out the island, but to date no new development has occurred.

Summer brings the rains to Mayaguana. Combined with heat and mosquitoes, it can get a little rough here. However, summer is the best time to go fishing.

GETTING THERE

Bahamasair (© 800/222-4262 in the U.S.; www.bahamasair.com) flies in here to a little airstrip. Flights depart from Nassau Wednesday and Friday at 9:15am and take approximately 2½ hours.

From Nassau, a mail boat, **MV *United Star,*** makes a stop at Mayaguana. For information, check with the dock master at **Potter's Cay Dock** in Nassau (© 242/393-1064).

WHERE TO STAY & DINE

Few other outposts in The Bahamas are as remote as Mayaguana, which is the main reason many visitors come—to get away from everything. Many visitors arrive by boat and just ask around for availability at one of the ultrasimple lodgings here. Some locals are willing to house you in one of their spare bedrooms for a rate that can be negotiated up or down to almost anything.

Baycaner Beach Resort   In operation since 1996, this is the only hotel on the island that can even lay a claim to being that. Its owner, Ernal Brown, is called "Shorty" by all the locals, and he's the man to see if you're one of the rare visitors who ever makes it to this part of the world. You can literally jump from your simply furnished bedroom right into the water. The bedrooms contain a comfortable bed and a scattering of wicker furnishings, along with a small air conditioner; each comes with a little, well-maintained bathroom. The lobby adjoins the dining room and bar, the latter popular with locals. You might have the dining room to yourself, however. Dig into that Bahamian staple of brown pigeon peas 'n' rice. Most meals feature conch—perhaps in a chowder or freshly made salad—and the inevitable grouper, the most popular fish caught off island. The hotel cook bakes fresh bread daily.

Pirates Well, Mayaguana, The Bahamas. © 242/339-3726. Fax 242/339-3727. www.baycanerbeach.com. 16 units. Sept–Apr $106 (£56) double; May–Aug $88 (£47) double. MC, V. **Amenities:** Restaurant; bar; limited room service; laundry service; scuba diving. *In room:* A/C, TV.

EXPLORING THE ISLAND

Abraham's Bay is the main town on the south coast, with an excellent harbor. The other little settlement on Mayaguana is **Betsy Bay,** secluded and lost in time. Wild corn and saucy hummingbirds share this spot along with some little sun-worn cottages. At **Pirate's Well,** goats are now the chief residents, although buccaneers used to roam past here. Locals still dream of finding buried treasure. The best views of the Mayaguana Passage can be had from both Betsy Bay and Pirate's Well.

Fishing is good on the island. Locals will often take you out on one of their boats, but you've got to ask around. In summer and early autumn, temperatures can soar beyond 100°F (38°C). Winters, however, are ideal, and it never gets cold here as it can in the north Bahamas.

Mayaguana might be called The Bahamas' "great outback" or "wild west." It's a rugged and salty environment. Sailing, deep-sea fishing, scuba diving, snorkeling, swimming, and walking are the main pastimes. The island is still too laid-back to have many organized outfitters. If you need to rent any gear or want to hire a guide for an organized outing, your best bet is to inquire at your hotel; the staff can usually hook you up with the right person.

6 Great Inagua ⟨★⟩

The most southerly and the third-largest island of The Bahamas, flat Great Inagua, some 64km (40 miles) long and 32km (20 miles) wide, is home to 1,200 people. It lies 527km (327 miles) southeast of Nassau.

This is the site not only of the **Morton Salt Crystal Factory,** here since 1800, but also of one of the largest nesting grounds for **flamingos** in the Western Hemisphere. The National Trust of The Bahamas protects the area around Lake Windsor, where the birds breed and the population is said to number 80,000. Flamingos used to inhabit all of The Bahamas, but the birds have disappeared from most other places. The reserve can be visited only with a guide. Besides the pink flamingo, you can see roseate spoonbills and other bird life.

Green turtles are also raised here, at **Union Creek Reserve,** and then released into the ocean to make their way as best they can; they, too, are an endangered species.

(Tours of the reserve are not well organized, and the operation is very informal, but if you're here, inquire about getting a look.) This vast windward island, almost within sight of Cuba, is also inhabited by wild hogs, horses, and donkeys.

Matthew Town is the chief settlement on the island, but it's not of any great sightseeing interest, although it has an 1870 lighthouse. Other locales have interesting names, such as Doghead Point, Mutton Fish Point, and Devil's Point (which makes one wonder what happened there to give rise to the name).

Little Inagua, 8km (5 miles) to the north, has no population and is just a speck of land off the northeast coast of Great Inagua, about 78 sq. km (30 sq. miles) in area. It has much bird life, though, and there are also wild goats and donkeys.

GREAT INAGUA ESSENTIALS

GETTING THERE   Bahamasair (© 800/222-4262 in the U.S.; www.bahamas air.com) flies to Matthew Town Airport from Nassau on Monday, Wednesday, and Friday at 9:15am. Flight time is approximately 2 hours.

You can also go by **mail boat, MV _United Star,_** which makes weekly trips from Nassau to Matthew Town (schedule varies). Call the **Potter's Cay Dock Master** (© 242/393-1064) in Nassau for details.

GETTING AROUND   **Taxis** meet incoming flights from Nassau. If you need a car, check with one of the guesthouses, but don't expect the vehicles to be well maintained.

FAST FACTS   The **Inagua Hospital** can be called at © 242/339-1249. The **police** can be reached at © 242/339-1263.

WHERE TO STAY

The choices of accommodations aren't great on this island, but most visitors are willing to forgo comfort to see the spectacular flamingos.

Morton Main House   The Main House is owned by Morton Bahamas Ltd., the salt people, whose employees often fill up all the rooms. Only five bedrooms are rented, and the furnishings are extremely modest, though everything is clean. Each unit comes with a small bathroom containing a tub/shower. Life here is casual and completely informal. You can order breakfast or lunch here—but no dinner. Unfortunately, it sits near a noisy power plant.

Matthew Town, Inagua, The Bahamas. © 242/339-1267. Fax 242/339-1265. 5 units. www.inaguamainhouse.com. Year-round $60–$85 (£32–£45) double. No credit cards. **Amenities:** Nonsmoking rooms. _In room:_ A/C, TV, iron, fridge, no phone.

Walkine's Guest House   Set 1km (⅔ mile) south of Matthew Town, this simple guesthouse has a blue exterior and rosy, shell-pink bedrooms. Your hosts are Eleanor and Kirk Walkine, who built their place in 1984 across the road from the beach. Rooms are very modest but spacious, with only racks to hang your clothes in lieu of a closet. Bathrooms are large, three containing a tub/shower.

Gregory St., Matthew Town, Inagua, The Bahamas. © 242/339-1612. 5 units, 3 w/private bathroom. Year-round $110 (£58) double. No credit cards. **Amenities:** Nonsmoking rooms. _In room:_ A/C, TV, coffeemaker, no phone.

WHERE TO DINE

Cozy Corner BAHAMIAN/AMERICAN   The most consistently reliable restaurant outside any of the guesthouses is this lime-green stone-built house 2 blocks from the sea. Your hosts, Rosemary Ingraham and her daughter Veronica, maintain a friendly bar where beer, rum punch, and gossip seem to be the staples of the town. Menu items include a simple roster of mostly fried foods that are almost always accompanied by french fries. Dishes include fried conch, fried chicken, burgers and "whopper burgers," plus whatever sort of fried seafood is available from local fishermen on the day of your visit.

William St., Matthew Town. ⓒ 242/339-1440. Lunch and dinner $7–$10 (£3.70–£5.30). No credit cards. Daily 10am–5pm.

EXPLORING THE ISLAND: PINK FLAMINGOS & MORE

The island's vast number of **pink flamingos** 𝒜𝒜𝒜 outnumbers its human population of 1,200. They're so plentiful on Inagua that some of them even roost on the runway of the island's airport, as well as at thousands of other locations throughout the flat, heat-blasted landscape.

Dedicated bird-watchers who are willing to forgo comforts usually trek inland to the edges of the many brackish lakes in the island's center. About half the island is devoted to a national park; the island's most viable industry involves distilling salt from the local salt flats.

To see the birds at **Inagua National Park** 𝒜𝒜 is reason enough to come here in the first place. Everyone entering the park must be accompanied by a warden, and reservations and a day pass costing $25 (£13) for adults and $10 (£5.30) for students must be obtained in advance. Get the passes either through The Bahamas National Trust in Nassau (ⓒ 242/393-1317 for information or reservations; www.bahamasnational trust.org) or by contacting one of the local wardens on Inagua, Henry Nixon, at ⓒ 242/339-1616. In addition to the park fee, you're expected to offer the wardens a large tip. Figure on about $50 (£27) a day, which is the usual payment. The best time to see our feathered friends is from November until June.

One of the best panoramas on the island is **Southwest Point,** lying 2km (1¼ miles) south of the "capital." From here you can see Cuba on a clear day because it lies just 81km (50 miles) to the west. The best vista of Cuba comes from the lighthouse here that dates from 1870—one of the last of a quartet of hand-operated kerosene lighthouses left in The Bahamas. The reefs off this point are treacherous, as many a captain learned when his ship was wrecked here.

Fun Fact **With Salt, Please**

Salt means a great deal to Great Inagua—not only for the Morton Salt Company's extensive operations (the company produces more than 1 million tons of salt each year), but also for the unique local wildlife.

First, seawater is pumped into the interior of the island and held by dikes. Great Inagua's salt ponds, about 80 of them, cover some 4,856 hectares (11,994 acres). As the water evaporates, it turns into heavy brine. The salt solidifies at night and melts during the heat of the day, and a crystallized bed forms at the bottom of the pond. In the final stage of processing, any remaining water is drained, and the salt is bulldozed into bleached-white mountains and shipped around the world for processing.

As the water evaporates from these salt ponds, brine shrimp concentrate and provide great meals for the island's colorful pink flamingos.

Index

See also Accommodations and Restaurant indexes, below.

RESTAURANTS

— I don't speak sign language.

A hotel can close for all kinds of reasons.

Our Guarantee ensures that if your hotel's undergoing construction, we'll let you know in advance. In fact, we cover your entire travel experience. See www.travelocity.com/guarantee for details.

*** travelocity*

You'll never roam alone.